GEOGRAPHY
IS DESTINY

ALSO BY IAN MORRIS

The Measure of Civilization:
How Social Development Decides the Fate of Nations

War! What Is It Good For? Conflict and the Progress of
Civilization from Primates to Robots

Why the West Rules—for Now: The Patterns of History,
and What They Reveal About the Future

GEOGRAPHY
IS DESTINY

Britain and the World:
A 10,000-Year History

IAN MORRIS

FARRAR, STRAUS AND GIROUX

NEW YORK

Farrar, Straus and Giroux
120 Broadway, New York 10271

Library of Congress Cataloging-in-Publication Data
Names: Morris, Ian, 1960– author.
Title: Geography is destiny: Britain and the World: a 10,000-year history / Ian Morris.
Description: First American edition. | New York : Farrar, Straus and Giroux, 2022. |
    Includes bibliographical references and index.
Identifiers: LCCN 2021061234 | ISBN 9780374157272 (hardcover)
Subjects: LCSH: Great Britain—Relations—Europe. | Europe—Relations—Great Britain. |
    Great Britain—Civilization. | Great Britain—History.
Classification: LCC D34.G7 M67 2022 | DDC 327.4104—dc23/eng/20220105
LC record available at https://lccn.loc.gov/2021061234

Our books may be purchased in bulk for promotional, educational,
or business use. Please contact your local bookseller or the Macmillan Corporate
and Premium Sales Department at 1-800-221-7945, extension 5442, or by email
at MacmillanSpecialMarkets@macmillan.com.

www.fsgbooks.com
www.twitter.com/fsgbooks • www.facebook.com/fsgbooks

1   3   5   7   9   10   8   6   4   2

Contents

INTRODUCTION

Fog in the Channel

When I was a boy, my grandfather told me – over and over again – that when he'd been my age, weather reports used to say 'Fog in the Channel – Continent cut off' (Figure 0.1). Like so many jokes, the humour was in the ambiguity. Was Grandad saying the country had gone to the dogs? Or that the English were comically self-important? Or both? Or neither? He never told. But forty-odd years on from the last time he shared it, the joke feels edgier. On 23 June 2016 the United Kingdom voted to leave the European Union. Before the week was out, the prime minister had fallen (the third of four Conservative premiers in a row to go over Europe), the Labour Party's Members of Parliament had voted no confidence in their own leader and $2 trillion of the world's wealth had evaporated. Not funny.

I decided to write a book about what had happened the morning after the referendum. I knew that hundreds of other authors would be making or had already made similar decisions, and the first books on Brexit in fact appeared within weeks. What made me think this one was worth writing anyway was that I suspected it would be rather different from the rest. Most Brexit books focus on just the seven years between David Cameron's announcement that he favoured a referendum in 2013 and Britain's actual departure in 2020. Some go back to 1973, when Britain joined the European Economic Community, a few to the late 1940s, when the first practical plans for European federation were floated, and a handful start with the Reformation or Spanish Armada in the sixteenth century. My claim here is that none of this is enough. Only when we look at the entire 10,000 years since rising, post-ice-age oceans began physically separating the British Isles from the European Continent do we see the larger patterns that have driven, and continue to drive, British history.

I am not suggesting that we will find foreign-policy rec-

Figure o.i. Reg Philips (1906–1980), steelworker, humourist and
occasional geographer, as he looked in the early 1930s.

ommendations or eternal truths about Englishness etched in the
rocks of Stonehenge. Archaeologists rightly mock people who say
such silly things. However, it is only on a multi-millennium timescale
that the forces driving Britain's relationships with Europe and the
wider world make themselves clear. Only when we put the facts into
this framework do we see why Brexit seems so compelling to some,
so appalling to others and where it might lead next.

Looking at the long run is hardly a new idea. Back in 1944 the
part-time historian Winston Churchill advised that 'The longer you
can look back, the farther you can look forward'. However, decades
then passed before full-time historians took much notice of his
advice. Only since the early 2000s have historians really warmed to
what we nowadays call 'big (or deep) history', studying trends span-
ning millennia and affecting the entire planet. Most big-history work,
including several books of my own, pulls back from the details of
what happened in particular times and places in order to tell a story
at the planetary scale. Here, by contrast, I want to turn the telescope
around, zooming in from the global to the local. History, after all, is
made by real people, and the broad-brushstroke stuff isn't worth the

pixels it's written in unless it helps us make sense of life as we actually live it. So, my plan here is to use the methods of big history to put post-Brexit Britain into the context of post-ice-age Britain's multi-millennium relationship with Europe and the wider world.

Even now, three-quarters of a century after Churchill, looking at the long term remains a minority activity. When, for instance, the highly respected historian David Edgerton said in his excellent book *The Rise and Fall of the British Nation* that 'Brexit is a recent phenomenon, with causes in the here and now', having 'nothing to do with deep history', he set off no storm of controversy; but I think he should have done. In what follows, I will try to show that Brexit in fact has everything to do with deep history, that only a long-term, large-scale perspective can make sense of it and that big history can even show us what Brexit might mean in the coming century.

The Thing Least Spoken Of

Two months and a day after the Brexit referendum, Nigel Farage, leader of the fiercely anti-European United Kingdom Independence Party (UKIP), surfaced in the unlikely setting of Jackson, Mississippi. He was there to speak in support of the Republican presidential candidate Donald Trump, even though, according to Britain's staunchly pro-European newspaper the *Guardian*, 'a quick survey of the crowd at random showed that eight in 10 people had never heard of Farage or Brexit'. Undeterred, Farage explained that Trump had invited him because UKIP had galvanised millions of ordinary people who 'believed [that] by going out and voting for Brexit they could take back control of their country, take back control of their borders and get back their pride and self-respect' – much as Trump saw himself doing in the United States.

Farage had been consistent throughout his campaign. Brexit was really about five things: identity (that is, who the British thought they were), mobility (who was moving into, out of and around the British Isles), prosperity (how rich the islanders were and how their riches were shared), security (how safe they were from violence) and sovereignty (who made the rules). Among these, Farage insisted, 'immigration was the absolute key'. Nothing else – not even cash – came close. 'Where we struck the chord', he explained, 'is yeah, our GDP may be going up through mass immigration, but who's benefiting? It's the big businesses getting cheap labour who are bene-fiting [. . . and there are] things in life that matter more than money.'

His audience liked what they heard. 'You've got to control the borders', a nurse from nearby Florence, Mississippi, assured the *Guardian*'s reporter. 'They say one in 50,000 [immigrants] might be a terrorist. But if I give you a jar of 50,000 M&Ms and tell you one is cyanide, are you going to take a big handful?' A good question, even if calculations by the libertarian Cato Institute suggest that the chance of a migrant turning out to be a terrorist is actually more like one in 29 million. What Farage saw, better than most, was that facts mattered less to the argument than values. The real question was not who the British were but who they *ought* to be, not who *was* moving in and out, getting rich or poor, being violent or telling Britons what to do but who *should* be doing all these things.

Plenty of people thought Farage was wrong. To the business website Forbes.com there seemed to be just three issues, not Farage's five, and while *Fortune* magazine agreed that five questions mattered, it chose five different ones. The BBC saw eight issues, the *Indepen-dent* and *Sun* newspapers ten each and the aggressively anti-European *Daily Mail* no fewer than twenty. Not to be outdone, the Europhile novelist Philip Pullman assured the *Guardian* after the vote that 'This catastrophe has had a thousand causes'. Exit polls suggested that even this was an underestimate: some people voted to go because they thought staying would win anyway; plenty claimed not to know why they voted as they did; and, defying all logic, 7 per cent of Farage's own party opposed leaving the European Union. After subjecting a dozen years' worth of opinion polls to a battery of statistical tests, the political scientists Harold D. Clarke, Matthew Goodwin and Paul Whiteley concluded in their book *Brexit: Why Britain Voted to Leave the European Union* that 'The narrow Brexit decision [. . .] reflected a complex and cross-cutting mix of calculations, emotions and cues'. They are clearly right; and yet Farage was right too, that his five factors captured enough of the issues people were thinking about for him to win.

In fact, Farage seems to have been righter than he knew. Big history suggests that identity, mobility, prosperity, security and sov-ereignty were not just the top concerns in 2016: they have *always* been what people worry about. In one of the oldest surviving written accounts of Britain the Roman writer Tacitus assures us that the locals were already arguing over them 2,000 years ago. As Rome dragged Britannia into its empire, says Tacitus, some Britons rejoiced in the sophistication and splendour brought by their violent conquerors while others saw everything Continental as decadent by definition. Rome exerted all its charms and soft power to make sure that the former viewpoint won out over the latter. As a result, Tacitus explains, 'Instead of loathing the Latin language, [Britons] became eager to speak it well. In the same way, our [Rome's] national dress came into favour, and the toga was everywhere to be seen.' However, he adds – sounding for all the world as though he were channelling the *Daily Mail* – although 'The unsuspecting Britons called such novelties civilisation', wiser men saw that 'they were in fact just part of their enslavement'.

In some ways not much has changed since then. In the first century as much as the twenty-first, Britons who embraced a wider world tended to think their own views were broad and enlightened whereas their opponents' were narrow and ignorant, while those who preferred the local to the global saw themselves as broad and democratic and their rivals as narrow and elitist. 'They're stupid, they're old, they're backward, they're racist' is how Farage claimed that cosmopolitan elites saw his (and, for that matter, Donald Trump's) supporters in 2016. Since antiquity, Europhiles have dreaded being dragged into the abyss by peasants with pitchforks while Europhobes have resented being told what to do by cliques of know-it-alls. Pro-Europeans mocked Michael Gove, a former secretary of state for education, when he told a television interviewer three weeks before the referendum that 'people in this country have had enough of experts', but he was speaking from a script written millennia earlier.

In other ways, however, everything has changed. Britons think quite differently about identity, mobility, prosperity, security and sovereignty nowadays from the way they did in Churchill's day, let alone in Queen Victoria's, Raleigh and Drake's or Julius Caesar's. Why so? Because, the big-history perspective seems to show, something else – something much deeper – ultimately determines how humans think about all five of these forces. That something else is geography.

In a sense, everyone already knows this. Asked in 2010 to name his favourite childhood book, the then prime minister, David Cameron, plumped for *Our Island Story*, Henrietta Marshall's engaging 1905 account of how insularity made the British (or, as she usually put

Figure 0.2. Setting the scene: locations mentioned in the Introduction.

it, English) character. In full agreement, the historian Robert Tombs opens his fascinating book *This Sovereign Isle* with the self-evident truth that 'Geography comes before history. Islands cannot have the same history as continental plains.' Quite so; yet there is more to geography than Cameron, Marshall or Tombs acknowledges. While Britain's physical form has changed rather little for thousands of years, with its coasts, rivers and mountains still more or less where they were when Stonehenge (Figure 0.2) was built, what that geography *means* has changed massively. The long-term view suggests that the geography's meaning consistently depends on two things: technology, especially the branches connected with travel and communication; and organisation, especially the kinds that allow people to use new technologies effectively. Because technology and organisation are constantly changing, so too is the meaning of geography, which, as it changes, transforms the meanings of identity, mobility, prosperity, security and sovereignty too. Brexit was just the latest round in an ancient argument about what Britain's geography means.

Farage (and almost every politician since Roman times) emphasised identity, mobility, prosperity, security and sovereignty because these are the main ways we directly experience the effects of geography. They are therefore what most of us, most of the time, care about, and what politicians, most of the time, talk about. But if we want to know *why* these forces affect us as they do, and where they might take us next, we have to dig deeper.

The ancient Greek historian Thucydides already knew this nearly 2,500 years ago. The most terrible event of his own times was a savage war that broke out between Athens and Sparta in 431 BCE; but when Athenians and Spartans analysed what was going on, he observed, 'the truest cause – the growth of Athenian power and the fear this produced among the Spartans – was actually the thing least spoken of'. Only when he put the events of his own lifetime into a perspective stretching back nearly a millennium, to the Trojan War, could he identify the truest cause. Just so, if we really want to know why Britons voted to leave the European Union in 2016 and what that decision will mean for the twenty-first century, we have to confront the thing least spoken of.

Three Maps

Like most geographical stories, mine is best told through maps. Three of them will do the bulk of the work, each representing one of the three broad stages through which Britain's relationship with Europe and the wider world has gone in the last eight millennia.

The first stage was by far the longest, filling a good 7,500 of these years. Figure 0.3, a map painted roughly seven centuries ago by a

Figure 0.3. The Hereford Map, painted by Richard of Haldingham and Lafford soon after 1300 CE. Following medieval conventions, the east (where Jesus would come again) is at the top, and the circle at the centre marks Jerusalem. The British Isles are the blobs squeezed in at the bottom left. Richard's map gives a good sense of the stage on which Britain's story was set in the 7,500 years between its separation from the Continent around 6000 BCE and John Cabot's trip to Newfoundland in 1497 CE.

man named Richard of Haldingham and Lafford, sums it up nicely. The map is big, more than 1.5 m across, and now hangs in a delightful display in a cloister of Hereford Cathedral. Much about it is peculiar to Richard's time and place, such as the conventions of putting east at the top, because that was where Jesus was expected to return, and Jerusalem in the middle, because that, of course, was the centre of the Christian world. Many of its details, however, would have made just as much sense at any time in the previous 7,500 years as in Richard's own age.

Chief among them is the smallness of Richard's world. Symmetry required that a circular map with Jerusalem at its centre include Africa and Asia, but as we move towards the top and right, details become thinner and more fanciful while sketches of mythical monsters multiply to fill in the blank spaces. For Richard, as for everyone who lived before him, Britain's stage was European and above all west European, limited to the lower left quadrant of the map.

Next, Richard saw Britain as being intimately involved with Europe. He drew the English Channel and North Sea no wider than the Rivers Rhine or Seine and narrower than the Nile. He certainly knew that the waters between Britain and the Continent could be dangerous; as recently as 1120, European politics had been capsized when a ship carrying the heir to the English throne went down in the Channel (admittedly, the crew had been roaring drunk). Yet Richard also knew that for every drowning there were hundreds of uneventful crossings. The Channel and North Sea were highways not barriers; Britain's proximity to Europe trumped its insularity.

Most striking of all, while Richard saw Britain as an actor on a European stage, he put it in the wings, not front and centre. Bigger, richer lands in the Mediterranean and Middle East – Italy, Egypt, Iraq, India – hogged the limelight. As we will see in the next few chapters, this was how it had been for millennia. For good and also for ill, every great transformation – from the coming of humans through the arrival of farming, metallurgy, writing, governments, empires and Christianity – had begun far away, on the other side of the Hereford Map. Each such upheaval created imbalances between the places where they began and everyone else, and the imbalances then evened out across space.

Just how this worked has been one of the enduring questions for archaeologists and historians. Antiseptic words like 'imbalances' and 'evening out' cover multitudes of sins. 'Imbalances' were in reality inequalities between societies, involving everything from wealth, knowledge and resources to numbers, efficiency and violence. Sometimes 'evening out' involved creativity and triumphs of the human spirit; at other times it was a matter of terror and slaughter. We will see multiple kinds of imbalance and versions of evening out in the chapters that follow, but one central fact is clear. For the first 7,500 years of their history the British Isles were pretty much the last place that goods, institutions, ideas and values invented on the other side of the map ended up, after arriving everywhere else first.

'Ended up' is the right term, because beyond Britain there was no more map. So far as Richard was concerned, the Atlantic Ocean was the edge of the world. To be sure, plenty of Europeans in his day knew this was not actually true; in the three centuries leading up to Richard's time, global warming had made the North Atlantic sufficiently passable for Vikings to sail all the way from Norway to Newfoundland. But Richard, like most educated men of his day, didn't much care. His ideas about geography came mostly from Greek and Roman writers, who harboured few doubts that, once out of sight of Europe's shores, sailors just fell off the edge of everything. 'Past Cádiz, into the darkness, we must not go!' the poet Pindar had warned Greeks in the 470s BCE. 'What lies beyond is not to be trodden, either by the wise or the unwise'; and the fearless few who ignored him generally either came home disappointed or did not come home at all. There was, the Roman geographer Strabo concluded five centuries later, no there there – just 'destitution and loneliness, while the sea goes on'.

The Hereford Map would have made complete sense to Pindar and Strabo, and, indeed, to almost anyone else in the seventy-odd centuries before Richard painted it. It still made sense nearly two centuries after him, when another Richard, England's third king of that name, was hacked to pieces on Bosworth Field in 1485. Another century after that, though, when Shakespeare wrote his play *Richard III*, the Hereford Map was beginning to look obsolete. 'All the world's a stage', the Bard assured the English (in *As You Like It*), and he was right. The curtain had risen on a new act in the drama, in which Britain effectively travelled from the edge of the earth to its centre. By 1902, when the geographer and explorer Halford Mackinder drew the second of the maps that sum up my story (Figure 0.4), Britain's

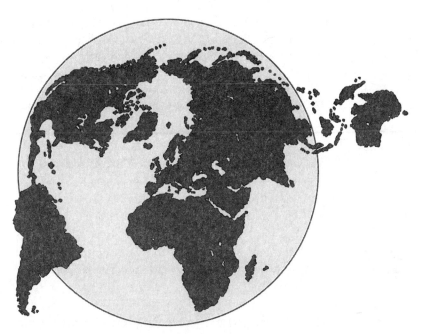

Figure 0.4. Mackinder's Map. Between 1500 and 1700 CE Britain replaced Jerusalem as the centre of the world, turned the oceans into highways and closed the English Channel. Yet by 1902, when Halford Mackinder summed up the new world order in this map, it was already passing away.

stage had expanded to take in most of the planet, and the country had recast itself in the leading role.

Two things had happened since Richard of Haldingham and Lafford's day. The first, beginning while Richard III's wounds were still fresh, was that Europeans began building ships that could fairly reliably cross oceans and come back again. The Atlantic was just as wide as it had ever been, but instead of being a barrier it was now turning into a highway to the world.

Portuguese, Italian and Spanish sailors were the first to burst the Hereford Map's boundaries (John Cabot, the first 'Englishman' known to have set foot in America, was actually a Venetian adventurer named Zuan Chaboto who had settled in Bristol). The reason it is England at the centre of Mackinder's Map, rather than Portugal, Italy or Spain (or even France or the Netherlands), is that the English excelled at combining the new maritime technology with new kinds of organisation. Ever since the Isles became islands, their proximity to the Continent had always trumped their insularity, because anyone who could reach the French side of the Channel could cross it to reach England too. The Hereford Map turned into Mackinder's because governments in London found ways to build fleets strong enough to prevent this. The Channel remained as narrow as ever, but if a Royal Navy could deny its use to enemies, insularity would trump proximity. Philip II of Spain, Louis XIV and Napoleon in France and Hitler in Germany all learned that if the Isles commanded the seas, the 34 km between Dover and Calais might as well be a million.

It is no accident that Shakespeare was the first writer, in the 1590s, to call England a

> . . . *precious stone set in the silver sea,*
> *Which serves it in the office of a wall*
> *Or as a moat defensive to a house,*
> *Against the envy of less happier lands,*
> *This blessed plot, this earth, this realm, this England.*

Chaucer and Malory never said anything like this, because it would simply have made no sense in the 1390s or 1490s. Only in Shakespeare's day did English governments start to become organised enough to turn the Channel into a moat defensive, and over the following century they pulled off one of the most audacious strategic pivots in history. In effect, they swapped their minor part on a European stage for the starring role on an Atlantic one; and, secure behind their wooden walls, they united the whole British Isles into a single state ruled from London while simultaneously creating an intercontinental empire.

For thousands of years imbalances of all kinds had been evening out from their Middle Eastern and Mediterranean starting-points until they reached Britain, but now Britain became the place from which people, goods and ideas rolled downhill. Britons pushed aside or exterminated populations in North America, Australia and (less completely) New Zealand, and, for good measure, took control of everything from Cairo to the Cape and Aden to Singapore. Even Jerusalem, the heart of the Hereford Map, was run by British officials for thirty years.

This was one of the most astonishing achievements in world

history, but – and this cannot be emphasised enough – it was also short-lived. Britain bestrode the world like a colossus, but only for 3 per cent of its 8,000-year history, as opposed to the 95-plus per cent of that history in which Britain was more like Europe's poor cousin. My grandad was born in 1906, only four years after Mackinder drew his map, but by the time Grandad died, in 1980, Mackinder's cartography was as out of date as Richard of Haldingham's.

The first act of Britain's drama, which took the Hereford Map as its stage, gave way to the second between 1500 and 1700, because ships that could cross entire oceans dragged much of the world on to a new stage, which Britain came to dominate. During Grandad's lifetime the second act, performed on Mackinder's Map, gave way to a third for similar reasons. New technologies – telegraph lines and oil-fired engines, container ships and jet planes, satellites and the internet – shrank space even more than sixteenth-century galleons had done. Just as had happened in the seventeenth and eighteenth centuries, people responded by creating new organisations – the United Nations, World Trade Organization and, of course, European Union – to take advantage of the changed meanings of geography. Across the last hundred years the novel technologies and institutions have tied so much of the world together, making the stage so big and so crowded with actors, that Britain has been shoved out of the limelight.

Some theorists like to say that our new, networked world no longer has centres and peripheries like the stages of the first two acts, but the third of my maps (Figure 0.5) suggests otherwise. This is a clever (if slightly disorienting) piece of cartography, allocating space to each nation in proportion to how much of the world's wealth it generates* rather than the physical area it occupies. This Money Map shows that the planet now has three centres: in North America, Western Europe and East Asia. Rather than being king of the hill, as it was in Act II, Britain finds itself perched at the edge of one of the three modern mountains of money. Actors in Beijing, Brussels and Washington, DC, are the ones who matter most on this new stage. The English Channel and the oceans are still there, but are no longer moats defensive. They have been shrunk to insignificance by precision-guided missiles and almost instantaneous information flows.

---

*As calculated by the United Nations in 2018 at purchasing power parity rate, which compensates for differences between countries in the cost of living.

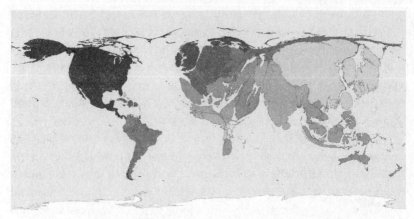

Figure 0.5. The Money Map: three mountains of money in North America, Western Europe and East Asia dominate everything. This disorienting map allocates to each country an area proportional to the amount of the world's wealth it generated in 2018. Britain still has a speaking part on this new stage, but is no longer the star.

If the rise of European and American mountains of money around 1900 twisted Mackinder's Map out of shape, the rise of the Chinese mountain since 2000 burst its bounds altogether. 'The size of China's displacement of the world balance is such that the world must find a new balance', Singapore's prime minister, Lee Kuan Yew, observed in 2012. 'It is not possible to pretend that this is just another big player. *This is the biggest player in the history of the world.*'

Geography's new meanings have overturned established ideas about identity, mobility, prosperity, security and sovereignty. The changes are roiling not just Britain but the entire West. For a quarter of a millennium the nations around the North Atlantic have been the world's centre of gravity. Life was not easy for everyone in the West (my grandad, a steelworker, knew this well), but even so, it was easier – especially for white, middle-class men – than for anyone else. Only in the last thirty years has that really begun changing. Life remains easier in the West than for the rest, but not by as much as it used to be. Fifty years from now, it may no longer be easier at all. The West's superiority no longer feels effortless. The world is more competitive; old ways of doing things cannot be relied on. No wonder Westerners are anxious.

In the 1930s, while the curtain was still coming down on Mackinder's Map, the great British novelist George Orwell already worried that the end of empire would 'reduce England to a cold and unimportant little island where we should all have to work very hard and live mainly on herrings and potatoes'. That didn't happen: Britain still boasts the world's sixth- or ninth-biggest economy (depending on how we count) and probably its fifth-strongest fleet (behind the United States, China, Russia and Japan), and is one of just nine nuclear powers. It has the second-largest haul of Nobel Prizes on the planet, and in 2018 the Soft Power 30 index ranked it number one in the world for its 'ability to achieve objectives through attraction and persuasion'. (It lost the top spot to France in 2019, having been made less appealing by interminable Brexit wrangling.) Britain remains a major actor, even if it no longer stands centre stage. The Royal Navy cannot defend the home islands' shores or commerce. The empire is gone, most of Ireland is gone and in 2014 Scotland came within half a million votes of going too.

A generation after Orwell, the American secretary of state, Dean Acheson, caused outrage by musing that 'Great Britain has lost an empire and has not yet found a role'. Two generations after Acheson, the search is still on. Should Britain be sheltering in the shadow of the American mountain? Or would it do better somewhere on the slopes below Brussels? Or climbing up towards Beijing? Alternatively, could it carve out an independent path between the three peaks? Or then again, could it collaborate with the old English-speaking Commonwealth to heap up a fourth hill of its own? Or try to play several of these roles at the same time? Or even write itself an entirely new role?

By 2016 Britons faced a burning question, but the one on the ballot that summer – 'Should the United Kingdom remain a member of the European Union or leave the European Union?' – was not it. Seen from a big-history perspective, the Brexit debate has simply been a distraction. The twenty-first century will be about Beijing, not Brussels. The real question is where Britain – and, for that matter, the rest of the West – will fit best on a world stage that is tilting eastwards.

A Fourth Map

One of the things that makes this question so difficult to answer is that there is arguably no such thing as 'Britain'. There are 6,390 or so separate islands off Europe's north-west coast, about 150 of which are currently inhabited; and while geography unites their destinies, it also divides them. I therefore want to introduce a fourth map (Figure 0.6), which will have as much claim on our attention in what follows as my first three.

No two isles are exactly the same, but a pair of divisions have been particularly important. The most obvious is between the two largest islands, Ireland and Great Britain (that is, England/Scotland/Wales). Rising sea levels after the Ice Age put water between Ireland and Scotland around 9000 BCE, but the land that became Ireland had been geologically distinct from Great Britain for millions of years before that. Ireland forms a kind of basin, with old sandstone and granite uplands in the north and south ringing a sandy, clayey, boggy and lake-filled depression in the middle.

The second geographical fault line runs through Great Britain, roughly from the mouth of the River Exe in Devon to that of the Esk in Yorkshire. It divides the low-lying, warm and dry (by British standards, anyway) south-east, with its fertile fields of soft, young soils, from the older, harder slate and shale uplands of the colder, wetter north and west. There is a wonderful description of this boundary in one of Jan Struther's *Mrs Miniver* essays (for my money, the most English – or perhaps I should say the most south-eastern and upper-middle-class – stories ever written). Motoring north across the Exe–Esk line in the 1930s, she said, brought her family

> out of the plain at last and climbing up into a completely different country, a country of small steep tumbled fields, rough stone walls, crying sheep, skirling plover, and lonely farmhouses sheltered by clumps of sycamore [. . .] presently the bones of the earth began breaking through the grass in rocky scars and outcrops; and higher still there were no fields at all, but only the bare moors.

That is exactly it.

Geography is unfair: other things being equal, the populations living on north and west Britain's thin soils and Ireland's heavy, wet ones have always been smaller and poorer than those on south-east Britain's fertile soils – which, in turn, have been smaller and poorer than the populations on the even better soils of the West European

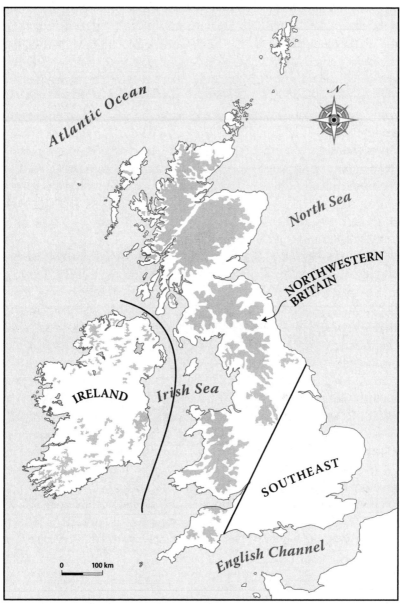

Figure 0.6. Rocks of ages: the three major geographical zones of the British Isles – the fertile lowlands of south-eastern Britain, the poorer highlands of the north and west and the basin of Ireland. Land more than 200 m above sea level is shown in grey.

mainland. As early as 1932, when British archaeology was just getting going, the pioneer Cyril Fox saw what this meant. 'It is the tragedy of British prehistory and history', he explained, 'and the key thereto, that the most habitable and most easily conquerable areas are adjacent to shores whence invaders are most likely to come.' The consequence, he concluded, was that 'In the Lowland [south-east] of Britain new cultures of continental origin tend to be *imposed* on earlier or ab-original culture. In the Highland [north and west], on the other hand, these tend to be *absorbed* by the older culture.' Thus has geography driven identity, mobility, prosperity, security and sovereignty. Most of the time England's history has been about dealing with what comes its way from the Continent, while that of Wales, the north and the West Country, of Scotland and of Ireland, has been about dealing with what comes their way from England.

I grew up in the Midlands city of Stoke-on-Trent, just above the line dividing the south-east from the north and west. It is a betwixt-and-between kind of place in what geographers call the Midland Gap, a 50-km-wide valley between Wales's Cambrian Mountains and northern England's Pennine range – definitely not south-eastern but not exactly northern or western either, and in the 2016 referendum a whopping 69 per cent of people in Stoke-on-Trent voted to go. Journalists took to calling Stoke the 'Brexit capital'. When the parliamentary seat for Stoke Central (where I'd lived as a teenager) fell vacant in 2017, UKIP fancied its chances so much that Paul Nuttall, who had just replaced Nigel Farage as party leader, stood for it himself. He lost (the seat had gone Labour in every election since its creation in 1950; only in 2019 did it turn, to the Tories), but still picked up a quarter of the votes.

I left Stoke-on-Trent in 1978, and have now passed more than half my life overseas, chiefly in Chicago and California. Whether that has broadened my perspective on Britain's place in the world or left me hopelessly out of touch, you will be the judge; but I also spent much of the year leading up to the 2016 referendum as a visiting professor at the London School of Economics, tucked away among the monuments, theatres and restaurants of the Borough of Westminster.* This has to be one of the most international neighbourhoods

---

*I would once again like to thank Manny Roman, Arne Westad and Mick Cox for inviting me, Emilia Knight, Bastiaan Bouwman, Christopher Coker and everyone

on earth (students kept telling me that LSE stood for Learn to Speak English), a place where ideas about identity, mobility, prosperity, security and sovereignty seem to share more with San Francisco than with Stoke-on-Trent. Exactly reversing my home town's vote in 2016, 69 per cent of Westminsterians wanted to stay.

So different are the regions in Figure 0.6 that we might hesitate to lump them together under the label 'British'. Between 1916 and 1923, at least 5,000 people died in bloody disagreements about whether Ireland was British, and in my own lifetime another 3,500 have been killed – more than in the 11 September attacks on the United States – over whether even Ireland's north-east corner should be considered so. In earlier centuries, more still died in similar arguments over Scotland and Wales.

Not surprisingly, plenty of people shun the B-word altogether. The journalist Eddie Holt even suggested in 2006, only partly in jest, that since 'the islands in question are huddled around a body of water [. . .] known as the Irish Sea, it seems only common sense to take the logical leap. Nobody, surely, could have any difficulty with the Irish Isles?' To avoid such arguments, officials in Dublin and London speak just of 'these islands' when they draw up joint documents. The historian Norman Davies, having written a fine thousand-page monograph about this part of the world, says he toyed with 'the British and Irish Isles', 'Europe's Offshore Islands' and the 'Anglo-Celtic Archipelago' as titles, before settling on the studiedly neutral *The Isles*.

I often borrow Davies's term in this book, but also use 'Britain' and 'British Isles' as shorthand for the entire archipelago. I have two reasons for this. First, the names are just so familiar that avoiding them feels pedantic. They go back to the oldest surviving discussion, written around 330 BCE, in which the Greek philosopher Aristotle (or perhaps one of his pupils) says that 'The two biggest islands, Albion [Great Britain] and Ierne [Ireland], are called the British Isles'. The Greek word he uses, *Brettanikai*, probably came from a Celtic word, *Pretani*, meaning 'the painted ones' or 'tattooed people'. Because some Britons were still dyeing themselves when Julius Caesar came and saw them in 55 BCE, Romans took to calling the province they created in modern

else at LSE IDEAS for making my visits to London so engaging and entertaining, and the students in my seminars, especially Jared McKinney and Jeff Kempler, for their insights and company.

England and Wales 'Britannia'. No author mentions skin painting after about 100 CE or tattoos after 400, but the name stuck.

The second, and more important, reason is that despite all the ways in which geography divides the Isles, its unifying force is ultimately greater. Calling the islands 'British' no more implies that all 6,390 of them should be ruled from London than that the people who live in them should still be painting themselves blue. The shared label 'British' just acknowledges a fundamental fact, forced on us by geography: that, much as they might quarrel, the people of the Isles are all in this together.

A Road Map

As historians have been doing since Thucydides' day, I make my case by telling a story, showing how one thing led to another. I begin in the centuries leading up to 6000 BCE, when rising seas were separating the Isles from the Continent. The first half of the book (Part I, 'The Hereford Map') takes us to 1497 CE, when Cabot showed that the Hereford Map was not in fact the whole stage; and its main point is that Britain's history was always driven by the geographical fact of being a cluster of islands at the Continent's furthest edge.

Part II, 'Mackinder's Map', looks at how the roles open to Britain were revolutionised as its stage expanded to take in the Atlantic and Indian Oceans. This takes nearly one-third of the book, although the years it describes – 1497–1945 – comprise barely one-fortieth of our story. This was, in many ways, the most extraordinary part of Britain's history, but that is not the only reason for the disproportion. Brexiteers often talked in 2016 as if Mackinder's Map were somehow the world's natural state, to which it would default once Britain shed its Continental entanglements. But that thinking was mistaken. Geography had to take on very particular meanings for Mackinder's Map to be possible, and by 1945 those meanings had passed away for ever.

Part III, 'The Money Map', covers just one and a half centuries, and even that only by dint of devoting much of Chapter 11 to things that haven't happened yet. I make no attempt here to refight the 2016 referendum. Instead, I ask what the 10,000-year-long logic governing Britain's place in the world tells us about where the Isles will go next – because, while the past is not a very good guide to the future, it's the only one we've got.

Part I

THE HEREFORD MAP, 6000 BCE–1497 CE

1

THATCHER'S LAW, 6000–4000 BCE

Catch-22

'We are inextricably part of Europe,' Margaret Thatcher told Britain in 1975. 'Neither Mr Foot nor Mr Benn' – the chief Brexiteers of the day – 'nor anyone else will ever be able to take us "out of Europe", for Europe is where we are and where we have always been.'

This may sound odd, given Mrs Thatcher's later reputation as the arch-enemy of European integration, and some historians do wonder whether she really meant it. After all, she had just taken over a Conservative Party whose biggest recent success had been taking Britain into the European Community; now that a Labour government was putting this achievement to a referendum, honour surely required her to defend it. Yet, whatever Thatcher's inner qualms (to which we will return in Chapter 10), her advice to the nation on the eve of the first Brexit referendum laid bare, as well as anyone has ever done, the fundamental facts of Britain's position. So compelling is her claim – that *Britain is inextricably part of Europe and cannot be taken out of it, for Europe is where Britain is and where it has always been* – that I am going to call it Thatcher's Law.

Like all scientific laws, Thatcher's has exceptions. Britain has not really 'always been' in Europe, because there has not always been a Europe to be in. Our planet has existed for 4.6 billion years, but shifting continental plates only began creating what we now call Europe about 200 million years ago. That caveat aside, however, Britain was very literally part of Europe for 99 per cent of these 200 million years, because the Isles were not islands at all but one end of a great plain stretching unbroken from Russia to an Atlantic coastline lying 150 km west of modern Galway (Figure 1.1). For want of a better name, I will call this huge, ancient extension of the Continent 'Proto-Britain'.

During the multiple ice ages which filled much of the last 2.5 million years, glaciers sucked so much water out of the oceans that

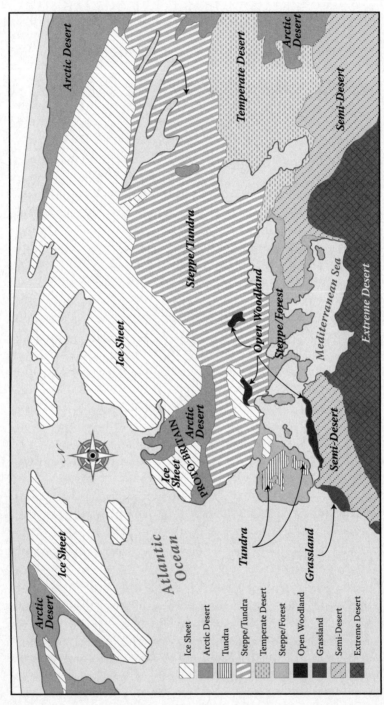

Figure 1.1. The expansion of Europe: coastlines and glaciers at the coldest point of the last ice age, around 20,000 years ago.

what we now know as the North Sea and Eastern Atlantic were largely above sea level. At the coldest point, 20,000 years ago, temperatures averaged 6 °C cooler than today. Ice sheets up to 3 km thick covered much of the northern hemisphere, trapping 120 million billion tons of water and leaving the sea level 100 m lower.

Nothing could live on the glaciers that blanketed the future Scotland, Ireland, Wales and northern England at the coldest points of the last ice age, and the tundras which stretched 150 km or more beyond their southern edge were scarcely more welcoming. At some points ice locked up so much moisture that barely one-fifth as much rain fell as nowadays and the air carried ten to twenty times as much dust. Even more than the cold, this aridity meant that very few plants could grow in Proto-Britain, and so there were very few animals around eating them, and no people at all eating anything.

The first human-like apes (anthropologists argue endlessly over how to define 'human') evolved on East Africa's savannahs around 2.5 million years ago, immediately creating the original geostrategic imbalance. The pattern that we will see over and over again in this book, of imbalances arising in one place and evening out across space, is therefore as old as humanity itself. In this case the evening out took hundreds of thousands of years, as proto-humans migrated into previously humanless parts of Africa. However, in another pattern that we will keep seeing, new imbalances were created as fast as earlier ones evened out, because new kinds of humans went on evolving, whether back in the original East African homeland or from interbreeding among the humans spreading into Asia and Europe. By 1.5 million years ago, people who could communicate in complicated ways – even if what they did was not exactly talking – had fanned out as far as Indonesia, China and the Balkans. Only during warmer, wetter breaks in the ice ages could they work their way further across Europe, but in one of these periods, nearly a million years ago, the first proto-humans wandered into Proto-Britain.

The evidence comes from a tangle of footprints on a muddy tidal riverbank at Happisburgh (pronounced, because this is England, 'Hazebruh') in Norfolk (Figure 1.2). After being buried by drifting sand, the mud hardened, preserving the tracks until 2013, when storms washed away the material covering them. Within two weeks the waters had washed away the footsteps too, but that was long enough for archaeologists to pounce and record every detail –

Figure 1.2. The British stage, 1,000,000 BCE to 4000 BCE (on a map showing modern coastlines).

earning, quite rightly, *Current Archaeology* magazine's 'Rescue Dig of the Year' award.

There is no way to date a footprint, but we do have two techniques for fixing in time the mud into which those ancient feet sank. We can get a rough sense from magnetised particles in the mud, because every 450,000 years or so the earth's magnetic poles reverse direction. When the Happisburgh mud was laid down, a compass needle would have pointed towards what we now call the South Pole, suggesting that the mud is close to a million years old; and we can sharpen that up with the second technique, looking at fossils (above all, voles' teeth) in the sediments, indicating a date 850,000–950,000 years ago.

The excavators speculate that a little band – perhaps five people, some of them children – made their mark on this ancient strand while gathering shellfish and seaweed for a meal. We do not know what kind of proto-humans they were, since they left no bones behind them. The earliest fossils of Proto-Britons are in fact only half as old as the Happisburgh footprints: a shinbone and two teeth found near another ancient riverbank at Boxgrove in Sussex, belonging to a tall, muscular, forty-something Heidelberg Man (in a tradition going back to the nineteenth century, archaeologists divide pre-humans into categories called 'So-and-So Man' – often named, as in this case, after the place where the first example was found [Figure 1.3]).* These creatures – strangely like us, yet strangely not – evolved about 600,000 years ago, probably in Africa, and were ancestral to both Neanderthals and ourselves.

Following another long-standing tradition, this Heidelberg Man's excavators christened him Roger, after the volunteer who dug him up. The prehistoric Roger apparently lived during one of the balmier breaks in the ice ages, when Proto-Britain was even warmer than the Isles are now, and rhinoceros and elephant roamed across southern England. A simple climatic pattern shaped what Proto-Britain's geography meant. During warm, wet breaks in the Ice Age, such as Roger's day, imbalances created by new kinds of proto-humans evolving in Africa or Europe would keep evening out until they reached the edge of the world along the Atlantic; but in colder, drier phases,

---

*Those who prefer their gendered language to be Latin call Boxgrove Person a *Homo heidelbergensis*.

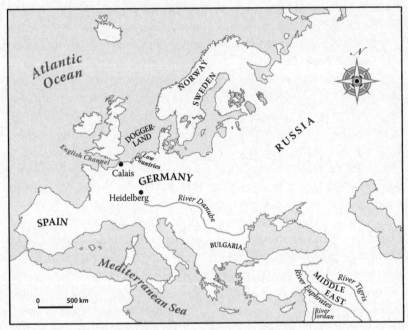

Figure 1.3. The European stage, 1,000,000 BCE to 4000 BCE
(on a map showing modern coastlines).

geography did what Michael Foot and Tony Benn could not. Ice and
dust turned Proto-Britain and much of the rest of the territory north
of the Alps and Pyrenees into uninhabitable wastelands, effectively
taking them out of Europe.

However, there was a complication: while global warming could
make Proto-Britain part of Europe, *too much* global warming, like too
little, could take it out again. Around 450,000 years ago, the collapse
of a melting glacier in what is now the North Sea released a vast lake
of frigid water which had been trapped behind it. For months on
end, more than a million tons of water rushed through the breach
every second of every day, gouging valleys and distinctive, teardrop-
shaped hills into the floor of what is now the English Channel. The
tsunami blasted through the high chalk ridge that had linked modern
Dover and Calais, carving out the depression we now call the English
Channel and turning Proto-Britain into Proto-British Isles.

In this dramatic fashion insularity entered Britain's story and
created a climatic Catch-22. When the Isles were warm enough to

live in, the English Channel would be full of water, and, whatever their other skills, Roger and his kind could not cross 34 km of open sea. But when Europe got cold enough for falling sea levels to turn the Channel into a land bridge, it was usually too cold for anyone to cross it and live in Proto-Britain. Climate amended Thatcher's Law: the Isles could only be part of Europe when, like Baby Bear's porridge in the Goldilocks story, they were neither too hot nor too cold but just right. Ice in the Channel and water in the Channel both cut Britain off.

So far as we know, the long period between about 400,000 and 225,000 years ago saw no Goldilocks moments. Britain remained empty of proto-humans until a brand-new imbalance emerged: the evolution of Neanderthals about 300,000 years ago, either back in the African core or somewhere on the European frontier. Hardier and cleverer than Heidelberg Men, they could cope better with the cold. Eighteen of their teeth show that they had migrated as far north-west as Pontnewydd in Wales by 225,000 years ago. For the next 250 centuries they made Proto-Britain's tundras their hunting grounds (their bone chemistry reveals that they were prodigious eaters of red meat). They disappeared only when, somewhere around 160,000 years ago (the dating is still unclear), a new megaflood – even bigger than the first one – carved the English Channel even deeper. Cut off from Continental reinforcements, Britain's Neanderthals went extinct, and there are no certain signs of humans in the Isles until temperatures again hit a Goldilocks spot some 60,000 years ago, cold enough for the waves to withdraw from a land bridge but warm enough for Neanderthals to migrate north-west as far as Derbyshire. Beyond that, not even they could go.

Brexits and Bre-Entries

To a Neanderthal, Thatcher's Law would have sounded ridiculous. It was just not true that Britain was inextricably part of Europe. Rather, it cycled in and out, and, whether through being too warm or too cold, was out more often than in. What eventually broke this pattern was the evolution of us – fully modern humans, with the intellectual abilities to innovate in technology and organisation and thereby to manage the meanings of geography.

Around 300,000 years ago, at roughly the time the first Ne-

anderthals appeared, our own version of humanity – *Homo sapiens*,
'Wise Man' – was also evolving in Africa. It remains unclear whether
the first *Homo sapiens* really were wiser than Neanderthals, but by
100,000 years ago their descendants definitely were, which created
a geostrategic imbalance that evened out faster than any before.
Turning right as they left Africa, *Homo sapiens* had reached Australia
by 60,000 years ago; turning left, they crossed the land bridge into
Proto-Britain around 43,000 years ago (there is some debate over the
age of Britain's oldest *Homo sapiens* remains, three teeth and a chunk
of jaw from Kents Cavern in Torquay).

The newcomers looked, walked and talked exactly like you or
me – so much so that the first scholar to excavate one of their skeletons (William Buckland, Reader in Geology at Oxford University),
at Paviland in south Wales in 1823, could not credit how old it was.
Buckland was a scrupulous scientist, and the fact that he found a
mammoth's skull next to the bones should have been a clue that they
were really ancient. However, Buckland was also a devout Christian, convinced that the Bible ruled out the possibility of humans
living alongside extinct animals. Certain that the mammoth dated
from before Noah's flood and the human from after it, he reasoned
that gravediggers had dislodged an antediluvian relic, creating the
misleading impression that the person and the pachyderm were contemporaries. Since the Roman army had built a camp near Paviland,
Buckland also reasoned that the skeleton dated to Roman times; and
since it was adorned with red ochre and ivory jewellery, he reasoned
further that it was a woman. In one last piece of reasoning he concluded that, since this 'Red Lady of Paviland' (as he named her) was
a woman wearing cosmetics and living near a military base, she was
probably a prostitute.

Rarely has a line of reasoning been so wrong. Radiocarbon
dating, which allows physicists to fix the date of any organic object
less than 50,000 years old from the balance between different isotopes
of carbon in it, suggests that, far from practising the oldest profession
in the first few centuries CE, the Red Lady was actually a forager who
lived around 31,000 BCE. And, thanks to better understanding of skeletons, we are also sure that the lady was a man.

By the time the Red Gentleman went to meet his maker, Britain's
Neanderthals had long since gone to meet theirs. Some archaeologists think that immigrant *Homo sapiens* hunted Neanderthals into

extinction or outcompeted them for food; others, that climate change or disease did the job. Either way, modern humans had Proto-Britain to themselves for the next 20,000 years, until the ice took Proto-Britain out of Europe again. By 20,000 BCE temperatures had reached the lowest levels on record. Glaciers buried everything except England and Ireland's south coasts, and even these were too cold and dry to inhabit. *Homo sapiens* abandoned not just Proto-Britain but almost everything north of the Alps.

Predictably, when things warmed up again after 15,000 BCE, humans migrated back into Proto-Britain. Recent advances in extracting and analysing ancient DNA suggest that the first settlers spread northwards from Spain up the Atlantic coast, advancing all the way to Edinburgh by 11,000 BCE; but two centuries after that, bitter cold once again drove everyone out of Proto-Britain. Another 1,200 years passed before it was warm enough for immigrants to return. First came plants, with scrawny birch, willow and aspen trees spreading northwest to join the grasses and shrubs which had been all that could live on the ice-age tundra. By 8000 BCE hazel had arrived too, and by 7000 BCE forests of oak, elm and alder covered much of Proto-Britain, especially the south-east. Deer, elk and wild horses and pigs colonised these woods, along with the predators who ate them – brown bears, wolves, wild cats and, of course, us.

I say 'us' advisedly. These newcomers, advancing from the Balkans, Italy and Spain as the glaciers retreated, are the first Britons whose DNA can still be detected in Islanders' bodies today. We have known this since 1996, when the geneticist Bryan Sykes extracted fragments of ancient DNA from one of the teeth of Cheddar Man, a prehistoric Briton who was excavated in 1903 after being buried in a cave in Cheddar Gorge just over 10,000 years earlier. Sykes enlisted a local schoolteacher named Adrian Targett to help him gather DNA samples from people living around the site, so he could measure how much the gene pool had changed since prehistory. To his delight, he found one definite descendant of Cheddar Man: Targett himself, who lived less than a kilometre from Cheddar Gorge.

By 2019 geneticists were also able to show that Cheddar Man, this oldest of Englishmen, had had 'blue/green eyes, dark brown (possibly black) hair and dark or dark-to-black skin'. Modern Britons' pale pigmentation and sensitivity to the sun seem only to have spread through the gene pool in the last three or four millennia. All the same,

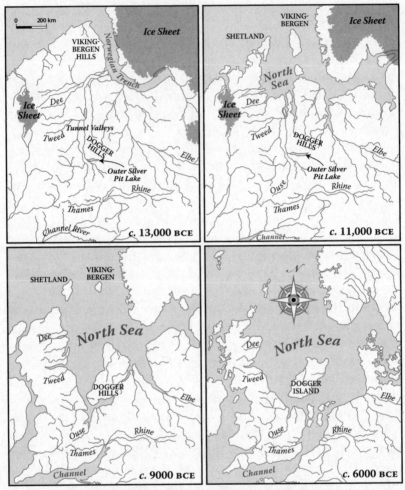

Figure 1.4. Paradise regained and lost: retreating ice sheets
exposed fertile new territory, but as sea levels rose, much
of it was drowned (top left, 13,000 BCE; top right, 11,000 BCE;
bottom left, 9000 BCE; bottom right, 6000 BCE).

says Targett, 'I can definitely see that there is a family resemblance' to
the latest reconstruction.

When Cheddar Man's ancestors migrated into Proto-Britain,
the far north and west were warm enough to live in but still linked
by land to the rest of Europe, but this only lasted a few centuries. By
9000 BCE rising, post-Ice Age oceans had flooded a channel between

Proto-Ireland and Proto-Scotland, and the waves of what we now call the North Sea were encroaching on the 100,000 km² plain which geologists know as Doggerland. By 6000 BCE the waters of the English Channel had drowned the valleys between France and England (Figure 1.4). In any earlier time this would have taken Proto-Britain back out of Europe, but modern humans now rose to the challenge. Neanderthals' replacement by *Homo sapiens* had made all the difference in the world.

As had happened 425,000 and 160,000 years earlier, there were tsunamis of awe-inspiring violence, but the main force washing away the land bridge between Britain and the Continent was the almost invisible, millimetres-at-a-time, creep of rising sea levels. This gently turned dry land into mud, forests into bogs, bogs into rivers and finally rivers into a narrow sea. For several generations it would have been difficult to say whether England was joined to the Continent or not, giving Proto-Britons plenty of time to adapt to increasing insularity. They resisted extrication from Europe with a tool that shaped all subsequent British and Irish history: the boat.

Archaeologists know little about the earliest boats, because the only way a hull can possibly be found is if it: (a) was abandoned somewhere no oxygen could reach it; (b) lay undisturbed for thousands of years; and (c) was rediscovered by someone who realised that this particular piece of wet wood was special. Given the odds against this, our information is patchy, although the world's two oldest known boats do come from just this period and just this part of the planet. Both are split, hollowed-out pine logs about 3 m long, one from a riverbank in the Netherlands and the other from a similar setting in northern France. Both were carved around 7000 BCE. However, only the most reckless mariner would have risked paddling either across the Channel. No log-boat substantial enough to stay afloat on the open sea is known before 4000 BCE – perhaps, some botanists say, because only then was the weather warm enough to support trees big enough to make seaworthy canoes.

Fortunately, the absence of evidence for Channel-crossing boats is not evidence of absence, because we know people were sailing the north-western seas before 4000 BCE. The pattern of settlement along the coast of Norway after 9800 BCE, for instance, makes sense only if people were moving by water, and huge cod and haddock bones from some sites in Brittany and Sweden could only have got there if fishermen were operating far out from shore. Further afield, people

Figure 1.5. Rulers of the waves: a gold model of a hide boat, or currach, buried at Broighter, County Derry, in the first century BCE. It would take a miracle for real examples of such flimsy boats to survive for archaeologists to find, but they were probably common in British waters by 6000 BCE.

had crossed from south-west Asia to Cyprus by 10,000 BCE, and on the other side of the world they were reaching Pacific islands a full 40,000 years earlier. Even if we cannot find their boats, Proto-Britons were definitely crossing the narrow seas.

Sailors may have stabilised logboats with outriggers, like modern Polynesian canoes, which would account for the rows of holes drilled along the sides of some Danish hulls. However, more likely than not, sailors around 6000 BCE were crossing the English Channel in hide boats like the currachs that can still be seen today on the Irish Sea. Such flimsy vessels stand little chance of surviving for us to find, but in the third century BCE the Greek historian Timaeus reported that Britons were making six-day sea crossings in them. They probably looked like Figure 1.5, a magnificent gold model buried in Ireland in the first century BCE. By then, sailors had probably been crossing the British seas in such vessels for millennia.

By 6000 BCE water in the Channel was no longer enough to extricate the Isles from the Continent. Boats had made the narrow sea a highway instead of a barrier. While Britain remained the edge of the world, it could not be taken out of Europe altogether. For the next 7,500 years the Islanders' story would be one of learning to live with what came their way from the Continent as one imbalance after another evened out towards the Atlantic.

Land of the Free

Post-Ice-Age Britain had a lot in common with contemporary Continental societies, but almost nothing in common with subsequent British history. Technology and organisation were primarily responsible for this. Archaeology tells us a lot about the former (although less about the latter). We know that this was a world without metal: everything we excavate – tools, weapons, ornaments – was made from stone, bone, shell or wood. The products could be surprisingly effective (the archaeologist Francis Pryor tells an excellent story in his book *Britain BC* about a butcher near the site of Boxgrove happily slicing joints of meat with prehistoric flint blades), but they also had limits. Just try digging holes using an antler as a pick or a shovel made from a cow's shoulder blade. The vast numbers of excavated animal bones and carbonised seeds also show that that this was a world without farming. Everyone who lived in Britain before about 4000 BCE survived by hunting wild animals, fishing and/or gathering wild plants.

Moving from technology to organisation means interpreting archaeological finds through analogies. The good news is that nineteenth- and twentieth-century colonial administrators and academics encountered plenty of hunter–gatherers still using stone-age technologies; the bad is that there are nevertheless huge differences between modern foragers and their prehistoric predecessors. Most obviously, prehistoric foragers had the most fertile places on earth as their hunting (and gathering) grounds, but modern foragers were long ago driven into the forests, deserts and jungles that no one else wanted. It also seems that no modern hunter–gatherer society is so remote as to escape the impact of industrialisation. One of my enduring memories of spending time in Tanzania in 1986 is of standing behind a young Maasai hunter, his spear over one shoulder and his kill over the other, while he drank a bottle of Coke and waited for a bus to take him home after a hard day chasing game. Cheddar Man did not have such options.

Arguments over how far modern analogies illuminate prehistory can be heated, but a few conclusions are probably safe. One is that Stone Age technology typically required hunter–gatherer societies to be fragmented, fluid and flat, just like more recent ones: fragmented, because populations were tiny and separated by wide spaces; fluid, because they were highly mobile; and flat, because they could support only minimal variations in wealth and power.

Modern foraging societies, using simple technologies in hostile environments, rarely average more than one person per square kilometre, and regularly need 10 km^2 of forest or scrub to support a single hunter or gatherer. Britain around 6000 BCE was more fertile, and certainly had enough plants and animals to feed denser crowds. But how dense? Lacking agreed-on methods of calculation, archaeologists hesitate to guess, but Barry Cunliffe suggests that 'the population may have reached several hundred thousand' by 4500 BCE. Reasoning back from what the population would be in Roman times, that strikes me as a bit high; but even if only 100,000 people lived in the Isles' 313,000 km^2, there would be almost one body per 3 km^2. Although we cram 675 people into the same space today, this would have been a madding crowd by modern hunter–gatherers' standards.

Recent foragers typically lived in tiny bands of just a dozen or so wanderers, constantly moving around territories a few dozen kilometres across as they followed migrating animals, spawning fish and ripening plants. They regularly walked 5,000 km a year (as compared with 300 for the average twenty-first-century Briton), but rarely went more than 50 km at a time from their home bases. Judging from the size of excavated campsites and the kinds of foods consumed, most prehistoric foragers were just as mobile; and if this is right, their low density and high mobility will have had direct consequences for how they organised themselves.

Their identities, like those of modern hunter–gatherers, were probably complicated. Tiny modern bands typically have a strong sense of their own specialness, buttressed by complicated stories about what makes them unique; yet biology requires them to belong to larger networks too, because the genetic consequences of breeding in a pool containing fewer than fifty potential mates are disastrous. Swapping gossip and goods with larger groups can also be a matter of life and death. In ancient times, as in modern, the wise forager would probably identify most strongly with a few close kin while preserving (or inventing) ties to more distant relatives and friends who might be scattered over thousands of square kilometres.

Some archaeological finds from prehistoric Britain hint at such links. Tools made from mudstone, bloodstone and pitchstone (wonderful names) show up scores of kilometres from the minerals' Hebridean sources, perhaps passed as gifts at festivals from one pair of hands to another until they broke or wore out. Objects made from Devonshire slate turn up 300 km away in Essex; several styles of English stone arrowheads and bone harpoons have their best parallels in Germany; and plenty of coastal communities kept up contacts with the Continent well after the Channel formed. Most remarkable of all, three ivory ornaments found alongside the Red Gentleman of Paviland have striking parallels in Russia.

What all this means is, admittedly, anyone's guess. After all, the fact that most of the world's bras are nowadays made in Guangdong does not mean that women everywhere feel Chinese (I will return to this issue in Chapter 11). But one site, Star Carr in Yorkshire, looks as though it must have hosted festivals bringing people together from far and wide to express some kind of shared identity. It sprawled over an area the size of two or three football fields, making it eighty times bigger than any other Proto-British campsite, and was visited repeatedly between about 8770 and 8460 BCE. The groups congregating here might have been hundreds strong. Around 8500 BCE someone built a tepee 3 m across – the oldest building known in Britain – and a 30-m-long wooden platform, from which they tossed ornaments, weapons and entire deer carcasses into a lake. Some of the celebrants dressed up, for who knows what disturbing rites, in slasher-movie-type masks, crudely carved from the skulls of red deer (Figure 1.6).

There was a lot to like about the foraging life. Studies of human skeletons and food scraps suggest that post-Ice-Age Britons usually enjoyed healthy, tasty and varied diets. In the twentieth century foragers rarely needed to spend more than ten hours hunting or gathering each week, despite living in barren settings; in prehistoric Britain the pickings must have been even easier. Finally, ancient hunter–gatherers, like modern ones, probably shared the wealth very evenly. Mobile modern foragers find it difficult to assert ownership over the wild plants and animals on which life depends, and if someone does manage to accumulate material goods, he or she is hard-pressed to drag them around the countryside every time the band moves on. As a

Figure 1.6. Prehistoric Halloween? A mask carved from a red deer skull around 8600 BCE, found at Star Carr in Yorkshire.

result, archaeologists find no rich burials from early Britain or Ireland (although, admittedly, they find few burials of any kind), let alone luxury homes. Britain's earliest houses, like the Star Carr tepee, were actually quite big: some huts were as much as 6 m across, framed with tree trunks 30 cm thick and probably covered with turf or thatch. Each site seems to have had just one such wigwam, which looks as though it sheltered the whole band rather than a single Stone Age plutocrat. Only after 7000 BCE do we find multiple huts on a single site, Mount Sandel in Northern Ireland, but even these are all much the same size.

But there were things not to like too. 'The inherent vice of capitalism', Churchill once said, 'is the unequal sharing of blessings; the inherent virtue of socialism is the equal sharing of miseries.' Prehistoric foragers – whom Marx and Engels saw as the very model of primitive communists – had a lot of misery to share. Tasty as their diets may have been, telltale marks in their tooth enamel show that seasonal shortages made malnutrition commonplace. They were also extremely poor. Their campsites are littered with thousands of chips of stone from making tools, but their only other household goods were baskets, mats and an animal skin or two for clothes. (There was no weaving in Britain before 2500 BCE, and cloth remained rare until 1500 BCE.)

I use the phrase 'extremely poor' deliberately. The World Bank defines extreme poverty – as compared with everyday, run-of-the-mill poverty – as an income equivalent to less than US $1.90 per day. The global economy's greatest triumph since the 1990s has been to lift more than a billion people, mostly Asians, out of extreme poverty; its greatest tragedy, to have left another billion – including all surviving hunter–gatherers – mired in that miserable condition. Converting prehistoric standards of living into dollar incomes is at best tricky and at worst slightly absurd, because too much (such as buses and Coca-Cola) is incommensurable; but judging from what archaeologists dig up, prehistoric foragers were even poorer than modern ones. The economist Angus Maddison was probably not far wrong in guesstimating premodern hunter–gatherers' incomes at the equivalent of around $1.10 per day.

Hunter–gatherer sovereignty seems to have had the same glass-half-full/glass-half-empty quality as their prosperity. Twentieth-century anthropologists never encountered rulers or ruled among foragers. In one classic story, a hunter in 1970s Botswana – irritated by an academic's endless questions about chiefs – eventually told him: 'Of course we have headmen! In fact, we're all headmen . . . each one of us is headman over himself!' Because they probably lived in larger groups than foragers in the twentieth-century Kalahari Desert, post-Ice-Age Britons might also have had more powerful headmen, but judging by the scarcity of finds that could reasonably be construed as symbols of power and inequality, headmen were not powerful enough to change the basic rules of modern bands. Good talkers generally get their way more than the inarticulate, the old more than the young and men more than women, but no one is really in charge. Decisions affecting everyone tend to be made through interminable discussions, dragging on until no one has the energy to argue any more; and no band ever rules another. Personal sovereignty is paramount.

One downside of modern hunter–gatherers' easy-going attitude towards sovereignty is that institutions of all kinds are weak, especially those for resolving disputes. Anthropologists argue over just how violent modern foraging societies are in the absence of law courts and police, but a growing number of studies suggest that in the twentieth century as many as one hunter–gatherer in ten met a bloody end. In twenty-first-century nation-states, by contrast, even when all the world's murders, wars and related horrors are bundled together, just 1 person in 140 dies violently. In Scandinavia, the safest place of all, barely 1 in 100,000 does so, despite what Nordic *noir* murder mysteries might lead us to believe.

Arguments also rage over whether modern statistics are relevant to the past, but as a case in point we might just return to Cheddar Man. He was shuffled off this mortal coil around 8300 BCE by two powerful blows to the left side of his head, of just the kind that a right-handed assailant would deliver with a stone axe. Even more alarmingly, when excavators dug into layers of earth beneath his body, they found human long bones deliberately smashed with rocks, a prised-open ribcage, a jawbone scarred when someone had used a stone blade to saw off a tongue plus a neck chopped in ways suggesting its owner had been beheaded while lying face-down. At least five skulls (one of them taken from a three-year-old) had been scalped and turned into drinking cups.

Little about Cheddar Man's identity, mobility, prosperity, security and sovereignty would have surprised his contemporaries on the Continent; yet far away, in the Middle East, changes had begun that would destroy everything about this way of life. By 6000 BCE, when the English Channel formed, new ways of life had arrived everywhere from Greece to the Danube Valley, and 2,000 years after that the revolution reached Britain's shores. And it was all driven by that most dangerous of forces: foreign food.

Down on the Farm

There was not much foreign food in Stoke-on-Trent when I was a lad. Even Indian cuisine, already a staple in cosmopolitan places such as Bradford and Birmingham, was unusual. So, when my mother served up a curry for a family dinner in the early 1970s, she knew she was being daring. It contained nothing as exotic as cumin or coriander (let alone curry powder), but even so, my grandad – his face set in disapproval – appeared to be chewing each grain of rice individually to make sure it was safe to swallow. The whole family frowned on pitta bread, and I did not encounter souvlaki or hummus until I made my own way to the Mediterranean in 1980.

That said, people in Stoke certainly had the option of seeking out an Indian or even Middle Eastern meal rather than an English one, but prehistoric foragers did not. Of necessity, they ate whatever was available locally. So, while Middle Easterners hunted wild sheep, goats and gazelles and gathered seeds from wild wheat and barley, Britons stalked wild elk, deer and horses (mammoths had gone extinct 2,000 years earlier) and collected water chestnuts, acorns, hazelnuts (a single storage pit excavated on the Scottish island of Colonsay contained 100,000 hazelnut shells) and wild apples and pears.

Almost as soon as the last ice age ended, these differences began changing the world. The upheaval started in the Middle East. The plants and animals growing there were special, particularly the wild wheat and barley which flourished in an arc linking the headwaters of the Rivers Jordan, Euphrates and Tigris. These were annual grasses, sprouting, producing seeds and dying in one season. When a plant ripened, its rachis (little stalks attaching individual seeds to the main body of the plant) would weaken, and, one by one, its seeds would fall to the ground. There, their protective husks shattered and they germinated. At least, that is what almost always happened, but a few plants – just one per one or two million normal plants – had a random mutation on a single gene which strengthened the rachis and the husk. When these seeds ripened, instead of falling to the ground and shattering they simply stayed where they were.

Until humans came along, this did not matter. Mutant seeds would die without reproducing; random genetic variations would generate roughly the same number of mutants the following year. If our ancestors had been like cattle, just coming along and eating wild wheat and barley off the stalk, the mutations still would not have mattered, because the mutant seeds would have passed through people's guts along with the normal ones with no consequences. But everything began to change the moment an unknown woman (in modern foraging societies women do most of the plant-gathering, and things were probably the same in prehistory too), realising that wild cereals grew better in some spots than others, took the obvious step of deliberately planting seeds in these places.

Mutant plants would be slightly over-represented in her garden, because some of the normal seeds would already have fallen before she got to them, but every last mutant would still be attached to the plant, waiting for her to come along. Every time she replanted seeds, the proportion of mutants would increase slightly. The process was so slow that it would have been invisible to the actors involved, but after a couple of thousand years, instead of one mutant plant per field of one or two million normal ones, harvesters had *only* mutant wheat or barley. Botanists call this process domestication, meaning the genetic modification of one species to create a new one which can only survive if another species (normally us) continually intervenes in its reproduction.

Domesticated seeds are distinctive, and start turning up on archaeo-logical sites near the Rivers Jordan, Tigris and Euphrates dating as early as 9500 BCE, just after the last ice age ended. Even a millennium later, they were still quite rare, but the finds suggest that by 8000 BCE roughly half the wheat and barley in the Jordan and upper Euphrates valleys had tough rachis and husks. By 7500 BCE virtually all plants did. While women were taming plants, men (probably) were doing the same with animals. The genomes of sheep, goats and cows respond to selective pressures in just the same ways as those of wheat and barley, and the more that foragers managed their prey, the more they turned wild animals into domesticated ones and turned themselves from hunters into herders. This too took millennia, but by 7000 BCE shepherds had channelled their flocks' reproduction to breed bigger, calmer beasts.

By 4000 BCE plant and animal domestication had converged in the ox-drawn plough, using domesticated beasts of burden to plant much larger areas than was possible using hand-held hoes. Fields of carefully managed, domesticated wheat and barley that waited for farmers to come along and harvest them now yielded dozens or even hundreds of times more calories than equivalent areas of wild plants. People steadily turned more calories into more of themselves. Before farming was invented, the world's population had doubled every 10,000 years or so; after, the doubling time fell to 2,000 years. In 9600 BCE there had been one or two Middle Eastern foragers per square kilometre; by 3500 BCE there were four or five farmers, and in some spots twenty or thirty.

Archaeologists often call this drawn-out process the 'agricultural revolution', because it turned almost everything upside down. Most immediately, it affected mobility, shrinking the forager's wide world of multiple campsites and hunting or gathering grounds into the farmer's narrow one of a fixed house and fields. (Shepherds' worlds were somewhere in between.) Women felt this even more than men. Walking thousands of kilometres every year, as female foragers typically did, was all but impossible for mothers with multiple small children to move around. Women therefore typically bore just four babies over a reproductive lifetime, two of whom, on average, grew up to make babies of their own. Farm wives, by contrast, delivered six or seven infants, of whom perhaps three lived into adulthood.

Given that a girl reaching puberty probably only had another twenty years to live, these fertility rates meant that most women spent their entire adult lives pregnant and/or minding small children. Historians and anthropologists have documented huge differences among the world's farming societies, but almost all of them developed similar sexual divisions of labour and mobility. Broadly speaking, male farmers commuted from a fixed home to plough equally fixed fields, while their wives and daughters commuted no further than a stream or village well, instead spending most of their time indoors doing all the threshing, sifting, grinding and baking required by farm foods and the equally endless organising and cleaning needed to maintain a year-round home. Domestic drudgery took over women's lives, and male and female identities grew more unequal as well as more separate. Men, literally the breadwinners, took charge of almost everything. So obvious did these decisions come to seem that we know of no society practising plough agriculture that ever did things differently. Patriarchy was born.

Inequality permeated life. Turning wild valleys into fertile fields required thousands of hours of work – felling trees, weeding, ploughing, manuring, digging wells – which farmers might hesitate to invest unless they were confident they could keep the fruits of their labour. This made property rights all-important. It is difficult for foragers to convert success at hunting or gathering into forms that can be passed on to the next generation, but once ownership has been established, it is difficult for farmers *not* to pass on prosperity. A boy whose parents bequeath him broad, well-maintained acres has a huge head start over one who inherits nothing, and if this fortunate son finds an equally favoured girl to marry, their own offspring begin life even further ahead.

Economists often measure inequality on a scale called the Gini coefficient, giving out scores from 0 (meaning that everyone in a society owns exactly the same amount) to 1 (meaning that one person owns everything and no one else has anything). On average, hunter–gatherer societies score around 0.25 for the distribution of the tiny amount of property they possess, while the sophisticated farming societies that have left written records average around 0.85 – about as unequal as it is possible to get if the poorest are to stand much chance of avoiding starvation. (For comparison, Britain's score in 2019 was 0.75.)

The palaces and royal tombs excavated by archaeologists show that the rich definitely got richer, but whether the poor became poorer depends on what we take 'poorer' to mean. In one important sense the answer must be yes: despite producing more food than foraging, farming also produced more mouths to feed, and empty bellies regularly outran the food supply. The result was that most people's diet, health and life expectancy declined as they shifted from foraging to farming. Eating lots of cereals gave peasants cavities in their teeth; living cheek by jowl with farm animals gave them tuberculosis, influenza, dysentery and smallpox (just as 'wet markets' for live animals in our own time seem to have given us Covid-19); and endless, repetitive labour in fields and farmhouses gave them arthritis.

Yet there is another sense in which farming made the poor richer. With their bigger populations and more sophisticated divisions of labour, farmers produced more – and better – material goods than foragers. Excavations on Middle Eastern foragers' campsites typically find traces of flimsy shelters and scatters of broken stones and bones, but those on farmers' villages find brick houses with stone foundations and tiled roofs, plastered walls and paved floors. Inside them are tools and ornaments (initially still made of stone and bone, but after 3000 BCE made of metal too), all the paraphernalia for weaving clothes and so much pottery that you have to wonder what people were doing with it. On one dig I directed on Sicily we catalogued over a million pieces of broken pot. Angus Maddison – the economist I mentioned earlier, who estimated that premodern hunter–gatherers' living standards were equivalent to incomes of about $1.10 per day – calculated that the typical figure for peasants was more like $1.50–2.20, which strikes me as consistent with the archaeological evidence. To borrow the World Bank's categories again, ancient farmers were poor, but normally not *extremely* poor.

Less equal identities and prosperity went along with less equal forms of sovereignty. There was not much point in accumulating broad acres and building grand homes if you had to plough or clean them yourself, so the rich needed to mobilise more labour than their families could or would provide. However, menial labour was rarely productive enough in agricultural economies for employers to be able to pay wages that would attract any sane person to work for them. In almost every farming society on record, the powerful found the same solution: use violence to lower the cost of labour. So long as the cost of feeding, clothing and housing workers plus enforcing their obedience added up to less than the cost of hiring them through free markets, then debt-bondage, serfdom and/or slavery were efficient tools for would-be employers. The powerful made the weak an offer they couldn't refuse: work for me, because however miserable the conditions are, they are better than being beaten or murdered.

The mighty rarely phrased things so bluntly, for the very good reason that the cost of labour fell even further if the poor could be persuaded that doing as they were told was good for them. Without exception, Middle Eastern monarchs tried to sell this idea by claiming that they had more in common with gods than with their fellow mortals. The world's oldest political text, produced in Egypt around 3100 BCE, even says that the pharaoh Narmer *is* a kind of god, the living incarnation of Horus. Nowadays most of us suspect that rulers who say they are superhuman are actually deranged, but 5,000 years ago the gulf between a pharaoh in his palace and a peasant in his hut was wide enough to make such claims credible. And who would not want to believe in the justice of a lord who insisted that he was merely a shepherd, tending his mortal flock on behalf of his own divine masters?

It took 6,500 years to get from the first farmers to Narmer, but the lot of early Britons was very different. For more than five millennia after the Ice Age ended, all Islanders remained foragers, moving from camp to camp and answering to no one – not because they were lazier than Middle Easterners, or more democratic, but because of the genetic cards nature had dealt them. The plants and animals they preyed upon were simply less amenable to domestication than those in the Middle East. Multiple regions of the world were endowed with domesticable resources (rice and pigs in East Asia; sorghum south of the Sahara; maize, potatoes and llamas in the Americas), albeit in lower concentrations than the Middle East, and foragers in these places all ultimately became farmers. Britons, however, could have gathered acorns till the end of time without ever creating a domesticated, high-yielding oak tree, because oak's DNA does not work that way. Good luck, too, domesticating elk or deer. Hazelnuts, apples and pears have been domesticated, but the genetic modifications involved were so complicated that they were not mastered until Roman times. Of Britons' main food sources, horses alone were domesticated early on (around 4000 BCE), but only on the steppes of Kazakhstan, where the animals had originally evolved.

With suitable resources so scarce, British hunters and gatherers would probably never have invented agriculture for themselves. Other things being equal, they might even now be roasting wild chestnuts and spearing elk on the banks of the Thames and Tees. But Thatcher's Law meant that other things were not equal.

The Counterscarp

In the early days of archaeology, 150 years ago, nearly everyone in the field had read the classics at school. Herodotus, Caesar and others had described how great migrations – by the Greeks and Romans themselves but also by Celts, Germans and Huns, and later on Anglo-Saxons and Vikings – changed the course of history. Not surprisingly, when they grew up and started excavating the past for themselves, archaeologists tended to see signs of immigrants everywhere. By the 1920s and 1930s enough evidence had accumulated to suggest that farming (as well as monument-building, metalworking, writing and plenty of other ideas) had begun in the Middle East, reaching central Europe later and the Isles later still. Almost all archaeologists agreed that migrants had carried these innovations from south-east to north-west.

Academics, however, are paid to argue, and by the 1960s some archaeologists were asking whether the story really was so obvious. Farming, monument-building, metalworking and writing had definitely been invented independently in the New World, so could they not have been invented multiple separate times in the Old World too? Anthropologists had shown that customs could spread without people moving much at all, through trade and copying; and radiocarbon dating (a new scientific technique, invented only in 1949) suggested that Stonehenge was much too old to have been built – as had been widely assumed – by immigrant architects from Greece. If even Stonehenge was a local development, daring spirits asked, might it be that the whole notion that migrations explained everything was wrong? It had been convenient for men like Caesar or the rulers of nineteenth-century Europe's empires to imagine that people like themselves had always been sitting in the driver's seat, but now, in an age of decolonisation, other explanations seemed to make more sense.

Thus began one of the biggest (and, on occasion, nastiest) arguments in modern archaeology. Because it will resurface several times in the next few chapters I want to go into some detail here, at our first encounter with it. When I was an undergraduate, back in the late 1970s, archaeology's great and good still generally pooh-poohed non-migrationist theories as faddish stuff and nonsense, but by the 1990s almost everyone in the field had quietly switched sides. 'A basic equation has grown up in the minds of some archaeologists,' one observer noted rather sadly, 'between any model of the past involving population movement and simple-mindedness.'

To scholars still making that equation, my talk of 'imbalances' emerging in one place and then 'evening out' across the map must seem particularly simple-minded, but the fact is that new scientific methods are bringing such simple-mindedness back into style. Better techniques for extracting DNA from ancient skeletons have done most to put migration back on the agenda, even if interpreting the new data remains controversial. Some of the conclusions that geneticists reached in the 1990s were decisively disproved in the 2010s, and many theories current in the 2020s will doubtless seem equally silly twenty years from now. However, other new methods also point to high mobility. One, called stable-isotope analysis, suggests that a lot of people grew up in places with one kind of geology but died and were buried in places with another. Our bodies build bones and teeth from the plants and animals we eat, which have absorbed carbon, oxygen, nitrogen and strontium from the water they drink; and the isotopic form of each element varies according to the particular rocks the water flowed over and dissolved. So, if the isotopes in an adult's teeth (which have generally formed and been sealed in enamel by the age of twelve) differ from those in his/her bones (which keep renewing throughout our lives), s/he must have grown up in one place but died in another. Putting these and other new methods together, it looks as though archaeologists (I include myself among the guilty) were altogether too quick to erase mobility from the past – or, more precisely, to define 'mobility' too narrowly, dismissing the possibility of large-scale, long-distance migration.

Why they (we) did so is an interesting question. Science is not the only lens through which scholars see the past. It cannot be a coincidence that archaeologists stopped talking about migration in the 1960s, just as race became taboo in polite circles, then started again in the 2010s, just as nationalists put it back on political agendas. Political correctness must explain part of the pattern. But only part: critics of migrationism won followers from the 1960s onwards because they persuaded honest scholars that many older theories were not only borderline racist but also crude, slipshod and downright naïve about the relations between genes, identity and what archaeologists dug up. Similarly, champions of migrationism won followers back in the 2010s because they convinced a new generation of equally honest scholars that the latest techniques – and the balance of common sense – showed that people in the past really did move around, in large numbers and over long distances. The new techniques do not mean that migration explains everything, just as older ideas did not mean that migration explained nothing. They just mean we must take each case on its merits.

In the case of the spread of farming across Europe, the merits of migrationism now seem overwhelming. I will turn to the genetics in a moment, but at root it is a matter of mathematics. A valley turned over to farmland can often support ten to a hundred times as many people as one used for hunting and gathering. So, as Middle Easterners became farmers, they multiplied; and as they filled up the valleys they had been born in, they went forth to find new ones. From these, they went forth again, and again. The poor, the desperate and the bold struck out in search of new pastures to put under the plough, carrying their domesticated seeds and herding their animals along with them.

Like Middle Eastern refugees in the 2010s, people fleeing misery and/or seeking opportunity millennia ago took two main routes to Europe: one by sea across the Mediterranean and one by land through the Balkans (Figure 1.7). Again like modern refugees, they normally found that, whichever route they took, the new pastures already had people in them. However, at that point prehistoric and modern immigrant experiences diverged. In the 2010s resident Europeans massively

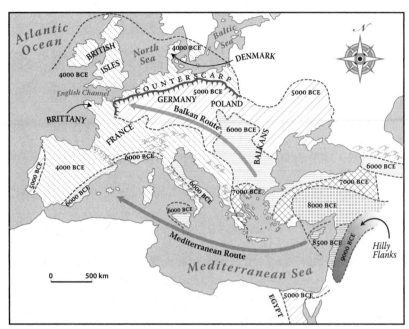

Figure 1.7. Going forth: the northward and westward expansion of farming from the Middle East to the British Isles, 9500–3500 BCE.

outnumbered Middle Eastern arrivals and were far more organised, but in ancient times the reverse tended to be true. Little by little, Europe's aboriginal hunter–gatherers were pushed towards hard choices.

One option for the locals was just to ignore the new arrivals. Sometimes this seems to have worked, especially when – as often happened – foragers and farmers preferred different kinds of territory. Foraging typically worked best in woods and wetlands, and farming on well-drained slopes whose light soils could be turned by early farmers' primitive hoes and ploughs. One study of bone chemistry suggests that foragers and farmers lived alongside each other in parts of Germany for 2,000 years, the former hunting wild game and fish and the latter consuming domesticated protein. However, as hunters and herders on multiple continents would find when European farmers reached their shores in modern times, coexistence was not always easy. 'The white man comes and cuts down the trees,' a Comanche told a Texan in the 1830s, 'building houses and fences, and the buffaloes get frightened and leave and never come back, and the Indians are left to starve, or if we follow the game we trespass on the hunting grounds of other tribes and war ensues.' Worst of all, immigrants would just keep coming. Even if they initially stayed off land that might be second-best for them but meant everything to local hunter–gatherers, eventually they encroached on it anyway.

Some foragers therefore chose another course. So long as there was more forest behind them, they could simply run away. However, this too was only a temporary fix. Sooner or later, new generations of land-hungry farmers, consistently outbreeding the foragers, would catch up with them. Tearing up the soil, burning forests and scaring off game, they would keep pushing until hunters and gatherers were penned into miserable places the farmers did not want – or left with nowhere else to go.

If flight was unattractive, foragers might instead fight, hoping that if they raided enough farms, burned enough crops and killed enough cattle, the intruders would give up and go away. But this seems to have been the path least taken. Archaeologists have found little evidence of violence along the farming frontier; typically, several centuries would pass after the arrival of agriculture before burned and/ or fortified farming villages become common. Some sites contain pits holding the casually dumped bodies of mutilated men, women and children; there is even evidence of torture and cannibalism. Given the timing, these probably represent farmer-on-farmer fighting, not hunter-on-farmer raiding. Perhaps there were just too few foragers for force to be effective.

Finally, if hunters and gatherers could not live with, run from or fight off the newcomers, they could join them, giving up their wandering ways and settling down to till the soil themselves. This process probably spanned generations – not a dramatic, one-time leap from collecting nuts to ploughing fields but a slippery slope towards a new way of life. As newcomers kept coming and pressure on resources kept growing, a foraging family might decide to spend a little less time walking between stands of wild plants and a little more time gardening and tending particular plots. In the twentieth century CE anthropologists in Africa, Amazonia and New Guinea regularly found that farmers using Stone-Age technology remained quite mobile, typically burning a clearing in a forest, working it until the soil's fertility declined and then moving off to burn a new clearing somewhere else. People perhaps behaved similarly in prehistoric Europe. Only as population pressure mounted would they start weeding gardens, then hoeing them and eventually ploughing and manuring – by which time they were just as much a farming family as any immigrants carrying Middle Eastern genes.

Someone, somewhere, probably tried out every imaginable variation on these basic themes, and the shift from foraging to farming must have been messier than a map like Figure 1.7 makes it look. Ferriter's Cove, a hunter–gatherer campsite on the Irish coast, perhaps illustrates this. Around 4350 BCE someone there tossed out several bones belonging to a domesticated cow, despite the absence of any other trace of such animals within 600 km. These bones probably arrived inside joints of smoked or salted beef, carried across the sea as souvenirs by some intrepid traveller, only to fall as flat with locals as my mother's curry did with my grandad. No one got excited enough about genetically modified foreign food to import living, breathing livestock or to domesticate local wild cattle. Foragers went on in their ways; agriculture remained a road not taken.

Every little region must have had its own tale, but they all ended the same way. Resistance was futile, because eventually weight of numbers always told. No more than 20 per cent (and perhaps more like 10 per cent) of modern European DNA goes back to foragers like Cheddar Man. All the rest belongs to later immigrants. 'History to the defeated / May say Alas but cannot help or pardon', W. H. Auden wrote during the Spanish Civil War. Alas for the hunters and gatherers of Europe, the victims of a process of evening out.

Yet if numbers made farming an irresistible force, they also, on occasion, made foraging an immovable object, because agriculture's advance paused, everywhere from France to Poland, around 5200 BCE (Figure 1.7 above). After expanding for a millennium at an average speed of over a kilometre a year, the farming frontier ground to a halt just 80 km short of the English Channel and North and Baltic Seas. There it would stay for the best part of a thousand years.

This is the earliest known example of what was to become one of the most important patterns in Britain's history: an outer rim of defences, of whatever kind, which could block unwelcome processes of evening out by preventing them from reaching the Continental shores opposite England. The first person to talk about such a barrier seems to have been William Cecil, Queen Elizabeth I's most influential adviser, who warned her in 1567 that allies in the Low Countries and Germany constituted 'the very counterscarp of England'. Elizabeth, seeing that preserving a counterscarp of allies might be the safest way to keep Spanish power away from the North Sea coast and therefore away from the Isles, scraped together the cash to send English troops to help Dutch rebels. The same strategic principle still held in 1949, when Britain's future prime minister, Harold Macmillan, told the Council of Europe that 'Britain's frontier is not on the Channel; it is not even on the Rhine; it is at least on the Elbe'. Neither Cecil nor Macmillan knew that such counterscarps had already been Britain's bulwark against invasion for 7,000 years.

To be sure, a counterscarp in 5200 BCE was very different from one in in 1567 or 1949. There were no queens or prime ministers to organise alliances in the Stone Age. The prehistoric counterscarp was what scientists call a self-organising system: no one is in charge, but order emerges out of chaos anyway. The arrangement of billions of cells to create bodies and that of thousands of ants into colonies are classic examples of self-organising systems. So too was the coalescence of hundreds of little foraging bands around 5200 BCE into a kind of hunter–gatherer superorganism, collectively strong enough – even though no one was telling it what to do – to hold back the evening out of agriculture.

Archaeologists have identified similar episodes in prehistoric Egypt, Thailand, Korea and Japan. What they all have in common is a particular kind of geography. In each case, farming stopped advancing when it reached the edge of a watery (usually coastal but occasionally riverine) hunter–gatherer cornucopia, whose wetlands overflowed with wild foods, especially shellfish. The foraging campsites these regions supported – regularly marked by mounds of billions of discarded whelk, oyster, cockle and scallop shells – were among the biggest, richest and most abundant that archaeologists have found anywhere in the world.

In these uniquely favoured environments so many foragers could support themselves that the numerical advantage that famers normally enjoyed was reduced or even reversed. In some hunter–gatherer camps in Brittany and Denmark archaeologists also find graves containing polished stone jewellery and weapons, commonly interpreted as symbols of political power. These densely settled, affluent foragers may have had true headmen, whittling away the farmers' advantages in political organisation too. Without anyone intending it, a foraging counterscarp effectively put Thatcher's Law on hold around 5200 BCE. Secure behind it, insular hunter–gatherers went on in their wandering ways for another thirty-odd generations.

It is not entirely clear why, around 4200 BCE, the counterscarp ultimately collapsed. Some archaeologists think the weight of farmers pressing against it became unbearable, others that incentives changed on the foragers' side of the line, making farming more attractive. Whatever the answer, the consequences for Britain were catastrophic. In 1940, when German tanks breached Britain's counterscarp in the Low Countries, Churchill promised the nation that 'We shall fight in France, we shall fight on the seas and oceans [. . .] We shall fight in the fields and in the streets, we shall fight in the hills; we shall never surrender'. But in 4200 BCE, none of these options was available. Once the counterscarp collapsed, the game was up. No hunter–gatherer Churchill organised Britons to defend the Channel crossings against advancing farmers. Even if there had been such a person, little skin boats were not physically capable of mounting patrols against raiders and denying them the use of the sea. When the counterscarp went, so too did every acre of farmable land behind it, all the way to the Atlantic.

Under the Plough

A month before the 2016 referendum, Robert Shrimsley, a journalist at the *Financial Times*, decided to poke some fun at the doomsday rhetoric flourishing on both sides of the Brexit debate. The coming week, he speculated, would begin with a speech from David Cameron warning that 'a vote to leave "could see us plunged into World War III by Thursday"'. When that failed to scare people, Cameron would add that 'Britain could be plunged into the fourth world war as soon as the third world war has ended'. Boris Johnson, Shrimsley speculated, would respond with his own speech 'in front of a large cave in Wiltshire where he says British people will be forced to live once all the immigrants come to take their homes. He adds that British citizens may not even get the best caves as these will all be given to Bulgarian families.' Not to be outdone, Nigel Farage would then pose outside the same cave, 'saying that it will not even be offered to Bulgarians as the entire population of Turkey will be living in it'.

Figure 1.8. Argonauts of the Atlantic: likely paths of immigrants bringing farming, voles and shrews to the British Isles, 4200–3500 BCE.

Ridiculous – except that when Thatcher's Law resumed its operations after 4200 BCE, Shrimsley's scenario was pretty much what came to pass. In the space of two centuries immigrants whose ancestors had left the Middle East a couple of thousand years earlier and had then migrated across Europe seized not only all the caves (not that people lived in them any more) but also almost every other scrap of land in the Isles. Studies of DNA suggest that newcomers replaced roughly three-quarters of the native genetic stock in the centuries after 4200 BCE and fatally undermined the other quarter's wandering way of life. It was a hunter–gatherer Armageddon.

Dragging cows, sheep, pigs and bags full of wheat and barley seeds on to skin boats, the boldest Continental farmers had paddled across the Channel to the Thames estuary by 4100 BCE. There they prospered, raising big families and moving inland. More immigrants came to Kent, and even braver souls set out from Brittany, crossing 200 km of open sea to pass Land's End and enter the Irish Sea (Figure 1.8). Nor were people and livestock the only animals on the move: starting around 3800 BCE, the bones of furry little rodents known as Orkney voles appear on sites in the Scottish islands. These have close genetic kin on the Continent but none in Britain, almost certainly meaning that they got to the Orkneys as stowaways on boats coming directly from southern climes (ultimately, Spain). Another rodent, a kind of pygmy shrew that evolved in the Pyrenees but is otherwise known only from Ireland, probably made a similar move at just this time.

Once they had sailed the seas to reach the Isles, farmers tended to be much less mobile than indigenous foragers, although there was, as usual, great variation. Isotopic analysis of skeletons from Hazleton North, in Gloucestershire, suggests that the first farmers there did regularly relocate over short distances, but other farmers put down roots in a single spot. The best evidence comes from weeds, about which we know a lot, because every time a Stone Age farm wife cleaned her oven, fragments of burned bread – full of charred seeds – would end up in rubbish pits, neatly packaged for archaeologists to excavate. These seeds show that when early farmers harvested their fields, they brought home not just wheat and barley but also cleavers, ribwort plantain and wild oats, species of weed that only flourish in continuously cultivated fields – meaning that farmers were staying put for years at a time.

Some settlers, particularly in Ireland and Scotland, also built sturdy timber-and-thatch farmhouses, again implying that they had no plans to leave any time soon. These were usually vaguely rectangular, divided into several rooms and roughly the same size as British homes in the 2010s CE (about 100 m²). Compared with foragers' huts, they were luxury accommodation, and the objects found inside them confirm that farmers were more prosperous than the foragers they replaced. Houses filled up with goods – above all pottery for cooking, drinking and storage. Before 4200 BCE there was no pottery in the British Isles; by 3800 it was almost everywhere.

These farmers were certainly dirt poor, but were not *extremely* poor, as the foragers they replaced had generally been. Immigrants imported from the Continent the knack of polishing stone axes rather than just chipping them into shape, producing more effective tools for chopping down trees to clear fields for farming. Seeking superior stone, they applied European mining methods, sinking shafts 15 m into the chalk of the South Downs to reach the richest veins of flint – no small achievement for diggers armed only with bone, stone and wooden tools.

Building farmsteads and mining flint were more complicated jobs than anything foragers had attempted, but they were just the tip of the iceberg. Hardly anything British hunter–gatherers had done made much of a mark on the landscape (I will come back to one extraordinary exception in Chapter 2), but after 4000 BCE farmers began altering the earth with enormous, eye-catching monuments. These came in two main kinds – those for the living (which contain no burials) and those for the dead (which do) – but both typically involved digging ditches, sometimes kilometres long, and heaping up great piles of soil. Archaeologists find almost nothing inside most of the monuments for the living, and few were well sited for defence. So, because we have no better theories, we generally assume that they were for gatherings – although why people congregated at them and why they felt the need to dig such long ditches remain mysteries.

Monuments to the dead provide more clues. Foragers rarely took much trouble over deceased relatives, disposing of them so casually that archaeologists hardly ever find them. After 4000 BCE, though, farmers in Britain came up with more than a dozen different types of tombs, mostly based on Continental models. Some contained great slabs of stone; others were heaps of dirt. The kind that archaeologists

Figure 1.9. The collective will: Belas Knap long barrow, Gloucestershire.

call 'long barrows' could be 100 m long. A thousand long barrows still survive, and there must originally have been many more. A medium-sized long barrow took about 7,000 hours to build (ten adults working full-time might throw one together in a few months), big ones twice as long. It was an astonishing outpouring of energy.

We have to wonder why Britain's farmers (and their ancestors on the Continent) thought this was such a good idea. One possibility, popular in the nineteenth century, is that the monuments challenged foragers' 'everyman-a-headman' theory of sovereignty and identity. Visiting long barrows that have been restored to something like their original glory, such as Belas Knap in Gloucestershire (Figure 1.9), it is easy to imagine overseers cracking whips as gangs of slaves toiled under leaden skies, emptying buckets of mud on to a growing mound celebrating the glory of a mighty king. But this idea has few followers nowadays, largely because nothing looking even vaguely like a royal burial has been found under any barrow.

Most archaeologists suspect that, far from celebrating the inequality that inevitably seems to accompany farming, monuments for the dead actually undermined it. The bodies under the mounds had often gone through complicated cycles, being buried until the flesh rotted and then dug up, dismantled and deliberately mixed together.

Sometimes they were then dug up a second time and carried off to a final resting place somewhere else altogether, making room for a new generation of dead. It is hard to get much more communal than this. Perhaps, one interpretation runs, mound-building, bone-mixing and ditch-digging were all mechanisms to defuse the tensions – both within and between communities – created by rising inequality. Monuments may have helped create new identities and sovereignties, connecting the builders and users to the particular places that they farmed rather than the broader landscapes that hunter–gatherers moved around. Communal tombs may even have acted to signal specific groups' ownership of land that their own ancestors had laboriously reclaimed from the wild.

If so, they only partly succeeded, because violent disputes were not rare. In our own age roughly 1 Briton in 5,000 dies violently (better than the global score which I mentioned earlier in this chapter, of 1 in 140, but worse than the Scandinavian, of 1 in 100,000), but an alarming 1 in 50 of the skulls found in early farmers' tombs in Britain and Ireland have depression fractures on the left side, just like those which killed Cheddar Man thousands of years earlier. Stone arrowheads have been found mixed among the bones of about a hundred skeletons, a few of them embedded in vertebrae and ribs. Sometimes we even find signs of large-scale fighting. One poorly preserved but well-excavated site, at Hambledon Hill in Dorset, was attacked three separate times in two centuries, each marked by burned buildings and hundreds of arrowheads (the oldest bow found in England, made of yew like those Henry V's archers had at Agincourt, dates to around 4000 BCE). The final attack, around 3400 BCE, destroyed Hambledon Hill altogether. One man, apparently carrying a baby in a sling across his chest, was hit by an arrow and then buried when a burning rampart collapsed on him.

As on the Continent, most of the evidence for violence dates long after the farmers' arrival, but, given how little hunter–gatherer DNA survived this process, I find it hard to picture the replacement as peaceful. I mentioned a few pages ago that Continental foragers and farmers sometimes lived alongside each other for millennia, but the single case of cohabitation known from Britain, revealed by new biomolecular techniques on Oronsay in the Hebrides, lasted only a couple of centuries. For Britain's aboriginal foragers the counterscarp's collapse after 4200 BCE seems to have meant uncontrollable mobility, the collapse of security, the loss of sovereignty and the end of their ancient identities. Alas.

In his 1926 book *On England*, published just fourteen years before his own age's counterscarp came crashing down, Britain's prime minister, Stanley Baldwin, mused that 'the one eternal sight of England' was 'of a plough team coming over the brow of a hill, the sight that has been England since England was a land'. He was wrong. Plough teams only appeared half-way through Britain's history, and, far from being eternal, their arrival was among the greatest disruptions the Isles have ever known. What is eternal about Britain is not agriculture but the relentless logic of its geography.

2

EUROPE'S POOR COUSIN, 4000–55 BCE

By 4000 BCE the pattern that would dominate Britain's history until 1497 CE was already in place. Anchored at the edge of the Hereford Map, the Isles were Europe's poor cousin. They were the last place that new ways of life reached after arising far away in the south and east and evening out across the entire Continent. Because of Thatcher's Law, every innovation did in the end arrive, but Britain typically lagged centuries or even millennia behind the Middle Eastern and Mediterranean trendsetters.

The pace varied. By 3500 BCE flows of people, goods, institutions and ideas from the Continent into the Isles had slowed, and they remained slow for four centuries. After 3000 BCE they did more than just slow, and people in northern and western Britain developed their Continental inheritance in ways that rivalled anything in mainland Europe itself. There was perhaps another interlude before 2000 BCE, and different archaeologists have identified various further interruptions, mostly shorter, all the way down to 300 BCE.

Each episode had its own sets of causes and consequences, but all were part – perhaps an inevitable part – of the larger process of the evening out of imbalances. Once a novelty had spread all the way to the Atlantic, regardless of whether it was demographic, economic, political or cultural, the differences between Britain and Europe became less pronounced, and the pace of movement from south-east to north-west slowed – only to resume as the next great innovation approached the Isles.

Across the 4,000 years following the arrival of farming, a second feature of Britain's relationship with Europe and the wider world made itself felt. While agriculture had been invented thousands of kilometres away in the Middle East, the people who actually brought it to Britain's shores after 4200 BCE came from no further away than what we now call the Low Countries, northern France and northern

Spain. By the first century BCE, however, traders and armies were coming all the way from Italy; and another century after that, Continental rulers arrived too. The stage was expanding.

NG10 the Great

It took farmers just four centuries to fill up every arable nook and cranny in the Isles, ploughing and planting their way forwards at an average speed of over 1 km a year. The hunting-and-gathering world died before them, and when the onslaught finally stopped, around 3700 BCE, it was because it had reached the edge of the earth.

Agricultural immigration created new identities. To judge from the archaeological evidence, there was at first a widely shared insular culture: everywhere they went, farmers carried with them more or less the same styles of stoneworking, potmaking and burial brought from the Continent by their ancestors. They often kept up long-distance links with their European homelands too. As a result, on sites dating before 3800 BCE, archaeologists find broadly similar kinds of axes and arrowheads, bowls and tombs, everywhere from the Isle of Wight to Scotland. They sometimes even turn up beautiful polished axes made from a stone called jadeitite, quarried in the Alps and passed from hand to hand for 1,500 km or more.

This open, inclusive world lasted only a few generations. Once the agricultural frontier reached the ocean, unity broke down. Smaller regional identities formed, each setting itself apart from its neighbours by doing things its own way. Exchanges across the English Channel slowed too; the last jadeitite axe we know of from Britain was buried with great care next to a wooden track (dated by tree rings to 3807 or 3806 BCE) across the marshes of Somerset (Figure 2.1). For all we know, farmers in Britain forgot that they had ever been immigrants (a recurring theme in British identity). By 3500 BCE few any longer visited the monuments built during the centuries of expansion. In some places people sealed up the entrances to the communal tombs containing ancestral bones – perhaps, some archaeologists suspect, deliberately separating themselves from their past.

Deeper changes may have fuelled the new identities. Between about 4100 and 3500 BCE Britain's population had boomed as immigrants rushed in, ploughed up the virgin soil and raised families. We can only guess at numbers, but population perhaps tripled, to surpass

Figure 2.1. The British stage, 4000–55 BCE.

300,000 (roughly one person per square kilometre) by 3500 BCE. These were the crowds that built the great monuments; but over the next half-millennium much of the Isles saw numbers fall back by perhaps 50 per cent.

Specialists argue over what happened. The climate had cooled and turned wetter since 3700 BCE, so perhaps farming became less productive. Or perhaps the first farmers – no conservationists –

over-exploited the soil. But whatever the causes, some of the consequences are clear. First, farmers turned from planting high-yielding but finicky wheat to lower-yielding but hardy barley; and then, by 3200 BCE, they stopped even bothering with barley. In place of cultivated grains, people shifted back towards gathering wild plants. Evidence from weed seeds and pollen (recovered by drilling cores into ancient lake beds) suggests that, as they abandoned their fields, forests grew back. Sturdy houses, built to stand for generations, disappear from the archaeological record.

Britons did not, however, go back to being egalitarian foragers. Rather, the first unambiguous evidence for chiefs comes from just these centuries. The old 'everyman-a-headman' collective tombs were replaced with smaller grave mounds, covering just one or two dead. Some tombs held elaborate grave goods. A few of these look like symbols of political power, including crude stone versions of the kind of mace still used in British royal coronations.

If archaeologists are right to see the dead in these tombs as chieftains who wielded new powers, their authority probably came from an equally new source: control over livestock. Excavated bones indicate that Britons were turning to ranching, driving herds of domesticated cattle from one wooded valley to the next. In modern pastoral societies, lucky and/or skilful herders can get rich quick if their flocks multiply, earning honour (perhaps enough to merit burial with stone maces) by feasting their followers with beef, butter and milk. The downside, however, is that bad luck and/or decisions can make them poor just as quickly.

Stanley Baldwin's eternal England this was not. Paradoxically, the most Baldwinesque bits of the Isles were some of the Scottish islands and parts of Ireland, where the population kept rising, grain was still planted and solid houses were being built. This was one of the few times in British history when the south-east's geographical advantages over the north and west were not just evened out but actually reversed. If you wanted to see wealth, power and sophistication between 3400 and 3000 BCE, you went to Orkney – or, better still, to a 5-km stretch of the River Boyne just an hour's drive north of modern Dublin.

The explanation perhaps lies in contact with the Continent. Movement back and forth across the English Channel slowed after 3800 BCE, but mobility along the western waters connecting Portugal,

Figure 2.2. Megalithic missionaries? The Tagus–Orkney axis, *c.*3000 BCE.

Galicia and Brittany to the Isles' hillier fringes (Figure 2.2) was, if anything, accelerating. Remarkable things were happening along the Continent's Atlantic coast. Near the mouth of the River Tagus, where Lisbon now stands, people were clustering by 4500 BCE into permanent villages a hundred or more strong. They were sufficiently well organised to build 3-m-thick stone fortifications studded with towers, and buried what were surely chiefs in huge stone tombs with lavish grave goods, including ivory from North Africa.

Further north, even odder things began going on in Brittany. At Locmariaquer, a picturesque inlet near Quiberon Bay (a place of immense strategic importance, as we will see later in this chapter), someone persuaded his fellows to quarry a 20-m-high, 350-ton stone stele and, as befitted early farmers, to carve a giant image of a plough on it.* They then dragged it 5 km and stood it up outside a communal tomb. The dragging alone would have required a work gang of at least 2,000 men, and the whole operation looks like an extreme example of the kind of collectivist zeal we saw among British farmers in Chapter 1. But what are we to make of the subsequent decision, taken within just a generation or two, to topple this and other huge stone stelae and smash them? Or to reuse the fragments to build a series of tombs holding just one or two corpses, accompanied by beautiful grave goods and their own elaborate monuments?

Over the next thousand years, tombs made of massive stone slabs (which archaeologists call megaliths, from the Greek words *megas* and *lithos*, 'big stone') spread all along Western Europe's shores. In the 1950s some scholars suggested 'megalithic missionaries' had inspired them, sailing along Europe's coastlines and preaching new notions about the afterworld. In place of older, egalitarian ideas about identity and sovereignty, says this theory, the prophets taught that a small elite (presumably including themselves) had privileged access to the supernatural and could ensure the gods' goodwill – so long as everyone else built them great stone monuments and generally did as they were told.

Like so many theories involving long-distance mobility, this one fell out of favour in the 1970s, but new radiocarbon dates now prove that Bretons did build the first megalithic tombs and that the custom then spread by sea, while new genetic evidence shows that, when megaliths reached the Isles, they were linked to new kinds of ruling families. The scale of some of the tombs, especially in Ireland's Boyne Valley, had always made this seem likely. Three genuinely giant-sized tombs were raised at Dowth, Knowth and Newgrange shortly before 3000 BCE. Each boasted a mound originally 100 m across and 20 m high. The Newgrange mound alone contained 200,000 tons of rock, was adorned with megaliths and was surrounded by a carpet of chunks of sparkling white quartz which would have been visible from kilometres away when it caught the sun.

Even if the work was spread across a generation, the amount of labour that had to be mobilised suggests to some scholars that

---

*Given the patriarchal leanings of most early farming communities, it seems unlikely to have been *her* fellows.

more hierarchical forms of sovereignty and identity were taking hold, and that impression is only reinforced by what lay under the huge mounds. At Newgrange a 15-m, stone-lined passage led to a cross-shaped chamber with an 8-m-high vaulted ceiling. In a smaller chamber off to one side, archaeologists found two adult skeletons plus burned bones from at least three more people and body parts of dozens of deer and elk. Knowth was almost as impressive. It had two passages and chambers, one of them (cross-shaped, like Newgrange) containing a big carved stone bowl surrounded by several cremations and rich dedications, including an elaborate flint mace-head. (Dowth is too badly disturbed for us to say much except that it had two stone burial chambers.)

Whatever the dead of Newgrange, Knowth and Dowth had done to make themselves so important – as important, apparently, as the great men of the Tagus and Brittany, and more important than anyone in the Isles had ever been before – meant that merely super-sizing their tombs was not enough. Going far beyond this, the buriers actually tried to fuse the great ones' bodies with the core principles of the cosmos itself. The Newgrange tomb was positioned precisely so that for a week either side of 21 December – the shortest day of the year – the rising sun's first rays shone through a slot above the grave mound's entrance and straight down a long stone passage, where, for seventeen magical minutes, they lit up a triple spiral carved on the central chamber's back slab (Figure 2.3). At Knowth the setting sun struck directly down the tomb's passage on 21 March, one of the two days each year with exactly equal amounts of light and dark, to illuminate one of the burial chambers; and on 21 September, the other such day, it repeated the feat in the other chamber. Once again, Dowth is too poorly preserved for us to work out its alignments, but the arrangements at Newgrange and Knowth cannot be accidents. These tombs were celestial hotspots, where, at the most meaningful moments of the year, the sun itself touched the last resting places of men and women who were more than mortal.

In fact, a new DNA study reveals, at least one of the men buried at Newgrange – prosaically labelled 'NG10' – really was different from the rest of us. When scientists sequenced his genome, they found 'multiple long runs of homozygosity, each comprising large fractions of individual chromosomes' – meaning, in English, that NG10's parents were first-degree kin: either brother and sister, or, even more

Figure 2.3. Seventeen minutes of magic: the burial chamber at Newgrange, where, around 3000 BCE, the rising sun at the winter solstice would light up NG10's final resting place.

creepily, father and daughter or mother and son. For good biological reasons, almost every society treats incest as an abomination – unless one family seems so far above everyone else (godlike, in fact) that only its own members can provide worthy mates. Ancient Egyptians, Incas and Hawaiians felt this way about their rulers. So too, apparently, did the prehistoric Irish.

Sadly, we will never know what went through people's heads when they built the Boyne tombs 5,000 years ago. One of the great no-nos in archaeology, in fact, is over-identifying with the people whose lives we dig up – even though we all do it. When I was excavating a religious site on Sicily a few years ago, I found that if I stood in the sun long enough I could almost see the ancient worshippers hacking gigantic red deer apart on their altars, dancing around with the antlers on their heads and smashing wine cups to the ground. Sometimes I even dreamed about them. Moved by much the same spirit, I cannot help feeling that those moments when dawn turned the Newgrange triple spiral to gold were ones of divine miracle and mystery. In those instants, did mortals thrill with the certainty that the gods walked among them again? Did their priests then whisper, long and low, words too sacred for commoners to hear? Did blessings overflow, and was the world thereby renewed for another year?

Well, maybe. At the very least, the archaeological facts shout out that these were magical places, designed to make dreams and visions merge with the waking world. All three tombs were decorated with swirling carvings of mazes, zigzags and spirals, which, like so much of the psychedelic art of the 1960s, were painted in garish colours. Several psychologists have likened the designs to images produced in the eyes and brain by 'flickering light, hallucinogenic fungi, and migrainous syndromes' (as one scholar rather soberly puts it).

This had to be intentional. Archaeologists have found seeds of opium poppies on multiple sites (we found them on the site I excavated in Sicily too), and psychologists studying modern-day evangelical Christians have observed that people who try hard to hear God's voice and immerse themselves in communities of the like-minded can train themselves to be hypersensitive to what they experience as authentic messages from beyond. Possibly (although, once more, who knows) combinations of narcotics, dramatic solstice or equinox ceremonies and other-worldly art enabled shamans before 3000 BCE not only to alter their awareness to the point where they were hearing voices but also to use their experiences to mobilise their communities to build these magnificent monuments as portals to another world.

Even before Newgrange was finished, related ideas were spreading up the western waters to the Isles' northern tip. A dozen major and many more minor mounds and monuments crowded the shores of the Loch of Stenness on Orkney, which seems to have had its own astronomical associations. The grandest, the tumulus of Maeshowe, was on a par with Newgrange, concealing an equally outsize central chamber, built so carefully that you can barely slide a piece of paper between some of its stone slabs.

From Portugal's scorched hills to northern shores where the pale summer sun barely sets, an extraordinary spiritual unity seems to have prevailed after about 3200 BCE. The Newgrange mound and its psychedelic carvings precisely echo finds from Brittany, while the Knowth flint mace-head has its closest parallels on the banks of the Tagus. Smaller similarities are too numerous to list. These men and women, dispersed along 2,000 km of Atlantic coastline, must surely have known each other and probably intermarried, even if we do not – yet? – have direct DNA evidence for it. With good reason does the archaeologist Barry Cunliffe speak of 'a shared system of beliefs [. . . a] widespread set of symbols and a sophisticated cosmology', or even a distinctive 'Atlantic mind-set'.

Little at Locmariaquer or Maeshowe would have surprised NG10. However, any time he or his counterparts wandered even a few kilometres inland, they would have found themselves in an utterly alien world. Many of us worry today about a growing gap between the great mass of mere mortals and an internationalised and (metaphorically) incestuous elite, flitting between the luxury hotels and Michelin-starred restaurants of London, New York and Singapore or gathering for closed-door festivals of self-congratulation in the picture-book-perfect Alpine resort of Davos. Something similar, it seems, was going on at the edge of the Atlantic 5,000 years ago. The great men and women buried along the banks of the Boyne and shores of Stenness had more in common with those around the Tagus than with the ranchers in their own backyards, who conspicuously lacked the cosmopolitan mindset of megalithic missionaries. Ours is not the only age to have Davos Men.

Jerusalem

I was invited to Davos once. It was surreal. The conference invitation asked me whether I would be bringing my own security detail and helicopter. That was a first for me. But no sooner had I swelled with pride at becoming one with the global elite than my daydreams were dashed. Immediately upon arrival, I discovered that there was more than one kind of Davos Man. Every attendee had been invited to grand-sounding dinners and parties, but some had been invited to *grander* dinners and parties, in roped-off piano bars from which lesser mortals were pointedly excluded. Even our name badges were ranked, with top people getting sparkly globes ('disco balls', we envious types called them) on theirs.

It was a good lesson in some timeless truths – that the competition to join the top people is nothing compared with the competition between the top people, and that the way to win that competition is by making yourself like other glitterati, but also distinctly different. If the Atlantic elite around 3000 BCE was anything like the Davos elite of today, and I strongly suspect it was, that's what its members most wanted to do. It was not enough to build another Newgrange, like the Maeshowe mound on Orkney: you needed something equally grand but also distinctive. And so, in the years around 3000 BCE, elites along the western edge of the British mainland came up with a kind of monument that no one else had: the henge. Henges were Stone Age disco balls.

Henges developed slowly, initially in Wales and Wiltshire, out of older traditions of digging circular ditches around cemeteries. They are named after the most famous example, at Stonehenge, which in its turn got its label from an Anglo-Saxon word meaning 'hanging stone'; but – in the kind of terminological tangle that archaeologists seem to enjoy – when experts call a monument a henge, they're not talking about stones at all. Instead, 'henge' means any monument involving a round(ish) ditch.

Like any good disco ball, henges combined novelty with well-established elite traditions, most notably the combination of astral and funereal functions. As early as the 1720s (CE), visitors had observed that, if they stood at the centre of Stonehenge, they could watch the sun rise on 21 June exactly through the henge's main entrance; and Stonehenge's 150–200 burials (there is debate over the original number) also make it the biggest cemetery known from third-millennium BCE Britain. The deceased were mostly adults, and had all been burned, with their remains – bundled in bags – interred in and around a ring of fifty-six standing stones (Figure 2.4: the huge sarsen stones that now dominate Stonehenge were added later, around 2500 BCE). Hardly any of the burials contained grave goods, but the handful of finds does include a beautiful polished stone mace-head and a little clay stand for burning something. Incense? Drugs?

What makes henges so significant is that they are the first unambiguous example of a regional imbalance beginning with innovations in the northern/western parts of the Isles and then evening out south-eastwards, reversing the usual pattern. Stonehenge, in fact, was a transplant from the west in a very literal sense. In all kinds of ways

Figure 2.4. O come, all ye faithful – worshippers streaming into a snow-covered Stonehenge around 2950 BCE, as imagined by the artist Peter Dunn. The fifty-six bluestones stand just inside the ditch and embankment. The upright timbers in the centre are archaeologically attested, although their purpose is unknown.

it is an odd henge, and only two other henges, both slightly earlier, really look much like it. The first is just a day or two's walk away, and happens to lie right under Max Gate, the house where Thomas Hardy wrote several of his 'Wessex' novels in the 1880s–90s. The site (nowadays known as Flagstones) was not excavated until a century later, but Hardy's gardener did uncover a sarsen stone from the buried henge. At one point Hardy even interrupted his regular writing to dash off a note describing a prehistoric burial that they had dug up. His neighbour also found a clay incense / drug burner, the only parallel in Britain to the one from Stonehenge.

If Flagstones were the only Stonehenge lookalike, we would probably assume that its details were just local Dorset peculiarities. However, the second Stonehengy site is 275 km away, at Llandegai in north Wales, and is just one of a whole string of Welsh connections.

Geologists have known since the 1920s that Stonehenge's original fifty-six upright stones were bluestones, quarried in Wales; and research since 2011 has even pinpointed their sources, around Craig Rhos-y-felin in the Preseli Hills. For a while, archaeologists speculated that advancing Ice Age glaciers might have pushed these bluestones all the way to Wiltshire without human intervention, but their geology now makes it certain that people deliberately relocated the 200 tons of rock to Stonehenge. The builders really, really wanted these particular stones. Nor do the Welsh links end there: stable-isotope studies suggest that four of the dead at Stonehenge were actually Welsh immigrants.

The archaeologist Mike Parker Pearson, who has been digging around Stonehenge since 2003, has a theory pulling all these details together. Stonehenge, he speculates, was built 'by communities moving eastward and settling on Salisbury Plain', where they formed 'a ruling elite family, perhaps even of [Welsh] origin'. Noting that the main evidence for quarrying bluestones at Craig Rhos-y-felin actually dates two centuries before Stonehenge, he has revived another theory from the 1920s: that these stones originally stood in a monument in Wales, which migrants dismantled, dragged to Wiltshire and reinstalled at Stonehenge. He has even found the original location, Waun Mawn. 'Such an act', he suggests, 'could have served to merge two sacred centres into one, to unify two politically separate regions, or to legitimise the ancestral identity of migrants moving from one region to another.'

This might sound like a lot to read into a few rocks, but such repurposing of sacred stones was actually quite common. In 2009 Parker Pearson's team found traces of a dismantled bluestone henge (which, with admirable parsimony, they christened Bluestonehenge), just a couple of kilometres from Stonehenge. Nor were the bluestones Stonehenge's only antiques: on either side of its south entrance the builders heaped up piles of cows' skulls which were already two centuries old when they reached the site in 2950 BCE. Ranchers tend to have strong feelings about their cattle, and we might wonder whether these were hallowed heirlooms, perhaps relics of some now legendary feast held back in Wales in the immigrants' great-great-great-great-grandparents' days.

For thousands of years, people, goods and ideas had been moving from south-east to north-west, but if Parker Pearson is right (and I think he is), after a century or so in which the Isles' grandest centres had clustered around the Irish Sea and in the Orkneys, a powerful Welsh clan reversed this flow. Just why it was Wiltshire they moved to is anyone's guess, although there is one obvious explanation: Stonehenge lies on the most direct overland route between the Irish Sea and the English Channel, and would have been just the place for trading goods between the two networks. However, even if this is right, it begs a second question: if profit drew immigrants to Wiltshire, why did they go to the trouble of building a Stonehenge – and, for that matter, even bigger monuments? In 2020 geophysical prospectors announced the discovery, right next to Stonehenge, of a second giant monument. Contemporary with Stonehenge, it consists of dozens of gigantic pits, forming a circle almost 2 km across. The circle is the biggest earthwork known from prehistoric Europe, and at its centre was the continent's biggest settlement, Durrington Walls. At one point, up to 4,000 people (possibly the Stonehenge construction crews?) had lived here; and after they moved away, a henge four times bigger than Stonehenge was built over its ruins. Newgrange had been a celestial hotspot, but Stonehenge went way beyond that.

The first person recorded as asking why Stonehenge was there was an English cleric named Henry of Huntingdon, who confessed in his *History of the English* (1129 CE) that 'no one has been able to discover by what mechanism such vast masses of stones were elevated, nor for what purpose they were designed'. Yet the Welsh scholar Geoffrey of Monmouth, writing just seven years later, was sure he had the answers. The stones, he announced in his *History of the Kings of Britain*, ultimately came from Africa, but prehistoric giants had transported them to Mount Killaraus (perhaps in County Kildare) in Ireland to build a 'Giants' Ring'. There the stones stayed, Geoffrey claimed, until the fifth century CE, when the British king Ambrosius decided to build a monument to mark the graves of heroes killed by his wicked rival Hengist (we will meet these characters again in Chapter 4). Ambrosius' advisers urged him to recruit the wizard Merlin, who was hiding in Wales. Merlin promptly magicked the Giants' Ring from Ireland to Wiltshire.

Almost any time we can check Geoffrey's stories against external evidence he is wildly wrong, and his 3,500-year error in dating Stonehenge hardly inspires confidence. However, he – like the people in our own time who enjoy dressing up as druids, camping out at Stonehenge and annoying archaeologists by objecting to their plans to excavate – did grasp an important truth. Stonehenge was more than just a convenient spot for a market on the overland route between the Bristol and English Channels. It was, above all, a profoundly sacred place.

In 2008 geomorphologists working with Mike Parker Pearson discovered just what had made this spot so special. Stonehenge stands on chalky subsoil crisscrossed with what geologists call periglacial features, basically crevices formed by water seeping into cracks and then freezing, which splits the rock further – then thawing, refreezing and repeating the process over and over again. Most periglacial features are tiny, but just outside the entrance to Stonehenge is a set of truly enormous cracks, up to 0.5 m wide and 150 m long. And they're not just big: if you stand at the centre of the henge to watch the sun set on the winter solstice, the grooves guide your eye directly to the spot where it disappears below the horizon. Doubtless I am over-identifying again, but surely it must have seemed that the gods had singled this spot out, scouring signposts into the soil itself so mortals could not miss the critical moment when the sun disappeared and the longest night of the year set in.

Nature had marked this place as what the Romans would call the *axis mundi*, the 'pivot of the world', where nature and the supernatural join hands. It was a kind of Insular Jerusalem, God's chosen spot on earth. Around 1300 CE, Richard of Haldingham and Lafford would tuck Britain away at the edge of the Hereford Map and put Jerusalem in the middle, but Stonehenge's builders were bolder. They put their magical stone circle, and the bodies of their ancestors, at the centre of the universe.

At some point, probably long before Stonehenge was built, people took pickaxes made from antlers and dug parallel ditches alongside the periglacial features, making them even more visible. And that was not all. Just a few yards away, local volunteers examining an area into which the Stonehenge visitors' car park was being extended discovered something even more surprising: one of the oldest monuments ever found in Britain – indeed, as I mentioned in Chapter 1, almost the only one erected before farming began. Around 8000 BCE, five millennia before the bluestones arrived, hunter–gatherers set up what seems to have been a row of pine totem poles, each nearly a metre thick and perhaps 10 m tall. For all we know, hunters had sensed this spot's sacredness ever since the ice retreated.

When the Welsh immigrants arrived around 2950 BCE, this holy of holies, where heaven and earth met, was already crowded with ancient barrows, enclosures and other monuments, which doubtless added to its lustre. In the 1950s the great archaeologist Gordon Childe speculated that carnivals held here at the summer solstice had drawn thousands of herders. He imagined them creating some sort of sacred peace, like the Olympic truces in ancient Greece. Perhaps the cattle-herding chieftains even forged a degree of political unity in discussions within the stone circle. Some specialists also wonder whether the wide distribution of a single style of pottery, known as Grooved Ware, marked a shared identity across much of southern Britain.

A new Britain was taking shape. Between 4200 and 3700 BCE Continental farmers had swept away the old hunting-and-gathering world, only for their own social order to disintegrate too after 3500 BCE. Five centuries after that, European ideas were shaking the Isles up again, spreading over the western waters as far as Orkney before being carried by Welsh migrants back to the south-east, to take root at Stonehenge. For the first time in its history Britain was no longer exactly Europe's poor cousin. By the time Stonehenge's giant sarsen stones were hauled into place around 2500 BCE – the time when Egyptian builders were working on their Great Pyramid at Giza – the circle was part of the most spectacular religious landscape outside the Mediterranean world. At the edge of the earth, Britons had created their own distinct version of the European Stone Age.

And yet we must keep some perspective. Stonehenge was great, but the Great Pyramid was greater. It used over 2,000 times as much stone as Stonehenge, and was, until 1883, the world's tallest building (even now, it remains the heaviest). Older imbalances had largely evened out at the edge of the world, but an entirely new one had already been created back in the old Middle Eastern core and begun to work its way north and west.

The Killers

This imbalance began with technology. People in metal-rich regions of the Middle East had been tinkering with shiny copper pebbles since well before 7000 BCE, and by 5500 BCE craftsmen in ore-bearing mountains in both Iran and the Balkans had discovered that, if they heated these pebbles to 1,083 °C, the metal in them would melt. From there it was a short step to pouring the molten metal into moulds to make glittering jewellery and sharp (but rather soft, and therefore easily bent or blunted) tools and weapons.

In the 1960s, around the time archaeologists began asking whether migration really had played an important part in prehistory, they raised similar questions about technology. Perhaps, some suggested, our modern obsession with technology makes us exaggerate its significance to the ancients. Maybe trusty old stone axes were every bit as good as high-tech copper alternatives; perhaps the real appeal of metal was its novelty and shininess, not any imagined efficiency. Half a century on, however, what these speculations actually seem to show is how little most archaeologists know about chopping things down. When Phil Harding, from Channel 4 television's *Time Team*, tested the theory by taking a copper axe to a tree, he learned within seconds that it was both easier and faster to use than stone – easier because it was lighter, and faster because while a woodsman with a chunky stone axe has to hack a broad swath through a tree trunk, a thin copper chopper only needs a narrow one. Copper-armed lumberjacks did have to stop every few minutes to pound their blunted blades back into shape (using a stone hammer – old technologies never die), but that was a small price to pay.

Given copper's advantages, an industry was quickly born. The Balkans took an early lead: between 4800 and 4300 BCE a single cluster of mines at Ai Bunar in modern Bulgaria produced more than 500 tons of finished metal. That made millions of axes and daggers. By 3300 BCE copper had spread as far as the Alps. (The famous 'Ice Man', whose frozen body was found in a mountain pass in 1991, was carrying a copper axe.) Five centuries later it was in the region around Lisbon in Portugal.

Some suspiciously thin, V-shaped cuts made in the chalk at Stonehenge and Durrington Walls around 2470 BCE make Mike Parker Pearson wonder whether copper axes had already reached Britain by then, and actual metal objects and signs of mining appear by 2400 BCE. The old, hard rocks of northern and western Britain were full of ores, and as soon as prospectors realised there was copper (not to mention gold) in them there hills, they fanned out across the west to dig it up. On Ross Island in Lake Lough, County Kerry, they struck it rich. Burrowing 15 m underground, they extracted so much ore that for the next five centuries four out of every five copper axes in western Britain and nineteen out of twenty in Ireland were cast from Ross Island copper (we know this because the ore is rich in arsenic, making it easy to identify in the lab).

'That the first copper workers were immigrants is difficult to refute', says Barry Cunliffe, because the elaborate Ross Island mines appear abruptly, with few signs of earlier experiments, and look exactly like mines in Brittany (as does the pottery the first miners used). By the 1920s archaeologists regularly asserted that the Isles were in fact overrun around 2400 BCE by Continental 'Beaker Peoples', so-called after a distinctive kind of pot found in their graves. Armed with new-fangled copper weapons, the theory ran, invaders had seized western metals from backward, stone-armed Britons who had no idea of the wealth they were sitting on.

This theory required a leap of faith, because pots are not people and there are endless possibilities other than migration for why European ceramic styles might have entered the Isles. By the 1970s many archaeologists suspected what actually crossed the narrow seas was an idea or a lifestyle rather than a wave of immigrants, and that human mobility was limited to a handful of specialists, hired to run mines for a native elite. Perhaps British over-achievers – the kind of people who officiated over ceremonies at Stonehenge – saw and liked how elites were now living in the more hierarchical societies on the Continent, and started imitating them.

The new theory fit the facts then available quite well, but since 2015 the facts have changed. First came a study of ancient DNA showing that large numbers of Central Asians (perhaps speaking early versions of today's Indo-European languages) had migrated westwards across Europe after 2800 BCE. In 2016 another DNA study confirmed large-scale Continental migration into Ireland around the time mining began on Ross Island; but the real bombshell came in a paper published in 2018, providing genetic evidence not only that copper-carrying immigrants entered England around 2400 BCE but also that their descendants replaced a staggering 90-plus per cent of the local gene pool.

This seems to prove that major migrations did take place, and the question now is how such a demographic replacement worked. One possibility is that there were relatively few immigrants but that they bred faster than the locals, producing an extreme outcome over twenty or thirty generations. Other archaeologists think that, rather than being outbred, native populations collapsed. *Yersinia pestis*, the bacterium behind the Black Death, is endemic among Central Asian rodents, and a remarkable 7 per cent of the skeletons in the 2015 DNA study had probably died of the plague (albeit a milder version than the one we will meet in Chapter 5). Nor should we forget violence. In 1898 the poet and politician Hilaire Belloc would joke (tastelessly) that the British Empire always won because 'Whatever happens, we have got / The Maxim Gun, and they have not'; in 2400 BCE immigrants had got metal axes and daggers and the natives probably had not. The fact that weapons became such popular grave goods in Britain after 2400 BCE perhaps indicates that the men buried with them wanted to be seen as killers.

The richest of all British Beaker burials, dating around 2330 BCE and barely an hour's walk from Stonehenge, included – along with two gold hair ornaments, decorations made from boars' tusks and five of the eponymous beakers – three copper knives of Spanish style plus flint arrowheads, wristguards of the kind archers use to protect themselves from their bowstrings and a cushion-stone for hammering copper and gold. Its occupant, usually known as the Amesbury Archer, was an immigrant aged about forty who, his isotopes suggest, had grown up around the Rhine or Alps. A second grave, alongside his, is just as interesting: it held the body of another man, about twenty years old, who wore gold ornaments just like the Amesbury Archer's and also shared with him an unusual genetic anomaly of the feet. The two men were probably father and son, although the youth's strontium isotopes show that he differed from his dad in one big way: he was a local Wiltshire lad.

One obvious interpretation is that the Amesbury Archer was one of the Continental immigrants who started arriving after 2400 BCE. Masters of metalwork, they came to get rich, perhaps as leaders of warrior bands, and stayed to rule (the *Daily Mail* even called the Amesbury Archer 'The King of Stonehenge'). Curiously, rich Beaker burials are conspicuously rare in the actual mining regions of western Britain and Ireland, which leads some archaeologists to conjecture that mines like the one on Ross Island belonged to absentee owners who preferred to live – and be buried – in the lusher lands of the south-east. When my own father began working in a north Stafford-shire coal mine in 1943, just before his fourteenth birthday, its owner also lived in the south-east and rarely showed his face at the pit. Some things never change.

It may not be an accident that the grandest grave of the age was so close to Stonehenge (or that a grave found just a kilometre from the henge in 2021 included what may be the head of another ceremonial stone mace). Stonehenge remained Britain's most important religious centre, even as immigrants replaced the people whose Welsh ancestors had built it. The site's role, however, was changing, and was probably doing so even before the newcomers arrived. Stonehenge's users stopped burying their dead among the bluestones after 2400 BCE, and began laying them instead in the ditch around the monument. Parker Pearson wonders whether, half a millennium after the bluestones were set up, no one any longer felt much personal connection to particular founders or stones. The dead of Stonehenge, he suggests, had merged into a kind of blurry ancestral collective, disconnected from the everyday world. The very last burial inside the henge was made around 2250 BCE, three generations after the Amesbury Archer arrived, and strikes Parker Pearson as a ritual statement that the old days were done. It was of a young man, who, like the Amesbury Archer – but unlike any other body inside Stonehenge – had been buried without first being burned. He is often called the Stonehenge Archer: he wore a wristguard and had been shot from several directions with at least three arrows. Was he a scapegoat, sacrificed in a ceremony that ritually declared the book of the Stonehenge dead closed? (Alternatively, was he just killed in a shoot-out or a hunting accident?)

How far the newcomers saw themselves as breaking with the native past and how far they felt like its inheritors remain unclear. On the one hand, people kept on visiting Stonehenge; on the other, by 2250 BCE they had upstaged Stonehenge with very different, and even bigger, monuments. One of these, Silbury Hill, was an astonishing, quarter-million-ton man-made mountain. One excavator estimated that it took 500 workmen fifteen years to heap up. Sadly, erosion and a careless excavation in 1776 have destroyed most traces of whatever went on on top of the hill, adding to the difficulties of saying what it meant to anyone. Possibly its differences from Stonehenge show that new identities were emerging; equally possibly, its location – barely 25 km from Stonehenge, surrounded by Wiltshire's ancient monuments – shows that the immigrants sought connections to the past.

Or we might combine the theories, seeing Silbury Hill as a statement that new rulers had taken control of the old gods and ancestors.

We just cannot say, but we are on firmer ground in thinking that the rush of immigrants after 2400 BCE had slowed to a trickle by 2000 BCE. Evening out had once again spawned new forms of identity, prosperity and sovereignty (not to mention inequality). Gaps between rich and poor were widening, especially in southern and eastern Britain, where a minority was being buried under increasingly enormous barrows. Among those chosen few, even fewer – Bronze Age Britain's 1 per cent – went to meet their makers amid displays of wealth beyond the Amesbury Archer's wildest dreams. The richest graves continued to cluster in Wiltshire, but other parts of the south and east were now producing plutocrats too. One mound, at Raunds in Northamptonshire, was topped with a stack of 185 cattle skulls, whose bodies would have provided 40 tons of meat – enough for thousands of Texas-sized steaks. Whether these came from a single spectacular funeral feast or a string of annual dinners in honour of a great ancestor we cannot say, but by any standards this was conspicuous consumption.

Ranching obviously still thrived, but this elite's lavishness increasingly rested on something new or, depending on how we look at it, very old: farming. After 1,000 years in which few Britons grew crops, wheat and barley returned around 2400 BCE and became steadily more important. By 1500 BCE England had become Baldwin country at last. Pollen from lake beds shows that trees were retreating, probably because farmers made war on forests with their copper axes. Agriculturalists marked out fields with ditches and stone walls, some of which have survived for 4,000 years. (As so often, the best evidence comes from sites with wonderful names. Who could resist digging in a place called Windy Dido?)

Farming was helped by global warming. Temperatures may have been as high around 1500 BCE as they are today, leading to longer growing seasons and higher yields. More food meant more babies and, most important, more babies surviving to adulthood, which perhaps pushed the Isles' population above half a million in 2000 BCE and to twice that number a thousand years later. Even so, hungry mouths did not consume everything: prosperity crept up too, seen in sturdier house foundations, more abundant pottery and metal tools inside dwellings and pits and barns for grain outside them.

Figure 2.5. Casting off: an artist's reconstruction of Ferriby Boat 1, built about 1800 BCE and found on the banks of the River Humber in 1937. Twelve metres long and powered by oars and perhaps a sail, it was made from planks of oak 10 to 20 cm thick, lashed together with yew and caulked with moss.

Even though migration slowed by 2000 BCE, cross-Channel commerce did not. Logboats had become much bigger since 4000 BCE (unwise as it sounds, some Danish examples even had open fireplaces on board), and by 2000 BCE vastly superior vessels were in any case available. Specialists call these sewn-plank boats. They were typically 10–15 m long and powered by oars, although one hull found at Ferriby on the River Humber (Figure 2.5) may have had a sail. They were made by shaving oak into smooth planks (an insanely time-consuming exercise until carpenters had metal tools) and then lashing them together with twisted yew withies and caulking the planks with moss, animal fat or beeswax.

Sewn-plank boats could carry more cargo further with less likelihood of sinking than log- or skin boats, and in the centuries after 2000 BCE so many people and things were crossing the Channel in both directions that finds from either side of it look more alike than ever before. This was especially true of flashy copper and gold jewellery. The archaeologist Timothy Darvill even speaks of a cross-Channel 'original bling society' in these years.

Over the centuries the bling-wearers turned themselves into a true aristocracy, lording it over peasants. Chiefs built great timber roundhouses, ringed by moats and palisades. One, at Thwing (another fine name) in Yorkshire, had a ditched enclosure as big as the circle of Stonehenge. Increasingly, however, the grandest chiefs clustered in the south-east, which had the richest farmland and shortest trade routes to the Continent. A great, slow revolution had been completed. Before 3500 BCE population and prosperity had also been concentrated in the south-east, but by 3000 BCE, when most Islanders had shifted from growing cereals to herding cattle, the centres of gravity had migrated north and west to Ireland and Orkney. They were pulled south again (perhaps by Welsh migrants) to Wiltshire by 2900 BCE, but by 1500 BCE Continental immigrants had dragged them to where they have mostly stayed ever since, in and around the Thames Valley.

Thanks to their proximity to Europe, these lords of the south-east were also the first to benefit from other Continental innovations. Since 2200 BCE British smiths had learned from Europeans to mix tin into their copper to make bronze, a much tougher metal, and around 1600 BCE central European metalworkers worked out how to cast bronze hard enough to make long blades that would not bend on impact. The new weapons – and the tactics they allowed – spread quickly in every direction, changing how men fought. Out went arrowheads and copper daggers; in came big bronze spearheads for thrusting and swords for slashing, shields for protection against both and great war horns for rallying troops above the battle's din. No more did skirmishers pepper distant enemies with arrows or jump out from ambushes for dirty deeds with deadly stilettos; what mattered now were heavy blows, traded face to face, on altogether bloodier battlefields. All across Europe, skulls sliced by swords and pelvises shattered by spears attest a new ferocity in fighting, which made its way into the Isles after 1300 BCE.

Chiefs accumulated other new kinds of bronzes in addition to weapons, such as big buckets for serving beer or mead and cauldrons and hooks for boiling meat. Like a lot of archaeologists, when I look at these weapons and feasting vessels, I immediately think of the proud and violent heroes we meet 2,000 years later in the Old English epic *Beowulf* – such as Scyld Scefing, the 'scourge of many tribes, a wrecker of mead-benches, rampaging among foes' – or even of the doomed hero of the medieval *Song of Roland*, blowing his battle horn Olifant until the veins in his temples burst. And perhaps we are right to think this way: the kitchen wares and weapons seem to speak of similar bands of brothers in arms, roaring drunkenly in their wooden halls, sharing plunder, meat and slave girls and weeping for their dead.

Another hint that these warriors felt differently about themselves from the archers of earlier ages comes from where we find their weapons – not interred in individual graves but tossed by their thousands into rivers (particularly the Thames), fens and bogs. This too was behaviour imported from the Continent, and apparently arrived with new ideas about the gods. Designs scratched on rocks and metal suggest that people still put the sun at the centre of their beliefs, as they had done in the age of Newgrange. Judging from these carvings, however, the sun had mutated. Shedding its links with the godlike dead, and its association with astronomically aligned monuments at solstices and equinoxes, it became a divinity who, as he sailed overnight through a watery underworld, demanded gifts to entice him back to the sky for a new day.

The sheer quantity of bronze consigned to the deep – probably enough to arm and adorn every man, woman and child in the British Isles – makes some archaeologists wonder whether other motives were also at work. While some offerings were masterpieces fit to delight any god, many were second-rate, broken or even just chunks of scrap metal and slag. Perhaps, these archaeologists suggest, we should see an analogy with the native societies of Canada's Pacific coast. Here, Europeans discovered in the nineteenth century CE, chiefs would call feasts at which they wantonly destroyed food, valuable blankets and carvings. Some even burned down their own homes. This madness appalled administrators sent from Ottawa but was actually perfectly sane: chiefs got much of their power from controlling the supply of prestigious goods, and so, the scarcer these goods were, the more powerful those who had them became. Since the 1970s some British archaeologists have argued that bronze worked in similar ways for chiefs who could control the trade in copper and tin. By tossing away hundreds of tons of the stuff, they were having their cake and eating it, simultaneously staying on the right side of the gods and ensuring that their followers still needed them to supply even more copper and tin.

As usual in prehistoric archaeology, we cannot know if these guesses are right. Only the biggest pattern, of the gradual evening out of the imbalances generated by Continental Europeans' invention of better bronze weapons and new ways of fighting, seems certain. Prosperity and power within the Isles were consolidated in the south and east; copper and tin continued being mined in the west – and in the background, as so often, yet another imbalance created in the Middle East was already rolling north-west towards the Isles.

Celtic Dawn

'Would that I had died sooner or been born later', the Greek poet Hesiod complained around 700 BCE, 'for now is truly a race of iron. Men have no rest from labour and sorrow by day or from dying by night, and the gods give them heavy burdens.'

Contemporary British and Irish chiefs would have known exactly what he meant. Iron, which reached the Isles right around the time Hesiod was singing, was yet another gift from the eastern Mediterranean. Smiths in Egypt had been smelting iron since 4000 BCE, but it was such an ugly and brittle metal that they rarely bothered with it. The nineteen iron items buried with the pharaoh Tutankhamun in 1327 BCE were almost certainly chosen for their novelty value, and the metal remained in practical terms very much second-best to bronze.

What made iron's fortune was the fiery destruction, around 1200 BCE, of nearly every Middle Eastern palace outside of Egypt. Why this happened is one of ancient history's greatest mysteries, but in the chaos that followed, the long-distance trade which had brought copper and especially tin to the East Mediterranean's great cities dried up. With bronze now in short supply, Cypriot metalworkers discovered that if they heated, quenched and hammered iron, they could work carbon into it until it became almost – but not quite – as good as bronze. However, iron ore could be found almost everywhere in the Middle East while copper and tin could barely be found at all; so, 'almost as good' became easily good enough. In Cyprus, Greece and Israel, iron largely replaced bronze for weapons and tools, becoming what archaeologists call the 'working metal' by 1050 BCE. The new technology reached Italy around 900 BCE, Germany and France a little before 700 BCE and the Atlantic coast a century later. Its spread then slowed, perhaps because Cornish mines were still producing copper and tin, but by 300 BCE iron had also triumphed across the Isles.

When archaeologists first identified this pattern, about a century ago, they overwhelmingly assumed that migration must explain it, and, often being well versed in Greek and Latin literature, felt confident they knew who the migrants were: Celts. According to the Greek historian Herodotus, people called Keltoi lived around the headwaters of the Danube in the fifth century BCE, and by the first century BCE Julius Caesar observed that central France was inhabited by 'people who are called Celts in their own language but Gauls in ours' (that is, Latin). In 1582 the Scottish scholar Edward Buchanan proposed that since the dialects spoken in Scotland, Ireland, Wales, Cornwall and Brittany were so similar, they must all descend from Caesar's ancestral Gallic/Celtic tongue; and soon after 1700, two more scholars – the Breton monk Paul-Yves Pezron and the Welsh polymath Edward Lhuyd – independently proposed that Continental immigrants had brought these Celtic languages to Britain.

Archaeologists then closed the circle by pointing to an intricate, flowing artistic style invented around 600 BCE (Figure 2.6) and known as the La Tène culture, after a Swiss lakeside site where some fine examples had been found. La Tène is barely 150 km from the sources of the Danube, where Herodotus placed the Celts, and over the course of three centuries La Tène art – not to mention iron – spread westwards into the Isles. So, iron-armed Celts must have migrated between 600 and 300 BCE from Switzerland to Britain, taking their languages and curvilinear art with them.

As in the arguments over the spread of farming and copper, scholars from many fields attacked this migration theory in the late twentieth century, and, given the importance of Celtic identity in modern Britain (to which we will return in Chapters 7–11), the arguments have been especially heated. This time, though, DNA has not ridden to the migrationists' rescue. A massive study in 2015 found little genetic basis to Celtic identity. The similarities between Celtic languages are real enough, but there is no reason to explain them through migrations after 600 BCE. In fact, there are grounds for thinking that precursors of Celtic languages had been spoken along Atlantic coasts from Spain to Orkney well before the first millennium

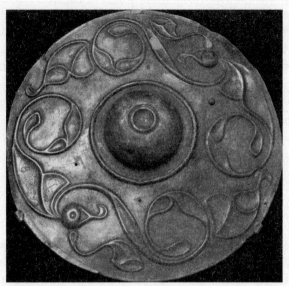

Figure 2.6. Killers with good taste: a bronze shield boss made around
200 BCE and found around 1849 in the River Thames at Wandsworth.
It shows two highly abstract birds, with open wings and trailing
tails. Hundreds of hours of delicate hammering allowed a warrior
to go into battle with an artistic masterpiece on his arm.

BCE, and had perhaps begun evolving in the intense maritime interactions that produced Newgrange around 3000 BCE. Herodotus' claim
that the Celts came from the headwaters of the Danube may actually
be consistent with this, because he actually thought that the Danube
rose in the Pyrenees, not the Alps (a detail generally ignored in the
nineteenth century).

It now seems that trade and copying did more than migration
to bring iron and La Tène art to the Isles, while Celtic languages
were largely locally grown. However, that did not stop the evening
out of iron from south-east to north-west being hugely disruptive.
'Cheap iron democratised agriculture and industry and warfare
too', the archaeologist Gordon Childe concluded back in 1942. What
he meant was that merchants who had sunk everything into pack
animals and warehouses to move copper and tin around, not to
mention chiefs whose positions rested on controlling these networks,
faced ruin when people turned to locally available iron ores. New

men overthrew old elites, and security collapsed in much of the Isles after 500 BCE. Huge efforts went into fortifying everything from farm-steads to foodstores. Some 3,000 hill forts have been identified, often in eminently defensible positions, and many more must have existed. Some were girdled by double or triple ditches and ramparts along with towers, elaborate gates and hornworks which forced attackers to expose their right sides (unprotected by the shields on their left arms) to slingstones and arrows.

Despite so much defence spending, plenty of hill forts were sacked. The most carefully excavated example, Danebury in Hamp-shire, was burned to the ground just before 500 BCE. It was rebuilt with even bigger fortifications soon after, but torched again in the first century BCE. Before the final assault, slingstones had been stacked for easy access just inside its wooden gate; after the sack, about a hundred bodies, most of them scarred by cuts and thrusts from iron swords and some hacked apart, were dumped in pits around the site.

Violence was apparently much on people's minds. Burials with arms and armour became popular after several centuries when they had been rare, as if mourners once more wanted to project martial ideals of manhood. Throwing weapons into water now fell out of favour, but much more gruesome kinds of worship flourished. Pride of place goes to ritualised murders, culminating in dumping the dead in bogs, where the acidic peat preserves them disturbingly well. Gel survived on the hair of one Irish example; another's skin was in such good shape that his fingerprints could be taken.

Hundreds of these bog bodies are now known. A few go back to the Stone Age, but there was a great upsurge in ritualised violence around 750 BCE all across northern Europe. And what violence it was: its victims – men, women and a few children – were beaten, stabbed, strangled, hanged, garrotted, beheaded and cut in half. Throats were cut, nipples slashed and backs broken. Overkill was the name of the game: the most famous bog person (Figure 2.7), a first-century CE corpse known as Pete Marsh (so-called not after his discoverer but because he was found in a peat marsh: archaeological humour is nothing if not obvious), had been murdered in three different ways (clubbing, garrotting, throat-cutting). The Old Croghan Man, buried in a bog near Dublin around 250 BCE, went one further: before being triple-killed (stabbed, beheaded, cut in two), he had been tortured.

It is the stuff of slasher movies, and I defy anyone to stand before

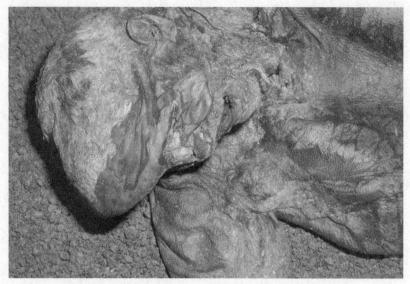

Figure 2.7. Murder in the mud: Pete Marsh emerges from a peat
marsh at Lindow Moss in Cheshire in 1986, perfectly preserved
by the acidic bog after being sacrificed in the first century CE.

Pete Marsh's flat, leathery corpse in the British Museum without
wondering whodunnit. The Roman writer Tacitus' comment that in
Germany around 100 CE 'cowards, shirkers and those who disgrace
their bodies are pressed down under a wicker hurdle into the mud of
a bog' may be relevant; so too the fact that, when pathologists looked
inside Pete Marsh's stomach, they found (in addition to DNA from
E. coli) mistletoe pollen. The druids, the most important priests in
Britain and Gaul, revered this as a sacred plant, and were also famous
for gruesome rituals (they 'drench their altars in the blood of prisoners and consult their gods by means of human entrails', Tacitus said).

But Britons did not need help from druids to be bloodthirsty.
Their chiefs, Roman writers say, enjoyed decorating the gates of hill
forts with skulls on pikes, hanging heads from their ceilings and even
indulging in occasional cannibalism. Calculated terror may have been
one way for chiefs to grind down rivals to increase their own power,
which would help explain why big hill forts like Maiden Castle and
Danebury got bigger still by 400 BCE while little ones around them
tended to disappear. Some archaeologists think that great chiefs were

forging coherent territories of 10 to 20 km², each dominated from a single stronghold. In the south-east, more distinctive pottery styles may also reflect the consolidation of political identities.

Three broad patterns of security, prosperity and perhaps sovereignty took shape. From the Thames to the Humber most people in eastern England lived in undefended villages of a few dozen houses, many of them better built and furnished than ever before. Further west, all the way from Cornwall to the Hebrides, they sheltered in poorer but strongly defended hill forts and farmsteads. On the other side of the Irish Channel, however, it is hard to know what was happening. The later royal centres of Tara, Navan and Knockaulin were all occupied by 300 BCE, which might mean that sovereignty was being concentrated; yet few sites at all have been found outside them, which might mean that Ireland was growing poorer, emptier, less stable and more isolated.

Left to their own devices, British chiefs might have battled away until just a handful were left standing, extending their sovereignty over thousands of square kilometres and cementing security by killing everyone who argued. Seven or eight centuries later, Celtic-speaking kings might have reigned over broad territories from great hill forts like South Cadbury in Somerset. And this is, in fact, more less what happened, but not because the chiefs had been left to their own devices. Instead, another imbalance between the Mediterranean world and the distant British Isles was now evening out across Europe.

The Human Face of Evening Out

So far, we have been concerned with technologically based imbalances, such as the effects of agriculture, copper and iron, but the imbalance that evened out across Western Europe in the late first millennium BCE – government – was organisational. The world's first real kings (rulers able to raise taxes, impose laws and wield so much force that they can simultaneously slaughter and protect their subjects) had clawed their way to power in the Middle East after 3500 BCE. Government changed almost everything, for both good and ill, but governments' greatest gift to historians was their obsession with writing things down. Mesopotamian and Egyptian governments developed systems of symbols for recording taxes and spending, and by 3000 BCE these systems were sophisticated enough for kings to use them to celebrate conquests, merchants to monitor accounts, astronomers to track the movements of the stars and poets to pre- serve words of beauty. Writing puts a human face on the past.

Societies with governments were normally more powerful but less equal than those without. Chiefs whose neighbours turned them- selves into kings tended quite quickly either to be taken over by these royal rivals or to survive only by creating similar governments of their own. Either way, the long-term outcome was the same: whether because the stronger conquered the weaker or the weaker became stronger so they could stand up to aggression, government spread. In our own day every scrap of land on the planet is claimed by some government or other.

However, all this took time. Fifteen hundred years passed before states expanded from their homelands in Mesopotamia and Egypt as far as Crete in the west and the oases of Central Asia in the east (Figure 2.8). Governments needed another three or four centuries to swallow up mainland Greece, and even in 1400 BCE the chiefs of Sicily and southern Spain could not really be called kings. The process of expansion was also fitful, and sometimes went into reverse, most spectacularly when the palaces of the eastern Mediterranean went up in flames around 1200 BCE. Proper governments, able to build palaces and write things down, withered or disappeared almost everywhere outside Egypt, only reviving again after 950 BCE, when a new Assyrian Empire, based in what is now northern Iraq, gobbled up most of the Middle East.

Empires like Assyria needed resources – food, metals, timber, people – on a whole new scale, which meant that trade typically went before the flag as merchants fanned out beyond a kingdom's borders to suck commodities into its ravening marketplaces, enriching them- selves in the process. Sailors from Phoenicia (roughly the coast of modern Lebanon) were already trading in the western Mediterra- nean before 900 BCE, but upped their game enormously in reaction to Assyrian demands for tribute. Seeing the gains to be made as mid- dlemen, they set up permanent colonies in Sicily, Sardinia, southern Spain and – most famously – at Carthage in North Africa, carrying government right across the Mediterranean. Hard on their heels came Greeks, piggybacking on Phoenician efforts and slotting themselves into commercial networks wherever they could; and in reaction to both, locals created kings and built cities for themselves.

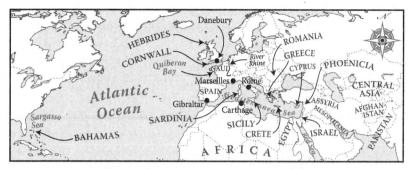

Figure 2.8. Trade and the flag: kings, merchants and explorers draw
Western Europe into a Mediterranean orbit, 3500–200 BCE.

Increasingly mobile explorers, traders and raiders pressed on.
Around 600 BCE an Egyptian pharaoh funded a boatload of Phoenicians to sail and row around Africa, just to see if it could be done.
Setting off from the Red Sea and keeping the coast to starboard, they
returned after two years via Gibraltar. A century later, sailing in the
opposite direction, a skipper named Himilco set off from Carthage to
explore the Atlantic. What little we know of him comes from a pain-
fully bad poem called *The Sea Shores*, written nearly nine centuries
later by a Roman official named Avienus. For reasons now unclear,
Avienus took it on himself to convert old sailors' almanacs about the
Mediterranean and Atlantic coasts into verse. The results varied from
the ponderous to the ludicrous, but Avienus was a learned man and
consulted what he calls 'things published long ago in the secret annals
of the Carthaginians' – including an account of Himilco's four-month
adventure on the Atlantic Ocean.

Himilco almost certainly got as far west as the wide Sargasso Sea,
just a few hundred kilometres short of the Bahamas. Here, he said,
'No breezes propel a craft, the sluggish liquid of the lazy sea is at a
standstill [. . .] seaweed floats in the water and often after the manner
of a thicket holds the prow back.' But getting to the Sargasso Sea
and back would not take four months, even if a boat got stuck in
the doldrums – which leaves historians of a romantic disposition free
to guess at where else Himilco went. We simply do not know, but,
fuelled more by wishful thinking than anything else, some writers
speculate that he went to Cornwall looking for tin. The sad truth is
that there is not a scrap of archaeological evidence for Phoenicians

in England, and no matter how much we torture Avienus' already tortured Latin, there is no way to make *The Sea Shores* put Himilco there either.

Half a dozen Greek pots did make their way to Britain during the sixth and fifth centuries BCE, which may – or may not – mean that actual Greeks carried them. According to the first-century-CE Roman geographer Pliny, 'tin was first imported [to Italy] from the Tin Island by Midacritus', which – again – may, or may not, refer to a Greek trading with Britain. Even if it does, we know nothing else about Midacritus. The first flesh-and-blood Mediterranean visitor to Britain of whom anything can be said was Pytheas, from the Greek colony of Marseille.

After arriving in the 320s BCE, Pytheas wrote, he 'traversed the whole of Britain accessible by foot'. He must have been a remarkable man, but sadly, *On the Ocean* – the book in which he described his journeys – was lost long ago (Pliny is in fact the last author we know of who read it). Sadder still, when ancient authors do mention his book, they mostly do so to mock it. Greeks apparently found Pytheas' tales just as tall as Venetians would find Marco Polo's when he came home from Cathay in the 1290s CE. Marco's *Travels* were only written down because he dictated them to a cellmate while he was in prison. Let us hope Pytheas was at least spared that indignity.

The details surviving about *On the Ocean* are not very informative. Pytheas said that Britain was cold, that the sun did not shine much (especially in the north) and that northern summer nights were very short. British societies, he said, were simple but populous and ruled by kings and aristocrats. Although he was in the Isles around the time that the Danebury hill fort was sacked, Britain struck him as rather peaceful (possibly he just meant relative to his native Greece, which was not saying much). He observed that Britons lived in timber houses and drank beer and mead. He also saw a circular temple, where, locals told him, the sun god Apollo lived during the summer. Excitable archaeologists sometimes suggest this was Stonehenge, but the rest of what Pytheas says implies that it was a henge much further north (perhaps in the Hebrides).

After Pytheas left, darkness falls again. Mediterranean governments had a long reach by the 320s BCE – Alexander the Great was rampaging through Afghanistan and Pakistan after overthrowing the Persian Empire in the very years that Pytheas was in Britain – but they had no interest in Western Europe. No Mediterranean ruler could (or cared to) project power into Europe's interior.

This only began to change after 200 BCE, when Roman armies pushed inland into Spain's interior and Italian traders opened up Gaul. Efforts to resist the former and profit from the latter partly explain why inland Western Europeans began flocking together in cities of several thousand and bowing to rulers of their own. Some adapted the Greek alphabet to record their languages and minted their own gold coins based on Greek designs. The Greek explorer Posidonius, who spent several years in this part of the world, was initially shocked at Gallic chiefs who decorated their front doors with enemies' heads and would happily hand fellow tribesmen to slave traders in exchange for five-gallon jars of Roman wine. However, the Greek geographer Strabo tells us, Posidonius not only got used to the hanging heads but even came to admire chiefs like Luernios, who, around 150 BCE, turned the Arverni tribe into a real kingdom (Figure 2.9). Luernios ruled 'from the Rhine to the Atlantic', said Posidonius, in part by attracting allies with grand feasts, at which he served the best Italian wines.

From this point on, Greek and Roman writers provide sufficient detail for us to be able sometimes to see evening out from European as well as Mediterranean perspectives. Luernios' ambitions had trapped the Arverni in what scholars of international relations call a 'security dilemma'. He created a kingdom largely because he feared Rome's growing presence in Gaul, but Rome then increased its presence in Gaul because it feared that Luernios' kingdom was strong enough to hurt its interests; and other Gauls, fearing both Luernios and Rome, began organising too. Caught in this spiral of suspicion, in 125 BCE the Greeks of Marseille asked Rome to protect them against increasingly effective raids by the nearby tribes. Rome's leaders, who counted Marseille as an ally, agreed; and, having defeated the raiders, the Romans decided that they had better build a fort to keep everyone safe. This, however, so alarmed the Arverni that Luernios' son Bituitos formed a federation to keep Rome at bay – which so alarmed Rome that in 121 BCE it sent an army, complete with elephants, to kill Bituitos. Having done so, Rome annexed his kingdom, plus Marseille and everything between the Alps and the Pyrenees. To this day, the region is known as Provence, from its Latin name, *provincia*, 'the province'.

Figure 2.9. The tribes of Gaul, according to Posidonius and
Caesar. The territory under Roman rule in 58 BCE is shaded.

Many Gallic chiefs found annexation by Rome an unattractive
prospect. Over the next two generations more and more of them
turned themselves into kings to oppose it – even though men who
would be kings had to spend so much money bribing their fellow
tribesmen into accepting their leadership against the shared enemy
that they often found themselves deep in hock to Roman moneymen.
'Not a single coin changes hands in Gaul without being entered into
the account books of some Roman', the lawyer Cicero would observe
in 73 BCE.

Rather than creating a counterscarp that would shield Britain
from Mediterranean imperialism, the Gallic chiefs who scrambled to
turn themselves into kings to resist Rome actually pushed the ten-
tacles of government and big finance towards south-eastern Britain
even faster. Gallic gold coins appeared in the Thames Valley before
150 BCE, and ambitious British chiefs were minting their own versions

by 125 BCE. Soon after 100 BCE coins appeared in Dorset too, in the hinterland of a new port at Hengistbury Head, and jars of Italian wine passing through this fine harbour were lubricating elite parties all over south-eastern Britain.

Coins and wine jars are much rarer on British sites than on Gallic, but some wealthy south-easterners seem to have fallen in love with the lifestyles of their more sophisticated peers on the Continent. As so often, foreign food led the way. (The dried-out remains of a bunch of imported Mediterranean figs turned up at Hengistbury Head.) It seems that south-eastern elites were also entranced by fancy European fashions. Complicated brooches of Continental type were showing up in their graves before 100 BCE, probably meaning that the fine robes favoured by Gallic nobles were arriving with them. (For women, *chic* meant tunics worn over long-sleeved bodices; for men, the evidence is less clear.) Rich south-easterners began aping Roman and Gallic standards of grooming, buying bronze razors to shave their faces, tweezers to pluck out stray hairs, tiny bronze spoons for scooping out earwax and little mortars and pestles for grinding make-up. Top people were cleaning up their act.

Behind these cosmetic changes, though, Continental styles of organisation were penetrating Britain too. Julius Caesar, probably writing in 58 BCE, says that 'within living memory', a certain Diviciacus, king of a tribe called the Suessiones and 'the most powerful man in Gaul', also 'controlled a large part of Britain'. Whether Diviciacus achieved this through conquest, dynastic marriage or attracting clients with lavish gifts, Caesar does not say. However, Caesar is very clear that, after years of raiding southern Britain, another group of Gauls, whom he calls Belgae (a generic name for tribes in or near what is now Belgium), also started stealing British land. 'Having come to raid,' he says, 'they stayed to sow.' By the 50s BCE chiefs in south-east Britain – whether Belgic immigrants or natives reacting to them – were copying the Gallic model so closely that they too were becoming kings.

Caesar Is Coming

Kings were something the Gauls created for themselves, not an imitation of Roman ways, because Rome, famously, did not have them. Instead, Rome left government to the Senate, a super-rich elite of about 600 men, who took turns being elected to the top jobs. Senatorial politics, however, was literally a matter of life and death, and it was the Senate's vicious internal dynamics that finally pushed government into Britain.

The central character in the story was Julius Caesar. Bullying, charming and bribing his way through the minefields of Roman politics, Caesar had by 59 BCE shoved his way to the front of the pack, but only at the cost of taking massive loans to fund his political campaigns. Now, desperately indebted and with creditors closing in, he made a secret deal with other powerbrokers which gave him command of an army in the Balkans. His idea was to use this to make war on a kingdom in what is now Romania, winning not only prestige but also the loyalty of his troops and enough plunder to recoup his fortunes. But when, as an afterthought, the Senate added the Roman province in southern Gaul to his command, Caesar saw new possibilities.

During the previous decade, many of Gaul's tribes had clumped into two broad alliances, one led by the Arverni, who had been fighting Rome since Bituitos' day sixty years earlier, and the other by a tribe called the Aedui. Because Arvernian chiefs remained resolutely anti-Roman, most Aedui leaned towards Rome, hoping to leverage the empire's friendship to help them dominate their Gallic neighbours. But soon after 60 BCE, things went horribly wrong for the Aedui. Caught between the Aedui and their Roman friends, Arvernian chiefs sought allies of their own. They hired 15,000 Germanic mercenaries to invade Aeduan territory – which the Germans did, but then, seeing how rich the pickings were in Gaul, they refused to go home. By 58 BCE they seemed set to steal everything, not just from the Aedui but from the Arverni too.

Smelling weakness, other Germans joined in. The Helvetii tribe, who lived around Geneva, found themselves squeezed between German and Roman aggression, and one of their leading men, named Orgetorix, persuaded them that they should migrate through Aeduan territory to find a better place to live. In a panic, the leading man among the Aedui, a druid named Diviciacus (a different Diviciacus from the one mentioned a moment ago), asked Rome for help; but in truth, Caesar now discovered, a much more devious plot was being hatched behind the scenes. Unknown to Diviciacus, his own brother Dumnorix was conspiring with Orgetorix to create such chaos among both the Aedui and the Helvetii that Dumnorix and Orgetorix could launch coups, making themselves kings and then dividing the whole of Gaul between them.

I am going into such detail about the backroom politics (and there was, in truth, even more happening than this) because here we really begin to see what 'evening out' meant on the ground. Dumnorix and Orgetorix wanted to turn themselves into great men by building bigger, stronger Arvernian and Aeduan states to resist Rome; Diviciacus wanted to do something similar by building a bigger, stronger Aeduan state in collaboration with Rome; and Caesar wanted to make himself the greatest man of all by swallowing Gaul into a bigger, stronger Roman Empire. Which scenario won out mattered very much to these four men, but in a sense it mattered rather less to the net result. Whoever came out on top, bigger, stronger states would keep spreading north-west from the Mediterranean, bringing kings, coins and towns to the coast across from Britain.

Almost any Roman proconsul would have done the same as Caesar when faced with the Helvetian migration in 58 BCE. Doing nothing risked letting the Helvetii ruin Rome's ally Diviciacus or even invade the Roman province, meaning disgrace and possibly death for the proconsul. Defeating the Helvetii, on the other hand, would bring the glory and plunder needed for scrambling up the greasy pole of Roman politics. An easy choice. What made Caesar special, though, was the pace at which he pushed things along. (Caesar always said that *celeritas*, 'speed', was his watchword.) Rather than just smashing the Helvetii, he went on in the next two summers to smash every anti-Roman alliance in Gaul. 'Because of these achievements', he crowed, 'a thanksgiving of fifteen days was decreed. This had never been granted to anyone before.'

Had Caesar not been given the Gallic command in 59 BCE, or if his senatorial 'friends' had let him down, or if he had lost a couple of key battles early on, the advance of government across Gaul would have been slower; and had Caesar been beaten badly enough, perhaps even leaving his bones in some Gallic forest, Rome might well have dropped the conquest of Gaul altogether. The empire, after all, abandoned conquering Germany after an army was annihilated in an ambush in 9 CE. But not even this worst-case (from the Roman perspective) scenario would have stopped government spreading. After the German disaster, the Roman historian Cassius Dio recounts, people beyond the Danube formed their own governments anyway. 'The barbarians adapted themselves to the Roman world', he explained. 'They set up markets and [. . .] as long as they learned our habits gradually and under supervision, they did not find it difficult to change their life, and they became different without realising it.'

Whoever ended up taking government to the English Channel – Caesar, some later Roman general or a great Gallic king – would then have had to confront just the same problem Caesar actually faced in 56 BCE: that, far from being a barrier, the Channel was a highway. The basic issue had not changed since farmers flooded across the Channel when the foraging counterscarp collapsed in 4200 BCE. No one could command the sea, so anyone with access to one shore could cross to the other.

If anything, the problem was even worse in the first century BCE than it had been in the forty-second, because shipbuilding had improved so much. Caesar reports that Gallic ships 'were made to suit the size of the waves and the weather. The ships were built entirely of oak, to withstand any force or rough treatment. The cross-timbers supporting the deck were made of beams a foot thick, with iron nails as wide as a man's thumb.' Such ships made crossing the Channel so easy that every time Gauls were defeated they could just sail off to their kinsmen in southern Britain and then bring British fighters back to Gaul to continue the struggle. For any government in Gaul the Channel was a wide-open flank. The only way to close it was by controlling both shores, giving Gaul a counterscarp of its own and preventing enemies from setting sail in the first place. So that became Caesar's plan.

His first step, in 56 BCE, was to move against the Veneti, a tribe living on the south coast of Brittany. They had the strongest fleet in Gaul, making a Channel crossing with the potentially hostile Veneti at his rear a huge risk. Caesar therefore sent his legions to bring them to heel – but every time he besieged one of their fortified villages, they just embarked on their boats and moved to the next one. Caesar, always practical, built a fleet of his own, but now found that the kind of galleys that worked well in the Mediterranean were useless against Atlantic sailing ships. 'Our ships were unable to harm theirs by ramming them (they were so strongly built) or, because of their height, to aim missiles at them with any success', Caesar lamented. 'For the same reason, it was difficult to board them with grappling irons.'

Catching the Veneti in Quiberon Bay, the magnificent Breton harbour that has always been the key to the western approaches to the English Channel, Caesar's sailors adapted quickly. Rigging up long poles with hooks on one end, they rowed their galleys up to the enemy ships. Using the hooks to grab the ropes that tied the yardarms on the Veneti vessels to the masts, they rowed away hard, pulling down the sails. It worked, and with the enemy warships now sitting ducks, groups of Roman galleys surrounded each, tossing grappling irons at its high decks until one finally took and marines could swarm onboard. Even then, most of the Veneti might still have escaped had the wind not dropped at the vital moment. 'By nightfall', Caesar tells us, 'almost none of their number had reached land.' Taking no chances, Caesar killed the Veneti's chiefs and sold almost everyone else into slavery.

Now the undisputed master of the Gallic coast, Caesar turned his eyes across the water. Little British kings, terrified at the prospect of Roman intervention, scrambled to turn themselves into bigger kings. Just as had previously happened in Gaul, civil wars broke out between pro- and anti-Roman factions. When Cassivellaunus, the anti-Roman ruler of the strongest tribe in the south-east, defeated his neighbours and murdered their king, the late king's son Mandubracius fled across the Channel begging Caesar to reinstate him. How could Caesar say no? Agreeing, he explained to his enemies in the Senate, would be honourable and glorious; refusing would be cowardly and dangerous. Once again, an easy choice (particularly, Caesar's sharp-tongued critic Cicero adds, because the conqueror had a rather inflated idea of the plunder available in Britain).

Late in the summer of 55 BCE Caesar sent one of his Gallic allies across the Channel 'to approach what communities he could, and urge them to choose loyalty to the Roman people'. His message: 'Caesar is coming. Soon.'

3

EMPIRE, 55 BCE–410 CE

Snafu

Caesar did come, and, having seen, he conquered. Or he said he did, anyway. In reality, right from the start, everything that could go wrong did. Caesar's problem was what the great military thinker Carl von Clausewitz would later call *friction*: 'everything in war is very simple', Clausewitz observed, 'but the simplest thing is very difficult'. Soldiers in our own times use the blunter term 'snafu' – situation normal, all f – d up.

The campaign of 55 BCE was one long snafu from start to finish. Commius, the envoy Caesar sent ahead to win the Britons over, was clapped in chains the moment he stepped ashore. A delay in coaxing the horses on to Caesar's cavalry transports made them miss the tide, and when they did get within sight of Britain, the wind changed and scattered them all over the Channel. Next, Caesar's ships turned out to be too big to get close to shore, so the poor bloody infantry had to plunge into neck-deep surf in full armour and claw their way on to the beach, probably at Pegwell Bay in Kent (Figure 3.1). Even Caesar had to concede that 'This was the one action in which [my] previous good fortune was found lacking'.

Once ashore, Rome's veterans made short work of the actual fighting, but without cavalry they could not pursue the fleeing Britons, who lived to fight another day. Even worse, not understanding the Channel's tides, Caesar left his ships where a powerful storm could smash them. After a little more skirmishing he cut a deal with the locals, crammed his men into hastily repaired hulls and got out of Britain the moment the weather permitted.

The next summer, 54 BCE, Caesar was back, with three times as many men (including cavalry), custom-built landing craft and a diplomatic offensive to parallel his military one. Initially Britain's

Figure 3.1. The British stage, 55 BCE–410 CE.

south-eastern tribes rallied around Cassivellaunus, the rising anti-Roman king mentioned at the end of the last chapter, but the alliance unravelled when it became clear that neither standing and fighting, hitting and running nor hunkering down in fortresses would make Caesar go away. With nothing to show for tens of thousands dead, wounded and enslaved, Cassivellaunus sought terms. Caesar declared another victory and sailed away.

It had not been Caesar's finest hour, and he would probably have come back again in 53 BCE, had a great Gallic uprising not prevented him. And yet he had done enough. His campaigns were wildly popular back in Rome, where the Senate decreed a twenty-day festival of Thanksgiving – even more than the celebrations for his conquest of Gaul – because, as a later Roman writer explained, 'what was previously unknown had been revealed to sight and what had formerly been unheard of had become accessible'. Caesar had dragged Britain on to a larger stage, dominated by Rome.

He had also given Gaul a British counterscarp, leaving behind a federation that historians normally call the Eastern Kingdom (Figure 3.2), under the same Mandubracius whose flight from Cassivellaunus in 56 BCE had given Caesar his justification for invading. Such client kings – 'friendly kings', Romans called them – were the empire's favourite method of control, and giving Mandubracius this job was probably Caesar's plan all along. He could have conquered and garrisoned the whole of Britain's south shore, but that would have cost a fortune, whereas Mandubracius didn't. In return for a title, some fancy gifts and vague promises of Roman support, Mandubracius bullied the neighbouring chiefs into refusing refuge to Gallic rebels, closing Caesar's open flank and achieving Rome's strategic goal on the cheap.

Mandubracius gained from the arrangement too, but it also came with costs. First, a client king was by definition Rome's man. Every local rival could rally opposition to him simply by posing as the defender of tradition against wicked Continental ways. The Eastern Kingdom's rulers therefore had to embrace Europe, relying on Rome to save their thrones (and skins). By the 20s BCE kings were minting coins based closely on Roman designs and being buried at Colchester and St Albans with heaps of Continental imports. One tomb, which perhaps contains the cremated remains of Mandubracius' royal descendant Tasciovanus (who ruled roughly 25–10 BCE), included imported Italian horse fittings, eighteen big jars of wine, a silver medallion of the emperor, a suit of Roman chain mail and bits of what might have been a throne. Another grave contained imported surgical instruments; another still, a Roman board game set up ready to play.

Figure 3.2. Peoples and regions on the British stage, 55 BCE–410 CE.

Romanomania infected only a cosmopolitan few, but their demand for expensive imports was enough to draw Gallic traders away from Hengistbury Head in Dorset – the favoured destination for the previous fifty years – and towards the Thames estuary. The new ruling class created Britain's first real governments, eroding the organisational imbalance between south-eastern Britain and the Continent while increasing that between south-eastern Britain and regions further north and west. By the 20s or 30s CE the Eastern Kingdom seems to have been taking territory away from its less centralised neighbours. The chiefs of these tribes – Dobunni, Durotriges, Corieltauvi and Iceni – reacted just as the Arverni, Aedui and Helvetii had done in Gaul three-quarters of a century earlier, scrambling to create kingdoms of their own either to resist Mandubracius or to compete with him for Rome's friendship.

A second problem for client kings was that they served entirely at the pleasure of their Roman patrons. Clientage was basically an endless negotiation. On one side, a 'friendly' king would try to get away with as much as he could without provoking Rome into replacing him with a more pliable man or annexing his kingdom; on the other, Rome tried to squeeze its 'friends' as hard as it could without driving them to revolt or leaving them so weak that less friendly rivals would kill and replace them.

Some clients excelled at this tightrope act. The grandmaster was Herod, king of Judaea at the time Jesus was born, but Commius, despite his bad start as Caesar's ambassador in 55 BCE, proved almost as adept.* As a client king in Gaul, he pleased Caesar so well that the great man enlarged his kingdom and exempted it from taxes. Commius therefore stood by his friend when other Gauls revolted in 53 BCE; but when it began to look as though Caesar was losing, Commius rebranded himself as a nativist, joined the uprising and became one of its leaders. Caesar turned the tables and crushed the revolt after all, whereupon its other chiefs threw themselves on his mercy, but Commius was either cleverer or more desperate. He fought on alone for three years, becoming such a nuisance (he almost killed one Roman commander in a dramatic horseback fight) that Caesar's lieutenant Mark Antony offered him a special deal: Commius could rule a newly formed 'Southern Kingdom', so long as he promised to 'live where he was sent and do as he was told' (with the proviso that he would never have to lay eyes on another Roman). He reinvented himself once again as the very model of a friendly king, living to a ripe old age in his capital near Chichester, issuing coins in his own name and dining off Roman crockery.

---

*The Bible says that Herod lived for at least two years after Jesus' birth, but other ancient sources make it certain that he died in 4 BCE – meaning, many historians conclude, that ancient scholars' calculations were mistaken, and Jesus was actually born around 7 BCE.

No would-be leader in south-eastern Britain could afford to ignore Rome, but it was still up to individuals – from the Isles to Italy – to decide what the details would look like. Clients regularly acted up, and at least two would-be friendly kings had to flee their homelands and seek protection from Caesar's nephew Augustus, who had made himself Rome's first autocrat after winning the bitter civil wars that followed Caesar's murder in 44 BCE. Annoyed beyond measure that 'the people would not come to terms with him', Augustus considered new military interventions in Britain in 34 and 27–26 BCE.

These storms blew over, largely because Augustus had better things to do than spend money annexing British kingdoms, but after 37 CE a new ruler, known by his nickname Caligula ('Little Boots', from the bootees he wore with his soldier suits as a boy), felt differently. Caligula's hobbies included dressing up as a god, appointing his horse to a top job in the government and engaging in sexual antics that shocked even the worldly Roman elite. Sleeping with his sister was the least of his foibles.* Unsurprisingly, Caligula had his critics, and, deciding that the best way to repair his reputation was through feats of arms, the troubled young monarch sought a soft target. Right on cue, probably in the year 38 CE, Cunobelin, the ruler of Britain's Eastern Kingdom, fell out with his son Adminius, who – predictably – asked Caligula for help. Cunobelin then died, leaving the Eastern Kingdom to Adminius' squabbling brothers, and Caligula made the convenient decision that justice demanded an intervention on Adminius' behalf.

But what a strange intervention it was. Given that no one despised Caligula quite as much as the rich, educated aristocrats who wrote the only accounts of him that survive, it is hard to be sure how much we can believe of what they say; but they tell us that, after assembling an invasion force in the spring of 40 CE, Caligula cancelled the mission without warning and instead ordered his men to collect seashells as spoils of an imaginary victory over the Ocean.

---

*It perhaps serves Caligula right that he is best remembered nowadays for the extraordinary film from 1979 bearing his name, which has the distinction of being the only feature film ever produced by the adult magazine *Penthouse*. As well as boasting a screenplay by Gore Vidal and a cast including John Gielgud, Helen Mirren, Peter O'Toole and (playing the man himself) Malcolm McDowell, it also featured several Penthouse Pets in live sex acts, which the backers added to the film after the actors and director thought production had finished. Even so, I suspect Caligula would have thought it tame stuff.

We can only wonder what Adminius thought of all this, but it turned out not to matter much. Caligula was dead within a few months, murdered (not before time) by his own guards. His replacement, Claudius, was a different sort of oddball – an academic – but despite being somewhat saner than Caligula, he needed military glory just as much. Adminius' brothers in the Eastern Kingdom unwisely chose just this moment to invade the neighbouring, pro-Roman Southern Kingdom, and when its long-serving client king fled to Rome, Claudius too found it convenient to conclude that justice demanded action. In April 43 CE he massed 40,000 men at Boulogne and, after a last-minute glitch when the troops baulked at boarding the ships, the invasion was on.

Cymbeline's Nose

In the short run, at least, Claudius did a much better job than Caesar at securing Rome's open flank. His main force landed unopposed, probably near Richborough in Kent. Twice the Eastern Kingdom's warriors barred its way at river crossings (one on the Thames, the other unidentified), and twice they fled when specially trained German detachments swam across in full armour. According to Shakespeare's play *Cymbeline* (the seventeenth-century spelling of Cunobelin), the Eastern Kingdom roared defiance at Rome. 'Britain is / A world by itself', says King Cunobelin's stepson, 'and we will nothing pay / For wearing our own noses.'

In reality, some of Cunobelin's relatives were perfectly ready to negotiate over their noses. Claudius was offering a deal: give up your sovereignty and some of your identity, he said, and accept more immigration from the Continent, and I will increase your prosperity and security. In case the presence of his legions was not sufficient incentive, Claudius himself rushed across the Channel as soon as word of the victory on the Thames reached him.

Claudius' critics were most amused that he (and the elephants he took along for a victory parade through Colchester) only stayed in Britain sixteen days, but that was enough. At least eleven native kings surrendered. Claudius annexed the Eastern Kingdom and fired Cunobelin's family, but he reinstated and even rewarded other men. The new master installed in the Southern Kingdom showed his enthusiasm for Rome by building a spectacular villa at Fishbourne, replete with mosaics and marble statues in the height of Continental style. Others received huge cash gifts, which they were encouraged to spend beautifying their villages. Within a decade, St Albans, Colchester and Bath all boasted vaguely Roman-looking stone temples and bathhouses.

Just what Claudius had in mind when he decided to outdo Caesar by annexing parts of Britain has never been clear. Capturing Colchester had given him his glory, and some historians think he only ever intended to set up a buffer zone of client kings in the lowland southeast, leaving the hilly north and west to their own devices. If so, his plans did not survive contact with reality, for, just like Caesar when he arrived at the English Channel a century earlier, Claudius discovered that victory simply led to further wars. Within four years of the invasion his men had been drawn into messy fighting in the Welsh mountains. 'Battle followed battle', the historian Tacitus grumbled, 'most of them guerilla fights in woods and bogs. Some were accidental results of chance encounters; others were planned with calculated courage, for hatred or plunder. Sometimes engagements were ordered by commanders; sometimes they knew nothing of them.'

Some scholars speculate that Claudius had always intended to cross from south-east to north-west because he knew that the northwest was where Britain's mineral resources lay. Romans certainly wasted no time in grabbing them: they were digging up lead at Charterhouse in the Mendip Hills as early as 49 CE, and within two decades miners had reached Prestatyn, a little seaside town on the north coast of Wales where my sister and I used to go on caravan holidays with our grandparents in the 1960s. Roof tiles and lead ingots stamped 'Twentieth Legion' show that the army initially ran Prestatyn's mines, several associated workshops and a little bathhouse, and the same seems to be true of most Welsh mining towns in the next half-century.

Other scholars blame this move not on greed but on mission creep, caused by the ever-present security dilemma. Not all of southeastern Britain's kings surrendered in 43 CE, and one – Cunobelin's son Caratacus – fled to Wales, which he used as a base for raiding Rome's allies. After chasing him up hill and down dale for several years, the legions finally massacred his followers and captured his wife and daughter. But Caratacus fought on. Fleeing now to the Brigantes in northern England, he tried to raise them against the aggressors. Their queen, Cartimandua, instead handed him back to the Roman governor, but Caratacus still refused to concede. Impressed, Claudius pardoned him and his family. Queen Cartimandua, however, had a tougher time. When her husband rejected her pro-Roman policies, she divorced him and took up with his shield-bearer. The Brigantes split into pro- and anti-Cartimandua/Rome factions, which were soon at war. Now the Roman army found itself dragged into fighting in northern England as well as Wales.

Whatever Claudius had sought in 43 CE, it was surely not this quagmire, and when he died eleven years later, his successor Nero seriously considered pulling out of Britain completely. Alternative futures branched: if Nero had brought the boys back home, leaving behind just a couple of client kingdoms like Caesar's, south-eastern Britain's integration into Europe would have slowed drastically. There is no way it would have stopped altogether: I speculated at the end of the last chapter that if Caesar had not pushed to the English Channel in the 50s BCE, the south-east might in any case have ended up looking like the parts of Germany just beyond the frontier, and I suspect something similar would have happened in Britain if Rome had withdrawn in the 50s CE. And in any case, the difficulties that Augustus, Caligula and Claudius had encountered trying to get British client kings to do as they were told were, if anything, getting worse. If Nero had cut and run, the most likely scenario was that some future emperor would have felt compelled to invade again.

In the end, says Nero's biographer Suetonius, the emperor stayed the course because evacuation 'would have reflected badly on the glory won by his adoptive father Claudius' – no small thing for a new ruler worried about his bona fides. Nero doubled down, betting that if he pushed just a little further north and west, he would find a stable frontier. He appointed aggressive governors to wage scorched-earth wars and root out the druids, around whom resistance rallied ('the Iron Age equivalents of the Muslim Mullahs', the archaeologist Francis Pryor calls them). The druids' sanctuary on the island of Anglesey – another holiday favourite when I was a boy – had become a refuge for anyone fleeing Rome's advance, so it had to go, despite an impassioned defence. 'The enemy lined the shore in a dense armed mass,' Tacitus says, 'among them black-robed women with tangled hair like Furies, waving torches. Close by stood druids, raising their hands to heaven and screaming terrible curses.' Even veteran legionaries flinched – but sprang ashore from their flat-bottomed boats anyway, and hacked down druids, Furies and all, finally burning their sacred groves.

Rome pursued its usual good-cop/bad-cop strategy, trying to resolve security problems cheaply by weakening local identities. On the one hand, officials discredited indigenous opponents; on the other, they offered local bigwigs opportunities to join a wider and more sophisticated world, lining up alongside like-minded groups from as far afield as Italy and Egypt. Tacitus understood exactly what was going on, and despite being a consummate insider – his father-in-law, Agricola, governed Britain for six years – was deeply ambivalent about it. In a famous assessment, a few words of which I quoted in this book's introduction, he describes how Rome

> gave private encouragement and official assistance to the building of temples, public squares and good houses [and] educated the sons of the chiefs in the liberal arts [. . .] The result was that instead of loathing the Latin language they became eager to speak it well. In the same way, our national dress came into favour and the toga was everywhere to be seen. So, the population was gradually led into the demoralising temptations of arcades, baths and sumptuous banquets. The unsuspecting Britons spoke of such novelties as 'civilisation', when in fact they were only a feature of their enslavement.

Conquest brought an ancient version of globalisation. For a favoured few, foreign money and luxuries eroded local attachments. But then as now, winds from the wider world could blow cold as well as hot. The financiers and officials who funded British rulers' new villas, hot baths and *haute cuisine* were, naturally, interested first and foremost in their own well-being; and when a credit crunch in the late 50s CE set off a string of bankruptcies back in Italy, they called in their loans, including staggering sums advanced to social-climbing chiefs. Nero's adviser Seneca, a philosopher noted for his exquisite moral refinement, demanded immediate repayment of 10 million denarii – enough to feed everyone in the British Isles for a least a couple of months. Worse still, Nero's financial agent in Britain suddenly announced that the gifts emperors had made to chiefs were really just loans, which had now fallen due.

Britons who had bet on Rome were abruptly brought low, and

no amount of toga-wearing or Latin speechifying could save even the highest from ruin. The Iceni tribe learned this the hard way. Their king, Prasutagus, had been a good friend to Rome, even naming Nero along with his daughters as his co-heir. But when Prasutagus died in 60 CE, Romans on the spot ignored these subtleties and simply stole everything not nailed down (and much that was nailed down). Prasutagus' widow, Boudica, they stripped, shamed and flogged; his daughters they raped; his nobles they evicted from their estates.*

That Boudica, her family and the Icenian aristocracy were angry enough to eat the Romans raw is understandable, but so too, it seems, were tens of thousands of poorer Iceni and neighbouring Trinovantes. 'They could not wait to cut throats, hang, burn and crucify', says Tacitus. With the Roman army busy 400km away killing people on Anglesey, there was no one to stop the rebels from storming Colchester, formerly the capital of Cunobelin's Eastern Kingdom but now remade as a retirement town for Roman veterans. Its straight streets and neat little shops full of imported pottery, wine and fish paste stood out like sore thumbs among the native villages, and its great stone temple of the deified emperor Claudius, over 30 m long and faced with alabaster and marble, was something from another world. The rebels torched it all.

On the main street – today's High Street follows the same line, several of its shops reusing Roman walls as foundations – the firestorm was so intense that it melted glass. Archaeologists found the baked bones of Romans caught in the blaze scattered through the ashes. Survivors fled to the great temple, only to die in turn when the rebels stormed it two days later. A huge bronze head found near by may once have graced its statue of the emperor, hacked off and then tossed into a river (to honour the ancient gods?).

Although archaeology is a science of ifs, buts and maybes, the thick, black, burned layers excavated at Colchester leave little doubt about the rebels' rage. Lashing out at the symbols as well as the sources of Roman power, they dug up immigrants' graves and scattered their bones. As if to advertise that they would nothing pay for wearing their own noses, the rebels even took time to hack the noses

---

*The spelling Boadicea, still normal when I was in school, is just a misreading of Boudica – a Celtic name more or less equivalent to Victoria – in a manuscript of Tacitus. No ancient author ever called her Boadicea.

Figure 3.3. No longer wearing his nose: the tombstone of Marcus Favonius Facilis, an Italian centurion (junior officer) in Rome's Twentieth Legion, set up at Colchester in the 40s CE and defaced in 60 CE.

off the sculptures on foreign-looking tombstones in the veterans' cemetery (Figure 3.3), before marching on the new Roman capital at London and burning that too.

Now the rebels had to face a new, and tougher, question: what next? The stage they were acting on now extended all the way to Italy, and despite taking their country back, the rebels had no obvious strategy for exiting the empire. They didn't even have a plan for fighting the main Roman army, which was rushing back from Anglesey. If by some miracle Boudica did defeat it, perhaps the empire would withdraw, as it had done from Germany fifty years earlier. More probably, though, Rome would just send another army. Anyone who doubts Rome's determination to show rebels that resistance was futile should visit Masada in Israel's waterless Judaean Desert, where, just a decade after Boudica, the army built a 125-m-high dirt ramp and dragged a siege tower up it to crush the last few supporters of a Jewish revolt.

As it was, Boudica's revolt ended in a massacre, not a miracle. Tacitus says that when the army caught up with her somewhere in the Midlands – perhaps near Mancetter in North Warwickshire – it killed 80,000 Britons for the loss of just 400 of its own (Boudica poisoned herself). In reality the Britons' losses must have been smaller, but Roman troops then went on a rampage so murderous that it shocked even Nero. In an effort to lower the temperature, he fired the senator governing Britain, but the province's agony was just beginning. Banking on capturing Roman grain supplies, the rebels had launched their campaign without taking time to plant their fields. Far more Britons now starved than had died by the sword.

The revolt forced Romans to ask again just what they thought they were doing here, at the edge of the world. Ancient writers say that 70,000 Roman soldiers and civilians died in the revolt, and all call it a 'disaster', but none even hints that Nero considered retreat. Rather, successive governors spent a decade rebuilding trust. Not until the mid-70s CE did local worthies display renewed enthusiasm for identifying with Rome, but once hearts and minds had been won back, Silchester and St Albans started looking as Roman as anything on the Continent. The rebuilt Colchester boasted not only a theatre but also a *Ben Hur*-style chariot-racing track (so far unique in Britain). Only then could the empire return to the question – on hold since the attack on Anglesey in 60 CE – of how much of Britain it needed to control to give Gaul a viable counterscarp. Pulling back to the Channel would solve nothing, and simply stopping along the line of the south-east / north-west geographical boundary had already failed. Rome needed to project its power across this line – but how far?

Tacitus' father-in-law, Agricola, appointed governor in 77 CE, was charged with finding an answer. Everyone agreed that the province would be insecure unless it included what we now call Wales and northern England. Agricola's predecessors had already ended the Brigantian civil war and devastated Wales. Agricola returned to Anglesey to flush out a druid revival, then in 79 CE marched at least as far north as the River Tees. In 80 CE he suggested setting the border between the Firths of Clyde and Forth, running through modern Edinburgh and Glasgow (Figure 3.4), and in 81 CE he told the emperor that he could take and hold Ireland with just 10,000 men.

Since 1996, when an amateur archaeologist found a mass of Roman material at Drumanagh, near Dublin, there has been speculation that Agricola did in fact send troops across the Irish Sea, although Tacitus does not mention it. If so, it could only have been a scouting

Figure 3.4. Looking for a counterscarp: Agricola's campaigns, 77–83 CE.

party, for in 82 CE Agricola instead launched a major invasion of Scotland. His army built forts almost as far north as Aberdeen. The largest, at Inchtuthil, covered 22 hectares. It was the single biggest construction job in the Isles since Silbury Hill, 2,500 years earlier, absorbing 16 million man-hours, 150,000 tons of stone, 20,000 tons of timber, 4,500 tons of clay roof tiles and 12 tons of iron nails. (When the fort was abandoned, more than a million nails were buried in a single pit, presumably to keep the locals from scavenging them.)

Agricola finally brought the northerners to battle in 83 CE, probably near Bennachie in Aberdeenshire. After slaughtering them, he at last had an answer to the question of where to stop: the Ocean. Only by conquering everything, he reported to the emperor Domitian, would Rome find a secure frontier.

It is tempting to see here a moment when a single man's decision made all the difference to Britain's history. If Domitian had followed Agricola's advice, his generals would have brought towns and coins, harbours and roads, villas and slavery to Scotland and Ireland as well as England and Wales. Nothing Rome could have done would have made the north-west as flat and warm as the south-east, of course, but the importance of the line between these zones would nonetheless have been greatly diminished. For several centuries, at least, the Isles might have had a significantly different future.

But Domitian did not take Agricola's advice. According to Tacitus, this was because he was jealous of his general's success and wanted to diminish his glory. Perhaps so: Domitian was famously unpleasant, notorious for bragging about torture techniques he had invented. Yet envy was not the whole story. It was the emperor's job to see the big picture, and in the early 80s CE that picture was turning distinctly dark. Domitian had begun re-deploying men from Britain to defend the River Rhine even before Agricola's victory in 83, and when he pulled the best troops out of Britain two years later, they went straight to plug gaps in the crumbling Danube frontier. Seen from the centre, the Rhine–Danube line mattered a lot more than Caledonia, and if the only way to preserve the former was by giving up the latter, then so be it. If Domitian had refused to bow to this strategic logic and had purchased Caledonia at the cost of Continental collapse, whoever replaced him (he was murdered in 96, and it could easily have happened sooner) would surely have done so, pulling the army back into increasingly settled forts along the Rivers Solway and Tyne.

Similarly, had the emperor Hadrian not decided in 122 CE to convert these forts into a continuous wall, on which 10,000 men would labour in wind and rain for the next fifteen years, a successor would have taken the decision instead. Another emperor in need of glory in the 140s CE pushed the frontier back northwards to the Clyde–Forth line which Agricola had once favoured, and in 208 CE a big army marched further north still. But none of these adventures lasted long. The hard fact was that Domitian and Hadrian had called the issue correctly. The right place for Rome's counterscarp was along a line between Carlisle and Newcastle. In the long run, no alternative worked as well as putting the frontier there. Scotland and Ireland were too difficult, too expensive and just too far away to bring into the empire. Their people could keep their noses, but England and Wales – the new province of Britannia – would be Roman. Not even such a very important person as a Roman emperor could overrule the vast impersonal forces of geography.

The Military–Urban Complex

What Rome offered Britons was prosperity and security; what it took in return was control over mobility and sovereignty – which, intentionally or not, combined to transform identity.

The biggest change was the unification of what would later be England and Wales under a single ruling class, whose members – governors, imperial agents, legionary commanders and a host of other officials – were without exception immigrants, drawn from a super-rich Continental elite (overwhelmingly Italian to start with, then more Gallic and Spanish). Rome's 600 or so senators – just 0.001 per cent of the empire's population – monopolised the best jobs, with a few thousand 'knights' (originally so-called because they were rich enough to own horses, but by the first century CE the equivalent of billionaires) filling the next level down. No Briton ever sat in the Senate, and, so far as we know, only two even became knights. A colonialist raj made most big decisions in Britain and referred the biggest decisions of all back to Italy.

Initially, the army that guaranteed Britannia's dependence was also all-immigrant, chiefly German, with rather more Italians in the officer class. It was recruiting Britons by the 60s CE but, following standard practice, shipped them overseas (mostly to the Rhine and Danube) to serve. However, the army loved enlisting veterans' sons, and so over time its ranks filled up with men born in the military retirement towns of Colchester, Gloucester and Lincoln. Although only two known tombstones explicitly name Britons serving in their home province, by 200 CE most troops were probably native-born, whereas bone chemistry confirms that most bodies in the cemeteries of first-century Gloucester and the great legionary fortress of York had been foreign-born.

Skeletal isotopes also suggest that immigrants, including Africans and Asians as well as Continental Europeans, were even commoner in London. Out of all the merchants named on inscriptions, in fact, only twenty sound British; most were Gallic or German. Even craftsmen (the literate ones, at least) were often immigrants, especially in the first century.

The educated men who took the top jobs in the new province were brought up to believe that they had earned their privileges by providing *Pax Romana*, 'Roman Peace'. This, astute Romans recognised, did not come cheap. Incorporation into the empire was violent, and suppressing revolts like Boudica's – which many provinces experienced a generation or so after their conquest – could be more violent still. But after that, the theory ran, civilisation, secure borders and law and order would pacify and enrich even the most turbulent natives.

Needless to say, theory and practice did not always coincide. Roman writers list eight wars in Britain in the 150 years after Agricola's campaigns. At least three (and perhaps as many as five) were fought chiefly north of the Wall, but others were waged within Britannia; and given the casual way the authors mention these conflicts, we should probably assume that others went unrecorded. It also says something that at least thirty towns built defensive earthworks in the second century, rather than relying on the army to protect them.

Sometimes, in fact, the army was the problem, not the solution. Among hundreds of letters found at Vindolanda near Hadrian's Wall, preserved by being dumped into the urine-soaked, oxygen-free mud of a latrine, one is from a trader seeking justice after a centurion beat him up. 'Because I couldn't complain to the prefect Proculus on account of his illness,' he wrote, 'I appealed to the military police and the other centurions in his unit, with no result. Accordingly, I beg Your Mercifulness' – probably the governor – 'not to let me, a man from overseas and an innocent one, about whose good faith you may inquire, be bloodied by rods as if I had committed some crime.'

What should we make of this? On the positive side, it shows that civilians did have ways to seek redress from the army; on the negative, the writer's complaints apparently went unheeded, even though the kind of man who could write a letter in Latin would surely have had friends in moderately high places (his references to his good name and foreignness may be hinting at this). We can only wonder what military occupation meant to the humblest *Brittunculi* – 'little Brits', as another Vindolanda letter condescendingly calls them.

Subjection to Rome clearly carried costs, yet the fact remains that massacre sites, burned villages, bog bodies, creepy skull cults and even burials with weapons all but disappeared from Britannia by 100 CE while continuing beyond the empire's borders. We cannot really quantify it, but it seems likely that Britons were more secure in the second century than ever before – and, Romans insisted, richer. 'Who does not now recognise', the geographer Pliny asked in the 70s CE, 'that thanks to the majesty of the Roman Empire [. . .] standards of living have made great strides? Or that all this is owed to trade, and the common enjoyment of the blessings of peace?'

Although Pliny never visited Britain, it was probably just the kind of place he had in mind. Infrastructure boomed as governors spent tax money not just on the famous Roman roads but also on bridges and ports. They issued charters for markets, regulated trade practices and standardised weights and measures. Coins, rare even in the south-east before 43 and unknown almost anywhere else, show up on Welsh and northern farmsteads a century later.

Even the gods smiled on Roman Britain. A boom in funding for research on climate change since the 1990s has produced rich records of ice cores, tree rings, pollen from bogs and lakes and remains of plants, animals and insects. On the whole, these data suggest that Europe had been warming up since about 200 BCE. In our own age, when global warming is such a threat, one of its few silver linings is that it will turn much of Russia and Canada into farmland; and 2,000 years ago the Roman Warm Period (as climatologists call it) raised a similar prospect of higher agricultural yields in northern Europe, where the biggest problem for farmers was the shortness of the growing season.

However, one of the lessons of recent research into the history of climate change is that the weather rarely directly *causes* people to do anything. Rather, it moves the goalposts, and people react as they will. Sometimes what used to work no longer does; at other times it still works but something else works better still. Either way, those who just plod along as if nothing is happening pay a price. The secret of success in the Roman Warm Period was to pour effort, investment and innovation into the land – exactly the things that the arrival of

Roman capital, institutions and agricultural know-how encouraged. With all this going on, it would be remarkable if prosperity had *not* risen after the Roman conquest.

At the crudest level, the fact that Britannia's population doubled between the first century and the fourth – from roughly 2 million to 4 million – shows that the economy grew, although it does not tell us whether it grew fast enough to make people richer as well as thicker on the ground. In situations where income statistics are as rare as they are in Roman Britain, economists often just look at how tall people are. Stature is genetically determined – short parents, short children – but reaching your full potential depends on being well fed in your growing years, which, in the absence of anything better, can serve as a rough proxy for income.

Until quite recently, our only evidence was the geographer Strabo's comment that he once saw some British slaves on sale in Rome who were 'taller than the tallest there by as much as half a foot, although their legs were bowed'. Archaeology now shows that his sample was misleading (or perhaps that he was just confused). Britons were indeed taller than Italians, but only by a couple of centimetres, and were not noticeably bandy-legged. More to the point, their stature barely changed in antiquity, with men's average heights fluctuating between 168 and 171 cm and women about 5 cm shorter. That should hardly surprise us, because even in rich countries there are few examples before the twentieth century of nutrition improving enough to add 10 cm on to heights (although, as we will see in Chapter 5, it could happen). Almost everyone in antiquity was short and skinny. Yet in other ways standards of living clearly did improve, even if the rising tide lifted some boats more than others. Who you were, and when and where you lived, made all the difference.

In his farewell address in 1961, President Dwight Eisenhower warned Americans to 'guard against the acquisition of unwarranted influence, whether sought or unsought, by the military–industrial complex'. Roman Britain was a very different place, but it had an equivalent: a 'military–urban complex'. Thanks to the unusual size of Britain's garrison – 10 per cent of the empire's troops guarding 4 per cent of its people – a military–urban complex acquired just the kind of influence Eisenhower worried about, and used it to control the economy's commanding heights.

The two groups at this complex's heart, soldiers and city folk, had barely existed in the Isles before 43 CE. Pre-Roman Britain had plenty of warriors but no soldiers in the sense of full-time salaried professionals, and while it also had numerous settlements with a few hundred residents, there were no real towns where thousands of people carried on activities distinct from those of the countryside. After the conquest, soldiers and city folk remained rare; even if we count (as historians usually do) soldiers' families and other dependants in the military category and set the bar for a town as low as 1,000 people, neither group had more than 100,000–200,000 members (2.5–5 per cent of Britannia's total headcount) in the second century, and both actually shrank in the third. However, they still made a difference.

Each group was, in certain ways, a society apart. Soldiers on Hadrian's Wall had more in common with brothers-in-arms defending Syria than with villagers just a few kilometres away. For one thing, all soldiers spoke Latin and quite a few wrote it too (although sometimes so badly that modern scholars struggle to work out what they were trying to say). It would be surprising if even one British civilian in ten could read a simple sentence, but hundreds of distinct hands have been identified in the tablets from the military base at Vindolanda. One commanding officer was an elegant stylist, regularly dropping literary allusions, and even non-commissioned officers might turn to verse. One Italian at Wroxeter wrote himself this epitaph:

> *Titus Flaminius, son of Titus, of the tribe Pollia from Faventia*
> *Aged forty-five, of twenty-two years' service*
> *As soldier and eagle-bearer of the Fourteenth Legion 'Gemina'.*
> *I did my bit, and now here I am.*
> *Read this, and be either more or less lucky in your life,*
> *For the gods cut you off from both wine and water*
> *When you enter the underworld.*
> *So, live with honour while you have time.*

In their letters the soldiers seem very conscious of being banished to the farthest fringe of the empire. They grumble constantly about the weather and food, asking their families to send warm socks. In one delightful letter Claudia Severa, a commander's wife based near Carlisle, invites Sulpicia Lepidina, married to Vindolanda's commander, to her birthday party, but much of the time officers' wives

Figure 3.5. Mod cons: a latrine with running water in a fort at
Housesteads on Hadrian's Wall, pictured by artist Philip Corke.

were apparently bored and lonely. Some soldiers relieved their own
loneliness by taking British wives, one of whom, named Regina,
was immortalised by her Syrian husband, Barates, on an elegant
tombstone. Others turned to prostitutes. Barates perhaps did both –
Regina, he says, had been his slave before he made an honest woman
of her – but Gaius Valerius Iustus of Chester was more typical in
mourning his wife, Cocceia Irene, as 'most chaste and pure'.

The government wanted to keep its troops happy, so it paid them
well. A first-century legionary earned 300 denarii per year at a time
when the average income was 200 denarii for an entire household.
The army laid on entertainment (in 2018 excavators found a pair of
leather boxing gloves at Vindolanda) and filled barracks and garrison
towns with all the modern conveniences (Figure 3.5). Long before
Napoleon pointed it out, Romans knew that an army marched on
its stomach, and made sure that the troops got the food and drink
they wanted. When Britons ate meat, it tended to be small amounts
of mutton, but excavated animal bones show that soldiers ate prodigious helpings of pork and beef. Many of the hillier parts of the

province must have turned into pig farms and cattle ranches to feed soldiers' insatiable stomachs.

A parallel army of traders grew up, working year-round to lug millions of gallons of Spanish olive oil and French wine to Hadrian's Wall and Wales. In our own day it no longer seems strange that helicopters rush Diet Coke, light beer and Thanksgiving turkeys to forward operating bases in distant deserts, but in ancient times it required a logistical revolution and massive government spending to provide equivalent support. By the second century this cost something like 25 million denarii per year, which, in a province whose gross domestic product was probably 200–250 million denarii, made the military a very important economic sector indeed.

The army's presence both stimulated and distorted the British economy, fuelling the rise of the second group that reaped the benefits of conquest: urbanites. The army needed specialists – white-toga workers – to raise money, move imports around and generally get things done. Since this required literacy and numeracy, rare skills at first among the natives, it meant even more immigration; and since it was hard to run a Roman province from a village, cities were required too.

Some were built on sites like Colchester and St Albans, where chiefs had ruled before the Romans came, but the greatest of them all grew almost from scratch, at London. Before the 40s CE, London had been a place of no particular importance. But as imperial armies marched west, floating their supplies up the Thames, this spot – the only place where the river was both deep enough for huge grain ships to dock and narrow enough to be bridged with Roman-era technology – suddenly became very important indeed. Tree-ring dating shows that efforts to drain the swamp between Ludgate Hill and Cornhill had begun by the year 48 CE, and the first street grid and little jetties along the river were probably also in place by then.

The city grew quickly and higgledy-piggledy. Archaeologists have found more than 170 structures built before Boudica's revolt – itself marked by a thick, burned layer detected in no fewer than fifty-six excavations – but none of them bears any mark of officialdom. This was a bottom-up boomtown, 'crowded', Tacitus says, 'with traders and their wares'. Most of the food these merchants and moneymen consumed – including grapes, opium poppies, coriander and figs – was shipped in from the Continent, as were the plates they ate it off.

Figure 3.6. Boomtown: wagons crossing the Roman bridge and
merchant ships unloading at London's docks around 100 CE,
as imagined in a model in the Museum of London.

The banks of the Thames soon bristled with wharves and warehouses
(Figure 3.6), and Latin, the language of commerce, filled the air.

From the very start London was unlike anything else in the
country. It was a Mecca for money, power and foreigners, and its
twenty-first-century banks, just like Colchester's shops, rest on
Roman foundations. In 2016 archaeologists clearing a site for the
Bloomberg Finance Group's new European headquarters found 400-
plus wooden tablets, saved from decay by being dumped in the now
subterranean Walbrook Stream. Several of them preserved traces of
Latin words, handwritten by businessmen's secretaries whose iron
styluses had pressed clean through the beeswax covering the tablets
to scar the wood underneath. The oldest, probably written in the 40s
CE, contains advice to a lender: 'They are boasting through the whole
market that you have lent them money', it says. 'Therefore, I ask you
in your own interest not to look shabby [. . .] you will not thus favour
your own affairs.'

Creating cities meant building tens of thousands of houses. Millions of tons of stone were quarried and carted around; whole forests

were cut down and milled into lumber; iron was mined and cast into nails; clay was dug up and fired into billions of bricks and roof tiles. Someone had to make all the pots, pans and tools excavated in these houses, as well as the shoes, clothes, blankets, tables and chairs, which don't normally survive. The labour involved is mind-boggling: by one calculation, the single (not particularly big) job of putting a wall around Silchester involved 100,000 wagon trips, moving 20,000 tons of stone to the building site. The Romans, in effect, built the equivalent of thousands of Stonehenges.

Isotope analysis suggests that in the second century between a quarter and a third of the populations of Gloucester, Winchester and York (and more in London) were still immigrants – but two-thirds to three-quarters of the townsfolk were therefore natives drawn in from the countryside (or their descendants). Some will have been slaves who had no choice, but most must have actively decided to relocate. Either way, by the year 200 CE at least one Briton in twenty had made the move.

And what a shock it would have been. Before the invasion, no community in Britain had more than a few hundred residents, but by the second century there were dozens of towns with a few thousand. Lincoln and York had 10,000, London three times as many. While this doubtless seemed very small beer to civil servants banished to this backwater from the city of Rome, where a million people lived, for a significant slice of Britain's population, moving to town was like visiting another planet. An entirely new identity, that of the urbanite, took shape.

Town life was less cosmopolitan than army life, but much more cosmopolitan than country life. For 8,000 years Britons had mostly lived in roundhouses, but Romans liked houses with corners, chiefly of a long, narrow type known to archaeologists as 'strip houses'. These looked rather like the 'shotgun shacks' of American sharecroppers (so-called, tradition has it, because if you fired a shotgun through the front door you would hit everybody in the building).

The food was different too. Everyone but the rich lived largely on bread, but moving to town meant exchanging the traditional luxuries of mutton, butter and beer for something more like the military package of pork, oil and wine. Excavated food remains suggest that townsfolk consumed less meat and Mediterranean imports than soldiers, and that the smaller the city a person moved to, the less like a soldier's his or her diet would be; but all the same, even the poorest townsperson knew what these foreign foods tasted like.

City folk even looked different. In the first century CE most peasants wore simpler versions of the new fashions which the rich had adopted from the Continent a hundred years earlier. This, as I mentioned in Chapter 2, involved tunics over long-sleeved bodices for women, held together with lots of brooches, and while we know less about men's clothes, they clearly wore a lot of brooches too. By the second century, though, urbanites had moved on, adopting another new style from across the Channel. Both sexes now sported wide-bodied 'Gallic coats' under cloaks which looked like a kind of ancient hoodie. Judging from the frequent finds of little iron nails around the feet of skeletons, this outfit went with leather hobnailed boots. Women's Gallic coats were longer than men's and worn with lots of underskirts, but both sexes abandoned brooches. The brooches found in graves, however, suggest that villagers stuck with the old ways for generations longer.

New arrivals from the countryside were doubtless mocked for their dirty fingernails and unfashionable clothes, but there were consolations: public baths, theatres, chariot races and gladiator shows, plus, of course, the foreign food. Like everywhere else in the empire, wages were higher in towns than in the country. Two recent studies, one looking at bones and the other at teeth, suggest that in some ways, towns – big enough to have urban amenities and clean water but not yet big enough to become petri dishes breeding murderous microbes – were healthier places to live than farms. However, a third study, looking at Dorset alone, drew the opposite conclusion.

Close to 10 per cent of Britons had found a place in the military–urban complex by 200 CE and were, on the whole, more European, more secure and more prosperous than the pre-conquest population. The historian Richard Saller estimates the increase in per capita consumption at around 25 per cent. Bearing in mind all the caveats about conversions mentioned in Chapter 1, we might think of living standards rising from the equivalent of about $1.50 per person per day to something nearer $2. People were still horribly poor, but for anyone living so close to subsistence, a raise of 40–50 cents per day would have made a world of difference. For the military–urban complex, at least, Rome delivered on its promise of prosperity.

The 90-Plus Per Cent

But what of the 90-plus per cent outside this charmed circle? For many years country folk were the silent majority of Roman Britain, their farmsteads and villages little studied compared with more glamorous forts, cities and especially villas. Villas – the country estates of the rich – are easy to spot, and as late as the 1950s made up half of all the known Roman sites. The twenty or thirty grandest were on a scale that the Isles would not see again until the eighteenth century. One palatial residence at Woodchester in the Cotswold Hills had at least sixty-four rooms, organised around two or three courtyards and sprawling over an area the size of two football pitches. It had central heating, glass windowpanes and gloriously painted walls. Crawling on their hands and knees, craftsmen had pressed 3 million little stone cubes into wet concrete to create its 1,000 m^2 of mosaic floors.

But since 1990, when a ruling known as Policy Planning Guidance 16 required developers to fund archaeological study in advance of building projects, the picture has changed completely. Archaeologists found so many small rural sites that by the 2010s villas comprised less than 2 per cent of the total. More than 100,000 Roman-era sites are now known, chiefly rural and poor. This abundance means that no single site can be typical, but by putting a few together we get some sense of what happened among everyday country folk.

Whitton, a farmstead in Wales, is a good example. We archaeologists tend to fall in love with the sites we dig, but even Whitton's excavators admitted that it was a 'humble and windblown habitation' (although a few pages later, feeling brighter, they dignified it as 'small and moderately prosperous'). It began life around 30 CE as a cluster of timber roundhouses with a well, enclosed – as was normal in this uncertain corner of the Isles – by a stockade and deep ditch. In the 60s CE the central hut was rebuilt twice as big (Figure 3.7), but nothing was added in stone until the 130s CE.

After that, changes came thick and fast. A masonry farmhouse was added and then expanded, decked out with painted plaster walls, a roof of clay and sandstone tiles, a hypocaust block for central heating (although this was apparently never turned on) and even a few glass windowpanes. The defensive ditch was filled in, and in its final phase, around 300–340 CE, the main house was six times the size of the original version – or more, if Figure 3.8 is correct to give it two floors. Only a handful of the farmers' pottery came from outside

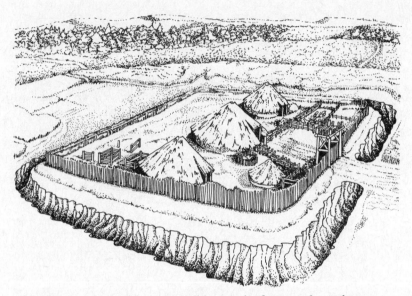

Figure 3.7. 'Humble and windblown': the farmstead at Whitton,
south Wales, in the 60s CE (reconstruction by Howard Mason).

Britannia, but they did have a bronze wine ladle (which, the excavators thought, 'shows a nice touch of refinement'). Only two coins
turned up in the first-century levels, but in the third century the
family lost thirteen, probably meaning that the farm now belonged
to a partly monetised economy. And also a literate one: the 200-plus
fragments of iron and bronze found in these levels included not only
ornaments, farm implements and tools for working iron and leather
but also five styluses for writing on wax tablets.

The excavator at my second site, Marshfield in the Cotswold
Hills, thought it 'relatively unremarkable' too. The first building here,
soon after 50 BCE, was a small roundhouse, with religious as well as
domestic functions. It was rebuilt, slightly larger, around 50 CE, with
painted plaster walls. After that, little changed until 250, when the
roundhouse was demolished to make way for a rectangular, multi-
room stone building three times as big. Around the year 360 another
renovation tripled the farmhouse's size again. Like Whitton, fourth-
century Marshfield had some sandstone roof tiles (a stone roof for
the whole building would have weighed an alarming 28 tons) and
probably two floors. Again like Whitton, while the pottery was

Figure 3.8. 'Small and moderately prosperous': Whitton in the early fourth century (reconstruction by Howard Mason).

overwhelmingly local – a mere 2.6 per cent was imported – an iron stylus points to literacy and the coins (one each from the first centuries BCE and CE but more than thirty from the third CE and over 120 from the fourth) to increasing engagement with monetised markets. The animal bones suggest that the farm specialised in raising sheep for wool. This generated enough money for its owners to buy oysters, carried 30 km from the Bristol Channel, even if, the report points out, the shellfish were four or five years old. 'By this age', the excavator cautions, 'oysters are getting a bit tough.'

My final example is Stowmarket in Suffolk, on the other side of the province. Here, excavations ahead of house-building found two round, timber farmsteads, built in the first century BCE. They were replaced in the second century CE by rectangular masonry buildings ('of fairly low economic status', the excavators conclude), which lasted until the early fourth century. The original roundhouses were quite big, but, as at the other sites, the stone buildings were much bigger and included not one but two little bathhouses, which perhaps afforded the residents as much fun as Californians nowadays get from their hot tubs. Once again, floors were paved, walls plastered and roofs tiled, but imports remained rare. So far as we know, nothing foreign entered the house at all before 150 CE, but broken jars betray

a taste for Spanish olive oil in the late third century. Like the Marshfield family, the Stowmarketers enjoyed their oysters, carried 40 km
to the farm. These oysters were young and tender, and the range in
their sizes suggested that they were caught wild, not farmed. The
excavators were also able to carbon-date the discarded shells. Just two
oysters got there before the conquest, but seventy-four were thrown
out in the century after 150 CE and a whopping 1,037 in the hundred
years after that.

Despite the differences between these sites, there is a definite
pattern. Little changed down on the farm in the first century of
Roman rule, but hints of growing prosperity and connections with
the broader world appear between 150 and 250 and expand massively
by 350. The Roman elite recognised this; while they still called the
natives Britanni, the word no longer implied that they were painted
barbarians. Britanni were now just people living in Britannia, and
Romans had to find a new word for 'painted people' – Picti – to deni-
grate the natives living north of the Wall (who did, apparently, still
tattoo themselves).

Neither the Picti nor the inhabitants of Ireland (whom Romans
called Scotti and Attacotti) saw anything like the rising living standards
of Rome's British subjects.* This suggests that Roman organisation –
rather than some force like climate change, which operated on both
sides of the border – was the main motor of economic growth. Scotland's single-roomed roundhouses and Ireland's ring forts were no
richer in the fourth century than in the first. Imports (including Roman goods) were so scarce that some historians wonder whether
Rome's advance actively underdeveloped Britain's north and west,
pulling trade routes away from them. Dunnicaer, a ragged hamlet
on a finger of rock projecting into the North Sea, is a good example.
On sites within Britannia the fine, red-glossed Roman pottery known
as 'Samian Ware' is ubiquitous, but Dunnicaer yielded just a single
fragment, heavily worn after being passed from hand to hand for a

---

*The Scots enter history in a notoriously confusing way. According to their own
tradition (although historians are nowadays sceptical about it), they began as a
group of tribes in Ireland and then migrated around 500 CE to the south-west part
of what we now call Scotland. There, under their great chief Fergus Mór, Scotti
created the kingdom of Dál Riata, growing in power until, by the twelfth century,
the whole country was called Scotland.

couple of centuries, perhaps as a talisman of the great world beyond. A few pieces of Roman glass also turned up, each as old and worn as the Samian potsherd.

As the military–urban complex pulled trade towards London, the western waters which had been so active through much of prehistory fell strangely quiet. Before Rome came, Ireland's contacts with the Mediterranean had been vigorous enough for the skull of a North African Barbary ape to end up in a religious building at the later royal centre of Navan, dated by tree rings to 95 or 94 BCE; but after the conquest such exotic items disappeared. Roman finds are actually commoner at the 3,000-year-old tomb at Newgrange than anywhere else in Ireland. Coincidentally or not, Roman objects also turn up around the prehistoric monuments of Orkney and at Stonehenge – where, for reasons now unknown, people dug pits all over the place and even left behind someone's head.

The demographic, political, economic, cultural and intellectual imbalances between the Roman south-east and native north and west widened with each passing century. Figure 3.9, bundling all the Marshfields, Stowmarkets, Lincolns and Londons together, suggests that people at every level of Britannia's housing market were building bigger in 350 than ever before. Since 4200 BCE the average house size in most parts of Britain had hovered around 100 m² (much the same as today), but in Britannia under Roman rule it more than doubled, to roughly the size of the average modern American home. The province's economy grew by something like 150 per cent between 50 CE and 350, lifting its gross domestic product from the equivalent of about $1 billion in 1990 values to some $2.5 billion (as compared with England and Wales's $2.8 trillion in 2019).

Many, perhaps most, among the 90-plus per cent eventually saw some income gains. To be sure, the rate at which Roman Britain's economy grew – about 0.3 per cent per annum – was trivial compared with the 7–10 per cent per annum that developing economies regularly manage today. Yet this remains one of the biggest booms in history before the Industrial Revolution. Because of this, economic historians often wonder whether a military–urban complex commanding just 10–15 per cent of the economy was really enough to drive so much change. Perhaps, they suggest, the complex was merely a starter motor, and Britannia's economic performance was in fact a function of Thatcher's Law. What mattered most was

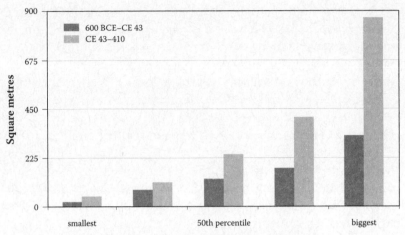

Figure 3.9. Homes fit for subjects: growth in every category of housing in Britannia, 600 BCE–410 CE.

what came Britannia's way from the Continent, even when that was catastrophic.

Creative Destruction

First came a series of Old-World-wide pandemics, beginning in the 160s CE. They were probably related to smallpox, although we currently have no ancient DNA to confirm this. In an age without face masks, where only the wealthiest could afford social distancing, disease killed perhaps a quarter of the population in some parts of Europe and Asia. Empires in China and Persia collapsed in the 220s, and although Rome hung on, Germanic immigrants filled the vacuum left by the dead.

People had been crossing the empire's frontiers ever since the empire existed, mostly young men looking for temporary work inside the rich empire or hoping to sell northern goods for a profit. Most of the time this benefited everyone. Yet when opportunities presented themselves, neither Roman residents nor immigrants were always fussy about using force to rob one another. As a result, the borderlands were rough places, and managing this volatility was one of the army's main tasks. On the whole, peasants, guest workers and soldiers rubbed along together well enough, but when the army lost its grip, as it did in the third century CE, things could abruptly break down. Employers could become slave traders, selling their workers into bondage; jobseekers could become bandits, looting undefended villages. If things got bad enough, complete families or even entire tribes might move in to steal the land itself.

It is unlikely that any of the immigrants from the 160s CE onwards were actively trying to overthrow the empire. However, if an emperor wanted to hang on to his throne and keep taxes coming in, he would regularly need to send out armies strong enough to chase trouble-makers off or bully them into behaving. This created a whole new problem: an army powerful enough to accomplish this might also be powerful enough for its commander to turn it around, march on Rome and grab the throne for himself – which is exactly what general after general did, plunging the empire into repeated civil wars. In the forty-nine years between 235 and 284, Rome had forty-three rulers. The plague killed one, Germans a second and a revitalised Persian Empire a third (after keeping him in a cage for several years, then flaying him and hanging his skin on their capital city's walls). Rival Romans killed the other forty.

Being at the edge of everything, Britain avoided the worst of this violence, but when in 260 CE a clique of Gallic generals decided they could do a better job at defending their province than the central authorities, the armies in Britain and Spain joined them. The empire scared the mutinous troops back into the fold in 274, only for British officers to walk out again in 276. Their resolve collapsed after six years, when their leader was poisoned, but in 286 Britannia declared independence a third time and held out for a decade. Britain was inside the empire for just six of the thirty-six years between 260 and 296.

The third-century walkouts were very different from Boudica's. All were led by non-British generals, objecting not to Continental rule but to ineffective rule. If emperors back in Rome cared more about the Rhine and Danube frontiers than about the distant north-west, Britons asked, why keep sending them British money? In 2016 some journalists detected echoes of Brexiteers' rhetoric in the events of 286, but the analogy is actually a poor one. The European Union is a federation of willing participants, which members can leave just by deciding to do so (even if they thereby condemn themselves to years in legal purgatory). Rome, however, was an empire, and when members tried to leave, Rome killed them, burned their homes and crucified their families or sold them into slavery. Force made 286 utterly different from 2016.

Because of this, when Carausius (an admiral recently sent to Britannia from what is now Belgium) seized power in 286, he insisted that he was not really rebelling. By keeping taxpayers' money local and spending it on their security, he said, he was just defending the north-west while his 'brothers' – as he presumptuously called emperors based in Rome – looked after the Continent. No one believed him, but it was what rebels were expected to say.

Few ancient writers mention Carausius, but those who do say that his greatest problem – indeed, the reason he was sent to Britain in the first place – was that the province now faced a new kind of security threat, coming from the sea. For two centuries the empire had given Britain an impregnable counterscarp. By controlling the entire Continental coast from Gibraltar to the mouths of the Rhine, it put Britain's shores out of range of German raiders, whose ships were not reliable enough for journeys directly across the North Sea; and while there were Pictish and Irish pirates aplenty, a small Roman fleet was enough to deter them. But this was now changing. Archaeology has revealed that people along the North Sea coasts of Germany and Denmark – later called Angles, Saxons and Jutes, although we cannot be sure what they called themselves in the third century – were building better boats (Figure 3.10). Their sturdy new ships turned the southern reaches of the North Sea into as much of a highway as the English Channel, exposing Britannia's east coast to raiding as well as trading. The stage on which Britain's story played out was expanding, and over the next several centuries new actors would drag Britannia out of its old Mediterranean-centred orbit and into a new one, around the North Sea.

Late twentieth-century historians often suggested that ancient writers exaggerated the scale and threat of rising mobility, but emperors at the time certainly thought they needed to respond. By 250 Rome had reorganised both sides of the Straits of Dover into a single command called the Saxon Shore. Small coastal forts were replaced with massive new ones, able to survive sustained sieges, along with watchtowers to give early warning of raids. Intercepting enemies at sea remained a forlorn hope, but if (or, more realistically, when) Germanic raiders landed, these strongpoints would at least pin them down until a new, consolidated fleet, based at Boulogne, could be called in to take them from behind.

Figure 3.10. Pirates of the North Sea? Nydam 2, a 20-m-long ship found in Jutland in 1863, dated by tree rings to the 310s and now on display in Gottorf Castle, Germany. It carried a crew of about thirty, and its overlapping planking probably made it seaworthy enough to cross the North Sea to England's east coast.

This was the force Carausius was sent to command in 286, and he did such a good job that the emperor got greedy and demanded a bigger share of the plunder from captured pirate ships. When Carausius refused, the emperor ordered his execution. Small wonder, then, that Carausius rebelled. But, having done so, he carried on doing his job, now spending the silver that British taxpayers no longer sent to Rome on new ships and even mightier forts for the Saxon Shore (Figure 3.11). Tellingly, he also built coastal castles between Cardiff and Lancaster, because Pictish and Scottish pirates in the Irish Sea were growing as bold as Germans. A coastguard of forty-oared patrol boats mentioned by a later writer, with sails, crews and rigging all in camouflage green, was probably also his creation.

Like every other third-century revolt, Carausius' ultimately failed, but by the time Rome got Britannia back under control in 296, it was obvious that the old way of doing things was over. Strategists decided that if neither the Saxon Shore nor Hadrian's Wall could reliably keep raiders out, the only option was defence in depth. Out went traditional legions massed along the frontiers; in came smaller, locally recruited militias, tasked not with winning battles but with acting as speed bumps, delaying intruders until mobile field armies (mostly Germans, mostly mounted), held deep in reserve – like the fleet at Boulogne – could ride to the rescue.

Figure 3.11. Planning for the worst: the massive walls and towers of the Roman fortress at Portchester. Most of what we now see was built in the eleventh century but reused the foundations laid by Romans around 290. The D-shaped towers are typically late Roman.

For Britannia, the consequences were huge. Its garrison shrank by half, spelling disaster for merchants who had grown rich supplying it; and the soldiers who did remain, mostly local-born, simply did not want as much wine and oil as the old immigrant force. Traders and financiers went bankrupt, wiping out much of the reason why British cities existed. Jobs disappeared and townsfolk drifted back to the countryside. Between 250 and 300 two-thirds of London's buildings were abandoned.

In York and Lincoln, the old inner cities similarly turned into slums. Urban amenities – baths, aqueducts, basilicas, theatres – were left to decay or even torn down. At Wroxeter the basilica was never rebuilt after a fire around 300; blacksmiths took over the one at Silchester. At St Albans the theatre was refurbished around the same time but soon after turned into a garbage dump. Of the fifteen major public baths in Britannia in the year 200, only nine were still open in 300 and none in 400.

This destroyed the old military–urban complex, but its destruction was creative. In earlier days immigrant soldiers and professionals had sent much of their pay back to the Continent to buy imports, but now indigenous soldiers and sailors spent their cash locally on mutton, butter and beer. This made the fourth century a golden age for small towns with just a thousand or two residents. Manufacturers fled the crumbling cities and set up shop in these places, now supplying farm-steads like Whitton as well as the military and urban markets. Farmers did not have much to spend, but there were nearly 4 million of them, and by 360 CE British agriculture was doing so well that the province became a net exporter of grain to the empire. Small-town craftsmen and shopkeepers prospered by selling peasants cheap, locally made but Roman-looking pots, roof tiles, tools and styluses. After 300 CE the 90-plus per cent in the countryside finally saw rising prosperity.

The rich – or more precisely, the *nouveaux riches* – prospered too, finding new ways to tap into the rents and taxes paid by the majority. Some bought up entire abandoned city blocks and turned them into pleasure parks. They effectively privatised what had been public goods by building personal bathhouses and theatres in gated communities and increasingly lavish villas. This looks like a deliber-ate choice. On the one hand, as manufacturing departed and cities stopped generating wealth, the rich felt less need to spend money on public amenities. On the other, some of the elite started seeing public baths and arcades as positively unwelcome reminders of old lifestyles that were now being swept away by the latest great innovation rolling from south-east to north-west across Europe: Christianity.

There had, of course, been Christians in the Middle East even before Rome invaded Britain in 43 CE, but the good news spread slowly. The first references to British Christians only come after 200, and Brit-ain's first saint, Alban, was probably not martyred till 305. Things got easier for Christians after 313, when the faith was legalised, and the very next year Britannia sent three bishops and a priest to a council in Gaul; but even so, unambiguous archaeological evidence for British Christianity remains rare until late in the fourth century. Britain did not produce a home-grown heretic – the real sign of having arrived in Christian circles – until 380, and even he promptly left for greener pastures in Italy.

This pattern, though, is probably just what we should expect, given the hesitancy Britons had shown about Continental religions even before the Word reached their shores. My own first experience

Figure 3.12. Unclassical: the second-century CE temple at Coleshill,
near Birmingham, as imagined by Michele Angel based on a
reconstruction by the archaeologist Malcolm Cooper.

of digging at a 'Roman' temple, back in 1979, was rather typical of
this. My college textbooks had told me what Roman temples should
look like, but this – the site was at Coleshill, near Birmingham – was
not it (Figure 3.12).* Classical proportions and marble columns were
nowhere to be found. In fact, we didn't find much of anything at all.
Even the stone blocks from the foundations for the very un-Roman-
looking square shrine had been dug up and carted away for reuse in
the Middle Ages, leaving just empty 'robber trenches' where walls
had once been. The most exciting moment of the season was when
the foreman's dog started a dig of his own in the middle of the sacred
precinct.

Having been slow to come to Britain, Christianity was especially
slow to reach the 90-plus per cent in the countryside (not without
reason did early Christians derive their word *pagani*, 'pagans', from the

---

*I would once again like to thank the Birmingham University Field Archaeology
Unit and Professor Martin Carver, the excavation director, for giving me this
opportunity and for doing their best to teach me to dig.

Latin *pagi*, 'peasants'). A huge cemetery of 1,200 late fourth-century graves at Poundbury in Dorset, however, shows that it did eventually arrive. The burials abound in the usual depressing details – half the population was dead by the age of five and most of the rest by forty, the men aching from years of digging and pushing ploughs, the women half crippled by housemaid's knee. Almost all Poundbury's people were short, thin and crawling with worms. But what makes this sickly crew significant is the dullness of their graves. In some sections of the cemetery all were laid out flat on their backs in uniform rows, with heads pointed east and almost no grave goods. This was how good Christians were supposed to go to meet their maker. Not everyone burying at Poundbury worked from this rulebook – some apparently remained stubbornly pagan – but even here, far from the trendsetting centres, plenty of bereaved families followed the same fashions as sophisticates in Rome or Carthage. Some even adopted the ultra-Christian rite of packing coffins with plaster, unintentionally preserving the dead so well that we can even see how they did their hair – men, long at the back and combed forward in a fringe (one older gentleman dyed his with henna and combed it over a bald spot); women, in elaborate coils, braids and twists, the fanciest dos surely requiring help from a lady's maid.

By 350 the identities of the 90-plus per cent were at last turning European. We might even say, with the historian Robin Fleming in her fine book *Britain after Rome*, that Britannia 'was as Roman in the fourth century as any other place on the planet'.

The Centurion's Song

And then, all of a sudden, it wasn't. Roman Britain ended not with a whimper but with a bang. In the half-century between about 360 and 410 its cities were abandoned, its industries imploded and its wealth evaporated. This time there was nothing creative about the destruction. Britannia finally and irretrievably crashed out of the Roman world.

In the 350s, while the owners of the little farm at Marshfield were still busy tripling its size and snacking on oysters, British iron production began falling sharply. Iron is the kind of thing few of us think about until we don't have any. Once, on an excavation I was on in Greece, we couldn't find the key to our tool shed at the start of the season. Trying to turn over sun-baked soil without steel tools quickly taught us the merits of metal. Our problem went away the next day, when the key turned up, but in fourth-century Britain there was no such easy fix. Iron kept on getting rarer, and life kept on getting harder. Even the humble iron nail, Fleming observes, 'grew scarce in the 370s, and by the 390s nails for coffins and hobnailed boots were simply no longer available, so the British slipped in the mud and buried the people they loved directly in the cold, hard ground'.

Bronze and silver coins also became scarce after 350, with the last known examples dating to 402. By then even pottery – the ancient equivalent of plastic – had disappeared from much of the province as kilns went out of business. For archaeologists this is a real nuisance, because we depend on ceramic styles to date (and often even to identify) ancient sites. My abiding memory of the first excavation I ever visited, some time around 1974 in the car park of a pub in Stafford called the Red Lion, is of the directors arguing over whether what was supposed to be a fifth-century site had actually yielded even a single object definitely of that date. Fourth-century Britons had made so much pottery that fifth-century Britons churned up broken pieces of it every time they dug a hole; and because fifth-century Britons made so little pottery of their own, it was well-nigh impossible to tell which layers on the site dated before 400 and which after. What is a nuisance for archaeologists, however, was surely a catastrophe for ancient Britons. In 350 Britons had been more prosperous than ever before; by 400 their grandchildren had lost all the economic gains of the Roman period. Even the most basic goods were disappearing.

Small towns, where craftsmen were churning out millions of pots and nails before 350, became ghost towns by 400. Residents were pouring energy into building defensive walls, moats and towers, but their forges and pot-banks fell silent, their drains silted up and their houses tumbled down. So far as we can tell, new house construction was rare after 375, and when it did happen, crews regularly looted stones for foundations and timber for beams from older structures (such as the temple at Coleshill).

Cities seem to have fared worst. Here too fortification flourished – defence contracting was clearly the industry to be in – but most digs suggest that suburbs were already being abandoned in the 350s and city centres too by the 370s. There is, however, some debate. Few fifth-century literary sources survive, and fewer still talk about Britain, but one, Constantius' *Life of St Germanus*, implies that St Albans was still a functioning city in 429. At Wroxeter, the only urban site where a large area has been excavated carefully, quite ambitious buildings were still being constructed around 450. Because these were made of wood, not stone, they are harder to spot than their Roman predecessors – which means, says one school of thought, that we have just failed to find structures built after 350.

Not so, says another school. While conceding that a few cities bucked the trend (St Albans still had piped water in the 420s, and at least some people hung on at Silchester and Winchester), these scholars see an unambiguous overall pattern. On site after site, excavations show waterpipes clogging, ramshackle huts encroaching on once tidy Roman streets and the rich walking or running away from their mansions. Directly above the ruins of the final buildings archaeologists often record thick layers of what they call 'dark earth'. Its vague name reflects our vague understanding of what it is, although it sometimes contains pollen from the kinds of plants normally found on waste ground. York, one of the grandest Roman towns before 350, seems to have turned into a marsh and was colonised by froghoppers, odd little insects that thrive in wetlands, as well as breeds of beetle that only live in tall grass.

A town can die in a heartbeat. In his wonderful book *The World Without Us*, the journalist Alan Weisman describes visiting Varosha, a tourist town stranded for thirty years in the demilitarised zone that has divided Greek and Turkish zones on Cyprus since 1974. 'Casement windows have flapped and stayed open, their pocked frames empty of glass', Weisman writes.

> Fallen limestone facing lies in pieces. Hunks of wall have dropped from buildings to reveal empty rooms, their furniture long ago somehow spirited away [. . .] In the meantime, nature continues its reclamation project. Feral geraniums and philodendrons emerge from missing roofs and pour down exterior walls. Flame trees, china berries, and thickets of hibiscus, oleander, and passion lilac sprout from nooks where indoors and outdoors now blend. Houses disappear under magenta mounds of bougainvillaea. Lizards and whip snakes skitter through stands of wild asparagus, prickly pear, and six-foot grasses [. . .] At night,

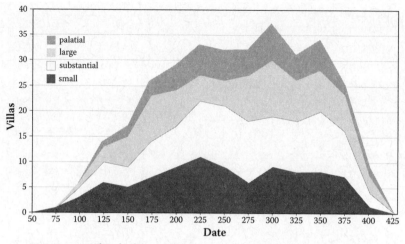

Figure 3.13. The decline and fall of the country house, 375–425 CE.

the darkened beachfront, free of moonlight bathers, crawls with nesting loggerhead and green sea turtles.

By the 420s London and Lincoln perhaps looked like muddier, drearier Varoshas, where – as the archaeologist Simon Esmonde Cleary pictures it – increasingly wretched squatters hung on among 'acres of tumbled buildings gradually disappearing under weeds and scrub and surrounded by the mute circuit of the town walls'. Nor were the old elite's sumptuous villas doing any better. No new ones were built after the 370s, and the existing ones were by then falling to bits. As roofs leaked and wet plaster crumbled, owners just walled up decaying rooms and let entire wings go to the dogs. Soon after 400 the last of the great and the good gave up camping out in their tumbledown palaces (Figure 3.13).

Britannia looks almost as though it fell victim to some ancient version of Pol Pot, the Cambodian dictator who, convinced that cities were seedbeds of capitalism, ordered his soldiers to drive every urbanite into the countryside in 1976 to fend for themselves. By 1979 all of the rich and a quarter of the poor had starved or died of disease. But fifth-century Britannia apparently had it even worse: as well as all of the rich, more than three-quarters of the poor disappear from sight. The number of known farms and villages – the places where most Britons lived – initially declined more slowly than that

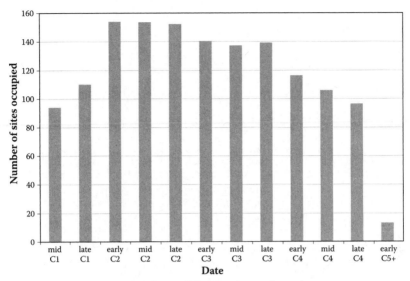

Figure 3.14. Darkness falls: numbers of rural sites in England and Wales, 50–450 CE, as reported in the flagship journal *Britannia* between 1969 and 1996.

of cities and villas, but after 400 the 90-plus per cent largely vanish too (Figure 3.14).

Once again, counterarguments are possible. Since the coins, fine pottery and masonry buildings that disappeared after 400 are precisely the things that make earlier Roman sites so easy to identify, post-Roman Britannia possibly looks more Pol Pottish to the archaeologist than it really was. The rich definitely endured because, despite the difficulty we have in digging them up, the handful of surviving fifth- and sixth-century texts keep mentioning them. Yet it still takes a lot of imagination to see the half-dozen generations after 360 as anything other than disastrous. Since the 1970s historians have grown uncomfortable with the traditional label 'dark age', because they do not want to make value judgements; but I confess to being at a loss to know what else to call these terrible times. The fifth century brought the people of Britannia poverty, violence and shorter lives. If that is not a dark age, I don't know what is.

So, what happened? Until recently, the outlines of an explanation seemed clear enough. Britain's story was just the local version of what happened all over Western Europe. Since the third century,

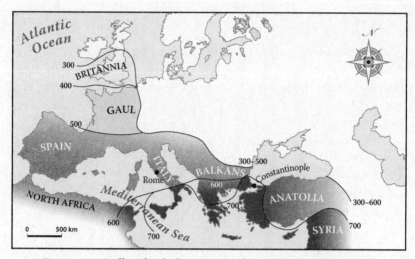

Figure 3.15. Rolling back the state: a schematic map (there is no way to be very precise) of the tidal wave of state failure that rolled from north-west to south-east across Europe, pushing the outer frontier of classical civilisation back from the British Isles around 300 to the Middle East (by then largely under Islamic rule) by 700.

population had been rising faster outside the empire than inside it, and societies beyond the Danube, Rhine and Tyne had learned to organise themselves better. Immigration blurred demographic imbalances, as pull factors (shorter growing seasons in northern Europe, making southern Europe more attractive) combined with push factors (the cooler weather driving nomads westwards off Central Asia's steppes, which in turn drove the Germanic peoples nearer Rome's frontiers westwards across them) to catalyse immigration into the empire. Never having worked out how to raise armies big enough to manage mobility without their commanders rebelling, Rome struggled to respond. In 378 disaster overwhelmed the government when thousands of Gothic immigrants in the Balkans, having been cruelly abused by officials, annihilated Rome's last viable field army. In 410 the Goths sacked Rome itself.

By then, local grandees had stopped waiting for Roman rescuers who came late or not at all. They took charge themselves, fighting immigrants and bandits, cutting deals with them and keeping tax revenues local. Quite often the men on the spot were Christian priests, stepping in because the church was the only large-scale organisation still functioning. Even so, they could not save everything, and hungry masses abandoned cities and the economy imploded as long-distance trade ground to a halt. The chaos transformed both sovereignty and identity because the empire became irrelevant. When in 476 a Gothic king deposed the emperor in Rome and didn't bother to replace him, few even noticed. Britannia left the empire because there was no longer an empire to belong to.

After millennia in which ideas and institutions had rolled from south-east to north-west, a great, slow-motion tidal wave of state failure now washed back the opposite way (Figure 3.15). Britannia was the first province to be swept away, its Roman-ness evaporating after 400. Gaul had followed by 500, Italy, North Africa and Spain by 600, the Balkans and Anatolia by 700 and Syria and perhaps Egypt too over the centuries that followed. It was, Edward Gibbon observed in 1781, 'an awful revolution, which will ever be remembered, and is still felt by the nations of the earth'.

Gibbon's judgement stood for nearly two centuries, until it fell foul of academics' dislike of ancient migrations in the 1960s–70s. Perhaps, Roman archaeologists suggested, the Germanic-style burials that began appearing inside the empire after about 300 CE represented not hordes of immigrants but locals copying German styles. Being 'German' was no more genetically hardwired than being Roman; identity was something people actively constructed. Revisionists recognised that dozens of eyewitness accounts survive of Germanic immigrants flooding across Rome's borders, but these often sound as overwrought as our own age's panics about Central American migrant caravans or Polish plumbers. Perhaps Roman writers were equally politically motivated.

But then came isotope analysis and ancient DNA. All the usual caveats apply – methods are still maturing, the data remain uneven, many interpretations are possible – but overwhelmingly the findings suggest that a lot of people were moving into and around the empire in the fifth and sixth centuries. Older visions of entire nations migrating were certainly oversimplified, and no two imperial provinces had exactly the same experience; but while Roman eyewitnesses may have misunderstood, distorted or exaggerated migration, they didn't just make it up.

Looking at the map, the obvious explanation for why Britannia was the first province to buckle is that it was more geographically exposed to rising mobility and declining security than any other part of the empire. Britannia had potentially mobile neighbours on three sides – Scots and Attacotti in Ireland, Picts beyond the Wall and Saxons and Franks in coastal Germany. Until the third century, when would-be raiders started building ships that could turn the seas into highways, this geographical vulnerability had been manageable; and even after then, Britannia could usually cope so long as its elite worked with the central authorities in Rome. But there was the rub. They didn't.

'Britannia is a province rich in usurpers', St Jerome complained in the 410s. No British rebellions are recorded between 306 and 350, coinciding exactly with the province's boom years, but after that, internal strife became the norm. In 350 rebels in Gaul offered Rome's throne to Magnentius, a commander in Britain, who fought his way to Italy and killed the emperor before the emperor's brother killed him in turn. Magnentius was not himself British, but some of the local elite had backed him, so the new emperor sent an official named Paul – 'inscrutable, baby-faced and hyper-vigilant', says the contemporary historian Ammianus Marcellinus – to root them out. Paul, though, 'went far beyond his instructions, descending like a raging river on the bodies and goods of many men and spreading ruin and destruction'. When Britannia's governor threatened to resign if Paul did not suspend the purge, Paul trumped up charges against him too. The terrified governor tried to kill Paul; when he failed, he killed himself instead.

Things were spinning out of control, and by the time Paul dragged his victims off to torture and death in Rome, the British elite was in disarray. After half a century of managing its own security without calling on Continental reserves, it needed four regiments to rush across the Channel through midwinter storms to fight incursions in 360. They restored order, but Ammianus says that raiding began again within four years.

As Romans saw it, their great advantage had always been that border raids were basically large-scale larceny, and because there was little honour among thieves, small imperial forces could defeat much more numerous enemies by fighting each robber band separately. With luck and skill they could even 'use the barbarian to pacify the barbarian', as a Chinese strategist (China faced some similar problems) labelled it in the third century BCE: smooth talking and large bribes could persuade potential enemies to fight each other rather than raid the empire. But these strategies fell apart in the 360s, because the Scots, Attacotti, Picts, Saxons and Franks discovered a second principle familiar to Chinese strategists: that of 'befriending the distant while attacking the near'.

A millennium later, Scots would build an 'Auld Alliance' on this principle, using friends in France to neutralise England by attacking it from two directions. England itself would go on to use the strategy repeatedly against France by seeking friends in Germany, Austria, Italy and Spain. The idea was older than either Scots or English knew, though. In 367, says Ammianus, the Saxons, Picts and Scots formed a 'Barbarian Conspiracy' to encircle Britannia. Attacked from three sides at once, its militias simply ran away. In the south, Franks and Saxons killed the general commanding the Saxon Shore forts, and, Ammianus continues, 'looted, burned and slaughtered all their captives'. In the north, Picts besieged the troops on Hadrian's Wall and 'roamed free, causing great destruction'.

In the nick of time Rome's general Theodosius dashed across the Channel with 2,000 troops and caught up with the invaders before they could sack London. In classic counter-insurgency style, he then rebuilt militia and intelligence services and hunted down the armed bands infesting the countryside. 'Theodosius' popularity was so great', says Ammianus, 'that he was escorted to the straits by a large crowd [. . . and] was received at the emperor's headquarters with joy and great praise.'

Historians often suggest that Ammianus exaggerated because, by the time he was writing, Theodosius' son (another Theodosius) had become emperor. Ammianus certainly seems confused over details, and, tellingly, despite his talk of victories, the situation kept degenerating. No one was keen to live outside city walls. The roads were unsafe and falling apart, residents were fleeing farms and small towns as fast as they could and trade was disappearing. Worse still, the more that insecurity eroded the prosperity needed to pay taxes, the less inclination Rome's rulers felt to use their dwindling stocks of men and money to provide security for a distant province that was losing value by the day. Naturally, the less Rome spent on protecting Britannia, the more its neighbours preyed on it, the more the British elites looked out for themselves and the less they identified as Romans.

Our evidence is poor – not many Romans were writing history

in the empire's dying days – but we do know that Picts and Scots returned in 382. Reserves already on hand stopped them, but the following year the reservists' Spanish commander Magnus Maximus (a wonderful name, meaning in Latin 'Great-Greatest') rebelled against the emperor – who was perhaps his cousin – and marched his men off to Italy, where he met his death. The troops who went with him never came back.

Most writers in the fifth and sixth centuries agreed that Magnus' adventurism 'left Britain deprived of all its soldiers [. . .] and the flower of its youth'. If the picture they paint – of a nearly defenceless province in constant uproar – is anywhere near the truth, it is no wonder that the economy came undone or that the surviving remnants of the British elite lost patience with the inattentive empire. Judging from the complete absence of coins dated after 402, Rome simply stopped paying the handful of troops left in Britain. 'Throwing off Roman rule', says the Greek writer Zosimus, Britons 'lived independently, no longer subject to Roman laws'. For a few months in 406 an actual native-born Briton took charge, only to be murdered, whereupon his assassin took a leaf from Magnus' playbook and marched what was left of the army off to Gaul to claim the imperial throne in 407. These troops never came back either.

When I was a schoolboy, the version we learned of these events differed little in essentials from 'The Roman Centurion's Song', a paean to England which Rudyard Kipling had put into the mouth of one of the men of 407:

> *Legate, I had the news last night – my cohort ordered home*
> *By ships to Portus Itius and thence by road to Rome.*
> *I've marched the companies aboard, the arms are stowed below;*
> *Now let another take my sword. Command me not to go!*
>
> *[. . .]*
>
> *Here where men say my name was made, here where my work was*
>   *done;*
> *Here where my dearest dead are laid – my wife – my wife and son;*
>
> *[. . .]*

Legate, I come to you in tears – My cohort ordered home!
I've served in Britain forty years. What should I do in Rome?
Here is my heart, my soul, my mind – the only life I know.
I cannot leave it all behind. Command me not to go!

Nothing brings the end of the empire alive for twelve-year-olds quite like this, but frankly the poem has little to do with the realities of 407. Kipling's stark contrasts between Romans, Britons, Picts and Saxons no longer really existed. A century of restless mobility had remade identities in the borderlands. Unlike Kipling's Italian centurion, the soldiers who marched away were local lads, and, more than that, many had Irish, Pictish or German parents. Some of these immigrants had been invited into the empire, serving in its armies in return for land; others had just pushed their way in. Plenty of fourth-century burials in southern England would have looked completely at home in Germany or the Low Countries, and by 400 settlers in Cornwall, Wales and western Scotland were commemorating their dead with what archaeologists call ogham stones, gravestones inscribed with Old Irish names in a peculiar script which used only straight lines.

All that was solid melted into air in those turbulent times, and, with no central army to oppose them, Saxons plundered the south and east coasts at will in 408. Despairing, local elites now begged Rome to return, but with Gaul and Spain in chaos and Germanic war bands about to storm his capital, the emperor Honorius had other things on his mind. In 410, Zosimus says, Honorius 'sent letters to the cities of Britain advising them to look to their own security'. The empire had concluded that Britannia was more trouble than it was worth.

4

THE ORIGINAL EUROPEAN UNION, 410–973

Post-Colonial Britain

'Long years ago we made a tryst with destiny, and now the time comes when we shall redeem our pledge', Jawaharlal Nehru announced as he led a newly independent India out of the British Empire in 1947. 'At the stroke of the midnight hour, while the world sleeps, India will awake to life and freedom. A moment comes, which comes but rarely in history, when we step out from the old to the new.'

We have little idea what Britons said as they left the Roman Empire in 410, but it was surely nothing like this. It may not even have been obvious that Britain really had left the empire: *Roma*, after all, was *aeterna*, and despite walking away plenty of times before, Britannia had always come back. But not now. What made 410 different from 260 (or 276, or 286, or 350) was that Rome itself had changed. The empire no longer provided Britain with a counterscarp against Continental raiders and invaders. No longer could Roman reserves rush across the Channel to bail out Britain, because there were no Romans left in Gaul to ride to the rescue; and soon enough there was no empire left either.

When India and Pakistan left the British Empire, they endured months of violence, years of migrations and decades of painful reorientation to a post-colonial stage. When Britannia left the Roman Empire, the same set of disasters lasted fully five centuries. Thatcher's Law remained in force, and once the Roman counterscarp had gone, the south-east, closest to the Continent, was exposed to the full force of Germanic mobility. Security and prosperity collapsed; sovereignty and identities were overturned. The north and west, by contrast, may actually have been better off after 410 than before. By 500 the organisational and intellectual imbalances between Britain's south-east and its north and west had evened out so much in the latter's favour that the Isles' centre of gravity was migrating towards Ireland, for the first time in 3,500 years.

But what geography took away, it eventually restored. The same proximity to the Continent that had dragged the south-east down in the fifth and sixth centuries lifted it back up in the seventh and eighth. The south-east – regularly known as 'England' after the ninth century [/] – joined an extraordinary new association, which I will call the Original European Union. Once again Rome was at its centre, but the new Rome was very different from the old one. Insofar as Rome now oversaw an empire, it was one of what social scientists call soft power: the kind that comes from being respected and admired, unlike the hard power of armies and economics, in which the ancient Roman Empire had excelled (although it certainly had plenty of soft power too). The Original European Union, like the modern one, had only minimal force at its disposal but massive moral suasion. The monks and other missionaries who served its rulers – the Catholic bishops of Rome – did not get their way by killing people and breaking things. Instead, they set up committees which searched tirelessly for consensus, talking until everyone agreed that submitting to God's will (as defined by Rome) would be better than arguing any more. The committees could certainly make life unpleasant for awkward people who refused to go along, but they could never call in the legions.

Submitting to the new Rome's soft power meant bartering identity and sovereignty for prosperity, security and sophistication, but most Britons were apparently happy enough with this deal for almost a thousand years. Yet it did have limits. 'The trouble with soft power', the historian Niall Ferguson once mused, 'is that it's, well, soft'; and the original European Union, like the modern one, found that honeyed words wouldn't always work with people who would rather fight than talk. This created two new dynamics. First, violent Scandinavian pagans who mounted hard-power challenges to Catholic Roman authority sometimes managed to drag the Isles' stage around to face more towards the Baltic than the Mediterranean (Figure 4.1); and second (often in response to the first dynamic), Islanders eventually created indigenous governments with enough money and military might to see off these challenges.

Between the seventh century and the tenth a new Britain emerged out of the post-colonial wreckage. It was ruled by native kings not distant Roman emperors, but it lodged in a European Union focused on Rome. For much of this time Catholic Britain remained Europe's poor cousin; yet within Britain a reunited England clawed its way

Figure 4.1. The European stage, 410–973.

back towards levels of population, prosperity and security not seen in six centuries, and brought the Celtic lands further under its shadow than ever before. The Islanders had found a new way to relate to Europe, and to each other.

Once and Future Kings

'Alas!' complained Gildas, an otherwise unknown sixth-century cleric, at the beginning of his short book *On the Ruin of Britain*. 'The subject of my complaint is the general destruction of everything that is good, and the general growth of evil throughout the land.' But 'Alas!' is also what modern historians often say on confronting Gildas's strange work. It is pretty much the only ancient account we have of Britain after Rome abandoned it, but it is hard to know what to make of this text. Four-fifths of the booklet is Biblical commentary, and even when Gildas actually talks about Britain, he sounds more like an Old Testament prophet than a scholar, casting Britons in the role of sinful Israelites and pagan invaders from the Continent as an angry God's scourge for his ungrateful people.

Gildas seems to be saying that, after a series of disasters, the leading Britons wrote to Rome's top general (probably in 446), begging him to bring the army back. 'The barbarians drive us into the sea', their letter said, but 'the sea drives us back on the barbarians. Between them, two kinds of death face us; we are either slaughtered or drowned.' Unfortunately, with Germanic war bands rampaging all over Western Europe and Attila the Hun besieging Constantinople itself, Britain was a low priority, and the empire never wrote back.

The next year, says Gildas, 'the proud tyrant Vortigern, leader of the Britons', decided that the only option was to revive the old strategy of turning one enemy into a friend and getting this friend to fight his other enemies. Vortigern therefore offered a deal to two brothers named Hengist and Horsa. They had just fled to Britain with three ships from the land of the Angles (which formed the angle where Germany and Denmark met). If the Angles would protect the rest of Britannia from raids, Vortigern promised, they could have the Isle of Thanet in the Thames estuary (Figure 4.2) as a new home. Hengist and Horsa agreed, and more Angles joined them, until there were too many for Vortigern to control. Not that he tried too hard: having fallen in love with Hengist's daughter Alice, Vortigern offered Hengist the whole of Kent (Figure 4.3) in return for her hand.

Hengist accepted, then turned on Vortigern anyway, sending him scurrying to a fort in Wales. Massacres, miracles and magic ensued, say Gildas and later writers, and for the next forty years raiders looted as they liked and settled all over what came to be called (after the Angles) England. Those Britons who were not slaughtered or enslaved, Gildas lamented, retreated 'to the mountains, precipices, thickly wooded forests, and to the rocks of the seas' of the north and west.

For many years archaeologists mostly concluded that, perplexing as Gildas's account was, it generally seemed quite consistent with the material record. Houses, burials and styles of dress in fifth-century England were all distinctly Germanic, sometimes so much so that they can be tied to specific regions (Jutland fashions were popular in Kent, north German in East Anglia). Even in the fourth century churches had been hard to identify archaeologically, but in the fifth century they disappeared, while male graves regularly included very un-Christian swords and spears. The first archaeologist to dig up a fifth-century village, in 1922, thought it fitted perfectly with Gildas's vision of brutish invaders: 'The bulk of the people', he concluded,

Figure 4.2. The British stage, 410–973.

Figure 4.3. Regions on the British stage, 410–973.

'were content with something that hardly deserves a better title than that of a hovel [. . .] with bare head room, amid a filthy litter of broken bones, of food and shattered pottery.' A century on we know that this site – Sutton Courtenay in Oxfordshire – was not even particularly poor; in 2009 *Time Team* archaeologists found one of the biggest Saxon royal halls yet known among its huts.

From the 1970s on, however, the now familiar doubts about migration narratives surfaced. Archaeologists began wondering whether people whose hovels couldn't even keep out the rain could possibly have conquered England in the way Gildas describes. Perhaps, revisionists suggested, what really happened around 450 was that a few tiny bands of bedraggled Continental refugees, fleeing violence at home, washed up in south-east England and tried to make new lives for themselves. Far from running in terror before them, Britons looked at the immigrants' shacks and realised that huts requiring no iron nails or stone foundations would be very practical for them too in their impoverished, post-Roman state. The more that the children and grandchildren of people who had considered themselves British, Roman and perhaps Christian began living like Germans, the more they began talking, dressing, burying and worshipping like them too. Gildas had mythologised England's turn against God into a story of mobility, sovereignty and security, but it was really one of identity and (lack of) prosperity.

This theory certainly makes sense of some of the evidence. Take the two Oxfordshire cemeteries of Queenford Farm and Berinsfield, barely a kilometre apart. The former, used in the fourth century, had classic Roman-style Christian burials; the latter, used in the fifth, had thoroughly Continental, pagan burials. Yet when anthropologists looked at the teeth from the two cemeteries, they found that a whole cluster of genetic anomalies occurred at similar rates in both sites. That can hardly be a coincidence, and in 2014 isotopic studies confirmed that the Berinsfield dead were locals. Queenford Farm's Britons apparently stayed put, learned the immigrants' ways and had babies who became Berinsfield's Anglo-Saxons.

In the last few years geneticists have also weighed in. In this case, their results favour a compromise, neither ignoring Gildas's near-contemporary account nor believing everything it says. Early efforts to calculate how much Saxon blood flows in modern Britons' veins foundered on the fact that there have been constant comings and goings across the North Sea during the last fifteen centuries (my mother's ancestors came and went between the Netherlands and England multiple times between 1860 and 1910), but in 2016 scientists succeeded in extracting DNA directly from fifth- and sixth-century skeletons. Around Cambridge, an area that probably saw especially heavy settlement, Anglo-Saxon genes replaced 38 per cent of the local pool – less dramatic than the 75 per cent replacement around 4200 BCE, to be sure, let alone the 90–95 per cent around 2400 BCE, but significant all the same.

More DNA studies are needed, but extrapolating from what we already have, it looks as though a million or so Britons stayed where they were in the fifth and sixth centuries and reinvented themselves as Anglo-Saxons, while maybe another half-million-plus were killed or chased away. Gildas overdramatised, but the reality was dramatic enough. Miserable caravans of British refugees retreated deeper into the dissolving Roman Empire, settling in such numbers in north-west France that the peninsula which Romans had called Armorica was renamed Brittany, complete with bishoprics of Cornouaille (Cornwall) and Domnonée (Dumnonia, the Roman name for Devon). Others Britons founded a kingdom in the Loire Valley and an abbey of Santa María de Bretoña in northern Spain. Most, though, trudged through the rain and mud north towards the Pennines and west into Cornwall and Wales.

Once there, refugees joined the locals in converting old Roman forts and even pre-Roman hill forts into homes for hundreds of people (at Cadbury–Congresbury, in Somerset, maybe a thousand). One tombstone commemorates a 'king of Gwent' in south Wales, and bards composed magnificent Welsh-language epics about bejewelled lords, riding forth to hunt in glittering armour and presiding over elegant feasts. At the hill fort that later became Cadbury Castle great men gathered in a timber feasting hall twenty times the size of the typical Saxon house, their drinking cups and wine having been brought all the way from Constantinople. They drizzled Mediterranean olive oil over their dinners, for all the world as though the Roman Empire were still a going concern.

Britons in the west worked hard to hang on to their Roman heritage. Classical scholars accustomed to Cicero's lean, spare prose often find Gildas's flowery version tiresome, but he and other clerics were clearly still spending years mastering Latin literary style. Some Britons tried to remain Roman by robbing old graves in search of antique vases and glass vessels to grace their dinner tables, while others took titles and names evoking older identities. One man claimed on his tombstone to be a 'citizen of Gwynedd', just as Britons formerly boasted of being citizens of Rome. Another, buried at Whithorn in Galloway, was named Latinus. More tombstones inscribed in Latin – over 200 – have been found in Cornwall, Wales and the Pennines from the period 450–650 than from the centuries of actual Roman rule.

These 'sub-Romans', as archaeologists often call them, fought hard to defend their kingdoms. According to the Venerable Bede (a much better scholar than Gildas), who wrote an *Ecclesiastical History of the English People* in the eighth century, German raiders united under single warlords in the 490s and twice more in the 560s. Britons responded in kind, led first by a man rejoicing in the ultra-Roman name Ambrosius Aurelianus (Gildas called him 'the last of the Romans'), and then, say some authors, by Arthur, the immortal Christian king.

Arthur is an enigma. Neither Gildas nor Bede mentions him; his first appearance is in the pages of a very peculiar *History of the Britons* written around 830 by a Welsh author usually known as Nennius. 'Then [around 500] it was', Nennius announces without explanation or preamble, 'that the magnanimous Arthur, with all the kings and military might of Britain, fought against the Saxons.' Nennius describes 'a most severe contest, where Arthur penetrated to the Hill of Badon. In this engagement, nine hundred and sixty fell by his hand alone, no one but the Lord affording him help.' In the tenth century a chronicle called the *Annals of Wales* added the detail that at 'the Battle of Badon [. . .] Arthur carried the cross of our Lord Jesus Christ on his shoulders for three days and nights and the Britons were victorious'.

It is odd that eleven generations passed after the Battle of Badon before any author mentioned Arthur, and odder still that ten more generations then passed before his story took on much of the shape known today. Geoffrey of Monmouth, the fantasist of the 1130s whose stories about Stonehenge we encountered in Chapter 2, was the first to mention Merlin, Camelot, the illicit love of Lancelot and Guinevere and Arthur's magical removal to the Isle of Avalon; and while Nennius and the *Annals of Wales* each devote just a few lines to Arthur, Geoffrey fills up fifty-four pages (in the Penguin translation) with his deeds, which, he says, included conquering half of Europe. Twenty years later another poet added the Round Table and the Sword in the Stone, and in the 1180s another still introduced the Quest for the Holy Grail. The full Arthurian package, with its brooding sense of loss and impending doom, only arrived in the 1460s, a thousand years after Arthur's own day, in Thomas Malory's 525-page *Morte d'Arthur*.

Usually historians find that the sources written closest to a king's lifetime say most about him and that information is lost as time passes. When this pattern is reversed, we tend to be suspicious. It is certainly possible that Geoffrey of Monmouth discovered ancient texts, now lost, that included all the details later listed by Malory. It is also possible that Gildas and Bede knew plenty about Arthur but just didn't happen to mention him, or that later writers embellished an original kernel of truth into more elaborate stories. Or it could be that Welsh bards in Nennius' age invented Arthur out of thin air to give themselves a suitably heroic and Christian ancestor.

Short of stumbling across an eyewitness account of King Arthur, which is never going to happen, it is hard to know what sort of evidence could resolve this argument, but in 1998 something rather remarkable did turn up in excavations at Tintagel (Arthur's birthplace, according to Geoffrey of Monmouth). It was a small piece of stone, inscribed in the sixth century with the more-or-less Latin phrase *patern- coli avi ficit artognou*. This probably means something like 'Artognou, descended from Patern[us] Colus, made this' (or 'had this made'). 'Artognou', coming from Celtic words meaning 'bear' and 'to know', might be translated as a personal name like 'Wise Bear' – and could plausibly have been latinised as Artorius and then anglicised as Arthur. The excavators, rightly, insist that this does not prove that a man remembered as King Arthur began his career at Tintagel as a chief named Wise Bear; but on the other hand, if Wise Bear really was Arthur, this is as close to proof as we are ever likely to get.

The arguments will go on, but what matters most for the story in this book is less whether Arthur really lived than what he came to stand for. As we will see in the next two chapters, Welsh, Scottish and even English ideologues for centuries to come would look back to the heroic Arthur, appropriating, elaborating on and fighting over him as the founding father of identities they wished to claim. Only after England absorbed Wales and Scotland into a United Kingdom did the struggles really die down. Arthur was perhaps the greatest Briton who never lived.

But not the greatest Irishman. Across the Irish Sea the mantle of collective ancestor was laid on the shoulders of an almost equally obscure fifth-century figure, Patrick. Patrick definitely existed – two texts written by him survive – but they are remarkably uninformative (the historian Thomas Bartlett jokes that Patrick invented 'the well-known Irish tradition of "whatever-you-say-say-nothing"'). He was born in northern England, perhaps around 410, and his father was a sub-Roman official who probably lived near Carlisle. Patrick was kidnapped by Irish slavers at the age of sixteen before being born again as a Christian while herding his owner's sheep. Six years later he escaped, only for God to send him a dream in which the Irish cried out, 'We beg you, holy boy, to come and walk again among us.' Inspired, Patrick returned to Ireland to preach.

Specialists dispute every detail of Patrick's story, but the canonical version says that, after arriving in Ireland in 432, he faced down a pagan high king and his druids at Tara and then founded a distinctive Irish church. On the Continent, bishops based in towns called the shots, but Ireland had no towns. With its population of perhaps half a million divided between thousands of petty chiefs, each ruling a mere handful of ring forts, there was no one to take charge except little groups of self-directed monks – who, with the zeal of converts, threw themselves into spreading the Word with a vengeance.

In the sixth century, when Anglo-Saxon England was pagan and largely illiterate, Irish monasteries became centres for Biblical scholarship. Bede says 'there were many in England, both nobles and commons, who [. . .] retired to Ireland for the sake of religious studies'. Irish monks simultaneously flowed the other way on *peregrinatio* ('walkabout'), carrying their learning back across the Irish Sea to enlighten Britain's remaining Christians as well as its pagans. The most famous missionary, Columba (Colum Cille in Irish), founded a monastery on Iona in the Hebrides and emulated the great Patrick by confronting a Pictish king and his chief druid in 580. The silence of our sources suggests that this did not go well, but just a decade later another monk, Columbanus, began a still more ambitious walkabout, setting up a string of monasteries in France and Italy.

No century in Britain's post-Roman history is as poorly understood as the fifth, but we can certainly see that the end of empire transformed the meanings of the Isles' geography. Mobility surged upwards, prosperity and security slumped down, and old forms of sovereignty and identity disintegrated. South-eastern Britain was dragged off the Mediterranean stage and attached to the north European homelands of its latest immigrant population, while the Celtic north and west retained (or reinvented) a strong sense of connection with the vanished Roman world. The journalist Thomas Cahill exaggerated when he called his bestselling book about this period *How the Irish Saved Civilization*, but he had a point. The Britons and Irish lit a remarkable beacon on the furthest western edge of the fading empire. There, among the ruins, Rome's inheritors hung on, waiting for Arthur to come back and save them.

Rome Returns

Instead, it was Rome that returned, although its second coming was very different from its first. This time Rome's heralds were not Caesar's legions but an Italian monk named Augustine and a mere forty of his fellows. The reconquest began, Bede tells us in a famous but far-fetched story, when a group of boys 'with fair complexions, handsome faces and lovely hair' caught Pope Gregory I's roving eye as he strolled through a slave market in Rome in 597. Learning that they were pagan Angles, Gregory announced 'Good, for these Angles [in Latin, *Angli*] have the faces of angels [*angeli*], and should share in the gifts of the angels in heaven'. After further wordplay, says Bede, the punning pope resolved to bring Britain back to Rome.

He would do so not by compulsion but by persuasion. Government had collapsed in much of Western Europe in the fifth century and revived only slowly across the sixth. In the interim, bishops were often the only men in a position to organise much of anything, and while they rarely had armies to enforce their commands, they had something potentially even more powerful: the ability to save or damn men's eternal souls. Bishops who could persuade Christians that they alone dispensed salvation were mighty men indeed, and by 500 a Mediterranean Big Five – the bishops of Alexandria, Antioch, Constantinople, Jerusalem and Rome – had pulled ahead of the rest. Jostling jealously with each other as well as with local players like the Irish monks, each set about saving more souls than anyone else.

Arab conquests took Alexandria, Antioch and Jerusalem out of the race in the seventh century, and in the eighth Rome and Constantinople gradually stopped talking to one another. By then the bishop of Rome – the pope – had won out in the west. Popes claimed that God alone could decide who was a king, and that it fell to them, as God's representatives, to announce His choices. Rome was in effect demanding for itself a slice of the sovereignty that chiefs like those in Anglo-Saxon England were currently trying to build up. Nor was that all: bishops also got very good at persuading warlords that only the church could save their souls, with the result that great chunks of some communities' wealth passed into Italian priests' hands as sweeteners to attract divine favour. Even before 500 King Childeric of the Franks, who had taken over much of the old Roman province of Gaul, complained that 'My treasury is always empty. All our wealth has fallen into the hands of the Church. There is no one with any power left except the bishops. Nobody respects me as king: all respect has passed to the bishops in their cities.'

This sounds like a bad deal for men who would be kings, yet joining Rome's European Union had its attractions. Like twenty-first-century Brussels, sixth-century Rome lacked hard military and economic power, but the fundamental goodness of its teachings gave it plenty of the soft sort. Rome was offering a deal: in return for surrendering some sovereignty, kings would receive a different sort of sovereignty, because only those who basked in Rome's approval looked legitimate. Rulers who accepted the one true God's endorsement could tap into the sanctity of traditions stretching back to the Roman Empire; those who did not would be cast into the outer darkness. To warrior chiefs, still struggling to pull away from a roiling mass of warlords and turn themselves into real kings, this was an enticing proposition. Even such a *realpolitik* ruler as Childeric's thuggish son Clovis could see that, if handled well, conversion could pay off. He submitted to Rome and then leveraged his new legitimacy to turn France into the greatest post-imperial kingdom in the west. Imbalances between Francia and southern England grew rapidly until, in a rerun of what had happened in the first century BCE, Clovis's descendants claimed kingship over southern England too. English chiefs scrambled to resist by becoming kings in their own right.

The most successful was Aethelbert, a warrior who had cowed his rivals in Kent and was now trying to persuade more of England to bend the knee. In the early 580s he signalled his claim to specialness by marrying Bertha, a Christian princess from France. Bertha not only connected Aethelbert to the Frankish ruling family but also brought with her to Kent an authentic European bishop; and he, presumably helped by immigrant Frankish craftsmen, turned a Roman ruin just outside Aethelbert's capital of Canterbury into a church of St Martin. This was probably the first all-stone building constructed in England in nearly two centuries.

The missionary Augustine made a beeline for Aethelbert in 597. When Aethelbert accepted the pope's offer, making himself just as legitimate as any Frankish king, Augustine pressed on into Essex (named after the 'East Saxons' who had settled there). Its king too converted, building a wooden church for St Paul in a corner of the largely deserted ruins of Roman London. But then the mission slowed: the further Augustine got from the Continent, the more cautious local kings became, and when he reached Wales in 603, he was firmly rebuffed by Britons who were already Christian. Backed up by learned Irish monks, the Welsh saw no need for Italians to tell them what God wanted.

Augustine also discovered that kings had a bad habit of picking and choosing the bits they liked in Rome's message, and even of exiting the Christian union when it suited them. When the kings of Kent and Essex died, both in 616, their sons returned to their old gods, and Augustine's panicky successor prepared to abandon the English mission altogether – until St Peter came to him in a dream and whipped the fear out of him. According to Bede, the chastened archbishop 'went to the king [of Essex] as soon as morning came, drew back his robe and showed him the welts from his blows. The king was amazed [. . .] he banned all idolatry, gave up his unlawful wife, accepted the Christian faith and was baptised. Thereafter he promoted the interests of the church to the best of his ability.'

The most famous find in Anglo-Saxon archaeology, the Sutton Hoo ship burial, may well reflect another king's wobbles over the Word. By the time the site was excavated, in 1939, the acidic, sandy soil had long ago dissolved the body buried here, but the excavators did find blackened sand and iron rivets left behind by the rotted hull of a wooden warship (Figure 4.4) and a spectacular but puzzling hoard of grave goods sitting on top of it. Some were unmistakably Christian, such as a pair of silver christening spoons, one inscribed *Paulos* and the other *Saulos* (the two names that the Bible gives St Paul); but others were equally unmistakably not. The magnificent helmet, mail shirt and sword found with the spoons had no place in a God-fearing

Figure 4.4. Shadows of things past: excavators in 1939 exposing iron rivets and stained sand in Mound 1 at Sutton Hoo, all that survived in this acidic soil of a 90-foot-long ship buried in the 620s. This (probably) contained the body of King Raedwald of East Anglia, a wobbly Christian.

man's grave. Nor did the human sacrifices (recovered by more careful excavators in the 1980s) that surrounded the burial.

Imported coins date the burial firmly in the 620s, and most historians think it belonged to Raedwald, who ruled the East Angles in those years and does indeed seem to have been conflicted over Christ. Bede says that after being 'initiated into the mysteries of the Christian faith in Kent', Raedwald 'was seduced by his wife and certain evil teachers'. Ever after, 'he seemed to be serving both Christ and the gods whom he had previously served'.

Yet Raedwald was among the last Anglo-Saxon kings to remain in two minds. Every time a ruler found Jesus, the benefits of following his example snowballed a little more for others. Only Christian kings could marry other Christian kings' daughters, and only Christian kings could tap into the church's booming wealth and diplomatic networks. Saints (most prominent seventh-century Christians ended up being sanctified) acquired enough influence to topple kings; getting on the wrong side of them, the historian James Campbell suggests, was 'the equivalent of a witch-doctor's curse'. Some kings waxed so enthusiastic about Jesus that after converting they abdicated and became monks – which, while bad for their own careers, boosted those of their heirs. Most monarchs had converted by 650, and those who resisted found themselves frozen out of all the meetings and marriages that mattered. The last pagan king, on the Isle of Wight, switched sides in 686.

And so it was that England gradually joined the Original European Union, its kings exchanging some of their hard-won sovereignty for membership of a bigger, more sophisticated club. The truth was, seventh-century kings *needed* the church. Immigration was slowing down as population growth eased in Germany and Denmark, leaving local chiefs with no one to fight but each other; and as the winners of these wars swallowed up the losers, their enlarged kingdoms began requiring the kind of literate, numerate administrators that only the church was producing.

Further north and west, we see the same processes working at smaller scales. Ireland's biggest chiefs bundled lesser lords together into clusters that were later called 'fifths', based in Ulster, Leinster, Munster, Connacht and Meath. The Uí Néill clan even leveraged its control of Tara to claim high kingship over all of Ireland, albeit without much obvious success. A vivid poetic tradition grew up around the wars, cattle raids and treacherous feasts of heroes such as Queen Medb, Cú Chulainn and Niall of the Nine Hostages. Sadly, these stories are probably as fanciful as the Arthur epics. Flesh-and-blood Irish kings seem to have been a more prosaic lot, worrying about alliances with scholars at abbeys like Armagh – or even about becoming abbots themselves – rather than cattle-rustling.

Rulers in Wales and the north seem to have had similar concerns to those in Ireland. Recent excavations at Rhynie in Aberdeenshire show that Pictish chiefs were building increasingly elaborate fortresses and decorating their tombs with life-size statues, and written sources suggest that the notion of having a single Pictish high king was gaining traction by 600. In the same years the seven or so tiny chiefdoms of post-Roman Wales shrank down to just Gwynedd and Powys.

One of the main reasons that government grew faster in England than in the north and west was that Francia rebuilt the old Continental counterscarp, bringing the French side of the English Channel under its control around 600 and the mouths of the Rhine around 680. Raiding and migration now more or less stopped, and with the Franks themselves too busy fighting each other to colonise or conquer southern England, the Anglo-Saxon kingdoms could grow much faster than their northern and western rivals.

Trade came roaring back after three centuries of disruption. Like so much else, the revival began in Francia, where busy little boats had never really stopped carrying grain, wine, pots and metalwork along coasts and up rivers. Ambitious (or desperate) skippers started trying their luck across the Channel too, and informal markets sprang up on beaches from Hamwic (Southampton) to Ipswich. By 750 the benefits of London's location, which had been anything but obvious since the Romans left, had lured several thousand people back there. Avoiding the ruins of Londinium – perhaps because its rotting Roman quays made river access difficult – they set up shop a mile upstream along the Strand, in those days still just the muddy little beach implied by its name. Much of today's West End, stretching from Covent Garden's piazza to Selfridges on Oxford Street, was soon packed with the timber huts (even now, few were yet building in stone) and open-air workshops of Lundenwic.

Britain's north and west had nothing like these towns, which galvanised the south-east. Ever since their arrival, the richest Saxon chiefs had got that way by killing and robbing people. Fierce warriors signed up to serve even fiercer ones, and as the latter turned into kings, they rewarded the former by making them lords and giving them estates. When not fighting, kings and their war bands would travel between their properties, consuming all the meat and mead on site then moving on to the next spot. It worked well enough, but had the drawback of being difficult to scale up. By 650, though, markets were putting new options on the table. Instead of just turning up and eating everything, a king or lord could install an agent on his farm, confiscate the lion's share of its output and then take his cut to Norwich or some similar market to swap for more durable goods. Continental merchants wanted food and drink (and slaves) to sell in the cities back home; Anglo-Saxon elites wanted Continental ornaments, clothes and weapons to distinguish themselves from their poorer peers. Everybody gained, except the slaves.

Kings also realised that, if they posted armed men at the markets, they could 'protect' everyone trading there and charge them for the privilege. Kentish kings imposed 10 per cent tolls at Lundenwic in the 660s, and by 700 rulers were using another Continental idea – coinage – to make extortion easier. The oldest coins dug up at Ipswich and other markets are imports, but kings found new opportunities to skim off profits by minting their own money and requiring merchants to use it. Offa, who ruled the great Midland kingdom of Mercia from 757 to 796, issued perhaps 10 million thin silver pennies, and the kings of East Anglia even decorated their own issues with pictures of Romulus and Remus, the legendary founders of Rome.

This was what made men who could read, keep records and organise things so useful. Fortunately for kings, the church was keen to provide them – in fact, more than keen, since clerks were powerful agents in Rome's ongoing argument with Celtic monks over whether the Anglo-Saxons would lean towards Italy or Ireland. Rome, with its immense resources, usually had the upper hand, but the Irish fought a good fight. Several Anglo-Saxon kings had found Christ while in exile in Celtic lands and had brought Irish ways of doing things back to England with them, and in 635 missionaries from Columbanus' Celtic monastery on Iona skipped around to England's east coast to found an even greater institution on Lindisfarne. Five years later they opened another at Hartlepool, from which missionaries fanned out across England.

Some of the differences dividing the Irish and Italians, such as which precise bit of his head a monk should shave, now seem like arguing for the sake of it, but others – especially how to calculate the date of Easter – were very serious indeed. I have to admit that Easter's arrival takes me by surprise most years, but seventh-century Christians knew that celebrating the festival at the wrong time endangered the immortal souls of everyone on earth. The matter finally came to a head in a great synod at Whitby in 664, where Oswy, king of Northumbria, sided with Rome. For the next 900 years few seriously doubted that God came to England via Italy.

Pouncing on this opening, the pope sent a new man, Theodore, to Canterbury to straighten English Christianity out. Theodore looked like an odd choice: at sixty-eight, he was ancient by seventh-century standards, and as a Greek refugee from Tarsus in Turkey (recently overrun by Muslim conquerors from Arabia) he seemed completely out of place in a backwoods place like Canterbury. However, Theodore was an inspired pick. He travelled constantly, teaching church law, holding councils and above all setting up schools – which, as well as turning out literary giants like Bede, provided crowds of lesser clerics to staff kings' counting houses. Some of the documents they produced still survive, including what appears to be a tribute list for Mercia, recording private wealth in surprising detail. Theodore in effect supplied Anglo-Saxon kings with civil servants; and then as now, bureaucrats had a *Yes Minister* tendency to turn the politicians they supposedly served into pawns. Theodore's parchment-shuffling protégés did more than anyone to establish the principle that no king was king without the say-so of Rome's man in Canterbury.

Trading some sovereignty for administrative capacity made the Anglo-Saxon kings more prosperous by far than either their predecessors or contemporary rulers in the north and west, and one of the first things they did with their newfound wealth was to hire better fighters. Some historians think that the poem *Beowulf*, the undisputed masterpiece of Old English literature, offers a window on to their brutal world. The text – probably written in England in the eighth century but set in Scandinavia in the sixth, told by a Christian narrator but describing resolutely pagan heroes – is difficult to interpret, but revolves around Hrothgar, king of the Danes, whose idyllic life of killing people and drinking with his followers in the great wooden hall of Heorot has been ruined by a monster named Grendel. None of his men dares face Grendel, so, at huge cost, Hrothgar hires the Swedish adventurer Beowulf, who duly kills both Grendel and his even scarier mother. Loaded down with loot, Beowulf then heads home to rule his own people, finally meeting his end fighting a dragon for yet more treasure.

No archaeologist has yet identified a dragon's lair, but Beowulfian swords-for-hire were real enough in seventh- and eighth-century England. With their help, the rising powers of Mercia and Northumbria pushed their borders up to the ancient boundary between the lowlands and highlands. Building ships, Northumbrians then went further still, raiding Anglesey and the Isle of Man. But this proved a step too far: a landing in Ireland went horribly wrong in 684, and the following year Picts ambushed and killed the king and much of his army. The Northumbrians decided – like the Romans before them – that conquering the north and west was too much trouble. Geography asserted itself, and imbalances evened out roughly along modern England's borders with Wales and Scotland.

By then, the Anglo-Saxons' understanding about sovereignty with Rome's European Union had transformed England. Offa of Mercia conceded to a papal legate in the 780s that he would 'let kings be lawfully chosen by the priests and elders of the people', and in return he earned the support he needed to create a kingdom that came up to Continental standards. For the first time since Stonehenge, the English perhaps built something bigger than anything equivalent on the Continent: Offa's Dyke, a 200-km-long, 8-m-high earth bank and 2-m-deep ditch. (I say 'perhaps' because some archaeologists think that some or all of it was actually built in the fifth century, presumably to keep Saxons out of Wales.) Charters called Offa 'king of the English', and the mighty Frankish king Charlemagne, who was pushing his empire deep into Germany and Italy in these years and would soon be crowned as emperor by the pope himself in Rome, actually considered marrying his daughter to Offa. Rather than bullying Offa, Charlemagne wrote to him as his 'dearest brother'.

The Anglo-Saxons had arrived. While still at the edge of everything – and still smaller and poorer than ancient Britannia – Mercia and Northumbria were respected members of a European community of kingdoms, complete with learned monks, fearsome armies and rich towns. The stage on which Britons operated once again stretched all the way to the Mediterranean, and England's prosperity attracted traders from ever further afield.

So it was that in 789 three boats from Scandinavia sailed into Portland harbour in Dorset, 'the first ships of Danish men which came to the land of the English', as a chronicler inaccurately put it (they were actually Norwegian). Once the ships had beached, a local reeve rushed down to invite the sailors to come to the royal hall at Dorchester, probably to haggle over what cut the king would take from their cargo. The Norwegians killed him.

The Robbers

Wicingas, people came to call them – 'the robbers'. 'Never before', the Anglo-Saxon scholar Alcuin lamented, 'has such terror appeared in Britain as we have now suffered from a pagan race, nor was it thought that such an inroad from the sea could be made.' Alcuin said this because for most people in the eighth-century Isles piracy had sunk to the level of background noise, thanks to the Frankish counterscarp in Europe. The only imbalances that seemed to matter were those coming up from the Mediterranean, tying Britain into the European Union. But now, out of the blue, Norwegians upended the strategic balance.

This was made possible by beautiful, practically unsinkable ships

Figure 4.5. Run for the hills: the prow of the Gokstad Ship,
built around 890, capable of carrying forty or so Scandinavian
terrorists/traders all the way to Constantinople or Canada.

like the one shown in Figure 4.5. These made crossing the North Sea
vastly easier, and over the next three centuries would carry Scandinavians all the way to the Middle East and the coasts of Canada. Given
a fair wind, a longboat leaving Bergen could beach in the Shetland
Islands two days later, then cruise down through the Hebrides to enter
the Irish Sea from the north (Figure 4.6). A ship could only carry thirty
or forty armed men, but that was thirty or forty more than the typical
village had on hand. The Vikings could land on almost any beach,
loot the first village they found, kill anyone who argued and be long
gone by the time a distant king could arrive with help. The Frankish
counterscarp was thus outflanked, exposing every coast in the British
Isles – in fact, every coast in north-west Europe – to robbery.

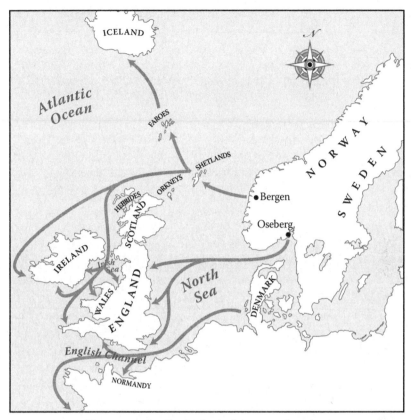

Figure 4.6. Outflanked: ninth-century longboats
render the Frankish counterscarp irrelevant.

That said, Alcuin was being slightly alarmist. There were very
few Viking ships in the eighth century, and he overreacted to a
handful of acts of extreme violence – much as we tend to do today
over terrorists, despite knowing that they kill far fewer people each
year than cars. By the 830s, however, raids were getting bigger, and
after 850 Vikings came in war bands thousands-strong, some of them
capable of overthrowing kingdoms. Ever since, Vikings have been
an archetype of brutality. We still speak of going 'berserk', from a
Norse word, and in the Second World War the Nazis called one of
their most vicious Waffen SS divisions the *Wiking*. Even so, in the late
twentieth century Vikings received the kind of academic makeover
that we saw several times in Chapters 1–3, with scholars suggesting

that they were neither as numerous nor as terrifying as Anglo-Saxon authors claimed. Debates focused particularly on the 'Blood Eagle', a horrifying ritual in which, some sources say, Vikings chained a victim face-down, sliced the flesh off his back, prised his ribcage open and then pulled his lungs out and draped them over his shoulders to look like the wings of an eagle. Anglo-Saxon sources assert that at least two of their kings died this way, but revisionists point out that we have only their word for it. The Vikings produced beautiful art and poetry, managed far-flung trade networks and sailed to America. Should we really believe it when their rivals call them mass murderers?

It's a fair question, but on the whole, we probably should. The revisionists are right that archaeologists sometimes assume too readily that every burned monastery or dump of dismembered corpses is the work of Vikings. They are also right that many Viking military camps were too small to hold more than a few dozen men. That said, there really are a lot of sacked ninth-century sites and massacre pits, often from just the places the literary sources say Vikings destroyed, and some Viking camps were enormous. One, occupied over the winter of 872–3 at Torksey in Lincolnshire, could easily have held 5,000 warriors and their families. DNA also adds some sense of scale. The Scottish islands (conveniently close to Scandinavia, and lacking strong kings to defend them) feature prominently in Norse sagas, and at Jarlshof on Shetland Norwegian-style longhouses replaced homes in the multi-roomed Pictish tradition.* DNA studies suggest that 23 to 28 per cent of genetic material in the Shetlands is Scandinavian.

Ninth-century Vikings enjoyed the same kind of advantages in mobility and force as Angles, Saxons and Jutes had held in the fifth, creating a military imbalance that once again threatened to drag Britain out of its Mediterranean/Christian orbit into a Baltic/pagan one. To Alcuin, Viking attacks on monasteries, beginning at Lindisfarne in 793, looked like a deliberate strategy, rejecting the European Union's soft power and undoing its achievements – although we should perhaps bear in mind what the American hoodlum 'Slick Willie' Sutton said when asked in the 1960s why he robbed banks: 'That's where the money is.' Vikings may have felt the same way about monasteries.

---

*The site's name is as thoroughly Scandinavian as anyone could ask for, but it was in fact only bestowed in 1814, by the Romantic novelist Sir Walter Scott.

The church and West European kings had no effective answer to fast-moving gangs of robbers striking at the edges of their world. In time-honoured tradition, therefore, men on the spot – local lords and abbots – took matters into their own hands, stopping paying taxes to the centre and spending the money on private armies instead. Established kingdoms unravelled astonishingly quickly. By 885, when King Charles the Fat failed to turn up to relieve a Viking siege of Paris, even the mighty Frankish Empire was effectively a dead letter. In 911 his relative Charles the Simple decided that his best option was to buy off the Norse chief Rolf the Walker (so-called, we are told, because he was too overweight to ride) by giving him the rich lands that would come to be called Normandy.

Normandy will feature prominently in Chapter 5, but it matters at this point in the story too, because its transfer to Norse control had two major effects. First, it broke the Franks as major players on the European stage, with immense consequences for Britain; and second, it revealed how the Vikings would ultimately be tamed. Ignoring Christianity and the European consensus was all very well for robbers, but the moment Viking chiefs settled down to enjoy what they had stolen, they faced the same problems as seventh-century Anglo-Saxons. Running kingdoms required literate administrators, which only the church could provide; brokering diplomatic deals took marriages into Christian royal families; and earning respect depended on building Christian churches and monasteries. The only way Rolf the Walker could seal his deal over Normandy, in fact, was by being baptised (although the human sacrifices at his funeral suggest that the new faith's subtleties sometimes eluded him). In this classic clash between hard power and soft, the Vikings learned that praying with Christians paid better dividends than preying on them.

But that all lay in the future. Right now, instead of rolling over like the Charleses Fat and Simple, British kings fought back against the Vikings – and also against each other, because standing up to Scandinavians usually meant consolidating larger kingdoms within Britain. After Vikings smashed a Scots–Pictish alliance in 839, the Scottish king Kenneth macAlpin (in Gaelic, Cináed mac Ailpín) battered other Scots, Picts and Britons until they entered a united front against the Scandinavians. As his unified kingdom of Alba took over the Highlands, macAlpin worked to build a shared identity, rooted in the Gaelic language and a 'Stone of Destiny' at Scone – which, legend held, the first Scots immigrants had carried over from Ireland centuries earlier. Alba could not dislodge Norwegians from the Orkneys or Shetlands, but neither (despite another great victory in 876) could the Vikings destroy Alba. Natives and Norse would share the north.

Ireland reached a similar place by a different route. Here the chaos of tiny chiefdoms and constantly shifting alliances made it harder for a macAlpin to emerge, but also made it harder for invaders to take control. Even when a charismatic high king could convince the clans to work together – such as Máel Sechnaill, who drove the Norwegians out of Dublin in 849 – unity never lasted long. But the Vikings were divided too; it was Danes, not Norwegians, who retook Dublin in 851, and the two nationalities feuded furiously from then on. While Norsemen could not be stopped from fortifying Wexford, Waterford, Limerick and, above all, Dublin, neither could they make much mark on the interior. Concluding that the pickings might be better in Iceland than in Ireland, many Vikings headed off to this new frontier in the 880s (mitochondrial DNA suggests that they often took Irish wives with them).

Wales's fate depended heavily on Ireland's. Once the Vikings had taken Dublin, Wales's un-plundered monasteries became tempting targets. Rhodri the Great, the Welsh equivalent of macAlpin and Sechnaill, united much of the country against the threat, but his kingdom collapsed when Mercians killed him in 877 (in this messy world everyone was fighting several wars at once). Place names and DNA suggest that plenty of Scandinavians settled in south-west Wales, but when the Vikings moved on from Ireland to Iceland, they mostly moved on from Wales too.

The richest robbing was to be had in England, and there the outcome was more dramatic still. Anglo-Saxon kings more or less held their own until 865, when a 'Great Host' (as our sources call it) descended on Northumbria. York fell in 866, to be joined to Dublin in a new Viking kingdom controlling both sides of the Irish Sea. Over the next five years Vikings set up a puppet ruler in Mercia and overthrew the Northumbrian and East Anglian kingdoms, possibly bloodeagling their monarchs. It looked alarmingly like a rerun of the end of the Roman Empire. Trade dried up, towns were abandoned and almost every library in Viking-controlled territory burned. London had become a ghost town even before the Great Host occupied it in 871.

The Vikings had come to London after rampaging through Wessex, the last Anglo-Saxon kingdom left. The Viking chief Guthrum had defeated Wessex's army five times, killing its king and bullying his inexperienced, twenty-two-year-old brother Alfred into paying him a massive bribe to go away. But Alfred did not get peace for his time: it was standard Viking practice first to rob a victim, then to demand more and finally, when there was nothing left to extort, to steal the land itself.

Alfred paid further bribes in 876 and 877, but in January 878 Guthrum switched to the endgame. Alfred's men ran away and the king himself fled into a swamp at Athelney, where, his biographer Bishop Asser says, 'He had nothing to live on except what he could forage'. It was the stuff legends are made of, and the most famous story about Alfred – that he burned the loaves that a peasant woman had told him to watch while he hid in her hut – is exactly that. Like so many of the Arthur stories, it is not mentioned until long after the king was dead, and then grew in the telling for centuries before reaching the form we know today.

But this is the only way Alfred resembles Arthur. Britons had been waiting for nearly four centuries for the Christian King Arthur to return from the magical Isle of Avalon and drive out the pagan Anglo-Saxons; but now the Christian Anglo-Saxon King Alfred returned from the marshes of Athelney and drove out the pagan Norse. From their hideouts Alfred and a growing band of desperadoes harried Guthrum's Vikings for months and then, in May, rode to Egbert's Stone (probably a monument from the age of Stonehenge, although which one is unknown). 'There', Asser says, 'all the inhabitants of Somerset and Wiltshire and all the inhabitants of Hampshire – those who had not sailed overseas for fear of the Vikings – joined up with him. When they saw the king, receiving him (not surprisingly) as if one restored to life after suffering such great tribulations, they were filled with immense joy.' Their morale sky-high, Alfred's men caught the Vikings two days later at Edington, and in hours of face-to-face killing with spear and axe, broke their line. After two weeks besieged in his camp, Guthrum accepted Christianity and withdrew to East Anglia.

What truly made Alfred the Great great (Figure 4.7), though, raising him above the macAlpins, Sechnaills and Rhodris, was not Edington. It was what he did next. He had learned that the secret of Norse success was mobility. Because Vikings could come and go as they pleased, no victory over them could be final. When bested, they sailed away, but at the first sign of weakness they came back. Alfred had to constrain their freedom of movement. And yet none of the obvious options – recreating the Saxon Shore forts, conquering a counterscarp in Scandinavia, controlling the seas in the modern sense of bottling up Viking fleets in their harbours – was practical, given his limited resources. He could not fight the Vikings on the seas and oceans or even on the beaches. However, he could fight them in the fields, in the streets and in the hills, by filling the countryside with strongholds. These burhs (the root of the modern word 'borough') would be proper towns, not just places of refuge. Their sturdy walls often reused Roman defences, and, placed a day's walk apart, they either forced the Vikings to stop moving and besiege them or, if raiders bypassed them, provided bases from which to harry the intruders and pin them down.

Getting burhs built required Alfred to be a great talker as well as a great fighter. Since he could afford neither to build them nor to pay the 27,000 militia – a vast number for ninth-century Wessex – required to man them, he needed to convince his lords and bishops that the pain of these 'common burdens' was less than the pain of Viking rule. Not everyone agreed, because, despite being scary, the Vikings were nevertheless people the lords could do business with. Some towns under Viking rule, such as Lincoln and Stamford, were positively booming, and a low-tax Viking state might be a pleasanter place for a rich man to live than a high-tax Anglo-Saxon one.

Alfred's genius lay in seeing that these issues of mobility, prosperity, security and sovereignty were ultimately about identity. His subjects had to *want* to pull together. He also saw a way to make that happen: he would rebrand himself as a uniquely Christian king. 'Before everything was ransacked and burned', he wrote, 'there was a great multitude of those serving God'; but now, 'what punishments befell us when we ourselves did not cherish learning nor transmit it to other men! We were Christians in name only, and very few of us possessed Christian virtues.'

Alfred called for an intellectual revolution. Instead of just educating a few more monks, he wanted to make every man in Wessex a new kind of Christian. All must learn to read, to experience the Word directly; all key Christian texts must be translated into Old English for

Figure 4.7. Cometh the hour, cometh the man: the 'Alfred Jewel', a late ninth-century gold, enamel and rock crystal ornament found barely 5 km from Athelney and inscribed 'Alfred had me made'.

them; and Alfred himself must spearhead the effort. On fire, Alfred made the Viking war a holy war, recruiting top European scholars (including Asser) to teach him enough Latin to put the classics into his own words.

Alfred was centuries ahead of his time. No other ruler would even imagine mass literacy for nearly another millennium. He failed, but what mattered was that his subjects rallied behind him. The *Anglo-Saxon Chronicle* says that by 886, when Alfred retook London, 'all the English people submitted to him, except those who were in captivity to the Danes'. Fifteen years after supposedly burning the loaves, Alfred had not just saved Wessex; he had begun turning it into England. People who formerly felt Kentish, Mercian or Northumbrian increasingly called themselves Angelcynn, the 'English kind', hailing from Englalonde. At least for official purposes, Wessex's version of Old English began replacing earlier centuries' smorgasbord of dialects.

When the Norse again tested Alfred's England, in the 890s, his burhs worked. He used them the way Rome had used its Saxon Shore forts seven centuries earlier, slowing raiders down while ships brought up reserves to trap and destroy them. Typically, Alfred threw himself into the job, personally designing new warships which were twice as big as Viking vessels and carried more marines. A description survives of one battle they fought in 896 in shallow coastal waters, in which they captured every Viking ship but one. After that, Vikings stopped coming.

Norsemen still controlled northern England when Alfred died in 899, but he had turned the tables much more than contemporary kings in Scotland, Ireland or Wales. He had rediscovered the magic formula of fortresses-plus-ships, found ways to pay for it and, above all, had bound his subjects to him in a shared sense of godly Englishness. With their southern and eastern coasts increasingly secure, his successors turned north and west, pushing burhs across the land, building a hundred ships and sending them to the northern tip of Scotland. By the time Alfred's grandson Athelstan recaptured York in 927, breaking the axis with Dublin which had made the Irish Sea a Viking lake, Wessex was not just turning into England: it was turning into Britain, promising/threatening to bring all of the Isles under one man's rule.

Horrified, Vikings from Dublin, Scots from Alba and Britons from the northern kingdom of Strathclyde set aside their differences in 937 to form a grand alliance, only for Athelstan to smash this too in a great battle at the so far unidentified site of Brunanburh. 'Never on this island before [was] such killing,' said a chronicler, 'no, not since from the east the Angles and Saxons, as we are told in ancient books full of wisdom, landed after sailing the broad seas [. . .] Five young kings lay on the battlefield, put to sleep by swords.' Athelstan only slightly exaggerated in stamping his coins *rex et rector totius Britanniae*, 'king and ruler of all Britain'. From Winchester to Dublin and Scone every petty monarch bent the knee.

The last of the Viking pirate kings – the magnificently named Eric Bloodaxe – was killed in 954, and most historians see the reign of Edgar 'the Peaceful' (959–75) as the Anglo-Saxons' high tide. There had been a remarkable turnaround. In the fifth century Britannia had been the most fragmented and impoverished part of the former Roman Empire; in the tenth the lands south of the River Tees were perhaps the biggest bloc in Western Europe obeying a uniform law code, spending the same coins, speaking more or less the same language and paying taxes to a single king. Edgar's subjects had not forgotten Mercia, Kent or Cornwall, but they now identified more with England.

Historians of modern Britain often treat Queen Victoria's Diamond Jubilee pageant in 1897 – 'brazen, plumed, arrogant, and self-righteous', says one – as a metaphor for her country's imperial hubris, but in their own way the celebrations that Edgar staged in 973 were even more outrageous. From the beginning of his reign he had been keener than any earlier king to claim to rule *Dei gratia*, 'by God's grace', and illustrations of him on manuscripts increasingly likened him to Christ. In his twenty-ninth year – as chroniclers remarked, the same age at which Jesus began his ministry – Edgar cast off all half-measures, and had himself crowned at Bath in a ceremony that explicitly linked him with the Son of God. This was heady stuff, but he followed it up with an even grander piece of propaganda, summoning lesser kings from all over the Isles to Chester. After swearing to be his 'co-operators', six (or eight – sources disagree) selected monarchs each took an oar and rowed Edgar across the River Dee. It was probably no coincidence that Bath and Chester were two of the best-preserved Roman sites in England: there, among the ruins, Edgar sent an unambiguous message. He had restored Britannia's ancient faith and even ruled the waves. The king had returned.

Catching Up

The kingdom he came back to was, to be sure, weaker, poorer and less polished than fourth-century Britannia, but any way we look at it the gap had shrunk. After falling from about 4 million people in the year 350 to barely 1 million in 550, its population was back up to 2 million (and growing) by 950. In Roman times one Briton in every ten or twenty lived in a town of 1,000 or more people; in the sixth century hardly any did, but in the tenth the proportion was back up to 5 to 10 per cent. Similarly, London, which peaked at perhaps 30,000 residents under Rome but was almost empty when Augustine arrived in 597, had 20,000 in Edgar's day.

Household wealth rose more slowly. After shrinking from an average size of around 150–200 m² in the fourth century to barely 30 m² in the fifth, houses grew again, but even in the tenth century they averaged only 50–60 m^2. Plenty of fourth-century farms had had paved floors, plastered walls and roof tiles, plus occupants who broke and threw away huge amounts of pottery. Fifth-century Saxons, by contrast, were so miserably poor that it can sometimes be difficult to identify their homes at all, and tenth-century Angelcynn, while they were better off than that, remained poorer than Romans. Hardly anyone built in stone. The English had crude (and hard for archaeologists to date) pottery and few coins, styluses or other signs of involvement with a wider economy. The one possible exception to this generalisation is the site of Flixborough in Lincolnshire, where excavators recovered 15,000 artefacts, including glass windowpanes, iron tools and twenty-seven styluses. Some archaeologists think that Flixborough shows that poor preservation, not actual poverty, explains the dearth of finds on other sites, but most suspect that Flixborough was actually an unattested monastic or royal site, not a peasant village at all.

The Anglo-Saxon economic boom, like the bigger Roman one, coincided with an episode of global warming. More sunshine again meant longer growing seasons and probably higher yields, as well as allowing crops to be grown further north and higher on hillsides; but in both the Roman and the Medieval Warm Periods people had to figure out how to take advantage of nature's bounty. Both times this turned out to be by pouring capital and labour into the land. Anglo-Saxons, like Romans, cleared forests, weeded and manured fields, built roads, bought animals and then reorganised society to exploit new opportunities.

On the face of it, the cold, wet north and west seem like the places that would benefit most from warmer weather, and we do see evidence of economic expansion in both. Mawgan Porth, for instance, a clifftop hamlet in Cornwall, was sufficiently connected to larger markets for its excavators to find a silver penny and a fine non-local jug, while monastic workshops at Portmahomack, deep in Pictish north-east Scotland, were producing quantities of metal, glass, wood and leather, and perhaps vellum.

It was the south-east, though, that did best. Up to a point, the explanation lies in its richer soils, denser populations and greater resources, but English kings' success at shutting out the Vikings mattered too. Risk is the enemy of investment, and the best bet for a family that expects Vikings to rob it is to sell its surpluses, buy silver and gold and bury them in the garden until needed. This is why metal-detectorists find so many hoards dating from the troubled half-millennium between 350 and 850 (it is Saxon gold that obsesses the heroes of the wonderful BBC comedy *Detectorists*), and why excavators find so few signs of farmers sinking their savings into agricultural improvements. But when rulers are able to control mobility, provide security and strengthen sovereignty – as the Romans had done, and as the Anglo-Saxons now did – investing for the long term is a better bet; and that is precisely what thousands of English farmers began doing after the 870s.

Sometimes, as at Yarnton in Oxfordshire, we can trace what happened in detail. Environmental archaeologists working here found that dung beetles, which feed off cow and horse manure, largely disappeared from the fields around Yarnton in the late ninth century, being replaced by bugs of kinds that flourish in meadows. A minor detail, except that it means that someone had spent thousands of hours digging drainage ditches to turn the village's muddy pastures into hay meadows. This had a downside for Yarntonians, because it meant that if they left their animals to graze freely between February and June, the beasts would trample the valuable hay growing in the new meadows; but the upside was that the meadows now produced enough fodder for Yarntonians who could afford to buy it to feed their cows and horses in stalls over the winter.

Conveniently for owners, stalled livestock relieve themselves where they stand, making it easy to transfer the fertiliser to their fields. By 900 Yarnton's fields had been colonised by kinds of weeds that do well in soils disturbed by heavy ploughing, while weeds that like to be left alone more or less disappeared. At the same time, evidence appears for strains of wheat and barley that flourish in heavy clay soils. The excavators conclude from all this that farming expanded from the light, dry soils of the hillsides, which had been favoured all over England since the fifth century, into the tougher clays of the valley bottoms, which had barely been touched since the Romans left. These soils needed more manure, heavier ploughs (of the kind Roman farmers had used but which had disappeared since 400) and more oxen to pull them. Fortunately, stalling animals provided the manure while meadows provided the hay to feed more oxen. All that a wealthy farmer had to add to capitalise on climate change was a lot more labour.

Population growth provided part of this labour, but pushing

workers harder provided even more. 'Oh, I work very hard', the learned abbot Aelfric imagined a ploughman telling his master in one poem:

> I go out at daybreak driving the oxen to the field, and yoke them to the plough. For fear of my lord, there is no winter so severe that I dare hide at home; but the oxen having been yoked, and the share and coulter fastened to the plough, I must plough a full acre or more every day [. . . and] I do more than that, certainly. I have to fill the oxen's bins with hay, and water them and carry their muck outside.

'Oh, oh!' cries his lord. 'It's hard work.'

But the lord made him do it anyway, and, to ensure that such ploughmen did as they were told, lords all over England remade the countryside. The huge, rather inefficient collective farms into which Saxons had divided much of Britannia after the conquest had been declining since about 650, as lords squeezed more from their land to sell in the new market towns. After 850, though, these rambling estates disappeared completely. Seeing the gains to be made from increased investment and closely supervised labour, landowners broke their broad acres into dozens of smaller farms of 50–100 hectares. These they leased, sold or even gave to smaller fry known as thegns.

Lords did not do this out of charity. It was easier to supervise improvements and workers on small estates than on huge ones, which often made it worthwhile for a thegn to pay more for land than a lord could make by working it himself. Smart lords were therefore happy to part with property. Even giving it away might be profitable, if the gift had enough strings attached. A thegn would typically rent out most of his property to tenants but hang on to some, the demesne, to work personally. Some used slaves for this, although with a healthy man priced around £1 (roughly the price of eight oxen, perhaps one-fifth of the typical thegn's annual income), not including accommodation, food and supervision, chattels were not cheap. In the tenth century most thegns found it cost-effective to free their slaves in exchange for labour dues, and then work their demesnes by hiring hands only when they needed them.

Between about 850 and 900, in some parts of England, groups of ten to fifty families began clustering in villages. Nowadays we tend to think of villages as being timelessly English, like Baldwin's plough teams eternally coming over the brow of a hill; but before the ninth or even the tenth century few English lived in villages (by which I mean settlements of a hundred or so people). Scattered farmsteads had always been more common, complemented in Roman times by small towns of a couple of thousand souls and a few cities up to ten times bigger. But in the ninth and tenth centuries villages began to appeal because living together simplified some of the tasks that now needed to be done. Pulling a plough through clay soil is hard, calling for as many as eight oxen, but few peasants could afford even one. The answer, of course, was to share, with multiple families each paying for part of an animal and taking turns using them all; and sharing was so much easier for neighbours living on the same street than for homesteaders scattered across hundreds of hectares. Living cheek by jowl also allowed villagers to avoid the costs of stalling oxen in winter, because they could agree to leave a block of fields fallow each year so their animals could graze on its stubble. Everyone gained – the poor got free fodder, while those who could afford to stall their beasts could add their share of the manure dropped by the cattle on the common land to their carefully harvested supply of private fertiliser.

Bringing people together solved a lot of the problems of country life. It made it easier for communities to police woodcutting, thereby preserving a mix of big, old trees for lumber and little, new ones for fuel. It also made it economical to build one big, modern water-mill to exploit a stream rather than lots of cheap but inefficient little ones. Again, everyone gained: a payment to the mill-owner allowed a poor family to buy back weeks of wifely labour, while the mill-owner earned a guaranteed income from villagers who needed his services.

So far as we can tell, peasants organised much of this themselves, bottom up. The more productive an estate was, though, the more rent its thegn could potentially charge his tenants, so thegns also got involved, supervising the animals allowed on fallow fields, patrolling the woods and raising capital to build mills. Anxious to oversee everything at once, they moved their own families into the new villages alongside their cottagers, tenants and slaves. Soon no settlement was complete without its manor house, often next to the church (Figure 4.8). Thegns whose estates flourished spent heavily on fancy façades and stylish gatehouses.

Figure 4.8. Tradition: the twelfth-century village of Wharram Percy
in Yorkshire, as imagined by archaeological artist Peter Dunn.
At the top right, just behind the church, is the manor house.

Thegns raised the cash to pay for such fripperies by selling agricultural produce at the nearest burh, which, following Alfred's design, normally contained a royal mint. To attract trade (which could, of course, be taxed), most burhs had their broad main streets double as market places, crowded with craftsmen. At Thetford, a little burh in Norfolk, archaeologists found a metre-thick layer of iron slag in the backstreet where blacksmiths dumped waste from their forges at the end of the day.

As well as its villages and burhs England also had a handful of well-placed cities (mostly on the same sites as Roman ones) linking regional economies and connecting them to traders from the Continent. Best placed of all was London, and as security improved, its geographical advantages reasserted themselves. In 889 Alfred began moving people back inside the old Roman walls which can still be seen in today's City of London. He opened a mint, and a charter from the same year mentions a new market inside a stone building (perhaps the old Roman bathhouse). Tree rings show that in 890

Londoners began pushing new piers into the Thames at Queenhithe, which was probably less crowded with rotting docks than the earlier Anglo-Saxon city around the Strand. Around 1000 they replaced the collapsed Roman bridge across the river and opened docks big enough to fit Continental ships – although, revealingly, their carpentry remained crude by Roman standards, and woodworkers had to use small planks from young trees or timbers recycled from ancient shipwrecks, not the mighty two- or three-century-old oaks Romans had exploited.

The principal way in which the Anglo-Saxon economy differed from the Roman, especially in London, was that under the empire the financial, commercial and political elites had overwhelmingly been immigrants, while under Edgar they were native-born. When England had joined Rome's European Union in the seventh century, its religious specialists had also been Continental immigrants; but by the tenth century they too had been Anglicised. England's home-grown great men, though, carried on acting as if they were Continental, because sophistication was still something imported from Europe.

Wine, the favourite tipple in Romano-British cities, made such a comeback that Edgar's heirs gave special privileges to Frankish merchants who could guarantee its supply. Edgar himself scandalised conservatives by aping the long silk robes that Germans wore, but within a century England's richest men were all doing the same. The silk kings wore was literally priceless: the only worms that could produce it belonged to the Byzantine emperor in distant Constantinople, and imperial silk was never sold on the market. The only way to acquire it was as a gift from German kings, who had received it from popes, who had in turn had it as a present from the emperor himself. Fortunately for English fashionistas, however, second-tier Byzantine silk weavers expanded production in the tenth century, and by Edgar's day anyone (anyone prosperous enough to get to Rome, that is) could buy bolts of almost royal quality. Silk regularly turns up on digs in London and Lincoln, and in York it made up fully 25 per cent of the stock in one tailor's shop. From the great cities silk scarves made their way to Dublin and ribbons to Winchester. Soon every thegn on the make was demanding the stuff. Illustrations in manuscripts show men in short tunics with flared skirts, edged at the collars, cuffs and hems with bands of coloured cloth which was probably silk.

To be sure, thegnly families mostly wore wool, but wool was

what largely paid for the imported silk. Mercian wool was already being exported from London in the seventh century, and by the tenth this was a major trade. Thegns could squeeze cash out of otherwise unproductive land by putting sheep on it and selling the fleeces to urban merchants, who then exported the wool to cloth manufacturers in Flanders. We have no figures before the thirteenth century, but by then England boasted 10 million sheep, outnumbering humans by more than two to one. England in Edgar's day was already finding a profitable niche supplying raw materials for Continental industries.

Some tenth-century townsfolk had caught up completely with their Roman predecessors, wearing copper and lead jewellery and leather shoes, using shop-bought pots and paying for them with coins. They had houses with glass windows, and the richest lived as elegantly as Continental elites. In the eighteenth century an Italian ambassador would unkindly remark that 'in England there are sixty different religious sects, but only one sauce', but in Edgar's time English sauces impressed even French epicures. English architecture was equally imposing. More than one-third of the space in Winchester, Alfred the Great's old capital, was occupied by palaces, monasteries and cathedrals. One church boasted an organ with 400 pipes, requiring two men to play its keyboards plus seventy more to pump air through its pipes. Norwich had forty-nine churches, and in every town in the land literate clerics struggled to save souls from the corrupting luxuries offered by equally literate merchants.

In every way we can count – population, prosperity, urbanisation, monetisation – tenth-century Englalonde was catching up with where Britannia had been six centuries earlier, even if in many of the ways that can't be counted – identity, sovereignty, culture – it looked entirely different. Instead of being subject to a distant imperial capital, it was now a proud partner in a European Union of souls (albeit one run from the same distant capital). Thatcher's Law still held, of course, and the Isles remained very much part of Europe. When the counterscarp provided by ancient Rome's legions and walls fell, the Isles had been exposed to every wave of immigrants washing in from the Continent, but the Catholic union had eventually tamed the wilder spirits of Germany and Scandinavia. Wealth and sophistication carried on rolling downhill from the commanding heights around the Mediterranean towards the Atlantic peripheries, but by the tenth century this slope seemed shallower than ever before, while that between England and the Celtic periphery was getting steeper. England might still be Europe's poor cousin, but not to the degree it had once been. Thanks to this evening out and the power vacuum left by the Frankish Empire's breakdown, tenth-century English kings could realistically talk about turning themselves into British ones. It had taken half a millennium, but the Isles were finding a new role on the European stage.

5

UNITED KINGDOMS, 973–1497

The United Kingdom of the North Sea

Edgar's new vision, of a United Kingdom of Great Britain and Ireland centred on the Irish Sea, barely outlived him. In its place, rulers would unite kingdoms of very different shapes across the next half-millennium. Each linked England to a different body of water: the North Sea, the English Channel and the eastern Atlantic. Some lasted a generation or two, others a century or two, but none permanently solved two fundamental problems – how to deal with what came their way from the Continent, and how to manage England's Celtic neighbours. It would take five or six centuries to find a solution, and seven to realise it, in the form of a United Kingdom that could close the English Channel while opening the Atlantic and mastering the north and west. But in 973 all that was beyond anyone's reckoning.

What undid Edgar's vision was God, who worked His mysterious way through the calendar. Some readers might remember the 'y2k' panic of 1999. At midnight on 31 December, fearmongers fretted, the entire global economy would implode, because the millions of computers that used only two digits to represent the year on their clocks would crash when the end of the second millennium caused them to reset to a row of zeros. A few easy fixes deflected that bullet, but the y1k crisis which unfolded in the year 999 could not be solved so simply. When better for Jesus to return, the faithful were asking, than on 31 December 999, the moment that the millennium arrived? This was exciting but also alarming, because how could He be anything but appalled when He saw that the church's upper ranks were packed with the dissolute, ill-educated younger sons of bloody-handed barons? So, what better fix to apply than to purge such sinners from the priesthood? And who better to do it than Christendom's purest, most learned scholars?

This was not a new problem. Cleaning up the church had been

Figure 5.1. The European stage, 973–1497.

a popular idea for centuries. After all, who wanted to trust his or her immortal soul to clerics who, even if well born, might be drunks, sexual predators or – as a later cleric grumbled – could not tell Judas Iscariot, Jesus' betrayer, from Jude the Apostle, Jesus' brother? Yet church reform was also complicated. Most of the keenest, cleverest reformers had studied on the Continent, particularly at Cluny in Burgundy (Figure 5.1). Allowing the pope to appoint such men as abbots or bishops in England would mean handing even more sovereignty over to Rome, and any king might baulk at that. Plenty of popes baulked at the idea too, given that they themselves were usually political appointees, their education and morals not above question. The last thing they wanted was to promote earnest academics who might embarrass them. So reform stalled – until y1k hit.

As the millennium neared and anxiety rose, kings looked for ways to spin reform to their advantage. One obvious plus was that its immediate costs would fall less on them than on the mightiest (and therefore most threatening) families in their kingdoms, whose younger sons would be the ones squeezed out of plum church positions. Kings, barons, bishops and pontiffs manoeuvred madly, trying to nudge reformism in directions that would simultaneously make them look holy, undermine their enemies and not cost too much. In England, Edgar jumped on the reform bandwagon in a big way, supporting learned Europeans against rivals nearer home. Most of his protégés got appointed, but the victims of his purge did not go quietly. 'Strife threw the kingdom into turmoil', one of the English reformers recorded. Reform 'moved shire against shire, family against family, prince against prince, ealdorman against ealdorman, drove bishop against the people and folk against the pastors set over them.'

By making church reform a weapon against his rivals at home, Edgar threw away Alfred the Great's most valuable legacy: England's sense of religious unity around a truly Christian king. That unity had been the key to driving the Vikings out in the 870s, and its breakdown in the 970s was the key that let them back in again. Lords who thought their king was stealing their lucrative church livings were understandably hesitant about risking their necks to save him, especially now that the Norse claimed to be Christians too.

The rot spread rapidly. In 991, just sixteen years after Edgar died, his son Aethelred 'the Unready' confidently sent his army to intercept a Viking host at Maldon (Figure 5.2), only for one of his lords to defect, betraying the royal host to slaughter.* Now unable to raise enough men even to defend Alfred's burhs, Aethelred fell back on the old tactic of bribing the Vikings to stay away, only to find – as the poet Kipling famously put it – that 'once you have paid him the Dane-geld / You never get rid of the Dane'. Like so many Viking warlords before him, Sweyn Forkbeard (another awe-inspiring name) first drained Englalonde's finances and then decided to swallow the country whole.

The fighting that followed was confused and confusing, in part because so many English turned their coats so often. The worst offender, Eadric the Grasper, cut private deals with Danes, murdered or blinded Anglo-Saxon rivals, defected with his army to the Vikings in 1015, defected back to Aethelred in time for the decisive battle in

---

*Aethelred's nickname *Unraed* actually meant 'Ill-Advised', but the modern mistranslation 'Unready' fits him even better.

Figure 5.2. The British stage, 973–1497.

1016 and then defected a third time in the middle of the fight. Victory, and ultimately Aethelred's throne, went to Sweyn's son Cnut – who, probably wisely, promptly murdered Eadric.*

---

*Cnut used to be spelled Canute. Rather than being a copying error, as in the use of Boadicea / Boudica, Canute was the French spelling of Cnut, which became popular in England after the Norman Conquest.

Cnut is mostly remembered as a man unwilling to bend to reality, thanks to a story that he once ordered the tide to stop coming in. When it ignored him, he jumped up, shouting 'Let all men know how empty and worthless is the power of kings! There is none worthy of the name but He whom heaven, earth and sea obey.' Hanging his crown on a crucifix, he refused to wear it again. However, when this story was originally told (about a century after Cnut's death), its point was that he deliberately got his feet wet to show his foolish courtiers how even kings must bow to the implacable force of God and his oceans. Cnut was in fact a man of vision as well as violence, and understood well what geography meant. The sea ruled the land. Edgar's idea of a United Kingdom of Great Britain and Ireland could only work if it was secure against external threats, above all those from Scandinavia; and the only way to attain that end was by uniting a kingdom around the North Sea, giving England a Scandinavian counterscarp (Figure 5.3). Denmark was the place 'from where the most harm came to you', Cnut told England's lords, but 'from now on, no hostility shall ever come to you from there, as long as [both] are justly ruled by me'. True to his word, he destroyed a Danish pirate fleet bound for England in 1018.

Cnut really earned his nickname 'the Great'. His crackdown on Viking raids did wonders for English security and prosperity, not least by ending the Danegeld, and, after initially purging Anglo-Saxon powerbrokers and enriching his Scandinavian followers, he worked to solidify identity by marrying Aethelred's widow and confirming English lords in their church positions. Nor, as a usurper in need of legitimacy, did he forget Rome. His personal piety was rather relaxed (he long maintained two wives), but he judiciously added to the church's wealth and showed respect by making the long trip to Rome to kiss the ring in 1027. The downside of all this, though, was that it kept Cnut crisscrossing the North Sea throughout his reign. One moment he was bullying Danish warlords to stop raiding, the next he was bribing unreliable allies such as the Anglo-Norse Godwineson family to keep the peace in England. Run ragged, he dropped dead at about forty, perhaps from a stroke.

Some historians see Cnut's kingdom as a brilliant solution to the North Sea's strategic problems, which, with just a bit more luck, might have lasted centuries. Others suspect that it was always doomed, because no successor could have kept up Cnut's frenetic

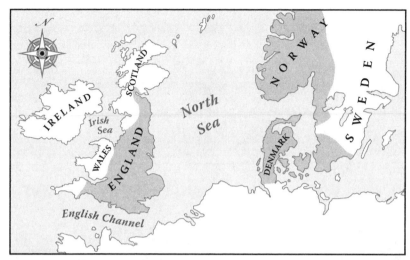

Figure 5.3. The United Kingdom of the North Sea as it looked around 1030.

pace. Others still consider it a solution to a problem that was actually solving itself. Cnut worked hard to reduce Viking raids on England, but Ireland, Wales and Scotland also suffered fewer raids after 1000 than before, despite being outside Cnut's United Kingdom. The fact was, Scandinavian population growth was slowing and Norse pirate kings increasingly wanted to become respectable Christians. Even without Cnut's counterscarp, mobility across the North Sea was declining from existential threat to background noise.

The United Kingdom of the North Sea limped on until Cnut's last son died in 1042, whereupon his supposed friends the Godwine-sons crowned Aethelred the Unready's last surviving son, Edward, after saddling him with a wife from their own clan. Edward, however, stubbornly refused to produce a son – nicknamed 'the Confessor', he was reputedly too godly to consummate his marriage – and when he died, in 1066, five men claimed the crown. Since their claims ranged from the weak to the laughable, all hell broke loose. Possession being nine-tenths of the law, Harold Godwineson, who conveniently happened to be at the Confessor's bedside when he died, got in first, despite having no royal blood at all (his claim was based on being married to Edward's sister). Immediately, Norway's King Harald, a former Viking mercenary nicknamed 'Ruthless', invaded Yorkshire

Figure 5.4. Regions on the British stage, 973–1497.

(Figure 5.4), basing his claim on a private arrangement with Cnut's youngest son. It is hard to say which of these thugs was worse, but Harold made the question moot by killing Harald in battle.

Three days later, Duke William of Normandy landed at Hastings.

The United Kingdom of the English Channel

In one way William was just another Viking adventurer come to steal England's throne. I mentioned in Chapter 4 that the Frankish king Charles the Simple had bribed the Norsemen to stop raiding his kingdom in 911 by giving them lands along the English Channel. Over the next hundred years, so many Norsemen settled there that people started calling their new home Normandy; and well before 1066 they had assimilated so thoroughly that observers often used 'French' and 'Norman' interchangeably. In that way Duke William was a thorough Franco-Norse hybrid, and his vision of a United Kingdom rested on a very different geographical vision from Cnut's.

His claim to England's throne, though not strong, was no weaker than anyone else's. His aunt had successively married both Aethelred and Cnut. According to the duke's spin doctors, Edward the Confessor had also chosen William as his heir, and Harold Godwineson, in a vulnerable moment, had actually agreed. Best of all, the pope supported William's claim. Papal approval worked something like a United Nations resolution today, valuable but not decisive unless enforced by arms; but once William defeated and killed Harold at Hastings, it clinched the deal.

Like Cnut, William saw the sea as the centre of everything, but he was thinking about the English Channel, not the North Sea (Figure 5.5). He also went about uniting his kingdom in an entirely different way. In a classic line in his play *Indian Ink*, Tom Stoppard imagines an ageing, archconservative Englishwoman telling a young Indian 'We [British] were your Romans, you know. We might have been your Normans.' We will return in later chapters to the accuracy of this claim, but her point – not lost on the Indian ('Did you expect us to be grateful?' he shoots back) – is that the Normans were horrible masters.

The closest analogy for what William did to England might be what the Nazis planned to do in 1940. While the Battle of Britain was still raging overhead, the SS prepared a pamphlet – usually called *The Black Book* – of instructions for occupying the Isles. Every British male aged between seventeen and forty-five would be conscripted for forced labour on the Continent and nearly 3,000 prominent figures taken into custody, mostly by the Gestapo. 'My dear – the people one should have been seen dead with!' the novelist Rebecca West quipped to Noël Coward when the list was published in 1945, but it was no

Figure 5.5. The United Kingdom of the English
Channel (and its enemies) around 1100.

laughing matter. The man in charge, Franz Six, went on to make his
name murdering Jews in Russia.

Far from exterminating England's Jews, William actually brought
the first Jews into the country, but in other ways his kingdom was just
as vicious as the Third Reich. He cut down the entire Anglo-Saxon
elite and enslaved everyone else. Within twenty years only four of the
country's big landowners were English. The ninety or so next-richest
Anglo-Saxons had been expropriated or murdered, and so too most
of the 15,000–20,000 thegns. When the English realised what was happening and rose up in revolt, Norman armies devastated Yorkshire.
Hundreds of thousands starved in this 'Harrying of the North', and
as far away as Worcestershire roads were lined with refugees' emaci-
ated corpses. Even one of William's staunchest supporters lamented

the 'helpless children, young men in the prime of life and hoary grey-beards perishing alike from hunger [. . .] such brutal slaughter cannot remain unpunished'.

William confiscated all the land in England, giving nearly half to an immigrant elite of 8,000 knights and keeping one-sixth for himself. In return, his knights promised to fight in his wars, each knight bringing a retinue of lesser men to whom he had given some of the land he had received, each lesser man bringing along even smaller fry and so on – although not all the way down to the bottom of the pile, where the English were. Norman rule was apartheid: by definition, all English were unfree, their lives worth less than those of Normans. Any time a suspicious death was noted, the nearest village had to pay a fine – unless they could prove the victim was merely English, in which case nothing happened. French was the language of the free, English the tongue of servility. William of Malmesbury (a Norman) put it plainly: 'England has become the residence of foreigners and the property of strangers.'

Resistance was futile, thanks to new military technology imported by William. Anglo-Saxons had been fighting Vikings since Alfred's day, and were very good at it, but they had ignored two innovations spreading up from the south-east: heavily armoured cavalry (William's knights were worth their weight in gold at Hastings) and castles. The burhs, which had turned the tide for Alfred, had been walled towns, but eleventh-century castles – 'private fortified residences', one specialist calls them – were different. With a central keep small enough to be defended by just a few dozen men, a well-built stone castle on a hill gave even minor lords an almost impregnable base from which to project power (Figure 5.6). Castle-building had begun in earnest in Italy around 950, but Edgar and other Anglo-Saxon kings had refused to let lords of doubtful loyalty build them. Eventually, Norman kings would wish they had done the same, but in 1066 William needed to let his carpetbaggers do whatever it took to control their new estates. Within a generation they had built 500 castles, typically just 15 km apart. Rebels had nowhere to run to, nowhere to hide. In fact, we hear of no more rebels after 1071, when the last freedom fighter – Hereward the Wake, who waged a guerilla war with Danish support in the boggy East Anglian Fens – disappeared from the historical record.

William launched an all-out assault on English identity, but the tiny numbers of his Norman followers limited what he could do. In

Figure 5.6. Forward Operating Base: Bamburgh Castle in Northumberland, built around 1080. Riding out from its squat central keep, Norman knights dominated the surrounding countryside (used with the kind permission of the Tyne & Wear Archives & Museums).

the church, one of the main battlegrounds, he could replace almost every bishop and abbot with immigrants, but lower down the hierarchy little changed. Monks and parish priests continued copying Old English literature and honouring English saints, and as late as 1154 we hear of villagers in Somerset fighting off a French abbot who tried to take the body of the miracle-working hermit St Wulfric (a good English name) to his monastery at Montacute (an equally good French name).

Up to a point, William could live with this resistance, so long as his new religious leadership found ways to work with Rome. Reformists now dominated the church, and popes were undermining kings' sovereignty aggressively. In 1075 Pope Gregory VII shocked everyone by announcing that, rather than negotiating with Germany's emperor Henry IV about appointing bishops in his territories, he would simply pick them himself. Panicking about so much church land passing into potentially unfriendly hands, Henry responded that if the pope could appoint his bishops, he, in his role of Defender of the Faith, could appoint the pope – 'not now pope', he called Gregory, 'but false monk [. . .] I, Henry, by the grace of God, together with all our bishops, say to you: Descend! Descend!' But Gregory did not descend. Instead, he took the nuclear option, excommunicating Henry, thereby releasing all Germans from any religious obligation to obey him. This was soft power at its hardest. Henry's barons abandoned him, and within a year the king was reduced to kneeling barefoot in the snow outside an Alpine monastery for three days, begging the pope's forgiveness.

Henry's path was not one William wanted to take, so he trod carefully, conceding enough popery to keep Rome quiet but not enough to compromise control of his kingdom. Noting that no Anglo-Saxon king had ever convened a proper reforming synod, William's Italian (but very loyal) archbishop of Canterbury, Lanfranc, called five of them. Lanfranc even invited papal legates to chair the first two. William gave reformers what they wanted, banning clerical marriage, founding thirty-four reformist monasteries and handing great chunks of England to monasteries based in Normandy. He appointed hardcore reformers from leading Continental schools, so long as they stayed on message – and the message was that God had sent the Normans, like the Saxons and Vikings before them, to punish England's sins.

There were some tense moments, but, by and large, William managed the Italian threat to his sovereignty adroitly, and he was lucky with other foreign threats. Not until the 1130s, when King Louis VI finally brought his unruly vassals under control, would a great power rise from the ashes of the old Frankish Empire, but Cnut's insight that England was indefensible without a Scandinavian counterscarp still applied. William was reduced to paying Danegeld when a Viking fleet entered the Thames in 1070, and by 1085 it looked as though not even that would save him. Cnut IV (Cnut the Great's grandnephew), whose claim to England's throne was at least as good as William's, mobilised the biggest Viking fleet ever seen. Disaster was averted only when Cnut's own men murdered him, whereupon the Danes fell to fighting each other rather than trying to recreate a United Kingdom of the North Sea.

Eager to avoid having to fight on every front at once, William largely left the Celtic world alone, even though, by bringing Continental organisation to the south-east, he had sharply increased imbalances of wealth and power with the north and west. Norman England had towns, coins, castles, cavalry and a reformed church; the Celtic fringe did not. As Normans saw it, the Welsh were just 'barbarous people [of] untamed savagery', the Scots 'worthless [. . .] with half-bare buttocks' and the Irish 'so barbarous, they cannot be said to have any culture at all'. Like Rome a millennium earlier, William could have conquered the Celts had he wanted to; but because – again like Rome's emperors – he saw few profits in expansion and had more pressing concerns elsewhere he left them alone.

But his barons didn't. Nine centuries after the Norman Conquest, when friends asked the American president, Lyndon B. Johnson, why he never fired his interfering FBI Director J. Edgar Hoover, he said, 'It's probably better to have him inside the tent pissing out, than outside pissing in'. William felt the same about his barons. Better to have them facing outwards, waging private wars against Celts, than looking inwards, waging private wars on each other (or, God forbid, on him). So, when border barons built castles on Welsh mountains, William did nothing, and when they killed the Welsh warlord Rhys ap Tewdwr and seized most of Wales in 1093, William's son Rufus did nothing either.

There is a little-known coda to LBJ's law of micturition, formalised by an (unnamed) Conservative minister in 2016. 'It doesn't matter where the pissers stand', he confided to the journalist Tim Shipman. 'The piss always gets into the tent eventually.' 'Twas ever thus, and in 1095 Rufus found himself awash in it after all. Welshmen still called themselves *Brytanyeit*, Britons ('Welsh' was an English term, from the Latin *Vallenses*, 'Borderers') and for six centuries had been waiting for King Arthur to return and reclaim his lands. Now, aroused by Norman aggression, multiple factions convinced themselves that one or another of their many leaders really was Arthur come again. 'Fiercely they threaten us', the Norman poet Gaimar lamented,

> [Saying] that in the end they will have it all;
> By means of Arthur they will win it back;
> And this land all together [. . .]
> They will call it Britain again.

Rufus, suddenly alarmed, resolved (said a Welsh writer) 'to destroy the inhabitants so completely as not to leave even a dog to piss against a wall'. But he didn't, because the Welsh just melted away into the hills, ambushing Norman columns as they raced to keep up. Powerless against these guerillas, Rufus built a few castles to keep out what urine he could, waged a war of words against Welshmen's Arthurian boasts and turned back to things he cared more about.

The ensuing Welsh–Norman verbal jousting over Arthur is probably why we now have so many stories about the once and future king. The subtlest propagandist was our old friend Geoffrey of Monmouth, who codified and/or invented many Arthurian legends in the 1130s. Geoffrey walked a fine line, identifying with a Welsh town yet devoting his career to Norman service. His studied ambiguity over Arthur's identity perhaps explains his book's success.

Geoffrey was hardly the only propagandist at work. In 1191 monks at Glastonbury Abbey – near, but not in, Wales – announced that they had found Arthur's and Guinevere's bodies. Arthur's, they said, was immensely tall, with at least nine healed wounds, plus a tenth, over his right eye, not healed. Gerald of Wales, another cleric who called himself Welsh but spoke French and worked for Norman kings, claimed that Guinevere's blond hair, still 'plaited and coiled with consummate skill', was perfectly preserved when her tomb was opened, but when 'a silly, rash and impudent' monk jumped into the grave and grabbed it ('female hair', Gerald helpfully pointed out, 'is a snare for the feeble-minded'), it crumbled to dust. Who knows what the monks actually dug up; but whatever it was, the Normans made clever use of it. 'In their stupidity', Gerald continued, 'the Britons [Welsh] maintain that he is still alive. Now that the truth is known [. . .] the fairy-tales have been snuffed out.' The propaganda war tilted the Normans' way: Arthur's steadily expanding story was appropriated for England.

Managing the northern frontier proved harder. Before 1066 identities in what we now call Scotland were even more fragmented than in Wales. There were Scots in the Highlands and Norse in the north and islands, while some in the south-west still self-identified as Britons and some in the north-east as Picts. Northern politics, says historian Alex Woolf, was largely 'a catalogue of men with strange names killing each other'. Even when the names are not strange, as in the case of Macbeth (more properly, Mac-Bethad mac Findlaích), the killing went on anyway. Macbeth won the Scottish throne in 1032 by killing his predecessor on the battlefield, only to be killed in turn by his own successor. In between, he married Lady Macbeth after burning alive her first husband, who had murdered Macbeth's father. Well might Shakespeare have Lady Macbeth ask, 'will these hands ne'er be clean?'

Normans handled their unstable northern frontier much like the Welsh one, fighting when necessary but otherwise ignoring it – until, in the 1120s, the Scots' King David pre-empted them. Rather than waiting for Norman barons to push in and steal his land, he decided to invite them in himself and just give it to them. In return, they would build him castles, create a French-language courtly culture and kill other Normans who muscled in without invitations. It was a cunning move, largely evening out the military imbalance with England and making Scotland a much tougher adversary than Wales.

Ireland, furthest away, was the easiest place for Norman kings to ignore, which they did for a full century, but eventually baronial pissing embroiled them there too. When two Irish chiefs fell out over the high kingship in 1169, the loser found friends among the Normans looting Wales. The Norman Earl of Pembroke, 'Strongbow', joined him the next year, and within a month took Waterford and Dublin. The year after that, Strongbow married into Irish royalty. Back in London, the Norman king Henry II realised that Strongbow was no longer inside an English tent pissing out: he was about to set up his own tent, as king of Ireland.

That just couldn't be allowed to happen. No subject could carve out his own little empire and proclaim its independence. So, much as he wanted to avoid being sucked into a Celtic quagmire, Henry *had* to make Strongbow's realm part of his own. On a vastly larger scale than anything Strongbow himself could do, Henry killed and looted his way across Ireland, abolishing the high kingship, building castles, shipping in Norman settlers and calling a council to bring local Christianity into line with Rome. Then, having adjusted the tent pegs so Strongbow was back inside, he headed home to deal with bigger problems. Ireland was left looking rather like Wales, with some parts run from royal castles, others answering to virtually independent Norman barons and others still under native kings, while Henry just tried to stay out of their feuds.

The reason Norman kings would not invest time or energy in the north and west was that what really mattered to them was keeping the two sides of the Channel together. Like Cnut, William was constantly going back and forth across the water at the heart of his kingdom. Of the 170 months he reigned, he spent 130 in Normandy. His sons were his main concern. The rule of thumb for medieval monarchs was to have an heir and a spare, because having either too few or too many sons guaranteed civil war, but even when they got this right, Norman monarchs still had trouble. William the Conqueror had had two heirs, but to prevent them killing each other he bequeathed the lands he himself had inherited (Normandy) to Robert, his eldest, while Rufus, the next son, received those he had conquered (England). When William died in 1087, the United Kingdom of the English Channel therefore split, and Rufus only reunited it by fighting. When Rufus died in 1100 it split again, and Henry I again reunited it violently. But when Henry died in 1135, things really went wrong.

Henry had had an heir and spare, but the heir drowned in 1120 and the spare, Matilda, was female. England had never had a queen, and most barons thought the crown should pass over Matilda's head to her two-year-old son. Another faction, though, launched a coup to install her cousin Stephen as king. Events then moved quickly. After promising to back Stephen, the pope got cold feet. Matilda prepared for war. Stephen's supporters started defecting to her, which left him too poor to buy their loyalty back. Wales rebelled, Scots plundered the north and government imploded. Within a few years every baron had his own tent. 'Each great man built himself castles and held them against the king, and they filled the whole land with these castles', said the *Anglo-Saxon Chronicle*. 'They filled them up with devils [. . .] and men said openly that Christ and His saints slept.' Sovereignty disintegrated. Suddenly, horrifyingly, the United Kingdom of the English Channel dissolved into Anarchy in the UK.

In some counties one-third of the land was too devastated to be taxable in 1150; in Leicestershire it was over half. 'You could easily go a whole day's journey and never find anyone occupying a village', the *Anglo-Saxon Chronicle* complained. Chroniclers probably exaggerated, but by Stephen's death in 1154 royal income had fallen by two-thirds, Wales was gone and Scotland controlled the north. Barons and bishops ignored the king whenever it suited them, and, worst of all, Normandy was largely lost. William the Conqueror's strategy of uniting a kingdom around the English Channel had failed as fully as Cnut's of uniting it around the North Sea.

The United Kingdom of the Atlantic Coast

In its place, Matilda's son Henry inherited (literally) a much more ambitious strategy. Almost everyone had ignored the infant Henry when the throne had fallen vacant in 1135, but, by managing not to be murdered in the next nineteen years, he became (via his mother) Duke of Normandy and King Henry II of England, and (via his father) owner of Anjou, Maine and Nantes. By marrying Duchess Eleanor, he also acquired Aquitaine. Without killing anyone, young Henry had traded the broken United Kingdom of the English Channel for a vastly bigger United Kingdom of the Atlantic Coast, running from the Pennines to the Pyrenees (Figure 5.7) – if he could enforce his claims.

There was the rub. Despite holding legal title, Henry's writ did not run far. Two decades of civil war had shattered England's coherence. Danes had begun raiding again in 1138, and would keep doing so until 1366. Some sort of Anglo-Norman identity was emerging within England, but Henry's new subjects on the Continent had no part of this. His possessions didn't even have a collective name until 1887, when the historian Kate Norgate started calling them the Angevin Empire, after Anjou. This was indeed the core of Henry's inheritance, and, as Norgate recognised, his empire was more Continental than English. Henry could understand English, but spoke only Latin and French. His enmities were European too. The marriage to Eleanor which had given him Aquitaine had only come about because King Louis VII of France, Eleanor's first husband, had obtained papal approval to set her aside for not delivering a son (her view: 'I have married a monk, not a king'). Louis thought that saddling Henry with a barren wife had been a diplomatic coup – until she produced six sons and three daughters. Hell hath no fury like a monarch mocked, and hurting Henry became Louis's life's goal.

It needed a man as energetic as Cnut or William to make these arrangements work, but Henry was up to the job. He threw himself into wearing down England's anarchists. One by one, he killed the worst and clawed back privileges from the rest, until even his barons eventually tired of anarchy. He then launched into reforming his varied lands' laws and stabilising their currencies. Within a decade royal revenues were creeping back up.

There was no way to do this without stepping on Roman toes, so in 1162 Henry decided to strengthen his negotiating position with

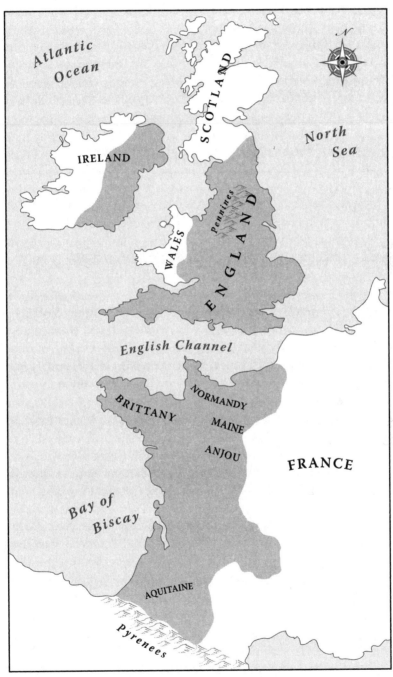

Figure 5.7. The United Kingdom of the Atlantic Coast in 1162.

the pontiff by engineering the election of a talented friend, Thomas Becket, as archbishop of Canterbury. Becket's brief was to deliver papal approval, however grudging, for consolidating the kingdom; but no sooner was Becket in the job than he searched his soul and found an arch-reformer within. Instead of acting like William the Conqueror's archbishop Lanfranc, Becket actively took Rome's side against Henry's power grabs. King and churchman each accused the other of bad faith, until Becket finally appealed over Henry's head to God Himself. The archbishop issued an Interdict, effectively cutting England off from Heaven. Church services were suspended; no bells could be rung; no one could get married, receive absolution (except on their deathbeds) or be buried in consecrated ground. Henry boiled over, raging to his barons 'Will no one rid me of this turbulent priest?' (or something along those lines) – whereupon four of them, assuming that tantrums at the top count as orders, hacked Becket to pieces before the altar in his own cathedral.

Becket's murder was an unmitigated disaster. The pope excommunicated Henry and sent legates to take over his kingdom. The hard edge of Roman soft power was revealed again. No ally now wanted to stand with Henry; even his wife, Eleanor, went back to her ex-husband, Louis of France. To hold on, Henry agreed to signal his submission to papal authority by kneeling before Becket's tomb and submitting to a mock whipping from Canterbury's monks – by which time Louis and Eleanor had overrun much of his Continental property.

Henry hung on, but when he died, in 1189, the United Kingdom of the Atlantic Coast ran into the same problem as every organisation that depends on a single leader's energy to keep it going: what to do when he's no longer around. Henry's elder son Richard ('the Lionheart') had energy aplenty but cared less about running his ramshackle kingdom than about winning glory and papal approval fighting Muslims in the Holy Land. Even so, an absentee monarch was better than his replacement, King John, who took over in 1199. Modern historians are often kinder to John than contemporaries were, but he was probably the worst king England ever had (no monarch has named a son John in the eight centuries since him). In an age when personal connections were everything, John was impulsive, lustful and sadistic (when a former friend evaded paying his taxes, John starved his wife and son to death). One after another, his allies defected. In 1204 Normandy went over to France, and when John gathered troops to counterattack, his advisers, one chronicler recorded, threatened to 'detain him violently, lest [. . .] seeking to recover the land that had been lost, he would lose what he still had'. John gave in, 'weeping and wailing'.

Nor did John learn from the past. Instead, he reran Henry's failed strategy of trying to handle Rome by appointing a crony as archbishop of Canterbury. Appalled by John's nominee, Canterbury's monks appealed to the pope – and not just any old pope but Innocent III, the savviest, least innocent pontiff in Rome's history. A century of reformism had greatly enhanced the church's moral authority, and Innocent wielded soft power as a terrible weapon. Offering to mediate between John and the Canterbury monks, he cunningly proposed a compromise candidate who was an academic superstar (appealing to the devout) and English (appealing to patriots) but who had also spent twenty years in France and was therefore unappealing to John. John's veto left Innocent able to pose as having no choice but to excommunicate the king, which had probably been his goal all along. This was politicking of a high order.

Innocent drew up letters deposing John in 1212, and the king's enemies in France, Scotland and Wales – and, of course, in England itself – fell over themselves volunteering to enforce them. But then John did something no one had expected: he wrote to Innocent, abdicating. For six centuries English kings had worried about Rome undermining their independence, but John now gave it away. However, his letter continued, the pope could not rule England himself – so why not give it back to John to run for him, as a fief?

John's unconditional surrender was a masterstroke. If he became the pope's man, attacking him would be an attack on Rome too – so if the French king invaded, he would be excommunicated instead of John. John had snatched victory from the jaws of defeat. However, just months later, he snatched defeat back again. The troops he rushed across the Channel to join a German alliance against France and win back Normandy blundered into a massacre at Bouvines in 1214. John's barons, most of whom already hated him, went on strike.

Refusing to fight for John or pay his taxes, they demanded that he sign the famous Magna Carta. This began as a straightforward baronial wish-list, but as the lords cast around for supporters, they added the protests of allies as diverse as London merchants, Norman gentry and even peasants, which is why the charter is mostly remembered as proto-democratic. John was appalled but signed anyway, confident that his new best friend the pope would release him from his word. Innocent actually went one better, excommunicating the inconvenient barons; but before Innocent's letter reached them, the barons had already declared John deposed and offered the crown to the French king Louis's son (yet another Louis), who had a tenuous claim through his wife.

Sovereignty had dissolved. No one was sure whether the pope, the barons, John or Louis was in charge. Hoping to fix the problem with force, Louis invaded in 1216. Half the country went over to him, and when John obligingly dropped dead (according to one chronicle, from overindulgence in peaches and cider), Louis, now the obvious king, stood poised to take over an even grander version of the United Kingdom of the Atlantic Coast. That was the last thing the pope wanted, so Innocent intervened once again and excommunicated Louis. With no English archbishop now willing to crown him, Louis could do nothing when a papal legate quickly anointed John's nine-year-old son as Henry III. Further Italian officials rushed across the Channel to run what was left of the old United Kingdom. Comprehensively outmaneouvred, Louis went back to Paris.

The big winner in all this was Rome's European Union. It had more or less turned England into a protectorate, not so different from the situation Greece found itself in after its 2010 debt crisis. Even after the papal legates went home, England remained locked in as the pope's ally against France's growing strength. This was a disaster for England, because the loss of its counterscarp in Normandy had exposed its coasts to French raids and made it easier for Scottish and French kings to co-operate. Henry's disaffected barons declined to help their boy-king defend his last Continental toeholds.

Henry hatched increasingly elaborate and expensive schemes to win back his inheritance. Unable to compete head to head with France, he built ever wider networks of allies, expanding England's stage into Castile and Savoy. In 1251 he and the pope cooked up an even grander scheme to outflank France. Sicily, like England, was a papal fief, its ruler chosen by Rome; and the pope now offered Sicily to Henry's nine-year-old son. It looked like a win for everyone. The pope would gain a friend in Palermo; Henry would put a powerful new foe in France's rear (Figure 5.8). Thinking bigger still, Henry

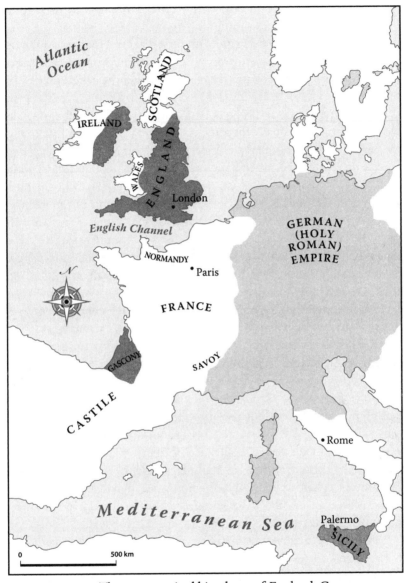

Figure 5.8. The not-so-united kingdoms of England, Germany
and Sicily in 1258. (The borders with France are those
formally recognised by the Treaty of Paris in 1259.)

then borrowed heavily to bribe his brother's way on to the throne of the ramshackle organisation known as the Holy Roman Empire, which, nominally at least, ruled much of central Europe. France, facing encirclement, made terms with Henry and the pope. For a few dizzy months Henry seemed to have overturned the entire European order.

Henry was being as clever as John, and as foolish. His barons had warned him that papal offers meant nothing without muscle and money to enforce them, and Henry had neither. Months of haggling merely exhausted the pope's patience, and in 1258 the European Union billed Henry £90,000 – three times his annual income – for expenses incurred in the Sicilian affair, with excommunication as the penalty for non-payment. His strategy (if that is not too kind a word for it) in ruins, Henry now asked his barons for a bailout. Instead he got a coup. The barons demanded that he call a 'parlemenz' and follow its instructions, and when he broke his word, the kingdom slithered back into anarchy. At some points barons kept Henry a virtual prisoner, at others the pope put England back under legates. Twice things reached such a pass that the French king was asked to arbitrate.

Henry more or less won the civil war that followed, but hardly anyone still thought that the old United Kingdom of the Atlantic Coast could function. England's strategic problems appeared to be insoluble. Henry's son and heir, Edward, ran away from them, following in his great-uncle Richard's footsteps by leading the last ever crusade to retake Jerusalem for Christendom. Still in the Holy Land when his father died in 1272, Edward decided on a diplomatic reset. On his way home, before even being crowned, he pointedly stopped in Rome to signal submission to the pope and then in Paris to cement peace with France. After that, he quietly dropped all talk of reuniting a kingdom along the Atlantic coast.

The central problem was that Thatcher's Law, that the Isles could not be taken out of Europe, still held. This made a Continental counterscarp crucial for England's security; but enforcing sovereignty and building identity across such diverse places had proved impossible. Edward therefore concluded that England had to find new ways to deal with what came its way from the Continent – with profound consequences for the lands to its north and west.

Boom . . .

Edward had only one tool for managing Thatcher's Law: diplomacy. He therefore cast himself as the great peacemaker. Norway's king, who had made trouble in the Isles as recently as 1263, was persuaded to stay away, and Edward burnished his reputation by brokering peace between France and Aragon. At home he threw himself into conciliating critics, meeting with parliaments twice a year to hear grievances and promoting trial by jury to settle disputes. Parliaments became places to negotiate taxes, particularly on trade, and above all on the burgeoning wool trade. By 1290 Edward was making four times as much from taxes as from royal land, which had been the cash cow of earlier kings. Collecting these taxes did call for an expensive bureaucracy (Edward's household accounts for the year 1285–6 alone fill 250 pages in the standard modern edition), but the pen-pushers and clever Italian bankers he hired more than paid for themselves.

Edward's income rose largely because England's national income – indeed, Western Europe's as a whole – was rising too. Thanks to the longer growing seasons of the Medieval Warm Period, populations had roughly doubled between 1000 and 1300, to 4–5 million people in England, 1–2 million in Ireland, another million in Scotland and 300,000 in Wales. The Isles were now more crowded than they had been under the Roman Empire.

Farmers drained hundreds of square kilometres of fen in Lincolnshire and East Anglia and chopped down even more of the royal forest, putting the reclaimed lands under the plough. They made their ploughs more efficient too: horses cost more to feed than oxen, which had long made them unattractive as draught animals, but Middle Eastern innovations – iron shoes, which reduced friction, and collar harnesses, which quadrupled horses' pulling power – were now making horses worth the outlay. Just one English draught animal in twenty had been a horse in 1086, but by 1300 one in five was, and horses were colonising farmland in the north and west as well. As a little bonus, farmers found that the extra horse manure meant they only had to leave one-third, rather than one-half, of their fields fallow each year. One immigrant monk from Flanders gushed that in England

There stretch before you the most fertile fields, flourishing meadows, broad swaths of arable land, rich pastures, flocks dripping with milk, spirited horses and flocks. It is watered by fountains of leaping spray, bubbling streams, notable and excellent rivers, lakes and pools crowded with fish and birds and coming and going of boats, all well suited for cities and people. Groves and woods are in leaf, field and hill full of acorns and woodland fruit, rich in game of all kinds.

I mentioned in Chapter 3, when talking about the Roman Empire, that premodern societies rarely increase their food supply fast enough to make much difference to adults' height. Eleventh- and twelfth-century England was exceptional in this regard: both sexes were, on average, 4 cm taller in 1200 than they had been in 1000, and would have towered over their Roman predecessors. They were living more comfortably too; average house sizes doubled between 850 and 1200, regaining the Roman (and modern) size of 100 m^2. These were substantial properties. By one estimate, a decent-sized timber-framed farmhouse would consume 333 mature trees. Construction also improved, with stone foundations and paved floors becoming common. Twelfth-century freemen's longhouses might strike us today as dark, smoky and unsanitary (Figure 5.9), but they were roomy and typically kept so clean that archaeologists find little in them. Fortunately, probate records and excavated garbage pits hint at steadily rising standards of living. Even middling peasants might have candles, board games and the odd imported majolica jug.

These were boom times, although by 1200 easily reclaimable land was running out. As in most of the booms we will see in this book, intensifying competition skewed how the fruits of growth were shared. In the long run, rising population and productivity normally favour landowners – people who buy labour and sell food – over landless labourers who do the opposite. The bigger you were, the better you did; so, by 1200, great men were buying back the lands they had been selling off since the ninth century to work them with hired hands. Few profited as mightily as the bishop of Worcester, whose income quadrupled between 1280 and 1310, but everywhere the wealth pyramid grew higher and steeper while competition at the top grew fiercer. There had been 200 or so English 'tenants-in-chief' (barons and earls) in the year 1200, and by 1300 the boom had made almost all their descendants richer; but even so, 120 of them had fallen out of this top group and been reduced to the rank of knights.

Figure 5.9. Hearth and home: artist Peter Dunn's reconstruction
of a timber-and-thatch longhouse at Wharram Percy in
Yorkshire, shared by people, dogs, cows and smoked hams.

Knights, meanwhile, had also fallen in numbers but risen in wealth.
The 4,500 knights in 1200 had dwindled to 1,250 a century later, the
several thousand missing men becoming mere esquires and gentlemen – men who mattered in their counties but, despite their new
wealth, no longer part of the charmed courtly circle around the king.

As the top of the social pyramid became narrower and richer
in the thirteenth century, the bottom became wider and poorer.
Because the number of labourers looking for work grew so much,
daily wages stuck for generations at one penny, even as inflation ate
away the penny's value. The smallest homes in thirteenth-century
villages were truly wretched – one-room huts measuring often just
4 m², built of whatever came to hand, which might be just a few
wooden beams laid on the ground, walls of cob (a mixture of clay,
straw, dung and animal hair) and thatched roofs. The whole lot would
rot every twenty to thirty years. Fewer than half the tenants on the
bishop of Winchester's estates owned even one cow, and one study

estimates that in wheat-growing areas 93 per cent of the cottagers' calories came from bread or pottage (oat-and-bean gruel).

The cheaper hired labour became, the less benefit there was in buying slaves, who virtually disappear from legal documents after 1200. The other side of the coin, though, was that fully half of 'free' thirteenth-century peasants were unable to make ends meet, and bound themselves to local lords as villeins, typically working part of each week on a lord's demesne. Because courts were only open to free men, this meant surrendering their legal protections. Lords regularly charged them fees such as the merchet, paid when a villein's daughter married (the notorious *ius primae noctis*, a lord's right to deflower his villeins' brides, is probably fictional). In return, villeins got a minimal safety net, putting them well ahead of those at the very bottom – masterless men – who were just one bad harvest away from disaster. In 1258, the chronicler Matthew Paris tells us, when 'a measure of wheat rose to fifteen shillings [. . .] the dead lay about, swollen and rotting, on dunghills, and in the dirt of the streets'. In the thirteenth century freedom really was just another word for nothing left to lose.

These were the years when Robin Hood and his Merry Men, outlaws who robbed the rich and gave to the poor, entered English mythology. Their story may have begun with one Robert Hod, a refugee from the archbishop of York's courts (Robert and Robin were interchangeable names, like Henry/Harry or Richard/Dick). The man sent to seize Robert/Robin's goods in 1225, Eustace of Lowdham, was the acting sheriff of Nottingham (he earned tenure in 1232) and was particularly busy around Barnsdale, a place prominent in the earliest Robin Hood stories. 'We will never know for certain', says the prominent Hoodologist David Crook, but he suspects that Robert Hod was actually an alias of a thuggish bandit named Robert of Wetherby. Perhaps, Crook concludes, 'we may look for the origins of the legend of Robin Hood in those summer days in 1225 when the sheriff of Nottingham's men hunted Robert'.

Eustace caught Robert and hanged him with a length of chain, but the idea of Robin Hood lived on. Over the next century or so, as life kept getting harder for the poor, plenty of real-life desperadoes ran off to places like Sherwood Forest. Even more went to London, including another mainstay of English legend, Dick Whittington. Few runaways fared as well as either the fairy-story Dick (who had a magical cat) or the real-life Sir Richard Whittington (who was elected lord mayor of London four times), but even the worst-off won a chance of escaping starvation. Admittedly, one reason why London always needed more labourers was that its fetid conditions killed so many (not until 1309 did it occur to its good burghers to penalise people for voiding their bowels in the streets), but the city kept growing anyway. The reason was the same as in Roman times: a big, rich kingdom needed hundreds of administrators, merchants and other specialists to run it, and they in turn needed thousands of builders, dockworkers, shopkeepers, brewers, bakers, prostitutes and servants to look after them.

London had 25,000 residents when the Normans arrived but 40,000 by 1200. By 1300 some 60,000 were crammed into the couple of square kilometres inside its ancient walls, with another 40,000 in suburbs beyond them. London was now two or three times the size of Roman Londinium. It was still only half as big as Paris and would barely have made the top thirty in Italy, but by British standards urbanisation was running riot. Norwich, Bristol, York and Winchester each had over 10,000 occupants; another twenty towns had 5,000. In all, perhaps one English person in six now lived in a town, well above Roman levels. New towns sprang up everywhere (the future giants Liverpool and Leeds both began in 1207). In William the Conqueror's day there had been no real cities north of York, but Newcastle was now growing rapidly and Scotland's King David I granted Edinburgh and half a dozen other settlements municipal status in the 1120s. He added Glasgow in 1136. A century later Cardiff, Carmarthen and Haverford also had populations over 1,000.

Just like Roman peasants, the country bumpkins drifting into thirteenth-century towns encountered strange sights, smells and tastes. Country folk ate mostly bread, root vegetables, cheese, curds and onions, usually home-grown and -cooked. In towns, however, few houses had ovens, so street food was standard fare. Poems describe cities ringing with cries of 'Hot pies, hot!' and, less appealingly, 'Hot sheep's feet!' Alcohol was available on every corner. Alehouses specialised in thick, filling and highly alcoholic brews; taverns, often boasting catchy names and signage, offered wine to a more discerning set; and inns rented out rooms. Belying modern England's reputation for hostelries of the *Fawlty Towers* type, these inns were famously warm and welcoming. Continental visitors were delighted by landladies who kissed and embraced them. And business was good: thirteenth-century York, with a population of 13,000, had 1,300 hotel rooms.

Most townsfolk lived in two- or three-roomed houses with a cesspit at the back. Walls were clay, roofs thatched and floors of clay or beaten earth with a covering of rushes, to be dumped outdoors when fouled. Life revolved around a central hearth in the parlour, although by 1300 the hot new idea in interior design was the chimney, set in a tiled fireplace against a wall, plus the fireproof tiled roofs that chimneys required. Below this level of affluence, the poorest people might inhabit hovels even nastier than those in villages, crammed down dark, narrow alleys choked with garbage and evil-smelling mud; above this level, richer types had sturdy, two-storeyed timber houses on stone foundations, with deep cellars and 'jettied' upper floors overhanging the street to maximise space.

Once in a while, archaeologists get lucky and find a good garbage pit that puts flesh on these architectural bones. In the 1280s, for instance, on Cuckoo Lane in Southampton, a rich merchant named Richard of Southwick buried his charred possessions after a fire. His family had lived well, tippling from delicate glasses and eating off imported plates, watching the rabble through glass windows and playing with pets that included a Barbary ape (although, judging from well-preserved parasite eggs in Richard's cesspit, everyone was crawling with worms).

Hundreds of thousands of migrants exchanged the countryside for towns' mixed blessings. Not surprisingly, the bigger the town, the wider its gravitational field. Barely one in ten of those who relocated to little Stratford upon Avon moved more than 25 km. Even middle-sized Exeter drew half its immigrants from within 30 km and five-sixths from within 100. To pull in actual foreigners, British (almost always, English) cities needed money, and so London – 'queen of the whole kingdom', one twelfth-century writer called it – was again the great attractor. Because most English wool moved through the city, Continental merchants and moneymen could make fortunes there shipping out fleeces (by 1300, some 8 million per year) and shipping in silk, spices, building stone and anything else the English elite wanted. Above all, that continued to mean wine: Bordeaux alone sent 25,000 barrels of claret every year. Norman, French, Flemish and German merchants had settled in London before 1066, and, as England's stage widened, Italians, Spaniards, Portuguese and Norwegians joined them in the thirteenth century. Foreigners moved to other cities too as they developed import–export businesses: seventeen English towns had Jewish moneylenders by 1190, and even tiny Truro in Cornwall had a German cobbler in the fourteenth century.

Medieval immigrants tended to be professionals, boosting prosperity by greasing the wheels of commerce. They therefore came, unlike the Anglo-Saxons in the fifth and sixth centuries or the Norse in the ninth, in numbers too small to have any measurable impact on British DNA. However, they did affect identity, not by blurring boundaries between Islander and Continental but by providing targets against which Britons – especially the English – could define themselves.

The Jews were the extreme case. William had brought Jewish financiers to England in 1070 because he saw, as did several contemporary rulers, that it could not hurt to surround himself with moneymen who not only lacked local friends but were also, because of their biblical baggage, unlikely to win any. However, it only took a generation for the calculus to change. Beginning in the Rhineland and France, popular enthusiasm for crusades to expel Muslims from Jerusalem spilled over into generalised anti-Semitism and persecution of local Jews. When Richard the Lionheart was crowned in 1189 and announced his intention of becoming England's first crusading king, Londoners celebrated by burning thirty Jews alive. The following year, northern lords, several of whom owed money to Jews, whipped up a mob and trapped 150 in York Castle. Fearing the worst, fathers cut their wives' and children's throats, then the rabbi cut the men's throats and finally his own. Those who offered to convert to Christianity were murdered by Christians anyway.

Conspiracy theories went viral. Jews were accused of poisoning wells and sacrificing Christian babies. Other foreigners became suspect too, charged with conspiring with the Jews to corrupt England's kings. Parliament accused Italians of introducing usury and sodomy into England; assaults on foreigners mounted, and rumours took hold that kings were taxing true Englishmen into ruin (or into flight to Sherwood Forest) to enrich sinister Europeans. In 1255 Henry III tried to look tough on foreigners by executing nineteen Jews on the absurd charge of kidnapping and crucifying a Christian baby ('Little St Hugh', he was called), but he still lagged behind the popular mood. When his barons rebelled three years later, they demanded in the name of 'the community of England' that 'all foreigners be put to flight from your face and ours as though from the face of a lion'. Xenophobia became respectable. 'Whoever did not know the English tongue was despised', one chronicler said, and no wonder, with Henry's French wife at one point mustering an army across the Channel to invade England to free him from his baronial captors. Rebellious lords called on patriots to defend their homeland against enemies without and traitors within. 'The response', says historian David Carpenter, 'was overwhelming and the atmosphere [. . .] perhaps rather like that in England in 1940.'

Xenophobia accelerated longer-term trends in identity, above all the consolidation of the Isles into four geographically rooted communities – English in the lowland south-east, Welsh and Scots in the highland west and north and Irish across the water. William the Conqueror's apartheid regime in England faded away. France's conquest of Normandy in 1204 confronted the Anglo-Norman elite with a choice between being French, thereby keeping their Norman estates, or being English, keeping their English ones, but in reality most Normans had already been absorbed into the English majority. Normans outside the courtly elite had been marrying Englishmen and -women from the start. 'Nowadays', the king's treasurer conceded around 1178, 'when English and Normans live together and marry and give in marriage to each other, the nations are so mixed that it can scarcely be decided (I mean in the case of freemen) who is of English birth and who Norman.'

Closer to the top, apartheid lingered longer. All kings until 1204 spent most of their days in France, and in 1250 one baron still called French the language that 'any gentleman should know'. The elite proved adept at mobilising xenophobia as a political weapon while remaining more or less French. Simon de Montfort, the Little Englanders' leader in the civil war of the 1250s, was French to the bone and barely spoke English; and when King Edward, who banished England's Jews altogether in 1290, assured Parliament that 'the English tongue, if [the French king's] power is equal to his malice, will be destroyed from the earth', he had to present his case in Latin to lords who debated it in French.

Even so, by the 1270s most of Edward's peers spoke English at home and had to hire tutors to teach their children French and Latin. A century later the English they spoke sounded at least something like the modern version, as did the Gaelic and Welsh being spoken to the north and west. Geoffrey Chaucer, John Barbour and Dafydd ap Gwilym had already given these three tongues their first literary giants.

Stronger national identities helped Edward draw the English together against what came their way from France, just as nationalism helped Llywelyn ap Gruffudd in Wales and Robert Bruce in Scotland unite followers against what came their way from England. Ireland's more fragmented politics made unity trickier, but even there by 1366 the Statutes of Kilkenny would subsume myriad older identities into a simple opposition between *Gaedhil* (natives) and *Gaill* (English settlers). Yet through it all, the formation of new identities was a contradictory business. Even as lines between England, Wales, Scotland and Ireland clarified and hardened, English writers began suggesting that some Scots and Welsh were not so bad, at least when compared with the French. (The Irish remained unacceptable.) In south Wales and the Scottish Lowlands people were living in cities, using coins to buy wine and sell wool and getting married – sometimes even to English people – in decent church services. 'The whole barbarity of [Scotland] was softened', an English saint observed. An English knight went further, saying Wales 'might very easily have been thought a second England'. King Edward agreed, and in 1277 set out to make it so.

. . . and Bust

Wales was a higher priority for Edward than for any earlier English king. It was all very well, he found, trying to manage Thatcher's Law through diplomacy rather than force, but so long as Scotland and much of Wales and Ireland lay beyond his control, England effectively had an open back door. Since England no longer had a Continental counterscarp, French forces could walk through this any time they liked, supporting an invasion of England with supplies from the north and west. Closing this back door suddenly seemed urgent. The good news was that the lack of a counterscarp meant that Edward, unlike earlier kings, could not be called away from the Celtic fringe to defend it; the bad was that French kings liked England having an open back door, so attempts to close it might provoke just the invasion Edward wanted to prevent. Edward's patient diplomacy meant that France and Rome in the end merely offered to mediate when he invaded Wales in 1277, even when he surprised everyone by staying in the field month after month until he starved Prince Llywelyn the Last (surely the saddest epithet ever) out of his mountain fastnesses. Edward then built a chain of state-of-the-art castles across Wales and in 1284 pronounced it 'a land annexed and united to the crown of England'.

Scotland needed subtler handling, but luck was on Edward's side. Between 1281 and 1286 accidents and illnesses carried off the Scottish king's three sons and then the king himself. Edward arranged for his own five-year-old son to marry the surviving six-year-old heiress. His luck ran out when she too died in 1290, but Edward just threw his weight behind one of fourteen competing claimants. 'He had it in mind', he announced, 'to subdue Scotland to his authority, just as he had recently subjugated Wales.'

Such talk evoked the United Kingdom of Great Britain and Ireland that King Edgar had pursued three centuries earlier, and Edward, capitalising on the growing strength of English identity, pushed nostalgia whenever he could. After so many Williams and Henrys, Edward was the first Norman king to bear a traditionally English name, and he assiduously associated himself with both the Anglo-Saxons and King Arthur. He reburied in grand style the bones that Glastonbury's monks said were Arthur's and Guinevere's, and staged self-consciously Arthurian jousts and feasts at Winchester, King Alfred's ancient capital. His crown, he claimed, had once been Arthur's, and it was probably Edward who commissioned a huge round table, dated by tree rings to 1250–80, which can still be seen in Winchester Castle's Great Hall.

'Now the islanders are all joined together', an English chronicler crowed,

> *There is no king, nor any prince, in all these countries*
> *Save King Edward, who has united them thus.*
> *Arthur never held these fiefs so fully!*
> *Now all he has to do is prepare his expedition*
> *Against the King of France, and conquer his inheritance.*

This was too much for France's King Philip, ominously nicknamed the Iron King, who struck first. Fighting broke out in 1294, and the next year Philip and a dozen Scottish lords concluded what came to be called the 'Auld Alliance', decreeing that an English attack on either was an attack on both. Immediately French ships plundered Kent, while William Wallace – the hero of Mel Gibson's film *Braveheart*, released on the Auld Alliance's 700th anniversary – raised Scotland in revolt.

Edward's barons were as unenthusiastic about this war as they had been about his father's fight for a United Kingdom of the Atlantic Coast, but they became downright hostile when Edward died in 1307. His son, another Edward, simply had no idea what to do, and was soon fighting – and losing – separate wars not only against France and Scotland but also against his own barons, his French wife and her boyfriend. In the north the terrifying Robert Bruce usurped the Scottish throne, annihilated an English army at Bannockburn and talked of uniting a kingdom of the Celts. As he held discussions with Welsh rebels and sent a fleet to Ireland, Scottish scholars conveniently unearthed 'prophecies of Merlin', predicting that 'the Scottish people and the Britons, by which should be understood the Welsh, shall league together and have the sovereign hand and their will'.

Robert's problem was that this was not quite what the new French king, Louis the Quarrelsome, had in mind. He was not fighting a United Kingdom ruled from London just to create one ruled from Edinburgh instead, so the stronger Robert became, the less Louis supported him. The perfect outcome, in his eyes, was for England and Scotland to bludgeon each other to a standstill while he got on with more serious matters on the Continent. Every misery that engulfed the Isles suited him nicely, such as a summer in 1315 so cold and wet that crops rotted before they ripened. Seven horrendously lean years ensued. In 1316 it rained 150 days without a break, making fields so muddy that knights could not fight. Oxen and expensive horses starved, leaving nothing to pull ploughs. Then the bees died, leaving nothing to pollinate plants. Then the people died too: hunger, damp and disease had carried off a million English by 1322.

All these evils afflicted France and Scotland too, but they suited French strategy nicely, at least until 1336, when a new king, Philip the Fortunate, overplayed his hand. Alarmed by a more assertive English king (the third Edward in a row), Philip dispatched to Scotland the biggest force to invade Britain since the Romans. Edward III saw it off, but the threat scared his barons into actually supporting their

king. For centuries they had resisted kings who wanted them to pay
for wars that would close England's back door and/or rebuild a Continental counterscarp; but now, they conceded, their king had a point.
Parliament voted funds for Edward to hire German allies to encircle
France just as France's allies in Scotland encircled England. When the
Germans took his money and did nothing, Edward raised the stakes.
His mother's father had been king of France, which made his claim
to France's throne stronger than its actual king's – so why not press
it? Why not go beyond even a United Kingdom of the Atlantic Coast
by uniting the English and French crowns, setting the counterscarp
on the Rhine? So began the on-again, off-again Hundred Years' War.

This was just the sort of issue where the pope's voice would once
have been decisive, but times had changed. When Pope Innocent
deposed King John in 1212, he did so knowing that two centuries of
church reform had given the European Union suffocating soft power.
People wanted to want whatever the pope wanted, so when he excommunicated a king, that king was finished. However, Rome's Achilles'
heel was that soft power quickly becomes self-defeating. Christians
followed the pope because he was God's vicar, but the more they did
what he said and the stronger a pope became, the harder it was to
believe that he really shared Christ's humility (let alone his poverty).
Clergymen lower down the ladder found they could win more points
with their flocks by being Eurosceptics, criticising papal corruption,
than by following the European Union's lead.

Edward therefore felt perfectly safe pressing his claims by force.
His troops, seasoned by years of fighting the Scots, won a string of
victories – Crécy, Sluys and Poitiers over the French, Neville's Cross
over Scotland – without parallel since Alfred's day. Yet even with the
French and the Scottish kings chained in his dungeons, Edward could
still not convert battlefield success into political success. Frenchness
had taken on the same kind of strength as Englishness, Welshness,
Scottishness and Irishness, and whatever Edward's claim to the French
throne, no one would grant that he could kill his way on to it.

Conventional warfare having failed, Edward took to terror. He
launched great smash-and-grab raids, burning, raping and looting
strips tens of kilometres wide across the French and Scottish country-
sides, yet no amount of pain seemed enough to end the war. Not even
Yersinia pestis, the bubonic plague, could do that. The Black Death
arrived in Marseille in January 1348, carried by fleas in the fur of rats

travelling in the holds of ships coming from Sicily (and before that, from the Black Sea). Traders and raiders then took the rats (and fleas) by barge and cart across France, bringing the 'Great Pestilence' to Weymouth in Dorset by June. Victims' groins and armpits filled with black, oozing, stinking pustules. At least half of those infected died. On its heels came a mutation which could be transmitted by droplets of moisture on the breath. This killed almost everyone who caught it.

Nothing brings home the differences between the fourteenth century and our own quite as effectively as the Black Death. During the 2020 lockdowns, social distancing and face masks kept the death rate from Covid-19 below 0.1 per cent of Britain's population. Fourteenth-century rulers of course lacked such tools; but they also seem not to have cared. Rather than withdrawing the plague-bearing armies that were ravaging France and Scotland and relieving their weakened subjects from paying taxes to support them, Edward intensified both activities. The population of England and Wales crashed from 4.8 million in 1348 to 2.1 million in 1400 and just 1.9 million in 1450 – lower than when Caesar had invaded. London shrank from 100,000 residents to 20,000 in a single generation. The plague wiped out nearly 3,000 villages (which is one reason why archaeologists know so much about medieval England). Actual plague pits remain rare, but DNA confirms that one was found at Thornton Abbey in Lincolnshire in 2016 (Figure 5.10), probably from a village so overwhelmed by death that local monks took charge of its corpses.

In another difference from our own age, while Covid-19 hurt the poor more than the rich, the Black Death did the opposite. For generations, dense populations had driven wages down and profits up, but after 1348 emptier landscapes did just the opposite. Lords, desperate to retain their increasingly scarce workers, forgave villeins' labour obligations, increased pay and even set up retirement schemes. The cleverest landlords adapted, buying more horses to augment their surviving ploughmen's efforts or switching from grain to sheep, which required less labour. As the bishop of Winchester's human flock shrank, his woolly one grew, from 22,500 in 1348 to 35,000 in 1369. Some owners turned poor land over to rabbits, which required no supervision at all. Skilled estate managers became important men. By 1354 the grand Lord Berkeley was regularly dining with his reeve, which he assuredly didn't do before 1348.

In the cold language of economics, mass mortality shifted the

Figure 5.10. Bring out your dead: a plague pit dating to around
1350, excavated in 2016, at Thornton Abbey in Lincolnshire.

land:labour ratio in peasants' favour. (In plainer English, the scarcity
of workers meant that the poor enjoyed a century of broad-based
prosperity that would not be surpassed until 1850.) Average heights
had fallen by 4 cm between 1200 and 1350, but by 1400 these losses had
been made up. In city and country alike, real wages doubled by 1450,
with the sort of results we see in Figure 5.11, comparing the sources
of calories consumed by harvesters in Norfolk in 1256 and 1424. Before
the pestilence workers lived largely on barley bread, cheese and butter;
after it meat and ale (on average, three pints per day) dominated their
diets, with bread eaten only when they wanted it. Before 1348 alehouses were rare outside towns; by 1400 every village had its pub.

Not that life was all beer and beef after 1348. Landlords pushed
back against uppity serfs, and thousands of those who had survived the pandemic died in political violence in France in 1358 and
England in 1381. Buffeted now by riots and insurrection as well as
war against each other and mass mortality, both kingdoms teetered
on the brink of dissolution. Powerful clans turned northern England
into two virtually independent states, Ireland slid out of royal control
and Scots plundered Anglesey. In 1399 barons deposed and probably

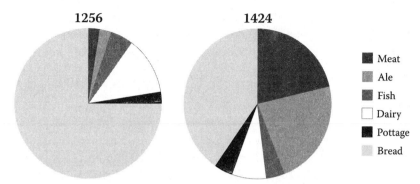

Figure 5.11. Before and after: the transformation of harvest workers' diets at Sedgeford, Norfolk, between 1256 and 1424.

killed another English king. In 1400 Arthur was resurrected again, this time in the person of a Welsh lord named Owain Glyndŵr. Glyndŵr descended from royalty on both sides and went nowhere without a personal seer who kept up a stream of Merlinesque prophecies. English garrisons fled before Glyndŵr's banner of a golden dragon on a white field, and in 1405 he convened Irish, Scots and Breton ambassadors to discuss a United Kingdom of the Celts. He signed a treaty with France, haggled with the pope and plotted with English malcontents to carve up the entire Isles. Things got so scary that Parliament banned Welsh minstrels from London. 'These were attempts', the historian Miri Rubin observes, 'to rethink the map of England and the relations between the components of the British sphere. Root-and-branch change seemed possible.'

The operative word, though, is 'seemed'. Geography was stubborn. Money, men and organisational capacity remained concentrated in the south-east. No United Kingdom of the Celts could work without France, the only player with the resources to balance England – but to the French the Celts remained a sideshow, to be patronised when convenient and dropped when not. Making matters worse, France's king was stark, staring mad. (Some days he sincerely believed he was made of glass; on others he forgot he was married with children, which was a real problem for dynastic diplomacy.) His bewildered barons split into two factions before 1405 was out, and, far from helping Glyndŵr, each offered to restore England's counterscarp in return for assistance against its rivals.

Henry V came to the throne in 1413 knowing perfectly well that these offers were really just invitations to take sides in an upcoming French civil war. Rather than joining either faction, he exploited the confusion to slaughter most of the French elite at Agincourt. Then, choosing the most promising-looking set of survivors, he haggled them into conceding his claim on their throne. When he died of the 'bloody flux' (the graphic fifteenth-century name for dysentery) in 1422, his infant son – predictably, Henry VI – was crowned in Paris as king of both France and England. But the feuding French factions soon reconciled, and within a generation drove the English from their entire country, excepting Calais.

A hundred years of war had won England less than nothing. By 1453 the country was back not merely where Edward I had been in 1272, with no counterscarp and an open back door, but where Henry III had been in the 1260s, with civil strife (what we now call the Wars of the Roses) tearing it apart. Scotland and much of Ireland broke free, English trade collapsed and French corsairs raided the southern coast. The Isles seemed stuck into a long-term, boom-and-bust pattern, cycling every century or so between a United Kingdom, which controlled England, parts of its Celtic hinterlands and the opposing Continental coasts, and Anarchy in the UK.

The new round of infighting ended in 1485, when yet another Henry, the Seventh, used French money and troops to kill his rival Richard III and seize his throne. Henry dropped all claims to a United Kingdom, except for Wales, which he claimed by right of having as much Welsh blood as English in his veins. After landing in Wales, he marched on London under the sign of the Red Dragon of Cadwaladr, an ancient Welsh ruler linked to King Arthur, and took a wife from the opposing faction in the recent civil wars. She was pregnant within days, and they named their son Arthur. It was mythmaking of the first order; but then, with no counterscarp and his Scottish and Irish back doors wide open, Henry had no other cards in his hand.

Unless something came up.

All the World's a Stage

Educated Europeans had known since Aristotle's day that the world was round. Rather than falling off its edge, sailors who headed west from Ireland would find themselves in what Greeks had called

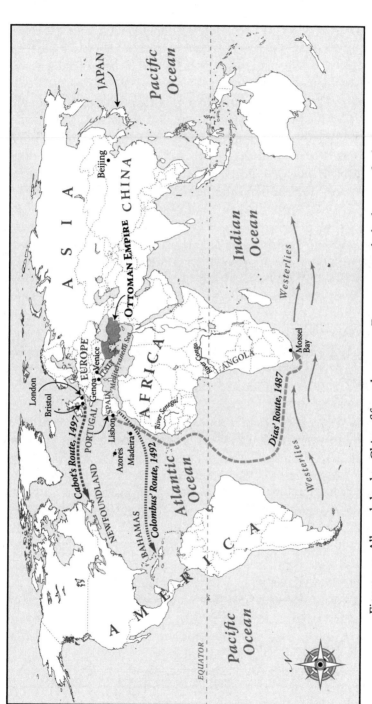

Figure 5.12. All roads lead to China: fifteenth-century Europeans explode the Hereford Map.

'Ocean', a vast, watery waste girding the inhabited world. It covered half the planet: had Richard of Haldingham and Lafford intended his Hereford Map to be seen from both sides, the back would have been an empty blue disk.

Educated Europeans also knew that the routes their merchants currently followed to the riches of the east, across the Mediterranean and Middle East or Central Asia (Figure 5.12), were therefore not the only ones. They could also, in theory, sail west to go east, cutting straight across Ocean. Or they could head north, around the top of Europe, or south, around the bottom of Africa (assuming, that is, that Europe and Africa had tops and bottoms). All seas led ultimately to the wealth of Asia. However, a third fact that educated Europeans knew was that the earth was roughly 36,000 km around, which meant that getting to the east by going west, north or south would involve journeys too long to be profitable. Whatever was possible in principle, in practice the Mediterranean and steppe routes were the only games in town.

It was therefore a real setback when Turkish invaders overran the Middle East during the fifteenth century and raised the tolls on silk, spices and other oriental luxuries passing through their empire. Equally bad, they sold trading monopolies to Italian merchants who added even more surcharges. Western Europe's importers began looking harder at oceanic routes and new kinds of ships which might cut travel costs. The most promising design was the caravel, a small, shallow vessel based on Mediterranean fishing boats, combining square sails for speed and triangular lateen sails for beating into headwinds. Portugal and Spain, better placed than anyone for sailing south down the west coast of Africa, led the way, often hiring Italians, the maritime experts, as skippers. Portuguese ships reached Madeira in 1420, the Azores in 1427 and the River Senegal, offering access to African gold mines, in 1444. They crossed the equator in 1473 and sailed into the mouth of the Congo in 1482.

No Westerners had come so far since the Phoenicians, twenty centuries earlier, but there progress stalled, because headwinds south of the Congo were too strong for caravels or the bigger versions called carracks to tack against them (the Phoenicians had used galleys, which could be rowed into the wind). But Bartolomeu Dias found the answer just five years later. As he struggled south along the Angolan coast, storms blew him westwards into open ocean. When

Figure 5.13. The boat that tore up the Hereford Map: a replica of
John Cabot's 50-ton caravel the *Mathew*, built in 1997 to celebrate the
500th anniversary of his voyage from Bristol to Newfoundland.

the gales died, thirteen days later, Dias realised that different winds –
the Westerlies – were now blowing him south-east. After a month
out of sight of land, he made landfall at Mossel Bay, near today's Cape
Town. His crew (understandably) refused to press on, but Dias had
proved that Africa did have a bottom. By following Dias's strategy of
volta do mar, 'returning by sea', European ships could swing out into
the Atlantic, bypass the African headwinds and be blown into the
Indian Ocean.

Portuguese sailors had effected the biggest geostrategic revolution of all time, and other European monarchs scrambled to catch up.
All manner of crazy schemes got a hearing, but few were crazier than

the pet project of the Genoese adventurer Cristoforo Colombo, anglicised as Christopher Columbus. Flying in the face of expert opinion, Columbus calculated that China was only 3,860 km west of Lisbon, and spent years looking everywhere from Venice to London for sponsors for a shot straight across the world-encircling ocean to Beijing. In 1492, the third time Columbus asked her, Spain's Queen Isabella put up the money, perhaps more to get rid of him than anything else. If so, she failed, because he was back a year later claiming that he'd been to the land of the Great Khan, which was pretty much where he'd predicted. (His first mistake was that China hadn't been ruled by a Mongol khan for over a century; his second, that he'd actually been to the Bahamas.)

England's Henry VII was one of the monarchs who had turned Columbus down. Annoyed, he now gave an Italian of his own, the Venetian Zuan Chaboto (who became known as John Cabot), permission – but not money – to seek a route from Bristol to China, preferably one shorter than Columbus's. Bad weather ruined Cabot's first effort, in 1496, but the next year his little caravel *Mathew* (Figure 5.13) carried him all the way to icy Newfoundland, which he decided was Japan, and home again.

Cabot's claim tore up the Hereford Map. No longer were the British Isles tucked away at the edge of the world. Newfoundland was not, obviously, Japan; but all the same 1497 marked the beginning of Britain's journey to the centre of the earth. The curtain was going up on a new act in the drama.

PART II

MACKINDER'S MAP, 1497–1945

6

ENGLEXIT, 1497–1713

Act II

It took over 200 years for Britain to exchange its supporting part at the edge of a European stage for the lead role at the centre of an Atlantic stage. Columbus and Cabot had shown that there was more to this world than dreamed of in the Hereford Map, but it would take technological and organisational revolutions for Europeans to be able to sail across the Atlantic reasonably easily, moving raw materials from west to east and people the other way. Only in the late seventeenth century did geography really change its meanings. After being a land of immigrants for over 7,500 years, the Isles became one of emigrants, overwhelmingly heading to North America – and one that forced other people to emigrate too.

Creating new organisations (such as the slave trade) to exploit the new geography was, if anything, even more of a challenge than creating the technologies that had transformed the map. Increasing mobility offered prospects of increasing prosperity, if rulers were willing to accept merchants and mariners into the elite; and rising prosperity promised (or threatened) to transform both security and sovereignty, because governments that worked out ways to tap into the new Atlantic economy could use its wealth to overwhelm rivals who failed to do so. Governments in London outperformed their Continental rivals at these tasks. They created the world's most efficient 'fiscal–military state' (historians' term for governments that married markets to military might), using it to build fleets that could put Thatcher's Law on hold by closing the English Channel to enemies. Finally, secure behind their watery defences, they turned the Isles into a United Kingdom of Great Britain and (most of the time) Ireland. At last, Britain's root-and-branch rethinking of mobility, prosperity, security and sovereignty advanced and even required new identities, more Insular and less Continental. In the 1530s England left

Rome's Original European Union. Scotland followed in the 1550s and one corner of Ireland after the 1570s. The rest of Ireland did not, with consequences that have haunted Britain ever since.

There was never really a master plan for this. No one in 1497, and precious few even in 1597, foresaw what the new geography would mean. But by 1697 a growing group within Britain's elite did see both how the map was changing and what they needed to do to take advantage of it. For better and for worse, they began moving Britain from the edge of the Hereford Map to the centre of Mackinder's.

The Pope's Bad Son

King Henry VII definitely didn't see what the new geography meant. Initially he gave Cabot just a £10 tip for finding 'Japan'. He subsequently improved on this, but only as far as making Cabot's pension twice what a skilled labourer earned. Henry was notoriously mean, but parsimony on this scale demands an explanation, and the obvious one is that his spies, famous for their efficiency, had heard rumours that Cabot had not been to Japan at all.

Tantalising hints survive that Bristol's fishermen had been trawling North American waters since the 1460s and knew that they held little but cod and ice (Figure 6.1). One theory even says that Bristolmen knew American shores so well that they named them after Richard Amerike, Bristol's chief customs officer. There is no actual evidence for this, however, beyond the remarkable coincidence of the names, and most historians – surely correctly – trace America's name to Amerigo Vespucci (like Cabot, an Italian expat, but this time domiciled in Spain). Realising as he sailed down Brazil's coast in 1501 that this couldn't possibly be Asia, Vespucci concluded that the planet really was as big as the experts said and that he was looking at a previously unidentified continent lying between Spain and China. By 1507 mapmakers had decided he was right, and were calling the new world America.

And so, informed opinion concluded, Cabot had changed nothing. The British Isles remained the edge of the world (the world that mattered, anyway). Because America didn't matter, proximity to Europe still trumped Britain's insularity; and because the dreams of grand United Kingdoms had all failed, England's story would still be about what came its way from the Continent, while Wales's, Scotland's and Ireland's were about what came their way from England.

Figure 6.1. The American stage, 1497–1713.

Like Edward I back in 1272, who had also inherited an England lacking a counterscarp, almost bankrupt and with its back door wide open, Henry had no viable option except compromise. He therefore cut what deals he could with France and Scotland, and sought marriage alliances with Spain. The biggest excitement of 1497, in fact, was not Cabot's discoveries but the betrothal of Henry's son Arthur to Catherine of Aragon (Cabot didn't even make the number two spot, which went to a bloody uprising in Cornwall [Figure 6.2]). Arthur's marriage mattered so much that, when he died shortly after the wedding in 1502, Catherine was hastily re-betrothed to his younger brother, another Henry (number eight). Just in case, the boys' sister Mary was additionally promised to Charles, heir to the Spanish throne.

Figure 6.2. The British stage, 1497–1713.

In both Madrid and London the hope was that tighter ties between the two would deter French kings from threatening either. Instead, Henry VIII's marriage to Catherine drove him to take England out of the Catholic European Union altogether. He did not mean to do this, any more than David Cameron meant to take Britain out of the modern European Union in 2016; but both men did it anyway. Thus does fortune make fools of us all.

If Cameron's Brexit has any parallel in history, Henry's Englexit (to coin an unlovely new word) is surely it. The two episodes certainly differed in endless ways, but what unites them is that these are the only occasions when parts of the Isles have walked away from a Continental empire of soft power (as opposed to Britannia's multiple exits from Rome's empire of hard power between 260 and 410). Each exit was driven by – and deepened – arguments within the Isles over identity, sovereignty and geostrategy. Each had major consequences for prosperity, brought on a constitutional crisis and took longer to resolve than anyone expected. Finally, each was an unintended consequence of diplomatic dances going back decades.

Henry did not start out as a revolutionary. If anything, he was so old-fashioned as to be almost reactionary. He ached to be another Henry V, solving England's problems on the battlefield – or, better still, to equal his brother's namesake King Arthur. Henry had the legendary king's fake Round Table at Winchester repainted, and imagined himself, like the lost Arthur, as a perfect Christian king. He was 'the pope's good son', he insisted, who 'will always be with his holiness and with the Church, from which I mean never to depart'. So, when the pope promised to support Henry's claim to the French throne if Henry would attack its current aggressive occupant, Henry leaped into action.

This was a mistake. England had fallen steadily behind France in the century since Agincourt. Its population was now just one-sixth of France's and its income barely one-tenth. France had also stayed up to date in the newfangled military art of gunnery, while England's army remained wedded to the longbow. Henry VII had understood this, and avoided wars, but despite (or perhaps because of) his father's views, Henry VIII invaded France anyway in 1513. A fiasco ensued, achieving only the capture of two towns which even Henry's own chancellor called 'ungracious dog-holes'. Henry's one consolation was that France's trump card, the Auld Alliance, also backfired. Scotland was even smaller, poorer and worse armed than England, and when its king, as stubborn as Henry, attacked regardless, he fared even worse. He, three bishops, eleven earls, fifteen lords and 10,000 of their troops were butchered in driving rain at Flodden Field. Scottish power was broken for a generation.

Henry never entirely gave up on force, even after another march on Paris petered out in the mud, but he recognised that he had to let his clever chancellor, Thomas Wolsey, try other methods too. One was a more muscular version of Henry III's Sicilian strategy of the 1250s, encircling France by having Henry stand for election to the German throne (which would have made him Emperor Henry VIII as well as King Henry VIII) while Wolsey simultaneously stood for election to the papal one. When neither bid succeeded, Wolsey unveiled Plan B: foreshadowing the balance-of-power strategies we will see in Chapter 7, he would get Spain and France competing for England's friendship. This quickly worked, and, without killing anyone, Wolsey brought a measure of peace to Western Europe. A grateful pope made him a cardinal and showered Henry with honours, but rather like Winston Churchill in the Second World War, Wolsey soon learned that cleverness alone could not permanently beguile bigger, richer allies. It was his efforts to square this circle that ultimately pushed England out of the Catholic European Union.

This came about not because of some coherent strategy to remake English identity but because of entanglements between traditional diplomatic concerns and webs of ambition, miscalculation and, in the end, money. For 400 years England's main rival had been France, but Spain was now supplanting it. When Catherine of Aragon married Prince Arthur in 1497, her homeland was already a major power, but twenty years later it was a superpower. Iberians had been in the forefront as Western Europe's stage began expanding across the Atlantic. Other Europeans had lost interest when it became clear that the Atlantic was not a short cut to Asia, but Spaniards had found new sources of prosperity in the New World. First, they looted the Aztec and Inca empires, then they shipped African slaves to America to dig up that continent's silver and used it to pay for their wars in Europe. At the same time a string of clever diplomatic marriages also started paying off, and Spain's King Charles – Catherine's nephew – inherited Austria, southern Italy, the Low Countries and much of Germany (Figure 6.3). Europe had seen no concentration of territories like this since the Roman Empire.

Landing Charles as an in-law was a two-edged sword. If Henry and Catherine worked well together, Charles could be the best friend England ever had; if they didn't, he could equally well be its worst enemy. No one expected sixteenth-century royal spouses to be best friends, but Henry and Catherine's relations grew dangerously frosty as years passed without the arrival of a son. The marriage produced

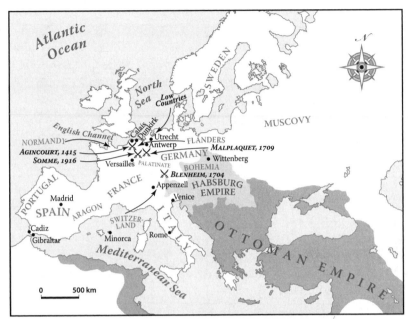

Figure 6.3. The European stage, 1497–1713 (showing the frontiers of the Habsburg and Ottoman empires as they were around 1700).

a daughter, Mary, but the last time a woman had inherited the crown, in 1135, anarchy had ensued. Provoking Spain was risky, but doing nothing seemed riskier still; so, with Catherine approaching her fortieth birthday and a son looking ever less likely, Henry began talking about trading her in for a younger, more fertile model. It had never felt right, he now claimed, that he had married his brother's widow. The church had only allowed her second marriage because she had sworn that Arthur had not consummated the first, but this, Henry now convinced himself, was not true. So, if the pope would just agree that a mistake had been made, Catherine could be shipped back to Spain and everyone could get on with things.

Henry had reasons to expect Rome to help moderate Charles's reaction. The pope currently needed England more than ever, not just to balance France but also to fight against a frightening new heresy. Over the previous hundred years Rome had slowly clawed back some of its lost soft power, but the German professor Martin Luther had recently reopened all the old wounds by insisting that reading the

Bible carefully showed that faith alone, not the intercession of the church, was what saved souls. At first, Luther carefully avoided pointing out that privatising soul-saving robbed Rome's European Union of much of its point, but within five years princes and peasants alike had concluded that Luther's theology justified resistance to Rome, violent when necessary.

Luther had admirers in England, but Henry stood by the pope. 'We are so much bounden unto the See of Rome that we canny do too much honour unto it', he announced, even writing an anti-Lutheran *Defence of the Seven Sacraments*. Yet successive popes, confident of squeezing even more concessions from Henry, found reasons to delay giving their good son the annulment he wanted – until, in 1527, disaster struck. Spanish mercenaries, nominally on Charles's payroll but in reality unpaid for many months, sacked Rome to recoup their wages, capturing the pope in the process. It was embarrassing for Charles that his men had behaved so badly but also rather convenient, because with the pope now the 'guest' of Catherine's nephew, Henry could forget about getting rid of her.

Not even Wolsey could negotiate this away, so Henry fired him, bringing in younger, more radical men. The issue, they assured Henry, was really one of sovereignty. In the beginning, they insisted, popes had merely been bishops of Rome and every king had been sovereign over his own realm, including its clerics. But after 1066, they continued, popes had made a power grab, claiming (without justification) that St Peter had given them sovereignty over everyone. It was time for Henry to take back his country – whereupon his own Church of England could give him his divorce, without interference from a lot of foreigners.

There was much for Henry to like in this theory, but it would require the pope's good son to turn bad, making a U-turn followed by a hard exit from the European Union. Neither of these appealed at all, so Henry persevered with petitioning the captive pope; and in 1532 the French king, currently wanting Henry as an ally against Spain, agreed to lobby on his behalf. Annulment now seemed so imminent that Henry's girlfriend, Anne Boleyn, who had spent the last six years refusing to sleep with him, relented. Secretly exchanging wedding vows, the happy couple consummated their passion. Immediately, Anne was with child.

This was awkward. The French king, embarrassed to find himself haggling on behalf of a bigamist, backed out, leaving Henry, still hitched to Catherine, desperate for a solution before his baby emerged a bastard. So it was that a witches' brew of accidents, sex, competing agendas and unintended consequences – odder even than the twists and turns of the 2010s – tumbled England out of the European Union. Henry's new fixer, Thomas Cromwell (the disturbingly sympathetic anti-hero of Hilary Mantel's *Wolf Hall* novels), bullied and bribed a sceptical but instinctively Europhobe Parliament into agreeing that since Henry had no superior but God, appeals to Rome against his decisions were illegal. A compliant archbishop of Canterbury now concluded that Henry had never really been married to Catherine, making his unborn son, rather than the illegitimate Mary, his heir. When the baby arrived, however, he turned out to be a she, Elizabeth; and to cap it all, the pope announced early in 1534 that, no matter what Henry said, England was still part of the European Union. Opinions from Canterbury didn't matter. Henry was still married to Catherine. If he ignored this, he would be excommunicated, and if he ignored that, the whole weight of the Spanish Empire would come down on him.

When Kings John and Henry III had been in similarly tight spots in previous centuries, they had knuckled under, but with the church's soft power now so much weaker, Henry VIII bluntly asserted independence from the pope. Everything now came down to a single question: who ruled, Westminster or Rome? Just three days after the pope's pronouncement, Parliament answered with the Act of Succession, denying the pope any say in who sat on England's throne. Eight months after that, in November 1534, an Act of Supremacy declared Henry 'Supreme Head on Earth of the Church'. England had left the European Union.

Like the modern Brexit, Englexit did not have to happen. It raises some of the most interesting what-ifs in English history. If Arthur had lived longer; if Henry had married someone else instead of Catherine (at one point he had broken off their engagement); if Wolsey had been luckier; if even one pope had been more reasonable in the 1520s; if Anne Boleyn's virtue had held out longer . . . the list goes on. Even after 1534 Englexit could still have been reversed, or at least softened. By 1537, in fact, with Catherine and Anne both dead and Jane Seymour (wife number three) having produced a son, the main issues had resolved themselves. Papal lawyers duly crafted a face-saving deal.

Most kings would have taken it, and much of the blame/credit for Englexit must be laid at Henry's door for saying no. But not all of it. Almost any English monarch would have done at least some of what Henry did. In fact, by the 1550s Scotland, France, the Low Countries, Sweden and many German states had all either renegotiated their membership of the European Union or exited altogether – not because their rulers needed divorces but because national identity, conflicts over sovereignty, the attractiveness of Luther's ideas and, above all, money pushed them down the same path. For a millennium the Catholic church's local franchises had been sucking resources out ' of their host kingdoms; by reclaiming those franchises, kings could take that cash back. No one knows exactly how much Henry and his carpetbaggers walked off with in the 1530s, but in real terms it dwarfed the notorious £350 million per week that Brexiteers promised to take back from the European Union in 2016. Lands and dues confiscated from monasteries added about £120,000 to the king's annual income (roughly equal to his entire revenue at his accession), but even more came in from looted gold, buildings, cattle and every other kind of property. This was simply seized and sold off.

In a way, the looting was extremely orderly. Bureaucrats drew up lists; monks and nuns were pensioned off, sometimes generously; elderly and infirm church staff got extra benefits. In other ways, though, it was a free-for-all. Insiders like Cromwell made fortunes, and even peasants got payouts. 'The poor people thoroughly in every place be so greedy upon these [monasteries] when they be suppressed that by night and day [. . .] they do continually resort as long as any door, window iron or glass or loose lead remained in any of them', one of Cromwell's men complained. While still a schoolboy, I excavated for several weekends at just the sort of site he was talking about, Hulton Abbey in Stoke-on-Trent. It had been an undistinguished House of God, whose monks were mostly shepherds and coal miners, but even so, it was better built and furnished than the villages around it. When Henry's men closed it in 1538, the locals carried off everything, including the stones from its walls. Its very location was then forgotten until farmworkers chanced across its foundations in 1884.

This much plunder could turn even a pope's good son into an Englexiteer – and make him suspect that no fate was too terrible for stubborn, self-righteous Remainers who got in his way. Henry, not known for anger management, had four particularly annoying critics hanged until almost dead, then cut down so their bowels could be slowly pulled out before their own eyes. Even then, some of them still called on their Roman God, so the hangman silenced them by stuffing their severed genitals down their throats.

Violence begat violence. Even Henry took fright when 10,000 northerners marched on London in 1536, singing

Christ crucified!
For thy wounds wide
Us commons guide!
Which pilgrims be . . .

Falling back on that oldest of royal expedients, lying, Henry offered whatever it took to get the pilgrims to go home, then hanged them by their hundreds. He (apparently seriously) proposed rewriting the Sixth Commandment to give kings permission to kill commoners, but not even his lickspittle archbishop of Canterbury could swallow that. Overruling the pope was one thing; overruling Moses was too much.

With a different king on the throne, Englexit might have been softer, but it could equally well have been harder too. Truly wild alternatives to Catholicism were bubbling up in Europe. Real Christians, some said, must live like the apostles, renouncing all oaths and violence and therefore refusing to serve the state in any way. Others, convinced that the end days had come, ignored laws altogether, condoning anarchy and free love. Wildest of all, some radicals claimed that women could have opinions – whereupon one such, a serving girl from the pretty Swiss town of Appenzell, announced that she was the New Messiah and would soon give birth to the Antichrist.

Henry, who had always fancied himself a theologian, saw no reason why exiting the pope's European Union must mean turning radical. Better, he thought, to stay soft, preserving most Catholic doctrines and ceremonies and keeping open the possibility of an eventual deal with the European Union. After all, leaving had immeasurably complicated England's already difficult geopolitics. Thatcher's Law still applied, and the bigger, stronger and richer Catholic powers on the Continent now had even more reasons for hostility. But when Henry died in 1547, the men who advised his ten-year-old son Edward

Figure 6.4. One way to reach consensus: Bloody Mary burns
Master John Rogers, Reader at St Paul's, 4 February 1555.

decided that hardening England's exit was the way forward. They
imposed a uniform Book of Common Prayer on all worshippers,
ripped the beautiful carved rood screens out of hundreds of churches
and smashed their stained glass – only for their course to be abruptly
reversed when Edward died in 1553, leaving the throne to Mary, his
staunchly Catholic half-sister (Catherine of Aragon's daughter).

It looked like Henry VIII's worst nightmares had come true.
Leavers and Remainers knifed each other in Whitehall; 'Bloody
Mary' burned more than 300 Protestants (Figure 6.4); and, when she
married the heir to the Spanish throne and took England back into
the European Union, 3,000 Protestants marched on London. They
dispersed only when Mary herself faced them down.

But even then, England's re-entry, like Henry's original exit,
was softer than it might have been. In the 2010s most Britons found
the four-plus years of turmoil between the referendum and their
eventual departure exhausting, but by the time Mary died in 1558,
England had endured a quarter-century of out-and-in. Some sort of

compromise, papering over the cracks, seemed increasingly desirable. Consequently, although Mary's half-sister and successor, Elizabeth, immediately took England back out of the Union, she too drifted towards Henry's have-your-cake-and-eat-it hopes, taking back sovereignty and money but trying to remain on speaking terms with Catholic Europe. Catholic Europe, however, had other ideas.

Beyond the Counterscarp

Seen from Rome, the real problem after 1534 was that Englexit, like the 2016 Brexit, emboldened Leavers all over Europe. England must therefore be seen to suffer for it, *pour décourager les autres*. There were plenty of opportunities to stir up trouble. England was small, weak and divided. Most of its people did not even know what Englexit was, and there were nowhere near enough churchmen competent to explain it to them. In Worcester in 1560 less than one preacher in five had studied the new ideas at university, and the archdeacon of Leicester reckoned in 1576 that barely twelve of his ninety-three clergy were up to the job of expounding scripture correctly.

The Church of England therefore urged Englexiteers to make education the path to both saving souls and getting on in life. The number of Members of Parliament (henceforth, MPs) who had soaked up the new thinking at Oxford or Cambridge almost tripled between 1563 and 1593. The rich channelled charity towards politically correct grammar schools, teaching approved ideas to boys of the middling sort – boys, in fact, like William Shakespeare, who attended Stratford Grammar in the 1570s. In towns, even the poor might learn their letters and some scripture. A remarkable two-thirds of London's labourers and male servants had done so by 1600. Something like Alfred the Great's idea of a literate, Christian England was finally emerging. In the countryside progress was slower: endowed schools proliferated (Lancashire had just three in 1480 but twenty-eight in 1600), but well under one villager in ten could read the Bible in Elizabeth's reign. With the new faith remaining a closed book to most people, Englexit's enemies concluded – possibly correctly – that if they just won over a few thought-leaders, the country might yet come back to Rome.

But how to do this? The quickest road was the highest, so France and Spain both dangled royal suitors before Elizabeth. Marrying back into the faith, they hinted, would be good for England's security and prosperity and, given the uncertainty over what Protestantism even was, might not matter much for identity. She was sorely tempted, even at the risk of putting Catholic cuckoos in the nest, but, after agonies of indecision, declined.

Where love failed, money might work. Elizabeth's finances depended heavily on taxing cloth exports, and when Spanish authorities banned English cloth from its main foreign market in Antwerp, it hurt. However, rather than pressing Elizabeth to soften Englexit, merchants sought out fellow Protestants in the Netherlands or opened entirely new markets. Some sailed down the west coast of Africa, buying gold and slaves; a Muscovy Company was founded to trade English wool for Russian fur; and despite the collapse of Cabot's delusion that Newfoundland was Japan, the hardbitten adventurer Martin Frobisher set off in the 1570s to see whether there might yet be a short cut to Asia around the top of America. In the 2020s global warming is finally opening such a route, but all that Frobisher found was glaciers and iron pyrite, fool's gold. Yet still the queen chose sovereignty over prosperity.

Frustrated again, the European Union reached out directly to England's most committed Remainers, the unrelenting remnant of its Catholic population. Seminary-educated priests began slipping into England to rally the faithful in 1574, followed in 1580 by Jesuits, the shock troops of the Catholic Counter-Reformation. Encouraged, a few English Catholics (especially in the north and west) defied their queen and burned for it, but most went the other way, trying harder than ever to show that they put England before Rome.

Welsh Catholics disappointed Rome too. Anti-Englishness had softened since Glyndŵr's day, and the legal fusion of Wales and England, begun in 1535, encouraged Welsh elites to make friends and look for advancement in London. Most important of all, a smart decision to translate the Bible into Welsh in 1563 snapped links between nationalism and Rome. Slowly, Protestantism became as Welsh as singing.

Scottish Catholics had much greater potential to make Englexit so miserable that no one would want to emulate it, and its Catholic rulers were happy to oblige. In 1558 Mary, Queen of Scots, married the heir to the French throne. However, Scotland had Protestants too, who took up arms to prevent the Auld Alliance reactivating. France sent an army to quash them, England sent another to throw the French out and Scotland's Protestants announced their own Scexit from the European Union in 1560.

Scexit plus Englexit did not add up to Brexit, though, and this apparent diplomatic disaster actually suited Rome rather nicely. Scotland's Protestants were mostly Presbyterians, who believed that ordinary elders, not aristocratic bishops, should run the church. Since England's bishops struck them as being almost as decadent as papists, compromising with Canterbury was very unattractive. Instead, the Presbyterians made an Auld Alliance of their own, linking arms with even more radical types – Baptists, and worse – in Germany and Switzerland. England now had a complete mess in its backyard, almost guaranteed to cause conspiracies and costly wars. Best of all (for Rome), while Scotland's church was emphatically out of the Catholic union, its queen remained in; and if Elizabeth died childless, Mary would have the best claim on her throne. Englexit might yet be reversed, or at least turned into civil war.

Any or all of this might have come to pass, had it not been for Mary herself. The Queen of Scots was just too colourful – and too cursed by bad advisers, bad luck, bad judgement or perhaps all three – to fit into anyone's plans. After an ear infection killed her French husband, she decided to marry her stunningly unsuitable cousin. Seven months later this new husband was involved in murdering – right in front of Mary – the man who, it was widely believed, had already replaced him in her bed. Another seven months after that, the husband was dead too, in an explosion generally blamed on Mary and yet another lover. In quick succession Mary abdicated, married the boyfriend (in a Protestant ceremony) and lost a short civil war with her Protestant subjects. Husband number three now fled, went mad and died. Having made Scotland too hot to hold her, Mary escaped to England and sought Elizabeth's protection – but then tried to talk any French, Spanish or papal agent who would listen into helping her kill Elizabeth and seize the throne. Elizabeth still baulked at executing her own cousin, but her royal advisers did it for her.

Mary's demise left Ireland as the Catholics' last best hope. London's grip there barely extended beyond the Pale, a fortified patch around Dublin which had been established as the zone of English settlement in 1488, and efforts since Henry VIII's day to change that had only made matters worse. When sent the king's greetings in 1528, the

Gaelic lord Brian O'Connor of Offaly reputedly asked 'What king?' Even as Henry was signing the Act of Supremacy in 1534, Irish chiefs were lining up to join Spain and the pope in fighting their shared heretical enemy.

The English response was basically to try to turn Ireland into another Wales, but by appointing himself head of a Protestant Church of Ireland, Henry only drove Catholicism and Irishness together to oppose Protestant Englishness. Henry bribed chiefs to adopt English titles and become his subjects, but they took his money and carried on conspiring. English accounts make sixteenth-century Ireland sound like twenty-first-century Afghanistan: every deal was frustrated by 'treachery and breach of fidelity'. Not even Trinity College, founded in Dublin in 1591, could teach Ireland's elite to feel English.

With persuasion clearly failing, London turned to ethnic cleansing. As early as the 1530s lawyers had floated schemes 'to *plant* young lords and gents out of England' on land confiscated from Irish monasteries, swamping Ireland with immigrants. Not much progress was made until the 1570s, when a poorer class of English Protestants began making 'plantations' in Munster and Ulster, leading to violence shocking even by Ireland's standards. The pope now embraced Catholic resistance and funded a thousand mercenaries to invade Munster, marching under his banner and singing 'The Pope Above'.

Seen from Rome, Ireland's troubles were a godsend, soaking up more English manpower and money than Scotland ever did. But even so, they were hardly driving England back into the fold, and popes began talking to Catholic kings – particularly Spain's – about more forceful resolutions to Englexit. Two developments favoured this. The first was the balance of power. For decades, any time France moved against England, Spain had come to England's aid, and vice versa. But in 1562 French Catholics and Protestants went to war with each other. Three million French lost their lives, paralysing the country for four decades and leaving Spain's King Philip free to move against England if he wanted to.

That 'if' was the second thing that changed. With an empire stretching from Italy to the Philippines (which were named after him), Philip had a lot to juggle. Turkish advances in the Mediterranean, rebellious Italian city-states, aggressive German Protestants and opportunities in America were all usually higher priorities than reversing Englexit. Or at least they were until 1568, when resistance to imperial taxes and religious repression merged in the Spanish-ruled Netherlands into a full-blown Dutch exit. As Philip poured troops in, the conflict became a classic security dilemma: Philip feared that unless he invaded England, Elizabeth would help the Dutch, and Elizabeth feared that unless she helped the Dutch, Philip would crush the Netherlands and then invade England.

The pope pushed Philip to defend the faith; the Dutch asked Elizabeth to be their queen; war seemed inevitable. Horrified by her lack of options, Elizabeth turned to new counsellors, men thinking outside the box – or, more accurately, outside the Hereford Map. England's future, they urged her, was on the high seas. They were a new breed: after Cabot no Englishman had gone back to America until 1528 and none crossed the equator until 1555. Until the 1560s few, if any, had the skills to get to the Caribbean without a Continental pilot. But then, making up for lost time, West Country pirates became slavers, smuggling Africans past Spanish customs officials and selling them into misery in the New World's silver mines. Business was good, yet some – John Hawkins, Francis Drake, Walter Raleigh – could not help wondering why they were wasting time selling the odd boatload of slaves to silver miners when they could be stealing the silver itself.

After being dug up at Potosí in what is now Bolivia, Spanish silver was shipped up the Pacific coast to Panama and then carried on mules across the isthmus to Nombre de Dios, to be loaded on a flotilla to Cádiz. The heavily armed flotillas were tough nuts to crack – only one was ever captured complete, by Dutch pirates in 1628 – so in 1571 Drake landed at Panama to attempt a great (mule) train robbery. After missing the shipment in the dense jungle, he turned bandit, organising runaway slaves into a robber gang. Two years later they pulled off the heist of the century.

In 1577 Drake was back with an even bolder plan, to sail around the bottom of America, enter the Pacific and seize the silver before it even reached Panama. In the end he only caught one ship, and to avoid Spanish patrols had to come home the long way around, crossing the entire Pacific and Indian Oceans and sailing back up the west coast of Africa. But when he reached Plymouth, his loot weighed in at 26 tons of silver, worth about £600,000 – a forty-seven-fold return on his backers' initial investment. With her share, the queen paid off England's entire foreign debt and still had £42,000 left in change.

This, Elizabeth's new advisers insisted, was the way to fight Spain.

The last fragment of the counterscarp had vanished in 1558, when France retook Calais after 212 years of English rule; but that did not matter, said Drake and other navalists, because technology had changed the meaning of geography. Instead of clinging to the edge of the Hereford Map, England now sat in the centre of Mackinder's, astride long, vulnerable sea lanes linking Madrid to its mines. Instead of waging ruinously expensive wars to rebuild a Continental counterscarp, Elizabeth could cut off Spain's silver supply. Plunder would make war pay for itself.

The technology that made this possible was the galleon (Figure 6.5), a bigger and better-armed version of the little caravels which had taken Columbus and Cabot to America in the 1490s. Galleons could do two things for England, said the new naval strategists. First, as Drake showed in the 1570s, they could open the oceans, projecting power all the way to the Americas; and second, as Drake's rival John Hawkins showed, they could also close the Channel. In 1586 Hawkins kept a squadron at sea for three months, blockading Portugal's ports. He insisted he could do the same in the English Channel, preventing Philip from invading England before English attacks on his silver supply broke his power. For thousands of years the only way to stop invasions had been by building a counterscarp on the opposite shore; but now, navalists claimed, ships could actually rule the waves. Insularity could trump proximity. Thatcher's Law could be broken; the English wouldn't have to be part of Europe if they didn't want to.

Elizabeth liked this. Ships were expensive, but counterscarps cost even more. In her very first speech to Parliament she had argued that a good fleet would be 'the strongest wall and defence that can be against the enemies of this island'. Yet the problem remained that, despite heavy spending on shipbuilding, no one knew whether the new strategy would actually work. Bitter debates divided her counsellors, and when Philip of Spain finally attacked, in 1588, Elizabeth hedged her bets. On the one hand, she unleashed Raleigh and Drake to plunder Philip's shipping and singe his beard by descending on his main port at Cádiz; but on the other, she sent 8,000 men to shore up a counterscarp in the Netherlands.

Military historians still argue over which mattered most in 1588, the fleet or the army. Elizabeth's naval preparations certainly paid off: although outnumbered by Spanish ships, the English had more of the fast, well-armed galleons, with bold, experienced crews. Their cannons

Figure 6.5. Beyond the Hereford Map: Sir Francis Drake's high-tech galleons loitering with intent between sea monsters and Santo Domingo (Dominican Republic), New Year's Eve, 1584.

were crude, able to fire only one to one-and-a-half shots per hour, but the Spanish cannons were even cruder, managing just one to one-and-a-half shots per *day*. Not surprisingly, the English had the better of it when the fleets closed, and the Spaniards scattered in disorder.

And yet, more conventional strategists claimed, that was beside the point. To invade England, the Spanish army in Flanders had to get on board the Armada, but that was harder than it sounded. Up-to-date warships had deep hulls, which meant that they needed deep-water ports. There were some excellent ones along the coast between Dunkirk and Antwerp, but thanks in part to the soldiers Elizabeth had sent to the counterscarp, these were in Dutch hands. If the Spanish troops climbed into flat-bottomed barges and rowed out to join the Armada on the open sea, nippy little Dutch caravels would sink them. Philip's admiral could not come into shore; his general could not go out to sea; and so, after much dithering, they called the whole thing off – not because of the fleet but because of the counterscarp.

We will never know whether one, both or neither strategy was decisive. Philip himself blamed his defeat on the English weather, while Parisian bookmakers put it down to disorganisation, offering six-to-one odds against the Armada even reaching the English Channel. Philip's commanders blamed his over-complicated plan, which required them to get through the Channel, defeat England's fleet, rendezvous with the army in Flanders and finally deliver it to London. 'We are sailing against England in the confident hope of a miracle', one senior officer grumbled. Everything had to go right.

Yet even when nothing went right, the battered Armada might still have salvaged something but for Mary, Queen of Scots. Had she held on to her throne until 1588, she could have let the Spaniards in through the back door and perhaps won England's throne for herself. As it was, her son James VI was by 1588 a sound Protestant (not to mention Elizabeth's most plausible heir). With nothing to gain from a Spanish invasion, he bolted the back door firmly. By the time the Armada rounded Cape Wrath and reached Ireland, it was in no condition to invade anyone.

The English struck a medal to commemorate their triumph. In mockery of Philip's pretensions to be the new Caesar, it read *venit, vidit, fugit*: 'He came, he saw, he ran away.'

The Great Rebuilding

The year 1588 was a defining moment for English identity. Regardless of the military historians' arguments over what really happened that summer, the men who fought never doubted that they had saved England from the Antichrist. The Armada entered legend – Drake coolly playing bowls as the galleons sailed by, fireships scattering Spaniards in the night, Elizabeth rousing her troops at Tilbury ('I have the body of a weak, feeble woman, but I have the heart and stomach of a king'). Factual or not, these stories lived on, enshrined in a new kind of English, a language fit for heroes. In their struggle to convey God's Word in ways everyone would understand (even 'a boy that driveth the plough', said William Tyndale of the first great English-language Bible), poets and preachers reinvented the English tongue in the sixteenth century. Bringing a connoisseur's ear and his own touch of magic to the way people talked in the 1530s, Tyndale turned 2,000-year-old Greek and Hebrew texts into ringing, unforgettable

English. 'Let there be light.' 'Blessed are the peacemakers.' 'A stranger in a strange land.' 'Eat, drink and be merry.' 'Let my people go.' All these expressions are Tyndale's. Without him, Winston Churchill and Martin Luther King would have been lost for words.

Where Tyndale blazed the trail, others eagerly followed. The Book of Common Prayer, composed largely by Archbishop Thomas Cranmer in the late 1540s, at first enraged conservatives with its plain style and simple rhythms. Some took up arms against it; kings hazarded crowns to defend it. But who can now imagine anything more English than its reassuring cadences? 'Lighten our darkness, we beseech Thee, O Lord [. . .] defend us from all perils and dangers of this night . . .'

English was changing faster than ever before, and it only stood to reason that a literary language good enough to express God's very essence had other uses too. London's first permanent, public theatre opened in 1576, and over the next thirty years a crowd of geniuses – Christopher Marlowe, Thomas Kyd, Ben Jonson – trained this powerful new weapon on the darkest recesses of the soul. None, though, matched Shakespeare, who not only added 1,700 new words to the English language but also moved men's hearts with little more than monosyllables. 'Once more unto the breach, dear friends, once more', demanded his Henry V, 'Or close up the wall with our English dead . . . Cry "God for Harry, England, and Saint George!"'

The new English language moulded a new English identity, looking back to Agincourt but also out across the oceans. Shakespeare's description of England in 1595 as a 'precious stone, set in the silver sea, / Which serves it in the office of a wall' would have sounded ridiculous even fifty years earlier. But now, secure behind what Shakespeare called their 'moat defensive', the new Englishmen felt empowered to remake the world as they liked it. They would lock the back door by absorbing Scotland and Ireland, break Spain by cutting off its silver and terrorise the Continent with 'descents' upon its coasts, burning and looting. They might even, as Shakespeare hinted in *The Tempest*, draw in the world beyond the Hereford Map.

Everything seemed possible on the stage and on the page. A generation after the Armada, in his treatise *Mare Clausum* (*The Closed Sea*), the lawyer John Selden even tried to give legal force to Shakespeare's rhetoric. 'The King of Great Britain,' he argued, 'is Lord of the Sea flowing about', which gave him the right to exclude others from his waters. But England's rulers, aware what a close call 1588 had been, were not so sure they could enforce any of this and filed *The Closed Sea* away, unpublished.

The technology might exist to close the Channel against rivals, but the organisation needed to raise enough money to apply that technology effectively did not, and no amount of enthusiasm, inspiration or legalese could change that fact. Elizabeth could not afford to pay the sailors who chased off the Armada, never mind pursue the Spaniards to destruction. Efforts in 1589 to exploit the victory came to nothing, because private investors, without whom the fleet could not sail at all, diverted it to more profitable but strategically pointless targets. 'Our half-doing', Elizabeth's spymaster-in-chief lamented, 'doth breed dishonour and leaves the disease uncured.' Philip built a new Armada, bigger than the first, and would have invaded in 1596 had storms not intervened. The next year nature saved the day once more when Spaniards tried to seize Falmouth in Cornwall.

England had successes too, burning Cádiz again, but the hard fact was that the moat defensive would remain unreliable until the crown could organise the kind of fleet it needed. Lacking that, all Elizabeth could do was commit even more troops to the counter-scarp, to keep the Spaniards from the deep-water Flemish ports, and also to Ireland, where the back door flew open in 1595. The Irish lord Hugh O'Neill – 'the Great O'Neill' – marched to the sacred Stone of Tullyhogue (according to tradition, blessed by St Patrick himself), proclaimed himself prince of Ulster and offered an Irish crown to Philip of Spain. In 1599 rebels shattered an English army at Roscommon; in 1600 the pope classified their war against Protestants as a crusade; and in 1601 Spaniards landed at Kinsale. Finally, in 1603, came the catastrophe against which neither moats defensive nor counter-scarps could protect: Elizabeth died childless.

The worst-case scenario, in which the UK descended back into anarchy, did not transpire. In fact, not only did the English welcome Scotland's King James as their ruler but their Continental counter-scarp also held and starvation and violence once again wore down Irish resistance. Certainly, England's position remained tenuous. Rather than turning Ireland into a new Wales, Protestant plantations had made Ulster a source of endless disorder, and James's optimism about blending his separate Anglo-Welsh, Scottish and Irish inherit-ances into a United Kingdom of Great Britain and Ireland proved fanciful. Back in 1560 Elizabeth's adviser William Cecil had urged that 'joining the two kingdoms [of England and Scotland], having also Ireland knit thereto, is a worthy consideration', but when the opportunity arrived, few English or Scots wanted a marriage on equal terms (no one asked the Welsh or Irish). James unilaterally declared himself 'king of Great Britain' and promoted a 'Union Jack' flag combining the symbols of England and Scotland (but not Ireland or Wales), but his efforts, he grumbled, only brought him 'long disputations, strange questions, and nothing done'.

The reason Cecil had thought a United Kingdom of all the Isles so desirable was that Continental kings had 'of late so increased their estates that now they are nothing like what they were, and yet England remains [. . .] without accession of any new force'. French and Spanish kings were finding novel ways to tap their subjects' wealth. From the Atlantic to China populations were at last regaining their pre-Black-Death levels, and farmers were once again clearing forests, draining bogs and squeezing livings out of marginal lands. All this meant that there were more people and resources for kings to tax – but also more people, with more resources at their disposal, to resist royal demands.

As in all earlier boom times, those already rich gained more than the poor, but this time around, three new forces added to the miseries of those at the bottom. One was inflation: wages were rising, but the mountains of silver dug out of the New World meant that prices were rising faster, eroding labourers' purchasing power. Second, the centuries of global cooling which climatologists call the 'Little Ice Age' were shortening growing seasons and reducing yields, wiping out the gains most families had enjoyed after the Black Death. In England torrential rain ruined several harvests in a row in the 1540s, 1550s and especially the 1590s. Prices spiked; the bloody flux carried off thousands; the poorest rioted, then starved.

The third force was perhaps the cruellest. Once upon a time, charity had been a virtue, and clothing and feeding the destitute an obligation. But as the poor and their problems multiplied in the sixteenth century, they developed a serious image problem, morphing in the eyes of the better off from deserving recipients of alms to dangerous agents of disorder. The more authorities told communities to help the needy, the more that duty bred resentment. The weaker the hungry appeared, the more threatening they might be – to the point that accusing poor, socially isolated widows and spinsters of conspiring with the Devil against their more prosperous neighbours started to seem entirely reasonable.

Witchcraft was an old worry, but after millennia of being just background noise it now became an obsession. In the worst years, between 1570 and 1630, Europeans executed perhaps 50,000 witches, 90 per cent of them women (before the 1550s witchcraft had been gender-neutral). In England witchcraft was not defined as a statutory offence until 1542, but by the 1580s more than one-eighth of all criminal defendants in Essex (admittedly, an extreme case) were charged with it. Scotland was even worse. A spectacular mass trial in 1590 so alarmed King James, whose name was on a list of the witches' targets, that he wrote a philosophical treatise *On Demonology*. When Shakespeare looked north of the border for *Macbeth* in 1606, witches around a cauldron struck him as a perfect opening scene.

Even more than usual, rulers from Moscow to Madrid had to fight to keep the unruly masses in their place. Most of the time landed elites – squeezed between royal and rural violence – sided with their kings, surrendering their influence over law- and tax-making in return for state support against the peasantry. After 1614 no French king felt a need to summon the Estates General, the assembly that they supposedly had to consult on taxation, until the revolutionary year of 1789. Theorists in Madrid and Paris increasingly agreed that God had given His kings absolute sovereignty, requiring no subject's consent.

In England, however, Parliament and men of property proved less pliable. New ideas about English identity, which made resisting royal greed look like a badge of Protestant honour, had a lot to do with this, and I will return to them in the next section; but new kinds of prosperity were perhaps even more important. Population growth, inflation and climate change might be driving the poor into increasing desperation, but many among England's 'middling sorts' (no one yet talked of 'middle classes') were prospering mightily from a new Atlantic economy and felt no need to knuckle under to royal pressure.

The original Atlantic economy, built by Spain and Portugal since 1492, had focused on extraction. Iberians were parasites, sucking wealth out of the Americas. The English, lower down the food chain, were parasites on the parasites, sucking wealth out of the Iberians by stealing their silver. By 1607 English adventurers felt ready to become parasites in their own right, founding James Fort (renamed Jamestown in 1619) to plunder Virginia's gold and spices. Virginia being noticeably short of both commodities, this went horribly wrong. Hunger and disease killed four-fifths of the would-be parasites during the winter of 1609–10.

James Fort might have ended then and there, had a new economic system not come to its rescue. Where the old Atlantic economy was all about stealing things in America and carrying them off to Europe, Virginia's new economy was about producing things better and cheaper than Europe could, and trading them. It began with a ship-wreck on the distant shores of Bermuda (the very disaster, in fact, immortalised by Shakespeare in the opening scene of *The Tempest*). While awaiting rescue, one survivor (John Rolfe, best known today for marrying Pocahontas, the daughter of a Native American chief) filled his pockets with seeds of local sweet tobacco. Columbus had seen Americans smoking in 1492, and although no English writer mentions the habit until 1565, by Rolfe's time it was all the rage among fashionable Londoners. Efforts to grow tobacco in England had failed, and the version that grew in Virginia tasted bad; so, Rolfe reasoned, why not steal Bermudan tobacco, plant it in Virginia and sell it in the home market?

It was an inspired piece of industrial espionage. Rolfe's first ship-ment reached England in 1614. It fetched just 3 shillings per pound, compared with 18 for proper Spanish weed, but his profits were still good. Soon everyone was copying him, and Jamestown became the latest Boomtown. Its population jumped from 104 in 1607 to 1,300 in 1625, 8,000 in 1640 and a whopping 25,000 in 1660, making it one of the biggest English towns anywhere. Mortality remained sky high and conditions miserable, but Englishmen flocked to Virginia anyway, gambling on getting rich before getting sick and dying. The bet paid off often enough for Englishmen to try it elsewhere in the Americas; and if they failed, they simply planted other crops. Settlers on Barba-dos began planting sugar cane in 1640. Sugar was already growing, and well, on Mediterranean islands, but it was perfect for the Carib-bean and soon proved even more profitable than tobacco.

The first American plantations looked rather like the ones recently created in Ulster, worked by indentured and mostly Irish labourers. Seeking a double dividend, English authorities in fact tried to rid the Isles of their alarming population of paupers by dumping them in America. However, planters quickly found a cheaper alter-native: African slaves. 'If we have no Negroes,' the magnificently

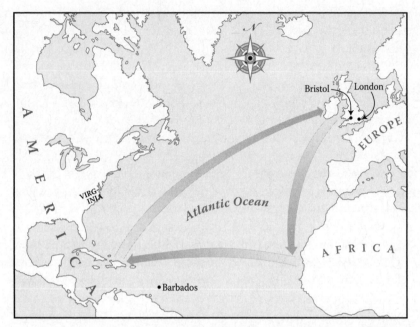

Figure 6.6. Triangular trades: the new Atlantic economy takes off.

named Malachy Postlethwayt observed in the eighteenth century, 'we can have no Sugars, Tobaccoes, Rice, Rum, etc. [. . .] it would be as impertinent to take up your Time in expatiating on that Subject as in declaiming on the common benefits of Air and Sun-shine.' In 1644 there were just 800 Africans on Barbados and 30,000 Europeans; by 1700 only 15,000 Europeans remained, but they owned 50,000 Africans.

In all, some 12 million Africans would be kidnapped and shipped across the Atlantic. Roughly one in eight died on the voyage, and another 4 million perished before even getting on board. This obscenity was the capstone in what historians call the 'triangular trades' (Figure 6.6), a moneymaking machine unlike anything seen before. By 1650 a merchant starting off in Bristol with a boatload of British manufactured goods – beads, blankets, guns – could sail to West Africa and swap his goods (at a profit) for humans. Sailing next to Virginia or Barbados, he could swap his Africans (profiting again) for tobacco or sugar; then, returning to Bristol, he could sell his New World drugs, buy more beads, blankets and guns, and – after netting a third profit – start the whole cycle again.

Godly Englishmen saw so few inconsistencies between their free-born, Protestant identity and trading in human misery that Puritans (as hardcore Protestants were now known) became prominent in the new Atlantic economy. These prosperous, self-righteous men proved infuriatingly hard for King James to intimidate, and, because their tobacco plants and sugar cane were scattered across thousands of farms and plantations rather than concentrated in one place (like the Spanish mines at Potosí), simply expropriating them was not an option either.

At first, James reacted by opposing tobacco completely. He tasked his governors in Virginia with talking growers out of planting it, and took time off from obsessing over witches to pen another book, *A Counterblast to Tobacco*. This weed, he insisted, was a 'filthy novelty [. . .] loathsome to the eye, hateful to the Nose, harmful to the brain, dangerous to the Lungs'. He had a point; but, as it became clear how lucrative the tobacco trade was, he gradually dropped his war on drugs in return for a cut of the profits. By the 1660s, one shilling in every pound of royal revenue came from tobacco.

Virginia planters got rich, and the Englishmen who organised the interlocking triangular trades got very rich indeed. Some, such as Edward Colston, a slaver whose statue was toppled into the River Avon by Black Lives Matter protesters in 2020, were based in Bristol, but overwhelmingly the new plutocrats lived in London. The city had 60,000 residents (the same number as before the Black Death) when Elizabeth took the throne in 1558, but 200,000 when James succeeded her in 1603 and an astonishing half a million in 1640. Its needs transformed much of England. Newcastle upon Tyne, for instance, turned into a major city in its own right by selling Londoners 100,000 tons of coal each year, and even in the countryside families able to connect to the new markets prospered by selling food and textiles to hungry and cold urbanites.

For most of the previous 7,500 years the Isles had been Europe's poor cousin, but the new Atlantic economy gave their geography (and that of the Netherlands, the other main participant in the triangular trades) new, and more prosperous, meanings. England's poor regularly knew hunger in the seventeenth century, but while Scots, Irish and Europeans other than the Dutch still had starving times ahead of them, England has (so far) suffered no further famines since 1597. English middling sorts in fact prospered so much that average incomes actually rose from the equivalent of about $2 per day in 1500 (roughly where they had been in Roman times) to $2.75 per day in 1600 and $3.60 by 1700.

We see the consequences very clearly in the archaeology. The great and the good rarely deigned to write about husbandmen's home renovation projects, but archaeologists speak of a 'Great Rebuilding' between 1580 and 1640, spreading from south-east to north and west. In tens of thousands of houses up and down the land, remodellers added upper floors to what had been cathedral-ceilinged single-storeyed halls, typically creating a living room and parlour downstairs and bedrooms upstairs. They added staircases (novelties at the time) and chimneys, porches and entryways, and they plastered walls and ceilings. William Hoskins, the archaeologist who identified the Great Rebuilding seventy years ago, concluded that houses became 'warmer, lighter, and larger: more fireplaces, windows glazed for the first time, more rooms and more differentiation between them'. Some were so well built that they still stand in their half-timbered glory (Figure 6.7). Nor were the changes just architectural; after 1570, Hoskins observed, 'there is more of everything and better of everything, and new-fangled comforts (like cushions and hangings) as well'.

As just one example among many, we might take Cowlam, a Yorkshire village partly excavated in 1971–2. Its name sounds Scandinavian, and Norman records say a lord lived there in the 1080s, but the oldest excavated houses date to around 1200. They were flimsy things, leaving merely rubbish pits and a few post-holes in the ground. No house plans could be reconstructed, and only a dozen or so pottery fragments were found. The fourteenth or fifteenth century, however, saw three sturdier, bigger houses built from wood or chalk blocks. Each was single-roomed, covering about 50 m^2; at least one had leaded-glass windows. The household finds, while still meagre, included a comb and knife handle carved from bone.

The Great Rebuilding then transformed Cowlam. A new farmstead and outbuildings were built over the earlier houses in the sixteenth century. The farm, twice as big as its predecessors, had two glazed windows and a central hearth and oven. Its seventeenth-century occupants left behind dozens of broken objects, including iron knives, hinges, scissors, scythes, a key, a cowbell and an ox-shoe, plus bronze and pewter spoons, a piece of a glass wine bottle and – something entirely new – nine pieces of clay tobacco pipes. The soil above the

Figure 6.7. Still standing after all this time: The Old
House in Hereford High Town, defying weather
and developers for four centuries.

buildings contained thousands more potsherds, some imported; one
was perhaps a urinal. More of everything and better of everything,
and newfangled comforts as well. Traces of this abundance trickled
down the social spectrum even as far as wretched hamlets like West
Whelpington in Northumberland, where the seventeenth-century
houses were tiny, covering less than 25 m²; but several nevertheless
had window glass and – like almost every archaeological site of the
seventeenth century – smokers' clay pipes.

The phrase 'An Englishman's home is his castle' seems to go
back to 1581, just as the Great Rebuilding was getting going, and was
enshrined in common law in 1628, as it was hitting its peak. Modern
Britons' image of themselves, as sturdy, sensible, self-sufficient people
in sturdy, sensible, self-sufficient houses, was born in these years. To
John Houghton, writing in 1677, it was obvious where the idea came
from. Because 'We have the most part of the trade of the World',
he rejoiced, 'many of our poor Cottagers['] children be turned Merchants and substantial Traders [. . .] our houses be built like Palaces,
over what they were in the last Age'.

New Jerusalem

King James's biggest problem was how to tap into this burgeoning wealth, but the solution his subjects favoured was: don't. Englexit had fed a new conceit that God was sending prosperity to the English because He had singled them out as a uniquely virtuous people. The kings He had set over such subjects therefore needed neither standing armies to police them nor palaces like Versailles or El Escorial to overawe them, and therefore had little need to tax them. Big, tax-and-spend governments were symptoms of popish decadence. Prosperity and identity combined to keep sovereignty decentralised.

This equation was hardly calculated to appeal to monarchs. What rendered it unworkable was the fact that diffuse sovereignty undermined security. As well as expecting kings to live within their means, Puritans also insisted that God wanted Protestant monarchs to stand up to the wicked Catholic European Union. Kings therefore needed soldiers and ships – which required big government and high taxes. A king who pleased God by resisting Rome must simultaneously displease Him by taxing his subjects; one who pleased Him by lowering taxes must simultaneously displease Him by cosying up to the Catholics.

As early as 1560, Queen Elizabeth's lord chancellor warned that her only viable path lay 'betwixt the Pope and the puritans', but as Protestant identities hardened, the path grew steadily narrower. Straying off it in Rome's direction might buttress security and prosperity but would dilute sovereignty and clash with the increasingly anti-Catholic identities of people who had grown up on the Armada legend, and that could prove fatal. Straying too far away from Rome and fighting popery on every front, by contrast, might energise Englishness and solidify sovereignty but threatened security and prosperity – which could also prove fatal.

Staying on course would have challenged any statesman, but James did himself no favours. His fondness for Continental luxury was all too obvious. He imitated Europe's elegant court cultures, built lavish Italianate palaces and hosted glorious masked balls. He also gave till it hurt, enriching handsome young 'favourites' beyond all measure. Money ran through his fingers like water, and his circle's 'prodigality and vanity of apparel, superfluity in banqueting and delicate cheer, deflowering of dames and virgins and other fruits of the French court' shocked staid Elizabethans.

James paid for this prodigality by cutting spending elsewhere. He ended Elizabeth's war with Spain, pardoned Irish rebels and left the fleet to rot. Fifteen years into his reign an inquiry found that only twenty-two of the forty-three warships on the books were seaworthy. Barbary pirates, operating from North Africa, regularly raided Cornwall, carrying 7,000 English off into slavery. Industrious, God-fearing taxpayers could be forgiven for wondering about James's priorities.

Yet when James finally strayed off the path, it wasn't entirely his fault. In an effort to soothe Protestant opinion he had married his daughter off to Frederick, ruler of a stretch of the Rhineland called the Palatinate. This was a popular move: Frederick was robustly Protestant, and the Palatinate also covered the flank of England's counterscarp in the Low Countries. But Frederick was ambitious, and in 1619 Protestants in Bohemia (roughly the modern Czech Republic) asked him to become their king.

James begged him to decline. Bohemia's Protestants were in revolt against their Catholic overlords, Austria's Habsburg dynasty, and as Bohemia's king, Frederick would immediately be at war not just with the Austrian Habsburgs but also with their kin in Spain. James knew that England's Protestants would expect him to fight for this godly cause and his son-in-law's new crown, but doubted that they would trust him with enough money to do the job properly. Ignoring James's advice, Frederick accepted Bohemia's crown, and events went just as badly as James had predicted. Catholic armies overran Bohemia and the Palatinate. 'Tears, sighs and loud expressions of wrath are seen and heard in every direction', Venice's ambassador to London recorded. It was a judgement, Puritans were saying, on James's lack of godliness. Popery was about to triumph, the Antichrist's arrival was imminent and the only hope was to build a morally pure New Jerusalem right now.

Puritans had two main ideas about how to do this. The first was to abandon England altogether and raise a city upon a hill in a New England across the ocean, but this seemed so risky that it found few takers. When the Pilgrim Fathers set sail on the *Mayflower* in 1620, most of the ship's 102 passengers were actually conventional economic migrants, fleeing crop failures, debt and disease, not religious refugees. According to the Puritan minister Cotton Mather, when one preacher in Maine told his congregation that 'the main end of planting this Wilderness [was] to approve themselves a religious people', he was sternly rebuked by a parishioner: 'Sir, You are mistaken [. . .] our main End was to catch Fish.' The original plan had in fact been to follow earlier economic migrants to Virginia, but storms drove the *Mayflower* ashore much further north. Unprepared for a New England winter, half of those who disembarked were dead within four months. The others survived only because Wampanoag tribesmen fed them and taught them to fish and farm.

The settlement's numbers stabilised, but its mission from God remained secondary until a larger group of Puritans arrived in 1630. Over the next decade 20,000 more arrived (although twice as many chose to go to Virginia and grow tobacco). British mobility had entered a new phase. For the next 350 years – until, in fact, 1987, the year I shipped out for America myself – emigrants from the Isles normally outnumbered immigrants into them, creating one of the biggest gene flows in history.

A second idea was to build a New Jerusalem in England itself. This was much more popular, convincing James that Europe's Catholics were much less threatening than home-grown Puritans. If he could marry his son Charles to a Spanish princess, he decided, the dowry he would extract might include not just enough cash to clear his debts but also the lands his son-in-law had lost in Bohemia and the Palatinate. It was consequently a disaster when negotiations stalled in 1623, but worse soon followed. In an episode much stranger than fiction, Charles, disguised in a false beard, took off for Spain to woo the lady in person, with only his boyfriend the Duke of Buckingham (who had previously been his father's lover) for company. What could go wrong did, culminating in Buckingham being caught in Charles's bedroom without his trousers.

Unsurprisingly, the mission failed. Charles, humiliated, abandoned his father's policies and accepted Parliament's demand for war on Spain, although the MPs, suspecting that Charles's judgement was no better than his father's, voted inadequate funds for it. As if trying to confirm their doubts, Charles abruptly married a French princess, hoping to use her dowry to pay his campaigning costs. This Catholic match appalled Parliament, and the dowry of course never materialised. Charles attacked Spain anyway, and then France too. Both wars were disasters, leaving Charles, says the historian Brendan Simms, looking 'strategically incompetent at best and malevolent at worst'. 'Our honour is ruined, our ships are sunk, our men perished,' a former royalist told Parliament, 'not by the sword, not by chance but [. . .] by those we trust.'

The bitter arguments over identity, mobility, prosperity, security and sovereignty merely masked a deeper debate over the meaning of geography – which remained, as ever, the thing least spoken of. On one side were men who took to calling themselves a 'Country' faction. Assuming that England's main strategic problem remained its proximity to Europe, they identified the pope as public enemy number one and strongly opposed royal policies. However threatening the Puritans might look, they insisted, Catholics were worse (think Bloody Mary). Anglicans must therefore make common cause against popery with Scottish Presbyterians and Dutch Calvinists; Ireland's Catholics must be crushed; and France and Spain must be fought. England's safety required a counterscarp, but the cost could be kept down by stealing Spanish silver. 'Cutting the Liver vein that supplies the body of Spain with such immense sums of money', leading merchants assured Charles, 'will humble them and give a general Peace and security so much longed for to all Christendom.' Emigration was therefore good, because it provided New World bases for intercepting Spanish ships as well as profits from sugar and tobacco (not coincidentally, the Country faction's leaders were often active in Atlantic trade). With taxes low, government lean and the church reformed, Jerusalem could be built at home.

The Country faction was opposed on almost every point by a rival 'Court' party. Assuming that insularity now trumped proximity, they argued that the real danger lay within. Home-grown Puritans were obviously worse than Catholics, so the king must curb the former in England, Wales and Scotland while making deals with the latter in Ireland. The world had changed since Elizabeth's day: France and Spain would not now invade, so England should make peace and forget about counterscarps. In fact, the counterscarp was itself now a threat, because Dutch merchants, despite being Protestants, were encroaching on England's trade. A friendly European Union could help England contain them, and softer identity politics would bring more security, prosperity and sovereignty. With peace on the Continent and money rolling in, Charles himself could live like a European king, ruling without having to ask his troublesome Parliament for money.

Charles greatly preferred the Court faction's theory, and for a while it worked. Good weather (and therefore harvests) helped, but he also hired clever lawyers and accountants, who doubled his income without asking Parliament for a penny. Charles built fast little frigates to chase Barbary pirates back to the Mediterranean and a huge, 100-gun flagship, the *Sovereign of the Seas*, to intimidate the Dutch. Income from taxes and trade tripled; Charles cleared his debts and had enough left over to fill his palaces with Continental paintings. 'I have never seen anything', the Dutch artist Rubens admitted, like 'the excellent pictures, statues and ancient inscriptions which are to be found in this court'.

Emboldened, Charles set his attack dog of an archbishop of Canterbury on the Puritans. Killjoys who complained about female actresses (Charles's French wife was a keen thespian) and public dancing (something else she enjoyed) were tried before a secret court, which sentenced even high-born Puritans to branding, lopping-off of ears and exposure in the stocks. Charles even decided that Scotland's undisciplined Presbyterians should renounce their spontaneous entreaties to God and submit to a proper prayer book, like England's.

Here his luck ran out. After correcting the prayer book's page proofs, a frugal royal printer recycled the paper, selling it to tobacconists to wrap Virginia leaf in. Soon every household in Edinburgh knew what Charles intended, and when the dean of St Giles' Cathedral rolled out the new rites, Puritans were ready. On cue, a hail of abuse, sticks, stones and stools drove the startled divine from his pulpit (Figure 6.8). Pledging to defend the 'true religion, liberties and laws of the kingdom *against all sorts of persons whatsoever*', Presbyterians proclaimed their own New Jerusalem.

Sending in troops only made matters worse for, despite his creative financing, Charles could not afford war. His underfunded army melted away before Scottish militias. Desperate, Charles begged Spain for a £300,000 bailout. When it fell through, he asked Parliament for money instead. But Parliament ignored him, unilaterally declaring peace with Scotland, impeaching his too-clever-by-half advisers and repealing his financial ploys. When Charles argued, MPs waged a media war, putting their case to the country in news-sheets sold in London taverns (like so much in this period, it is hard not to see parallels with the 2010s). 'Parliament is far too nimble for the king in printing', one of his supporters lamented. 'The common people believe the first story which takes impression in their minds.' Soon a mob of 15,000

Figure 6.8. Holy rollers: sticks, stones and stools rout
the dean of Edinburgh and end King Charles's hopes
of softening both Englexit and Scexit, 1637.

was demanding the execution of Charles's current favourite and half a million Englishmen signed petitions condemning royal misrule.

According to legend, it was Charles's French wife who roused him to attack his own Parliament. 'Go, you coward', she is supposed to have shouted. 'Pull those rogues out by the ears, or never see my face more.' One of the queen's ladies betrayed him before he even reached Westminster, and magistrates raised the militia against him. Charles – 'like to have been torn in pieces by the citizens', said one observer – fled to Windsor, then York. The New Jerusalem's birth pangs had begun.

Nasty and Brutish

They were painful. By 1651 violence, starvation and disease had carried off one in thirty of the English and Welsh (more than in either World War), one in fifty Scots and an appalling one in six Irish. Once fighting began, no one knew how to end it. 'If we beat the king ninety-nine times,' the Earl of Manchester conceded, 'yet he is king still, but if the king beat us once we shall be all hanged.' Yet it was also true that the king could hang his critics ninety-nine times over and Parliament would be Parliament still, and could not be forced to approve his taxes. Violence tore open every seam in the Isles without providing resolution. Whitehall broke with Westminster, south-east with north-west, city with country, high church with low. Towns, villages, families and even individual consciences split down the middle.

The struggle lurched in confusing directions. When Charles failed to check risings of Presbyterians in Scotland and Catholics in Ireland, Scots invaded both England and Ireland, Irish invaded Scotland and the English made war on each other. When his English subjects destroyed his armies, Charles asked Irish Catholics to attack England to save him. They wouldn't, so he fled to Scotland's Presbyterians, who sold him out, handing him back to England's Presbyterians. They, rather than deposing him, decided to restore him to power. Outraged that these 'Scottified' dealings were undoing its battlefield gains, the English Parliament's army went rogue, kidnapping Charles and marching on London. Radicals in the ranks, calling themselves Levellers, Diggers and Ranters, embraced communism and democracy and demanded New Jerusalem now. Charles, unfazed, carried on conspiring. He launched and lost a second civil war, whereupon General Oliver Cromwell mounted a military coup against king, Parliament and radicals. He purged MPs until only a rump remained, of men more or less willing to follow the army's orders. One of the first was that, if Charles would not do as he was told, Parliament should chop his head off – which, in January 1649, it did.

Decapitating a king broke God's law, but it also cut the Gordian knot entangling English sovereignty. Far from disintegrating into anarchy, England's government turned in the 1650s into what the philosopher Thomas Hobbes – who lived through the bloodshed – called *Leviathan*. What Hobbes meant by this was a ruler as terrifying as the Godzilla-like monster Leviathan in the Bible. 'On earth there is nothing like him', says Job in the King James Version; 'He beholds every high *thing*; he *is* king over all the children of pride.' Without a Leviathan-like state enforcing laws, Hobbes believed, there could only be 'continual fear, and danger of violent death; and the life of man, solitary, poor, nasty, brutish, and short'. Making England great meant having a Leviathan strong enough to scare its people straight, bullying them into pulling together to get things done.

Without Charles around to dispute sovereignty, Parliament turned itself into such a creature, raising its own taxes to pay for armies that could defend the hardest possible Englexit. The new burdens it imposed provoked outrage, not least because they were so like the ones Charles had imposed – and Parliament had opposed – in the 1630s. Some protesters, such as the Leveller William Walwyn, saw merely 'a pulling down of one Tyrant, to set up another, and instead of Liberty, heaping on ourselves a greater slavery than that we fought against'. But now that Parliament was embracing taxation, resistance remained disorganised and Leviathan reached deeper into people's pockets.

Some of the money went to pay for a properly professional army, which chased Charles's dashing but undisciplined cavaliers off the battlefield. Most of the cash, however, went to build magnificent modern galleons. At this point technology and organisation converged. Queen Elizabeth, lacking a Leviathan able to fund fleets for extended periods of service, had needed a lot of luck to close the Channel in 1588. By 1650, though, Cromwell had the income such a fleet required. Leviathan was beginning to be able to break Thatcher's Law at will. So long as there was money, insularity really could trump proximity, making imbalances, counterscarps and back doors irrelevant. England's leaders faced a novel question: secure behind a true moat defensive, what should they do next?

Cromwell felt strongly that settling scores with the Celts came first. He invaded Ireland within months of Charles's death, surpassing even the bloody standards of earlier English conquerors. One massacre at Drogheda left 3,500 dead, including the rebels' (English) commander, beaten to death with his own wooden leg. Catholics were chased off Ireland's best land and 10,000 were sold as slaves in the Caribbean. The population shrank by 200,000. Reading the runes, Scottish churchmen asked Charles's son – also a Charles – to return from hiding in France and proclaim a Presbyterian United Kingdom, but Cromwell struck first. He killed or captured 13,000 Scots in 1650 while losing just twenty of his own troops, then annihilated a second Scottish force a year to the day later. The younger Charles only escaped by putting on a dress and hiding in a tree (pubs beyond count and several warships have been named Royal Oak in its honour).

After the Celts, Cromwell assured Parliament, 'your great Enemy is the Spaniard'. In 1655, reviving Drake's strategy, he launched a 'Western Design' to seize Hispaniola (modern Haiti and the Dominican Republic) as a base for intercepting the Spanish silver fleet. In this it failed, but it did seize Jamaica and captured or sank ships in not one but two silver fleets. Cromwell followed up by sending an army back to the counterscarp in the Low Countries, and in 1659 – 101 years after losing its last Continental toehold at Calais – England annexed Dunkirk.

Cromwell, we might say, had won Elizabeth's wars. But that was the problem. His vision remained sixteenth-century, even though what would have counted as victory in the 1550s no longer did so in the 1650s. The stage had changed too much, and the actors had taken on new roles. Defaults and defeats had broken Spain, while the Protestant Dutch had evolved from being part of England's counterscarp to being challengers in their own right. While the English had been fighting each other, Dutch merchants had – in one political lobbyist's words – 'la[id] a foundation to themselves for engrossing the Universal Trade, not only of Christendom, but indeed, of the greater part of the known world'. Reluctant to concede that Protestants could be bigger threats than Catholics, Cromwell tried to neuter Dutch competition with protectionist laws and even proposed merging England and the Netherlands (in effect, a hostile takeover bid). But in the end he had to fight – and win – history's first all-naval war against them.

The longer the fighting continued, the more the grandees around Cromwell realised that the great man's domestic and foreign policies were outdated. Domestically, people were tired of taxes and New Jerusalems. Cromwell's wars had run up a £2 million debt, and his efforts to suppress 'drunkenness, swearing, profaning the Lord's day, and other wickednesses' at sword-point had been disastrous. But lessons had been learned. If the 1620s–30s had showed that kings could not rule like Leviathans without Parliamentary support, the 1640s–50s showed that Parliaments could not act as Leviathans without the legitimacy of an anointed king. Cromwell flatly rejected the obvious solution, of anointing himself as King Oliver, but the minute he was dead, discussions began about bringing back a monarch to lead a royal (but better-behaved) Leviathan. The only plausible candidate was the exiled son of the decapitated Charles I; so, with shockingly little fuss, Charles II rode back into London in 1660 and reinstated the Stuart dynasty. Fireworks, fountains flowing with wine and the street party of the century greeted him. Theatres reopened, maypoles were danced around and fun became fashionable again.

In foreign policy two points now seemed clear: first, that 'the undoubted Interest of England is Trade'; and second, that 'without a powerful Navy, we should be a Prey to our Neighbours, and without

Trade, we could neither have Sea-Men nor Ships'. Charles responded by tightening Cromwell's economic protectionism and building ships that could carry 100-plus cannons. His brother James, who gave more thought than anyone before him to running a commercial empire, strengthened colonial governors, supported land grabs (including seizing New York from the Dutch) and promoted men like Samuel Pepys – diarist, man about town and administrative genius – to rationalise the navy. By 1680 English merchantmen outnumbered Dutch, one-third of the crown's revenue came from charges on international trade and 300,000 English colonists occupied the American coast from Maine to the Carolinas.

Charles's vision was more global than Cromwell's but still saw the world more in terms of the Hereford Map than Mackinder's. And perhaps rightly so: given the continuing absence of a counterscarp and doubts over whether Parliament would fund enough ships to close the Channel, treating colonies and commerce not as ends in themselves but as means to fund action on a European stage made a lot of sense. Spain might be weakened, but the Dutch remained threats and France's dynamic new king Louis XIV was raising a Leviathan even more effective than England's. ''Tis incredible the money he hath, and is bestowing in making harbours', the Earl of Shaftesbury marvelled. Louis 'is grown the most potent of us all at sea'.

Puritans were convinced that Louis would build enough ships to reopen the Channel, invade England and restore popery, so, fearing his own subjects as much as the French (or Dutch), Charles built too. Costs exploded. Each modern ship of the line consumed 3,000 oak trees and the labour of 100 craftsmen, working twelve-hour shifts for eight months at a time. The royal docks became England's biggest employer. Even in peacetime the fleet ate up two-thirds of Charles's revenue, and yet, Pepys complained, 'The want of money [still] puts all things, and above all things the Navy, out of order'. No matter how much Leviathan raised, it was never enough. In 1667 England's unpaid sailors went on strike (literally so, striking sail so their ships could not move till they got their wages). The Dutch sailed into Chatham and torched the king's dockyards.

Like his father and grandfather before him, Charles was caught between the Scylla of wars he couldn't afford and the Charybdis of cosying up to Continental kings. His subjects mostly preferred Scylla, but, like his father, he steered for Charybdis anyway. 'The French [are]

Figure 6.9. Dedicated follower of fashion: Charles II models the
latest Parisian look, resplendent from periwig to shoes (probably
painted in 1670, the year he sold England out to France).

indeed generally hated to the devil by all English except the King',
one ambassador noted. In fact, critics said, Charles was 'altogether
Frenchyfied'. Everyone in court circles ate French food, drank French
wine, listened to French music and wore French clothes, including
the enormous new periwigs (Figure 6.9). But Charles, who had
grown up in exile in Paris, seemed more seduced than anyone by
France's sophistication. He shared his French-made bed with French
mistresses, at least one of them on Louis's payroll. His wife, though
Portuguese, was widely considered 'an adopted daughter of France'.
'A colony of French possess the court', one poet complained. 'Pimps,
priests, buffoons [. . .] fairy-like the King they steal away.'

This was not just xenophobia talking. Charles really did sell
England out. In return for a hefty subsidy of £342,000 per year he
secretly agreed in 1670 not only to join Louis in war against the
Dutch but also to rejoin the Catholic European Union – if necessary,
using French troops to ram popery down his own people's throats.

Historians often wonder whether Charles was just saying whatever it took to get Louis's gold, but his brother James was certainly serious. Rather than just leaning towards the Catholics, James actually became one; and since Charles had no legitimate heir (despite fathering fourteen bastards), this meant that England would soon have a Catholic king.

Relations with the Catholic European Union could still split the nation, but not in quite the same ways as before. The sort of men who would have joined the Country faction in the 1620s had now been rebranded as 'Whigs' (originally a term of abuse for extreme Scottish Presbyterians) – radicals determined to defend English Protestant identity even at the cost of overruling James's divine right to the throne. Whigs tended to be relaxed about non-Anglican Protestants and ready to live with (and often get rich serving) a strong Leviathan. Meanwhile, the old Court types had become 'Tories' (an equally insulting nickname for Irish Catholic bandits), insisting that God-given sovereignty overruled Protestant identity and that whatever the Lord gave – even a Catholic king – only the Lord could take away. Tories tended to identify strongly with the Anglican church, worrying more about non-Anglican Protestants and the threats Leviathan posed to their liberties than about the handful of Catholics left in England.

A century earlier, it would have been bizarre for committed Anglicans to be willing to tolerate a Catholic king, but by the 1670s, although James's conversion was the thing most spoken of, the argument was no longer really about Rome. A century of religious wars had killed almost everyone's enthusiasm for New Jerusalems, and the agreement that had ended thirty years of savage fighting in Germany – that each sovereign should decide his nation's religious identity, without outside interference – was proving widely popular. Louis neither expected nor particularly wanted James to share sovereignty with Rome; converting England was attractive only because it would leave James dependent on France. Rome's thousand-year-old European Union was ceasing to matter much in kings' calculations, even when they professed to be its servants. The pope himself complained that 'the French King makes not [. . .] war upon the account of religion, but only to tyrannise over his neighbours'.

The Whig–Tory confrontation was less about transubstantiation or the Eucharist than about attitudes to Englishness, Europe,

Leviathan and tradition, although this did nothing to lower the temperature. Rivals slandered, bankrupted, beat and murdered each other with extraordinary abandon. 'There were a hundred thousand men ready to rise in arms against Popery', the historian Hugh Trevor-Roper once observed, 'without knowing whether Popery were a man or a horse.' Reasonable men predicted imminent civil war, 'just as if the old Game was playing over'.

Fortunately, Charles II was a better politician than Charles I. When Whigs in Parliament allowed press censorship to lapse, freeing newspapers to abuse James, Charles did not fall into the trap of trying to muzzle the media. Instead, he hired hacks of his own. "Tis the press that has made 'em mad and the press must set 'em straight again', the royalist scribbler Roger L'Estrange advised. Tory newspapers began their long tradition of hiring the sharpest pens of the day – men like John Dryden – to get their points across.

Charles also undercut Whig anxieties by marrying off Mary, James's solidly Protestant daughter by his first wife, to the even solider Dutch Protestant William of Orange. James had a young (Catholic) second wife, but since she had produced no sons, Mary remained next in line after her father. Uniting her with the virulently anti-French leader of the Dutch war against Louis XIV was pure genius. William even had his own claim to the throne: as Charles's nephew, he was fourth in line, behind James, Mary and her younger sister, Anne. The country rejoiced.

Finally, Charles split Whig opposition by accusing zealots of seeking a veto over God's will (roughly equivalent to accusing a politician in the late 2010s of opposing the people's will). Not wanting to be tarred with this brush, most moderates agreed to hold their noses, hoping that a Catholic king, especially one with a Protestant heiress, could be managed. Even if he couldn't, they hoped, his rule would surely be less terrible than playing the old game over.

King over All the Children of Pride

Tories soon had second thoughts. Almost as soon as Charles died and James assumed the throne in 1685, the new king revealed a shockingly poor grasp of political realities. Acting more like his clumsy father than his sly brother, he appointed unpopular Catholics to top jobs (especially in Ireland) and invited a papal ambassador to his court. His supporters insisted they could live with this, but even they panicked when a baby arrived in his popish wife's belly and emerged, in June 1688, as a boy. Four of their ringleaders, fearing that a Catholic dynasty might overturn the delicate deal keeping England's peace, joined three top Whigs in begging William of Orange to do something.

William needed no encouragement. He was already waging a covert press campaign to swing English opinion against France, and anticipated that a coup would increase the pressure on James to co-operate. So, mobilising Dutch money, he hired a force four times larger than the Spanish Armada. He also had the luck of the devil: while English admirals argued about whether to fight for their Catholic king, a 'Protestant Wind' penned their ships in port, leaving the Channel open. Rushing across, William marched on London, insisting he was only there to defend English liberties. James's men started melting away. When even his daughter Anne joined her sister and brother-in-law's side, James melted away too.

No one had expected James's regime to implode so suddenly. Quickly caucusing, Parliamentary powerbrokers announced that James had abdicated (he hadn't) and that his nephew and daughter would jointly and smoothly succeed him (they were usurpers, installed by a foreign army). So began the series of shady back-room deals that Whigs celebrated as the Glorious Revolution.

William wanted one big thing, that England should step forth on the European stage, joining Austria, Spain and the Netherlands in a Grand Alliance to defend the counterscarp and pen Louis XIV within France's borders. This would require an English Continental commitment on a scale not seen since Henry VIII, or perhaps Henry V. To obtain this, William and Mary conceded the one big thing Whigs in Parliament wanted: a Bill of Rights surrendering the throne's 'power of suspending the laws or the execution of laws by regal authority without consent of Parliament' and of 'levying money for or to the use of the Crown without grant of Parliament'.

The experiences of the 1660s–70s had clarified the lessons of the 1620s–30s (that kings could not run Leviathans without Parliaments) and 1640s–50s (that parliaments could not run Leviathans without kings). What was needed was a hybrid Leviathan, 'the Crown in Parliament'. Parliament would make the decisions, but monarchs remained heads of state, with 'royal prerogative' – something which, a Parliamentary Select Committee conceded as recently as 2004,

Figure 6.10. The closed sea: English and Dutch fleets fight
the French to a standstill at La Hogue in 1692.

remains 'a notoriously difficult concept to define adequately'. In principle, royal prerogative means that MPs' decisions only become law
when the monarch says so; in practice, we have yet to learn what
happens if a monarch refuses, although Mike Bartlett's bewitching
2014 play *King Charles III* suggests that it would not end well.

The Crown in Parliament at first struggled to find its feet. A Jacobite (that is, pro-ex-King James) uprising in the Scottish Highlands
fizzled out, but unpaid English sailors went on strike again and James
slipped into Ireland to raise another revolt. William defeated him at
the River Boyne in 1690, but on the very same day a French navy battered the Anglo-Dutch fleets at Beachy Head. Had Louis been ready
to invade England, or had he even made invading England a higher
priority than sending yet more men to the Low Countries, little
would have stood in his way. But the moment passed, and a string
of naval battles off Normandy's coast in 1692 more or less closed the
Channel again (Figure 6.10).

Like Elizabeth a century earlier, William never doubted that England's security required a counterscarp as well as a moat. A quarter of
a millennium before American strategists articulated their 'domino

theory' of Soviet expansion, English thinkers had similar ideas: 'If Flanders be an accession to France, Holland must soon follow, and England next', one pamphleteer explained. 'They are like Nine-pins, the throwing down one carries the rest.' Tories often argued that naval warfare alone was enough to prop up the dominoes (and would pay for itself), but most Whigs – and William – preferred Continental commitment. The Whigs won, and by 1695 England had 45,000 men entrenched in the Flanders mud and was funding a further 20,000 Dutchmen, Danes and Germans.

The expense, £50 million by 1697 (a stunning 61 per cent of GDP), was sustainable only because Whigs introduced new ways of thinking about prosperity. Adapting Dutch ideas, they created an official national debt, owed not by the king but by the Crown in Parliament. A newly created Bank of England raised money by selling interest-bearing bonds, basically shares in the national debt, which could be freely traded on a stock exchange. The king could not default on this debt without Parliament's say-so, but Parliament now had incentives to raise taxes rather than resist them, because lenders could be convinced to accept low interest rates if Parliament guaranteed repayment from future tax revenues. Over a period of ten years government revenue mushroomed from £2 million to over £5 million, and the number of bureaucrats collecting it from 4,000 to 12,000. 'Credit makes war, and makes peace; raises armies, fits out navies, fights battles, besieges towns', observed Daniel Defoe, the author of *Robinson Crusoe* and other tales of off-the-Hereford-Map adventure. 'Credit makes the soldier fight without pay, the army march without provisions [. . .] and fills the Exchequer and the banks with as many millions as it pleases, upon demand.'

The war became one of attrition – both military, with the armies digging in and besieging each other's fortresses in the Low Countries, and financial, with each Leviathan waiting for the other to go insolvent. Both were close calls. Despite his naval defeats in 1692, Louis considered another invasion in 1696 but instead switched from big-fleet actions to choking England's Atlantic trade. Because England grew nearly all its own food, Louis's goal was not to starve it, as Germany would try to do in the twentieth-century world wars, but to bankrupt its merchants, whose profits – and therefore Leviathan's income – depended on overseas trade. State-sponsored pirates captured 4,000 English and Dutch merchantmen in this first Battle of the Atlantic.

As pain mounted, support for William's war ebbed, but Louis's cause collapsed faster. Defaulting on his debts and facing famine, he sued for peace in 1697. William held out for a better deal, but Tory allegations mounted that, in cahoots with a 'Moneyed Interest' of corrupt Dutch financiers and Whig war profiteers, he was putting his native Netherlands' interests ahead of England's. Defoe, a passionate Whig, saw only xenophobia here: 'the King', he said, was 'Reproached and Insulted by Insolent Pedants, and Ballad-making Poets [. . .] Only [. . .] for employing Foreigners, and for being a Foreigner himself.' But the Tories understood the national mood better. When given the choice, the one-quarter of Englishmen who had the vote backed a very 2010s-sounding Tory platform of rolling back the state and getting out of Europe.

The Tories disbanded William's standing army. Even the Crown-in-Parliament deal behind his new Leviathan was in danger until Louis overplayed his hand. Louis had welcomed peace in 1697, but changed tack when a run of unexpected inheritances and deaths left his grandson as the obvious candidate for the Spanish throne as well as the French. This would create a Continental super-state, potentially powerful enough to dominate the Channel and overwhelm England. Even Tories were aghast; but, rather than compromise, Louis raised the stakes still further by proposing that when England's King William died, which could not be far off, the crown should revert to the Catholic son of the exiled, recently deceased King James.

Faced with a traumatic trifecta – Jacobite uprisings in the Scottish Highlands, Franco-Spanish invasions of the Netherlands and a Catholic claiming the throne – British elites acted decisively. Few Scots and English were any fonder of each other than they had been a century earlier, when James I had proposed merging them in a United Kingdom of Great Britain, but in 1707 they negotiated a full-blown Act of Union. No one really liked it. There were riots in Glasgow, and after just six years a bill to dissolve the union came within one vote of passing. But the deal held: England locked its back door, Scots gained access to English markets and colonies and James I's Union Jack finally flew.

Britain's new ruler, Queen Anne, revived her brother-in-law William's Continental strategy on an even grander scale. Widening the war, her fleet seized Minorca and Gibraltar. The latter put England back on the European mainland for the first time since surrendering

Dunkirk nearly fifty years earlier, but in a new way. Gibraltar was a base to project naval power into the Mediterranean, not a counterscarp to keep France away from the Channel. Sweeping marches through Germany under the ultra-Whig Duke of Marlborough expanded the stage further still, exposing France's eastern flank rather than just defending the counterscarp fortresses. Even so, victory did not come, despite a battlefield triumph at Blenheim greater than anything since Agincourt. When another victory at Malplaquet in 1709 yielded little but 20,000 casualties – proportionately, more of Britain's population than the 60,000 losses on the first day on the Somme in 1916 – even Queen Anne asked 'When will this bloodshed ever cease?'

As in the 1690s, the war became a slogging match. Britain fared better this time against French privateers, committing the navy to systematic convoy duty in 1708, but even so, Tory complaints gained traction. Anne, they pointed out, had 170,000 troops – mostly foreign – on her payroll. Leviathan was bigger and taxes higher than ever. Inflation was rising and the economy in recession. When Anne fell out with Marlborough's wife, Sarah (the subject of the strange, but strangely fascinating, 2018 film *The Favourite*), Tories turned on the duke too, prosecuting him for embezzlement – probably justifiably, given that he and Sarah had made themselves two of Britain's first millionaires. With the great man gone, the Tories opened secret negotiations with Louis, who was more than ready to talk.

Whigs at home and Anne's Austrian, German and Dutch allies on the Continent urged her to fight on, confident that France was on its last legs, but her ministers signed a separate peace with Louis at Utrecht in the Netherlands in 1713. This Tory betrayal – as critics called it – unleashed anger well beyond what Brexit created in 2016. Whigs were as furious as Britons might have been if, on the eve of D-Day in 1944, the United States had abandoned the Grand Alliance and cut its own deal with Hitler. The moment the Whigs were back on top at Westminster they threw themselves into impeaching and imprisoning the guilty men who had sold out Britain's European friends for personal gain. Utrecht, they felt, had effectively turned the clock back to 1689, letting France live to fight another day and betraying a quarter-century of sacrifice.

They were wrong. Whatever Utrecht's moral failings, the fighting since 1689 had changed everything. Britain was war-weary in 1713, but France was starving and bankrupt. Britain was politically divided, but France was becoming ungovernable. Britain had repaid its loans and replaced its ships; France had not. Britain's Leviathan had broken France's. On earth there was nothing like him. After a quarter of a century of taxing, spending and killing, he was king over all the children of pride.

7

THE PIVOT, 1713–1815

Global Britain

Utrecht began the grandest strategic pivot in Britain's history. Tobacco, sugar and slavery had by 1713 been pulling Britain on to an Atlantic stage for a full century, but leaders in London still thought largely in terms of the Hereford Map: taxes earned from the triangular trades were spent on European struggles for identity, security and sovereignty against France, Spain and, in some people's minds, Rome. The Tories who sat down to negotiate at Utrecht, however, were working with a map that looked increasingly like Mackinder's.

This made it hard to share the Whig obsession with fighting France to the death. The obvious fact for a nation at the centre of the world, a poet from the Tory ranks concluded, was that 'On trade alone thy glory stands'; and so, he added, 'Be commerce then thy sole design / Keep that, and all the world is thine'. Who cares, Tories asked, if France, Spain or the pope flourishes? All that mattered was that no power on the Continent should have enough warships or merchantmen to challenge British commercial interests (let alone to invade the Isles). The way to ensure that was not by prolonging the Whigs' wars against France but by dividing Europe into equally matched alliances, in which every government was too busy worrying about the opposed alliance to find the time, energy or money to compete with Britain on other continents. Any time a state became too powerful, others (Britain in the lead) would defect to the rival alliance, guaranteeing – as the treaty of Utrecht put it – 'the peace and tranquillity of the Christian world through a just equilibrium of power (which is the best and most secure foundation)'.

This was a brutally transactional view of the world. 'We have no eternal allies and we have no perpetual friends', the foreign secretary, Lord Palmerston, would reflect nearly 150 years later; only 'our interests are eternal and perpetual'. Protestants, Catholics, even Muslims –

all could be allies, so long as they kept Europe occupied while British merchants, secure behind their moat defensive and sitting in the middle of Mackinder's Map, engrossed the trade of all the world. Between 1713 and 1815 Global Britain was invented.

Balancing Act

On the face of it, conditions did not look promising for Global Britain in the years just after Utrecht. Despite seventeen pregnancies, Queen Anne died childless in 1714, and many thought that her Catholic step-brother – James II's son – had the best claim to succeed her. To prevent this, Whig ministers had passed a law, still on the books in the 2020s, excluding papists from the throne; but as Anne's end neared, top Tories secretly approached James anyway. Only a last-minute Whig scramble ensured that Anne's more distant but soundly Protestant cousin George was crowned instead.

George was no one's idea of an Atlantic-first, Global Britain type. The kindest thing his minister James Stanhope ever found to call him was 'an honest, dull German gentleman'. George made it clear that he preferred his native Hanover (Figure 7.1) to London, going back whenever he decently could and insisting that Britain protect it. He detested Tories, showed no interest in strategy and never learned to speak English. Tories returned his dislike. Their newspapers baited him, reviving their seventeenth-century tradition of stoking public rage by hiring literary giants – Swift, Fielding, Pope, Johnson – who happily blurred distinctions between opinion and news. Violence was common: militiamen regularly had to read the Riot Act (passed in 1715) before firing on anti-Hanoverian mobs. On one occasion the government even deployed artillery against angry Anglicans in Norwich (Figure 7.2).

Yet, rather than coming apart under the strain, as they had done in 1642, British elites showed how much they had learned since then, closing ranks around the Crown in Parliament. No one wanted anarchy back. When the rabble rioted, their betters shot or hanged them with equanimity. The people's voice was steadily silenced: whereas nearly one Englishmen in four had the vote in 1700, barely one in six did by 1800. The whole of Scotland had only 2,662 electors. Plenty of seats had just a few dozen constituents, often happy to sell their support; and if bribing them became too expensive, politicians

Figure 7.1. The Euro-Mediterranean stage, 1713–1815.

could simply agree privately on who would run. Wiltshire held only one contested election in 105 years, Shropshire none at all in 109.

King George deserves some of the credit for holding the state together, thanks, says the historian David Scott, to his virtue of 'lack[ing] the imagination to blunder on the magnificent scale of some of [his] predecessors'. Most credit, however, goes to George's fixer-in-chief, Robert Walpole (Figure 7.3). Walpole was perhaps the most venal, scheming and corrupt prime minister the country ever had, but also the cleverest. A master of detail with a silver tongue ('while he was speaking the most ignorant thought that they understood what they really did not', Stanhope said), he shot to prominence in 1720 in the financial crisis known as the South Sea Bubble. As bad in its way as the 2008 meltdown, this threatened Britain's entire financial system and exposed sleaze in high places. Only Walpole proved equal to it, calming markets while also shielding from scandal not only the king but also his mistress and friends, all of whom had made fortunes. Unlike in 2008, heads did roll: after sacrificing the chancellor of the exchequer and the first lord of the treasury, Walpole took their jobs – and lucrative kickbacks – for himself.

Figure 7.2 The British stage, 1713–1815.

Above all, Walpole effectively ran a one-party Whig state which mostly pursued Tory policies. Tories won the popular vote in elections in 1727, 1734 and 1741, but gerrymandering gave Whigs majorities anyway. Drawing the obvious conclusion, flocks of Tories defected. The Whig party became a very broad church, in which ideology mattered less than having the right friends. In the historian J. H. Plumb's memorable phrase, 'The rage of party gave way to the pursuit of place.'

Figure 7.3. English colossus: Robert Walpole in a 1740 cartoon, balancing between France and Spain as he bestrides the narrow world.

Walpole enthusiastically co-opted the Tories' Britain-first, balance-of-power approach to Europe and the wider world, constantly making and breaking alliances to keep the Continent in equilibrium. Trade boomed. Twice as many British ships crossed the Atlantic in 1740 as in 1675, and by then half the world's international shipping flew the Union Jack. Legally declared imports had doubled, and exports had grown even more. Two-thirds of British government revenue came from taxes on trade, even if smuggling had increased more than anything. However, while sophisticated ministers in London might see Walpole's flipping and flopping as diplomacy of 'a very high level of conceptual flexibility' (the historian Brendan Simms's euphemism), to everyone else it looked like perfidy. Nor could ministers agree where the balance of power actually lay. Until the 1740s most British strategists thought that France's bankruptcy made Spain the main threat, and tried to retreat from Continental entanglements while plundering

Spanish possessions in the Mediterranean and Caribbean. Others insisted that staying in Europe to support Austria mattered more, while the king, apparently caring most about protecting Hanover, embroiled Britain in distracting disputes with Sweden, Prussia and Russia. Then, as French strength revived, the balance broke down altogether. Walpole found himself warning Parliament that Britain was 'at present without any one ally upon the Continent'. If this continued, he worried, 'the greatest part of Europe would unite against us'.

Some were fine with this. 'Under Queen Elizabeth, Sir', one of Walpole's many rivals insisted, 'we neither had, nor did we stand in need of Allies [. . .] Let us for once change our sneaking Conduct, and all will be well.' But as the balance broke down, Walpole was blamed. In 1742 his supporters abandoned him. Within months British troops were back on the Continent, fighting France, their king personally leading them into battle (the last time, to date, this has happened). They won a famous victory, but France soon won even greater ones. Austria was collapsing. Fortress after fortress fell. France, Walpole's successor wrote, was vanquishing all rivals on land and, once it had succeeded in this, 'by being absolutely disengaged from all expense on the Continent, would soon be able to be superior to us at sea'.

At this critical moment Britain's focus on investments across the Atlantic rather than European alliances suddenly paid off. A daring assault by British ships and American militias took the French fortress at Louisbourg, which guarded access to Canada. With Quebec and Montreal defenceless, France offered to talk. 'Bawling and huzzaing' (Stanhope's words) filled London. The deal finally hammered out in 1748 swapped Louisbourg for fortresses France had taken in Flanders, which infuriated Atlanticists, but the implications were momentous all the same. For the first time, British and French governments acknowledged that events in America could matter as much as those in Europe. The Tory *Gentleman's Magazine* offered its 15,000 readers an Atlanticist anthem, celebrating the goddess Victory's return to Britain via Canada:

> But not on Flandria's* hostile plain
> As we, mistaken, then besought,
> The British blood is spilt in vain,

---

* That is, in Flanders.

For not the British cause is fought.
Beyond the wide Atlantic sea
She rises first to crown our toils,
Thither to wealth she points the way,
And bids us thrive on Gallic spoils.

Whig grandees still sometimes accused those who put the Atlantic ahead of Europe of burying their heads in the sand and 'disregard[ing] all the troubles and commotions of the continent [. . .] to attend our commerce'; yet attending to commerce rather than Continental troubles and commotions was just what growing numbers of Britons wanted to do. The national mood was shifting.

Pudding Time

An easy, complacent age was shaping up for men who were willing to go along to get along. Balladeers called it 'Pudding Time':

When George in Pudding Time came o'er
And Moderate Men looked big, Sir,
My Principles I chang'd once more,
And so became a Whig, Sir.

These were self-confident, stately, magnificent days. A self-confident, stately, magnificent elite filled London's West End with elegant mansions and squares, sewers and street lights, piped water and pleasure gardens. It was a far cry from the angry identities of the seventeenth century: Vivaldi, Scarlatti and England's adopted son Georg Frideric Handel filled these perfect, harmonious homes and recital halls with equally perfect, harmonious music (*The Messiah, Zadok the Priest*). The great and the good colonised fashionable new suburbs like Kensington and in the countryside built on a scale not seen since the Romans. Capability Brown gave them exquisite gardens. Some are still there to stroll around, thanks to the National Trust and English Heritage. Back then, however, Arcadian strolling was not for plebeians. At Castle Howard, Sir John Vanbrugh flooded an entire village to improve his view; at Houghton Hall, the candles Walpole burned to illuminate a single dinner party could easily cost £15 – what a labourer earned in a year.

The gap between rich and poor widened, but the surprising thing is that it didn't widen even more. Measured on the Gini coefficient of inequality, which I described in Chapter 1 (where 0 represents perfect equality, and 1 means that one person takes everything), income inequality crept up from 0.47 in 1688 to 0.49 in 1751 (it had been about 0.45 under Rome). However, the 'extraction ratio' – a score developed by the economist Branko Milanović to measure the proportion of society's total surplus that the elite expropriate – actually fell. Roman elites had gobbled up a hearty 75 per cent of the available pudding, but the English managed just 57 per cent in 1688 and 55 per cent in 1759. The explanation: although the rich were eating more pudding, the pudding itself was growing so much faster that the poor ate more too (just not as much more as the rich).

A reorganisation of agriculture helped. There was a run of good weather, but farmers also found ways to squeeze more from the soil. The grandest in the land got involved; after being pushed out of government, one ex-minister earned the nickname 'Turnip Townshend' for his improving efforts. Better transport contributed too, making it easier to move food to consumers. Between 1700 and 1750, dredging lengthened England's navigable rivers by one-sixth. Five thousand kilometres of turnpikes (toll roads) were built, some as good as Roman roads. Travel times fell by 20–40 per cent.

More controversial was 'enclosure', which typically involved local grandees or MPs converting common land into private property and selling it, allowing buyers to consolidate larger estates. Figure 7.4 shows what happened in the not untypical village of Middle Claydon in Buckinghamshire, dominated by the Verney family. In 1648 local farms came in all shapes and sizes, but over the next seventy-five years a dozen big farms of 75–150 acres swallowed two-thirds of the land. By the 1750s just half that number of (even bigger) estates was left. Like many villages, Middle Claydon shed half its population between 1648 and 1722.

Those who had most, gained most; those who had least, lost most. Enclosure deprived tenants even of the possibility of topping up earnings by grazing a pig or two on common land. 'All I know', one told the agronomist Arthur Young, 'is, I had a cow, and an Act of Parliament has taken it from me.' Pushed out of villages like Middle Claydon, the poor drifted towards towns. Fortunately, towns were often eager to pull them in, because expanding trade made merchants

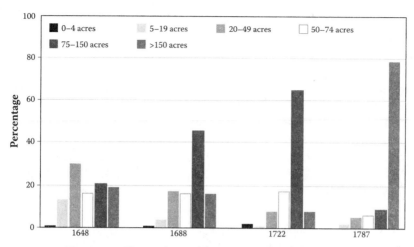

Figure 7.4. Slicing the pudding in Middle Claydon: the percentage of land in farms of different sizes, 1648–1787.

eager to hire workers to produce textiles, pianos, guns and anything else that could be sold overseas. Little 'manufactories' multiplied, often paying wages better than those back on the farm. The ruthlessly efficient farmers who had enclosed common land indirectly helped too: agricultural output rose by 19 per cent between 1690 and 1750, and food prices fell accordingly. Despite the disruption of their lives, most labourers were better off by the 1740s than their parents had been.

Construction boomed. Builders threw up tens of thousands of two-up, two-down brick and stone houses for new townsfolk, sufficiently sturdy that many still stand. A French observer marvelled that 'they have their houses well furnished, are well dressed and eat well; the poorest country girls [. . .] have bodices of chintz, straw hats on their heads and scarlet cloaks upon their shoulders'. A German pastor was equally impressed. English rustics, he said, dressed 'not as ours in coarse frocks, but with some taste, in fine good cloth [. . .] distinguished from people of the town not so much by their dress as by the[ir] greater simplicity'.

As always, rising prosperity required more organisers and bosses, who necessarily congregated in cities, which drew in still more people to build, serve and sell them things. London became a greater magnet than ever. By 1750 it was the largest city in Europe, with 675,000 residents. Far off in Asia, Beijing and Tokyo were bigger still, but there was nothing on earth, European visitors agreed, quite like London's shopping. 'The number of shops [. . . is] so far beyond that of any foreign city that it is to strangers a just matter of amazement', wrote Guy Miege, a Swiss observer. César de Saussure, also Swiss, thought the outlets on the Strand 'the finest in Europe'.

London was unique (only one other English town, Norwich, had even 30,000 residents), but its glories did trickle down to the shires. There was money to be made bringing urbanity to the provinces, and Bath and Brighton ('Piccadilly by the sea-side', William Wilberforce called the latter) both reinvented themselves as adjuncts of the West End, whither socialites could repair from the metropolitan whirl to refresh their jaded palates. All over England, newspapers, novels and style magazines were telling eager readers how to make their own Little Londons. Even gritty, no-name towns such as Birmingham opened bookshops and assembly rooms, where the middling sort could converse about essays in the *Gentleman's Magazine* and *Tatler*. Provincials' effrontery offended some sophisticates: 'I wish with all my heart that half the turnpike roads of the kingdom were ploughed up, which have imported London manners [. . .] I meet milkmaids on the road with the dress and looks of Strand misses', one admiral harrumphed. Yet much as Londoners might sneer at 'the wives and daughters of the most topping tradesmen v[ying] with each other every Sunday in the elegance of their apparel', provincials were building a new, homogenised, middle-class English identity.

Its most original feature was frenetic commercial energy. Arriving in Bristol, Horace Walpole (the prime minister's son) was astonished that 'the very clergy talk of nothing but trade and how to turn the penny and are in a hurry, running up and down'. Coming to Birmingham in 1741, the teenage William Hutton thought the locals 'possessed a vivacity I have never beheld: I had been among dreamers, but now I saw men awake'.

Exactly so, for another feature of the new Englishness was caffeination. Coffee was yet another drug imported from the Middle East. England's first coffee shop was opened in Oxford around 1650 by a Jewish immigrant named Jacob (or perhaps in London in 1652 by a Greek immigrant named Pasqua – accounts differ). Guy Miege, so impressed by London's retailers, soon thought coffee 'more common [in England] than anywhere else'. Taken (as it regularly was) with other, equally addictive imports – nicotine, sugar, cocoa – caffeine offered Englishmen an instant up for a penny a cup.

A battle was under way to define a new English identity, fit for people in the middle of Mackinder's Map. Older drugs (ale for the many, wine for the few) were chiefly depressants, hardly conducive to the wide-awakeness Hutton so admired, and if anything, England's alcoholic haze had been thickening. Beer, a Dutch import, had been replacing English ales since the fifteenth century. Ale and beer are both malt liquors, but beer includes hops (highly hopped modern 'real ales' are not really ales at all); and hops, which make a brew taste brighter, last longer and hold more alcohol, proved hugely popular. London malters were using them by 1424, and although some writers still considered beer a sinister Dutch import in the 1540s, within a century it was thoroughly naturalised. Samuel Pepys's diary shows that the English tradition of mocking French beer had begun by the 1680s.

By then a new Dutch drug, even more likely to sap energy, was challenging 'English' beer: gin. 'At first', Defoe says, 'like the Champagne and Burgundy, it was drank among the Gentlemen only', but when its price fell after 1720, distillers 'saw plainly that what was good for the High, was also good for the Low'. Rotgut it might be, but gin was mightily alcoholic. 'Drunk for a penny, dead drunk for twopence', the saying went. Saussure watched children falling down drunk, and a customs official reported that 'Young creatures, girls of 12 and 13 years of age, drink [gin] like fishes [. . .] there is no passing the streets for 'em, so shameless are they grown.' One mother was hanged for leaving her baby at a workhouse then reclaiming him after the governors had given him new clothes – whereupon she strangled him, sold his clothes and bought more gin with the proceeds.

Gin would soon be considered as English as beer, becoming the main battlefield in a war not so much *on* drugs as *over* drugs. As early as 1657 the caffeinated were celebrating how 'this coffee drink hath caused a greater sobriety among the nations, for whereas formerly apprentices and clerks with others, used to take their morning draught in ale, beer, or wine, which by the dizziness they cause in the brain, make many unfit for business, they use now to play the good-fellows in this wakeful and civil drink'. Not everyone thought this cause for cheer: 'coffee-houses', one critic wrote to a friend, made 'every carman and porter [. . .] a statesman. It was not thus when we drank nothing but sack or claret, or English beer and ale.' Nevertheless, caffeination made steady inroads into the older drunken nation. By the 1690s one tourist calculated that London had 3,000 coffee shops. Even quite small towns had one – or usually two, one Whig, one Tory. Anticipating Starbucks, owners provided comfortable surroundings and free newspapers. Customers stayed all day, talking politics, doing business and buying cup after cup of coffee.

In the 1650s coffee had still been considered 'a Turkish drink', so un-English, rhymed one traditionalist, that 'When coffee once was vended here / The Al-Koran did soon appear'. But, like beer and gin before it, coffee was soon naturalised, losing its English identity only when tea overtook it (when I was young, most people I knew considered coffee an American affectation). The first time an Englishman drank tea was in 1637, on a ship bombarding Guangzhou. It was still a novelty in 1660, when Pepys had 'a Cup of Tee (a China drink) of which I had never drunk before', but by 1750 the English consumed ten times more tea per head than coffee. Even at its peak of popularity, coffee had always been a tipple of urban middling sorts, but tea, so much easier to prepare, had universal appeal. Teapots and -cups show up on even the tiniest rural sites, and, judging from potsherds found in a recent excavation near the gates of St John's College, Cambridge, even the most elite of coffee houses were dealing mostly in tea by the 1740s (although patrons also consumed plenty of beer and wine).

At every level, one of the great appeals of tea and coffee was as lubricants for interactions of a kind that Georgians called 'polite'. 'Politeness' was a big idea in the eighteenth century, implying civility, reason, manners and tolerance, key concepts in a new Englishness. All these came easily to ladies and gentlemen who were mildly caffeinated, while people who were roaring drunk were more prone to 'Enthusiasm' – another big idea, evoking the religious and political rage of the previous century. 'Polite' people cared about commerce, science and the balance of power, not wrestling with the Antichrist or killing witches. (The witchcraft laws were repealed in 1731, although one last witch was apparently lynched in Tring in 1751.) They read the *Spectator* and the *Rambler* as well as, although not yet instead of, the Old Testament. Those who persisted in seeing themselves as sinners in the hands of an angry God could certainly flock to new, not quite respectable sects like Methodism, whose spellbinding orators preached personal salvation to huge crowds under the open skies; but the Church of England increasingly offered a decent, reliable God, served by sound, safe pastors. A 'vast epistemological effort' was under way, says the historian David Scott, 'that gradually moved religion from the realm of truth to that of opinion'. Eighteenth-century Englishmen or -women often had strong opinions, but keeping them polite was the main thing.

The Five Nations

Politeness was a broad, West European phenomenon, but that did not stop the English from believing themselves more polite than their neighbours to the south-east, and *much* more so than those to their north and west. More than ever before, members of England's prosperous, polite and self-confident elite convinced themselves that Continentals had more to learn from them than the reverse – and that rival identities within the Isles should be erased by pushing Englishness into the highlands and islands.

The results varied. Despite fears of being 'Englished out of Wales', the 300,000 farmers and herders scattered across the Welsh hills and valleys went on speaking their own language (Cornish, by contrast, died out around 1780). England's agricultural and urban revolutions barely touched Wales; Wrexham, its biggest town, had only 4,000 residents. The Welsh gentry, however, found much to like in Englishness. Most stopped giving their children Welsh names or sending sons to bardic schools. Some decamped entirely for England, only to rediscover their Welshness, albeit in novel forms, once they got there. Edward Lhuyd of Oxford, for instance, championed the theory that all the Celtic languages were related, while Welshmen in London launched a magazine and several societies promoting their identity. All celebrated King Arthur and the Welsh roots of 'Britain'. One society even had a song called 'We are the Aborigines', despite its founder being a clerk in the Admiralty and only one of its officers speaking Welsh. Another member, Edward Williams, took the bardic name Iolo Morganwg, dosed himself with laudanum (liquid opium) and started making up 'Druidic' poems. When sales took off, he established himself in London, where he stayed until he died.

Efforts to Anglicise the Irish were much less successful. Most of the settlers 'planted' in Ulster in the seventeenth century had been Scottish, and for the other three-quarters of Ireland's population, Irishness now basically meant Catholicism. This majority's lot had become much harder. In 1641 Catholics still owned two-thirds of the land, but by 1702 they held just one-sixth and by 1750 less than one-tenth. For them this was potato time, not pudding time. Famines killed half a million Irish in the 1720s and '30s, but the population still doubled between 1640 and 1750, thanks to this high-yielding crop (sometimes seasoned, to English observers' disgust, with jellied calf's blood). Rents tripled, and Protestant landlords saw little need to improve their estates in the English manner.

Some among the Irish Protestants strongly embraced Englishness, but England rarely hugged them back. Even an Irish lord chancellor worried that in London 'I shall be thought [. . .] (what of all things I would least choose to be) an Irishman'. Other Protestants reacted by appropriating anti-Catholicism as a distinctly Irish identity, policing their popish neighbours with a ferocity that many English found distasteful. Even the king called a 1719 plan to castrate Catholic priests caught proselytising 'ridiculous'. In Ulster the descendants of recent Scottish immigrants invented their own hardline British (not English) identity. To this day Ulster's Orangemen provoke Catholics with annual marches honouring King William's victory at the Boyne in 1690. And finally there was Dublin, which went another way entirely, turning into a trading town with 60,000 residents (second only to London) and a commercial elite that included Catholics as well as Protestants.

The sharpest identity issues of all were in Scotland. For twenty years after 1707 few Scots saw much benefit in the Act of Union, and although famine disappeared after the 1690s, the country remained poor and unruly. One Londoner, despite being hardened by his home town's stench, recalled spending a night in Edinburgh (justly nicknamed Auld Reekie) 'hid[ing] my Head between the Sheets; for the Smell of the Filth, thrown out by the Neighbours [. . .] come pouring into the Room'. Taxes rose, and duties on malt – vital for distilling whisky – provoked riots in 1725. Even in the cities older men routinely wore swords, which Englishmen had not done for generations.

But Scottish cities were changing. The Union threw England's empire open to Scottish merchants, and Glasgow's 'Tobacco Lords' made fortunes from transatlantic trade in the 1730s. The *Gentleman's Magazine* and *Tatler* arrived; 'at last', Lady Panmure boasted to her husband, 'old Reeky will grow polite with the rest of the world'. It did, and its New Town – full of streets and squares called Hanover,

George, Charlotte or Princes – still stands as perhaps the ultimate example of Georgian town planning.

Politeness was just the beginning. Scotland enjoyed an intellectual explosion unparalleled in British history. This owed something to long-standing cultural ties with France, more to the Presbyterian church's encouragement of mass literacy and probably most to the opening of England's cultural markets to Scotland's freethinkers. Scottish universities could certainly be stuffy – Edinburgh and Glasgow both turned the philosopher David Hume down for jobs – but thanks to the Act of Union, English buyers made Hume's books bestsellers. The streets were indeed, as the *Scots Magazine* put it, 'crowded with men of genius'. Scotsmen went south, changed their names and accents and turned into celebrities.

It was perhaps predictable that, with Anglicised intellectuals earning international acclaim, Scotland would produce its own Iolo Morganwg. In 1759 an unknown poet named James Macpherson astonished Edinburgh's academic elite with what he claimed were translations of previously lost epics by the ancient Gaelic poet Ossian, son of Fingal (Figure 7.5). Reactions were ecstatic. The Anglo-Irish playwright Thomas Sheridan said Ossian surpassed 'all the poets in the world, and [. . .] excelled Homer in the Sublime and Virgil in the Pathetic'. There were red faces all round when, within three years, Hume and others exposed Ossian as a scam, but so many Scots (and romantically inclined English) wanted to believe in him that Macpherson carried on making hay, rising to riches, high office and finally a tomb in Westminster Abbey.

The urge to believe was fuelled by anxiety that the new, Anglo-Scots urban culture was driving the old, impolite, Gaelic culture of the Highlands into extinction – which it was. London and Edinburgh elites, keen to civilise the wild clans, pushed roads (400 km of them between 1725 and 1740, another 1,200 by 1760) and redcoats into the mountains. Desperate Highlanders begged ex-King James's exiled heirs to come back and save them, and the heirs in turn begged anyone who might listen – France, Spain, Sweden, Russia, the pope – to kick in England's back door and raise Jacobite revolt. Six times their plots were exposed; twice more, in 1715 and 1745, violence erupted. But it was hopeless. 'If they have no foreign assistance', Stanhope calmly observed – and the moat defensive made sure they hadn't – 'there must be an end of them.' That came at Culloden, where British

Figure 7.5. Not quite polite: the wild, made-up bard Ossian calling
up his Gaelic gods, as pictured by François Gérard, 1801.

musketeers mowed down charging clansmen and then killed, raped,
robbed and burned their way across the north. After that, anyone
seen in 'Highland clothes' could be jailed for six months; a second
offence brought deportation. Instead of waiting to be ethnically
cleansed, tens of thousands of refugees took ship for the New World.

The world they found there was new indeed. As recently as 1690,
when one Colonel Cuthbert Potter had ridden from Jamestown to
New England, he had been attacked by hostile natives and French
pirates, insulted by loutish locals and thrown in jail by suspicious officials. But by 1744, when the Scots-born Dr Alexander Hamilton made
much the same journey, all that was history. America, like Edinburgh,
was growing polite, and instead of trying to arrest, rob or kill Hamilton, proud Americans showed him their civic buildings and made

urbane conversation. He even took 'a glass of good wine' with a Narragansett chief and his silk-gowned wife.

The thirteen American colonies were becoming a fifth British nation, to rank alongside the English, Irish, Scots and Welsh. Over 2 million British subjects lived there, a quarter as many as in the British Isles. Americans (from now on, I will use that word for migrants from the Old World to the New) had become more genetically diverse since 1650, as hundreds of thousands of Irish, Scots, Germans and Africans joined what had previously been an almost entirely English immigrant pool. Culturally, however, matters were more complicated. Each set of settlers brought its own baggage of identities and hatreds, and as the ratio of locally born white Americans to new immigrants shifted (four-fifths of white Virginians had been first-generation immigrants in 1668; by 1750, nine-tenths were American-born), these identities developed in new directions.

One direction was towards England. The richest Americans were as prosperous as almost anyone in the old country. The Penn family owned 40 million acres, and plenty of grandees along the Hudson River, known as 'feudal lords', held more than 1 million. Below them were great merchants such as the Browns of Providence, who traded tobacco and slaves; below them, much bigger groups of successful planters, businessmen and professionals. America had its own middling sorts, mostly farmers, as well as some desperately poor landless labourers. Overall, white America's income inequality and extraction ratios were remarkably similar to England's (the former, 0.46 on the Gini coefficient in America and 0.49 in England; the latter, 61 per cent as against 55 per cent).

Americans who could afford it built brick and stone townhouses and country mansions on Georgian lines. Out went stools and wooden bowls: in came English chairs and china, just right for taking tea while wearing imported wigs and waistcoats. A whole package of English politeness came with this. As a boy in the 1740s, George Washington practised his handwriting by copying 'Rules of Civility and Decent Behaviour' from an English manual, which taught him not to kill lice or spit into the fire in front of guests. Some Americans also adopted the English yearning for a more 'reasonable' God, while others – again like the English – reacted against His new mildness by flocking to hear evangelicals from the old country who toured the colonies imploring mercy from a still angry Lord.

In all these ways and more, Englishness swept America. In the following century the French traveller Alexis de Tocqueville would conclude that 'the American is the Englishman left to himself', distilled to his essence in the absence of interfering kings and bishops. But there were important differences too. Like the Anglicised gentries of Wales, Ireland and Scotland, Anglo-Americans formed a part-society, surrounded by people who did not – sometimes could not – share this identity. Some 400,000 people, roughly one American in five, were slaves, whose ancestors had recently been dragged from Africa. Most lived in the southern tobacco- and rice-growing states (South Carolina felt 'more like a negro country' than a British one, a visitor thought), but even on Manhattan island 20 per cent of the population was unfree. There had been no slaves in England for centuries. Churchmen sometimes grumbled that British industrial relations 'approached much nearer to that of a planter and slaves in our American colonies than might be expected of such a country as England', but not even Irishmen could be burned at the stake, as thirteen slaves were in New York in 1714.

Slavery was not the only way in which eighteenth-century America had more in common with medieval than eighteenth-century England. Eleventh- and twelfth-century Norman conquerors would have instantly understood America's violent, open frontiers. In the Middle Ages kings had regularly tried to stop their lords seizing Welsh, Scottish and Irish territories because the costs of defending these land grabs outweighed the benefits (which, in any case, flowed to the lords not the kings). But the barons seized land anyway, bringing a world of troubles on their kings' heads. Just so, in eighteenth-century America, kings and governors tried to stop settlers from drifting westwards, because that not only set off expensive wars with the natives but also made it harder to protect British colonies against French and Spanish rivals. But colonists, choosing mobility and prosperity over security, went west anyway.

Rather like the Anglo-Irish, Anglo-Americans looked not quite English to the English themselves – 'unworthy of the name Englishmen', Benjamin Franklin angrily concluded, 'fit only to be snubb'd, curb'd, shackled and plundered'. The historian Linda Colley uses an engraving published in London in 1774 (Figure 7.6) to sum up English condescension about American identity. Father Time, at the left, is delighting Britain's nations with a vision of their glorious future. In

Figure 7.6. The British nations: John Dixon's 1774 engraving *The Oracle*. Lit up in the centre (left to right) are Ireland, England/Wales, Scotland; on the right, neither polite nor English, is America.

the centre sit three fair, fashionably dressed maidens, representing, from left to right, Ireland, Britannia (standing for England and Wales) and Scotland. At the right, crouching beneath them, is a dark-skinned, scantily clad America, complete with bow and feathered head-dress. The point, says Colley, is that Anglo-Americans 'had yet to evolve a recognisable and autonomous identity of their own'. Being part of the picture and yet so different from the Islanders, they provoked 'profound uncertainty about the workings of the imperial relationship'. This was about to become a problem.

Narcissists

Britons were not alone in realising that geography had changed its meanings. Strategists in Versailles, like those in London, recognised that 'Commerce is the true source of the power of the state'; yet France had shown 'negligence and indolence' in this area. The problem, they concluded, was that French leaders had failed to notice that the Hereford Map was out of date. While France had been fighting Spain, Austria and the Netherlands in Italy, Germany and the Low Countries, Britain had achieved what one pamphleteer called a 'universal monarchy of the sea'. France had to face the facts of Mackinder's Map, which meant putting Britain at the centre of a global strategy.

Louis XV's ministers identified three objectives. First, France must isolate Britain diplomatically. That seemed possible. Britain's shifty balance-of-power tactics had alienated the other great powers, which only went along with London because they were even more scared of France than Britain. So, instead of invading everyone, France should make nice. Austria, Russia and Spain all reacted positively, and by 1756 only Prussia – terrified of being partitioned between Austria and Russia – remained pro-British.

With the prospect of having to fight another Continental grand alliance receding, France could turn to its second objective: the oceans. Louis's ministers therefore promoted export trades, which grew tenfold between 1720 and 1780. However, the Louisbourg crisis in 1745 had laid bare the harsh reality that, so long as Britannia ruled the waves (not coincidentally, 'Rule, Britannia' was composed in 1740), French commerce would always be vulnerable to the Royal Navy. Louis therefore poured money into his fleet, building new ships called 'seventy-fours', after the number of cannon they carried. Cheaper and faster than Britain's ships, these delivered almost as much firepower. If France kept on building, and if Spain joined France, their allied fleet might eventually outnumber Britain's.

But this was a big if. 'We must not flatter ourselves', French strategists realised, 'that we can long sustain the expense of a navy equal to theirs.' Their plan therefore had a third dimension: Indians, in both North America and South Asia. France would make allies in both places and persuade them to fight the British. Given the right incentives, North American 'Indians' (as Europeans still called them, despite knowing since 1500 that America was not Asia) could connect French colonies in Canada and the Mississippi Valley, encircling and then strangling Britain's colonies (Figure 7.7); and in India, where Britons had been trading since 1592, pro-French princes would shut

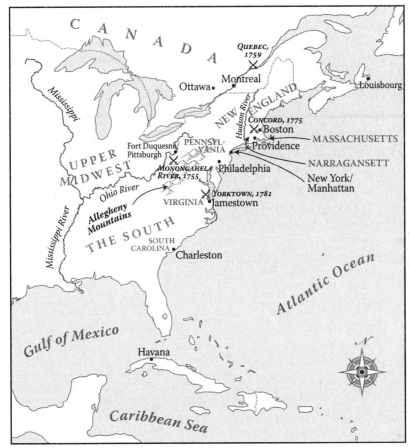

Figure 7.7. The North American stage, 1713–1815.

down British trading enclaves in Bengal and the Carnatic (Figure 7.8). If Britain took the bait, it would send ships and men to both of these peripheral theatres; and then, with Britain friendless and distracted by threats on every front, the *coup de grâce* – a cross-Channel invasion.

Winston Churchill was right to call the conflict that ensued 'the First World War'. Europeans had fought each other in America and Asia before, but never on this scale or with such consequences – even if, as in India, the participants did not always realise what was at stake.

There was certainly money to be made in India, not only from the spices which originally drew the Portuguese there but also from cotton, which became all the rage in England around 1700. 'It crept

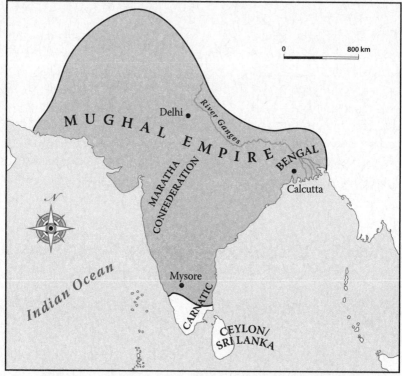

Figure 7.8. The South Asian stage, 1713–1815. (Frontiers of the
Mughal Empire are shown at their greatest extent, in 1707.)

into our houses, our closets, our bedchambers', Daniel Defoe wrote.
'Curtains, cushions, chairs, and at last beds themselves were nothing
but Callicoes or Indian stuffs.' A few men even made spectacular
fortunes, such as Thomas 'Diamond' Pitt, whose grand- and great-
grandsons will feature prominently later in this chapter. Arriving in
India in 1674, Pitt somehow or other – rumours spoke of murder and
dastardly deeds – acquired a 141-carat diamond, still widely considered the purest and fairest in existence. After paying £20,000 for it in
1701, he resold it in 1717 for £135,000.*

---

*Converting currencies across the centuries is a speculative business, but
according to the economist Greg Clark's calculations (https://measuringworth.
com/ukearncpi/), the purchase price was equivalent to about £3.25 million today,
and the sale price to £20 million.

But it was also clear that India was never going to become another America. The powerful Mughal Empire penned foreigners into tightly policed trading posts, which needed long-term, large-scale and high-risk investments to survive at all. Few traders found this attractive, so the Dutch, English and French governments each gave their merchants permission to form an 'East India Company' with monopoly rights. Freed from competition, these Companies could recoup their up-front investments by charging as much for their spices, diamonds and cotton as customers back home could pay – so long as the Companies agreed to fight their own battles (whether against the Mughals or one another), hiring private armies and navies rather than asking their home governments to commit soldiers and ships to protecting them.

This was where French strategists saw their opportunity. The Companies always inhabited a dangerous, murky *demi-monde*, but its risks – and opportunities – grew sharply after 1707, when the Mughal Empire began disintegrating. What few rules there had been went out of the window as the ex-empire's former princes and officials carved its carcass into fiefdoms of their own. The fighting and uncertainty were bad for the European Companies' profits, but on the other hand, they opened up new ways to make money. After all, men who would be kings needed cash and good soldiers if they were to fight each other, and, for a price, the Companies could provide both.

So it was that in the 1740s the British and French Companies each backed a rival candidate as nawab (ruler) in the Carnatic region, and this local conflict merged into their wider world war. Neither London nor Versailles much cared which nawab won, but France sent out a few warships to support its Company – whereupon Britain sent more. Louis was delighted. So what if a British candidate became nawab, so long as London wasted resources on this sideshow? Even better for Louis, the nawab of Bengal seized the British Company's base at Calcutta in 1756, cramming dozens of captives into a tiny cell, where many suffocated. Britain's Company went to war with him (or, more precisely, joined an ongoing civil war against him) to avenge this Black Hole of Calcutta. The British-backed side again won and installed its own nawab, but only at the cost of drawing still more ships, men and money away from Europe. Seen from Paris, this all looked very satisfactory.

If anything, the 'Indians' in North America were even more

helpful, doing most of the fighting in a war that left French forts
controlling the upper Ohio Valley. With the thirteen British colonies
failing to co-ordinate their defence, London again swallowed the bait,
sending two regiments of regulars across the Atlantic to be massacred on the Monongahela River by French Canadians and their native
allies. More tribes flocked to the French side, and British settlers in
the Virginia and Pennsylvania borderlands scurried back towards the
coast.

It had been centuries since Britain's enemies had pursued such a
coherent strategy, and the government was flummoxed. The Whigs
split, and out of their acrimony came a leader of a new kind – William
Pitt, a man whose power depended less on the favour of grandees or
the king (who loathed him) than on public opinion. In many ways
Pitt personified the worst of eighteenth-century politics: he was
obscenely rich (he was Diamond Pitt's grandson), utterly self-centred
('I am sure I can save this country and nobody else can', he told one
prime minister) and represented a parliamentary constituency with
only seven voters. Hume called him a 'wicked madman', yet even one
of Pitt's harshest critics conceded that 'I know nobody, who can plan,
or push the execution of any plan agreed upon, in the manner Mr Pitt
did'. Pitt got things done, and knew *what* to get done.

Pitt agreed with French strategists that the European and Atlantic stages were now linked, but whereas French plans involved using
America and India to distract Britain from the Continent, Pitt did the
opposite. 'America', he insisted, would be 'conquered in Germany'.
By giving Prussia money to hire enough troops to keep France busy,
he argued, Britain could clean up across the seas. It worked. For four
consecutive years British subsidies doubled Prussia's income, and
Prussia's king – Frederick the Great – smashed the Russian and Austrian armies opposing him. Louis XV felt compelled to intervene in
Germany. 'However inconvenient and expensive the German war is
for England,' Pitt reminded Parliament, 'it is more inconvenient and
more expensive for France.' To meet his bills, Louis stopped building
ships. His global strategy then disintegrated. 'No navy, consequently
no strength to resist England', an official agonised in mid-1758. 'The
navy has no more sailors, and having no money cannot hope to
procure them.'

Britain was in a very different position. The fiscal–military state
it had created between 1689 and 1713 left lenders confident that they

could loan Britain whatever it needed. Through thick and thin, the interest was paid on time, and Britain not only funded Prussia but also made its own fleet bigger and better. France had been fought to a standstill again.

With his larger strategy in ruins, Louis decided in 1759 that the only way to salvage anything was by gambling everything on a cross-Channel invasion. He ordered his Mediterranean and Atlantic fleets, currently blockaded in Toulon and Brest, to break out and unite at Quiberon Bay (where Caesar had defeated the Veneti in 56 BCE). From there they should sail north through the Irish Sea, drop an army at the River Clyde, raise a Jacobite revolt in Scotland, carry on around Cape Wrath and finally come back down Britain's east coast, picking up another army in Flanders and dropping it in Essex to march on London.

This was a lot to ask – more, even, than the Spain's Philip II had asked in 1588. Louis's Mediterranean fleet never got anywhere near Quiberon, and his Atlantic fleet had to make a mad dash towards the bay ahead of a ferocious storm, with Britain's ships right behind it. For any other fleets, at any earlier point in history, that would have been the end of the campaign, because neither navy had charts of this complicated coast and no one had ever fought a fleet action in such appalling weather. But this was a new age, and in Edward Hawke, who had joined the navy at fifteen and worked his way up through the ranks, the British had a new kind of commander. As the storm closed in, Hawke signalled a general chase.

Tossed by wind and waves, dodging jagged rocks, his ships crowded into the bay behind the French. 'I say', Hawke's account describes him yelling at his flagship's master amid the chaos, 'lay me alongside the French admiral.' When the veteran sailor sensibly replied that the cliffs were too close, Hawke shouted back, 'You have now done your duty in appraising me of the danger. Let us now see how well you can comply with my orders.' (We excitable, modern types might wonder whether this was actually what Hawke said, or just what he wished he had said; but this was, pray recall, a polite age.) Hawke told his captains to 'hold their fire until they can put their hands on their enemies' guns'. In the darkness, smoke and rain, captains could hardly do much else, but in the madness one French ship after another lurched between Hawke and his prey, only to be ripped apart by point-blank British broadsides. Hundreds of 24-pound iron cannonballs smashed through hulls, spraying the men inside with jagged oak 'splinters' (as sailors called them) big enough to tear off arms and heads. Gunners slipped and slithered in gore. With all order lost, the French turned to flee. The killing continued into the night, until the French flagship, still dodging Hawke, finally ran aground and was burned. 'All that could possibly be done has been done', Hawke wrote politely to the Admiralty.

Nothing in Britain's history, not Agincourt in 1415, not even the Armada in 1588, really compares with 1759. This was arguably the country's finest hour. Nor was it a desperate, backs-to-the-wall moment, like 1940, but one of triumph on every front. With the seas secured, Pitt redirected British funds across the Atlantic, where redcoats recaptured Louisbourg and, helped by American militias, secured the Ohio Valley by storming the crucial Fort Duquesne (renamed Pittsburgh in the great man's honour). Amid heroics to compare with Hawke's, Quebec fell that same year, Montreal in 1760, the last French base in India in 1761 and its remaining sugar islands in the Caribbean (plus Spanish Havana and Manila) in 1762. In France, said one merchant, 'all this came like a clap of thunder', while in Britain, Horace Walpole rejoiced, 'our bells are worn threadbare with ringing for victories'. A new song, 'Heart of Oak' (now the Royal Navy's official march), was a smash hit:

> *Come cheer up my lads, 'tis to glory we steer!*
> *To add something more to this wonderful year;*
> *To honour we call you not press you like slaves,*
> *For who are so free as the sons of the waves?*
> *Heart of oak are our ships, heart of oak are our men;*
> *We always are ready. Steady, boys, steady!*
> *We'll fight and we'll conquer again and again.*

No more was Britain Europe's poor cousin. Even the great rake Casanova, busy as he was with other pursuits, noticed as he traversed Britain in 1759 that 'the people have a special character, common to the whole nation, which makes them think they are superior to everyone else'. One British envoy in Germany actually wrote home that the glories of the 'wonderful year' had 'struck such an awe upon all foreigners, that they look upon us as a race of people superior to the rest of mankind'.

Britons perhaps held an inflated view of their own excellence even before 1759 (and arguably still do), but the 'wonderful year' seems to have given many of them a case of what the modern American general H. R. McMaster calls 'strategic narcissism' – 'a preoccupation with self, and an associated neglect of the influence that others have over the future course of events'. Nations that 'define the world only in relation to their own aspirations and desires', McMaster suggests, always come to grief.

So it was in 1760s Britain. So magnificent did recent events seem that some Britons – Tories, particularly – began wondering whether Pitt had really needed to spend all that money on Continental allies. Maybe, said some, power would have balanced itself anyway, because European states had an interest in shifting their alliances to obstruct France, even without British bribery. Others claimed that the subsidies had not actually distracted France at all. 'Supplying a French army in Germany', said one pamphlet, 'did not take one hand from one of the ports of France, their navy was not impaired by it, their marine and seamen were not lessened.' All that had really been needed, the implication seemed to be, was English heart of oak.

The new king, George III, agreed. He dropped Pitt ('a true snake in the grass') and Frederick the Great ('getting rid of him is what I most ardently wish'), and his ministers relentlessly bullied France and Spain and snubbed Austria. British diplomats made themselves so unpopular in the 1760s that Russia was the only country still willing to consider an alliance, but when Catherine the Great asked for a subsidy, she was firmly told that 'an alliance with Great Britain is too considerable in itself to want the assistance of money to render it valuable'. Not surprisingly, Britain soon had no friends at all.

Strategic narcissism was even more disastrous in America. As usual, everything came down to cash. Tories have always liked low taxes, and much of their anti-Pittism stemmed from the realisation that taxes would have to stay high through the 1760s to pay off the £133 million debt run up by Pitt's policies. Tens of millions of this had been spent in America, but, by tradition, Americans only paid taxes approved by their own assemblies. In their wisdom these taxed themselves at rates around one twenty-fifth of what Islanders paid; and, given that the thirteen colonies no longer needed protection against French Canada, most Americans thought taxes should fall even further.

That hope was dashed by a major uprising by the Odawa/Ottawa people, which so panicked colonial authorities that they made an infamous proposal to eliminate the rebels by sending them blankets infected with smallpox. Anxious to avoid further conflicts, London floated two ideas. First, since settlers' thefts of native land had triggered the revolt, Americans would be banned from moving west of the Alleghenies. Unfortunately, while strategically sensible, this ignored how Americans saw the map. Mobility was a colonist's God-given right; restricting it was tyrannical.

Second, even with mobility restricted, more troops would be needed for the settlers' security. Britain would foot most of the annual £200,000 bill, but proposed raising about £50,000 by extending 'stamp duties' – basically, a fee for official approval of any legal or business document – from the home islands to America. Seen from London, this too looked reasonable (even generous); but it meant a 50 per cent tax increase for most Americans, without their consent. This assaulted not just Americans' prosperity but also their assemblies' sovereignty and their freeborn identity. A king who demanded taxation without representation, the lawyer Patrick Henry argued, 'far from being the father of his people, degenerates into a Tyrant, and forfeits all rights to his subjects' obedience'.

This was fighting talk. A decade earlier not even French invasions had goaded the colonists into working together, but in 1765 they agreed to boycott British goods. Recognising that it would be well-nigh impossible to collect duties from angry subjects 5,000 km away, the government changed tack. In the past, colonists had accepted Britain's right to tax what came in by sea, so London replaced stamp duties with import duties. By this point even that struck Americans as outrageous, and well-organised gangs began tarring and feathering customs officials and pulling down their houses. Troops were deployed to Boston; fist fights with locals became commonplace. One snowy night in 1770 a gang surrounded a sentry, calling him a 'damned rascally Scoundrel Lobster Son of a Bitch' (an odd-sounding insult, but 'Lobster' was slang for a redcoat). Deeply offended, soldiers shot five Bostonians dead.

Everything Parliament did now looked sinister to Americans. Even an apparently clever plan in 1773 to break the boycott by relieving tea of every tax but one backfired; enraged at the sole remaining impost, protesters turned incoming shipments away from New York,

Philadelphia and Charleston and dumped 40 tons of leaves into Boston harbour. Trying to calm the storm, a group of New York merchants offered to pay for the losses, but King George's exasperated ministers now closed Boston's port, shut down Massachusetts's assembly, took tighter control of law, expanded British rights to billet troops and put the Upper Midwest under Quebec's control.

For ten years extremists had been warning moderate Americans that Britain was bent on undermining their identity and security and constraining their mobility, prosperity and sovereignty. These 'Intolerable Acts', as critics called the new laws, seemed to prove their point. Just as radicals had warned, Parliament appeared to be treating Americans the way Charles I had treated the English in the 1640s. Some Americans, like some English before them, felt duty-bound to resist. A Continental Congress in Philadelphia claimed that American assemblies had the same legal status as Britain's Parliament, and New Englanders stockpiled weapons. When British troops seized an arms cache in Concord, Massachusetts, the militia fired a shot heard round the world. By the time a Second Continental Congress sent an 'Olive Branch Petition' to King George, few congressmen still wanted to talk and George no longer cared to listen. America was exiting the United Kingdom.

The breach divided Americans and Britons against themselves as well as against each other. In some colonies, particularly New York (nicknamed Torytown) and the South, remainers outnumbered leavers. Even revolutionaries felt regret. 'Long did I endeavour', Benjamin Franklin wrote, 'to preserve from breaking that fine and noble china vase, the British Empire.' Thomas Jefferson agreed that 'We might have been a free and great people together'. Similarly, British opinion split along party lines, with some Tories favouring force against 'our unnatural children, the Americans', while Whigs often sympathised with this struggle against tyranny. 'Be the victory to whichever host it pleases the Almighty to give it', Pitt suspected, 'poor England will have fallen upon her own sword.'

Consequently, both sides waged war uncertainly. Had Britain armed New York's loyalists, turning the struggle into an American civil war, it might have won as early as 1776. Had it committed fully to military victory, rather than limiting its violence in the hope of bringing Americans to the negotiating table, it might have won around Philadelphia in 1777. Had Britain not been so diplomatically isolated,

France might not have joined the Americans in 1778, followed by Spain in 1779 and the Netherlands in 1780, and Russia might not have organised an anti-British League of Armed Neutrality. Britain would not then have needed to divert resources from fighting the rebels to defending the Channel and the Caribbean. On the other hand, had Congress backed its army more enthusiastically, it might have won sooner. Had its currency collapsed even faster than it did (by 1781 a horse cost $20,000), it might also have lost sooner.

Soldiers like to say that victory goes to whoever makes the last-but-one mistake, and in this case, it was a near-run thing. There were so many snafus, joked one wag, that any 'other General in the world than General Howe would have beaten General Washington, and any other General in the world than General Washington would have beaten General Howe'. But as it was, at the very moment that the revolution seemed most likely to fail, with the American army mutinying and France and the United States both going bankrupt, Britain's general Lord Cornwallis out-errored everyone by getting his army trapped at Yorktown. Even after his surrender Britain still had the ships, men and money to fight on, but Yorktown broke its political will. The narcissistic empire had defeated itself.

Much Too Big to Fail

Informed opinion in the 1770s had held that losing America would send the Isles back from Mackinder's Map to the Hereford version, driving Britons off their Atlantic stage and trapping them once more at the edge of a European one. Shortly before the rebellion Pitt even predicted that an American exit from the empire would tear Britain apart, by tempting every gentleman in England to sell up and relocate across the Atlantic. But shortly after it, his son (also named William, and also prime minister; to distinguish between the two, historians call them Pitt the Elder and Pitt the Younger) noticed something very different. India's value to Britain, he told Parliament, 'had increased in proportion to the losses sustained by the dismemberment of other great possessions' – by which, of course, he meant the American colonies.

There was no cunning plan to compensate for losing North America by conquering South Asia. For one thing, the entire Asian operation was in the East India Company's hands, not the government's, and 'John Company' (as it was known) consistently put short-term profits ahead of long-term strategy. Having ejected the nawab of Bengal in 1757, the Company had thought it only fair to demand that his replacement pay for the troops that propped him up, and over the next eight years top Company-men pocketed kickbacks totalling perhaps £2.5 million for 'facilitating' these deals. Lowlier staff also ran riot in the countryside, ignoring laws and extorting whatever they could. The Company's future governor-general Warren Hastings was shocked at 'the oppression carried out under the sanction of the English name'. It seemed like 'Every man who wears a hat, as soon as he gets free from Calcutta becomes a sovereign prince.'

British rapacity provoked resistance, and the Company had to fight another war in 1764 to clarify who called the shots in Bengal. After that, a new deal was struck. The Company would now pay the nawab an annual fee of £260,000, buying itself the right to assess and collect Bengal's taxes – which also meant taking over the country's courts, so it could settle disputes, and its policing, to enforce decisions. The Mughal emperor himself became a Company employee. The value of Company shares almost doubled, as did the taxes Bengalis paid.

John Company had morphed from a corporation with a security force into an army with a trading division. The Company was now effectively an independent state with 20 million subjects, more than twice as many as King George – yet also not an independent state, because it operated under licence from the British government. This, Company-men seemed to think, freed them from the obligations binding either states or companies. Such a 'vast exportation of coin [. . .] is carried every year to the country of England', the Indian scholar Ghulam Hussain Khan noted, 'that money had commenced to become scarce in Bengal'. The Company's officials carried off so much loot (the word itself being one of the things taken from Bengal at this time) that even Englishmen who had grown up in Pudding Time were shocked.

The Company was out of control. Back in Britain, outrage mounted over its venality. Between 1769 and 1771 roughly one-fifth of the Bengalis it administered starved or died from plague. The Company had not directly caused the rice harvests to fail, and its officers were at least partly right that their ability to lower the death toll was limited; when local princes tried to save their starving subjects in

1784–6 in the face of new harvest failures, one-fifth of the people again died. What really appalled British public opinion was less the Company's failure than its callousness. So many Bengalis were dying that John Company hired 100 men to dump their bodies into the Ganges, but its executives still sent home more than £1 million in personal profits in 1770–71. Its Council boasted that 'notwithstanding the great severity of the late famine, and the great reduction of people thereby, some increase [in revenue] has been made'.

The Company had become a problem – for British sovereignty, because the constitution had no room for 'a state in the disguise of a merchant', as the rising Parliamentary star Edmund Burke called it, but also for British identity. A polite people did not preside over famines. 'We have outdone the Spaniards in Peru!' Horace Walpole complained to a friend. 'What think you of the famine in Bengal, in which three millions perished, being caused by a monopoly of the provisions by the servants of the East India Company?' Pitt the Elder, always touchy about the shady Indian origins of his family fortune, worried that men who had corrupted Bengal would now corrupt Britain too. 'The riches of Asia have been poured in upon us,' he warned Parliament, 'and have brought with them not only Asiatic luxury, but, I fear, Asiatic principles of government.'

It would be nice to think that MPs were men of principle, but prosperity was what worried them most. In elite circles John Company's incompetence mattered more than its corruption. Even as the Company sucked vast fortunes out of Bengal it was going broke. By 1772 its assets stood at nearly £5 million, but its unpaid bills came to £1.6 million and its unfunded obligations to £9 million. So the Company came cap-in-hand to the Bank of England for a million-pound loan. The Bank had already sunk £5.5 million into John Company; if it went under, so would the Bank, leaving Britain unable to service the national debt.

Even more than the South Sea Bubble of 1720, the Company's crisis in 1772 evokes 2008. Gradually, Parliament – just possibly influenced by the fact that two-fifths of its members held Company stock – dismissed all other options until the only one left was an unprecedented, £1.4 million government bailout. The Company's clever accountants even thwarted the obvious step of separating its trading activities from its semi-governmental ones and nationalising the latter. Instead of sending its tax revenues from Bengal straight back to London, the Company started spending them locally on Indian cotton and silk, then selling the fabrics overseas, sending the profits back to Bengal and using them to pay for the next year's tax collection – thus ensuring, one politician lamented, that tax 'revenue was absolutely necessary to the conducting of the commerce, and that the commerce was essential to the collecting of the revenue'. Breaking up the Company was like unscrambling an egg.

Parliament set up supervisory boards, but not much really changed (sounds familiar?). Company-men kept extorting Indian wealth and sending it home (probably another £1.3 million between 1783 and 1793). Eager to channel public outrage to their own ends, politicians in London blamed all this on the Company's governor-general, Warren Hastings, impeaching him before the House of Lords for 'gross injustice, cruelty and treachery against the faith of nations'. After an eight-year trial he was acquitted. The Company kept waging wars, expanding its territory and getting bigger still; and, like Britons in the 2010s, those of the 1780s just learned to live with a corporation that was *much* too big to fail.

Politicians in London had much to answer for, but no one should be surprised that they acted as they did. Britain emerged from the American rebellion in 1781 owing £243 million (nearly twice as much as in 1776), and money had to be found to service this debt. Fortunately, Pitt the Younger (whom we should perhaps call Pitt the Youngest: he was only twenty-four when appointed prime minister in 1783) was also an administrative genius. The main task, he saw, was restoring Britain's credit. He made sure the Company shared its loot, and also committed millions to a Sinking Fund which paid a little off the national debt every single year. He made a cult of efficiency, abolishing countless sinecures and making government accounting less opaque. He undercut smuggling by slashing import duties (especially on tea) and bribery by raising administrators' salaries. Even more valuably, he encouraged Atlantic commerce. Because Americans still needed to export their tobacco, sugar, timber and cod, and to import most of their manufactured goods, there was actually little risk of Mackinder's Map turning back into the Hereford one. Transatlantic trade soon regained pre-revolutionary levels, and just kept growing. The tonnage of British merchant ships doubled between 1782 and 1788; ten years later, over half of Britain's exports went to the United States.

'Honest Billy's' reforms initially barely dented the mountain of debt, but what mattered was the message he sent taxpayers and markets. Money entrusted to him would be well spent. It would buy the navy the biggest dry docks in the world as well as ships sheathed in copper (so they ran faster) and the best cannons and gunpowder anywhere. With the cash left over, Pitt even improved the postal service.

France, by contrast, did none of these things, instead allowing its own debts from the American war to become unmanageable. A belated effort to increase tax revenues in 1789 split the elite and triggered popular revolt. The monarchy fell; France's public finance, army and navy all imploded. Pitt and his colleagues made pious noises about their eagerness to restore the rulers whom God had set over the French people, but in reality Louis's misfortune delighted London's strategists. 'I defy the ablest heads in England, to have planned [. . .] a situation so fatal to its rival, as that to which France is now reduced by her own intestine commotions', Pitt's foreign secretary crowed after the Bastille fell. Pitt went even further, assuring everyone in 1792 that 'there never was a time in the history of this country, when [. . .] we might more reasonably expect fifteen years of peace'.

War broke out almost exactly a year later, and lasted, on and off, for another twenty-two.

The Nearest-Run Thing

France's revolution divided British opinion even more than America's had done. 'How much the greatest Event it is that ever happened in the world!' cheered the Whig leader Charles James Fox. Like-minded crowds chanted 'No Pitt, No War, Bread, Bread!', booed the king and threw stones at 10 Downing Street and the royal carriage. Yet revolutionaries remained a minority. James Woodforde, a Norfolk parson, was more typical in calling protesters 'the most violent & lowest Democrats'. Edmund Burke's *Reflections on the Revolution in France*, roundly denouncing events in Paris, became a bestseller. According to Burke's friend Gilbert Elliot, war with France was a struggle 'between all the order and all the anarchy in the world'.

For the Woodfordes and Elliots, the Parisian New Jerusalem was all too reminiscent of their own country's seventeenth-century enthusiasms. Whatever Pitt did to suppress dissidents, including suspending habeas corpus, therefore seemed fine. France's revolutionaries, like England's in 1649, made themselves pariahs by beheading their king – and, in another parallel, thereby unleashed demons the likes of which few had imagined. A million Frenchmen volunteered to fight for liberty, equality and brotherhood.

This made the French war something entirely new. Unable to feed so many men under arms, France's government sent them across its borders to fend for themselves. There, untrained in forming neat lines and firing disciplined volleys like eighteenth-century professionals, they nevertheless overwhelmed the old-fashioned Austrian and Prussian armies with massed bayonet charges and cannonades. Radical young generals – most spectacularly, Napoleon Bonaparte – learned to get the most from these wild new armies. By 1796 they had overrun northern Italy, the Rhineland and the Low Countries – promptly making France's war very traditional as well as very new. Like Philip of Spain in the 1580s and Louis XIV in the 1690s, Bonaparte began building invasion barges at Dunkirk. All counterscarps and balances of power had collapsed. Even the Royal Navy, the last safeguard of insularity over proximity, was looking shaky, suffering five serious mutinies in 1797.

When England had fought France a century earlier, fears had regularly focused on the Scottish back door, but the Act of Union in 1707 (and subsequent ethnic cleansing of the Highlands) had slammed this shut. Now anxieties shifted to Ireland, just as when Spain had been the foe. Ireland's internal divisions had only grown more complicated across the previous thirty years, and in 1795 a religiously mixed but wholeheartedly republican Society of United Irishmen began covert talks with Paris. Thousands of peasants joined its armed wing, a secret society calling itself 'The Defenders'; in response, loyalists created their own armed Orange Order and the Anglo-Irish elite raised a yeomanry.

The United Irishmen threw the back door open in 1798, proclaiming a republic in County Wexford. Loyalist yeomen promptly crushed them, with a savagery that horrified the English lord lieutenant, despite his wartime experiences in America and India. 'These men have saved the country', he lamented, 'but they now take the lead on rapine and murder [. . .] the conversation, even at my table [. . .] always turns on hanging, shooting, burning, etc., and if a priest has been put to death, the greatest joy is expressed.' The fighting was

over long before French troops could usefully intervene, but it had
left 30,000 dead and had rattled the British. Pitt reran the script of
1707, pushing through a new Act of Union to bring Ireland inside the
United Kingdom of Great Britain.

Ireland, however, was not Scotland. Union made all Scots full
British citizens in 1707, but that did not happen in Ireland in 1801.
Many Irish Protestants bitterly opposed Catholic emancipation, and
King George agreed that lifting legal restrictions on Catholics – essential if the bulk of the Irish were to become British – would violate
his coronation oath to uphold the Anglican Church. The strategists
around Pitt were horrified; leaving Irish Catholics outside the Union,
one insisted, 'must imply alarming weakness in the British dominion
[. . .] for our foreign enemies to make use of'. Pitt resigned in protest,
but George was adamant. Force, not shared identity, would continue
to be what attached Ireland to England. 'Where is the consolidation?'
an Irish MP asked ten years later. 'Where is the common interest?
Where is the heart that should animate the whole?'

With Pitt gone, six successive administrations (including another
under Pitt) oversaw the war, but none found a way to turn older strategies – closing the Channel, funding Continental coalitions, grabbing
France's overseas colonies and waiting for Paris to go bankrupt – into
victory. However, they did stave off defeat. 'Let us be masters of the
[Channel] but for six hours', Napoleon boasted in 1804, 'and we shall
be masters of the world'; but that never happened, even when Spain
added its fleet to France's. Instead, the Royal Navy, enjoying the kind
of overwhelming superiority that American forces would boast over
conventional opponents two centuries later, annihilated the Franco-
Spanish fleets at Trafalgar in 1805, killing ten enemy sailors for each
British death. Tragically, one of the Britons who fell was their match-
less commander, Horatio Nelson; but even so, says the naval historian
Nicholas Rodger, Trafalgar gave Britain 'an unchallenged command
of the sea, in quantity and quality, materially and psychologically,
over all her actual or potential enemies, which she had never known
before'.

No rival would seriously threaten to reopen the Channel for nearly
a century, but Trafalgar was still not enough to win the war. Nor was
using sea power to seize France's colonies, because France had few
colonies left. Far from fighting to preserve what he did have, Napoleon (who had taken over the government in 1799) actually seemed

Figure 7.9. The New Rome: Napoleon's empire at its height in 1810, showing greater France (dark grey), areas administered by France (light grey) and its allies (horizontal lines), plus the battles that defined its limits.

eager to offload them, selling much of the American Midwest to the United States in 1803. Britain did seize Ceylon (now Sri Lanka) and the Cape of Good Hope from Napoleon's Dutch allies, but this did nothing to shorten the war; and when a British officer decided in 1807 – without orders – to seize Buenos Aires and single-handedly liberate Latin America from Spain, things went horribly wrong. Enraged locals killed or captured half his force; British merchants who had rushed to Argentina lost everything.

Funding Continental coalitions went even less well. Despite vast financial outlays, Britain found no new Frederick the Great. Its allies kept losing, and by 1807 Napoleon had shattered four successive coalitions. When he sat down that summer to talk terms with Russia (legend has it that the tsar's first words were 'I hate the English as much as you do'), he dominated Europe as no one had since Roman times (Figure 7.9).

Not even Louis XV in the 1750s came as close as Napoleon to breaking Britain's global position. Marginal notes in his books suggest that even as a teenager he understood India's strategic importance, and in 1798, while the Irish uprising still raged, he concocted a bold – even fantastic – scheme. He would make himself a new Alexander the Great, conquering Egypt and then marching east to team up with native princes and expel the East India Company. Taking with him maps of Bengal and a former French ambassador to the court of Tipu, the anti-British ruler of Mysore in India, Napoleon slipped across the Mediterranean, dodging British patrols. 'Having occupied and fortified Egypt', France's foreign minister announced, 'we shall send a force of fifteen thousand men from Suez to India, to join Tipu-Sahib and drive away the English.'

Egypt, Napoleon insisted, was 'the geographical key to the world'. And so it would be – but not until 1869, when the Suez Canal opened. Napoleon was also right that Egypt would one day drive away the British, but not until 1956 (at which point France was on Britain's side, and Britain had already lost India). In the real world of 1798 the logistical obstacles to invading India from Egypt were so extreme that many historians consider Napoleon's Indian Ocean strategy pure propaganda. In any case, the question became moot when the British fleet, with a derring-do worthy of 1759, destroyed Napoleon's ships at the mouths of the Nile. Bonaparte promptly abandoned his army in the desert and skulked home to France.

The danger, such as it was, was averted; but, just like the Irish crisis, it woke up British officials. Deciding that the French mercenaries with whom Indian princes had for several years been stiffening their armies were part of a larger Gallic plot, the Company struck. It killed Tipu on the walls of his capital in 1799, and four years later broke the Maratha Confederation's French-trained army at Assaye. 'I never was in so severe a business in my life', the British commander confessed, 'and pray to God, I never may be in such a situation again.' But in Assaye's wake, the Company swallowed up most of India. A visiting admiral was only half-joking when he said 'I fear we are aggrandising in this Country full as much as your friend Bony [Bonaparte] at home'.

Thwarted in India, Napoleon came up with a better idea. Britain had followed up its victory at Trafalgar by blockading Continental ports, much as it had done in every war since Elizabeth's against Spain. As Napoleon saw matters, though, Britain needed trade with Europe more than Europe needed trade with Britain. He controlled every major Continental harbour, and if the British wanted a blockade, he would give them one. 'I will conquer the sea through the power of the land', he wrote to his brother, proclaiming that 'No ship coming from England or the English colonies [. . .] will be received in any port'.

The consequences were immediate and brutal. British exports, worth nearly £41 million in 1806, fell to just £35 million in 1808. Five of Manchester's biggest firms went bankrupt in 1810. Work dried up, wages fell and the price of wheat rose by half. Unlike when Louis XIV had unleashed his privateers in the 1690s, England's booming population now needed to import food every year. As in the Battles of the Atlantic in 1915–17 and 1941–3, the spectre of famine was never far away in the early 1810s. Food riots convulsed England in 1811–12.

The Duke of Wellington famously called the Battle of Waterloo 'the nearest-run thing you ever saw in your life', but the economic war of 1807–12 was nearer still. Had Europeans not been so desperate for imported sugar, coffee and tobacco, Napoleon might have got his way – but instead, boycotting Britain just turned every smuggler on the Continent into England's ally. Everyone who could access the black market did so. Napoleon's wife was among the worst offenders, and his brother was so outrageous that Napoleon threw him off the throne he had given him. But the cause was hopeless. When Napoleon invaded Poland in 1807, his army had to buy British overcoats and shoes because no factory on the Continent could make enough.

Napoleon might still have won his trade war had Britain's financial institutions not proved so strong, its taxpayers so resolute and its financiers – especially the German-Jewish Rothschilds – so ingenious. Britain kept finding new markets (not even the disaster at Buenos Aires in 1807 could keep them out of South America). Despite boom and bust, the government's take from customs and excise tripled between 1793 and 1815, and other taxes grew even more. The Younger Pitt had introduced Britain's first income tax in 1797, and by 1815 the payout from it and new property taxes had swelled tenfold.

The money markets never lost confidence in Britain. The national debt quadrupled, but the government kept paying the interest – by 1815, £32 million per year – and attracting new lenders. In the end, money defeated Napoleon, just as it had defeated Louis XIV, XV and XVI. Napoleon's old-fashioned economic advisers only made things worse, assuring him that if he broke his own blockade and sold grain

PEACE AND PLENTY.

Figure 7.10. 'Peace and Plenty': Thomas Rowlandson's 1814 print says it all.

to hungry Englishmen after their disastrous harvest in 1810, Britain would eventually run out of gold. It didn't. Come what may, Britain could always borrow more.

By one calculation, British living standards fell by 1–2 per cent each year between 1807 and 1812, but French living standards fell nearly twice as fast, and it was Napoleon, not Britain's bankers and merchants, who cracked. Bonaparte succumbed to his own strategic narcissism, convincing himself that force was the way to stop rampant smuggling through Portugal and Spain. When he committed troops to both countries in 1807–8, an insurgency swallowed them up. Britain seized the opportunity this presented. By 1811 the Duke of Wellington had 100,000 troops in Spain – more than Marlborough had had in the Low Countries a century earlier – but Napoleon had committed 300,000.

By itself, this Peninsular War could never have broken France, but it was not by itself. In 1812, still believing he could enforce his blockade on Britain through violence, Napoleon invaded Russia too. It was too much: no amount of tactical brilliance could make up for the 500,000 men who disappeared in the snows. Two years later, the armies of yet another British-funded coalition (the seventh) entered Paris. Relief overflowed (Figure 7.10). Britain's church bells rang for victory; publishers printed so many bulletins that they ran out of ink. 'What overpowering events!' one patriotic cleric wrote to his friend. 'Surely there will never be any more news as long as we live. The Papers will be as dull as a Ledger and Politics as insipid as the white of an egg.'

Another bad prediction. Within a year Napoleon was back with a new army. Casting aside its now traditional role of paymaster to Continental coalitions, Britain took the lead in the fighting, meeting him head-on at Waterloo on the traditional counterscarp in the Low Countries. Even by the appalling standards of Napoleonic battles, this was a meatgrinder. One-third of each army, including almost every officer on Wellington's staff, was killed or wounded. Without even stopping to change his bloodstained uniform, the duke's aide galloped and sailed back to London, careening through the West End in a carriage with three French eagles sticking out of the window. He found the prince regent at a society ball, which broke up in pandemonium as revellers spilled out into the streets bawling 'God Save the King!'

'TOTAL DEFEAT OF BONAPARTE!' the *Morning Chronicle* trumpeted hours later. 'We stop the press to announce the most brilliant and complete victory ever obtained by the Duke of Wellington and which will forever exalt the Glory of the British Name.' For a century to come, Mackinder's would be the only map that mattered.

8

WIDER STILL AND WIDER, 1815–65

The World-System

Nine days before Waterloo, after months of debate at Vienna (Figure 8.1), delegates of all Europe's great powers (except France) issued a 'Final Act' describing what post-war Europe should look like. At Utrecht in 1713 a Continental balance of power had still been a radical Tory notion, but at Vienna in 1815 almost every statesman accepted it as the only way to avoid more wars like Napoleon's, which had left 5 million dead. It also gave Britain exactly what its leaders wanted: a solid counterscarp, a secure back door, a navy as strong as the next three or four combined and no rival even thinking about uniting the Continent as a prelude to challenging Britain at sea. Thatcher's Law had been suspended.

But not repealed. Although later writers would wax nostalgic about Britain being 'splendidly isolated in Europe' after 1815, statesmen at the time had no such illusions. Over the next fifty years the struggle to keep Thatcher's Law in check just deepened, rather than ending, Britain's role on the European stage. Playing its constantly changing part well also complicated Britain's efforts to exploit its position in the middle of Mackinder's Map; and its increasingly interlinked global markets in turn revolutionised identity, mobility, prosperity, security and sovereignty within the Isles.

The historian J. R. Seeley is sometimes mocked as a hypocrite for saying in 1883 that Britain had conquered 'half the world in a fit of absence of mind'. Yet there is a sense in which he was right. No one had a script for the role of lead actor on a global stage. The British were making it up as they went along. Without entirely understanding what they were doing, they responded to the changing meanings of geography in the half-century after Waterloo by improvising an organisation not only bigger, richer and stronger but also more delicately balanced than any empire seen before.

Figure 8.1. The Euro-Mediterranean stage, 1815–65 (1830 frontiers shown for the Habsburg and Ottoman empires).

Conventional maps of this empire, of the pink-coloured kind some of us still saw in our schooldays, simply don't do justice to what Victorian Britons built. So big and so new was this structure, sociologists and historians sometimes suggest, that it was no longer really an empire at all. It was a *world-system*, a multi-dimensional network of nodes and connections girdling the entire earth. It was the most intricate organism humans had ever created – yet no one was exactly in charge.

Great Games

Britain's initial priorities in 1815 were to pay down its debts and prevent France from spawning another Napoleon, and the best way to address both seemed to be by sharing the costs of occupying and overseeing the defeated enemy with Austria and Russia. This balance-of-power tactic inevitably raised a string of new concerns. A France that was *too* weak would leave Russia and/or Austria too strong, so, to balance against that, Britain built up Prussia as a counterweight. But a resurgent Prussia might pose a threat itself, so Britain also had to meddle constantly to prevent it (or Austria) from uniting the smaller German states. Every solution either created a new problem or complicated other pressing interests. In principle, Britain favoured the spread of liberalism in Europe, especially when it liberalised trade, but Russia's, Prussia's and Austria's autocrats saw only danger in so much freedom. As early as 1822 Britain, Austria and Russia had fallen out over the liberal uprisings rocking southern Europe from Lisbon to Athens.

Disputes remained manageable so long as liberals and conservatives alike put the balance of power ahead of principles, but geopolitics made inconstant bedfellows. In 1821 reactionary Russia covertly encouraged a Greek nationalist uprising against the Ottoman Empire, because weakening Turkey was one of its major goals, while liberal Britain, normally a champion of small nations, opposed the revolt because it wanted Turkey strong enough to keep Russia out of the Mediterranean. Britain then swung around to supporting Greek freedom, even lending the revolutionaries money. It soon emerged that the rebels were not liberals at all, but by then an independent Greece seemed like the best way to contain Russia, and Britain became its main cheerleader.

Geopolitics mattered even more on the counterscarp. British diplomats were horrified in 1830 when Belgians rebelled against the Dutch rulers imposed on them at Vienna fifteen years earlier, but when France supported the uprising and proposed partitioning Belgian territory – taking the French-speaking parts under Parisian control – Britain dropped its Dutch friends. The merits of an independent and intact Belgium suddenly seemed compelling, especially if ruled by a German prince who happened to be a British citizen (and whose nephew Albert would subsequently marry Queen Victoria). In a final diplomatic coup Britain convinced the Great Powers, including Prussia, to guarantee Belgium's borders and therefore Britain's counterscarp – with momentous consequences in 1914.

In 1830, however, Germany seemed the least of Britain's worries. Even France had taken second place to a new ogre: Russia. Russia had long been a concern, but a distant one. Now, however, it was getting too big to be balanced. It had twice as many subjects and six times as many soldiers as the Isles, plus territories stretching from Germany's borders to Japan's. In the eighteenth century Britain's European and Asian stages had in many ways remained distinct, with balancing driving the plot on the former and imperialism on the latter. Having

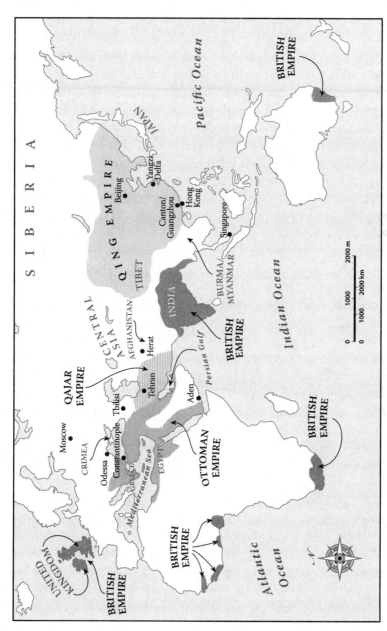

Figure 8.2. Playing the Great Game, 1815–65 (empires marked as they looked in 1830).

become a superpower by turning India into a Company state after the collapse of the Mughal Empire, Britain was now determined not to let the tsar do something similar in the visibly crumbling Ottoman, Qajar and Qing empires, all of which shared borders with Russia (Figure 8.2). Adding vast new territories to the British Empire was unthinkable, so successive British governments tried instead to prop up rickety Asian rulers as bulwarks against St Petersburg. This merged the distinct eighteenth-century European and Asian stages into a single nineteenth-century Eurasian one, on which Britons and Russians played out a deadly, twilight struggle between spies, assassins and (for reasons which will become clear) mapmakers. Kipling famously called it 'the Great Game'.

The early rounds focused on Turkey, where Russia had been trying for a century to reach the Mediterranean via Constantinople (which Russians took to calling 'Tsargrad'). Successive tsars put pressure on Turkey in the 1820s by posing as protectors of its Christian subjects (including the Greeks), and when the Ottoman governor of Egypt rebelled in 1831, France – which had kept up its Egyptian connections since Napoleon's time – amplified Russia's demands to partition the Turkish Empire. Britain's interests seemed certain to suffer, until the foreign secretary, Lord Palmerston, brokered a deal opening Turkey to Western European trade. This gave France reasons to support Britain in keeping Russia out, and by 1853, when Russia intervened to shield Turkey's Christians from religious oppression, France even joined Britain and the Ottomans in invading Crimea. The ensuing struggle is best remembered for military bungling and Florence Nightingale's efforts to introduce hygiene to hospitals; yet, badly as the war went for Britain, it went even worse for Russia, which subsequently left Turkey alone for twenty years.

Persia was a different story. At first seeing less at stake here than in Turkey, Britain ignored Qajar requests for help against Russian aggression, with the unsurprising result that the Persian shah and the Russian tsar made a deal. With Russian encouragement, Persia turned east in 1836, besieging the oasis city of Herat, known ominously as 'the Gate of India'. This got London's attention: what use were Britain's fleets if Persia opened a path to Herat and Russians could simply walk down it to Delhi?

In reality, a thousand kilometres of steppes, deserts and mountains separated Russia from Herat and another thousand separated Herat

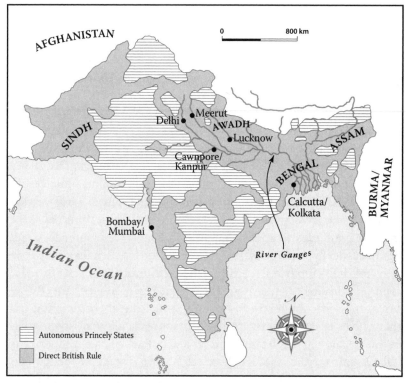

Figure 8.3. The South Asian stage, 1815–65 (1857 frontiers).

from Delhi (Figure 8.3), but four decades after Napoleon's Egyptian adventure Europeans still had no decent maps of Central Asia. Policy hawks in India therefore decided in 1839 to invade Afghanistan to make it a counterscarp for India. This was a bad idea, badly executed. Almost everyone involved died. To the men on the spot, however, it seemed eminently reasonable. The East India Company had solved most of its problems since the 1740s with force, and, despite frantic instructions from London telling them to stop, Britons dealt with local difficulties between 1819 and 1839 by shooting their way into Singapore, Burma, Assam and Aden. Legend has it that after ignoring orders not to invade the rich lands of Sindh in what is now Pakistan, one not so remorseful conqueror sent his classically educated superiors a single-word telegram which surely ranks as the worst pun of all time: '*Peccavi*', Latin for 'I have sinned' ('I have Sindh').

The Company was equally voracious where there was no con-
ceivable Russian threat. In 1848 it proclaimed that a 'Doctrine of
Lapse' allowed it to confiscate the lands of any client prince whose
heir was adopted rather than a direct descendant. Eight years later
it seized the kingdom of Awadh, which had an entirely legitimate
heir. This destroyed what little remained of local elites' trust. It was
no secret that Delhi, the sole remnant of the Mughal Empire, would
be next. 'It appears to me inexpedient to recognise any of the sons as
Heir Apparent', the British Resident told everyone.

For a century the Company had peddled the fiction that it was
really just an agency of the Mughal Empire, running India on the
natives' behalf. Company men played the part, often living just like
elite Indians. Scholarly types studied Sanskrit; others put on native
dress (a good idea in sticky Bengal), learned to love spicy food and
enthusiastically embraced Indian sexual mores. Britain's first Resident in Delhi reportedly promenaded around the city walls every
evening with his thirteen wives, each on her own elephant. By the
1820s, though, administrators coming out from the Isles often cast
themselves in very different roles. A more muscular Christianity was
in the air, along with heightened feelings of white racial superiority.
'Our Asiatic territories were given to us', one director preached, 'not
merely that we might draw an annual profit from them, but that we
might diffuse among their inhabitants, long sunk in darkness, vice
and misery, the light and benign influences of Truth.'

This 'moral regeneration of India', as one governor-general
called it, was not complete humbug. Mughal emperors had spent 150
years trying to stamp out suttee (the burning of widows on their hus-
bands' funeral pyres), but in 1829 the Company succeeded where they
had failed. However, even Indians who admired Britain rarely desired
compulsory Christian regeneration. 'The distant and contemptible
manner in which we are treated by the generality of English gentlemen', complained a pupil in Delhi's English College, 'wounds our
hearts and compels us to forget the blessings of English rule.' Britain's
first Resident (he of the thirteen wives) agreed: 'I fear we do not gain
much Popularity in the eyes of the natives by such degradation.'

The Company had suppressed worse discontent than this in the
past, but two further issues amplified it in the 1850s. One was hunger
in the countryside, where cheap British textiles were driving millions
of weavers out of business. The other, even more pressing, was anger

in the army. The Company issued its 300,000 native troops, many of them already unhappy about racism and falling pay, new rifles plus ammunition which came pre-packaged in paper cartridges, greased to slide snugly down the gun barrels. All a soldier now had to do was bite the cartridge to release the gunpowder, then ram the slick package into place. But that was the problem: the grease ordered by the government was made from pork and beef, turning the cartridges into an equal-opportunity insult to anyone, Hindu or Muslim, who put such abominations to his lips. The offending lubricant was immediately withdrawn, but the insult lingered. A mutiny at Meerut was mishandled; rebellion spread to Delhi; and, to his surprise, the eighty-two-year-old Mughal emperor was sprung from semi-captivity and appointed its leader. Within weeks Britain had lost much of northern India.

For a while, 1857 looked as threatening as 1776, but the Mughal emperor was no George Washington. Peasants, soldiers, urban elites and princes each wanted different things, and when they failed to act together, British reinforcements steadily turned the tide. Fuelled by lurid newspaper accounts of a massacre at Cawnpore (modern Kanpur) and a bitter siege at Lucknow, even liberal Britons sanctioned extreme violence. Deep wells of hatred were unsealed, with vile deeds done on both sides. Some Britons justified their actions by pointing out that while rebels had murdered 1 in 7 of the Europeans in their country, they themselves killed at most 1 in 250 Indians – even though, South Asians responded, this meant that Britain had avenged its 6,000 dead by killing over 1 million Indians. Either way we look at it, it was a grim balance sheet, which destroyed any notion that Indians supported the empire. Parliament stepped in, finally abolishing the East India Company and Mughal Empire and taking direct control itself.

Above all, the insurrection* underlined the need to keep Asia's remaining empires stable, lest Britain be drawn into further bloodbaths. All eyes therefore turned to China, where the Qing dynasty had

---

*Few things get historians quite so agitated as names. The term 'Indian Mutiny', used for generations in Britain, is now widely considered to belittle the events. Indian, Pakistani and Bangladeshi historians usually speak of the First War of Indian Independence, while Western scholars try to get away with more neutral-sounding words like Uprising, Revolt or (the one most used in the 1850s) Insurrection.

been battling uprisings of its own for decades. So far, Britain's support of the Qing had been half-hearted. On the one hand, London wanted a China strong enough to resist Russian encroachment; on the other, it wanted one too weak to enforce protectionist policies. Since 1757 Western traders had only been allowed into a single port, Canton (modern Guangzhou), and almost the only thing Chinese officials would let them sell was silver. This quickly became a problem for the Company: demand for tea was booming at home, but the Company's bullion reserves were steadily shrinking. So, nothing if not ingenious, Company men found an appalling solution. Regardless of what Chinese officials wanted, Chinese people wanted opium; the world's best opium grew in India; so, the Company should sell Indian opium to Cantonese addicts able to pay in silver, use the silver to buy tea and then sell the tea back in Britain, profiting at every point. By the 1830s this bargain provided Chinese smokers with over 10 tons of opium every year (enough to keep 2–3 million users permanently high) and Britons with all the tea in China.

Now saddled with both an opium epidemic and massive outflows of silver, the Qing government declared war on drugs in 1839, seizing hundreds of tons of dope from foreign dealers and destroying it. But, instead of being sent to jail, British drug lords lobbied Lord Melbourne, the prime minister, to recoup their £2 million loss. Melbourne, a rather nastier character than the suave, witty version portrayed by Rufus Sewell in the television series *Victoria*, caved in and – despite facing simultaneous crises in Egypt, Persia and Afghanistan – dispatched a flotilla to Canton. Swatting aside Chinese defences, its threat to cut off Beijing's food supply convinced the Qing government not only to reimburse Melbourne's £2 million (plus interest and the costs of the campaign) but also to open five ports to merchants and missionaries and surrender Hong Kong as a base.

The parallels with British behaviour in eighteenth-century Bengal were hard to miss. In China, as in India, defeat at Western hands destabilised the native regime, emboldening Britons to demand further concessions. When the Qing finally refused to co-operate in 1856, an Anglo-French force marched on Beijing, just as the Company had marched on Delhi a century earlier. 'We might annex the Empire, if we were in the humour to take a second India in hand', its commander concluded; but by the time he reached the Forbidden City, in 1860, the Indian uprising had made that look most undesirable.

Rather than burning Beijing, which would surely have toppled the regime, the expedition contented itself with vandalising and looting the emperor's beautiful Summer Palace. Having humiliated the emperor, Britain then provided mercenaries (and loans to pay for them) to help his armies fight the rebels.

If the Qing had fallen, China would probably have become the stage for an even greater game than the one already being played from Tbilisi to Tibet, and that was not in Britain's interests. Moreover, Britain would not just have been playing against Russians; in China, they would also have faced Frenchmen and, increasingly, Americans. After annexing California in 1848, thousands of Yankees had crossed the Pacific, whether to chase whales, spread the Word or sell opium in Canton. Their government did its bit to help them, sending a fleet in 1854 to bully Japan into opening its ports. In much the same way that containing Russia had linked previously distinct European and Asian stages into a single Eurasian one, confronting the young United States now linked the entire Old-World stage to a New-World one.

New Worlds Called Forth

For over 10,000 years, since rising sea levels flooded the land bridge between Siberia and Alaska, the Old- and New-World stages had been almost completely separate. Only since 1492 had they been rejoined, entirely to the Old World's advantage. Humans, other animals, microbes, ideas and institutions had flowed westwards across the Atlantic, with horrifying consequences for American natives. The imbalances had still not entirely evened out in 1823, when the American secretary of state, John Quincy Adams, warned President James Monroe that Europeans intended to 'recolonize' the continent. 'Russia might take California, Peru, Chili [*sic*]; France, Mexico', he said. 'Great Britain [. . .] would take at least the island of Cuba for her share of the scramble' (Figure 8.4).

Adams was mistaken. Transatlantic balances still favoured Europe, but a Cuban colony was a burden Britain definitely did not want. The real appeal of America was its markets, and after colonists from the Rio Grande to Cape Horn started rising up against their protectionist masters in Lisbon and Madrid in 1820, British goods poured in. So long as Iberian imperialists could be kept out of the Americas, Britain's foreign secretary, George Canning, reasoned, there would be

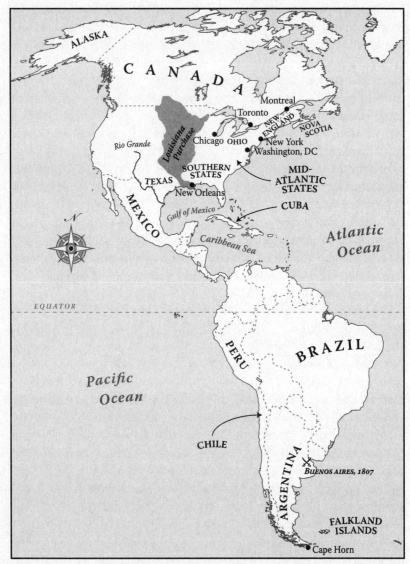

Figure 8.4. The American stage, 1815–65.

no need to repeat anything like the disastrous 1807 attempt to open Buenos Aires to free trade. So, when Monroe responded to Adams's warning by announcing that 'the American continents [. . .] are henceforth not to be considered as subjects for future colonization by any

European powers', Canning was delighted. The United States would now shoulder the burden of keeping imperialists out of America. 'The deed is done, the nail is driven', he wrote. 'Spanish America is free; and if we do not mismanage our affairs sadly, she is English. The Yankees will shout in triumph, but it is they who lose most.'

Britain hardly renounced the use of force in the New World after 1823. Between the 1830s and 1850s it occupied the Falkland Islands as a base to protect trade around Cape Horn and sent gunboats to secure investments in Peru, Argentina and Brazil. However, the main British actors on the American scene were now bankers and commissioning agents, not Royal Marines. Fanning out, they bought up coffee, sugar, hides and guano and lent Americans the money to buy British tea, textiles and iron. By 1850, 10 per cent of Britain's imports came from South America and the same proportion of exports went there, making it in both respects second only to India. It was immodest of Canning to say 'I called the New World into existence to redress the balance of the Old', but not entirely inaccurate.

Despite mutual animosity, Britain's role in North America evolved in similar directions. The United States' expansion required capital, which British banks happily supplied. Barings, the biggest, bankrolled Jefferson's Louisiana Purchase in 1803 and the spread of cotton plantations across the new territories. It meant huge profits for all involved, except, of course, the African slaves imported to do the work. The slaves' presence complicated Britain's role in America enormously. After two centuries in which abolitionists had been considered cranks, liberal opinion had now swung against human trafficking (but not against its fruits: Britons consumed more tobacco, sugar and cotton than ever before). In 1807 the British and American governments both banned the transatlantic trade, and in 1833 Britain went further, outlawing slavery across its entire empire. British interceptions of American ships suspected of slave-trading caused constant friction. One of the main American goals in annexing Texas in 1845 was the fear that if Britain got in first, a Texan colony would become a safe haven for runaway slaves.

But Britain's leaders had no such intentions, because land wars in the Americas were the last thing they needed. Britain also kept clear of the North–South Civil War, despite multiple approaches from the Confederacy. Anglo-American disagreements were quietly negotiated away until Canada was the one remaining source of friction. Initially, Americans and Canadians alike assumed that its annexation

to the United States was, as a Nova Scotian put it in 1824, the 'event
[. . .] which we all know must happen', but as years passed and it didn't
happen, the assumption steadily weakened. War scares did continue:
in 1837 Canadian troops killed an American inside the United States;
in 1844 James Polk ran for president on the slogan 'Fifty-four forty or
fight!', threatening war over the latitude of the American–Canadian
border; and in 1859 a British pig started a stand-off by wandering into
an American potato patch. But in the end there was just too much
space in North America for either London or Washington to fight
over borderlands that one prime minister bluntly called 'a few miles,
more or less, of miserable pine swamp'.

Such condescension was common. British politicians rarely took
Canada seriously. It was, said one peer, 'a last resource to people who
have ruined themselves at home [. . .] with scarcely a gentleman or
a good income among them'. Even that, though, was positive compared with the ways Britons saw some of the other outposts they
picked up in these years. When Captain Cook claimed Australia in
1770 (Figure 8.5), no one could think of anything to do with a continent of red sand and poisonous insects on the far side of the world
except dump convicts there. New Zealand, spotted in 1769, did not
seem fit even for that. Few Europeans except whalers, sealers and
missionaries went there, and Britain felt no need to claim the islands
until 1840. South Africa seemed to offer still less, although the Cape
of Good Hope at least had enough strategic rationale to justify the
presence of several thousand soldiers.

The thought that Canada, let alone Australia, New Zealand
or South Africa, might become settler societies comparable to the
pre-revolutionary thirteen colonies seemed laughable in 1815. The
problem, the colony-booster Edward Gibbon Wakefield observed,
was that 'A Colony that is not attractive to women, is an unattractive
colony'; and these rough and ready frontiers (which, for convenience,
I will call by their later name, 'Dominions') were not places anyone
wanted to raise a family. In fact, one colonial secretary admitted in the
1830s, most British politicians believed 'that we have no interest in preserving our colonies and ought to make no sacrifice for that purpose'.

This changed so quickly that by the 1860s the author Charles
Dilke was calling the Dominions 'Greater Britain', and arguing that
Britain's future lay with them. This transformation had been fuelled
by a massive upsurge in mobility. In one of the biggest gene flows in

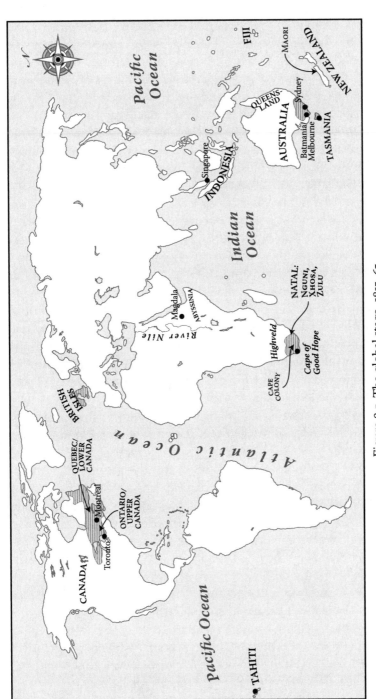

Figure 8.5. The global stage, 1815–65.

history, over 7 million souls departed British shores between 1815 and
1870. About 3 million went to the United States, but almost everyone
else headed to the Dominions. Their mobility created entirely new
kinds of British identity, challenged traditional ideas of sovereignty
and had major repercussions on prosperity and security.

Canada, with its pockets of fertile farmland, direct links to
American and British markets and established settlements, led the
way. Arrivals (mostly Protestant Irish, often entire families) doubled
between the 1820s and 1850s, turning Toronto and Montreal into real
towns. The latter was 'increasing hourly in population, wealth and
enterprise', the *Boston Recorder* warned Americans. In Australia the
visionary governor, Lachlan Macquarie, and 17 million imported
sheep turned a prison camp into a ranching economy: the 50,000 ex-
Britons, overwhelmingly convicts, of 1815 grew by 1861 to more than a
million white Australians, almost all free (the last boatload of jailbirds
arrived in 1868). Sydney and Melbourne (which originally gloried in
the name Batmania) became just as urban as Toronto and Montreal.
Distant New Zealand moved more slowly, only acquiring its first religious mission, permanent whaling station and agricultural colony
(which quickly failed) in the mid-1820s. South Africa was slowest of
all, receiving 5,000 British immigrants in 1820, but few more until gold
was discovered in the 1880s.

British governments still tried to ignore these far-flung outposts,
and when they did engage with them, it was usually for the same reason
they engaged with Asia's empires: fear of European rivals getting in
first. In the Dominions, France seemed more threatening than Russia.
In 1815, 320,000 of Canada's 800,000 Europeans were still descendants
of the French settlers conquered by Britain fifty years earlier, and in
Lower Canada (modern Quebec), the proportion reached 80 per cent.
Yet, despite violence in 1837–8, ex-Britons had outbred and out-immi-
grated ex-French by the mid-century. Anglo-Quebecois antagonisms
continued (and still do), but the risk of secession, let alone a French
invasion, grew ever more remote. Visits from French ships also
inspired alarms in Australia and New Zealand, and not just among
Britons: after a sighting in 1831 some of New Zealand's indigenous
Maoris petitioned the British king to become 'a friend and guardian
of these islands'. (They need not have worried: even annexing flecks
of sand like Tahiti almost exceeded France's capabilities.)

In South Africa the European rivals were Boers (or Afrikaners), hardscrabble farmers descended from Dutch and German settlers. When Britain took over the Cape, 20,000 Boers (plus their 25,000 African slaves) already lived there, and British immigration and breeding never caught up. The Boer majority's lifestyle – especially its embrace of slavery – struck most Britons as disgraceful, and the Boers remained resolutely uninterested in becoming British. Instead, after London outlawed slavery in 1833, 15,000 of them staged a Boer-exit. Taking their wagons beyond Britain's reach, they set up their own republics on the Highveld, where they could enslave whomever they liked. Embracing the old inside-the-tent-pissing-out principle, Britain extended its colony's borders in 1848 to bring the Boers back under the canvas, only to decide after six years that these people really were better left outside.

The Boer problem was not unique. All too many emigrants, British as much as Dutch, had gone overseas primarily to steal everything they could. They were outraged when governors, worried about the expense of garrisons or the rights of natives, told them to stop. 'Ah! Those good old times, when I first came to New Zealand', one colonist reminisced, 'before governors were invented, and law and justice and all that.' Like Americans in the eighteenth century, all Britain's overseas settlements eventually clashed with law, justice and all that, and in every case Britain found controlling opinionated emigrants thousands of kilometres from home a tall order.

Again Canada led the way. Separate uprisings roiled Ontario and Quebec in 1837. Neither amounted to much, but, wiser now than in 1776, London dispatched a team of grandees under Lord Durham to look into the rebels' grievances. Its recommendations combined the cynical – unite Quebec and Ontario, to smother French identity under the weight of British numbers – and the stoical, conceding more or less what Americans had wanted in the 1770s. Durham called this 'responsible government'. Let white Canadian men (French as well as British) elect their own government, he argued; its politicians would soon moderate their wild speechifying when they had to answer to voters for the results. Some in London resisted surrendering so much sovereignty to colonials, but there was an unassailable counterargument – what was the alternative? When opposing settlers, the Colonial Office conceded, 'we are almost always worsted'. Britain couldn't afford to refight an American Revolution on every continent. So, by 1845, Canada had responsible government.

London was more cautious when other Dominions demanded it. There were, after all, limits to how badly a Canadian government could behave. Its powerful American neighbour ruled out most land grabs, and Canada had not fought a serious war against First Peoples since 1816. In South Africa, by contrast, settlers had attacked the Xhosa and Nguni as recently as the 1830s–40s. In Australasia, Queenslanders were still raiding aboriginals, white Tasmanians had more or less exterminated their indigenous neighbours and New Zealanders were fighting the bloodiest war of all against the Maori, which dragged on until 1860. Yet once again, given the costs of trying to coerce its violent offspring, Britain yielded. Australia won responsible government in 1850 and New Zealand in 1852. South Africa took longer because, while its settlers did not share the Boers' fondness for slavery, they did not want to share the vote with Africans either. Officially, Cape Colony only received responsible government in 1872 and Natal in 1893, but representatives elected by whites were in fact deciding most issues before 1860.

New kinds of New Worlds were being called forth in the Dominions, filled with new kinds of Britons, mostly more prosperous and freer than they would have been back home. They created new identities, lifestyles and versions of the English language. Yet despite forging their identities in conflict with the old country, as Americans had done, the once rebellious white Canadians, Australians, New Zealanders and South Africans (Boers excepted) came to identify more, not less, with the Isles. We can only wonder how things might have gone if Britain had sent its American colonists a Lord Durham, rather than imperial narcissists, in the 1760s.

We do not have to wonder what would have happened to the various New Worlds' natives, though, because wherever Europeans settled, disaster followed. Indigenous numbers fell by one-third in Canada between 1815 and 1900, one-half in New Zealand between 1840 and 1896 and over four-fifths in Australia between 1788 and 1911. Only in South Africa, where white immigrants were rarer and locals had had longer to adapt to Eurasian diseases, did native numbers stay strong. But even there, the survivors lost their lands and liberty. The Maori had a proper treaty with Britain, but it didn't stop them being told, six years after signing it, that their property rights were 'a vain and unfounded scruple'.

What a dizzying contrast this made with the world of Henry

VIII, just three centuries earlier. In the 1540s an isolated and uncertain England had clung to the edge of a hostile Catholic Continent, surrounded by enemies and fearing for its very survival; in the 1840s a mighty and boastful Britain strutted a stage that girdled the world. People, goods and ideas rolled downhill from British heights to the masses huddled at its feet. For most people on the planet, history was now about dealing with what came their way from the Isles.

A Mighty Spirit

And what a lot of that there was. Depending on how we count, Britain's economy grew five- or sixfold between 1760 and 1860, and because the proportion of its products sold overseas roughly doubled, its exports expanded at least tenfold. There had never been such a boom. It revolutionised identity, mobility, prosperity, security and sovereignty, not only in Britain but also across most of the planet.

British commerce and agriculture – especially in England and the Scottish Lowlands between Glasgow and Edinburgh (Figure 8.6) – had begun an organisational revolution well before 1815. The sixty-four Parliamentary Acts of Enclosure in the 1740s had increased to 574 by the 1810s. Markets steadily expanded, the division of labour deepened and trades turned into professions. In 1760 a farmer with a sick horse asked his farrier what to do; a century later he called a college-trained vet. The first three-year course in animal medicine was offered in 1791, and the Army Board recognised specialised veterinary surgeons in 1796. By the 1820s not one but two veterinary journals were being published. The Royal College of Veterinary Surgeons was chartered in 1844, and an 1852 list of qualified vets contains 1,733 names.

Professionalisation infected every walk of life. Accountants, for instance, split into sub-specialities, one of which invented actuarial tables and became insurance agents. In 1783 five firms were offering life insurance; in 1844 it was 105. Banking went the same way. For every local bank operating in 1784 there were almost six in 1815. By then, paper money was circulating widely and was generally trusted, and capital was abundant enough for aspiring entrepreneurs usually to be able to borrow at interest rates below 3 per cent.

In the 1720s the world's most productive workers had been Asians, in Bengal and China's Yangzi delta, but by the 1770s parts of

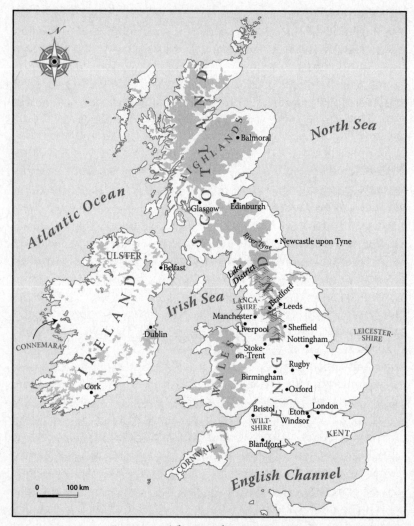

Figure 8.6. The British stage, 1815–65.

England had overtaken them. Yet somehow, other parts of the Isles remained so far behind that one-quarter of country folk were receiving welfare. English radicals usually blamed this on exploitative elites while English conservatives condemned feckless paupers, but in 1798 the curate Thomas Malthus suggested a disturbing alternative. The issue, he proposed, was not one of morality: it was one of mathematics. When population was low, land was plentiful and demand for labour strong. This drove wages up, while keeping rent, food and real estate cheap, because fewer people meant less demand. Overall, this was good for the poor and bad for the rich. However, high wages and cheap food allowed workers to feed their babies better, enabling more to survive – which pushed the population up, reversing the previous patterns. Wages now fell while rents, food prices and land values rose. This was good for the rich and bad for the poor, but would necessarily continue until enough of the poor starved, emigrated or stopped having children to bring population down again. Then, the whole cycle would restart. Good weather, agricultural improvements, cheaper transport and so on made differences at the margins, but that was all, and their effects did not last. This Malthusian Trap, as we now call it, was an iron law of political economy.

Eighteenth-century England fitted Malthus's model perfectly. After decades of stability the population had risen from 6 million to 9 million in the forty years before he wrote. Hard work and more skilful farming did increase food production, but by less than 10 per cent. All the gains of Pudding Time were eaten up. Wages fell, often by 10–20 per cent, while the real price of a loaf of bread doubled between 1740 and 1770 and then doubled again by 1800. Consumption of tobacco, sugar and coffee declined (although tea-drinking increased). Napoleon's embargo, bitter winters and poor harvests only added to the misery of the 1800s.

Perhaps one English person in five regularly went hungry, yet, in contrast to earlier centuries, few actually starved. As hard as times were, records of the heights of teenagers recruited into the army suggest that boys born after 1800 were actually taller – normally a sign of better childhood nutrition – than those born in the 1780s–90s. Historians debate the details, but it seems that the half-century after 1760 saw yet another bifurcation, with misery at the bottom but success for many in the middle, while at the top money flowed in. With land paying high dividends, whoever could do so bought more of it. Its price doubled across a century. In 1700 peers had owned about one-sixth of England's broad acres; by 1800 they held closer to one-quarter, and the 0.01 per cent pulled away from the other 99.99. It is against this background that we should judge characters like Jane Austen's Dashwoods and Bennets. They cling to their all-important gentility because they know that, if just one daughter makes the right marriage, all will be well – but if not, the whole family might sink into the mass of 'Nobodies' (defined by the novelist Henry Fielding as 'All the people in Great Britain except about 1,200').

Many hoped that once Napoleon was gone, tariffs and embargoes would wither, effectively adding all the land on the Continent to Britain's food supply and driving down the price of bread. This seemed so obviously good for so many that some made free trade an article of faith. 'Free Trade is implied in the primeval benediction God pronounced on Man', one Methodist minister insisted, and a governor of Hong Kong was even blunter – 'Jesus Christ is Free Trade, and Free Trade is Jesus Christ'.

The landowners who had done so well when Napoleon's trade war drove up the price of food grown on their land disagreed, however, and lobbied Parliament for protection; and since so many of these landowners were MPs themselves, Parliament obligingly passed a 'Corn Law' banning wheat imports until home prices reached exorbitant levels. Outrage against protectionism and the 0.01 per cent now turned ugly. When 60,000 protested at St Peter's Field in Manchester in 1819, the yeomanry killed at least eleven and injured 600 more. The government suspended habeas corpus. Conspirators came close to blowing up the entire cabinet in 1820, and there was talk of French-style revolution.

Salvation came from augmenting Britain's organisational breakthroughs with technological ones which extended the stage on which Britons acted, but in a direction few had anticipated: downwards. Right beneath their feet was an underground kingdom of coal. People had known about it, and been digging it up, for millennia; what changed now was how they used the energy trapped in fossil fuels. Until the eighteenth century coal was almost exclusively burned to heat houses and food, and demand had expanded as population growth ate away at Britain's other major fuel source, its forests. In 1700 Londoners had consumed 800,000 tons of coal, mostly shipped in from Newcastle upon Tyne, but they needed 1.5 million tons in 1750 and 2.5 million in 1800. Because coal, unlike trees, is non-renewable, the veins nearest the surface were quickly exhausted, and although shafts could be dug deeper, groundwater eventually flooded them all. Draining them, while possible (one ingenious pit owner yoked 500 horses to a bucket chain), was also ruinously expensive.

To the practical men who drank coffee, haunted provincial assembly rooms and ran coal mines the solution was obvious. They could burn some of the coal they dug up, use the heat released to boil water and channel the steam into driving pistons, and these pistons would pump the water out of their mines. But this was easier said than done, and not until 1698 did anyone actually convert principle into practice. The first working engine, the 'Miner's Friend', was cheaper than feeding 500 horses, but it was slow, could raise only 12 m of water and had a markedly *un*friendly tendency to explode. Worst of all, it was horribly wasteful. Because it used a single cylinder to boil water and then condense the steam, operators had to reheat it for every stroke of the piston. There was a lot of ingenious tinkering, but no engineer managed to convert more than 1 per cent of coal's energy into force. 'The vast consumption of fuel of these engines is an immense drawback on the profit of our mines', one owner complained. 'This heavy tax amounts almost to a prohibition.'

The breakthrough came in 1765, when a model of a steam engine made its way to Glasgow University. We academics have a certain reputation for being unable to make machines work, and so the device ended up in the hands of James Watt, the university's Mathematical Instrument Maker. Watt got it going, but its inefficiency offended his craftsman's soul – until, out for a walk one Sunday, he had a brainwave. As he told it, since 'steam was an elastic body it would rush into a vacuum, and if a communication was made between the [boiling] cylinder and an exhausted vessel, it would rush into it, and might there be condensed without cooling the cylinder [. . .] the whole thing was arranged in my mind'.

Separating the boiling and condensing chambers, then keeping the former hot and the latter cold (rather than constantly heating, cooling and reheating a single chamber) cut coal consumption by three-quarters. It was as brilliant as it was simple, even if, like so many inspired Scotsmen before and since, Watt had to relocate to England to capitalise on it. There, funded by the equally brilliant Birmingham manufacturer Matthew Boulton, he staged a grand public display of his engine, pumping 20 m of water from a mine in sixty minutes flat, outperforming older machines while burning just a quarter as much coal.

This was in 1776, a year of great events, but I would rank Boulton and Watt's exhibition above any of them. Almost immediately, manufacturers of all sorts saw what these engines might do, with cotton kings leading the way. When the East India Company began importing light, brightly coloured Asian calicoes in the seventeenth century, British wool merchants, seeing sales slump, had hit back by lobbying Parliament to ban the cloth. Raw cotton could still be imported and spun and woven in the Isles, but British spinners and weavers were much less skilled than Bengalis. In the 1760s the market for British cotton was just one-thirtieth of that for British wool.

Enter James Watt. For 10,000 years textile production had depended on nimble-fingered women (men less often) twisting wisps of fibre on to spindles. Through most of this time a spinster had needed 5,000 hours to produce a kilogram of yarn. The invention of pedal-powered spinning wheels in the twelfth century cut that to 2,000 hours, and in the eighteenth century, marvellous new machines with equally marvellous names (Hargreaves's jenny, Arkwright's throstle, Crompton's mule), powered by windmills and waterwheels, slashed that to just three hours – *if* the wind was blowing or the streams running. Now, however, steam engines could provide jennies and throstles with reliable, cheap energy regardless of the weather. The first fully steam-powered mill opened in 1785.

English machines spun cotton that was often as good as but *always* cheaper than Indian products. Costs collapsed, from nearly £5 per kilogram of finished cloth in 1786 to under £1 in 1807. Applying steam power to weaving as well as spinning in the 1830s made British cotton 200 times cheaper than Indian. As prices fell, demand boomed. Hundreds of thousands of men, women and (especially) children laboured in mills twelve or more hours a day, six days a week. Production soared from 3,000 bales in 1790 to 178,000 in 1810, and 4.6 million in 1860. Exports (many of them back to India, where cheap Lancashire cloth undercut local products) grew a hundredfold between 1760 and 1815, becoming the source of almost one-twelfth of the nation's income.

A consumer revolution began. Peasant women who had spent multiple weeks each year making clothes could now buy them for just a few days' wages. And that was just the beginning: steam power jumped from industry to industry, bringing more goods to mass markets. British ironmasters had learned how to smelt ores with coke (much cheaper than charcoal) in 1709, but had trouble keeping their furnaces hot enough – until 1776, when Boulton and Watt's engines solved the problem by providing steady blasts of air. Costs fell and sales soared. Despite wars and embargoes, pig iron output rose from

68,000 tons in 1788 to 325,000 in 1811. By 1850 half of the world's iron was made in Britain.

British mines were by then also producing half of the world's coal, sending it to steam engines at factories via another innovation: canals. The first industrial canal, built to carry coal to Manchester, opened in 1759. It cost an eye-popping £10,500 per mile but halved the price of fuel. Speculators had sunk £20 million into canals by 1815, opening great swaths of the countryside to the industrial economy. By then, though, canals were already old hat. In 1804 a Cornish engineer used a lightweight, high-pressure steam engine to propel a carriage along iron rails. Within a decade similar engines were powering paddleboats. A generation later, George Stephenson's famous *Rocket* was puffing between Liverpool and Manchester pulling a 13-ton load at 20 km per hour, and boats were paddling across the Atlantic.

Steam engines unleashed an energy bonanza. Britain's economy, already the world's most productive in the 1770s, was *by far* the most productive in the 1830s. The average English worker outproduced the average American or Dutchman by one-third and the average German by two-thirds. By 1850 British steam engines were producing energy equivalent to the labour of 13 million men – who, had they existed, would have eaten all the wheat grown in all the Isles. Instead, these 13 million phantoms ate coal. It was a miracle. 'The spinning jenny and the railroad', marvelled the novelist Charles Kingsley, 'are to me [. . .] signs that we are, on some points at least, in harmony with the universe; that there is a mighty spirit working among us [. . .] the Ordering and Creating God.'

Anno Dombei

Britain boasted just 2 per cent of the planet's population in the 1850s but operated 40–45 per cent of its modern, fossil-fuel machinery and produced roughly half its manufactured goods. Such an arrangement could operate only if Islanders found buyers for all the goods they made and sellers for all the goods (especially food) they needed; and so, between the 1810s and the 1860s, Britons set about turning the rest of the world into a network to meet and supply their needs. An organisational upheaval began that was every bit as astonishing as the technological one.

Mobility reached unprecedented levels. 'North America and

Russia are our corn fields', the economist William Stanley Jevons
announced at the end of this half-century.

> Chicago and Odessa are our granaries; Canada and the Baltic are
> our timber forests; Australasia contains our sheep farms, and in
> Argentina and on the western prairies of North America are our
> herds of oxen; Peru sends her silver, and the gold of South Africa
> and Australia flows to London; the Hindus and the Chinese
> grow tea for us, and our coffee, sugar and spice plantations are in
> all the Indies. Spain and France are our vineyards and the Medi-
> terranean our fruit garden; and our cotton grounds, which for
> long have occupied the Southern United States, are now being
> extended everywhere in the warm regions of the earth.

Such a world-system was impossible without an enormous merchant marine, and by 1860 every third trading vessel on the seas flew
the Union Jack. However, this massive mobility and the prosperity
it created would also be impossible unless Britain's traders could be
kept secure while they trucked and bartered on distant shores; and
for that, Lord Palmerston, Britain's prime minister, had an answer.
'Cudgels & Sabres & Carbines are necessary', he minuted in 1860,
'to keep quiet the ill-disposed People whose violence would render
Trade insecure.'

What this meant became very clear in 1850. Eighteen years earlier,
after winning its war for freedom from Turkey, the newborn Greek
state had rapidly run into debt. The Rothschilds, Britain's biggest
bankers, arranged a multinational loan, but by 1847 Greece was
defaulting again (there is no new thing under the sun). Its government
invited the financier Jakob Rothschild to Athens over Easter to discuss
more loans. Realising just in time that the Jewish banker might be
offended by the old Athenian tradition of lynching an effigy of Judas
Iscariot in celebration of Christ's resurrection, officials banned the
ritual, whereupon churchgoers, including a government minister's
son, expressed their righteous indignation by ransacking the grand
home of Don David Pacifico, a prominent Jewish merchant. Police
stood by and watched.

Don Pacifico demanded compensation, and when Greek authorities ignored him, the don – who held British citizenship by right, he
claimed, of being born in Gibraltar – appealed to London for support.

His story had its fishy elements (for one thing, he also claimed two different places of birth), but it was also convenient, because it gave Palmerston grounds to demand repayment of Greece's entire debt. When Athens defaulted again in 2009, it never crossed Angela Merkel's mind to send a gunboat, but in 1850 Palmerston sent a whole flotilla, which seized the Greek navy and blockaded Piraeus. Greece's king then did as he was told.

When Tories had first pushed balance-of-power strategies back in the 1710s, Whigs had condemned their perfidious politicking as un-English; now, Palmerston's 'astounding combination of audacity and mendacity' struck opposition Tories as equally inconsistent with British values. Palmerston, however, holding forth to the House for five hours, justified his actions with a radical redefinition of British identity. The real issue, he insisted, was not whether he or Don Pacifico was being honest. It was 'whether, as the Roman, in days of old, held himself free from indignity, when he could say, *civis romanus sum;** so also a British subject, in whatever land he may be, shall feel confident that the watchful eye and strong arm of England will protect him against injustice and wrong'. It was by now past 2 a.m., but Palmerston brought the House down. Conservatives as well as Liberals were on their feet, cheering, stamping and waving dispatch papers. Palmerston was right. Not Rome itself had been able to protect its people the way Britain could. With a British passport in his pocket, even the shady Don Pacifico could walk tall.

All this, thanks to the fleet which preserved the security of the world-system. Between 1857 and 1862, years when the government kept full records, merchants requested military muscle no fewer than 102 times. Backing them up cost money, and because ministers always needed to keep defence spending down, most fed the fleet by starving the army. By 1850 this was just one-fifth the size of France's. Such a tiny force made sense only if diplomats could defuse Continental and American conflicts before they required armies big enough to fight another Blenheim or Waterloo; and most of all, it required subtle and judicious use of the navy itself. Sometimes, sending a few gunboats (as at Athens in 1850) did the job. But when it didn't, the fleet had to

---

*Civis romanus sum, 'I am a Roman citizen', is an expression of Cicero's (*Against Verres* 5.37) which MPs of the 1850s would have encountered as schoolboys. It is best known from St Paul's borrowing in Acts 16:37.

act as a force multiplier, rushing reserves from one trouble spot to another so that little packets of troops could police enormous areas.

At the time Britons often ascribed their ability to maintain a global security system on such a shoestring to those most Victorian of virtues, pluck and grit. Both were displayed in abundance in actions all around the world, but neither would have helped much had Britain not possessed one more advantage – India. Even when British daredevilry was at its most extraordinary, as it was in Abyssinia (modern Ethiopia) in 1868, it was India that made it possible. The Abyssinian adventure had begun two years earlier, when the emperor Tewodros took nine Britons (including a baby) hostage. When diplomacy failed to free them, Queen Victoria gave Lieutenant-General Sir Robert Napier the grandiloquent order 'Break thou the Chains'. But that was easier said than done, because Abyssinia had no roads, railways or ports, so Napier, as plucky and gritty as anyone could ask for, built an artificial harbour – the ancestor of the Mulberries deployed on D-Day in 1944 – and towed it to East Africa. Some 13,000 troops, 26,000 labourers and 41,000 pack animals (including forty-four elephants) disembarked through it and, braving heat and hailstorms, carved a path over 500 km of mountain and desert to Tewodros's fortress at Magdala (Figure 8.7). This they stormed and looted. Tewodros shot himself with a silver pistol, a gift from Victoria in happier days. Of the 700 men who died that day, not one was British (although two died later of wounds). 'There was a fluttering of silk regimental Colours', said an eyewitness, 'the waving of helmets, and the roaring of triumphant cheers [. . .] and the hills re-echoed "God Save the Queen".' *Civis romanus sum.*

It was Englishmen and Highlanders who scaled Magdala's walls, but they would never have got anywhere near the citadel had tens of thousands of Indian infantry and animals not helped them. Britain used the Indian army as a strategic reserve, to be tapped whenever its eastern interests were threatened. The world-system would not have worked without this. Indian troops fought in Egypt in 1799, in China in 1840 and in Persia in 1857 (and would be back in Egypt in 1942). The Bombay Marine even patrolled the Persian Gulf on the Royal Navy's behalf.

Britain used Indian money to pay for its Indian reserve. India ran trade surpluses with Europe, Asia and America, but fully half its foreign-currency profits went to covering deficits with Britain. British

Figure 8.7. Pluck, grit and India: Indian elephants haul British
artillery through the wastelands of Ethiopia, 1868.

administrators stripped Indian markets of barriers against cheap,
machine-spun cotton from Lancashire's mills, and, despite having
introduced British consumers to cotton in the seventeenth century,
India became the biggest buyer of British cotton in the nineteenth.
Unable to compete on price on finished cloth, Indians turned to
growing cotton – and indigo, jute, opium and tea – for export, using
the proceeds to pay for the British imports. British administrators
put a further finger on the scale by pegging the rupee at rates that
favoured the pound, then having India borrow on London's money
markets to fund railroads which opened even more of the interior to
British goods. The world-system actively deindustrialised India's vast
economy, which produced one-quarter of the world's manufactured
goods in 1750 but just 2.8 per cent in 1880. Adding insult to injury,
Indians were billed not only for the salaries of the British soldiers who
policed them after the 1857 insurrection but also for the pensions of
the Europeans who administered them.

The world-system did bring benefits to India. South Asians
bought British goods because they were cheaper than local products;
Indian entrepreneurs could borrow at low interest; and by the 1890s

British-financed railways could sometimes even move food around fast enough to blunt the edge of famine. But all these advantages had costs. Large-scale earth-moving for the railroads diverted or dammed thousands of small rivers, leaving standing water where mosquitoes flourished. Malaria exploded, taking 20 million lives between 1890 and 1920 and ruining many millions more. One historian calls it 'death by development'. No one could pretend Indians were getting a good deal.

By the 1860s India was transferring tens of millions of pounds to Britain every year yet, even so, Britain ran an annual trade deficit of £100 million. With so many bills to pay, especially for imported food and raw materials, not even Britain's enormous exports (or rigging its relationship with India) could keep the books in balance. The world-system would not have worked at all, in fact, but for one last development, which contemporaries called the 'Londonisation' of commerce. Already by 1815 London was the easiest place on earth to raise money, find shippers, gather commercial information, hire agents and buy insurance. Britain's 'invisible' trade in services, already large in the eighteenth century, boomed in the nineteenth to meet the world-system's requirements. Confident that British governments would not stoop to confiscating their cash (which governments in less disciplined countries regularly did), merchants piled up mountains of money in London, for which bankers found outlets overseas. Britain's foreign direct investment probably hit £200 million in the 1850s, £700 million by 1870 and over £2 billion by the century's end.

Staggering fortunes were made, more than filling the gap between imports and exports. By the 1890s, in fact, Britain's balance of payments regularly ran a £100 million profit. Its factories, fleet and Indian Empire would not have been sustainable without invisible trade; but the invisible trade could not have worked without the factories, fleet and India. The world-system was a monstrous, complicated juggling act. No juggler could see more than a tiny part of the whole, or knew what anyone else was doing, and yet between them they remade the map. It truly seemed, said Dickens in *Dombey and Son*, his great novel of pride, prejudice and global commerce, that

> The earth was made for Dombey and Son to trade in, and the
> sun and moon were made to give them light. Rivers and seas
> were formed to float their ships; rainbows gave them promise

of fair weather; winds blew for or against their enterprises; stars and planets circled in their orbits, to preserve inviolate a system of which they were the centre [. . .] A.D. had no concern with anno Domini, but stood for anno Dombei – and Son.

Dickens vs Malthus

The world-system which the British made remade the British too. Britain's population almost doubled between 1801 and 1851, but its industrial production and exports rose even faster, which meant – contrary to Malthus's gloomy prognostications – that factory owners could use some of the money foreigners paid for cotton, coal and iron to pay workers just about enough to buy bread, even at the inflated prices guaranteed by the Corn Law. Britons went hungry but did not starve or stop having babies. Instead, they flocked into industrial cities until, for the first time, more than half of the English were urban. Birmingham grew from 71,000 souls to 233,000, Bradford from 13,000 to 104,000.

Villagers moving to cities had always found much to marvel at, but never as much as in the nineteenth century. Proud captains of industry adorned their home towns with superb civic buildings, paved and cobbled their streets and even illuminated them by piping coal gas underground to street lamps. Every self-respecting town centre in England soon had gaslight (Stoke-on-Trent, where I grew up, got its first gasworks in 1825), as did several in Wales, Scotland and Ireland. Yet barely had this vast coal-gas infrastructure been built than experiments in London with electric light were making it obsolete. In the 1830s Londoners could be whisked along well-lit streets in hired hansom cabs (traffic permitting); twenty years later they could catch horse-drawn buses; in the 1860s underground trains arrived.

However, nineteenth-century cities rivalled all earlier ages in squalor as well as grandeur. A million new houses were needed for the army of factory hands, but rare was the town that regulated them. Better-paid labourers, such as Sheffield's steelworkers, lived comfortably; despite Sheffield being 'dirty beyond the usual condition of English towns', an 1840s visitor noted, 'it is the custom for each family among the labouring population to occupy a separate dwelling, the rooms in which are furnished in a very comfortable manner'. In fact, he added, 'the floors are carpeted'. In Nottingham

Figure 8.8. 'Scampy living' in the shadow of Westminster
Abbey: the slums of Devil's Acre in London, 1873.

the typical working family around 1800 rented two or three rooms,
but most moved up to four or five when the lace trade boomed in
the 1820s. 'For a growing proportion of the labour force', the leading
historian of English housing concludes, 'there were both improving
housing standards and bigger surpluses over the necessities of life.'

But not for all. Where labour was cheap, as on Liverpool's docks,
building was 'scampy' (as people called it at the time). Even streets
were optional, with houses instead packed around 'courts' as little
as 2 m wide, squeezed into gaps between existing properties. The
typical 'back-to-back' type of the 1840s had three floors with a 10 m^2
room on each level, plus a separate, single-room dwelling in the cellar
for the poorest families of all (Figure 8.8). Several dozen people might
share such a building.

Observing 'basement floor[s] of thin, gaping boards placed within
six inches of the damp ground; with slight walls of ill-burnt bricks
and muddy mortar, sucking up the moisture and giving it out in the

apartments; ill-made drains, untrapped, pouring forth bad air', one district surveyor concluded that 'you scarcely need more causes for a low state of health'. The average English person in 1840 lived forty years, but in Liverpool, generally judged the least wholesome city, servants and labourers looked forwards on average to just fifteen (half dying as babies and few survivors living much past thirty). Such was Liverpool's grimness that even middling tradesmen averaged only twenty-two years and gentry thirty-five. In London too the masses' ills spilled over to infect the rich: cholera swept the metropolis in 1832, and coal smoke and fog combined into blinding 'pea-souper' smogs, so vividly described in Dickens's *Bleak House*, paralysing the capital and killing the elderly of all classes.

We might wonder why anyone exchanged the English countryside for the miserable world immortalised by Dickens, were the answer not so depressingly obvious. The countryside was even worse. Standards of living had barely budged since the Middle Ages. 'Picturesque and harmonious from the artist's point of view,' one traveller commented, 'cottages are in most other respects a scandal to England.' Even William Cobbett, no fan of industrialisation, recognised that in Wiltshire 'labourers seem miserably poor. Their dwellings are little better than pig-beds, and their looks indicate that their food is not nearly equal to that of a pig.' In Leicestershire he saw 'hovels made of mud and straw [. . .] Enter them, and look at the bits of chairs or stools; the wretched boards tacked together to serve for a table; the floor of pebble, broken brick, or of the bare ground; look at the thing called a bed; and survey the rags on the backs of the wretched inhabitants' (Figure 8.9).

People moved to cities because they could. For many, population growth meant that the only alternative to Dickens's world of urban misery was Malthus's world of rural starvation. Weep as we might for Little Nell or Tiny Tim (or for Dickens himself, packed off to a boot-blacking factory at the age of twelve), we should save more tears for people in those parts of the Isles that steam power and cities had not yet reached. When harvests failed in the Scottish Highlands in 1836, thousands confronted the ancient choice between starving at home or fleeing over the water. In Ireland a decade later it was millions.

Ireland was as Malthusian as a place could get. Thanks largely to potatoes, its population had grown faster than anywhere else in

Figure 8.9. *Et in Arcadia ego*: the interior of a
cottage near Blandford, Dorset, 1846.

the Isles, from 5 million in 1800 to over 8 million in 1820. But rural poverty went well beyond what Cobbett saw in England (Figure 8.10), and, because England's steam-powered cotton mills had undercut old-fashioned textile mills in Dublin, Belfast and Cork, Ireland was actually *de*-industrialising by 1840. So, when the fungus *Phytophthora infestans* arrived from America in 1845, turning plump, firm potatoes into inedible black slime, the ensuing 'positive check' – Malthus's euphemism for starvation – went beyond anything seen in centuries. Several thousand starved; typhus and dysentery killed a million; and even more took ship for England or America.

Sir Robert Peel, prime minister when the blight struck, tried to bring food to Ireland from India and poured money into public works so people had wages to buy it, but rural Ireland lacked the infrastructure for this to work. His successor, Lord John Russell, stopped even trying to act against what he called 'a famine of the thirteenth century acting upon a population of the nineteenth'. Some English Malthusians actually welcomed the working of the 'check': 'I have always felt a certain horror of political economists', the master of an Oxford college later said, 'since I heard one of them say that the famine in Ireland would not kill more than a million people, and that

Figure 8.10. Ultra-Malthusian: a tumbledown cabin
in County Donegal, late nineteenth century.

would scarcely be enough to do much good.' Not until 1997, 150 years
too late, did a British prime minister publicly express regret over the
inadequacy of the official response.

Such was Britain at mid-century. On the one hand, it ruled an
empire on which the sun never set; on the other, it left Britons to
rot and starve like medieval peasants. *The Economist* magazine,
founded in 1843, felt it 'a happiness and a privilege to have had our
lot cast in the first fifty years of this century', because 'the difference between the 18th and the 19th century, is greater than between
the first and the 18th'. They were right. The jurist Walter Bagehot,
however, saw in the same years just 'crowds of people scarcely more
civilised than the majority of two thousand years ago'. He was right
too. Truly, the essayist Thomas Carlyle concluded, 'The Condition
of England [. . .] is justly regarded as one of the most ominous, and
withal one of the strangest, ever seen in this world.'

The Starched Collar of Europe

The explanation, two observers of this scene concluded in 1848, was
that 'our epoch is more and more splitting up into two great hostile
camps, into two great classes directly facing each other: Bourgeoisie

354 Geography Is Destiny

and Proletariat'. These observers – Karl Marx and Friedrich Engels – certainly had an axe to grind, but that did not make them wrong. The pursuit of prosperity was remaking identity and driving demands for new kinds of sovereignty.

As Marx and Engels saw things, capitalism – by pushing the poor into factories – had 'pitilessly torn asunder the motley feudal ties that bound man to his "natural superiors", and has left remaining no other nexus between man and man than naked self-interest, than callous "cash payment". It has drowned the most heavenly ecstasies of religious fervour, of chivalrous enthusiasm, of philistine sentimentalism, in the icy waters of egotistical calculation.' But to what end? Having 'conjured up such gigantic means of production and exchange', Marx and Engels continued, capitalism 'is like the sorcerer, who is no longer able to control the powers of the nether world which he has called up by his spells'. Now that 'Masses of labourers, crowded into the factory, are organised like soldiers [. . .] The advance of industry [. . .] replaces the isolation of the labourers, due to competition, by their revolutionary combination.' The result: 'What the bourgeoisie, therefore, produces, above all, is its own grave-diggers.'

There were moments when they seemed to be right. When a million workers signed a petition demanding one-man-one-vote, Parliament rejected it; when 3 million signed a new version, that was rejected too. Panicky politicians jailed labour organisers or transported them to Australia. Rioters were shot; a botched attempt to assassinate Peel killed his secretary. Yet the proletariat did not bury the bourgeoisie, partly for traditional reasons (good weather produced bigger harvests and cheaper bread) but more so for new ones. Mining, manufacturing, building, trade and transport created 4.2 million new jobs between 1811 and 1861. Much of the credit also goes to the political elite. Seeing opportunities in the problems, Whigs (or Liberals, as they increasingly liked to be called) co-opted calls for revolution. These men were anything but socialists; the Whig cabinet that Earl Grey (he of the tea) formed in 1830 was perhaps the richest Britain ever had. Their idea was to create a coalition of country grandees and urban middle classes, transforming the Liberals from the party of finance and cosmopolitanism into the voice of a natural ruling class, which would keep both reactionary aristocrats and revolutionary proles in their proper places.

This ruling class, Grey decided, should contain the 800,000 men with assets yielding £10 per year – less than one British male in six, but twice as many as currently had the vote. The old aristocracy and many of the bottom 80-some per cent disagreed, and sometimes protested violently against Liberal plans. It took troops three days to reclaim the streets of Bristol from rioters. However, the mayhem concentrated elite minds on the need to do something, and, after three elections in two years, the Great Reform Act passed in 1832.

This changed how Westminster worked. Since about 1700 each monarch had picked a prime minister, whose job was to form a ministry, which, through patronage, persuasion or corruption, would try to translate royal wishes into Parliamentary acts. Eighteenth-century elections mattered, because a prime minister was no use to a king unless elected MPs would support him, but electors' voices were only one of several elements in the system. The Great Reform Act changed this, convincing MPs that a mandate from the people trumped royal wishes. So when William IV dismissed Melbourne and his Whig administration in 1834 and appointed the Tory Robert Peel in his place, Peel found himself unable to govern. No king tried that again. The last time an election was automatically held when a monarch died was 1837, and 1839 was the last time a ruler fired a prime minister (Peel again) just because she disliked him.

Peel drew the obvious conclusion: Tories (or Conservatives, as they were beginning to call themselves) must compete for the new voters' support. Just like the Whigs, they needed to reinvent themselves. Peel's plan was to preserve the Tories' image as the party of tradition, church and crown, but also to make them look business-friendly by appropriating the free-trade issue, formerly a Whig talking point. So in 1846 he out-liberalised the Liberals by repealing the Corn Laws. This, he knew, would split his party, because Tory landowners would never forgive the betrayal; but in the long run, he gambled, Conservatives would displace Liberals as the voice of the middle class, the people who were now remaking England in their own image.

For millennia the first thing a man had done on coming into money was to imitate the upper classes. Plenty still did so, but plenty more didn't. Self-made, self-assured and self-respecting, a new middle class asserted a new way of being British. The biggest bestseller of 1859 was not John Stuart Mill's *On Liberty* or even Charles Darwin's *Origin of Species*. It was Samuel Smiles's *Self-Help*, a how-to book for

the aspiring bourgeois. 'God helps those who help themselves', Smiles
reminded readers; 'Go thou and do likewise.' What mattered now
was not a man's background but his ability to get things done. 'The
spirit of self-help', Smiles explained, 'as exhibited in the energetic
action of the individual, has in all times been a marked feature of the
English character, and furnishes the true measure of our power as a
nation.' To be English, said Smiles, was to be down-to-earth, unlike
effete Continentals. On hearing a Frenchman praising the genius of
the inventor of shirt-ruffles, Smiles observed, a wiser Englishman
'shrewdly remark[ed] that some merit was also due to the man who
invented the shirt'.

Convinced perhaps by the millions of cotton shirts that England
now exported, foreigners increasingly agreed. *Self-Help* was translated
not just into every major European language but also into Japanese,
Arabic, Turkish and multiple Indian tongues. Egypt's khedive decorated his palace with sayings taken not from the Prophet but from
Smiles. Another foreigner, the Polish poet Juliusz Słowacki, agreed
that Englishness was now the epitome of the serious, stern, middle-
class style. 'If Europe is a nymph,' he wrote,

> *Then Naples is her bright-blue eye,*
> *And Warsaw is her heart [. . .]*
> *Paris is the head,*
> *London the starched collar.*

Queen Victoria was the perfect monarch for Smiles's starchy, hard-
working new world. (She gave a copy of *Self-Help*'s sequel, *Lives of
the Engineers*, to her German son-in-law as a wedding gift.) When *The
Times* compared Victoria to her three predecessors ('an imbecile, a
profligate and a buffoon'), it called her 'a ruler of a new type'. By
the admittedly odd standards of royalty, she was extremely normal.
She was happiest at Balmoral, her Highland retreat. 'They live here
without any state whatever', one extremely grand visitor recorded,
'like very small gentlefolk, small house, small rooms, small establishment' (it is, in fact, a castle with a seven-storey tower). Wags mocked
her stuffy 'Balmorality', but more thoughtful observers saw that it
brought 'the pride of sovereignty to the level of petty life'. When,
for instance, Victoria visited their city in 1858, the editors of the *Leeds
Mercury* enthused 'that she is a wife and a mother of so lofty a purity

and discharging her duties so well that she forms the brightest exemplar to the matrons of England'.

Seeing which way the wind blew, the great and the good Balmoralised themselves too. Out went cabinet ministers who fought duels (as two had done in 1809); even Palmerston's fondness for boxing, gambling and wenching became embarrassing. Instead, when the grandest aristocrat in the land said he got a job because he could not bear being 'a gentleman at ease', few now professed surprise. By 1908 Robert Baden-Powell – the founder of the Boy Scouts – was boasting without irony of Britain's 'stolid, pipe-sucking manhood, unmoved by panic or excitement, and reliable in the tightest of places'. Not everyone bought in, of course; wealthy young reprobates hardly went extinct, and fiercer, seventeenth-century-style enthusiasms clung on. But little by little, wildness went underground and pipe-sucking became cool.

The key, the educator Thomas Arnold saw in the 1830s, was to instil into the aristocracy's sons 'religious and moral principle [and] gentlemanly conduct', plus, 'thirdly, intellectual ability'. English schools had not previously been known for gentlemanly conduct; the militia had had to read the Riot Act to Winchester's boys in 1770. But Arnold set about making his school at Rugby an incubator for a new ruling class, fusing the old elite of birth with a new, Smilesian elite. 'It is only in England that this beneficial salutary inter-mixture of classes takes place', his son wrote (meaning, by 'classes', bourgeois and aristocratic). 'Look at the bottle-merchant's son, and the Plantagenet being brought up side-by-side [. . .] Very likely young Bottles will end by being a lord himself.'

Arnold's success in this department was perhaps limited (when a friend of mine taught for a year at Rugby in the 1980s, the old elite of birth seemed to be doing just fine), but a fictionalised version of Arnold in Thomas Hughes's novel *Tom Brown's School Days* really did change how the middle classes thought about schooling. In Hughes's fantasy version of Rugby, the 'fresh, brave school-life, so full of games, adventures, and good-fellowship' turned stubborn, headstrong Tom into exactly the sort of Christian gentleman that Balmoralistic parents wanted. *The Times* called *Tom Brown* 'a book every English father might well wish to see in the hands of his son', and, when it did reach thousands of boys' hands, headmasters responded by making life imitate art. In the 1870s a French visitor could leave

Eton convinced that 'Boys who learned to command in games were learning to command in India'.

Schools like Rugby taught boys to look, as well as act, sober and serious. Eighteenth-century Englishmen, keener on politeness than flamboyance, had already been moving away from the peacock finery of French courts, but in the nineteenth century an identifiably 'English' look – plainer, more functional and downright middle-class – altogether overthrew Continental claims to dictate the terms of fashion. Men's wigs, which had been shrinking since 1700, went out of style altogether after 1800. The most celebrated clothes horse of the age, George Bryan ('Beau') Brummell, boasted that 'I, Brummell, put the modern man into pants, dark coat, white shirt and clean linen'; but he was in truth just first among equals in a crowd of men busily reinventing the 'English' look. Newly fashionable tailors on London's Savile Row and Jermyn Street sold them sharply tailored bespoke suits, worn with Hessian boots, acres of starched white shirt and perfectly knotted cravats (Figure 8.11). Books appeared with titles like *The Art of Tying the Cravat* or, my personal favourite, *Necklothita-nia or Tietania, being an Essay on Starchers, by One of the Cloth*. Some 'dandified' the new look by adding garish waistcoats and impossibly high collars, but others simplified it to the point that looking 'respect-able' came within the reach even of skilled working men.

It was certainly a stretch for a factory hand to become a poor man's Beau Brummell, but it was becoming possible. In the late 1840s, just as Marx and Engels were writing *The Communist Manifesto* and Dickens's tales of the plight of the poor were winning their widest audiences, inflation-adjusted wages finally regained the heights they had attained three centuries earlier, just after the Black Death. And this was no short-term fluctuation: wages went on rising, doubling for most people between 1850 and 1900. Even at the century's end, the average English worker still made a miserable $4,500 (measured in 1990 US dollars, the standardised unit of historical accounting), but that was more than people earned anywhere else. Britons of all ranks were buying more stuff, giving Victorian parlours their charac-teristic clutter. Most importantly, they could afford more food. The typical working family only ate meat once a week, but men's daily intake rose from 2,350 calories in 1850 to 2,850 in 1900. Life expectancy increased in tandem, from forty years in 1850 to forty-eight in 1900.

Much of the improvement came from steadier employment

Figure 8.11. Men in black-and-white: the English look at its sharpest, 1856.

as markets matured, moderating the boom-and-bust swings of the Hungry Forties. Better machines and organisation increased the value added by each worker, and, rather than lose these gains if their employees went on strike, bosses and governments alike became readier to negotiate. Radical Whigs, worried about rapacious capitalists, made common cause with Tory landowners, eager to clip businessmen's wings, and pushed through a Factory Act, capping the working week for children under thirteen at forty-eight hours. Soon after, women and boys under ten were banned from working in mines. In 1867 the franchise was extended to most male householders (whether leasing or renting), roughly doubling the electorate. The next year countless little unions combined into a single Trades Union Congress, which demanded – and got – national 'Bank Holidays' for all workers. Most factories also granted Saturday afternoons off. In the 1870s the adult working week stabilised at fifty-six hours – a lot, but less than it had been. Left-leaning intellectuals formed Socialist Leagues and Fabian Societies in the 1880s; workers responded with a properly proletarian Labour Representation Committee in 1900.

Many Conservatives worried that workers were rising above their stations. Liberals often agreed, but tended to consider that a small price to pay for the literate, thinking labourers an industrialised nation needed. The first Education Act had been passed in 1837. Fourteen years later, typical upper- or middle-class boys still spent only six years in school and lower-class ones just four, but by 1870 England and Wales had enough state schools to accommodate every boy and girl under thirteen. Scotland received similar laws in 1872, although none was felt necessary for Ireland. By then, public health inspectors had been appointed, police forces created, capital punishment for nearly all non-violent crimes abolished and transportation to Australia ended. The Isles were becoming kinder, gentler countries.

Perhaps because they were being treated as more responsible and respectable, the poor started acting more responsibly and respectably too. Between 1850 and 1900 homicide rates roughly halved, and assault, theft and infanticide fell sharply. Even illegitimate births declined, although so did births of all kinds: following what seems to be almost a sociological law, as people got richer, they had fewer babies (births per marriage fell from six to four between 1860 and 1900) and invested more time and effort in each. Temperance was a harder sell, and a 'beer scare' in the 1830s evoked the gin craze of a century earlier, but drinking declined too after 1870. 'The English proletariat is becoming more bourgeois', Engels complained to Marx.

He was right that Britons increasingly saw themselves as law-abiding, tolerant, reasonable folk. Foreigners often found parts of this – such as kindness to animals – baffling, but cockfighting, bull-, bear- and badger-baiting and cruelty to cattle were banned all the same. The Society for the Prevention of Cruelty to Animals even bagged Victoria as its patron. Adopting the boarding-school obsession with team sports gave working-class men still more ways to be bourgeois (a Lancashire court was assured in 1851 that 'Wherever cricket is widely practised, crime is very light'). However, the middle classes remained cautious about this upward mobility. Cricket clubs carefully distinguished between 'gentlemen' (middle-class amateurs) and 'players' (salaried proletarians), giving each their own door to go out on to the field. Rugby football developed two distinct sets of rules, a 'union' variety generally preferred by more middle-class teams in the south and a 'league' version for plebeian players in the north. Association football began rather similarly, but in 1892 a Northern Football League of paid 'professors' swallowed up a Southern Football Association of 'gentlemen'. Soccer has been a bottom-up sport ever since, played and watched by 'lads' on their Saturday afternoons off. Newspapers were already deploring football hooligans in 1885, and vandalising trains – such a popular pastime for 1970s fans – made the press the following year.

Despite these momentous changes, what most concerned commentators was religious identity. 'We thank thee, O God, that we are not as other nations are', one preacher rejoiced in 1854, 'unjust, covetous, oppressive, cruel; we are a religious people, we are a Bible-reading, church-going people.' Yet when census-takers had asked in 1851, they found that on Sunday, 30 March, only half the people in England and Wales who could have been in church were (there was more church-going in Scotland, and much more in Ireland). Church-going was becoming a choice, not the centrepiece of English identity. (One London costermonger, asked by a reformer if he knew what St Paul's was, replied, 'A Church, Sir, so I've heard. I never was in Church.')

Even so, the mid-century anxiety over the decline of Anglicanism was overblown. Rather than becoming pagans, the English were redefining religion, as still important but a more private affair. Christmas is the prime exhibit. It remained a religious holiday, of course, but in the 1840s its focus shifted from the church towards the home, and it took on new forms, merging joy at Jesus' birth into a broader celebration of domesticity, kindness and abundance – the most important things to hold on to as the Industrial Revolution turned so much else upside down. There were new rituals (the goose, the gifts, the plum pudding) and wonderful, purpose-made Christmas 'carols', sung instead of everyday hymns. 'Once in Royal David's City', 'The Holly and the Ivy' and 'Good King Wenceslas' were all published between 1848 and 1853, and eighteenth-century songs like 'Joy to the World' and 'Hark! The Herald Angels Sing' were spruced up with jaunty new tunes in 1839–40. Only a couple of today's classics ('God Rest Ye Merry, Gentlemen' and 'The First Noel') are much earlier. A single year, 1843, saw the printing not only of the world's first commercial Christmas cards but also of Dickens's novella *A Christmas Carol* (which established 'Merry Christmas' as the standard seasonal salutation). The later 1840s brought the greatest innovation of all, the decorated pine tree. Estonians had been decking trees since perhaps 1441 and Lithuanians definitely since 1510, but Britons took no notice until Victoria's German husband, Albert, set one up in Windsor Castle in 1841. The

Figure 8.12. Christmas Balmoralised: family, love
and abundance around the tree, 1848.

habit went viral in 1848, when the *Illustrated London News* published a
drawing of the royals around their tree (Figure 8.12).

At first, new notions of Christmas were as controversial as
working-class athletes, and conservative Christians made worship a
metaphor for the larger 'Condition of England' question. Gladstone
and Disraeli, rival prime ministers in the 1860s, both made their
names in the 1830s with books on church and state. Some thought
salvation lay in the kind of muscular Christianity being promoted in
the public schools, which missionaries were carrying not only to India
and Africa (where Dr Livingstone's adventures began in 1852) but also
to England's inner cities; others gravitated towards the 'Oxford Movement', a kind of Anglicanism so high that it was hard to tell from
popery. The Movement's obsession with tradition positively cried
out for parody (in Thomas Love Peacock's novel *Crotchet Castle*, the
hero, a Mr Chainmail, insists that everything has been going downhill
since the twelfth century), but the joke faded when several Movement leaders openly embraced Rome. The pope seized the moment
to appoint Catholic bishops to England after a three-century absence.

Even though the Original European Union had been almost irrelevant for 150 years and there were hardly any Catholics left in England, this apparent assault on identity and sovereignty outraged public opinion. The prime minister denounced 'Papal Aggression' as an 'attempt to fasten [Rome's] fetters upon a nation which has so long and so nobly vindicated its right to freedom of opinion'.

The quirks of a few Oxford academics would probably have looked less unnerving but for English anxieties about Catholics fleeing the Irish famine. Historians often say that, if Spain was Napoleon's ulcer, Ireland was England's running sore. It could neither be excised from the Union, because of security concerns about the back door, nor absorbed within its new, starched-collar identity. London had belatedly given Catholics equal rights in 1829, only to find that this was no longer enough (if it ever had been) to reconcile them to the Union. Not one but two governments fell over Ireland in 1834, and when Peel himself – perhaps the best prime minister Britain ever had – was ousted by his party in 1846, it was over Ireland as much as economics. 'We have reduced protection to agriculture, and tried to lay the foundation of peace in Ireland,' he reflected; 'and these are the offences for which nothing can atone.' By the time Gladstone became prime minister in 1868, Ireland was again at the top of the legislative agenda. The Irish Republican Brotherhood had begun its first bombing campaign in England the year before.

Yet not even Ireland could puncture mid-century Englishmen's awe-inspiring self-regard. 'Why is it that an Irishman's, or a Frenchman's hatred of England does not excite in me an answering hatred?' the historian Thomas Babington Macaulay asked his diary. 'I imagine that my national pride prevents it. England is so great that an Englishman cares little what others think of her, or how they talk of her'. In fact, Palmerston told the House of Commons, 'there never was a period when England was more respected than at present [. . .] in consequence of her good faith, moderation and firmness'.

Macaulay and Palmerston beg for parody almost as much as the Oxford Movement, yet they had a point. Between 1815 and 1865 Britain reordered the earth to fit Mackinder's Map. When my grandfather joked in the 1970s about fog in the Channel cutting the Continent off, or Brexiteers waxed lyrical in 2016 about what Britain would achieve if it could just escape Brussels's snares, they were responding to the world as Palmerston had seen it, but that world was a fleeting one. When Palmerston died in 1865 (going out in style, with the immortal words 'Die, my dear doctor? That's the last thing I shall do!'), the great and the good who gathered to see him off solemnly agreed that his demise marked the end of an era. 'Our quiet days are over', a former chancellor said at the graveside. 'No more peace for us.'

9

THE NEW WORLD STEPS FORTH, 1865–1945

Strange Defeat

Palmerston's mourners were gloomy not because the world-system he had so vigorously defended was failing but because it was working too well. Britain still had the world's only significantly industrialised economy, and continued to prosper by producing cheaper and better goods and services than anyone else and by persuading foreigners to buy them. Foreigners of course needed to have money to do this, and since the surest way for them to prosper was by imitating Britain and industrialising, it made sense for British financiers to lend them the cash they needed to build up their own fossil-fuel economies (particularly since much of that money would be used to buy British machines, coal and expertise).

Such was the glory of free trade; and yet free trade also meant bankrolling the rise of rivals. American and German wars of unification in the 1860s–70s created huge internal markets (Figure 9.1), and British investment paid for factories to industrialise them and railways to unite them. By the 1880s American and German industrial productivity were both growing faster than British; in 1907 the United States had actually pulled ahead (Figure 9.2).

Hence the gloom. The men around Palmerston's grave were well aware that all previous shifts in the balance of wealth and power – from Rome to the Germans, Spain to France or France to Britain (Figure 9.3) – had ended in violence, and that the killing power of modern armies and navies guaranteed that this time would be worse. And so it turned out: the two world wars that Britain and its allies fought to beat back a German challenge killed at least 100 million people. Equally important, though, was a parallel war which Britain fought against an American challenge, in which no one died at all, because it went on in boardrooms, stock exchanges and factories. Waged on a titanic scale, it defined the first half of the twentieth

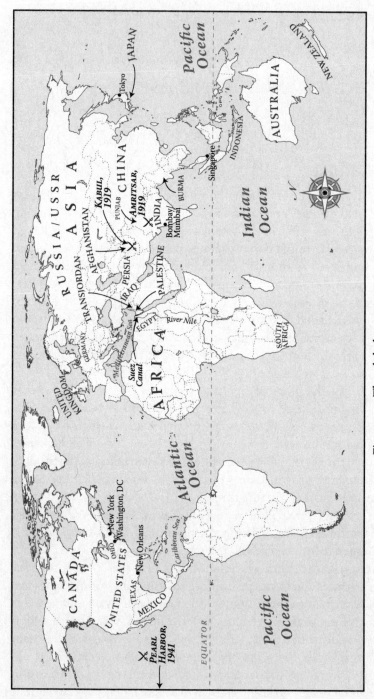

Figure 9.1. The global stage, 1865–1945.

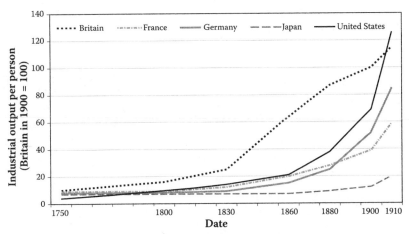

Figure 9.2. The Great Convergence: Britain prospers in
the nineteenth century, but others prosper faster.

century and ended in a crushing British defeat – but what a strange
defeat it would be.

Recessional

Investing and selling in Germany or the United States were very
different propositions from flooding India with goods or building
infrastructure such as the Suez Canal (opened in 1869) or the Bombay–
Calcutta railway (1870). Indians and Egyptians could not protect their
own industries against lower-cost British competition or stop real-
life Dombeys using canals and railways to cut their transport costs.
German and American governments, however, could – and did – use
tariffs and freight charges as weapons, buying from Britain only what
they wanted (coal, iron, machines) while making other imports more
expensive than locally produced alternatives.

Britain could have retaliated with tariffs of its own but rarely did
so, because its world-system depended on British consumers being
able to buy imports (especially food) cheaply so they could concentrate their efforts on more profitable activities (such as coal mining or
selling insurance). Foreign tariffs rigged markets against Britain, but
the Isles still had more coal than Germany, deeper funds of capital
than the United States and an overwhelming edge in workers with

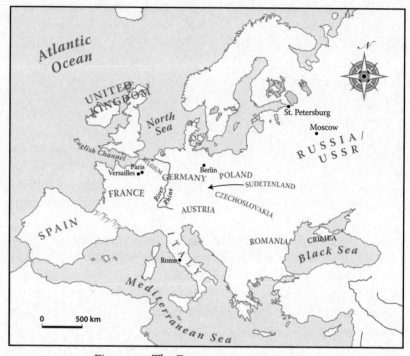

Figure 9.3. The European stage, 1865–1945.

that sixth sense – bred by generations of on-the-job training – for just when to close a valve or tighten a bobbin to keep engines and looms going.

Yet by the 1880s it was clear that, behind their tariff walls, Americans and Germans were finding ways around the Dombeys' advantages. Germany turned to technical education, teaching engineers enough science to design machines that burned less coal than Britain's. Americans invented management science. Instead of investing their own capital in family firms, entrepreneurs sold shares to raise cash and then hired professionals who restlessly innovated with time-and-motion studies, assembly lines and other newfangled ideas. All this book-learning struck Britons as faintly comical, but in cutting-edge industries such as optics and chemistry the appliance of science produced better results than going by feel. By the 1890s it was Britain – with its faith in self-help, muddling through and inspired amateurs – that was starting to look comical.

Many of the advances behind the new, high-tech industries actually began in British laboratories, but German and American industrialists regularly reaped the biggest benefits. In 1885, the very year that British mechanics perfected the mechanics of the bicycle, the German engineers Gottlieb Daimler and Karl Benz worked out how to burn petrol (hitherto a low-value by-product of kerosene, used in lamps) in lightweight internal combustion engines. Americans got rich by bringing the two technologies together. In 1896 automobiles were still so slow that hecklers yelled 'Get a horse!' at the first American car race, but in 1913 American factories would churn out a million vehicles. By then the Wright brothers, two bicycle mechanics from Ohio, had put wings on a petrol engine, mounted the contraption on a bicycle chassis and made it fly.

British bankers were still making money financing these activities, but Americans and Germans made more. In sheer size, the American economy overtook Britain's in 1872, and Germany followed in 1908. By 1913 even distant Japan – which had seemed so exotic, backward and simply funny when Gilbert and Sullivan wrote their comic opera *The Mikado* in 1885 – was catching up, and had an economy one-third as big as Britain's.

Free-traders insisted that a rising tide would lift all the boats, but by the 1880s it was becoming clear that some boats were rising faster than others – and that some economies were paying for their navies to add boats faster than Britain. In 1815 the Royal Navy had had more battleships than the rest of the world combined, but by 1880 it only just outnumbered the next three fleets (the French, Russian and American) and by 1910 scarcely the next two (the German and American). Worse still, foreign boats were getting better as well as more numerous. Defending its ability to police sea lanes and break chains was pushing Britain's bills up alarmingly.

The Isles had led the world in maritime technology for a century. London had sent the world's first all-iron gunship (the *Nemesis*) to China in 1840 and the first steam-powered battleships with screw propellers to Crimea in 1854, but its rivals quickly copied these. HMS *Warrior*, launched in 1860, was the biggest, fastest and heaviest-gunned ship on the seas, but within twelve months other navies were building guns that could pierce its 11-cm armour. Innovation begat innovation. HMS *Portsmouth*, launched in 1871, dispensed with masts and sails altogether, housing its guns in great revolving turrets;

Figure 9.4. Don't mess with England: two of the ten 12-inch cannons on HMS *Dreadnought* (launched 1906), able to hurl shells nearly 20 km. On top are two of its twenty-seven 12-pounder guns, for defence against nippy new torpedo boats.

the *Alexandra* (1877) carried tubes for newly invented torpedoes; and in 1900 Britain commissioned the first submarines (designed by an Irish nationalist in the 1880s, to sink British ships). HMS *Dreadnought*, launched in 1906 (Figure 9.4), was so fast and so well armed and armoured that it made every other ship on the seas obsolete – but for barely for a year, until Germany started a dreadnought of its own. In 1911 the young first lord of the Admiralty, Winston Churchill, switched the navy to oil-fired engines. These outperformed coal-fired boilers but also rendered Britain's immense coal reserves irrelevant. The fleet now needed to protect long sea lanes to Indonesian, Persian and above all American oil wells.

The national mood darkened from the 1860s onwards because rivals such as Germany and the United States were adopting and adapting British technologies and organisation to mount their own industrial revolutions, which were changing the meanings of geography and making it more difficult for Britain to stay in the middle of Mackinder's Map. To be sure, Britain remained for now the indispensable nation: its merchantmen, battleships, naval bases, foreign assets, capital reserves, communication networks, engineers and bankers still dominated the world. Its scientists and soft power were at their peak, and in 1897 even its bitterest enemies joined the celebrations marking Victoria's sixtieth year on the throne. But no one could doubt that the world was becoming more competitive.

Analyses took two very different forms. One focused on identity, arguing that Britons had lost their edge since 1870, as self-confidence yielded to self-doubt. In a hugely influential essay with the alarming title 'Disintegration', the Conservative supremo Lord Salisbury argued that, because Britain had granted most workers the vote, conflicts between 'masses' and 'classes' were inevitable. The result, he said, would be the dispossession of 'churchmen, landowners, publicans, manufacturers, horse-owners, railway shareholders, fund-holders' (odd bedfellows, but his point is clear). Ireland would then break away, followed by 'large branches and limbs of our Empire'. Other pessimists blamed decline on the loss of commercial energy. E. E. Williams's bestseller *Made in Germany*, written in 1896, foresaw British goods being swept from the world's shelves by better, cheaper, German wares, while W. T. Stead's *The Americanization of the World* (1901) predicted exactly what it said on the cover. Most shocking of all, Rudyard Kipling – the pre-eminent poet of empire – was moved by Victoria's Diamond Jubilee to pen an anguished 'Recessional', arguing that Britain had turned away from God and foreseeing only decline, fall and oblivion:

> *Far-called, our navies melt away;*
> *On dune and headland sinks the fire:*
> *Lo, all our pomp of yesterday*
> *Is one with Nineveh and Tyre!*
> *Judge of the Nations, spare us yet,*
> *Lest we forget – lest we forget [. . .]*
>
> *For heathen heart that puts her trust*
> *In reeking tube and iron shard –*
> *All valiant dust that builds on dust,*
> *And guarding, calls not Thee to guard –*
> *For frantic boast and foolish word,*
> *Thy mercy on Thy people, Lord!*

But other analysts saw only a simpler problem of security. From George Chesney's book *The Battle of Dorking* (1871) to William Le

Queux's classic *The Invasion of 1910* (a 'future history' serialised in the *Daily Mail* in 1906) some writers convinced themselves – and thousands of readers – that a German attack was imminent. Le Queux's story so unnerved public opinion that the chancellor of the exchequer, lord president, foreign secretary, secretary for war and first sea lord met sixteen times in 1907–8 to compile a report debunking him (a job that P. G. Wodehouse did much better in his 1909 parody *The Swoop! or How Clarence Saved England*).

Over at the Admiralty, men made of sterner stuff concluded that reeking tube and iron shard would just have to rise to these challenges. One idea, championed by the fiery first sea lord, Jackie Fisher, was that technology could keep the costs of closing the Channel within the nation's budget. 'My beloved submarines', Fisher promised, 'will magnify the naval power of England seven times more than present' – with the result, he speculated in 1905, that '[with]in three or four years of this, the English Channel and the western basin of the Mediterranean will not be habitable by a fleet or squadron'.

Fisher was a hundred years ahead of his time. In our own age submarines and anti-ship missiles do indeed close seas to enemy surface action (the US Seventh Fleet will not sail through the Taiwan Strait again in our lifetimes), but not in his. Admirals quickly learned to keep submarines out of torpedo range by surrounding their battleships with escort vessels, submarine nets and submarines of their own. The only way to keep the Channel as a moat defensive was by massing conventional warships there, just as in 1588. Fisher, converted now to the need for big-gun battleships, insisted that because 'Germany keeps her whole fleet always concentrated within a few hours of England, we must therefore keep a Fleet twice as powerful concentrated within a few hours of Germany'. The question was how to pay for it.

Diplomats identified an answer in the 1890s. In a pivot as sharp as that of 1713, Britain would rejig its nineteenth-century world-system to make it look more like the eighteenth-century balance of power, but now on a global scale. The first step was to recognise that Britannia did not need to rule every single wave herself. What she did need was a set of allies who could be relied on to police their own beats on her behalf, while she and a second set of allies focused on the one big thing, keeping the Channel closed.

The key to the first set of allies was the United States. Disagreements persisted over Canada, the Caribbean and free trade, but British governments refused to let them escalate. First came naval talks in which Britain treated the Americans as equal partners. Then, in 1893, London upgraded its legation in Washington, DC, to a proper embassy. Two years later it bent to American demands in a spat over Venezuela, and in 1901 it tacitly recognised the Caribbean as an American lake. Britain had quietly sloughed off responsibility for the western hemisphere. The next year, it went further, concluding a naval alliance – the first in its history – with Tokyo, making the north-west Pacific a Japanese lake. Fisher could now consolidate his Australia, China and Far East squadrons into a single Eastern Fleet at Singapore and bring five battleships back to the Channel.

As late as 1898, when British and French troops squared off across the Upper Nile, some strategists still thought France posed the greatest cross-Channel threat, but most eyes were turning to Germany. The Kaiser had very publicly sided with the Boers when British conspirators had bungled a plot to seize their South African gold mines in 1895. In 1899 fake news circulated about a Russo-Franco-German plan to attack while Britain was bogged down on the veldt, and in 1900 Germany launched a massive battleship-building programme. Quarrels with Paris over distant deserts and jungles now seemed trivial, and Britain's new king, Edward VII, as unlike his Balmoralistic mother as could be imagined, was packed off to Paris on a charm offensive. Since nothing charmed 'Edward the Peacemaker' quite as much as champagne, French cuisine and pretty women, the visit was a huge success. A 'friendly understanding', or Entente Cordiale, was struck in 1904.

The Entente freed up another six battleships from the Mediterranean, and two more followed when Britain agreed with its other old rival, Russia, that Germany mattered more than the Great Game. Far-flung navies had indeed melted away, and London had conceded that it could no longer run the sort of world-system it had managed fifty years earlier; but the Home Fleet had stayed one step ahead of its rivals. Reeking tube and iron shard still kept the Channel closed.

Greater Britain

To some strategists, reorganising the navy to meet the German challenge was merely the first step, because the truest cause of

Britain's security crisis was its loss of prosperity relative to rivals as its world-system increasingly mismatched geographical realities. Americans and Germans were exploiting these new realities aggressively, but opportunities beckoned for Britain too, above all in the enormous Greater Britain created by the millions of migrants who had moved to the Dominions. 'When we inquire into the Greater Britain of the future,' the historian J. R. Seeley pronounced in 1883, 'we ought to think much more of our [Dominions] than of our Indian Empire.' In the wide, open spaces of Australia, Canada and New Zealand (and perhaps South Africa), he said, 'you have the most progressive race put in the circumstances most favourable to progress. There you have no past and an unbounded future. Government and institutions are all ultra-English. All is liberty, industry, invention, innovation.'

Figure 9.5, a revealing (if disorienting) map published in 2009 by the historian James Belich, shows what Seeley and others had in mind. Greater Britain's boosters liked to point out how similar the settlement of Canada, Australia and New Zealand was to the American settlement of the expanses beyond the Appalachians. Britain and the United States, Belich observes, each had an 'old' core (the Isles for the former and the thirteen Atlantic colonies for the latter) containing what Belich calls a 'senior partner' (England for Britain, the Mid-Atlantic states for Americans), which provided most of the people, money and organisation for expansion, plus two 'junior partners'. In each system one of these junior partners (Scotland for the British, New England for the Americans) produced disproportionate numbers of businessmen and government officials, while the other – Ireland, internally split between Catholics and Protestants, and the Southern states, split between blacks and whites – provided 'the shock troops of settlement'. The tripartite 'Old Britain' and 'Old America' had each spent the nineteenth century creating new, larger versions of themselves, one across the oceans and the other across the Appalachians.

The two systems were similar in so many ways, but there was one all-important difference. Old and New America were both run from Washington, DC, while Old and New Britain had multiple responsible governments, each charting its own course. The solution, said Seeley, lay in new institutions, which would in effect draw the Dominions towards the Isles (as in Figure 9.5), so that 'Canada and Australia would be to us as Kent and Cornwall' (Figure 9.6). By pooling sovereignty

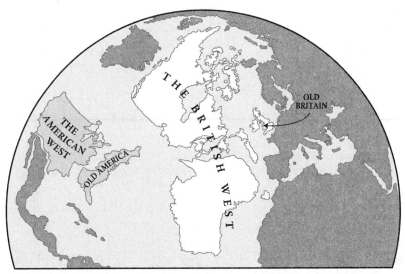

Figure 9.5. Belich's Map: historian James Belich's comparison, drawn in 2009, of Greater Britain and America. Canada, Australia and New Zealand have been dragged into the Atlantic to form a 'British West' in close union with 'Old Britain', much like the union between the original thirteen colonies of 'Old America' and the trans-Appalachian 'American West'.

in a union based on mobility and identity, the thinking went, this Greater Britain would reinvigorate the Isles' prosperity and simultaneously solve their security problems. If that could be accomplished, another historian concluded, this 'firm and well-compacted union of all the British lands would form a state that might control the whole world'. Greater Britain could become another United States, rendering understandings (friendly or not) with France, Russia and Japan unnecessary.

No one could fault this vision for lack of ambition. Britons have regularly revived it – most recently, in the wake of the 2016 Brexit referendum, as CANZUK, a union of Canada, Australia, New Zealand and the United Kingdom. However, the late nineteenth- and early twenty-first-century versions both ignored one crucial detail: Canadians, Australians and New Zealanders showed no interest in federation. In 1884 Gladstone concluded that imperial federation was 'chimerical if not a little short of nonsensical'; in 2019 Australia's former prime minister Kevin Rudd called CANZUK 'utter bollocks'.

Figure 9.6. The British stage, 1865–1945.

What kept Greater Britain alive after 1900 was the work of one man: Joseph Chamberlain. Of all the big personalities in early twentieth-century Britain's politics, 'Joe' (as he was universally known) was arguably the biggest. He was a cartoonist's dream, with his trademark monocle and orchid buttonhole, and had a wonderful backstory. Having started out as a shoemaker's apprentice, he rose to become a partner in a Birmingham firm that manufactured two-thirds of the world's screws, before becoming the city's most radical mayor. He then split the Liberals over Irish home rule, left the party, led the charge into the Boer War in 1899, became a fighter for imperial federation and finally split the Tories too.

'In a splendid isolation, surrounded and supported by our kinsfolk', Chamberlain thought, Britain could permanently stand aloof from Europe. However, he also understood that it would take a lot to convince the Dominions of federation's benefits. Chamberlain therefore raised the stakes, putting on the table the world-system's central premise: free trade. Most of the Dominions would love preferential trading rights with the Isles, so, Chamberlain asked, why not renounce the faith in free trade? Why not slap tariffs on everyone else's goods, giving Britain's colonial kith and kin the same kind of advantages that migrants across the Appalachians enjoyed within the United States?

This was bold. Some Conservatives embraced these ideas; others, including Winston Churchill, defected to the Liberals rather than betray Dombeyism. Outraged by Chamberlain's heresy, Liberals hit back with the catchy slogan 'Hands off the people's food!', arguing that imperial preference would effectively bring back the Corn Laws and, with them, expensive bread. They staged public bake-offs, contrasting wholesome, heart-warming Big Loaves from Free-Trade ovens with the miserable Small Loaves (the kind of crusts foreigners gnawed on) coming out of Tariff ovens. Unfazed, the *Daily Express* hired P. G. Wodehouse to write pro-Chamberlain doggerel, which proved so popular that it inspired a music-hall act.

Chamberlain redoubled his efforts. The average Briton in 1900 lived twelve years longer than his or her ancestors had done in 1800. The left-wing firebrand David Lloyd George had been talking for years about the need for old-age pensions, but his Liberal comrades had never found the money to pay for them, so Chamberlain outflanked them by insisting that the income from tariffs could cover the bill. The Liberals saw no option but to commit to funding pensions without tariffs. Their new star Churchill pledged to provide unemployment insurance too.

When the people spoke, in 1906, their voice was deafening. They wanted pensions and social security, but wanted free trade and dreadnoughts too. They gave the Liberals a huge parliamentary majority and the unenviable job of paying for their promises. Lloyd

George pulled a host of penny-pinching tricks, setting pensions at just one-quarter of a labourer's income and only paying out to those in their seventies (by which time most people were dead), but the budget still grew by 10 per cent. Having ruled out Chamberlain's indirect taxes on food, Liberals had no alternative to levying direct taxes on wealth – a 'People's Budget', Lloyd George proclaimed in 1909, 'to wage implacable warfare against poverty and squalidness'.

His implacable warfare was actually rather tame by modern standards. Income tax did shoot up, but only from 4 to 6 per cent. What enraged the landed elite was not that their estates were being taxed into ruination, but that they were being taxed at all. Yet even this limited redistribution almost failed, because by 1910 the Liberals could only muster the necessary votes in Parliament by enlisting the support of Irish Nationalists, whose price was the government's support for home rule in Dublin. The whole scheme, Conservatives could claim, was a plot against the Union. Redistribution and home rule meant 'the end of all', a former prime minister pronounced: 'the negation of Faith, of Family, of Property, of Monarchy, of Empire'.

When he finally pushed the package through, Lloyd George gloated that 'We have got them at last'. After millennia of facing down revolting peasants and confiscatory kings, the denizens of Britain's Downton Abbeys began a slow-motion descent into bankruptcy and dispossession. (Not coincidentally, the *Downton Abbey* television series starts in 1912, just two years after the People's Budget passed.) They took their time a-dying, to be sure, and there were still plenty of them hanging around Cambridge when I arrived there in 1982 – but far fewer than there had been in 1882. The People's Budget inaugurated the landlords' recessional.

The Liberals' triumph was very much a poisoned chalice. By succeeding in tying taxation to Ireland, the Conservatives inextricably commingled the issues of prosperity and identity and found a new stick with which to beat the Liberals. No sooner did Irish Nationalists demand their quid pro quo of home rule than the Tories rebranded themselves as a 'Conservative and Unionist Party', arguing that defending the Union was the greatest issue of the day. Banking that Englishmen still found the pope scarier than the Kaiser, they insisted that 'home rule' really meant 'Rome rule', and that only Conservatism could keep England's back door shut.

Unionism worked no better than the Liberals' Irish policies. In

March 1914 London's spies revealed that paramilitaries calling themselves the Ulster Volunteers were planning an armed uprising: but rather than the sinister Catholic Republicans invoked by Unionists, these insurgents were Protestants, and instead of shooting them, the king's army was helping them. Every one of the Ulster Volunteers' leaders was a former British officer, and dozens of serving officers threatened to resign their commissions rather than force 'Rome rule' on co-religionists. Seeing no better option, the government tried to compromise the crisis away by calling it a misunderstanding, but it wasn't. Just weeks later, two army officers helped smuggle nearly 25,000 rifles, mostly German, to the Ulster Volunteers. Armed by Britain's greatest strategic rival, Britain's greatest patriots – military men and Orangemen – were conspiring to burn the Union to save it. Far from forging an imperial federation with the Dominions, the Isles themselves seemed close to disintegration.

Business as Usual

In the summer of 1914, the novelist H. G. Wells observed, most Britons were 'mightily concerned about the conflict in Ireland, and almost deliberately negligent of the possibility of a war with Germany'. For three weeks after terrorists killed Austria's Archduke Ferdinand on 28 June, investors all over Europe kept on buying government bonds, usually a sign that they expect no international drama. Only on 18 July did bond prices slump in Paris, Berlin and St Petersburg. Now expecting a Continental conflict, investors moved their money to London, assuming that the land of starched collars would be safe. On the 29th they realised their mistake, and British bonds fell 6 per cent. On the 31st the stock exchange was shut 'until further notice'. The *Guardian* was still predicting peace on 3 August, but Britain declared war on the 4th.

In modern memory, the 'Great War' of 1914–18 stands out as the dawn of a new age. It was the first industrialised conflict, with aircraft, tanks and gas. It was also the first to be filmed. The actual footage – jerky, silent, grainy, black-and-white – looks anything but modern, but when digitally remastered by Peter Jackson for his magnificent film *They Shall Not Grow Old*, the teenage warriors of a century ago leap to life in colour. They move normally and even speak to us, their words deciphered by lip-readers and rendered by experts in their

Figure 9.7. The war to end all that had gone before:
business as usual breaks the world-system, 1914–18.

regional dialects. The effect is shocking, heart-rending. This was not
the war to end war, but it was the war to end all that had gone before.

Yet breaking with the past was the last thing Britain's leaders
intended in 1914. The war, Churchill promised, would be 'business
carried on as usual during alterations on the map of Europe'. It certainly began traditionally enough, in the slow-motion disintegration
of the Habsburg and Ottoman empires (Figure 9.7) – not, as many
strategists had expected, in clashes over new colonies in Africa. At
first, some newspapers even called it the 'Third Balkan War', although
that name lost favour as alliances dragged in Russia, Germany, France
and then Britain too. Yet this cascade of declarations of war was also
normal, being the logical consequence of all balance-of-power frame-
works since the eighteenth century. When Britain jumped in, its
reasons were equally old-fashioned. Germany could not be allowed
to dominate Europe, leaving it free to build an even bigger fleet, and
absolutely could not be allowed to conquer the Belgian counterscarp.

After entering the war conventionally, Britain fought it conventionally too. It funded a Continental coalition (France, Russia, Serbia
and eventually Italy and Romania) and sent a small expeditionary
force to the counterscarp. This followed a strategy Louis XIV would

have recognised, of digging muddy trenches in Flanders, measuring advances by metres and grinding the enemy down through attrition. The mass armies of 1916–18 were more novel but hardly unprecedented; they were just bigger versions of Marlborough's and Wellington's forces. And while the casualties inflicted by artillery and machine guns shocked everyone, the first day on the Somme in 1916 was proportionately no bloodier than Malplaquet or Waterloo.

As in most wars since the sixteenth century, Irish rebels tried to open Britain's back door and were savagely suppressed; and, as in most since the nineteenth, Britain aggressively protected its routes to South Asia. One army advanced from the Suez Canal to Jerusalem, while Indians invaded Iraq and (a newer twist) Australians and New Zealanders helped assault Gallipoli. Equally predictably, Britain's main effort was a naval blockade, strangling Germany while seizing its colonies and trade.

So far, so much business as usual. Yet the First World War *was* different, because of the United States. When Britain and France had blockaded each other back in 1806, both had claimed the right to intercept neutral ships suspected of carrying contraband to the enemy. This particularly hurt Americans, but there was little they could do about it. Thomas Jefferson hit back with his own embargo against both Britain and France, but American living standards promptly fell by 5 per cent per year (twice the rate of French decline, three times Britain's). The military solution attempted in 1812 worked little better. Andrew Jackson saw the British off at New Orleans, but redcoats burned the White House.

When British and German skippers started boarding American ships in 1914, however, things went very differently. The war had begun with a vast reversal on financial markets, as money which had for decades been flowing out of London in the form of overseas investments flowed back to pay for the fighting. Even so, selling off the family silver came nowhere near meeting Britain's needs. Staggering sums had to be mobilised, and the only people with that kind of cash were Americans. By late 1916 the banker J. P. Morgan had raised a jaw-dropping $2 billion for the cause. So, when the US Navy complained early in the war that Britain's blockade was 'untenable under any law or custom of maritime war hitherto known', London backed down rather than risk enraging its creditors. Germany followed suit in 1915, fearing that American anger at the sinking of the

liner *Lusitania* would drive President Woodrow Wilson to throw the
government's money, as well as Wall Street's, behind Britain.

Wilson, however, was playing a deeper game. Britain's dollar
addiction gave him leverage, which he hoped to use to pressure
the belligerents into accepting 'peace without victory' – an indeci-
sive outcome leaving Britain, Germany, France and Russia poorer
and weaker and the United States correspondingly stronger. The
problem, however, was that Morgan, a massive donor to Wilson's
Republican rivals, was in effect running his own pro-British foreign
policy. Morgan's Republican tail was wagging Wilson's Democratic
dog: American investors had so much riding on British victory that
they might yet drag Wilson into backing Britain to avert financial
meltdown.

Betting on being too big to fail, Britain ratcheted its embargo
back up, blacklisting American firms that traded with Germany. 'I
am, I must admit, about at the end of my patience with Great Britain
and the allies,' Wilson told his closest adviser. 'Let us build a navy
bigger than hers and do what we please.' Over the summer of 1916
Congress appropriated nearly $500 million to do just this and set up
an Emergency Fleet Corporation to bankroll the biggest merchant
marine on earth. And so it was that Wilson, not the Kaiser, broke the
British world-system. For centuries Britain had defeated Continental
rivals by outspending them, but those who live by the chequebook
can die by it too.

That autumn English anxiety turned to despair. Planning multiple concentric offensives for the following summer, the Allies asked
Morgan to raise a further $1.5 billion, but four days before the bond
was floated, the Federal Reserve Board advised Americans against
investing. Picking his moment perfectly, Wilson published a 'Peace
Note', effectively challenging the combatants to admit that the war
was pointless. The king broke down in tears. Sterling collapsed. By
the year's end, Britain had so depleted its reserves that its American
assets could cover only another three weeks of purchases. All the gold
in the Bank of England would only pay for another six. 'By next June
or earlier', the chancellor of the exchequer warned, 'the President of
the American Republic will be in a position, if he so wishes, to dictate
his own terms to us.'

Wilson had disrupted business as usual, but the shape of a
new business model remained unclear. Lloyd George hoped for an

Anglo-American joint venture, with the 'active sympathy of the two great English-speaking nations' meaning that 'the entire world could not shake the combined mastery we would hold over the seas'. When he eased himself into the premiership in December 1916, this became London's official view. In Washington plenty of Republicans liked the idea, but the American people were less sure. By the narrowest of margins, November's presidential election gave Wilson four more years to pursue peace without victory. Ultimately, however, neither London nor Washington mattered as much as Berlin. There, misreading American politics even more than Lloyd George, the Kaiser let his top generals convince him that, despite the fine talk, Wilson would never abandon Wall Street's investments. There would be an Anglo-American takeover – unless Germany won the land war first.

Germany therefore unleashed its submarines, hoping to turn Mackinder's Map back into the Hereford Map by closing the Atlantic to American materiel and men. In truth, though, Wilson was still reaching for peace without victory. Even when American sailors drowned, he refused to ask Congress to declare war, relenting only when German diplomats, assuming that intervention was inevitable, tried to divert American energies by encouraging Mexico to reconquer Texas. America went to war in April 1917.

For a full twelve months it looked as though the Kaiser had called the situation correctly. German submarines sank one-third of Britain's merchant marine; France's army mutinied; Russia collapsed; and for a few heady days in April 1918 the British army was on the run. 'With our backs to the wall', its commander ordered, 'each one of us must fight on to the end.' The line held. By May, 700,000 Americans were in France, Britain's naval blockade was finally starving Germany and a terrible new influenza was killing millions. The Kaiser's decision had been disastrously wrong. German soldiers surrendered in their tens of thousands; the Kaiser fled; revolution and civil war broke out. Peace came with victory after all.

10:10:6:3:3

But what a peace, and what a victory. Britain's triumph was not as great as in 1815 or 1763, but it was certainly comparable with 1713, more than meeting the nation's security goals in Europe. Victory left Germany weak but not *too* weak. French plans to dissolve Germany into its pre-1871 components would have gone too far for Lloyd George: with Russia's new Soviet rulers apparently set on spreading Bolshevism across the Continent, he preferred an intact Germany as 'a dyke of peaceful, lawful, patient strength and virtue against the flood of Red Barbarism flowing from the east' (Churchill's words). A not too weak Germany would keep France on its toes and therefore dependent on British goodwill. A nervous Paris would also do the work of building alliances in Eastern Europe, simultaneously encircling Germany and bottling up the Soviet Union. Mired in civil wars and ethnic cleansing, the Soviets and East Europeans were no threat to anyone but themselves. Viewed from London, this was all very satisfactory.

Asia was messier. Forced by the war to abandon its old strategy of propping up the Ottoman Empire, Britain eventually occupied Palestine, Transjordan and Iraq to protect its communications with India. In India itself, so many men – nearly a million – had served in the war that Lloyd George agreed in 1917 to accelerate the country's promotion to Dominion status. The flu then killed more people in India – perhaps over 12 million – than in any other nation, and Britain's part in partitioning the Ottoman Empire alienated tens of millions of Indian Muslims. The Raj seemed to have no response to the London-trained lawyer Mohandas Gandhi, by turns saintly and cynical, who catalysed the independence movement by bringing Hindus and Muslims together and preaching non-violent resistance. But resistance turned violent anyway. Appalled by his followers' brutality, Gandhi renounced them, only for Brigadier-General Reginald Dyer, convinced that he was facing an 1857-scale uprising, to gun down nearly 2,000 at Amritsar in 1919. Uprisings spread across the Punjab. The emir of Afghanistan invaded to support the insurgents; Britain rushed 300,000 troops to the frontier and sent airplanes to bomb Kabul.

By the time order was restored and Gandhi was locked up, a new question was dividing London. Surely, said some, imperial possessions were means, not ends. So long as they contributed to a world-system that benefited Britain, all well and good, but if their costs outweighed their benefits, Britain should abandon them and find new ways to flourish. If a new business model required rethinking identity, mobility, prosperity, security and sovereignty, then so be it. Some on the left, such as George Orwell (who served as a colonial policeman in

Burma, and hated the experience), positively welcomed such a rein-
vention, while some on the right were passionately opposed. Most
people, however, were unsentimental. The costs of empire seemed
to be rising and the benefits falling if an educated man like Gandhi,
who would have been a natural British ally thirty years earlier, now
saw nationalism as a better bet. The balance sheet had shifted.

Not even Ireland, that most ancient colony, now seemed necessary. For eight centuries it had been a back door that England had to
keep closed, whatever the cost, but by 1918 it was no longer obvious
who would walk through it. So, with another expensive, bloody guerilla war dividing opinion at home and alienating it in America, British
and Irish representatives drew an 'interim' line (still there a century
later) around six majority-Protestant counties in Ulster in 1921. The
Catholic south finally walked away. 'Only national self-preservation
could have excused [. . .] iron repression,' said Churchill, 'and no reasonable man could allege that self-preservation was involved.'

It was hardly a clean break, and the south fought a civil war of
its own in 1922–3, but if Ireland could go, was anywhere sacred?
Certainly not the Dominions, which were virtually independent by
1931. Yet many, Churchill included, thought India really was a matter
of national self-preservation. For them, the question was how, not
whether, to hold on. Judging that holding on would be impossible if
the 150,000 Britons on the spot lost the 300 million locals' goodwill,
most imperialists considered compromise the only route, but when
the army sacked Dyer over Amritsar, the backlash at home was ferocious. The hard-right *Morning Post* raised £26,000 for him. Churchill
tried compromising with the compromisers: while privately thinking
Dyer right to 'shoot hard', he let him go, but drew the line at appeasing Indian demands any further. But appeasement there was. India
won Dominion status in 1929, and by 1935 even a Conservative prime
minister, Stanley Baldwin, was calling Churchill's stand against Indian
responsible government 'quite mad'.

All these issues in the end came down to the one great secret of
the empire, revealed in 1916: that winning the military war against
Germany had meant losing a financial one against the United States.
As a proportion of GDP, the national debt was actually smaller in
1918 than in 1815, and the £1 billion Britain owed the United States
was roughly balanced by another billion which the other allies owed
to Britain; but France and Italy were broke, Russia's Bolsheviks

repudiated their debts and foisting Britain's bills on to Germany was pointless since the Germans could not pay. Having borrowed in dollars, Britain could not even inflate its debts away by printing money. London was left holding the bag.

When Napoleon fell, Britain had been the world's financial and shipping centre and its only industrialising nation, but by the time the Kaiser fell, invisible exports and income from overseas investments had collapsed and British industry, mobilised to manufacture guns and ammunition during the war, was making little that anyone wanted to buy. Forty per cent of government spending was going just to service the debt. John Maynard Keynes was almost unique among economists in urging further state spending to stimulate growth, but Lloyd George listened to more orthodox advisers and opted for austerity. He cut state spending, hiked interest rates and raised the basic rate of income tax (just 6 per cent in 1911) to 30 per cent in 1919.

Because deflation drove prices down faster than wages, those who had jobs generally benefited. By 1929 the typical wage packet went 10 per cent further than it had done in 1919. My grandad, a steelworker in Stoke-on-Trent, had married, started a family and rented a brand-new house – the end one in the terrace, no less – by the age of twenty-three. But the downside of the economy shrinking just as 5 million ex-servicemen came home was that one in six was left jobless. When employers cut wages, workers shattered all records for days lost to strikes. In 1926 a General Strike briefly paralysed the country.

Most industrialists thought that letting the pound depreciate against the dollar was the answer, making British goods cheaper for foreigners to buy. Financiers, however, preferred 'sound money', believing that a strong, stable pound would restore their credibility as the world's bankers. Churchill, now chancellor, worried about 'Britain possessing the finest credit in the world simultaneously with a million and a quarter unemployed', but, not for the last time, those in power chose finance over factories. American money was rushing into Europe's reviving economies, and so, to attract it to London too, Churchill overrode Keynes's objections and pegged sterling to gold at the pre-war exchange rate of $4.86. The result was constant balance-of-payments crises, as Britain haemorrhaged reserves to defend its overvalued currency.

With sterling, manufacturing and India – three of the pillars of the nineteenth-century world-system – so visibly shaken, it was perhaps inevitable that the fourth, the fleet, would come under pressure too. Far from reducing costs, the end of the war set off a naval arms race, with Britain, Japan and France scrambling to keep up with Wilson's shipbuilding programme. Britain could not afford this, but Wilson refused to compromise, even threatening 'another and more terrible and bloody war and England would be wiped off the face of the map'. British and American admirals almost got into a fist fight at the Versailles peace conference. However, many Americans, particularly Republicans, shared Lloyd George's dislike of Wilson's ambitions. It was fiscal conservatism as much as isolationism that swung the Senate against the Versailles treaties, and pledges to cut military spending helped Republicans win the White House in 1920.

When Republicans proposed bringing all the players to Washington to discuss naval reductions, Lloyd George leaped at the chance. Settling into seats their seats in Constitution Hall, three years exactly after the war ended, the delegates probably expected a day of conventional, conference-opening pieties. Instead, they got what one eyewitness called 'the most intensely dramatic moment I have ever witnessed'. Charles Evans Hughes, the new secretary of state, hit them with a detailed review of every major fleet, demanding that sixty-six battleships be scrapped. 'Hughes sank in thirty-five minutes more ships than all of the admirals of the world have sunk in a cycle of centuries', one journalist wrote. Warship-building, Hughes shouted, 'must stop!' Everyone rose to their feet in a 'tornado of cheering'.

Everyone, that is, except Britain's naval men. Hughes did not just want to eliminate their traditional superiority over the next two or three navies combined: he wanted Anglo-American parity. His '10:10:6:3:3' formula meant that for every ten tons of battleship or aircraft carrier flying the Union Jack or Stars and Stripes, there would be six under Japan's Rising Sun and three (actually, 3.3) each under the French and Italian tricolores. And, since the United States could concentrate its forces on just two oceans while Britain had interests in every stretch of water in the world, even parity would now be a pipe dream. To crown it all, Americans insisted that the Anglo-Japanese alliance should lapse too, so Tokyo could not act as London's agent in the Pacific.

Unattractive as all this looked from London, King George signed the Washington Naval Treaty anyway, because the only alternative was to lose an arms race and end up even worse off. It was some consolation that Republicans preferred keeping taxes low to building their full quota of warships (it is to Calvin Coolidge, who won the White House in 1924, that we owe the view that 'the chief business of the American people is business'), but even so, the hard fact was that the British world-system could not run at 10:10:6:3:3. The day the treaty was signed, 6 February 1922, was the Royal Navy's worst since its defeat by Louis XIV in 1690.

Turned Out Nice

At first, this did not seem to matter much. Mackinder's Map had rotated westwards to centre on New York City rather than London, but Britannia still more or less ruled the waves, markets boomed and the '20s roared. But that illusion only lasted seven years. Even now, economists argue over what caused Wall Street's meltdown in 1929, but its consequences are clear enough. Americans brought their money home from Europe; Europeans raised interest rates to attract it back; deflation returned. Orthodox economics held that once bankruptcies drove unemployment high enough, leaner, meaner businesses would thrive, but that didn't happen. Almost one-third of Britons, Americans and Germans had lost their jobs by 1933 and most economies were still shrinking.

Alone again, Keynes kept recommending public spending to boost demand, but the United States instead introduced 21,000 tariffs to protect its markets. Other governments followed suit. International lending dried up. By 1931 eighteen national banking systems teetered on the edge of collapse. In Britain sailors mutinied when public sector wages were cut to save money. Implicitly conceding that the pound was no longer the planet's preferred medium of exchange, London abandoned the gold standard, rushing to save what it could of its world-system by forming a 'Sterling Area'. Much as Chamberlain had wanted, tariffs now protected the empire (except Canada, which went with the Americans) against almost everyone else. In a fine irony, it was Joe's son Neville who wrote the new rules.

Recovery came quickly, although not evenly. India and the Dominions did well, their exports to Britain jumping sharply, but within the Isles the old south-east/north-west divide deepened. Coal, cotton and steel had made northern England the world's workshop in the nineteenth century, but in the twentieth, foreign competition undercut all these industries. Two-thirds of men in Jarrow were out of work, and things were not much better in the mines of south Wales and County Durham or the Tyneside and Clydeside shipyards.

George Orwell's *Road to Wigan Pier* is the most moving account of England in the 1930s, but it needs to be read alongside another classic, J. B. Priestley's *English Journey*. Little of the England Priestley saw, especially in suburban London and Birmingham, resembled Wigan or Jarrow. New industries – plastics, electronics, aero engines – were making money and hiring. By 1937 unemployment was back below 10 per cent and wage packets were, in real terms, one-sixth fatter than a decade earlier. Nearly 2 million new homes were built between 1934 and 1938. Housing had been improving steadily since the 1890s, with governments insisting on proper streets of terraced or even semi-detached homes, not the old back-to-backs. Damp courses, kiln-fired bricks, tiled roofs and metal drains became standard, although toilets remained outdoors (my grandparents only moved theirs inside in 1968). Even poor neighbourhoods got piped water and gas. The first council (public) housing, London's Boundary Estate, opened in 1900. By the 1930s council houses and flats made up almost half of new construction. Belying their later 'whiff of welfare, of subsidisation, of [. . .] second-class citizenship' (so described by the Labour MP Anthony Crosland), these initially appealed across class lines. In 1931 London County Council classified one-third of renters on its Dover House Estate as skilled working-class and another third as white-collar; some even employed maids.

Home ownership boomed too, thanks to cheaper, longer-term mortgages. Those able to pay for added respectability built detached houses, ideally tucked away in their own gardens and stretching for kilometres along the roads leading out of crowded cities. Intellectuals such as E. M. Forster decried the 'red rust' of 'London's creeping', but suburbs were what people wanted. Solid semis multiplied; the bourgeois filled their 'Stockbroker Tudor' villas with telephones (numbers tripled) and their garages with cars (ownership doubled). By 1935, 5,000 cinemas were selling 20 million tickets every week; three-quarters of homes had a radio.

These were hints of things to come, of a more leisured, middle-class Britain. The south-east, at least, was vanquishing what reformists would soon be calling 'the five giant evils, of Want, of Disease, of Ignorance, of Squalor and of Idleness'. Most families had a breadwinner, a roof, decent clothes and reasonably regular meals. Women had the vote, and the 1931 census showed that most men over sixty-five had retired. Medical care remained patchy, but typhoid, cholera and tuberculosis, the great nineteenth-century killers, had been defeated. Infant mortality fell by one-third across the 1930s. No British statesman would have chosen a world at 10:10:6:3:3, but, to borrow a catchphrase from George Formby, the most popular comedian of the day, things had 'turned out nice again' after all.

Very Well, Alone

No one could say that of the Continent. Unable to revive prosperity by falling back on partners like the Dominions, Europeans toyed with sweeping revisions of sovereignty. France proposed a European Federal Union in 1930; Germany considered a customs union with Austria, hoping to draw Eastern Europe into its orbit too. Both failed, and, with governments now walling off their economies, talks on disarmament, borders and debt also collapsed. Everything the elected governments did seemed to make matters worse, and wilder, dictatorial notions gained traction. In Germany, far-right and far-left parties between them captured half the votes in 1932 (Hitler's Nazis twice as many as the Communists). National identities were coming apart. In France political rioting almost brought the government down; German street fighting was even worse; and Spain fell into civil war.

Britain's troubles paled by comparison. The British Union of Fascists never attracted more than 50,000 members and the Communists barely 10,000 (as compared to almost 450,000 individual Labour members and the Tories' 2 million). Events seemed to be confirming the superiority of Britain's 'stolid, pipe-sucking manhood, unmoved by panic or excitement' to the fractious, excitable Continentals. It was a sign of the times that Britain had to resort to 'national unity' coalition governments after 1931, but when German conservatives tried to unite their country by appointing Hitler chancellor and manipulating him from behind the scenes, he repaid them by abolishing democracy altogether after just two months in office.

Hitler turned Europe's crises of prosperity, sovereignty and identity into one of security. Few doubted the threat he posed. Having railed for years about an Anglo-American-Jewish conspiracy to reduce Germany to 'less than a Nigger state', he promised to conquer 'living space' for the German people in Eastern Europe. Just a year after his coup Britain's Defence Requirements Subcommittee judged Germany 'the ultimate potential enemy'. Another year after that, Hitler began rearming.

There was nothing new about a tyrant wanting to bind the Continent together by force, and the same tools that had stopped Louis XIV, Napoleon and the Kaiser – a balance of power to distract the aggressor, a counterscarp to block him and a fleet to bankrupt him – remained available. Admittedly, the biggest potential balancer – the United States – was disinclined to help and the Dominions were dubious, but France was eager, bringing with it Polish, Romanian, Czech and potentially Soviet allies to encircle Hitler. Even Mussolini, Italy's fascist dictator, was amenable. The counterscarp too looked solid, thanks to a Franco-Belgian military alliance and formidable fortifications along France's German border. Finally, the fleet could still close the Channel. Concentrating it in home waters would, the chiefs of staff conceded, 'expose to depredation, for an inestimable period, British possessions and dependencies, including those of India, Australia and New Zealand', but a grand new naval base at Singapore (planned but not yet built) should help. So too a naval deal with Germany, tying Hitler into the 10:10:6:3:3 formula at about 3.5.

But was this enough? Most military men suspected that air power, barely a factor in 1914, had now changed the equation. 'Modern aeroplanes', the *Daily Mail* warned, 'can eliminate all other forms of warlike action whether by land or sea', rendering fleets irrelevant. Airships had bombed London in 1917, and the bigger, faster planes of the 1930s might well be unstoppable. 'We thought of air warfare in 1938 rather as people think of nuclear warfare today', the future prime minister Harold Macmillan recollected in the 1960s. An aerial 'knock-out blow' was anticipated within hours of war being declared. 'Every town every street every house every occupant will be exposed', said the *Observer*, a newspaper for educated types. A Whitehall committee predicted 20,000 casualties for the first day of the war and 150,000 for the first week. The hard truth, Prime Minister Stanley Baldwin gloomily concluded, was that 'the bomber will always get through'.

This vision of modern war seemed to overturn Britain's established strategies. Since Elizabethan times rulers had been confident that, given a strong fleet, the Channel would be a moat defensive, even against enemies who controlled the Continent's shores. But if Hitler's planes could sink the fleet and leapfrog the Channel, the situation might resemble medieval or Roman times, when invaders could not be intercepted. The only way to stop enemies crossing the Channel in those days had been by denying them access to their own coastlines, so they could not launch ships at all. Thinking similarly, the chiefs of staff concluded that a Continental counterscarp was now 'even more important in the defence of this country than in the past [. . .] If the Germans were to succeed in over-running the Low Countries and in establishing air bases near the Belgian and Dutch coasts', they feared, 'not only London, but the whole of the industrial centres in the Midlands and the north, as well as our shipping approaching the coasts, would be within effective and even decisive range of air attacks, which owing to the short range, could be heavy, continuous and sustained.'

The implication was obvious: Britain must build a deeper counterscarp than ever before and defend it at all costs. 'The old frontiers are gone', Baldwin told Parliament. 'When you think of the defence of England you no longer think of the chalk cliffs of Dover; you think of the Rhine. That is where our frontier lies.' Yet acting on these insights proved difficult. A balance of power works only if its members are ready to fight, but British (and even more so French) voters were desperate to avoid repeating the First World War's bloodletting. There was also an economic angle. Industrial capacity was still recovering from 1929, and British factories could only start making weapons if they stopped making the export goods that paid for everything. Borrowing to cover costs might set off inflation without producing more weapons; raising taxes might additionally choke off growth. With prosperity and security in conflict, everything urged caution – which made it difficult for potential partners to trust each other. Italy and the Soviets soon distanced themselves.

Britain stalled by buying Hitler off. The way the decade ended has made appeasement a low, dishonest word, but it was actually a very British tradition. It seemed to be working in India in the 1930s and had worked in the Dominions since the 1830s; not appeasing the Americans had proved disastrous in the 1770s. Churchill mocked 'an appeaser [a]s one who feeds a crocodile hoping it will eat him last', but being eaten last was popular – and rightly so, so long as appeasement bought time to rearm to fight for the balance of power and the counterscarp. But by giving Hitler a free hand in the Sudetenland in 1938, Britain allowed him to break Germany's encirclement, defeating the whole purpose of the exercise. Seeing this, Stalin made terms with Hitler and the two dictators partitioned Poland. Only after all allies – real and hoped-for – had defected did Britain and France decide to fight.

Their plan, such as it was, followed a pattern set in 1702. Britain would send armies to the Continent while blockading its waters (as in 1914, borrowing cash and buying supplies transatlantically) and waiting for the foe's collapse. What undid the plan was that Hitler overran the entire counterscarp in just eleven weeks; what saved Britain anyway was that the experts turned out to be wrong about the bomber always getting through. The air force and fleet kept the Channel closed. There were terrifying moments, and the Blitz killed 60,000 Londoners, but Hitler never stood much chance of winning a battle of attrition in England's skies. British radar could see the Germans coming; German planes needed most of their fuel just to fly to and from their targets; and British aircraft, pilots and production were all superior. Between June and October 1940 the Royal Air Force lost 915 aircraft while British factories built 2,091 new ones; over a similar period, Germany lost 1,733 and added just 988. On 17 September 1940 Hitler postponed the invasion indefinitely.

It was, as Churchill said, Britain's finest hour – and his own. Nineteen forty was the new 1588, with Churchill casting himself as both Elizabeth and Shakespeare. He gave the British a new way to see themselves, as the few who stood alone, defying evil, all in it together (Figure 9.8). It was a remarkable achievement for a spendthrift, champagne-swilling descendant of dukes and heiresses. Churchill had always been a divisive figure; my grandad, a communist as well as a steelworker, repeatedly said that the main thing to know about him was that he had ordered troops to shoot striking miners at Tonypandy in Wales in 1910 (in fact he hadn't). Even by the standards of the 1930s, Churchill's scorn for Indians was exceptional, and plenty of Britons of that decade would have sympathised with the demonstrators who daubed 'was a racist' on his statue in Parliament Square in 2020. Yet, despite all this baggage, Churchill made himself the symbol of a genuinely British struggle in 1940. Before the Battle of Britain a Scottish Nationalist leader had told friends he would welcome a German invasion, Welsh nationalists had sent delegates to Berlin and Irish Republicans had planted bombs in London. But by the time battle was joined, with invasion appearing imminent, pollsters found that

Figure 9.8. Very well, alone. The greatest political cartoon
of all time (David Low, *Daily Mail*, 18 June 1940).

88 per cent of people backed Churchill. Eighty years have passed, but
listening again to his speeches from that summer, with the familiar
growl and the heavy pauses, I can only wonder what the other 12 per
cent were thinking. 'We shall go on to the end [. . .] We shall defend
our island, whatever the cost may be. We shall fight on the beaches,
we shall fight on the landing grounds, we shall fight in the fields and
in the streets, we shall fight in the hills; we shall never surrender.'

But never surrendering was not the same thing as winning. In his
first week as prime minister Churchill had asked 'What is our aim?'
and had answered: 'Victory – victory at all costs, victory in spite of all
terror; victory, however long and hard the road may be.' Yet the path
to victory was no clearer in 1940 than it had been after 1588 (or 1805).
Britain could blockade the Continent, raid its coasts, bomb German
cities and support guerillas, but none of these would break Hitler's
empire. Not even Hitler's decision to emulate Napoleon's invasion of
Russia, right down to a disaster at Moscow, did that. From the very
start Churchill pinned everything on the single strategy of fighting
on, 'until, in God's good time, the New World, with all its power and
might, steps forth to the rescue and the liberation of the old'.

God's good time – or rather, President Roosevelt's – came slowly, despite Roosevelt seeing more clearly than Wilson that Britain was America's counterscarp against Germany. Even when a 1916-style financial crisis gripped Britain, with its dollar reserves dipping below what was already owed to American manufacturers, Roosevelt remained dubious. 'They aren't bust', he assured advisers late in 1940. 'There's lots of money there.' That said, he did open the bottle-neck by removing 'the silly, foolish old dollar sign' from transactions, allowing the United States to lend or lease raw materials, equipment and munitions to Britain, including ships to carry them across the Atlantic. The details could be worked out later.*

In the end, the Lend-Lease Agreement provided £5 billion worth of material, more than Britain's entire pre-war wealth, for which Britain only paid £1.4 billion. It was, said Churchill, 'the most unsor-did act in history'. However, it wasn't charity. Roosevelt demanded fire sales of Britain's American assets at knockdown prices plus the surrender of naval bases and bullion (even sending warships at one point to carry the gold away). Britain also promised to dissolve the Sterling Area at the end of the war, making the pound freely convert-ible against the dollar and effectively conceding American financial mastery. This part of Lend-Lease provoked Churchill to draft a letter accusing Roosevelt of behaving like 'a sheriff collecting the last assets of a helpless debtor'. Wisely, he didn't send it.

When Japan attacked Pearl Harbor on 7 December 1941, Churchill first heard of it from his butler. 'Now at this very moment I knew that the United States was in the war, up to the neck and in to the death. So we had won after all!' he exulted. The immediate result was catastrophic for Britain's exposed East Asian empire, but Churchill remained upbeat, because, he told Roosevelt the next morning, 'I am expecting that Germany and Italy will both declare war on the United States'. This they obligingly did, Hitler reasoning that since 'the world war is here, the extermination of the Jews must be the necessary con-sequence' – which required defeating America and murdering its Jews too. 'Saturated and satiated with emotion and sensation', Churchill wrote, 'I went to bed and slept the sleep of the saved and thankful.'

The New World stepped forth even more forcefully than in 1917,

---

*Much later: after repeatedly refinancing, Britain made its final Lend-Lease payment in December 2006.

delivering an even more complete victory. It left Britain possessing not only the world's second-biggest fleet and third-biggest economy and army, but also a truly united kingdom. 'This is not a victory of a party or of any class', Churchill declaimed from a London balcony the day Germany surrendered. 'It's a victory of the great British nation as a whole.' Privation had pulled Britain's people together. The Ministry of Information had realised early on that 'People are willing to bear any sacrifice if a 100 percent effort can be reached and the burden fairly borne by all.' Even rationing became a symbol of fairness, that central plank in British identity. 'There could be no more powerful tribute to rationing', the Ministry of Food's official historian recorded, 'than the demands that, say, cake should be rationed.' When the Roosevelts visited Buckingham Palace, the First Lady was astonished to find 'a plainly marked black line in my bathtub above which I was not supposed to run the water'. The king did, in fact, write secretly to his ambassador in Washington to request soft American toilet paper, but what mattered was that everyone at least *appeared* to be pulling together. When a man shouted 'Thank God for a good King!' during one of George VI's regular visits to London's bombed-out streets, the usually tongue-tied monarch came straight back with 'Thank God for a good people!' Nineteen-forty was not 1640.

Yet the glorious triumph was also a strange defeat. The Second World War had cost Britain twice as much as the First and left its economy even more distorted. Many export markets had been lost and a quarter of the nation's pre-war wealth had gone. American money was the only thing standing between Britain and hunger in 1945, and when Harry Truman, the new president, abruptly ended Lend-Lease, Keynes had to be rushed to Washington to beg for $5 billion in emergency loans. He arrived in September fully expecting the Americans to recognise Britain's sacrifices by writing off much of its debt, but left in December understanding that Truman's administration was interested in 'influencing the future and not [. . .] pensioning the past'. In the future, they foresaw, Britain's sovereignty would be much diminished. Members of both Houses angrily objected to borrowing on terms that would leave victorious Britain so dependent – but the alternative, Labour MP Hugh Dalton reminded them, was grim. All the 'hopes of better times, to follow in the wake of victory, would be dissipated in despair and disillusion'.

PART III

THE MONEY MAP, 1945–2103

10

THE VERY POINT OF JUNCTION, 1945–91

Churchill's Map

After 1945 few believed that the world still looked like Mackinder's Map, but Churchill came to the rescue with a new geographical vision. The events of the next four or five decades repeatedly bore out his judgement. However, adjusting to the new realities proved painful indeed for Britain.

'As I look out upon the future of our country I feel the existence of three great circles among the free nations', he explained at Llandudno in 1948 (Figure 10.1). 'The first circle for us is naturally the British Commonwealth and Empire, with all that that comprises. Then there is also the English-speaking world in which we, Canada, and the other British Dominions and the United States play so important a part. And finally there is United Europe.' The point, Churchill continued, was that

> we are the only country which has a great part in every one of them. We stand, in fact, at the very point of junction, and here in this Island at the centre of the seaways and perhaps the airways also, we have the opportunity of joining them all together. If we rise to the occasion in the years that are to come it may be found that once again we hold the key to opening a safe and happy future to humanity, and will gain for ourselves gratitude and fame.

This was a bold vision, although, as Churchill was among the first to point out, alongside the three free circles was a fourth, unfree one, cordoned off by an iron curtain (Figure 10.2). The war had relegated Britain to a supporting role on the global stage. The relationship that really mattered now was between Soviet and American stars – and by the time Churchill spoke at Llandudno, that relationship had soured.

Figure 10.1. The British stage, 1945–91.

Even on the furthest left, few Islanders wanted to follow Stalin, who increasingly looked like the latest in the Spanish-French-German tradition of would-be Continental conquerors. Britain's shared cultural, strategic and financial interests with the United States made following Truman's lead vastly preferable. This consisted not of fighting or appeasing the Soviets but of containing them, blocking every Soviet move.

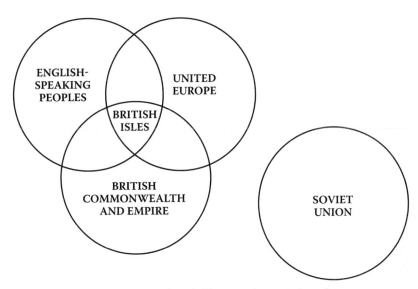

Figure 10.2. Churchill's Map: three circles of
freedom and the Soviet fourth.

Containment contained Britain too, because nothing prime ministers did, even domestically, could be allowed to compromise this approach to the Soviet circle. Consequently, when Truman asked his allies to step up following the Communist invasion of South Korea in 1950 (Figure 10.3), Britain's first Labour government faced difficult decisions.

In an election held just weeks after Hitler shot himself, Britons had astonished the world by replacing Churchill with Clement Attlee, a socialist committed to building a New Jerusalem of full employment and universal healthcare. But the world was wrong to be astonished: all along this had been what most Britons had thought they were fighting for (as one young woman told an interviewer, 'it's no good being a worker and voting for somebody who'll stand for the bosses'). What was more astonishing was how well Labour's programme worked. The population in poverty fell from 18 per cent in 1936 to 1.5 per cent in 1950, and by that decade's end diphtheria, tuberculosis and maternal mortality were all but abolished and the National Health Service was the country's most admired institution. Facing facts, Churchill's party committed to the welfare state too, and after it regained power in 1951, Labour's ex-chancellor happily

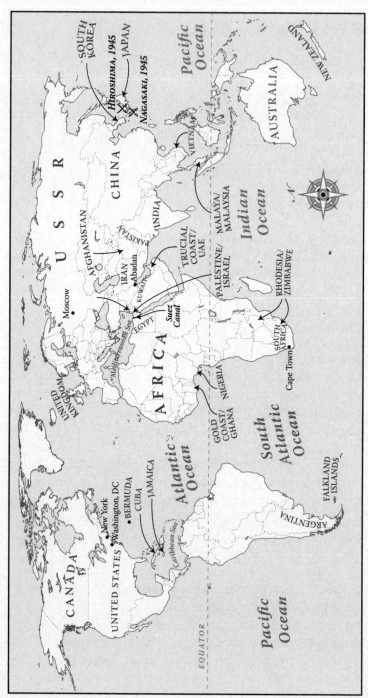

Figure 10.3. The global stage, 1945–91.

conceded that the Conservatives 'have really done exactly what we would have done'.

The great problem both parties had to face was how much the welfare state cost. Even with American loans, Britons had to tighten their belts more than ever after 1945. Bread was rationed for the first time in 1946; clothing remained restricted until 1949 and meat until 1954. British finances were so precarious that when Attlee fulfilled Churchill's promise to make sterling convertible into dollars in 1947, the pound collapsed so fast that exchanges had to be suspended after just six weeks. Now asked to send troops to Korea, Attlee found that not even pushing the standard rate of income tax to 47.5 per cent and the top rate to 97.5 per cent could cover the costs of New Jerusalem *and* rearmament. Forced to choose, he began charging patients for prescriptions, dentistry and eyeglasses rather than let Truman down. Two ministers resigned, but the government held firm. In fact, its larger-than-life foreign secretary Ernie Bevin regularly outdid the Americans themselves in anti-Stalinism. An alien in the suave world of diplomacy (he left school at eleven and famously told the king that he had learned his craft in 'the 'edgerows of experience'), he knew one big thing: that Soviets were nearly as bad as Nazis. Without Bevin, the North Atlantic Treaty Organization (NATO), committing Americans and Europeans alike to treating an attack on any signatory as an attack on all, might never have happened.

According to legend, NATO's first secretary-general (another Brit) said the organisation's goals were to keep 'the Russians out, the Americans in and the Germans down' (Figure 10.4). Russians out, for obvious reasons, and Americans in because Western Europe could not keep the Russians out by itself, even with Britain putting 80,000 men into an allied army defending a counterscarp on the Elbe. Only the Americans could provide a second, very different sort of counterscarp, because the fears of the 1930s had now become realities. Nuclear weapons really could annihilate entire cities. Greatly helped by his spies, Stalin was able to build an atomic bomb in 1949, just four years behind the Americans; by 1953 both superpowers had hydrogen (fusion) bombs hundreds of times more powerful than the weapons used at Hiroshima and Nagasaki. The following year Britain's civil service estimated that an all-out Soviet attack would immediately kill 9 million civilians, with another 3 million soon dying from radiation poisoning and 4 million more being disabled. The bomb transformed

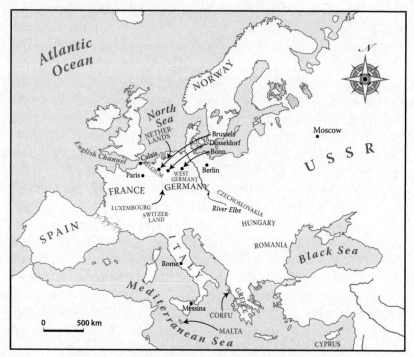

Figure 10.4. The Euro-Mediterranean stage, 1945–91.

Britain's security as much as the galleon had done in the sixteenth century.

No physical counterscarp could be deep enough to stop Soviet bombers reaching the Isles, so the only viable form of defence seemed to be deterrence, a virtual counterscarp created by threats of massive nuclear retaliation and mutual assured destruction. Despite the shocking expense of building a British bomb, Bevin never hesitated. 'We've got to have this thing over here, whatever it costs', he said in 1946. 'We've got to have a bloody Union Jack flying on top of it.' When the Americans tested the first hydrogen bombs, Churchill did not hesitate about getting them either. 'We must do it. It's the price we pay to sit at the top table.' The people agreed: 60 per cent had told pollsters they wanted atomic weapons; 58 per cent said the same about hydrogen bombs.

The point of British nuclear weapons was not actually to frighten Stalin. If Britain used all its hydrogen bombs, it could kill about 8 million Russians, which would hardly deter a country that had lost 20 million fighting Hitler. Only the Americans had enough bombs to push the death toll towards 100 million, which actually did frighten Stalin. The British bomb was really meant to worry Washington. A secret report explained in 1957 that 'by threatening to use our independent nuclear power [we can] secure United States co-operation in [situations in] which their interests were less immediately threatened than our own'. Most American presidents recognised Britain as their most important ally, but the knowledge that Britain could start Armageddon on its own if the United States failed to support it might stiffen the spine of any who wobbled. It was blackmail, but desperate times called for desperate measures.

The 'Germans down' part of NATO's mission was more complicated. In 1945 the Soviets and Americans had worried more about a German revival than about each other. Breaking Germany up reduced their anxieties, but when Stalin became the new bogeyman, Americans saw an opportunity: since money and men were short, why not have a new, pro-Western West Germany rearm and pull its weight? Politicians in Paris thought the answer was obvious: people who had invaded France three times since 1870 might well do it again. Instead of admitting Germany to NATO, they proposed forming a supranational European Defence Community, combining French, German and British forces. Many Americans liked this idea; most British were appalled. Not even Churchill, who had been promoting Continental integration since 1943, thought Britain should join. The Isles were supposed to be the junction between Anglophone, imperial and Continental circles, not part of the United Europe.

The European Defence Community fizzled out, but American support for federation only grew. When the United States unveiled its Marshall Plan in 1948, hoping to make West Europeans less sympathetic to communism by reviving their economies with massive cash infusions, the original idea was to channel dollars through a supranational organisation. Bevin proved too nimble, landing Britain's share while dodging federalist snares. The US secretary of state, Dean Acheson, then approached France's foreign minister, Robert Schuman. Since neither defence planning nor handouts had allayed French fear of West Germany, Acheson observed, why not merge the two countries' core industries, making war impossible for either? The German chancellor, delighted to be treated as a legitimate partner,

was all in favour; and, since Bevin could not sabotage what he did not
know about, the Franco-German deal was sprung on him as a *fait
accompli* in 1950.

The Schuman Plan (actually drafted by Jean Monnet, the founding father of European federalism) placed coal and steel under 'a new
High Authority, whose decisions will bind France, Germany and the
other countries that join'. Italy, Belgium, Luxembourg and the Netherlands promptly did so, but not Britain. Ninety per cent of Britain's
energy came from coal, and energy security seemed critical. 'It's no
good, we can't do it,' the deputy prime minister insisted, 'the Durham
miners won't wear it' – even though not wearing it exposed them to
competition from an enormous Continental cartel. This threatened
British prosperity, but staying out seemed necessary to defend Britain's sovereignty and identity against what Schuman called 'the first
concrete step towards a European federation'.

Federalists were thrilled. Europeans were doing what had never
done before, merging hundreds of millions of people into a bigger,
richer, safer superstate without forcing anyone into it with violence.
Britain's 'official mind' (as the journalist Hugo Young calls the inner
circle of politicians and senior civil servants), however, suspected that
Schuman was actually doing with committees what Hitler had tried
to do with armies. Even those who grasped the rather obvious differences between the Third Reich and the Coal and Steel Community
often likened Schuman's move to the Catholic church's sovereignty
grab thirteen centuries earlier – which is, of course, why I called the
medieval church the Original European Union. All six national representatives who signed the deal in 1950 were Catholics. One of Bevin's
top advisers called Schuman's Plan 'just a step in the consolidation
of the Catholic "black international" which I have always thought
to be a big driving force behind the Council of Europe'. In the early
1960s Labour's leader still feared being 'sucked up in a kind of giant
capitalist, Catholic conspiracy'. Thirty years later, Margaret Thatcher
sometimes saw Rome behind Brussels.

Popery was not really coming back (even if some Catholics did, on
the Coal and Steel Community's fiftieth anniversary, urge the Vatican
to canonise Schuman), but the Six who formed the Community were
indeed thinking rather like the Saxon chiefs who had accepted Rome
back in the seventh century. The Six hoped that surrendering some
of their sovereignty and blurring their identities would increase their

prosperity and improve security (mobility, at this stage, was not really an issue). Britain's twentieth-century rulers, however, saw little to gain from such a deal. 'This is something which we know, in our bones, we cannot do', said the Tory Anthony Eden, and Labour's National Executive insisted in a collective statement (sneakily titled 'European Unity') that 'Britain is not just a small, crowded island off the Western coast of Continental Europe [. . .] In every respect except distance we in Britain are closer to our kinsmen in Australia and New Zealand on the far side of the world than we are to Europe.'

Official wisdom even doubted that Schuman's Community would deliver on its bottom line of prosperity. Britain's industrial output in 1950 surpassed France and Germany's combined; one-quarter of world trade was in British hands; and most British exports went to imperial markets. Why sacrifice this position in Churchill's first circle to join a shaky, protectionist third circle, even if that pleased the American second circle? 'There is no attraction for us in long-term economic co-operation with Europe', one senior civil servant concluded. 'At best it will be a drain on our resources. At worst it can seriously damage our economy.' Even some of the Six suspected that staying out made sense for Britain.

Staying out also had the advantage of making it harder for the Six to accomplish much – which, some British diplomats hoped, would kill the merger. Instead, the Six upped the ante, calling a conference at Messina in Sicily in 1955 'to work for the establishment of a united Europe by the development of common institutions, the gradual fusion of national economies, the creation of a common market and the gradual harmonisation of [. . .] social policies'.

Paul-Henri Spaak, the Belgian foreign minister who led the charge, bent over backwards to involve Britain, but London just ignored him. Even a couple of years later a Gallup poll found that 39 per cent of Britons had never heard of the Common Market, while 12 per cent thought Britain had already joined. The only Messina getting much coverage in British newspapers in 1955, Young observes, was 'the Old Bailey trial of the Brothers Messina, charged with pimping and racketeering'.

The head of the British civil service insisted that Spaak's 'mysticism' would only 'appeal to European Catholic federalists', but still moved to nip it in the bud – not by boycotting Messina or sending a political heavyweight to crush Spaak but by dispatching a low-ranking economist, with instructions to walk out at the moment of maximum inconvenience. According to legend, although there is no actual evidence for it, the sacrificial civil servant abruptly stood up mid-meeting, announcing, 'Gentlemen, you are trying to negotiate something which cannot be negotiated. But if negotiated, it will not be ratified. And if ratified, it will not work.' And with that, or maybe with something else, Britain turned its official back on European integration.

In some ways, the arguments for staying out looked stronger in 1955 than they had five years earlier. The European Economic Community proposed at Messina went well beyond Schuman's Plan, particularly in its Common Agricultural Policy, which guaranteed prices for farmers. The Community would pay top franc, deutschmark or lira for anything farmers grew, whether it had buyers for the produce or not, selling surpluses overseas for whatever it could get and swallowing the losses. This was good politics in France, where one family in four worked the land, and even in West Germany (one in five), but not in Britain (one in twenty). British factory workers would be subsidising inefficient Continental farmers and paying more for their food into the bargain.

Yet the arguments for going in were stronger too. Above all, the Six were thriving. Figure 10.5 says it all: Britons were 11 per cent more productive in 1955 than they had been in 1945, but Germans were doing 28 per cent better and French and Italians over 140 per cent. This was not all Schuman's doing, of course. Recovery had begun before 1950, and Norway and Switzerland, which stayed outside the Community, were booming too. The reality was simply that Western Europe had resumed its pre-war growth. Even without knowing what the right-hand side of Figure 10.5 would bring, it was already obvious in 1955 that, the more Britain did to integrate its economy with Europe's expanding markets, the more it would prosper.

There was more than a whiff of 1760s-style strategic narcissism about Britain's refusal to face these facts. The historian Richard Weight draws a striking parallel between how Britons felt about Messina and how they felt about something they considered genuinely important: football. Britain never formed a national football team, believing for many years that the only people worth playing against were other Britons. French footballers founded an international federation in 1904, but Britain's four nations only joined fully in 1947 and, even then, largely ignored it. The World Cup began in

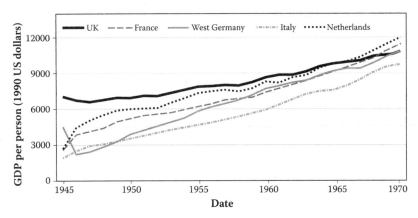

Figure 10.5. And the first shall be (almost) last: Britons get richer, 1945–70, but everyone else gets richer faster.

1930, but no team from the Isles entered for twenty years and interest remained minimal until 1958. When Continentals created the European Cup (a knock-out competition for national league champions) in 1955, the year of Messina, the English League banned Chelsea, the previous season's champions, from competing. By then, though, football had changed just as much as economics. A sports writer summed it up: 'In the beginning we were not the champions of the world – we *were* the world. Then we became, with the passage of time, not the whole class, but at least the top of the class. And now, let us face the truth, we are nowhere near the top.' He could just as well have been talking about geopolitics.

Rejecting a protectionist Continent to trade freely with the empire made distinctly less sense in 1955 than in 1950, because the empire simply mattered less. Britain now had more commerce with the European Economic Community than with the Dominions, and with every passing year the empire cost more, yielded less and became harder to reconcile with containment. Colonies such as Malaya and the Gold Coast (modern Malaysia and Ghana), which both had dollar-earning exports, were worth fighting for; and because nationalists in both countries were left-wing enough to be plausibly linked to Moscow, a case could be made to the Americans that suppressing them contributed to containment. In the rest of the ramshackle empire, however, the argument for holding on was less obvious.

Britain therefore took a new tack. First, it would redefine frightening freedom fighters who opposed imperialism as respectable
leaders who could form democratically elected governments, and
then it would grant them independence within an enlarged British
Commonwealth. If handled adroitly, the hope was, these new nations
would welcome British businessmen, soldiers and civil servants as
advisers, and even compete for British investment. The flags and
national anthems would change, but not much else (even the Queen's
picture would stay on office walls). The historian Ronald Robinson
perhaps overdid it in calling this the 'continuation of imperialism
by other and more efficient means', but turning the empire into a
fuzzier commonwealth looked like a viable path for avoiding George
Orwell's gloomy prediction (which I quoted in the Introduction)
that decolonisation would 'reduce England to a cold and unimportant little island where we should all have to work very hard and live
mainly on herrings and potatoes'.

Outcomes in fact varied. Having talked Indian and Pakistani
nationalists into Commonwealth membership, Britain abruptly
pulled out in 1947. 'Britain has fulfilled her mission', Pathé newsreels
breezily announced; 'It is for India herself now to make her destiny.'
Hindu–Muslim violence soon killed perhaps a million and displaced
8 million more. Britain withdrew just as abruptly from Greece, leaving
behind a civil war, and Palestine, where conflicts continue even today.
Elsewhere, a Cabinet committee concluded, few of the independence
movements seemed likely to become problems until the 1970s, and
Britain should hang on. Given adequate investment, some colonies
might even become profitable. Bevin thought that African minerals
'could have the United States dependent on us, and eating out of our
hand in four or five years'.

That was unrealistic, but Western Europe did start importing
oil from Kuwait and the Trucial Coast (now the United Arab Emir-
ates), both under British control. Consequently, when Mohammad
Mosaddegh, Iran's left-leaning prime minister, nationalised the
Anglo-Iranian Oil Company's refinery at Abadan – the biggest in the
world – in 1951, Attlee acted. Instead of gunboats, he sent spies, who,
working with Americans and Iran's shah, engineered a coup. The
oilmen, rebranded as British Petroleum, were soon back at work. A
precedent was set, and when Egypt's nationalist leader Gamal Abdel
Nasser cosied up to Moscow and nationalised the Suez Canal in 1956,

Washington and London agreed that he too had to go. However, they disagreed on tactics. While President Eisenhower felt that Suez 'was not the issue upon which to try to downgrade Nasser', Prime Minister Eden saw violent regime change as the only option.

Quite why Eden turned so Palmerstonian is still debated. He disliked Nasser personally. Having opposed appeasement in the 1930s, he could hardly now humour a Mussolini wannabe. He was ill. He was trying to fill Churchill's shoes. The list of motives is endless. And, to be fair, there were real similarities between Suez and situations like the Don Pacifico affair. Palmerston in 1850 and Eden in 1956 both enjoyed overwhelming military superiority, both were certain of their cause and both had convenient cover stories. Eden even had French support. So he acted.

But one difference mattered more than any of this. Palmerston had not had to worry about containment. 'I know Ike', Eden's chancellor, Harold Macmillan, assured him; 'He will lie doggo!' But given that Soviet tanks had begun crushing a Hungarian revolution the day before British and French paratroops dropped into Egypt and that Ike was up for re-election the day after, he couldn't lie doggo. 'At all costs,' Eisenhower told his secretary of state, 'the Soviets must be prevented from seizing the mantle of world leadership through a false but convincing exhibition of concern for smaller nations.' Eisenhower wanted to make that exhibition himself, so he hit Eden where it hurt: in the wallet. Panicky investors had been selling sterling for weeks, and Britain had already haemorrhaged £250 million propping it up. Eisenhower now refused to help until every British soldier left Egypt. Within thirty-six hours of landing, the Anglo-French expedition had achieved most of its objectives, inflicting 2,000 Egyptian casualties and destroying 260 aircraft for the loss of just 32 commandos and 3 planes of its own. But Eden now recalled it.

There had been imperial setbacks before. Afghans, Zulus and Japanese had slaughtered entire British armies. But there had never been anything quite like this humiliation. ('I am not sure I should have dared to start,' Churchill commented, 'but I am sure I should not have dared to stop.') Suez was, in a sense, the last battle of the world wars, where Britain paid the full price for losing its financial struggle with the United States. Over a hundred Tory MPs approved a motion accusing Eisenhower of 'gravely endangering the Atlantic Alliance', but the reality was harsher. Britain had embarrassed its paymaster and itself. 'There's nobody, in a war, that I'd rather have fighting alongside me than the British', Eisenhower said privately. 'But – *this* thing! My God!'

Pivoting Back

Six years after Suez, Dean Acheson famously offended millions of Britons by telling them that 'Great Britain has lost an empire and has not yet found a role', but this was not really news. Even before he resigned, Eden had observed that Suez *'has not so much changed our fortunes as revealed realities* [. . .] Surely we must review our world position and our domestic capacity more searchingly.' He was right. Britain's world position and domestic capacity had to be rethought *together*. Eden had not done this, and his successor, Harold Macmillan, only tackled the world position. It would take another thirty years to confront domestic capacity too.

With his tweeds, drooping moustache and languid one-liners, Macmillan (Old Etonian, ex-Guards) hardly looked like the man to make a global pivot, but behind his hammy exterior, said one rival, lay 'an infinite capacity for elasticity'. Just a decade earlier, a Ministry of Defence adviser had warned his masters that 'We are not a Great Power and never will be again. We are a great nation, but if we continue to behave like a Great Power we shall soon cease to be a great nation.' Macmillan understood, but calculated that the way to remain a great nation was by pretending to be a great power, acting as if nothing had changed while in fact changing everything. Jetting off to Bermuda, he repaired the Special Relationship with Eisenhower; in Moscow he talked arms control with the Soviet leader, Nikita Khrushchev; in Cape Town he announced the end of empire; and in Paris he asked to join the European Economic Community after all.

Macmillan needed to show Eisenhower that he knew his place, and Eisenhower, wanting British backing, was ready to believe him. However, Macmillan also needed to show voters he was no lapdog, and the two imperatives regularly clashed. The rapidly evolving nuclear counterscarp proved particularly tricky. Just a year after Suez, the Soviets launched Sputnik, a beeping, 75-kg satellite, demonstrating that they had missiles capable of delivering nuclear warheads anywhere on earth in under an hour. In 1959 Americans got their own rockets airborne, and the next year both sides worked out how to launch missiles from submarines, effectively making nuclear weapons invulnerable to surprise attacks. To Americans one obvious consequence was that Britain's bomber-delivered deterrent was now unnecessary, but to Macmillan it demonstrated that Britain needed rockets too. Fiascos followed. Britain's missile programme, said one journalist, became 'a paradigm of national impotence as the thrusting rocket failed to take off, failed to achieve its intended climax, blew up in mid-course, or found itself being withdrawn'. Unsatisfied, Macmillan wheedled Eisenhower and his successor, John F. Kennedy, into selling him American missiles – which they did, although Kennedy insisted on keeping all Polaris missiles under NATO control unless 'supreme national interests' intervened.

What counted as supreme national interests was never defined, but cases such as Suez clearly did not. When Cuba sparked a real crisis in 1962, Britain turned out to matter no more in Kennedy's counsels than ex-powers like Spain had in Palmerston's. It was hard not to wonder whether Americans would really risk New York to defend a counterscarp around Europe – or whether Britain should even want them to, given what it might mean. The BBC was probably right in 1965 to suppress *The War Game*, a mockumentary set in Kent during a fictional nuclear war. It won an Oscar, but the BBC kept it under wraps until 1985. It is the most disturbing film ever made. If war did come, the Ministry of Defence suspected, 200,000 soldiers would be needed just to keep order at home, but the United Kingdom might disintegrate anyway into a dozen military dictatorships run by regional commissioners.

Nobody wanted any of this, and in 1961 some 100,000 marchers descended on Trafalgar Square demanding unilateral disarmament, but even their leaders quickly realised they were making a mistake. 'We thought that Great Britain was still a great power whose example would affect the rest of the world', one said, whereas in reality, 'If we threw away our bombs, who'd notice?' Only the superpowers could end their own nuclear rivalry and, with it, the need for a nuclear counterscarp.

Fortunately, both superpowers were exploring their options. Soviet attitudes softened after Stalin died in 1953, and softened further when Richard Nixon's surprise trip to China in 1972 threatened them with encirclement. The Cuban crisis alarmed both sides, and by 1976, when the Soviet arsenal reached parity with the American (at around

25,000 warheads each), the United States had become less trigger-happy too. Both sides remained ready to use force (the Americans in Vietnam, the Soviets in Czechoslovakia), but they also agreed to limit nuclear and biological weapons. Cosmonauts and astronauts shook hands in space; long-term coexistence began to seem possible.

The softening trickled down to American allies. Cold Warriors like Bevin aside, Britain had rarely been as strict about containment as the Americans. While Washington reacted to communist infiltration of the government with executions, jail sentences and the dismissal of 10,000 suspects (another 15,000 resigned while under investigation), London hushed up the defection of two of its top agents and fired only thirty-five people (another twenty-five resigned). During the 1960s the two Germanys recognised each other's right to exist, a new generation of 'Eurocommunists' sought a middle path between Washington and Moscow, France withdrew its forces from NATO command and Britain relaxed containment even more.

Judging the pace was never easy. When the United States stumbled into another war of containment in Indochina in the 1960s, hardly anyone in Britain wanted to send troops, but with the economy again in dire straits, American officials promised that 'a British Brigade in Vietnam would be worth a billion dollars at the moment of truth for Sterling'. Harold Wilson, the Labour prime minister, recognised that 'we can't kick our creditors in the balls', but he couldn't kick his voters in the balls either; so he dodged, weaved and fudged, much like the 'friendly kings' who had ruled southern England on Rome's behalf 2,000 years earlier. He refused to put boots on the ground in Vietnam, but did promise not to devalue the pound (because the speculators attacking it might then turn on the dollar), close military bases in Asia (because the United States might then have to fill the gap) or increase public spending (which would eat up any American loan). Then, in classic client-king style, having landed his bailout, he kicked his creditors in the balls anyway. ('There are two things I dislike about Wilson', said one of his colleagues: 'His face.') Gambling that Johnson needed friends so badly that he wouldn't retaliate, Wilson broke his word on everything, especially Britain's expensive colonial commitments east of Suez.

Wilson deserved his reputation for slipperiness, but almost any prime minister would have done the same (and probably not as skilfully). Ten years earlier Macmillan had conducted an 'audit of empire' and concluded that, far from adding to the Isles' prosperity, the strain that most overseas possessions put on Britain's armed forces and reputation made them net liabilities. Touring Africa to see for himself in 1960, he asked the governor-general of Nigeria, 'Are these people ready for self-government?' The response: '"No, of course not." I said, "When will they be ready?" He said, "Twenty years, twenty-five years." Then I said, "What do you recommend me to do?" He said, "I recommend you to give it to them at once."' Sobered, Macmillan headed to Cape Town for the best-remembered speech of his career. 'The wind of change is blowing through this continent', he told the all-white representatives of South Africa's all-white electorate. 'We must all accept it as a fact, and our national policies must take account of it.' The South Africans walked out of the Commonwealth and Britain walked out of Africa.

Never had such an empire vanished so quickly, but, outside the far right, few in the Isles seemed to care. There was no electoral backlash, no violence. So, when Wilson ran out of money in 1967, he threw Britain's Asian territories overboard too. Everything east of Suez was to go within ten years, except a base in Hong Kong. Britain would 'cease to play a worldwide military role', the government announced. 'We shall increasingly become a European power.'

For 250 years Britain had schemed to keep the Continent divided while acting on a global stage, but having lost that role, opposing European unity no longer served much purpose. Macmillan had initially resisted this conclusion, making a bid soon after Messina to suffocate European federation by submerging the Six into a bigger customs union without the federalist zeal, but when this failed, he faced facts. 'For the first time since the Napoleonic era', he lectured his foreign secretary, 'continental powers are united in a positive economic grouping, with considerable political aspects, which, though not specifically directed against the United Kingdom, may have the effect of excluding us both from European markets and from consultation in European policy.' This new Continental system, he worried, could even 'replace us as the major ally of the United States'. He foresaw a 'grim choice', between isolation and betraying Britain's Commonwealth friends – but in the end this was no choice at all. By 1960 Britain bought 8 per cent of its imports from and sold 9 per cent of its exports to Australia and New Zealand, as against 15 and 16 per cent for the European Economic Community – and the gap was widening. Prosperity mattered more than shared cultural identity, Macmillan decided. The Dominions, like the Empire, must go. In 1961 Britain applied to join the European Community.

Macmillan's pivot towards Europe was the biggest strategic shift since the 1710s, but there was no echo of the party rage of Walpole's age. Some Conservatives worried that Macmillan wanted 'to surrender our independence to "Frogs and Wogs"', and Harold Wilson (not yet in office, so not responsible for his words) preached that 'we are not entitled to sell our friends and kinsmen down the river for a problematical and marginal advantage in selling washing machines in Düsseldorf'. Only one MP voted against Macmillan's plan. It was on the Continent that it ran into resistance. In 1963 France's president, Charles de Gaulle, announced that because 'England is insular', its entry would create 'a colossal Atlantic community under American dependence and leadership which would soon swallow up the European Community'. So the answer was *non*.

Four years later Wilson tried again. Debate over what the pivot might mean for identity, mobility, prosperity, security and sovereignty was even more muted than when Macmillan had applied, and de Gaulle said *non* again. Finally, in 1971, de Gaulle's successor, Georges Pompidou – currently more concerned about West Germany's softness towards the Soviets than about American stooges – invited another application, and Wilson's successor, the unusually Europhile and Americaphobe Edward Heath, was ready.

This time domestic divisions did emerge over the pivot, but they ran – in a sign of things to come – within, not between, parties. On the far right, Enoch Powell saw a 'life and death struggle' beginning, 'as surely about the future of Britain's nationhood as were the combats which raged in the sky over southern England in the autumn of 1940. The gladiators are few; their weapons are but words; and yet their fight is everyman's.' The far left was blunter, throwing punches and yelling 'Fascist bastard!' at Labour's leading pro-Marketeer. The atmosphere at the final Parliamentary vote was electric. 'See the Ambassadors' Gallery over there?' an attendant asked. 'Haven't seen it so full since we used to matter in the world.' But the result was never in doubt: the United Kingdom would enter the European Economic Community as of 1 January 1973. News was telephoned to Dover Castle, where Harold Macmillan lit a bonfire, answered immediately by one across the Channel in Calais.

Emotions ran high among the political elite. Jean Monnet told French television that 'This is what I have been waiting for during the last twenty-five years'. Heath outdid him: 'Forty years after my first visit to Paris', he reminisced, 'I had been able to play a part in bringing about the unity of Europe [. . .] For me personally, it was a wildly exciting moment.' Disagreement within Labour's leadership was so heated that Wilson had to promise a referendum – the first in Britain's history – over membership once Labour was back in power.

But when the vote came, in 1975, most Britons just shrugged. At one point, James Callaghan, Labour's foreign secretary, even told a radio interviewer that 'I am not pro, nor am I anti.'. Exasperated, the interviewer burst out: 'What are you doing on this programme? You're here to advise people to vote "Yes", aren't you?' His answer: 'I'm here because you asked me.'

Against this background, Margaret Thatcher's attitude, mentioned in Chapter 1, makes more sense. Despite formulating the Law that I named after her during this campaign, she admitted privately that she 'wished she didn't have to vote at all'. Almost unanimously – and almost unanimously half-heartedly – mainstream politicians said Britain should stay, leaving just a ragtag from the rightest and leftest fringes saying go. In 1974, one year after Britain entered, two-thirds of the Britons asked by pollsters had said they wanted to leave; another year after that, two-thirds voted to stay. An uncertain pivot was complete, and Britain had found a role – for now.

'Orrible Lot

Or part of a role. It had been obvious to Eden in 1956 that reviewing Britain's world position required reviewing its domestic capacity too, but Macmillan was not interested. To critics, he seemed much too satisfied with things just the way they were. The problem, a new generation of angry young men (and women) thought, was that Macmillan and his cronies stood for 'the Establishment', a hopelessly old-fashioned clique of grandees whose relatives cluttered up the top ends of Britain's professions. Such people, real or not, were such perfect foils that the early 1960s became the finest age for satire since Swift was in his prime (*Private Eye*, for instance, was founded in 1961). Seeing a market, Penguin Books published a series of slim paperbacks on British traditions called *What's Wrong with . . . ?*; and seeing votes,

Wilson pledged in 1964 'to make far-reaching changes in economic and social attitudes which permeate our whole system of society'. A new nation, he promised, would be 'forged in the white heat of this revolution'.

The moment seemed ripe for far-reaching change, even in the very fabric of the United Kingdom. The Union had been created in the eighteenth and nineteenth centuries to close England's back door to Continental enemies, leaving the Isles free to expand over-seas. Now, with no invasions imminent, the empire in retreat and containment having redefined geopolitics, the Union's point was less obvious.

The questions were sharpest in Ireland. The independent Repub-lic in the south was no longer London's problem, but many of the Catholics stranded on the British side of the 1922 dividing line were eager to rejoin their co-religionists. Twice as many Ulster Protestants, however, were determined to prevent that at all costs. Successive governments tried to buy off discontent by pumping cash into the province's industries, which, like those of Scotland and Wales, had been struggling since 1945. At first, it seemed to work: when hardly anyone supported its bombing campaign in 1962, the Irish Repub-lican Army (IRA) renounced violence. But the fact that Northern Ireland's Catholics disliked murder didn't mean that they liked the Union. Catholics overwhelmingly thought Protestants were hogging government aid, while Protestants often feared that appeasers in London were selling them out to popery. What, ministers wondered, were they to do with a place where a man of God could respond to pleas for bridge-building by saying that 'a bridge and a traitor are very much alike, for they both go over to the other side'?

Nothing, most concluded. In the whole of 1966, the year sectarian killings resumed, Parliament discussed Northern Ireland for just two hours. But outrage begat further outrage, and in 1969 a march cele-brating William of Orange's victories (in 1690) triggered three days of violence. No one could ignore that. Forgetting his own warning that 'I can get the army in but it's going to be a devil of a job to get it out', James Callaghan – now in the role of home secretary – sent troops to protect the Catholic minority. This, too, initially seemed to work. 'Kids were following you everywhere', said one soldier. 'Tea? There was too much tea – and buns and sandwiches.' Quickly, though, the army's position – standing between Republicans who were desperate to join a Republic that didn't want them and Loyalists whose loyalty to the Union required them to take up arms against it – became impossible, making the army the one thing that both sides (and their countless splinter groups) hated even more than each other.

By 1972 political murders averaged more than one a day. Its early optimism lost, the government interned suspects without trial. Some were tortured. On the streets nervous troops shot unarmed rioters. Discipline was cracking. When a Unionist general strike (backed by terrorist violence) virtually shut down Belfast in 1974, the army's commander warned that if ordered to break it, 'we would have said, "With great respect, this is a job for the police"' – even though, as he knew, 'the police were on the brink of not carrying out their duties'. After two weeks London gave in to the strikers' demands. 'A million British citizens, the Protestants of Northern Ireland', *The Times*'s Belfast correspondent wrote, have 'staged what amounted to a rebellion against the Crown and won with scarcely a shot being fired.' It was as bad as 1914. Perhaps, Wilson told an aide, it was time to 'consider "the unmentionable": British withdrawal from Northern Ireland'.

Republican terrorists had pushed London to this extreme by a relentlessly escalating violence. Republicans killed twice as many Loyalists as Loyalists killed Republicans. In 1979 bombs killed the Queen's second cousin and then Margaret Thatcher's closest adviser; in 1984 they almost killed Thatcher and most of her cabinet too. The endless reports of kneecappings, shootings and nail bombings were numbing. Even the images lost their power to shock: the weeping widows; the angry, red-faced politicians; and what one would-be mediator, whom terrorists duly tried to kill, called 'the hard men with the dark glasses, the balaclava helmets and pickaxe handles'. Most of us in England just wanted Northern Ireland to go away. Yet it wouldn't, in fact couldn't. Most Northern Irish wanted to stay British, and pulling the army out would probably mean civil war. It might even turn Belfast into a back door again, some thought, open to Soviet infiltration. So Northern Ireland had to stay in the Union.

Neither Wales nor Scotland had nationalists as violent as Ireland's, although Welsh terrorists did graduate from destroying postboxes in the 1950s to setting bombs in the 1960s and torching nearly 200 English-owned weekend cottages in the 1970s. No Welsh nationalist MPs were elected until 1966 and no Scottish until 1967; even in the 1970s barely one Welsh person in ten and one Scot in five wanted independence. But in both lands wages remained lower, opportunities narrower and lives shorter than in England. Majorities (slim in Wales, wide in Scotland) favoured some sort of home rule.

Welsh nationalists worried that lack of prosperity was undermining their identity. Wales, said one MP, was 'in danger of being no more Celtic in character than is the Lake District or Cornwall today. What military conquest has failed to do over two millennia is now being accomplished by the cheque-book invasion in two decades.' In Scotland, by contrast, nationalists hoped that an ocean of oil discovered under the North Sea would give them enough prosperity to reassert their identity. Accessing the oil stretched technology, skill and courage to their limits, but in 1978 black gold finally turned Britain's balance of payments black too. 'North Sea oil stands for nothing less than national survival', *Time* magazine cheered. But which nation? 'It's *our* oil', Scottish nationalists insisted, seeing a choice between being 'rich Scots or poor Britons'. London skirted that choice, instead offering elected assemblies in Cardiff and Edinburgh – and then talking both Welsh and Scottish voters into declining them (the former overwhelmingly, the latter only after sneaky procedural politics in Westminster).

Oil was a two-edged sword. On the one hand, it threatened to undo the Union by making exit affordable for Scotland; on the other, it could potentially fund a way out of economic difficulties for the whole of Britain. The nation's economic institutions seemed even more hidebound than its political ones, and although prosperity was rising, critics claimed that it needed to rise faster still. By the standards of any earlier age, gains had been impressive. By 1974 two-thirds of households had central heating and washing machines and nine in ten had fridges and televisions (with colour sets now outselling black-and-white). Macmillan was quite right to say in 1957 that 'most of our people have never had it so good'. My parents were just the kind of people he had in mind: both had left school at thirteen, my father to go down a coal mine and my mother to file papers in a local tax office. In the three years before Macmillan's speech they had met at a dance, married, moved into a semi-detached house, brought my sister into the world and acquired a car. I followed in 1960, as did a Ford Cortina in 1963, a detached house in a new suburb (Figure 10.6) in 1965 and a stereo in 1968 (*The Sound of Music* was our first LP). We became a two-car family in 1972, extended the house in 1973 and

Figure 10.6. The post-war dream in person:
the author in the half-built family home,
July 1965. The Ford Cortina is outside.

moved to a bigger place in a nicer neighbourhood in 1977. In 1979 my parents even took a foreign holiday – to Corfu, which they loved, despite sunburn, ants and a touch of food poisoning. My sister and I finished school and stayed in education beyond it. We were the post-war dream personified.

But despite millions of stories like ours, the graph in Figure 10.5 shows exactly why Britain's economic performance seemed so inadequate. Our house was filling with stuff, but houses in Common Market countries were filling with *more* stuff. In 1961 Macmillan's economic adviser confessed that 'Britain is now universally regarded as a country of very low growth'; by 1979 it seemed to Britain's ambassador in Paris that 'Our decline in relation to our European partners has been so marked that today we are not only no longer a world power, but we are not in the first rank even as a European one'.

Every pundit had a different explanation. The pound was

overvalued, said some, making imports easier to buy, exports harder to sell and payments harder to balance. Or possibly spending on stereos and holidays was soaking off capital which should have been invested. Britain spent too much on the army, or on welfare, or on both. Refusing to join the Six in the 1950s had sheltered British producers and left them uncompetitive. Managers were complacent; workers were lazy; teachers were Marxist moles; long-haired students wanted to be revolutionaries, not engineers; unions were greedy.

All of these arguments had merits. In 1979, when I was a long-haired student (reading archaeology, not engineering), I landed a summer job in a plastics plant. We were making an enormous sewage tank for export to a former colony in Africa, and I was given the job of drilling holes in the flanges of hundreds of separate segments so they could be bolted together at the other end. I drilled and drilled before it dawned on me that the holes didn't line up. We'd worked on the tank for weeks, but now it couldn't be assembled. It wasn't entirely my fault – I'd been given the wrong template – but anyone paying attention would have seen right away that something was off. Resigned to being sacked, I went to the boss to confess. He sighed, then sighed again, then told me to finish up and help him load it on the lorry. Down at the pub, a friend assured me that it could be fixed on arrival. Africans were good at that kind of thing, he said. I still couldn't shake the feeling that there went another customer who wouldn't be buying British again.

I have dozens more stories like this, as, I suspect, does everyone who worked in British factories or offices in the 1970s. Yet there had been plenty of such stories in Dickens's day too. My workmates and I spent our lunchtimes in the pub, but we never attained the falling-down drunkenness that nineteenth-century foremen constantly cursed. In the end, there is no way to know whether 1840s feckless-ness was worse than 1970s incompetence, although my grandad's stories about 1930s steelworkers and my dad's about 1950s miners make me suspect that continuities outweighed contrasts. What had really weakened between the 1840s and 1970s was not Britain's back-bone but its strategic situation. The slide had begun in the 1860s, as rivals like Germany and the United States industrialised; it accelerated after 1914, as Britain spent down its foreign assets, and turned into a rout after 1945, when the protected sterling area dissolved. What had worked in Disraeli's day didn't work in Wilson's. Eden had been right that remaining at the junction of the world's circles depended on Britain's domestic capacity as well as its world position.

The fate of the first men to face this is revealing. Seeing the difficulties, Macmillan's chancellor, Peter Thorneycroft, sat down with his ministers in 1957 and designed a package to pull the economy into line with Britain's changed position. They proposed slashing borrowing and spending, limiting pay rises, hiking interest rates and letting the pound float against other currencies. In the short term it would mean recession and unemployment, but longer term it promised growth more like France's or West Germany's. Macmillan neither adopted the plan, thereby losing votes, nor killed it, thereby losing investors' confidence. Instead, he strung the revolutionaries along while quietly undermining them, until, as he'd hoped, they resigned. Having his whole economic team quit at once should have been fatal, but he rode it out in classic style: heading to the airport, he calmly told reporters that his plan 'was to settle up with these little local difficulties and then turn to the wider vision of the Commonwealth'. He gambled – rightly – that voters would distinguish between Britain's world position and its domestic capacity, and rank the former above the latter. He looked statesmanlike, the rebels ridiculous.

This was tactically brilliant but strategically disastrous. 'The simple truth', Thorneycroft stressed in his resignation speech, 'is that we have been spending more money than we should.' He warned that 'it is the road to ruin', but rather than disappoint voters like my parents, Macmillan tried to match income to expenditure by spending even more. The idea, a more pliable chancellor explained in 1963, was that this would deliver 'expansion without inflation, expansion that can be sustained'. Instead, borrowing, prices and unemployment all rocketed, creating the chaos that drove Wilson to break his promises to Lyndon Johnson in 1967. When chancellors of both parties again tried to spend their way to growth in 1972–4, the results were even worse. Public spending rose by one-third, unemployment doubled and borrowing tripled. Inflation hit 27 per cent; the pound fell by one-third and the stock market by half. 'If I were a younger man', Labour's James Callaghan – now prime minister – mused in 1976, 'I'd emigrate.'

Instead, Callaghan did something almost equally unexpected. He faced reality. 'The cosy world we were told would go on forever', he explained, 'where full employment would be guaranteed by a stroke of the Chancellor's pen, cutting taxes, deficit spending – that cosy world is gone.' At best, it worked 'by injecting a bigger dose of inflation into the economy, followed by a higher level of unemployment as the next step'. At worst, it undermined investors' confidence. If 'the patience of our creditors [gets] exhausted', his chancellor had already warned, 'we would then face the appalling prospect of going down in a matter of weeks to the levels of public services and personal living standards which we could finance entirely from what we earned. I do not believe that our political or social system could stand that strain.' The lessons of Suez, or 1941, or even 1916, were finally sinking in. Sovereignty depended on prosperity. Britain must bow to the bankers.

Not so, said critics on Labour's left. Appalled by Callaghan's logic, they offered an 'Alternative Economic Strategy', rejecting the country's experiences since 1916. It was time to 'stop paying "danegeld"', said one minister, and tell 'the Americans and the Germans: if you demand any more of us we shall put up the shutters, wind down our defence commitments, introduce a siege economy'. Big firms would be nationalised. Protected by tariffs and capital controls, Britain would tax and borrow heavily to fund massive investment, producing full employment and rising living standards. This would mean breaking with the Europeans and Americans and abandoning the Common Market, NATO and nuclear weapons; but relations with the Soviets would improve, making counterscarps unnecessary.

All this meant that the 1975 referendum on Europe, like that in 2016, was about something much bigger than the question on the ballot. The real issue – and the thing least spoken of – was whether Britain's domestic capacity and world position could be better reconciled by continuing the two-decades-old pivot back to Europe or by imposing a siege economy and trying to make insularity trump proximity. Sticking to his guns, Callaghan pushed through the former, accepting bankers' demands for austerity and talking most union chiefs into moderating wage demands. Pandemonium broke out at Labour Party conferences. Delegates shouted down the chancellor, banned the bomb (again) and voted to nationalise the banks. But Callaghan got his way. Inflation fell by half in just twelve months; the economy started growing again; calls to break up the United Kingdom subsided. Optimistic that Britain's domestic capacity would soon align with its post-Suez world position, Callaghan promised that one more push, limiting wage increases to 5 per cent, could bring inflation down to Continental levels in 1979.

The 'Winter of Discontent' that ensued seemed to bear out Macmillan's belief that Britons could not tolerate austerity. With deep snow blanketing the country, 25 million working days were lost to strikes. Railways and road haulage were paralysed, imports piled up on docks and shops – even Marks & Spencer – ran out of food. Livestock starved. Callaghan considered deploying troops but baulked at turning the entire Isles into Belfast. Right-wing newspapers exaggerated strikers' malice ('Target for Today – Sick Children', bayed the *Daily Mail*), but pensioners really did freeze to death, hospital pickets really did turn cancer patients away and bodies really did go unburied. The ambulance drivers' spokesman told the *Daily Express* that if a strike 'means lives lost, that is how it must be'.

Observers of all sorts concluded that efforts to force domestic capacity into line with Britain's world position were tearing apart the national identity forged in 1940. 'That Britain has become such a scrounger is a disgrace', Henry Kissinger told President Ford in Washington. At home, even the lifelong trade unionist Frank Chapple was appalled. His shop stewards, he told a Callaghan aide, were 'a fucking 'orrible lot. In fact', he added, 'my members are a fucking 'orrible lot too.' Capitalising on the divisions, Margaret Thatcher warned the electorate that 'There are wreckers among us [. . . who] make me wonder what has happened to our sense of common nationhood and even of common humanity.' What the country needed, she said, was 'an acknowledgement of moral absolutes and a positive view of work'. Britain needed to rediscover its backbone.

The Great Unbuttoning

Opinions varied over when the rot had set in. Some thought it was just in the last generation. As recently as 1945 British studios were still making films like David Lean's *Brief Encounter*, a torrid love story in which nothing actually happens and no one says what they mean. Thirty years later, they were making *Confessions of a Window Cleaner*. Alternatively, perhaps the First World War had already broken British spirits thirty years before *Brief Encounter*. 'Your country was sort of a museum piece', the American journalist Ed Murrow said of 1930s England. 'You seemed slow, indifferent and exceedingly complacent

[. . .] your young men seemed without vigour or purpose.' Or perhaps the rot went deeper still. In a string of influential books the historian Correlli Barnett suggested it had begun in Samuel Smiles's age, as Victorian gentlemen put social justice ahead of wealth and power.

But despite their differences, most cultural critics agreed that British identity was changing at an extraordinary pace. In just five years, between 1964 and 1969, many of the rules that had guided upright behaviour for centuries went out of the window. All sorts of moral lapses – from homosexuality, abortion and attempted suicide to premarital sex, divorce and looking at pornography – were decriminalised, made easier or redefined as not being moral lapses at all (in England and Wales, anyway: homosexuality remained illegal in Scotland until 1980 and in Northern Ireland until 1982). Punishment softened: flogging for criminals (but not children) went in 1948 and hanging in 1964. Oddly, the one area where rules tightened rather than loosening was that iconic issue of the '60s, drugs. Cocaine and opium had been perfectly legal until 1920, but the number of banned narcotics more than tripled between 1950 and 1970.

Most of these reforms were unpopular. They belonged to the grand Victorian tradition of enlightened elites telling the great unwashed what to want. Very few people considered abortion, divorce or homosexuality acceptable. (When I was at school, in the 1970s, calling another boy 'queer' remained the fastest way to start a fight.) The reformists' main achievement, in fact, was perhaps the last thing they had intended: deference towards liberal elites collapsed, dragging them into the gutter with the rest of us. It was bad enough when news leaked in 1963 that the minister of war and a Russian spy were visiting the same prostitute, but then came stories 'that nine High Court judges had been engaging in sexual orgies [and] that a member of the Cabinet had served dinner at a private party while naked except for a mask, a small lace apron and a card round his neck reading "If my services don't please you, whip me".' When a slightly scaled-down version of the orgiastic judges story reached Macmillan, he was incredulous. 'One', he allowed, 'perhaps two, conceivably. But eight – I just can't believe it'.

He was right to harbour doubts, but many did believe, because there was so much circumstantial evidence. More Soviet spies turned up in high places, including Buckingham Palace. A home secretary resigned over corrupt property deals. The leader of the Liberal Party was charged with hiring a hitman to shoot his former gay lover (what most enraged opinion was that the gunman shot the lover's dog). The Queen's sister was photographed canoodling with a man eighteen years her junior.

The real change in the 1960s and '70s was not that the Establishment suddenly opened up to foreign agents, financial impropriety and politicians paying for sex – all had been common currency in the nineteenth century – but that the conspiracy of silence about such things collapsed. Letting the daylight in made it hard to take the toffs seriously. Even committed monarchists felt fine shouting 'We love you, Liz!' at Queen Elizabeth's Silver Jubilee in 1977. No one had said that sort of thing to Queen Victoria. By the 1970s the prime minister himself was asking his Cabinet to use first names.

The most visible change was in how people looked. John Lennon, who had as good a claim as anyone to be the face of the '60s, said that 'nothing happened except that we all dressed up'; but it would be fairer to say that we all dressed down (Figure 10.7). Britain ceased to be the starched collar of Europe. Swinging London unbuttoned its collar and even took off its tie. Some new looks blurred gender norms (men grew their hair, women cut theirs and put on trousers); others heightened them (neither miniskirts nor skin-tight jeans left much to the imagination). In different ways 1970s punks and 1980s New Romantics undermined even further conventional ideas about how boys and girls should look. But all the transgressors agreed on one thing: no more hankering for seriousness and sobriety. Starting among the young and lefty and then spreading up and out, people went out of their way to look *less* respectable.

There were stubborn rearguard actions. At my comprehensive school some younger teachers (beardy weirdies, we called them) daringly put on corduroy jackets and lectured us about apartheid, but most staff – who couldn't have been very old, although they acted it – seemed to think that resisting the rising tide of indiscipline was their main job. Uniforms were the favourite battlefield. Children can think of more things to do with ties than wrap them around their necks, especially when teachers can't cane them any more.

Clothes were even more of a minefield further up the social ladder. Harold Wilson found just the right look for a modern Labour prime minister, always in a suit, but a crumpled one, often concealed by a raincoat. Michael Foot, however, got it wrong. When he arrived to

Figure 10.7. We all dressed down: John Lennon, one of the
world's most influential men ('more popular than Jesus',
he joked), as he looked in 1964 (left) and 1969 (right).

honour the nation's war dead in 1981 in a casual coat and tartan tie,
even one of his own MPs said he looked 'as if he was taking part in
a demo rather than a solemn act of respect'. The *Daily Mail* offered
readers cut-out-and-keep Michael Foot dolls, which could be dressed in
assorted proletarian outfits – or, alternatively, in top hat and tails, 'like
the real leader of a real party'. As so often, though, the *Mail* overdid it.
Even among Tories, the patrician look was out. Margaret Thatcher's
blue suits, pussycat bows and immaculate coifs were aggressively
middle-class, and later leaders unbuttoned even more. David Cameron
regularly took off his tie, and Theresa May was interviewed wearing
leather trousers (although that upset almost everyone).

The pace varied, but the nation moved in one direction. Even my
mother caved in. Having banned denim from the house in the 1960s,
on the grounds that it was not only rough but also American, she
bowed to the inevitable in the '70s. Resistance was futile, because the
Great Unbuttoning *made sense*. For millennia those who could afford
it had aped the styles of kings and courtiers, the people with power
and wealth; and since Continental kings and courtiers generally had

more power and wealth than English ones, and English ones more than Welsh, Scottish or Irish ones, fashions normally rolled from Italy, Spain and France towards the Atlantic. What broke this ancient pattern in the nineteenth century was that London's dark-suited, bourgeois financiers and managers amassed even more power and wealth than most kings and courtiers, which prompted old elites – first in Britain, then everywhere else – to refashion their own identities in imitation of this serious-minded middle class. By the 1950s the coming class (above all in the United States) was clearly that of the affluent young workers buying all those houses, cars and appliances. It was therefore the common man's tastes – more casual, sexier, rougher, edgier – that the upper and middle classes rushed to emulate.

Europeans had been worrying about Americanisation since the 1890s, but in the 1950s American youth and affluence turned burgers, Coca-Cola, pop music, Hollywood and denim into an 'irresistible empire' (the historian Victoria de Grazia's phrase). Like most of the West, Britons simultaneously loved and resented this, but their position at the very junction of Churchill's circles coloured the Americanisation of British identity in two unique ways.

One British peculiarity was that a new kind of Europeanisation went alongside Americanisation. British sophisticates had been using Continental culture to distinguish themselves from the vulgar herd since before the Romans came. In some ways, that pattern intensified in the 1960s, exemplified by what the historian E. P. Thompson called the rise of 'the Eurostomach [. . .] of Oxford and north London', defined by its socially exclusive 'haze of remembered vacations, beaches, bougainvillea, business jaunts and vintage wines'. But cheap package holidays to Continental beaches, which began in 1950, opened Europeanisation to the lower orders too. By 1971, 4 million Islanders had burned their pale skins under the Mediterranean sun; a decade later it was 13 million. Penniless bohemians could now quaff table wine in Soho trattorias; young Mods on Vespas sipped espressos in shining coffee shops; and suburbanites bought Mateus Rosé and cooked coq au vin. Technologies of travel had changed what geography meant. By 1980 the average Briton drank a glass of wine every four days or so, and Dutch-style lager was popular enough for Britons to invent the lager lout. But gentler Continental habits caught on too. After not visiting the old country for several years, I was astonished in the mid-1990s to find my father hugging people. This was new.

The second way that being in the middle of Churchill's circles shaped British identity was Commonwealthisation (if there is such a word). As so often, foreign food led the way. Englishmen had been appreciating South Asian delicacies (especially kebabs, pilau and pickles) since at least 1689, and it was English cooks who created eighteenth-century India's first curries – thick, creamy, spicy and sometimes hot sauces, related to, but different from, local seasonings. Their popularity waxed and waned. In the 1880s, when British India had become a starchier, more segregated place, one cookbook said that 'the molten curries and florid oriental compositions of the olden time [have been] banished from our dinner tables'; but even so, the author admitted, a 'well-considered curry' remained a 'capital thing' for breakfast.

London got its first Indian restaurant in 1911. Bengalis opened dozens more in other cities in the 1930s, and by the 1960s most towns had one. Chinese cuisine followed a similar trajectory: immigrants from Hong Kong opened the first restaurant in Liverpool around 1900, but the big breakthrough again came in the 1960s, when Billy Butlin installed Chinese kitchens in his holiday camps (I first saw Chinese food in 1966, at his Minehead camp). By 1976 Britain had more Chinese restaurants than fish-and-chip shops. A century earlier, fish and chips had themselves been widely considered nasty, smelly Jewish imports (which, some speculated, had actually been introduced by the French), but were then naturalised – like tea, beer and gin before them – as defining elements of British identity. In the late twentieth century, Indian and Chinese food went the same way, until by 2001, a foreign secretary could call chicken tikka masala 'a true British national dish', as English as lager. Eleven years later, Food Network UK reported that it and stir-fry were Britain's most popular restaurant meals.

Commonwealthisation differed from both American- and Europeanisation in being rooted even more firmly in mass mobility. A million Americans had migrated into Britain during the war, but then went home again, and while the Italians, Maltese and Cypriots who came after the war stayed, they numbered barely 100,000. By 1980, though, there were about 2 million people of Caribbean or South Asian descent in the Isles, and they weren't going anywhere.

The first wave had come from the West Indies. Hurricanes in 1944 ruined thousands of farmers just at the moment the United States tightened its immigration laws. Britain, however, was hungry for cheap labour and in 1948 passed a British Nationality Act, offering passports to all Crown subjects. Almost immediately, the SS *Empire Windrush* brought 510 Jamaicans (eighteen of them stowaways) to London, and more ships followed. Britain had been a nation of emigrants for 350 years; 1958 was the first year in which immigrants, mostly Caribbean, outnumbered them. This continued until 1962, when Parliament restricted entry. When pollsters asked, two-thirds of respondents said they approved of limits, citing concerns about jobs and the loss of identity. Mick Jagger, almost as much the voice of the '60s as John Lennon, agreed: 'They just are different and they do act differently and they don't live the same.' Discrimination was widespread (a Ministry of Labour leaflet warned immigrants 'You must expect to meet this in Britain') and violence not unknown. Gangs attacked immigrants in Birmingham and Liverpool in 1948; fighting convulsed London's Notting Hill suburb for three nights in 1958.

By then, Caribbean immigration had slowed, but South Asian arrivals were accelerating. 'If I had the money to go, I wouldn't stay in this country', one Wolverhamptonian told his MP, because 'in fifteen or twenty years' time the black man will have the whip hand over the white man'. The MP, Enoch Powell, had been a brilliant classicist before going into Conservative politics, and combined a Thucydidean skill for seeing to the heart of matters with a tragic flaw, worthy of Sophocles, of going to extremes. 'Poor old Enoch', said one colleague, 'driven mad by the remorselessness of his own logic.' (Macmillan insisted on having Powell's chair moved in Cabinet meetings because 'I can't stand those mad eyes staring at me a moment longer'.) Powell had been one of the ministers who had resigned with Thorneycroft over inflation in 1957, and in 1968, seeing immigration as another issue that mainstream politicians were ignoring, took another last stand. 'Like the Roman', he announced, quoting the poet Virgil, 'I seem to see "the River Tiber foaming with much blood" [. . .] Only resolute and urgent action will avert it even now.'

The *Daily Mirror* called these 'the ravings of a sick hysteric', but one poll found that 74 per cent of Britons agreed with Powell. Other polls named Powell the most popular politician in the land. He said out loud what many were thinking about immigrants, even though in 1968 few Britons had actually met one. When my parents learned that Indians were buying the house next door, there were dark mutterings about strange smells and foreign ways; but when our new neighbour turned out to be a doctor, with a better-educated and frankly much nicer family than anyone else in our cul-de-sac, dark mutterings were officially banned. Friendships were formed. There was all-round sadness when the doctor got promoted and headed off for a better part of town.

Our neighbours were hardly typical immigrants, but neither were they outliers. South Asian newcomers regularly displayed that most Smilesian virtue, the urge to get on. Nearly half a century later I attended a dinner at Birmingham University where both the guests of honour – the university's newly sworn-in chancellor and the city's lord mayor – were Indian immigrants. When I'd enrolled there as an undergraduate in 1978, no one would have thought this possible.

The combination of Americanisation, Europeanisation and Commonwealthisation gave post-war British identities a distinct flavour. Unlike the rest of the West, Britons took American behaviour, added their own traditions, mixed in European and Commonwealth flavours and re-exported a new *Anglo*-American product to the rest of the world. For half a century this culture has constituted the true Special Relationship.

Take rock and roll. When it first broke on British shores in the 1950s, the *Daily Mail* warned readers that 'It is deplorable. It is tribal. And it is from America.' British musicians initially contributed little to the world's most important emerging art form, sending hardly any hits into *Billboard* magazine's American Top Twenty in the 1950s. (Lonnie Donegan, singing 'Rock Island Line' – an American song – was first, in 1954.) Yet in 1964 the Beatles took America and the world by storm. Certainly, there has never been another band like them; but Britain nevertheless produced dozens (hundreds) of shockingly good bands in the next half-century. In 1904 one German critic had unkindly called Britain 'the land without music', but by 1965 the *New Musical Express* could crow that 'We may be regarded as a second-class power in politics, but [. . .] we now lead the world in pop music!' Even the Parisian newspaper *L'Express* conceded that 'England rules over international pop music'.

And not just pop music. Besides chart-topping records, Britain has churned out world-beating films, fashions, children's stories, murder mysteries, television shows and computer games. A billion people watched the opening ceremony of London's 2012 Olympics, maybe the most uplifting spectacle ever staged. Britain even clawed back its influence over the world's top holiday, Christmas. I mentioned in Chapter 8 how, at the zenith of the world-system, Dickens and others reinvented Christmas as a semi-secular, ultra-English celebration of family, prosperity and generosity. The twentieth century, however, saw Americans capture it, along with so much else. Between 1934 – when both 'Santa Claus is Comin' to Town' and 'Winter Wonderland' were published – and 1960 – 'Must be Santa' – Americans enjoyed a golden age of non-religious Christmas songs. ('Jingle Bells', virtually the only American standard penned outside this quarter-century, is the exception that proves the rule; it was released in 1857 as a Thanksgiving song but repurposed for Christmas by Bing Crosby and the Andrews Sisters in 1943.) Americans conquered Yuletide cinema in the 1940s, with *Holiday Inn* (1942), *Christmas in Connecticut* (1945), the magnificent *It's a Wonderful Life* (1946) and *Miracle on 34th Street* (1947). On television the mid-1960s were the glory years, generating *Rudolph the Red-Nosed Reindeer* in 1964, *The Charlie Brown Christmas Special* in 1965 and *How the Grinch Stole Christmas* in 1966. Yet, just when American control of the world's most popular holiday (even among non-Christians) seemed total, Britain struck back. *Love, Actually*, released in 2003, gets my vote for the finest festive film ever made.

'Shiny, happy [. . .] insatiable in its optimism', one rather Grinchy critic grumbled, *Love, Actually* merely 'mastered the knack of making the parochial international, [. . . telling] audiences across the Atlantic almost exactly what they wanted to hear about the old country'. Yes, but is that so bad? Britain, says the historian Dominic Sandbrook, has 'embraced a new identity as the world's great dream factory'. Harry Potter, Bob Marley, Manchester United and the Spice Girls are probably not quite what Winston Churchill had envisaged, but these are the people who have realised his vision of a Britain connecting all the circles of the world. Their imaginative, unbuttoned, huggy identities would not have worked in the days when Britain was fighting Napoleon and conquering India, but those days are gone. Post-Suez realities required different kinds of people, and so Britons became them. Watching *Brief Encounter* and *Love, Actually* back-to-back, it is hard not to see how much has been lost – but hard too not to see how much has been gained.

No, No, Yes – or No

In some ways Margaret Thatcher might have agreed. While her political programme could be backward-looking and nostalgic, striving to restore the good old days, it was also ruthlessly pragmatic, jettisoning even the most hallowed traditions if they no longer worked. Perhaps it would be fairest to say she was selective. Despite constantly talking of shattering the cosy consensus that had dominated politics since the war, the main difference between her approach to Churchill's circles and Macmillan's was just that she usually went further. Only on domestic capacity did she seriously diverge, seizing the road not taken in 1957. Dusting off Thorneycroft's advice, she cut costs, raised interest rates, squeezed money out of circulation and tried (not always successfully) neither to print nor to borrow more of it. With less cash around, the thinking ran, the economy would shrink, bringing inflation down. Firms would go bust, but the survivors would be fitter. Even nationalised industries would have to become more efficient if there was no more money to give them, and investment would shift from manufacturing towards services, where Britain had more potential to prosper.

Parts of the programme definitely worked. Inflation, close to 20 per cent in 1980, fell by three-quarters over three years. Steady growth returned, hitting 4 per cent in 1983 and staying close to it until 1988, outdoing even the artificial booms of the 1960s–70s; and in financial services, Britain regained much of the ground it had lost since 1945. Terrified that anyone who could swap pounds for dollars would do so, every government since Attlee's had imposed strict capital and exchange controls. Ignoring bankers' complaints that 'We cannot have an international currency and deny its use internationally', politicians forbade Britons from taking or sending more than £50 per year out of the country.

Bankers had been finding ways around these restrictions well before Thatcher intervened. In the late 1950s, having decided (foolishly) that London's capitalists were marginally less wicked than New York's, the Soviets had parked their dollar reserves with them, whereupon none-too-fussy financiers lent these 'Eurodollars' overseas, charging fat fees. Changes in American tax laws in 1963 helped further, and when Arab oil magnates also banked their dollars in London in the 1970s (Japan followed in the 1980s), the City's Eurodollar market exploded.

Thatcher's contribution was to suspend exchange controls, giving all London bankers the same freedom to borrow and lend in dollars as that enjoyed by the happy few with access to Soviet, Japanese and American money. This, along with computerisation, set off a free-for-all. In a magnificent understatement, one insider admitted that 'There may indeed be some unsound banking here and there'; in truth, billions of dollars sloshed wildly in and out of London. A single rogue trader was able to bring down Barings Bank, but luckier speculators walked away with windfall profits and huge bonuses. A further ruling in 1986 lifted most remaining restrictions on banks, making London once again the most attractive place for foreigners needing financial services. On the back of mergers with American banks, the modern steel-and-glass, Gherkin-and-Shard, champagne-and-cocaine City was born.

This financial big bang was a godsend for the government. When added to profits from North Sea oil, it more than balanced Britain's books. Yet it was also a curse, because it took away the government's ability to control sterling's value just at the moment when guaranteed income from oil was making British currency attractive to speculators. The pound shot up from around $1.60 in 1976 to $2.46 in 1980, pricing many British exports out of markets. It was one thing to kill outmoded, inefficient industries, but the overvalued pound now murdered hundreds of perfectly healthy, export-oriented manufacturers.

This part of the programme to align domestic capacity with world position definitely did not work. Two million jobs vanished, mostly in the old industries based in the north. Even in the somewhat insulated Midlands, my ex-student friends and I all saw the insides of Jobcentres (with their depressingly cheerful orange signs) in the early 1980s. Rioters burned inner cities, adding more support to claims that deflation was politically impossible.

Backbenchers and ministers muttered and plotted, but two things saved Thatcher. The first was the Labour Party. Had it offered voters a plausible alternative, Conservatives would probably have reacted by ousting their leader and abandoning efforts to reform domestic capacity before the next election. Instead, Labour split. Its left revived the 'Fortress Britain' strategy, arguing that Churchill and Macmillan had misunderstood the meanings of geography, and that Britain should not be trying to bridge Europe and America. Within days of winning an election, they pledged, they would nationalise the economy's commanding heights, restore capital and exchange controls and impose workers' co-operatives. Within weeks they would take Britain out of the European Economic Community (not so easy, we now know), and within months would abolish the House of Lords, to prevent any rerun of its 1910 opposition to the People's Budget. Along the way, they would gut defence spending, ban the bomb, cast off American shackles, impose a wealth tax, mandate a thirty-five-hour week, restrict some imports, tax others and bring the City to heel. 'Comrades', their self-appointed leader Tony Benn advised, 'this is the very least we must do!'

Labour Party conferences degenerated into swearing, spitting, shouting and punching matches. Even on television, they were gripping affairs. Few were surprised when four centrist grandees left Labour in 1980, founding a Social Democratic Party committed to being neither Thatcherite nor Bennite (and to not swearing, spitting, shouting or punching). These seemed like such good ideas that by late 1981 all polls agreed that an immediate election would give the new party and its Liberal coalition partners a crushing majority.

The prospects looked grim for both major parties – until a second wild card repaired Tory fortunes, but not Labour's. It turned up because Mrs Thatcher, again following Macmillan, had quietly been distancing herself from the empire. Since opinion polls suggested that only 25 per cent of Britons (as opposed to 48 per cent in 1961) now considered the Commonwealth a high priority, Thatcher brokered a deal over Rhodesian apartheid, returned Hong Kong to China and decided, as one of many military cutbacks, to scrap the ageing icebreaker HMS *Endurance*, the navy's last ship in the South Atlantic. But that was too much distancing. Despite being little practical use any more, the *Endurance* had symbolised Britain's commitment to the Falkland Islands, which Argentina had claimed since the nineteenth century. In April 1982 its gruesome dictators – eager to distract attention from their criminality – interpreted the *Endurance*'s retirement as a green light to invade.

Everything about the situation screamed 'Suez'. Loading 25,000 troops on to ships at three days' notice and sending them 10,000 km into an oncoming South Atlantic winter screamed disaster-in-the-making. Thatcher knew it, but also knew that everything about surrendering screamed the end for her. So the task force had to go. A month later, I was in a pub in Birmingham when the television cut to an announcement that HMS *Sheffield* was burning after an Argentine missile strike. The place fell entirely silent. One by one, still not speaking, people started getting up and going home. Everyone understood. British identity had not changed completely since 1940. The task force had to go.

So many things could have gone wrong, but most of them didn't. For that, Mrs Thatcher could thank not only her troops and her luck (the most important thing for any commander, said Napoleon) but also her friends. Above all, what stopped the Falklands turning into another Suez was Ronald Reagan. Some American officials tried to enmesh Thatcher in compromises, but in the end, the president told them 'give Maggie everything she needs to get on with it'. Reagan claimed he 'would mortgage the Washington Monument, if necessary, to help get Margaret Thatcher re-elected'. Such were the rewards for prioritising the American circle.

Reagan and Thatcher saw eye to eye on many matters, especially her determination – again in Macmillan's mould, but going further – to face down the Soviet circle. The United States had been hardening its line since the Soviets had reopened the Great Game by invading Afghanistan in 1979, but even before this, Moscow Radio was calling Thatcher the 'Iron Lady'. She revelled in it. 'I stand before you tonight in my Red Star chiffon evening gown, my face softly made up and my fair hair gently waved, the Iron Lady of the Western world', she told her constituents in 1976. 'Yes, I *am* an iron lady. After all, it wasn't a bad thing to be an iron duke.'*

As it had been since Macmillan's times, managing the nuclear counterscarp was the trickiest Anglo-American issue. Thatcher closed a deal to replace Britain's Polaris missiles with the latest, hugely expensive, American Tridents, but was privately horrified by an American plan (widely mocked as 'Star Wars') to shoot down Soviet missiles with space-based weapons. British scientists doubted that it would work, but Thatcher worried that even the possibility would weaken Washington's commitment to a European counterscarp. To keep the Americans in, she let them put intermediate-range missiles on their bases in England, although that provoked millions to march once again to ban the bomb. Tensions ran so high in late 1983 that Soviet officials interpreted reports of British civil servants working overtime

---

*The Duke of Wellington's nickname.

as meaning that war was imminent. They cancelled leave and loaded live nuclear weapons on aircraft.

This was the closest call since the Cuban crisis in 1962, and it left both Reagan and Thatcher eager to engage the Soviet circle again. Fortunately for both, the leader the politburo appointed in 1985 was Mikhail Gorbachev – 'the sort of guy you can do business with', Thatcher's advisers thought. More fortunately still, after four decades, containment had finally boxed the Soviet economy into such a corner that Moscow found itself forced into a going-out-of-business sale. With his revenues falling just as the West ramped up another arms race, Gorbachev tried to revive growth by liberalising and holding an audit of empire. When this concluded (like Macmillan's British audit thirty years earlier) that imperialism did little for the Soviet economy, Gorbachev cut half a million men from the army, retreated from Afghanistan, scrapped his intermediate-range missiles and announced what some called the 'Sinatra Doctrine' – that each East European government must do communism its own way, without Soviet support against its own people. In June 1989 Hungarians rolled up the barbed wire along their border with the West; five months later, the Berlin Wall came down. The Soviet Empire had dissolved even faster than the British.

Against all reasonable expectations and without firing a single missile, the United States had won the Cold War. There were 70,000 nuclear warheads in the world, probably enough to kill everyone, but just a few hundred people got shot in 1989, mostly in Romania. The struggle ended with such a whimper, in fact, that few of us living through it initially grasped what had just happened. I certainly didn't, despite spending 1989 living in the belly of the beast, just a few minutes' drive from the White House – where the new president, George H. W. Bush, seemed equally unsure what was going on. Several advisers thought Gorbachev was tricking them into relaxing containment. But the Soviet Empire did disappear, and the nations within the USSR, seeing little point in their union without its empire (rather like some nationalists in the United Kingdom), did pull away from Moscow until the Soviet Union disappeared too.

The Soviet circle's implosion upended Britain's relationships with the other three circles, but with Europe most of all. Until 1989 Thatcher's Continental strategy was, like so much else, Macmillanite but beefier. The 1975 referendum had locked Britain into Europe and its trade-offs of identity and sovereignty for prosperity and security (at this point European mobility still wasn't a big issue). The only question was whether the trade-offs were worthwhile. On that, Thatcher's views were clear. Britain's contribution to Community coffers had ballooned from £100 million in 1973 to nearly £1 billion in 1979. Walking away was unthinkable (it was 'a matter of profound regret', Thatcher said, 'that much political energy in our country is still devoted to the hoary question of whether we should be "In" or "Out"'), but there was an option to 'withhold', suspending payments to Brussels. So Thatcher cold-shouldered the Community but stayed at the table until, in 1984, she browbeat the Eurocrats into returning most of Britain's money. This was, one diplomat thought, 'the most valuable financial agreement this country *ever* negotiated'.

This victory began what another aide called Britain's 'golden years' in Europe, when Thatcher herself pushed 'ostentatiously *communautaire*' proposals, even agreeing to dig a Channel Tunnel. Yet the more she advanced the Macmillanite agenda of merging Europe's markets but not its other institutions, the more the Continental federalists insisted that a single market needed a single currency, which meant merging almost everything. In fact, the European Commission's president announced in 1988, 'In ten years 80 per cent of the laws affecting the economy and social policy would be passed at a European and not a national level'. First, an Exchange Rate Mechanism would link Europe's currencies, then a European Monetary Union would replace all the guilders, drachmas and pounds. Meanwhile, the European Assembly would become a Parliament, legislating on everything from human rights to the environment, until – as federalists had been urging since 1950 – a United States of Europe emerged. The point of junction between Churchill's circles would be swallowed, and Britain with it.

Thatcher agreed that 'Our destiny is in Europe, as part of the Community', but doggedly insisted that such a destiny 'does not require [. . .] a European super-state exercising a new dominance from Brussels'. But the fall of the Berlin Wall upended everything. With the Russians definitely out, the Americans saw less need to stay in or to keep the Germans down. Within weeks, Bonn and East Berlin were talking reunification. This was France's worst-case strategic scenario, and its President Mitterrand warned Thatcher that West Germany was about 'to achieve what neither Bismarck nor Hitler could achieve'. Reunification, he told her, would require a Franco-Russo-British alliance to balance Germany; 'and then we would all be back in 1913'.

Before Europe could reach that point, though, it first had to relearn the lesson of 1916: that nothing worked without the United States. Bush had already decided that 'the center of gravity is at the heart of Europe and that isn't Britain, it's Germany'. So long as a united Germany stayed within the American-dominated world-system, Washington had no objections. Mitterrand therefore cut a deal: France would support reunification if Germany accepted a new European treaty, deeper union and a single currency. France's worst-case scenario now became Britain's, facing a Franco-German-American front alone.

For years, Thatcher's foreign secretary said, her attitude to European integration had been 'no, no, yes', as her instinctive suspicion gradually yielded to argument. After the Wall fell, however, it became – as she herself put it while fighting the Exchange Rate Mechanism – 'no, no, no'. Now that Germany was united, she lectured Bush, it must be contained, with Russian help; but no one was listening any more. One by one, her top ministers withdrew their support, and, when a nasty leadership struggle broke out, so did the rest of her parliamentary party. No, no, no was not enough, and out went the Iron Lady. Within three months her successor was telling the world 'I want us to be where we belong, at the centre of Europe'.

The circles had shifted. New maps were needed.

11

KEEP CALM AND CARRY ON, 1992–2103

The Pentagon's New Map

Nineteen-eighty-nine was America's 1815. After Waterloo the whole world had had to learn to live on Mackinder's Map and to deal with what came its way from Britain. Now it had to adjust to a map with America in the middle. An initial sketch of this map was unveiled in February 1992, just weeks after the Soviet Union had officially dissolved itself. Every two years the US government publishes a pamphlet called the Defense Planning Guidance. Typically, these are dull documents, designed not to rock boats, but this time the drafting committee did something reckless. It told the truth. 'Our first objective', it explained,

> is to prevent the reemergence of a new rival, either on the territory of the former Soviet Union or elsewhere, that poses a threat on the order of that formerly posed by the Soviet Union. This [. . .] requires that we endeavor to prevent any hostile power from dominating a region whose resources would, under consolidated control, be sufficient to generate global power. These regions include Western Europe, East Asia, the territory of the former Soviet Union, and south-west Asia [that is, the Middle East].

Like all such documents, this was promptly leaked to the press. Its directness provoked uproar, and the Department of Defense duly toned it down, but every American government since then has more or less followed it.

At the centre of the Pentagon's new map (Figure 11.1) was the United States itself, overlapping with everyone else. With one exception, the other circles did not overlap at all, interacting only via the essential nation. The sole exception, in Eastern Europe, was granted

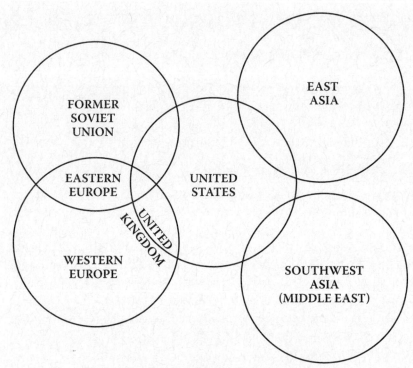

Figure 11.1. The Pentagon's new map: the world
as seen from Washington, 1992.

because allowing former Soviet satellite states to defect to Western
Europe looked like a cheap and easy way to keep Russia weak. No
one objected when Poland and Hungary applied to join the European Union in 1994 or when both, along with the Czech Republic,
sought NATO membership five years later. So well did this seem to
be working that in 2000 Vladimir Putin mused about bringing Russia
into NATO too.

The United Kingdom fitted very differently on the Pentagon's
map from on Churchill's. Rather than being the very point of contact,
linking everyone else, it seemed that the best it could hope for was to
be America's first port of call in Europe – although the reunited Germany's economic weight meant that not even that was guaranteed.
Britain's story in the thirty years since 1992 has been driven largely
by its efforts to come to terms both with this new map and with
how the new map has changed the rest of the world. This not only

makes sense of the often confusing events since the 1990s but also fits them squarely into Britain's full, 8,000-year history – which in turn, I believe, provides some insight into what the twenty-first century is likely to hold.

One thing Conservative and Labour governments alike agreed on in the 1990s was that, despite Thatcher's fall, Britain was not ready to be just another European country. Her successor, John Major, opted out of the 1992 Maastricht treaty's commitment to a single European currency (Figure 11.2), and despite his broad Europhilia, Labour's Tony Blair essentially followed suit on becoming prime minister in 1997 by announcing tough preconditions for Britain joining the euro. Like Major, Blair discovered that Britain's post-war Euro-indifference was morphing into Euro-anxiety as the full implications of the Pentagon's new map for identity, prosperity and sovereignty sank home. Many Conservatives who had been guardedly pro-European in the 1970s–80s now concluded that they had been tricked. As yet, single-issue Eurosceptic groups like the UK Independence Party (founded in 1993) won few votes, but politicians of all stripes were learning not to provoke the Europhobes. Some Tories – egged on by Mrs Thatcher – even began seeing advantages in befriending them.

The limits of Britain's Europeanness were exposed in 2003. The immediate cause came from a second of the Pentagon's circles, the Middle East, but the truest cause – which was, for once, much spoken of – was Britain's ongoing effort to remain the junction between the European and American circles. British attitudes to the Middle East had long been closer to Washington's than Brussels's, including a willingness to use force. Since its Islamic Revolution in 1979, Iran had regularly called Britain the Little Satan, as compared to an American Great Satan. 'The brutal truth', one American secretary of state reflected, was that when NATO went to war in Iraq and Yugoslavia in the 1990s, 'the only forces that counted were UK forces and US forces' (other officials added the Canadians too).

After the terror attacks of 11 September 2001, George W. Bush's administration in Washington concluded that a new counterscarp was needed against Islamism, and must be based as much in hard power – bombing, counter-insurgency, regime change, covert assassination and even torture – as in foreign aid, diplomacy and propaganda. Most West Europeans disagreed, and so, when Franco-German opposition threatened the American decision to invade Iraq in 2003, Bush reacted

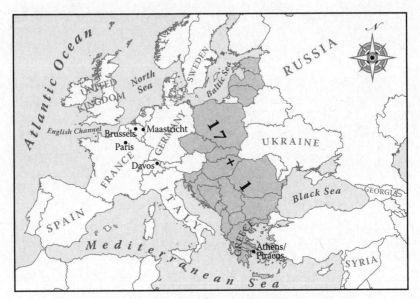

Figure 11.2. The Euro-Mediterranean stage, 1992–2103.

by trying to split Europe along very eighteenth-century, balance-of-power lines (Figure 11.3). Washington outflanked the 'old Europe' of Paris and Berlin by reaching out to poorer, weaker states further east; France and Germany outflanked these by reaching beyond them to Russia, Turkey and even China; and Blair saw a chance to reassert Britain's role as America's surest friend in Europe.

Thatcherite anxiety about handing sovereignty to Brussels was now swamped by a wider fear of surrendering it to Washington. This focused particularly on the danger that assisting the United States in its wars in Iraq and Afghanistan would undermine, not protect, the Isles' security. After all, critics claimed, it was home-grown terrorists – radicalised by Britain's involvement in what both Bush and Osama bin Laden had called 'crusades' – who got on planes with bombs in their shoes and who murdered fifty-two Londoners in 2005 (they were mistaken: al-Qaeda was heavily involved).

Talking heads often overreacted to the possibility that Islam was eroding British identity. The journalist Melanie Phillips, for instance, claimed in her book *Londonistan* that 'piggy banks have been banished from British banks in case Muslims might be offended' (not true). Steve Emerson, an American observer, called Birmingham (Figure

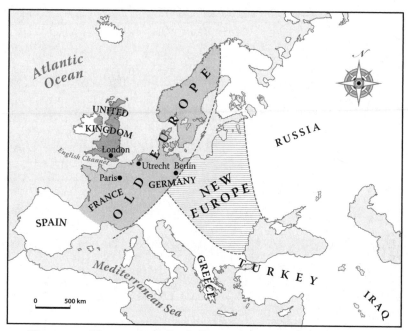

Figure 11.3. The new Utrecht: balance-of-power politics, 2003-style.

11.4) a 'Muslim-only' city, where 'Muslim religious police' beat up 'anyone who doesn't dress [in] religious Muslim attire' (not only not true but also, as Birmingham officials responded with admirably British understatement, 'a bit bonkers' too). Yet some radicals really were advocating Muslim-only zones under sharia law, and polls found that one-third of respondents thought they already existed.

Much less bonkers were worries that British identity was fraying along older lines. In 1998 the Good Friday Agreement finally ended Britain's war on Irish terror by loosening the bonds of the Union and conceding 'the birthright of all the people of Northern Ireland to identify themselves and be accepted as Irish or British, or both, as they may so choose'. The year before that, Wales (narrowly) and Scotland (overwhelmingly) had voted for their own parliaments. Even the English, who often seem embarrassed by their national identity ('it is always felt that there is something slightly disgraceful in being an Englishman', George Orwell thought), rediscovered its appeal.

The Celtic independence movements certainly energised English nationalism, but European immigration was definitely the main

Figure 11.4. The British stage, 1992–2103.

motor. Until the 1950s barely one English resident in thirty had been born overseas (Figure 11.5), and even in the 1970s Caribbean and South Asian arrivals only pushed that up to one in twenty. But between 2004 (when ten new countries, mostly Eastern European, joined the European Union) and 2009, immigrants boosted England's population by 700,000. More than one resident in eight was now foreign-born, a

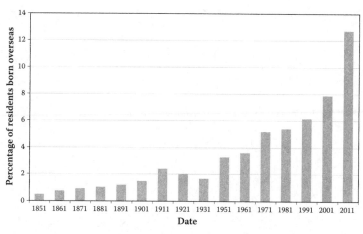

Figure 11.5. The Polish plumbers are coming: the percentage of
residents of England and Wales born overseas, 1851–2011.

level probably not seen in fifteen centuries, and by 2010 two-thirds of
babies born in London had at least one foreign-born parent. Anxiety
about immigration – and even blatant xenophobia – returned to
mainstream politics.

Each immigrant had his or her own reasons for relocating, but
prosperity was often the main attractor. The economy grew more
than 2 per cent each year between 1993 and 2007, while unemployment
fell from over 10 to under 5 per cent, despite anxiety over newcomers. As in most booms, inequality increased. Between 2001 and 2008
London bankers' bonuses tripled until, at £16 billion, they equalled
half the defence budget. However, state redistribution ensured that
even the lowest earners gained 10 per cent – despite, again, competition for jobs from immigrants. 'The boom and bust that for thirty
years has undermined stability', the chancellor, Gordon Brown,
announced, had 'end[ed] once and for all'.

The Money Map

What made Brown's claim look so believable in 1998 and so ludicrous
a decade later was the last of the circles on the Pentagon's new map,
East Asia. Britons had been active on China's coast since the seventeenth century, but even in the nineteenth, when steamships, railways

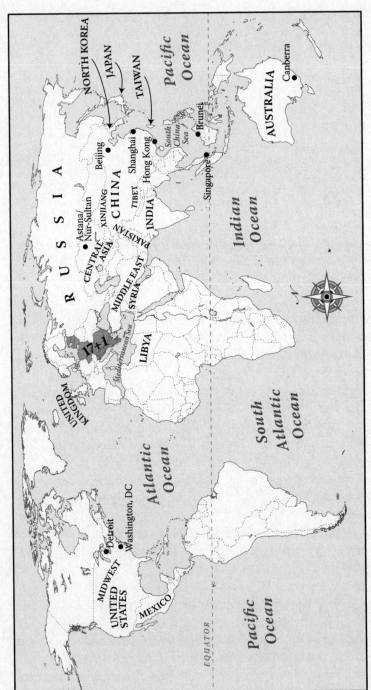

Figure 11.6. The global stage, 1992–2103.

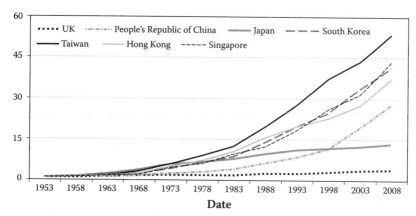

Figure 11.7. A lion among tigers: the ten-, twenty- and even fifty-fold growth of East Asia's economies, 1953–2008 (the vertical axis shows how many times bigger each country's economy was than in 1953). Chugging along at the bottom is Britain.

and the telegraph had drawn the Atlantic and Indian Oceans into a London-based world-system, the Pacific was still too far away, and too big, to be centre stage. Only since 1945 had that really changed, as container ships, jet aircraft and eventually the internet shrank the ocean – and by then, the fall of the Dutch, French and British empires and Japan's defeat had made the Pacific an American lake.

All Western economies profited from the expansion of the global economic stage into East Asia, but the 'Asian Tigers' (Hong Kong, Japan, Singapore, South Korea, Taiwan; Figure 11.6) that joined the American world-system profited most. Their economies grew faster than any in history (Figure 11.7), lifting a billion people out of extreme poverty (in the World Bank's sense, discussed in Chapter 1, of living on less than $1.90 per day). Japan's economy overtook Britain's in 1962 and West Germany's in 1967 to become the world's second-biggest.

A century earlier, self-doubt had consumed Asia's previously self-confident elites when Western ships shot their way into Eastern waters. In China the years between the 1840s and 1940s are still remembered as the 'century of humiliation'. Reversing this, the Japanese and Korean hi-fis, televisions and cars that now flooded Western markets in the 1970–80s set off extremes of handwringing. Michael Crichton's paranoid novel *Rising Sun* and Ezra Vogel's soberer, social-scientific

Japan as Number One both became bestsellers, even though the redraw-
ing of the map had in fact barely begun.

Despite tragic mismanagement while Chairman Mao was at the
helm, China's economy nevertheless tripled in size between 1949
and 1976; but in the forty-five years after Mao's death it expanded
another fortyfold. 'To get rich is no sin', Deng Xiaoping insisted as
he opened Special Economic Zones to attract foreign capitalists to
China's shores in the 1980s, and when Japan fell into recession in 1992,
the People's Republic seized its number-two spot. When Mao and
Nixon met in 1972, the average American worker had been nearly
twenty times more productive than the average Chinese. By 2000 he/
she was less than seven times as valuable, and by 2020 barely four
times. In 1972 China generated 4.6 per cent of humanity's wealth; in
2000 it was 11.8 per cent, and in 2020 it was 18.9 per cent – more than
any other country on earth.

China has remade itself since the 1980s. In the biggest migration
in history nearly 200 million people have moved from dirt-poor inland
villages to smoky, coastal cities. What this wrought has to be seen to
be believed. I once took a helicopter ride over Shenzhen on the south
coast. At first, we couldn't see the city at all through the sickly, yellow-
brown smog. Slowly, its skyscrapers, tower blocks and traffic-choked
streets emerged, and just kept emerging. They went on, and on, and
on – and Shenzhen is only China's sixth-biggest city. The fifth-biggest,
Guangzhou, was another half-hour's flight away. Hong Kong, where
we'd started our trip just fifteen minutes before, was the eleventh-
biggest, with a mere 7.5 million people. Living near the San Francisco
Bay, I thought I knew crowded landscapes, but coastal China is something else.

Hence the conclusion drawn by the Singaporean prime minister, Lee Kuan Yew, which I quoted in my introduction: that 'China's
displacement of the world balance is such that the world must find a
new balance'. China has replaced what remained of Mackinder's Map
with the Money Map, dominated by three great mountains of cash in
North America, Western Europe and East Asia. By some estimates,
Chinese-made goods fill 90 per cent of the shelf space in American
stores like Walmart; rare is the American who doesn't don at least one
piece of Asian underwear each morning. By 2018 over one-fifth of
American imports came from China, generating a jaw-dropping trade
deficit of $419 billion. Britain buys less than one-twelfth of its imports

from China and runs a deficit under $30 billion, but China is nonetheless Britain's third-biggest trade partner, behind the European Union and United States.

To understand what this has meant for Britain, we must follow the money. In the late nineteenth century British free-traders had reaped huge rewards by providing capital, goods and expertise for Germans and Americans to industrialise and join its world-system. In the early twenty-first, American free-traders did much the same with China, working with Beijing to keep Chinese exports cheap by pegging the renminbi to the dollar at a low rate. To hold the exchange rate down, China sank $1 trillion of its profits into US Treasury Bonds.

The US Federal Reserve took this Chinese money and lent it to American banks, which then made loans to ordinary folk (me included) against the security of real estate. In effect, poor Chinese workers lent money to rich Americans so they could buy more Chinese imports. Millions of Americans bought their first homes; millions more refinanced old ones and took out equity to spend on cars, holidays and Chinese underwear. Fortunes were made, albeit with two entirely predictable results. First, the flood of money drove house prices through the roof, making lenders ever keener to get in on the action; and second, these same lenders lowered their standards for loans as they aggressively hunted new borrowers. By 2004 one borrower in ten failed to provide some (sometimes, any) of the normal paperwork. By some estimates, one loan in thirteen couldn't conceivably be repaid.

Normally bankers who make bad loans go bust, but financiers found two clever (or maybe too clever) fixes. First, to avoid damaging their creditworthiness, banks kept these huge liabilities off their balance sheets by funding them with constantly renewed, short-term loans from other banks; and second, new computer algorithms sliced and diced millions of mortgages, repackaging them into bigger bundles. Plenty of the individual loans would fail, of course, but the idea was that good and bad borrowers would cancel each other out, making the bundles themselves safe. Then – the masterstroke – the bundles could be used as collateral for the short-term loans needed to keep the debts off the banks' books. Big banks regularly lent each other $40–50 against each dollar of notional mortgage debt put up as security, not worrying, for now, that the details of the actual mortgages were buried so deep in a matrix of interlocking corporate balance sheets that no one knew what any bundle was really worth.

Homeowners began defaulting in 2006, and defaulting in large numbers in 2007. That was not itself a threat to the world-system. Everyone knew it would happen. What turned it toxic was that banks got cold feet about renewing short-term loans to other banks on the security of mortgage-tainted collateral. Assets were worthless if no one would buy them or lend against them. In August 2007, when lenders lost confidence in the British bank Northern Rock's credit, it went from multibillion-pound business to ward of the state in just forty-eight hours.

A year later it was Wall Street's turn. When asked to allow Barclay's Bank to buy the Lehman Brothers brokerage, Britain's chancellor told the Federal Reserve that he would not 'import the cancer from US banks into Britain', but he was being disingenuous. The sickness had always been global, and the tumours in New York, London, Frankfurt and Beijing had metastasised well before September 2008. British banks owned American mortgage-backed assets supposedly worth $159 billion, while Germans held another $200 billion-worth and Chinese $400–500 billion. These sums, however, were trivial compared with the international bank-to-bank lending, supposedly secured by these inflated mortgages, which kept the whole system running (Figure 11.8). British banks were on the hook for trillions of dollars, and when confidence collapsed and the assets evaporated, efforts to keep the banks solvent burned through the nation's dollar reserves in just a few days. By 13 October, RBS, the world's biggest bank, was just hours away from going under. 'You'd have had complete panic', the chancellor later said. 'There was a grave risk of [. . .] a breakdown of law and order. We were that close to the brink.' Gordon Brown, now prime minister, acted decisively, nationalising RBS and Lloyds and committing £500 billion to keeping the banks open – over £7,000 for each man, woman and child in the Isles.

No mobs marched on Threadneedle Street that day, or in the weeks and months that followed, thanks to a quiet – indeed, secretive – decision by the US Federal Reserve to act as global lender of last resort. If foreign banks folded and dumped all their dollar-denominated assets at once, the American economy might go under. So the Fed offered European and a few other central banks unlimited borrowing rights in dollars. It is hard to say how much they handed out, because there are many ways to measure, but it was at least $10 trillion. Every cent was ultimately paid back, with interest, but the liquidity kept

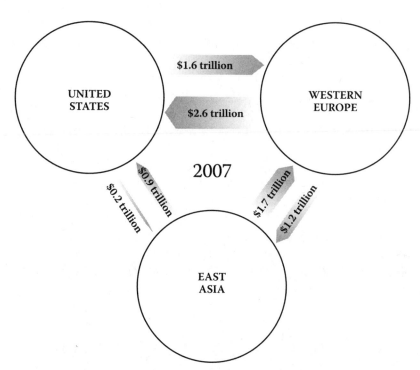

Figure 11.8. Pass the parcel: the multi-trillion-dollar flows
between American, European and Chinese banks that
kept everything moving till the music stopped.

the world's economy afloat until banks worked out what their assets
were actually worth. As it had done in 1916 and 1941, the New World
stepped forth to the rescue of the Old.

But this time, not just the New World. In 2009 China stepped
forth too. Western demand for imports slumped, wiping out perhaps
30 million Chinese jobs. Reacting rapidly, Beijing guaranteed its banks
from central funds and kept the economy going by spending over \$1
trillion on roads, railways and healthcare. And China didn't just avoid
collapse: its economy actually grew in 2009, by a whopping 9.1 per
cent. The knock-on effects of this kept much of the rest of the world
afloat. Far from dumping its dollar assets, Beijing bought another \$500
billion of Treasury Bonds in 2008–9.

When the heads of the world's twenty biggest economies gathered in London in April 2009, an unfunny new joke did the rounds.

'After 1989', it went, 'capitalism saved China. After 2009, China saved capitalism.'

Swivel-Eyed Loons

Salvation came at a cost. Over £1 trillion of Britons' personal wealth evaporated in the first year of the crisis, and successive governments – first Labour, then a Conservative–Liberal Democrat coalition – slashed state spending. The rich lost most, because they had most to lose, but they also bounced back fastest. Government austerity particularly hurt the elderly, the poor, the disabled and the older northern cities. Rates of bankruptcy, unemployment and suicide all jumped. One survey in 2012–13 found that the top one-fifth of Britain's families were, on average, worth 64 per cent more than during the previous survey, in 2005, while the poorest one-fifth were worth 57 per cent less.

In some ways London suffered most. Its financial sector, an outsize source of both prosperity and volatility, shrank every year from 2008 on. After a decade of this, Londoners' take-home earnings had fallen by 5.9 per cent, while the rest of the Isles had lost just 4.2 per cent. In other ways, though, London was relatively unscathed. Employment rebounded, and, fuelled by this and continuing immigration, so did the property market. My father's house in Stoke-on-Trent was worth more or less the same in 2015 as in 2005, while the typical London property had doubled in value. The average London family was 78 per cent richer in 2018 than in 2008, the average Tyneside household 12 per cent poorer. The old contrast between the prosperous, populous and cosmopolitan south-east and everyone else deepened in the 2010s.

London had been a world apart ever since the Romans settled there, but never more so than now. Londoners seemed rather proud of this. In 2014, 180,000 of them signed a mischievous petition 'calling on Mayor Sadiq Khan to declare London independent, and apply to join the EU'. 'Mayor Sadiq,' it asked, 'wouldn't you prefer to be President Sadiq?' Around the same time, taking a train with my niece from King's Cross station to her family home in Bedfordshire, I was startled awake by her mobile phone pinging and announcing 'You are now leaving the London area'. It seemed to be advising against it.

In much of the Isles, distrust of London elites intensified. The conservative *Daily Telegraph* suggested that '"London" has become shorthand for faraway people with no grasp of the nation's problems'. In Scotland demands for independence revived. Britain's prime minister, David Cameron, confident in the Union's strength, agreed to a referendum in 2011; but by mid-2014, when the vote was held, the mood had soured so much that the polls were for a while too close to call. In the end Scotland stayed, but millions in England were also wondering whether geography still meant what it had done before 2008. The *Telegraph* thought that the real problem with 'London' was that it had become indistinguishable from 'the faceless monster of Europe' – and that the solution was to break up the European Union, not the United Kingdom.

This would mean major changes to the Pentagon's map, not to be undertaken lightly; but the growing numbers of Eurosceptics were now feeling that, as well as promoting creeping federalism and untrammelled mobility, Brussels was just dangerously incompetent. Since 2009 it had taken on, and was losing, a war on three fronts, all of which might threaten Britain.

The first theatre of the struggle, in Greece, began as a problem of prosperity but soon came to be seen as a threat to sovereignty too. Greece had flourished since joining the European Union in 1981. I happened to be in Athens in December 2009, at the very moment the Greek government officially admitted that European integration had gone horribly wrong. Arriving at the spanking new Venizelos Airport two days earlier, I had been amazed at how much richer the country looked than it had done thirty years earlier, when I'd been a regular visitor. Athenians were now drinking espressos, not the traditional thick Greek coffee, boiled with the grounds in it. The old *periptera*, streetside stalls selling almost everything, were gone. Even Omonia Square looked clean. But now the government confessed that it and its predecessors had been lying about the scale of their debts. With tourism devastated by the financial crisis, Athens could not meet its interest payments.

Overnight, it felt as though the air went out of the country. The Greek debt, $297 billion, was small beer by the standards of 2008, but what made this molehill into a mountain was the European Union's utter inability to deal with it. The Union's founding document, the Maastricht treaty, explicitly banned Brussels from bailing out insolvent member states, leaving that job to commercial banks; but in the absence of a centralised government to bully them, Europe's banks had not recapitalised after the 2008 meltdown on anything like the scale of American institutions. Once again, dodgy collateral paralysed credit markets. 'There is virtually no interbank lending between European banks', Germany's finance ministry noted. Capital fled from risky European bonds to safer American ones, and by mid-2010 Italy too was having trouble servicing its loans. 'There are overall signs of an acute pending systemic crisis', the German report concluded.

No one was really in charge. With banks refusing to write off their loans, the Greek government unable to repay them, other governments unwilling to take the debts on and the European Central Bank banned from buying them, Brussels just wobbled on, month after month, doing enough to keep Athens from defaulting but not enough to resolve anything. Two years passed before the Central Bank committed to 'do whatever it takes to preserve the euro', regardless of treaties. This relieved the markets but horrified constitutionalists. 'To British eyes', said Daniel Hannan, a Member of the European Parliament and committed Brexiteer, 'the whole process seemed bizarre. Rules had been drawn up in the clearest language that lawyers could devise. Yet, the moment they became inconvenient, they were ignored.' This left Brussels looking unreliable on sovereignty as well as on prosperity.

The second front in Europe's crisis – Ukraine – added a security dimension. The Union's eastward expansion, begun in 1990, had continued, and in 2014 Ukraine took the first steps towards joining. Just months earlier, however, Russia had annexed the Ukrainian territory of Crimea and sponsored an insurrection in the Don basin. The European Union and United States censured Russia, imposed sanctions and held talks, but Russia took no notice. Brussels, it seemed, could not even mobilise its members to defend a prospective partner.

The third front in Europe's war, in the Mediterranean, began with problems of mobility. Middle Eastern refugees had been seeking asylum in Europe since the War on Terror began in 2001, but Syria's collapse into violence drove the number up well above 2 million in 2015–16. Migration on such a scale produced predictable problems. Some immigrants seemed uninterested in assimilation. Others (particularly in Germany) committed violent crimes. A handful were actual terrorists. But in the febrile atmosphere of 2015 British Eurosceptics interpreted the Union's inability to control mobility on its borders as a threat to identity, prosperity, security and sovereignty. Only 81,000 migrants – about one in thirty – made it all the way to the Isles, but Nigel Farage, the charismatic new leader of the UK Independence Party (UKIP), saw an opportunity. Brussels's incompetence, he told the *Telegraph*, had 'opened the door to an exodus of biblical proportions'. Middle Eastern terrorists, he continued, 'say they will use the migrant tide to flood Europe with 500,000 of their own jihadists. I think we'd better listen. Five hundred thousand may not be realistic. But what if it's 5,000? What if it's 500?'

UKIP steadily lured discontented, anti-metropolitan provincial voters away from the Tories, its support rising from one vote in thirty in the 2010 general election to one in eight in 2015. Campaigning for the Conservative leadership in 2006, Cameron had promised to stop 'banging on about Europe', because voters cared more about jobs, schools and the National Health Service. As late as 2013, according to one of his oldest friends, he still viewed grassroots Tory Europhobes as 'mad, swivel-eyed loons'. Faced by the threat from his right, however, he decided to humour the loons. Speaking at Bloomberg London that January, he agreed to an in/out vote on Europe. 'It is time for the British people to have their say.'

When Cameron shared his thinking with Nick Clegg, leader of the Liberal Democrats and his deputy prime minister in a coalition government, Clegg called him 'crazy' to take such risks just to win voters back from UKIP, but Cameron insisted that 'I have to do this. It is a party management issue.' His gamble struck Ken Clarke, the most Europhile Conservative MP, as 'reckless beyond belief'; but Iain Duncan Smith, a former Tory leader, saw method in Cameron's madness. With another election due in 2015, he said, 'I have no doubt that the thinking in Downing Street [. . .] was that the outcome was likely to be a coalition government and [. . .] that this referendum would be traded away.'

In fact, Cameron saw potential upsides in a referendum. Europe's crises since 2010 had revealed what wide gaps remained between London and Brussels on finance, federalism, foreign policy and national sovereignty. French and German politicians openly talked of taxing London's euro-denominated financial transactions. Britain needed to do something, and quickly, before treaty changes advanced too far. The threat of a referendum, especially one that might never actually happen, promised to kill two birds with one stone, rallying

Conservatives behind Cameron and signalling to Brussels that he was serious.

When I had an opportunity in 2018 to ask Nick Clegg about Cameron's strategy, he just laughed, giving the impression that the former prime minister's idea of long-term thinking had been wondering what to have for dinner as opposed to lunch. But some Conservative leaders were definitely thinking hard about the changing meanings of geography at the global scale. Concern was mounting in the early 2010s that Britain's relationship with the United States was no longer as special as it had been when Blair and Bush went to war together. Anglo-American co-ordination over the Syrian and Libyan civil wars was poor, and the *Guardian*'s Simon Tisdall was probably right to say that 'modern US presidents view Britain as a moderately useful client state, junior military partner and gateway to Europe'. In light of China's post-2009 advances, this struck some – especially Cameron's chancellor (almost, some said, his co-prime minister), George Osborne – as a good time to widen the circle of Britain's friends.

Osborne urged that 'Britain should run towards China', and financiers positively sprinted. London's HSBC (the Hongkong and Shanghai Banking Corporation, created in the heyday of the nineteenth-century world-system) floated the first non-Chinese renminbi-denominated bonds in 2012, and the City quickly overtook Singapore as the main clearing centre for renminbi outside the People's Republic. The Bank of England began renminbi sterling swaps with the People's Bank of China in 2013, and the next year Britain issued the first non-Chinese sovereign renminbi bond, valued at £300 million.

There was certainly some resistance to Osborne's goal of becoming China's 'best partner in the West'. The chancellor emphasised what China could do for British prosperity, but the prime minister worried more about identity, and especially human rights. He caused deep offence in 2012 by meeting with Tibet's Dalai Lama, in exile from China: 'They [the Chinese] like George but they don't particularly like David', one official told journalists. Cameron swallowed his reservations and accepted billions of pounds from the China National Nuclear Corporation for a new reactor, even though Americans had blacklisted one of the Corporation's units for diverting nuclear technology to military uses. Theresa May, the home secretary, was briefed by her special adviser in 2015 that her party's leaders were 'selling our

Figure 11.9. And I would rather be anywhere else . . . Xi Jinping
and David Cameron looking acutely uncomfortable over pints
of pale ale at the Plough at Cadsden. Soon after, the Chinese
company SinoFortone Investment bought the pub.

national security to China' – but upon becoming prime minister a
year later she approved the deal anyway. When Washington opposed
Britain joining the Asia Infrastructure Investment Bank, branding it a
Chinese challenge to American-sponsored institutions, Osborne and
Cameron took no notice.

The cosying up culminated in Xi Jinping's state visit to London
late in 2015. When I walked through Soho's Chinatown just a couple
of days after he left, it looked as though it had been quite a party.
Not content with a state dinner at Buckingham Palace, Xi had also
gone to the pub with David Cameron. Neither man looked entirely
in his element there (Figure 11.9), but China's ambassador still called
it the beginning of a 'golden time' (Cameron preferred 'golden era').
Britain was feeling its way towards a new role, securely within the
European Union but drawing on Chinese as well as American friendship to balance its relations with Brussels.

But then came the vote.

The End of the World

The referendum undid everything. Few had seriously expected Brexit to win: even Nigel Farage, as he cast his own vote, conceded that 'it looks like [staying in] will edge it'. When it didn't, the markets went mad, Cameron resigned and four years of political chaos began. No one, apparently, had thought about what to do next.

Initial reactions were extreme. Donald Tusk, the president of the European Council, told a German newspaper that 'As a historian I fear Brexit could be the beginning of the destruction not only of the EU but also Western political civilisation in its entirety'. As a long-term historian, however, I can't agree. Brexit mattered, but it wasn't the end of the world. It was just the latest move in an 8,000-year-long game. It deepened divisions and exposed dishonesty and incompetence within the ruling class; yet Britain had been just as divided, and its elites equally duplicitous, in plenty of earlier arguments over geostrategy. The infighting of the 2010s was mild compared with what followed the Peace of Utrecht in 1713 or the fall of the Palatinate in 1619, let alone the 1534 Englexit. No one tossed Theresa May in the Tower or stuck David Cameron's head on a pike, attractive though some readers might find such images. Were Boris Johnson and Jeremy Corbyn really wickeder than Walpole or Cardinal Wolsey? Probably not. Slippery as he may have been, the Brexiteers' strategist Dominic Cummings had nothing on Henry VIII's fixer Thomas Cromwell.

Political leaders had to scramble to improvise new policies in the late 2010s because Brexit abruptly scuppered all ongoing efforts to come to terms with the Money Map. Since the 1990s Western elites had been working with China. Floating in private planes above the three mountains of money, a new, more globalised elite – the notorious Davos Men – prospered mightily by linking the peaks together. British politicians had initially been slow to recognise the new reality; between 1997 and 2010 the two Labour prime ministers managed only three visits to China, as compared with ten for Germany's chancellors. But British financiers, technologists and manufacturers had run well ahead of the politicians, thoroughly entangling the nation's wealth with China's. Between 1989 and 2015, despite the 2008–9 crisis, most Britons saw their real incomes rise by half, even as globalisation simultaneously lifted a billion of the world's poorest people (mostly in Asia) out of extreme poverty. It was an extraordinary record.

But not a perfect one. The benefits of cheap Chinese credit and

underwear were widely spread, which sometimes made them difficult to see, whereas competition from low-wage Asian workers was
often concentrated in specific industries, turning some places into
black spots of bankruptcy and unemployment. All the talk of golden
eras was jarringly inconsistent with many families' post-2009 realities
of homes worth less than what they had paid for them and dead-end
jobs. Across much of the West, people whose living standards were
stagnating (or worse) or who just disliked globalism were being persuaded, or were persuading themselves, to blame their problems on
enemies of all kinds – foreigners, immigrants and especially Davos
Men. These citizens of the world, the argument ran, were too comfortable with mobility, lacked national identity, cared little about
security or sovereignty and only boosted prosperity for people like
themselves.

My wife's uncle Bob, an early supporter of Donald Trump,
explained the logic to me over coffee one morning in 2016. He lived
near the Mexican border in Tucson, Arizona. He didn't for a moment
believe Trump's claims that he would lock Hillary Clinton up and
make Mexico pay for a border wall, he said, but he did think that
Trump was 'the only politician who's ever said what I think'. A billion-
aire could lead an anti-Establishment crusade so long as he convinced
voters that the Establishment was not a clique of malefactors of great
wealth but a gaggle of over-educated metropolitans with suspiciously
flexible views on race, gender and religion. At home, such people
must be humbled; abroad, they must be shunned, no matter if they
claimed to be friends. And Trump was not alone in saying this. One
presidential candidate after another followed him, turning first on
the Trans-Pacific Partnership, the Transatlantic Trade and Investment
Partnership and the North American Free Trade Agreement, and
then on the United Nations, NATO, the World Trade Organization
and the European Union itself.

Britain had its own version of this. In England the obvious
scapegoats were Brussels and its claret-swilling, home-grown fellow
travellers who had done down Margaret Thatcher. Saving Thatcher's
legacy therefore required breaking Thatcher's Law and extricating
Britain from the Continent – just as, the thinking often ran, Britain had
extricated itself in 1940, 1805 and 1588. Britain must rebuild ties with
English-speaking peoples of the United States and CANZUK. The
platform bore more than a passing resemblance to eighteenth-century

Toryism, and Jacob Rees-Mogg, one of its leading proponents, in fact rejoiced in the nickname 'the Honourable Member for the Eighteenth Century'. When given their say in 2016, 47 per cent of English and Welsh voters wanted to stay in Europe, but 53 per cent wanted to go.

In the north and west, by contrast, the obvious scapegoat was England, and the obvious response was the ancient one of outflanking it by keeping it tied down in Europe. In Northern Ireland 56 per cent said stay and just 44 per cent go; in Scotland it was a crushing 62 to 38. These Celtic positions also had eighteenth- and nineteenth-century analogies, this time with Whig administrations. In an irony Gladstone would have appreciated, leaving the European Union raised the spectre of the United Kingdom's dissolution and the unification of an independent Ireland. But weight of numbers (as usual) favoured the lowlands, producing a national vote of 48 per cent for staying, 52 per cent for going. A near-run thing, but as Cameron had said all along, 'leave means leave'.

I will not refight the referendum here. That ship has sailed. I do want to emphasise, though, how little in either side's argument was new. The fact that many Remainers were relatively young, educated, prosperous and/or widely travelled did not mean they were all spineless, elitist and/or rootless, just as the fact that many Leavers were older, less educated, had lower incomes and were less well travelled did not mean they were all ignorant, racist and/or out of date. For at least 2,000 years, and probably for 8,000, Islanders who worried primarily about sovereignty while seeing mobility as a threat and identities as relatively fixed had tended to prefer insularity to proximity, while those who worried primarily about prosperity while seeing mobility as an opportunity and identities as relatively fluid had preferred proximity to insularity. The underlying strategic arguments had not changed.

But the details had, and the devil was in them. The Polish plumbers who migrated to England after 2004 had little in common with the farmers who arrived after 4200 BCE, the metal-users who came after 2400 BCE or the Anglo-Saxons and Vikings of the fifth and ninth centuries CE. Jean Monnet was not Adolf Hitler; Maastricht was not Munich; the twenty-first-century Brexit was not the sixteenth-century Englexit. The Armada was not coming, although Chinese underwear was.

Beyond Biding and Hiding

For more than thirty years after Mao's death Chinese leaders bent over backwards to accommodate their economic revolution to the Western world-system, even softening the way they described it from 'peaceful rise' to 'peaceful development', out of fears that 'rise' sounded threatening. The West welcomed China into the World Trade Organization and turned a blind eye to Beijing's regular infractions of its rules, confident that economic engagement would benefit everyone.

That confidence collapsed in the mid-2010s. According to legend, when Keynes was once accused of inconsistency, he retorted: 'When the facts change, I change my mind. What do you do, sir?' When the facts started changing in 2009, everyone started changing their minds. In the West, accommodating Chinese cheating began to feel like appeasement; in the East, submitting to American rules felt like extending China's century of humiliation. In the sunny 1990s Deng Xiaoping had warned his comrades to 'hide your capacities and bide your time', but in the 2010s Xi Jinping was less patient. Enough of biding and hiding, he told the politburo. It was time to 'make China's voice heard, and inject more Chinese elements into international rules'.

Diplomatic reshuffling began quickly. In 2011 Barack Obama flew to Australia, increasingly on the front line of Sino-American rivalry. In Canberra he announced a sweeping 'pivot to Asia', summarised by Hillary Clinton, his secretary of state, as involving 'strengthening bilateral security alliances; deepening our working relationships with emerging powers, including China; engaging with regional multilateral institutions; expanding trade and investment; forging a broad-based military presence; and advancing democracy and human rights'. This was not, Obama insisted, containment of the old anti-Soviet kind. However, while promising that 'we'll seek more opportunities for cooperation with Beijing', he added that 'We will do this, even as we continue to speak candidly to Beijing'.

Opinions differ on how much actually changed, but Xi responded two years later by flying to Kazakhstan's capital, Astana (since renamed Nur-Sultan), to say that it, in fact, now marked the front line. Chinese strategists had been complaining for decades that the 'Island Chains', two strings of American allies stretching from Australia to Japan, were Western tools for containing their country. In a bold move Xi outflanked these barriers. He announced a 'Belt and

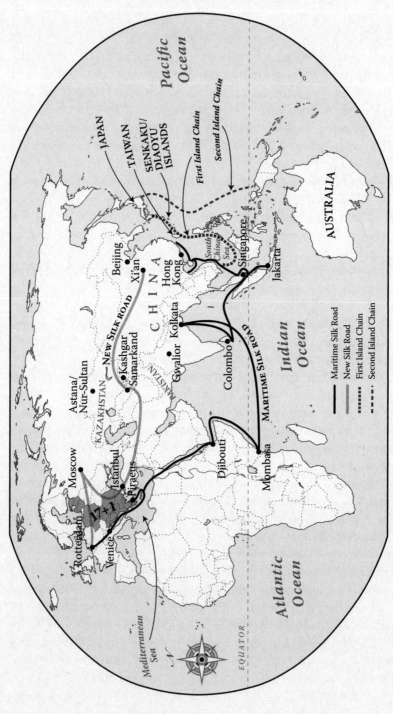

Figure 11.10. Outflanking the Pacific counterscarp: China's Belt and Road Initiative.

Road Initiative', pouring $4–8 trillion into road, rail and air links across Central Asia (Figure 11.10) to revive the ancient Silk Roads which had once linked China to Europe. An Asian Infrastructure Investment Bank was unveiled a month later, with $50 billion in seed capital (which Xi quickly doubled), augmented in 2014 by a Silk Road Fund with a further $40 billion.

The initial response was enthusiastic. Over 100 governments agreed with China's Xinhua News Agency in calling the initiative 'a bid to enhance regional connectivity and embrace a brighter future'. In the United States, however, Xi's move fuelled a backlash. As late as 2014 the journalist and strategist Robert Kaplan had felt that 'Whereas World War II was a moral struggle against fascism, the Cold War a moral struggle against communism, [and] the post-Cold War a moral struggle against genocide [and] terrorism [. . .] China, its suffering dissidents notwithstanding, simply does not measure up as an object of moral fury'. By 2019, however, Americans were telling pollsters that China was their greatest rival.

Moving China from the 'friend' to the 'enemy' column was one of the few things Republicans and Democrats agreed on after Donald Trump's election in 2016. Trump's administration not only imposed tariffs on Chinese goods to encourage American companies to bring supply chains home but also challenged China's legitimacy by accusing its technology firms of spying, calling out oppression in Xinjiang and Hong Kong and blaming Beijing for Covid-19. However, Trump also oversaw a broader rethinking of American policy, which in some ways echoed London's after 1713. Where Georgian Britain had replaced a multilateral, largely Protestant Grand Alliance against France with shifting, bilateral alliances designed to maintain a balance of power, the United States now stepped back from its multilateral, Cold War alliances with democracies. In their place, Trump sought new partners as counterweights to China, including Russia and India, while labelling the European Union the 'biggest foe globally right now'. The subsequent Biden administration disavowed such transactional treatment of allies, but, as Britain learned in the eighteenth century, balance-of-power politics have unintended consequences. On the one hand, worries over American unreliability encouraged Europeans to seek 'strategic autonomy', finding their own balance between Beijing and Washington; on the other, China seized the opportunity to woo long-standing American allies.

This war of words, ongoing as I write (in 2021), is being fought on two main fronts. The first is the Island Chains, where governments have tied themselves in knots to avoid having to choose between China, their most important partner for prosperity, and the United States, most important for security. Australia was among the first to feel the pain. In 2009 a government Defence White Paper had announced unambiguously that 'strategic stability in the region is best underpinned by the continued presence of the United States' – but, as the press gleefully pointed out, after that single sentence putting America first, the rest of the paper revolved around how to cosy up to China. Two years later I had the fascinating experience of speaking at a conference called by the Australian Strategic Policy Institute to straighten out the muddle before the next white paper was due. By the time I left Canberra, Australia's position seemed even less clear than when I had arrived, but when I returned in 2019, this time as a guest of the Australian Army, all ambiguity had gone.* Chinese assertiveness alarmed Australians even more than Trump's transactionalism. Falling in step with the United States, the country opened its own trade war with China, accused Beijing of spying and banned Huawei from its 5G communication networks. No Australian prime minister had set foot in China in three years, and almost everyone I spoke with, from civil servants to Special Forces officers, thought this was as it should be.

The second front is European. There China is exploiting not just Euro-American mistrust but also conflicts between trade-oriented northern governments, indebted southern ones, eastern ones tired of being criticised for human rights abuses and a British government tired of all things European. In 2012 China founded a '16+1' group to channel investment to sixteen Central and East European states, which became 17+1 when Greece joined in 2019. The sums involved were relatively small, but warning bells sounded nevertheless when a Chinese company bought Piraeus (the same Greek port Palmerston had blockaded during the Don Pacifico affair) and when Italy – not (yet) part of the 17+1 – signed on to the Belt and Road Initiative.

---

*I would like to thank (once again) Peter Abigail of the Australian Strategic Policy Institute, Lindsay Adams, Rick Burr, Peter Connolly, Lee Hayward and Al Palazzo of the Australian Army and everyone else involved in my trips for their many kindnesses.

Britain too became a target. 'Brexit is an opportunity for China', one official commented; 'once out of the European Union, Britain will need all the friends it can get.' The *Global Times*, a Chinese government mouthpiece, issued the barely veiled threat that 'becoming a follower of the US is not in line with the UK's aim for a Global Britain'.

In the early 2020s Europe is roughly where Australia – so far from God, so close to China – had been ten years earlier, desperately trying to avoid having to choose one superpower over the other. True to form, Brussels has hedged its bets. 'China', it pronounced in 2019, is 'a cooperative partner with whom the EU has closely aligned objectives', but also 'an economic competitor [. . .] and a systemic rival promoting alternative models of governance'. The result, it continued, 'is a growing appreciation in Europe that the balance of challenges and opportunities presented by China has shifted', heralding 'a further EU policy shift towards a more realistic, assertive, and multi-faceted approach'. By the convoluted standards of Euro-speak, this is fighting talk; yet before 2020 was out Brussels and Beijing had signed – despite intense American opposition – an investment deal that the European Commission called 'the most ambitious agreement that China has ever concluded'.

London perhaps acted true to form too. Having been slow to develop official ties with China in the 2000s, it was then slow to separate itself, welcoming Huawei into its 5G networks as late as January 2020. However, Britain then swung back towards the Macmillan–Thatcher–Blair tradition of following an American lead, announcing its own 'Indo-Pacific tilt' in its 2021 *Integrated Review of Security, Defence, Development and Foreign Policy*. While emphasing the possibilities for Sino-British co-operation, the *Review* also warned that 'China's military modernisation and growing international assertiveness within the Indo-Pacific region and beyond will pose an increasing threat to UK interests'. It is hard not to see parallels with the wild swings in Britain's European policy between the 1950s and 2010s.

These dilemmas are not going away. In her first week in the job, President Joe Biden's press secretary confirmed that 'Strategic competition with China is a defining feature of the 21st century'. If the competition's outlines remain obscure, it is probably, many analysts believe, because China is following what they often call the 'Gerasimov doctrine'. This strategy, named after the Russian army's current chief of staff, is one of deliberate unclarity, of blurry, grey movements in a fog of ambiguity. 'The emphasis in methods of struggle', Gerasimov observed, 'is shifting towards widespread use of political, economic, informational, humanitarian and other non-military measures.' American strategists nowadays talk less of sharply contrasted states of peace and war than of constant, multi-level 'campaigning', and China's actions in the South China Sea, where its coastguards, 'fishermen' and aircraft regularly harass other countries' oil rigs, fishing fleets and even warships, seem to fall very much under this heading. Ignoring the United Nations' law of the seas, Beijing has bullied its neighbours into private deals and has turned uninhabited rocks into artificial islands, complete with naval facilities and runways. None of this is war in traditional terms, but all of it infringes on the sovereignty of other countries. 'Overt use of force', Gerasimov advises, 'often under the guise of peacekeeping and crisis management, occurs only at a certain stage, primarily to achieve definitive success in the conflict.'

Britain and France, like the United States, have sailed warships close to disputed islands and reefs to demonstrate their refusal to be Gerasimoved. There is even talk of re-establishing a British base in the South China Sea, perhaps at Brunei or Singapore. However, pollsters find little enthusiasm for treating the Island Chains as new counterscarps. Britons do worry about China, but less so than Americans or Australians, seeing Russia (which poisoned three British citizens in Salisbury in 2018), North Korea, the Middle East and cyberattacks as more immediate threats. Come what may, including an American intervention against a mainland Chinese invasion of Taiwan, Britain is unlikely to fight. It might move an aircraft carrier from Aden to Hormuz to free an American carrier for service in the Pacific, but the actual shooting will fall to East Asians and (perhaps) Americans.

The RAND Corporation, an American think tank, has for decades been staging simulations of potential conflicts along the islands linking Japan to Singapore. These war games always used to end with American-led coalitions holding their own, but not any more. China's submarines, aircraft and especially missiles improved so much in the late 2010s that American carriers now need to stay nearly 2,000 km from China's coasts to be safe, rendering them largely ineffective. The most recent simulations, modelling conflicts set in the mid-2020s, generally saw the United States getting the worst of it.

Nothing could weaken the American world-system quite as

quickly as a military defeat in the Island Chains; nothing could weaken the Chinese Communist Party's legitimacy quite as quickly as a defeat of its own; and nothing could rush the entire world towards disaster quite as quickly as a serious defeat tempting either side to escalate to nuclear weapons. Given the stakes, only madmen would risk war. Rulers have taken plenty of wilder gambles in the past, but my own guess is that China will continue to play a long game in Taiwan, giving the lure of prosperity time to change opponents' thinking on identity, security and sovereignty. Given the alternatives, we should all hope I am right.

The long game is a long Chinese tradition. For 2,000 years premodern China's emperors used to call their realm *zhongguo*, the 'Middle Kingdom', because it sat at the centre of *tianxia*, 'All under Heaven'. Individual emperors might make mistakes but, left to its own devices, the geographical logic of a Middle Kingdom Map – with the Chinese *zhongguo* at its centre – would always assert itself. Seen from this perspective, modern China's 'century of humiliation' between the 1840s and 1940s was a mere blip, briefer in fact than such earlier aberrations as the Manchu and Mongol conquests. The world is now simply resuming its rightful shape.

In a pair of earlier books, *Why the West Rules – For Now* and *The Measure of Civilisation*, I tried to work out how fast the world might be moving towards a Middle Kingdom Map by calculating what I called an 'index of social development'. Basically, this measured Eastern and Western societies' abilities to master their physical and intellectual environments to get things done, going all the way back to the end of the last ice age. For many millennia the highest development scores were always in the Middle Eastern–Mediterranean region, but about fifteen centuries ago Chinese development pulled ahead. It stayed there for 1,200 years; but once Europeans burst out of the Hereford Map, Western scores came surging back. By my calculations, Western development overtook Eastern in the fateful year of 1776, pulling further and further ahead across the nineteenth and twentieth centuries – until, after 1945, the East began closing the gap again. If we project the trends of the last hundred years forwards, the arithmetic reveals that, other things being equal, Eastern development will once again catch up with Western in the year 2103.

This was a rather tongue-in-cheek prediction, given the number of things that might prevent other things being equal (global warming, pandemics, war, technology, domestic politics – the list is endless). Yet this crude projection has its uses, above all in forcing us to confront the elephant in the room: that Western dominion looks likely to last another generation, and probably another two, but not another three. Come 2103 (or thereabouts), the game will be up. For almost everyone on earth, the twenty-first century is going to be about learning to live with what comes their way from China.

Zeno's Dog

Some twenty-three centuries ago a Cypriot named Zeno moved to Athens and set up shop as a philosopher. His followers came to be called Stoics, because they met in a shady, colonnaded stoa around Athens's marketplace, where Zeno explained life to them in homely analogies. Imagine, he liked to say, that you are a puppy, tied to the back of a cart. Puppies have free will – in abundance – so, when the cart starts moving, you are able to decide what to do. You can trot along with the cart, enjoying your run and perhaps catching scraps dropped by the people in it; or you can race off in a different direction; or you can refuse to move at all, in which case you'll be dragged by the neck or even run over. None of us, Zeno insisted, is strong enough to ignore the vast impersonal forces that pull us around – but neither are we so weak as to lack all choice. We are neither fate's pawns nor its masters. The secret of success is seeing which way the cart is going and working out how to make the most of it.

Big history shows that geography is the key to working out what the cart is doing. We experience the cart's movement through its impact on identity, mobility, prosperity, security and sovereignty, but if we want to understand what is actually happening, we need to dig down to the maps. Only by observing how technology and organisation determine the size of the stage we act on can we, as individuals or communities, identify the most important actors and find the most rewarding role for ourselves. With varying degrees of success, this is what Britons have been doing for the entire 8,000 years since the Isles physically formed. For most of that time Britain's stage was limited to Western Europe and was dominated by actors off to the south and east. For people in what eventually became England, history was largely about dealing with what came their way from the Continent;

for those further north and west, it was about what came their way from England. The stage was stretched towards the Mediterranean by Rome, reoriented towards the Baltic after the empire fell and then enlarged enormously after Columbus and Cabot escaped from the Hereford Map, but at every point it has been up to Islanders themselves to work out which way to run, and how fast.

This is what the great strategic debates of the last half-millennium – over Catholicism, the balance of power, splendid isolation, imperial preference, the Atlantic alliance, the European Union – have all ultimately been about, and it is what arguments will continue to be about in the twenty-first century. After pulling the puppy westwards across the Atlantic for more than a century, history's cart is now heading east again. The question which should have been on the referendum in 2016 was not what to do about Brussels. It was what to do about Beijing.

What made the wrangling over Brexit such a disaster was that Leavers and Remainers consumed a crucial half-decade in arguing over resolutely short-term, superficial issues of identity, mobility, prosperity, security and sovereignty while leaving long-term geography least spoken of. That error allowed both camps to indulge in a shared delusion that Europe still filled the stage. The political scientist Kerry Brown tells a revealing (or perhaps horrifying) story about giving a public lecture on Anglo-Chinese relations shortly before the 2016 vote. 'The audience listened to news and analysis of the fundamental rearrangement of the power structures and realignment of geopolitical forces in the world they were living in with an almost preternatural calm', he says, while just metres away 'a debate on the UK and the European Union in one of the neighbouring rooms nearly ended in a riot'. History's cart was rolling eastwards, but Zeno's dog was running the wrong way.

At roughly the same time that Zeno was theorising in Athens, the authors of the Indian epic the *Mahabharata* – living through an era when hundreds of separate city-states in the Ganges Valley were being consolidated into a few empires – proposed that international relations are governed by a 'Law of the Fishes': that in times of drought the big fish eat the little ones. In the twenty-first century the whole world is consolidating. We are living through a megadrought. Today's little fish, a former deputy secretary-general of the United Nations observes, are 'start[ing] to think in a defensive way about blocs'. The best way to avoid being eaten by one big fish, governments are concluding, is by attaching themselves to another (hopefully less threatening) big fish. Yet this is just the moment, he adds, that Britain has chosen to cast itself 'adrift without a bloc'.

Consolidation is not a new story. A European fish has been eating Britain since 1973, and an American one since 1916. They have just been doing it quietly. Earlier big fish – Romans, Saxons, Vikings, Normans – tore into the Isles like Jaws, and Hitler or Stalin would have done much the same; but twentieth-century Washington and Brussels acted more like shoals of minnows. Little by little, they nibbled away at British sovereignty and identity until governments in London had less say over the Isles' prosperity and security (and, in Europe's case, mobility) than their counterparts in Washington and Brussels.

The 2016 debates focused obsessively on whether European nibbling was good or bad for Britain, but would have done better to ask whether it was good or bad relative to what a Britain outside the European Union would experience from China. Some analysts, particularly Americans, infer from Beijing's behaviour in Xinjiang, Tibet and Hong Kong that Jaws is again attacking. 'If we bend the knee now', Donald Trump's secretary of defense said in 2020, 'our children's children may be at the mercy of the Chinese Communist Party.' Other observers (particularly in China) insist that China barely even qualifies as a minnow. The real issue, says one financier, is that Westerners are 'so used to your supremacy. Your being treated nicely by everyone. It hurts to think, *Okay, now we have to be on equal footing to other people.*' Somewhere in the middle, and frankly much more convincing, is Kerry Brown's measured assessment that 'Chinese interests in the UK fall into three broad categories: investment, finance and intellectual partnership (the latter inclusive of technology and expertise)'. The accountants are coming – but there will be no Chinese Armada shooting its way up the Channel, no Boris Johnson rallying the troops at Tilbury. China will be a nibbler too.

Nibbling with Chinese characteristics will in many ways look rather like the American and European versions, particularly as regards prosperity. British incomes quadrupled in real terms between the first tranche of Marshall Plan aid in 1948 and voting to leave the European Union in 2016. Most economists expect Brexit to hurt prosperity (the Bank of England thinks the economy will be 3–4 per cent smaller by 2030 than it would have been otherwise), but its champions counter that a nation freed from Brussels will reinvent itself as 'Global Britain'. Rather than being 'confined to the immediate European hinterland as we see the rise of new powers', Boris Johnson suggests, 'we should make a new approach to policy-making, as regards China'. The plan is that by turning into what critics mock as 'Singapore-on-Thames' – a low-tariff, low-tax and low-regulation hub for global commerce – Britain will generate more than enough prosperity to offset the post-Brexit red ink.

Global Britain will very likely face fierce European competition for the same Chinese trade and American antagonism to leaning eastwards, and even if it weathers these successfully, the consequences may not be to everyone's liking. Not least, running to China seems certain to boost mobility, such a red line for Brexiteers. Some of the forces driving mobility are beyond Britain's control: the World Bank expects 140 million climate refugees to flee Latin America, Africa and Central and South Asia by 2050, with Britain one of their preferred destinations. But becoming Global Britain will also require further, smaller flows of skilled, highly educated immigrants from trading partners. These have, in fact, already begun. European migration to Britain fell by three-quarters between the Brexit vote and the coronavirus outbreak in 2020, but non-European migration increased enough in this period to cancel it out. Most of the newcomers were Chinese, and most of these Chinese were students. British law limits their postgraduate residence to two years, but fully half say they hope to stay longer. The students overwhelmingly settle in cities, chiefly London, and if Chinese business practices in other countries are any guide, tens of thousands of skilled professionals will follow in their footsteps. Some will end up in connected northern cities such as Edinburgh and Manchester, and a few, perhaps, in less connected ones; but Singapore-on-Thames will surely widen the gaps between the south-east and everywhere else.

Global Britain also seems likely to revive the kind of anxieties about sovereignty that dogged George Osborne's China policy in the early 2010s. Chinese diplomats regularly dismiss such concerns, arguing that its foreign policy is different from those of earlier great powers such as, Britain and the United States. While these nineteenth- and twentieth-century giants created unequal world-systems guaranteed by chains of military bases, China's foreign policies are

Confucian, and therefore non-coercive. However, calling a policy Confucian means no more than calling it Christian or Muslim. There is so much in the Bible, Koran and Confucian classics that these labels can cover almost any sin. Ancient and medieval Confucians had few qualms about using force for ends they deemed virtuous, and created profoundly hierarchical empires. It is hard to disagree with the strategist Robert Kaplan that, whatever its diplomats may say, in practice China is an 'über-realist power', pursuing advantage in ways that Palmerston would have recognised.

China has already shown what its influence might mean for the rule of law. In 2014 the Communist Party devoted a plenary session of its Congress to the topic. In Washington or London any such event would have involved discussions of how law constrains government action, but in Beijing it focused on the law's role in enforcing the Party's will – which Xi Jinping promptly extended into a call for 'the rule of law in international relations'. It was perhaps this kind of law that China's ambassador to London had in mind when he warned Britain in 2020 that 'We want to be your friend [. . .] but if you want to make China a hostile country, you will have to bear the consequences'. Being eaten by China may well compromise sovereignty much more than American and European nibbling did in the twentieth century. Like Australia in the 2010s, Britain in the 2020s may find itself having to choose between its established American security partner and an increasingly assertive Chinese economic partner.

The most extreme outcome would be a British decision to abandon the American alliance and make China its chief security partner. As of the early 2020s, this looks every bit as implausible as jumping ship from the American security system to the Soviet one did during the Cold War – but if China succeeds in breaking or even just outflanking the Pacific counterscarp, the shock to Britain's strategic assumptions will be as severe as anything since the rise of the German mountain of money in the late nineteenth century. Back then, Britain quickly converted its arch-rivals France and Russia into allies and started down the path towards a long-lasting Anglo-American partnership. So long as Palmerston's law – that Britain's interests are eternal while its friends are not – retains any force, it will be rash to rule out a similar strategic reshuffle within the next thirty years, turning China into an ally and the United States and European Union into rivals.

The biggest barrier to such a pivot might be identity. Shared history, culture and language bind Britain to the other English-speaking peoples, and the World Values Survey's 'culture map', compiled from thousands of responses to opinion polls, puts Britain and China at opposite extremes. Despite China's economic triumphs, its authoritarianism is just not very attractive overseas. The Soft Power 30 index (which defines soft power as 'the ability to achieve objectives through attraction and persuasion') ranked China twenty-seventh in the world in 2019, with a score of 51.25 out of 100, dragged down by widespread worries about its political system. Britain, by contrast, came in at number two, with 79.47 points, having lost its number one spot to France, largely over the seemingly endless Brexit wrangling. Efforts to project Chinese soft power in the West, such as the more than 500 Confucius Institutes established on university campuses, have had mixed results at best.

The British businessman Martin Sorrell once predicted that 'Chinese and computer code are the only two languages the next generation should need', but few Britons seem convinced, at least about the former. Out of more than 270,000 schoolchildren sitting A-level exams in 2018, only 3,334 took Mandarin. They slightly outnumbered the just over 3,000 takers for German, but Spanish and French each had twice as many students. Only one state school in twelve even offers Mandarin classes, but one in three independent schools does so – another sign, perhaps, of a prosperous, mobile, Sinophile and Europhile elite pulling away from everyone else, fragmenting current senses of British identity and opening spaces for alternatives.

'British identity' itself is, of course, a relatively recent invention, which hardly existed before the 1707 Anglo-Scottish Act of Union. Forging a sense of Britishness was crucial to the quest to close England's back door, but as that strategic imperative faded across the twentieth century, so too did the rationale for a shared insular identity. Polls suggest that half of all Britons expect Scotland to leave the Union by 2030, and almost half of Northern Ireland's population now favours reunification with the south. The geographical logic behind the Franco-Scottish Auld Alliance of 1295 and the Saxon-Pict-Scotti 'Barbarian Conspiracy' of 367 has not gone away. For Scotland and Ireland, and perhaps Wales too, climbing on to the European Union's mountain of money could be the most sensible way to deal with their bigger English neighbour. Isolated and encircled – if that is how things turn out – the English may well wonder whether climbing the Chinese mountain is their own best option, even at the cost of becoming what Kerry Brown calls 'a new kind of tributary state, economically, and eventually politically "owned" by China, undermining its own values, and driven purely by mercenary motives'. Unattractive as it sounds, this may be among the least bad strategies left by mid-century if England's freedom of manoeuvre keeps contracting.

But, as so often, 'if' is the operative word. There is more to life than money. Britons in the past regularly weighed identity, mobility, security and sovereignty more heavily than prosperity, and may yet do so again. And in any case, the most important decisions will be taken far from London. Perhaps the United States and European Union will come together to contain China. Or perhaps the Europeans will join China to undermine American hegemony. Or, unlikely as it looks in the early 2020s, Americans and Chinese may divide the world between them, leaving Europe out in the cold. Any number of intermediate positions are possible, each presenting its own opportunities and challenges. Britain might double down on its old American alliance, or offer itself as a new point of junction between American, European and Chinese circles. Then again, it might be tempted by something like the 'Fortress Britain' philosophy championed by Labour leftists in the 1970s (and again, some suspected, in the late 2010s). It could even return to the European Union. After all, that is what England did in 1553, nineteen years after its Englexit from the Original European Union – before exiting again just five years later.

There are always options, and if Britain's 8,000-year history teaches anything, it is surely that the Islanders in the past have risen to plenty of challenges bigger than this one. The first step is always to face the facts as they are rather than as we would like them to be. Every actor in the twenty-first-century drama confronts the same question: what would Zeno's dog do? Big history does not provide a pre-packaged answer, because that is not how history works, but it does force us to focus on the thing least spoken of – that the meanings of geography are changing faster than ever. As the global stage expands and tilts eastwards and the cart rolls across it, the time has come to recognise that Beijing, not Brussels, is the issue. Distracted by the Brexit debate, Zeno's dog has spent a critical half-decade running the wrong way.

In 1910, another moment when wealth and power were moving

rapidly from one part of the world to another, the American poet Ella Wheeler Wilcox sent a sharp message across the Atlantic:

> *England, awake! from dreams of what has been,*
> *Look on what is, and put the past away.*

The map has changed since Wilcox's day, but her point has not. Britain, awake. 2103 will be here sooner than you think.

12

CAN'T GO HOME AGAIN, 2017

In the spring of 2015, 'in the quiet before the presidential primary season', the journalist and strategic analyst Robert Kaplan decided to drive across the United States, 'to look at the America that exists beyond the reductions of television cameras and reporters' questions'. He wanted, he said, 'to see what is out there before I reflect on America's place in the world and construct a strategy for how to deal with it'. This would require drawing on both his journalistic and his strategic backgrounds, he explained. On the one hand, a 'journalist constantly talks to people; what they tell him helps shape his experience and perceptions'; on the other, 'an analyst thinks about what is not being said but what is obvious'. His plan, he decided, should be 'to overhear what people talk about when among friends and acquaintances – I want to understand their true concerns and preoccupations – and consider that along with everything else that I observe'.

In the summer of 2017, almost exactly a year after the referendum, I decided to do something similar in England, starting off in Remainer Westminster and dropping in on Brexiteering villages, towns and cities across the land. Having spent the last thirty years overseas, I hoped, I might even see the country with fresher eyes than locals who were already sick and tired of all the arguments. And, because this is still just about possible in England (unlike the United States), I would use public transport rather than a car. Nothing tells you more about people than how they behave on a bus.

That turned out to be an inspired decision. You see so much more through a train window than from behind a steering wheel. You see just how far unbuttoning has gone – the casual obscenity, the graffiti, the litter left on shared seats – but you also see how much survives of the spirit of *Brief Encounter*. Travellers still form orderly queues, wait their turn and thank each other. The young still offer their seats to the elderly. On one trip (admittedly, this was ten years earlier), my train was cancelled because someone had committed suicide on the line. As we all got off, one passenger grumbled loudly about the inconvenience. Another quietly reminded him that we should perhaps be thinking of the victim's family, or even of the train driver. Englishness can still be magnificent.

Predictably, one of my stops was Stoke-on-Trent. It is just the sort of place Kaplan had sought out in the United States, largely ignored by pundits until it was rechristened the 'Brexit capital' in 2016. Stoke is apparently endlessly forgettable. It is neither one thing nor the other, equally lacking in bubbling cosmopolitan elites and seething urban underclasses. It is just part of the rather dull lump in the middle of the country, where not many people want to go. When supporters of London's Chelsea Football Club wanted to show in 2021 just how much they opposed joining an elite European 'Super League', they made their point by carrying placards saying 'We want our cold nights in Stoke'. When the government announced that same spring that it planned to transfer some administrators from London to my home town, an editor at *The Times* thought that the appropriate way to word this was 'Hundreds of Home Office Civil Servants Face Being Moved to Stoke'. Stoke rarely sets pulses racing.

Stoke is a product of its geography. It lies just north of the line separating the flat, fertile, relatively warm and dry lowlands of the south-east from the broken, thin-soiled, cooler and rainier uplands of the north and west. It sits squarely in the Midland Gap, the 50-km-wide valley dividing Wales's Cambrian Mountains from northern England's Pennines (Figure 12.1). It has no particular strategic importance, and not much of note has happened there. On maps of archaeological and historical sites the Midland Gap is often a blank, left behind long before anyone thought up the term. That only really changed in the 1760s, when Josiah Wedgwood industrialised the region's ceramic production (Stoke is often called 'The Potteries') and canal-builders linked it to national markets.

Even then, Stoke remained stubbornly in between. It was certainly not rural, but neither was it an urban powerhouse like nearby Birmingham or Manchester. It was neither a cultural wasteland nor a trendsetter. It produced one great literary figure, the novelist Arnold Bennett, but he did his most important work in Paris. Nor did it excel in the thing the locals most cared about: Stoke City Football Club

Figure 12.1. The unremarkable middle: the city of Stoke-
on-Trent in the rolling countryside of the Midland
Gap, seen from Penkhull New Road, 2014.

('the Potters') was one of the twelve teams that founded the Football
League in 1888, but remains the only one never to have won the league
championship or the FA Cup. The greatest footballer of all time – Sir
Stanley Matthews – was a Potter but, like Bennett, had to leave Stoke
to win medals. (He was also a true Englishman, never once being sent
off or cautioned for foul play in his thirty-five-year career.)

What Stoke did have was a rock-solid working class, although its
core industries – pottery, steel, coal – were long dead by 2009. According to Stoke Central's former MP, Tristram Hunt, the recession had a
'Detroit-style impact'. A decade on, Stoke's unemployment rate was
pretty typical for England, but more than one job in five was classified
'routine', meaning driving, labouring or cleaning. So many houses
had been abandoned by 2013 that the city council started selling them
off for £1 each (although purchasers did have to commit £30,000
to renovations). Of the Potters who turned out for the referendum
(Stoke Central has one of the country's lowest voting rates), 69 per
cent said Go.

Yet the moment you leave the train station – a grand nineteenth-century pile – the 'left-behind' story starts feeling like a bad fit. The bus stops are still there out front (even if the great fume-belching red monsters of my youth have been replaced by nippy little electric vehicles), but much of Station Road has been taken over by taxis. Even on a quiet Wednesday morning I counted more than forty drivers waiting for fares, and they had a steady stream of takers. This was new: I don't remember seeing cabs at all in the 1970s, other than the odd one outside the faded North Stafford Hotel. They give a strangely prosperous first impression of the Brexit capital.

Crossing the Trent and Mersey Canal (one of the glories of eighteenth-century engineering) and climbing up Shelton Old Road somewhat dispels that perception. The little terraced houses along its side streets had never been the city's most desirable, but I now counted almost half of them boarded up, often tagged with graffiti. Steel bars protected their windows; barbed wire topped the walls where their backyards butted up to alleys. I spotted three men talking to themselves, one slumped against the door of the Redemption Community Centre. This was new too. Yet just across from this depressing scene was something else I'd never seen before: a brightly painted hostelry with a sign proclaiming 'Stoked', a gastropub specialising in Asian fusion cuisine. In my day it was a hostelry called 'The Black's Head'.

On his American journey Kaplan described himself as driving away from the East Coast's 'world of slim people on low-carb diets with stylish clothes [. . .] a world where both skin tone and sexual orientation are not singular but multiple, and celebrated for that' into a Middle America that was 'a vast and alternative universe all its own: of downtrodden, unpretty, unprogressive, often obese people, but there all the same'. England may be less extreme, but the similarities, like the people, are there all the same. The body shapes, the baseball caps and sagging tracksuits, the cigarettes and the sheer number of locals who apparently had nothing much to do all revealed Stoke-on-Trent as a different world from frenetic, wired London. On some streets I saw more police than shoppers, and every other outlet seemed to be a Poundsaver or similar bargain-basement outlet.

But once again there were surprising contrasts. In places richer than Stoke, residents regularly resist the creeping intrusion of chain restaurants and cafés, but in the Potteries these businesses feel like little embassies from more connected countries. Within a couple of minutes I saw not just a Starbucks but also representatives of the British chains Costa Coffee and Caffè Nero, plus a Potteries looka-like called Caffè Java. No one would mistake these for the equivalent places in Covent Garden or Mayfair – the staff and customers looked too much like Kaplan's 'vast and alternative universe' for that, as well as being too friendly – but there were still plenty of people paying £2 for an espresso. There was even a smattering of skinny hipsters connecting to the free wifi and talking excitedly about gadgets and foreign holidays.

All this was new too, and stepping back into the sunshine (perhaps also new, an upside to global warming), it struck me that the biggest change since the 1970s is that Stoke has had an upgrade. Potters have not entirely given up or been left behind. Stoke was a grim, rough town forty years ago, and much of that persists. However, it is also livelier, more colourful, more connected and – for many – more pros-perous than it used to be. Until Covid killed it in 2021, Stoke had its own literary festival. It still has a magnificent Monkey Forest, where you can sit around with macaques. It might all look provincial to Lon-doners, but people are making their own worlds, and enjoying them.

This being Britain, the ultimate test was of course the pubs. Most of the ones I remembered were still there, but cleaner and with a wider selection of fare on offer. The Alma, whither my sister and I would be dispatched half a century ago to fetch my grandad home for his Sunday dinner, had changed beyond all recognition. In the old days the fug of cigarette smoke made it hard to see across the bar to where a line of dark-suited steelworkers stood drinking their pints in silence. Now it is all primary colours and craft ales.

The Jolly Potters in Hartshill, where I used to drink myself forty-some years ago, was even more revealing. In the late 1970s it was a distinctly hard place, where the clientele of potters might be anything but jolly. Now, though, it positively shines. Its enthusiastic young landlady gave me a tour of the beer garden, children's play area, pizza oven and on-site ice-cream maker – all extremely new – and poured me a couple of very good pints of Bass.

Sitting in the garden, I followed Kaplan's advice to be 'a pas-sionate eavesdropper'. The afternoon drinkers were not angry or frightened about globalisation. They were not denouncing Europe, the government or anyone else. Like the Americans Kaplan over-heard, their conversations were about lost keys, babies and used cars.

Figure 12.2. Signs of the times: the Spode works, which closed
in 2008 after more than two centuries in business. The 'China'
sign above the window, memorialising Josiah Spode's discovery
of the secret of translucent porcelain – 'china' – here in 1813,
turned out to be prophetic in all the wrong ways.

No one sounded left behind – not even the parole officer explaining
at length on his mobile phone why his client had failed to turn up for
a job interview.

Having studied the pubs thoroughly, I weaved my way back
towards the station. According to the Domesday Book, England's
Norman conquerors had turned the slopes below Hartshill into a
deer park, from which it takes its name. In the 1970s the park was a
gigantic dumping ground for the city's pot-banks, piled high with tens
of millions of fragments of misfired bathtubs, plates and roof tiles.
(One of my first archaeological experiences was working on finds
excavated from a dump belonging to the Whieldon factory, where
Wedgwood had been apprenticed in the 1750s.) Since 2005, though,
Hartshill Park has been remade with funds from the National Lottery.
Well-groomed paths now curl through dense vegetation, opening up

Figure 12.3. Dream factory: Josiah Wedgwood brought up to
date at his works in Barlaston (what remains of Wedgwood
is now owned by the Finnish company Fiskars).

every so often on to little follies made from abandoned pot-banks. It's
a delightful, whimsical spot in the middle of the city. I was sad to step
out from its shade on to the main road. Almost immediately a shaven-
headed middle-aged man, fragrant with stale beer, lurched out of a
doorway. Glaring at me, he muttered something incomprehensible
but vaguely hostile and then stumped off up the hill.

Journalists venturing out from the metropolis to places like Stoke
tend to come back with stories of how the Thatcher years and a
decade of austerity destroyed warm, close-knit working-class communities. The reality is messier. Stoke today is not especially warm
or close-knit, but frankly, it never really was. Like so many English
towns, the authentic 1970s Stoke was rough, dirty and generally dull.
Those who could leave tended to do so. (My parents stayed, but
sometimes speculated about what might have been if they'd seized a
chance to emigrate to Canada in the 1960s.)

Britain's economy more or less doubled in size in the thirty years
after 1979, and, as in so many boom times, bifurcated along the way.
Places that could connect to the expanding global stage drew talent,

energy and capital away from those that couldn't. Stoke Central's dynamic MP Tristram Hunt, for instance, resigned his seat in 2017 to take one of the most metropolitan jobs imaginable, directing London's Victoria and Albert Museum. But bifurcation worked at the local level too: Stoke's famous old factories are all gone (Figure 12.2), taking thousands of mostly monotonous jobs with them, but a handful have been reinvented as dream factories (Figure 12.3) – unbuttoned, creative places, more about image and style than anything, and thoroughly at home in Global Britain. The last four decades have given the city some things to be sad about and others to be glad about. But regardless of whether Europe is to be praised or blamed for either, when asked in 2016 whether they wanted to stay or go, two-thirds of Potters concluded that leaving made most sense.

One detail sticks in my mind. Poking through the offerings on a street vendor's table, I found a perky little coffee cup with a picture of a bottle kiln on it. It seemed like a good souvenir of my trip back home. I picked it up and turned it over. Made in China, it said. I put it back and moved on.

ACKNOWLEDGEMENTS

No one can write a book without help from a lot of other people. This one would never have happened without the continuing support of Stanford University's School of Humanities and Sciences or the generosity of the Carnegie Foundation, which supported the early stages of my research with an Andrew Carnegie Fellowship.

I owe an enormous debt to Martin Carver, Nick Clegg, Simon Esmonde-Cleary, Ian Hodder, Phil Kleinheinz, Mark Malcomson, Brook Manville, Jared McKinney, John O'Brien, Josh Ober, Mike Parker Pearson, Neil Roberts, Steve Shennan, Brendan Simms, Kathy St John, Matthew Taylor and Greg Woolf. All read and advised on parts or even the whole of the book in manuscript form, although they should not be held responsible for what I did with their advice. Invitations to spend parts of the academic year 2015–16 as the Philippe Roman Professor of International Studies at the London School of Economics and part of the summer of 2019 as the Australian Army's Keogh Professor of Future Land Warfare shaped my thinking in major ways. I also benefited greatly from invitations from George Hammond (Commonwealth Club of California), Mark Malcomson (City Lit), Freddie Matthews (British Museum) and Katie Zoglin (World Affairs Council) to give public lectures for their organisations, and from Brendan Simms to attend the Centre for Geopolitics's online seminars.

Shan Vahidy was an exemplary and wise editor, Michele Angel drew the wonderful maps and charts, Penny Daniel saw everything through production smoothly and Valerie Kiszka untangled multiple muddles I created, as she so often does. Andrew Franklin at Profile Books and Eric Chinski at Farrar, Straus and Giroux patiently dispensed advice and kept the whole thing moving, despite my delays and abrupt changes of direction; and Sandy Dijkstra, Elise Capron and Andrea Cavallaro at the Sandra Dijkstra Literary Agency and Rachel Clements at Abner Stein provided the perfect amount of support. My thanks to you all.

NOTES

This section provides sources for all quotations in the text. For works of the last 150 years or so I normally provide page numbers; for older works, which have been reprinted in multiple versions, I give chapter references where appropriate. Translations from Latin and Greek sources are my own unless indicated otherwise. I cite speeches given in the House of Commons since 1800 from https://hansard.parliament.uk. All links were current as of September 2021.

Introduction

2: 'The longer': Winston Churchill (March 1944), https://www.oxfordreference.com/view/10.1093/acref/9780191826719.001.0001/q-oro-ed4-00002969.

3–4: 'Brexit is a recent phenomenon': David Edgerton, *The Rise and Fall of the British Nation* (2018), p. xx. 'a quick survey' and 'You've got to control the borders': https://www.theguardian.com/us-news/2016/aug/24/nigel-farage-donald-trump-rally-hillary-clinton. 'believed [that] by going out': Nigel Farage (24 August 2016), http://foreignpolicy.com/2016/08/25/when-donald-met-nigel/. 'was the absolute key', 'Where we struck' and 'They're stupid': Nigel Farage, phone-in interview hosted by JT on SuperTalk FM, Jackson, Mississippi (23 August 2016), http://www.express.co.uk/news/uk/703541/Nigel-Farage-UKIP-immigration-Brexit-vote-Donald-Trump-Jackson-Mississippi-US-President.

4: Issues in the Brexit vote: http://www.forbes.com/sites/johnmauldin/2016/07/05/3-reasons-brits-voted-for-brexit/#5d1ca6cc78c1; http://fortune.com/2016/06/14/brexit-britain-eu-vote-referendum-supporters/; http://www.bbc.com/news/uk-politics-eu-referendum-36574526; http://www.independent.co.uk/voices/brexit-eu-referendum-why-did-people-vote-leave-immigration-nhs-a7104071.html; https://www.thesun.co.uk/news/1278140/why-voting-to-leave-the-eu-will-save-our-sovereignty-rein-in-migration-and-boost-our-economy/; http://www.dailymail.co.uk/news/article-3653526/Undecided-Read-essential-guide-giving-20-reasons-choose-leave.html; https://www.theguardian.com/books/2016/jun/25/philip-pullman-on-the-1000-causes-of-brexit; http://lordashcroftpolls.com/2016/06/how-the-united-kingdom-voted-and-why/. 'The narrow Brexit decision': Harold Clarke et al., *Brexit* (2017), p. 146.

5: 'Instead of loathing': Tacitus, *Agricola* (98 CE), 21. 'people in this country':

Michael Gove MP (3 June 2016), https://www.youtube.com/
watch?v=GGgiGtJk7MA. *Our Island Story*: https://www.telegraph.co.uk/
culture/books/booknews/8094333/Revealed-David-Camerons-favourite-
childhood-book-is-Our-Island-Story.html.

6: 'Geography comes before history': Robert Tombs, *This Sovereign Isle* (2021), p. 1.

7: 'the truest cause': Thucydides, *History of the Peloponnesian War* (*c.*400 BCE), 1.23.

10: 'Past Cádiz': Pindar, *Nemean Ode* (probably 473 BCE), 4.69–70. 'What lies
beyond': *Olympian Ode* (probably 476 BCE), 3.44–45. 'destitution and loneliness':
Strabo, *Geography* (*c.*20 CE), 1.1.8. 'All the world's a stage': Shakespeare, *As You
Like It* (probably 1599), Act II, scene vii.

12: 'precious stone': Shakespeare, *Richard II* (*c.*1595), Act II, scene i.

14: 'The size': Lee Kuan Yew, from Graham Allison et al., *Lee Kuan Yew* (2013),
p. 42.

15: 'reduce England': George Orwell, *The Road to Wigan Pier* (1937), Chapter 10.
'ability to achieve': https://softpower30.com/what-is-soft-power/. 'Great
Britain has lost': Dean Acheson, speech at West Point (5 December 1962), from
Douglas Brinkley, 'Dean Acheson and the "Special Relationship"', *Historical
Journal* 33 (1990), p. 601. 'Should the United Kingdom': https://www.gov.uk/
government/topical-events/eu-referendum/about.

16: 'out of the plain': Jan Struthers, *Mrs. Miniver* (1939), pp. 59–60.

18: 'It is the tragedy' and 'In the Lowland': Cyril Fox, *The Personality of Britain*
(1932), pp. 39–40. 'the Brexit capital': http://www.newstatesman.com/politics/
staggers/2017/02/
stoke-central-election-brexit-and-other-issues-could-swing-vote.

19: 'the islands in question': Eddie Holt, *The Irish Times* (15 July 2006), http://
www.irishtimes.com/news/islands-in-the-stream-1.1031157. 'these islands': as
in the Good Friday Agreement (10 April 1998), https://peacemaker.un.org/
uk-ireland-good-friday98. 'the British and Irish Isles': Norman Davies, *The Isles*
(2000), p. xxii. 'The two biggest islands': Aristotle, *On the Cosmos* (*c.*330 BCE),
393b12.

1. Thatcher's Law, 6000–4000 BCE

23: 'We are inextricably': Margaret Thatcher, speech to the Conservative
Group for Europe (16 April 1975), https://www.margaretthatcher.org/
document/102675.

31: 'blue/green eyes': Selina Brace et al., 'Ancient Genomes Indicate Population
Replacement in Early Neolithic Britain', *Nature Ecology & Evolution* 3 (2019),
pp. 768–9.

32: 'I can definitely see': Adrian Targett, interview (7 February 2018), https://
www.dailymail.co.uk/news/article-5364983/Retired-history-teacher-believes-
looks-like-Cheddar-Man.html.

36: 'the population': Barry Cunliffe, *Britain Begins* (2013), pp. 127–8.

38: 'The inherent vice': Churchill, speech to Parliament (22 October 1945), https://winstonchurchill.org/resources/quotes/vice-of-capitalism/. 'primitive communists': Friedrich Engels, *The Origin of the Family, Private Property, and the State* (1972 [1884]), pp. 18–25.

39: 'Of course we have headmen!': Richard Lee, *The !Kung San* (1979), p. 348.

47: 'A basic equation': Peter Heather, *Barbarians and Empire* (2009), p. 19.

49: 'The white man comes': Spirit Talker/Muguarra to Noah Smithwick (Comancheria, 1838), from S. C. Gwynne, *Empire of the Summer Moon* (2010), p. 111.

51: 'History to the defeated': W. H. Auden, 'Spain' (1937), https://www.workersliberty.org/story/2011/09/09/spain-w-h-auden.

52: 'the very counterscarp': William Cecil, Baron Burghley (1567), from R. Wernham, *Before the Armada* (1966), p. 292. 'Britain's frontier': Harold Macmillan, speech to the Council of Europe, Strasbourg (August 1949), from Hugo Young, *This Blessed Plot* (1998), p. 113.

53: 'We shall fight in France': Churchill, speech to Parliament (4 June 1940). 'in front of a large cave' etc.: http://www.ft.com/cms/s/0/ec333342-2323-11e6-9d4d-c11776a5124d.html#axzz4LIRwSVeW.

59: 'The one eternal sight': Stanley Baldwin, *On England* (1926), p. 6.

2. Europe's Poor Cousin, 4000–55 BCE

65: 'megalithic missionaries': V. Gordon Childe, *Prehistoric European Society* (1958), pp. 124–34.

66: 'multiple long runs': Lara Cassidy et al., 'A Dynastic Elite in Monumental Neolithic Society', *Nature* 582 (2020), p. 385.

68: 'flickering light': Jeremy Dronfield, 'Migraine, Light and Hallucinogens', *Oxford Journal of Archaeology* 14 (1995), p. 272.

69: 'a shared system' and 'Atlantic mind-set': Barry Cunliffe, *Facing the Ocean* (2001), pp. 199, 155.

72: 'by communities' and 'Such an act': Michael Parker Pearson et al., 'Craig Rhos-y-felin', *Antiquity* 89 (2015), p. 1350. 'a ruling elite': Parker Pearson et al., 'Who Was Buried at Stonehenge?' *Antiquity* 83 (2009), p. 36.

73: 'no one has been able': Henry of Huntingdon, *History of the English* (1129), Book I, translated in Thomas Forester, *The Chronicle of Henry of Huntingdon* (1853), p. 7. 'Giants' Ring': Geoffrey of Monmouth, *History of the Kings of Britain* (1136), 8.10–12, translated in Lewis Thorpe, *Geoffrey of Monmouth* (1966), p. 196.

77: 'That the first copper workers': Cunliffe, *Britain Begins*, p. 201.

78: 'Whatever happens, we have got': Hilaire Belloc, *The Modern Traveller* (1898), Part 6. 'The King of Stonehenge': http://www.dailymail.co.uk/news/article-1180243/The-king-Stonehenge-Were-artefacts-ancient-chiefs-burial-site-Britains-Crown-Jewels.html.

82: 'the original bling society': Timothy Darvill, *Prehistoric Britain* (3rd edn, 2010), p. 197.

83: 'scourge of many tribes': *Beowulf* (probably eighth century CE), lines 4–5, translated in Seamus Heaney, *Beowulf* (2000), p. 3.

84: 'Would that I had died': Hesiod, *Works and Days* (*c.*700 BCE), lines 175–8.

85: 'people who are called Celts': Caesar, *The Gallic War* (*c.*58 BCE), 1.1.

86: 'Cheap iron': Gordon Childe, *What Happened in History* (1942), p. 183.

88: 'cowards, shirkers': Tacitus, *Germania* (*c.*98 CE), 12. 'drench their altars': Tacitus, *Annals* (*c.*110 CE), 14.30.

91: 'things published long ago': Postumius Rufus Festus Avienus, *The Sea Shores* (350–400 CE). 'No breezes': *Sea Shores*, lines 120–24.

92: 'tin was first imported': Pliny the Elder, *Natural History* (78 CE), 7.197 .'traversed the whole': Pytheas, *On the Ocean* (c. 320 BCE), quoted by Strabo, *Geography* (20s CE), 2.4.1.

93: 'from the Rhine': Posidonius, from John Collis, *The European Iron Age* (1984), p. 149.

94: 'Not a single coin': Cicero, *In Defence of Fonteius* (delivered 73 BCE).

95: 'within living memory' etc.: Caesar, *Gallic War*, 2.4. 'Having come to raid': Caesar, *Gallic War*, 5.12.

97: 'Because of these achievements': Caesar, *Gallic War*, 2.35.

98: 'The barbarians adapted': Cassius Dio (written *c.*230 CE), 56.18. 'were made to suit', 'Our ships' and 'By nightfall': Caesar, *Gallic War*, 3.13–15.

99: 'to approach' and 'Caesar is coming': Caesar, *Gallic War*, 4.21.

3. Empire, 55 BCE–410 CE

100: 'everything in war,' etc.: Carl von Clausewitz, *On War* (1831; ed. Michael Howard and Peter Paret, 1976), pp. 119–21. 'This was the one action': Caesar, *Gallic War*, 4.26.

102: 'what was previously unknown': Cassius Dio, 39.53.

104: 'live where he was sent': Caesar, *Gallic War*, 5.28.

105: 'the people would not come to terms': Cassius Dio, 53.25.

106: 'Britain is / A world by itself': Shakespeare, *Cymbeline* (*c.*1611), Act III, scene i, lines 14–16.

107: 'Battle followed battle': Tacitus, *Annals* (*c.*110 CE), 12.38.

108: 'would have reflected badly': Suetonius, *Life of Nero* (*c.*120 CE), 18. 'the Iron age equivalents': Francis Pryor, *Britain AD* (2005), p. 44. 'The enemy': Tacitus, *Annals*, 14.30.

109: 'gave private encouragement': Tacitus, *Agricola*, 21.

110: 'They could not wait': Tacitus, *Annals*, 14.34.

112: 'disaster': Tacitus (*Annals*, 14.29) and Suetonius (*Life of Nero*, 39), writing in Latin, called it a *clades*; Cassius Dio (62.1), writing in Greek, called it a *pathos*.

116: 'Because I couldn't complain': Vindolanda tablet 344 (*c.*100 CE), http:// vindolanda.csad.ox.ac.uk. I have modified the published translation slightly to make the sense clearer and have incorporated the addendum on line 7.

117: 'little Brits': Vindolanda tablet 164, line 5. 'Who does not now recognise': Pliny the Elder, *Natural History*, 14.2.

118: 'taller than the tallest there': Strabo, *Geography*, 4.5.2. 'guard against': President Dwight D. Eisenhower, Farewell Address (17 January 1961), https://www.ourdocuments.gov/doc.php?flash=false&doc=90&page=transcript and https://www.youtube.com/watch?v=8y06NSBBRtY.

119: 'Titus Flaminius': https://romaninscriptionsofbritain.org/inscriptions/292 (*c.*50 CE). Following Barry Burnham et al., 'Roman Britain in 1994', *Britannia* 26 (1995), 388–9, I read *aq(uilifer)* rather than *a(t)q(ue)* in line 3.

120: 'most chaste and pure': Gaius Valerius Iustus (*c.*200 CE?), https://romaninscriptionsofbritain.org/text/507.

121: 'crowded with traders and their wares': Tacitus, *Agricola*, 20.

122: 'They are boasting': http://www.bbc.com/news/uk-england-london-36415563 and Roger Tomlin, *Roman London's First Voices* (2016).

125–6: 'humble and windblown habitation', 'small and moderately prosperous' and 'shows a nice touch': Michael Jarrett and Stuart Wrathmell, *Whitton* (1981), pp. 164, 188.

126–7: 'relatively unremarkable' and 'By this age': Kevin Blockley, *Marshfield* (1985), pp. 185, 356.

127: 'of fairly low economic status': Kate Nicholson and Tom Woolhouse, *A Late Iron Age and Romano-British Farmstead at Cedars Park, Stowmarket, Suffolk* (2016), p. 183.

137–8: 'was as Roman' and 'grew scarce in the 370s': Robin Fleming, *Britain after Rome* (2010), pp. 22, 27.

139–40: 'Casement windows': Alan Weisman, *The World without Us* (2007), pp. 120–21. 'acres of tumbled buildings': Simon Esmonde Cleary, *The Ending of Roman Britain* (1989), p. 148.

143: 'an awful revolution': Edward Gibbon, *History of the Decline and Fall of the Roman Empire* III (1781), subchapter 'General Observations on the Fall of the Roman Empire in the West'.

144: 'Britannia is a province': Jerome, *Letters* (*c.*412 CE), 133. 'inscrutable' and 'went far beyond': Ammianus Marcellinus (*c.*380 CE), 14.5. 'use the barbarian' and 'befriending the distant': *Stratagems of the Warring States* (anonymous, third century BCE), from Dennis and Chang Ping Bloodworth, *The Chinese Machiavelli* (1976), pp. 111, 58.

145: 'looted, burned and slaughtered' and 'roamed free': Ammianus, 27.8. 'Theodosius' popularity': Ammianus, 28.3.

146: 'left Britain deprived': Gildas, *On the Ruin of Britain* (*c.*540 CE), 14. 'Throwing off Roman rule': Zosimus, *New History* (*c.*500 CE). 'Legate': Rudyard Kipling, 'The Roman Centurion's Song', in *A Child's History of England* (1911), https://www.poetryloverspage.com/poets/kipling/roman_centurions.html.

147: 'sent letters to the cities': Zosimus, *New History*, 6.10.12.

4. The Original European Union, 410–973

148: 'Long years ago': Jawaharlal Nehru, declaration of Indian independence, Delhi (15 August 1947), https://sourcebooks.fordham.edu/mod/1947nehru1.asp.

149: 'The trouble with soft power': https://foreignpolicy.com/2009/11/03/think-again-power/.

150–1: 'Alas!' etc.: Gildas, *On the Ruin of Britain*, 1, 20, 23, 25.

151: 'The bulk': E. Leeds, *Early Anglo-Saxon Art and Archaeology* (1936), pp. 25–6.

155–6: 'king of Gwent' and 'citizen of Gwynedd': tombstones quoted in James Campbell et al., *The Anglo-Saxons* (1982), p. 21.

156: 'last of the Romans': Gildas, *On the Ruin of Britain*, 25. 'Then it was' etc.: Nennius, *History of the Britons* (*c*.830), p. 50. 'the Battle of Badon': *Annals of Wales* (tenth century), Year 72, supposedly 516 CE.

157: 'Artognou': Rachel Barrowman et al., *Excavations at Tintagel Castle, Cornwall, 1990–1999* (2007), p. 199.

158: 'the well-known Irish tradition': Thomas Bartlett, *Ireland* (2010), p. 4. 'We beg you': St Patrick, *Confessions* (fifth century), 23. 'there were many in England': Bede, *Ecclesiastical History of the English People* (731), 3.27.

159: 'Good, for these Angles': Bede, *History*, 2.1. 'My treasury': Gregory of Tours, *History of the Franks* 6.46 (written *c*.590).

161: 'went to the king': Bede, *History*, 2.6.

162: 'initiated into the mysteries' and 'he seemed': Bede, *History*, 2.15.

163: 'the equivalent': Campbell et al., *Anglo-Saxons*, p. 94.

167: 'let kings be': 'Legatine Canons at Cealchythe' (785), in John Johnson, *A Collection of the Laws and Canons of the Church of England* I (1850), p. 273. 'king of the English': charters of Offa, in Campbell et al., *Anglo-Saxons*, p. 101. 'the first ships': Dorothy Whitelock, ed., *English Historical Documents* I (1978), p. 180. 'Never before': Alcuin, in Whitelock, *Documents* I, p. 776.

171: 'that's where the money is': William Sutton and E. Linn, *Where the Money Was* (1976), p. 160. This is often generalised as 'Sutton's Law' ('first, consider the obvious'), but Sutton denied ever saying it. In reality, he said, 'Why did I rob banks? Because I enjoyed it.'

173: 'He had nothing to live on': Asser, *Life of King Alfred* (893), 53; translated in Simon Keynes and Michael Lapidge, *Alfred the Great* (1983), p. 83. 'There all the inhabitants': Asser, *Alfred*, 55.

174: 'before everything' and 'what punishments': Alfred the Great, prose preface to translation of Pope Gregory I's *Pastoral Care* (*c*.890), translated in Keynes and Lapidge, *Alfred the Great*, 125.

175: 'all the English people': *Anglo-Saxon Chronicle* for 886, https://avalon.law.yale.edu/medieval/ang09.asp.

176: 'Never on this island': *Anglo-Saxon Chronicle* for 937. 'king and ruler': Tom Holland, *Athelstan* (2016), p. 37.

177: 'brazen, plumed': Jan Morris, *Heaven's Command* (1973), p. 21.

180: 'Oh, I work': Aelfric, *Colloquy* (c.1000), translated in M. Swanton, *Anglo-Saxon Prose* (1993).

184: 'in England': Francesco Caraccioli (1748–99), at http://www.bartleby.com/344/393.html. The statement is often attributed to Voltaire, but there is no reliable source for this.

5. United Kingdoms, 973–1497

188: 'Strife threw': Byhrtferth, *Life of St Oswald* (c.1000), from Campbell et al., *Anglo-Saxons*, p. 192. 'once you have paid': Kipling, 'Dane-Geld', from *A Child's History of England* (1911), https://www.poetryloverspage.com/poets/kipling/dane_geld.html.

190: 'Let all men': Henry of Huntingdon, *History of the English* (c.1140), 6.17. 'from where the most harm': Cnut, letter to the English (written 1019/20), from Timothy Bolton, *Cnut the Great* (2017), p. 130.

193: 'We were your Romans': Tom Stoppard, *Indian Ink* (1995), p. 17 (first performed 1993). 'My dear': Rebecca West, quoted in Noel Coward, *Future Indefinite* (1954), p. 92.

195: 'helpless children': Orderic Vitalis, *Ecclesiastical History* (c.1125), 2.196, translated in Marjorie Chibnall, *The Ecclesiastical History of Orderic Vitalis* II (1969), p. 233. 'England has become': William of Malmesbury, *Chronicle of the Kings of England* (1120s), 2.13, translated in J. A. Giles, *William of Malmesbury's Chronicle of the Kings of England* (1847), p. 253. 'private fortified residences': Charles Coulson, *Castles in Medieval Society* (2003), p. 16.

197: 'not now pope': Henry IV, letter to Gregory VII (24 January 1076), in Theodor Mommsen and Karl Morrison, eds, *Imperial Lives and Letters of the Eleventh Century* (1962), pp. 151–2.

198: 'barbarous people' etc.: from David Carpenter, *The Struggle for Mastery* (2003), p. 15. 'It's probably better': President Lyndon Baines Johnson (31 October 1971), http://www.nytimes.com/1971/10/31/archives/the-vantage-point-perspectives-of-the-presidency-19631969-by-lyndon.html. 'It doesn't matter': anonymous Conservative minister quoted by Tim Shipman, *All-Out War* (2016), p. 13. 'Fiercely they threaten us': Gaimar, *History of the English* (late 1130s), Epilogue, lines 245–51. Translated in Thomas Hardy and Charles Martin *Lestoire des Engles solum la translacion Maistre Geffrei Gaimar* I (1889), p. 214.

199: 'to destroy the inhabitants': Anon., *Life of Gruffudd ap Cynan* (c.1150), from John Gillingham, *William II, the Red King* (2015), p. 19. 'plaited and coiled' etc., Gerald of Wales, *Mirror of the Church* (1216), 2.8–9, translated in Lewis Thorpe, *Gerald of Wales* (1978), pp. 284–5. 'a catalogue of men with stange names': Alex Woolf, 'Scotland', in Pauline Stafford, ed., *A Companion to the Early Middle Ages* (2009), p. 260.

200: 'will these hands': William Shakespeare, *Macbeth* (probably 1606), Act V, scene i.

201: 'Each great man' and 'You could easily go': *Anglo-Saxon Chronicle* for 1137, https://avalon.law.yale.edu/medieval/ang12.asp.

202: 'I have married a monk': Eleanor of Aquitaine, from Richard Barber, *Henry II* (2015), p. 44.

204: 'Will no one rid me': attributed to Henry II, December 1170, but not attested in any contemporary source.

205: 'detain him violently' etc.: Ralph of Coggeshall, from Marc Morris, *King John* (2015), pp. 57–8.

209: 'There stretch': Goscelin of St Bertin, *History of the Transfer of the Relics of St Augustine* (1098/9), 51, from Robert Bartlett, *England under the Norman and Angevin Kings* (2000), p. 287.

212: 'a measure of wheat': Matthew Paris, *English History* (1250s) for 1258, translated in J. A. Giles, *Matthew Paris's English History* III (1852), p. 291. 'We will never know': David Crook, 'The Sheriff of Nottingham', *Thirteenth-Century England* 2 (1988), p. 68.

213: 'Hot pies!' William Langland, *Piers Ploughman* (late fourteenth century), Prologue, and 'Hot sheep's feet!' London Lickpenny (early fifteenth century), from Ian Mortimer, *The Time Traveller's Guide to Medieval England* (2008), p. 9.

214: 'queen of the whole kingdom': *The Deeds of King Stephen* (c.1150), from Carpenter, *Struggle for Mastery*, p. 43.

216: 'the community of England': *Annals of Tewkesbury* for 1258, from Andy King, *Edward I* (2016), p. 15. 'Whoever did not know': *St Albans Abbey Chronicle* for 1263, from Carpenter, *Struggle for Mastery*, p. 376. 'The response': Carpenter, *Struggle for Mastery*, p. 379. 'Nowadays': Richard FitzNeal, *Dialogue of the Exchequer* (c.1178), from Carpenter, *Struggle for Mastery*, p. 5. 'any gentleman should know': Walter of Bibbesworth (c.1250), from Carpenter, *Struggle for Mastery*, p. 9. 'the English tongue': Edward I, writ summoning Parliament (30 September 1295), from William Stubbs, *The Constitutional History of England* (1875), p. 129.

217: 'The whole barbarity': Saint Aelred of Rielvaux, *Life of David, King of the Scots* (c.1153), from Carpenter, *Struggle for Mastery*, p. 16.

218: 'a land annexed': Edward I (1284), from Carpenter, *Struggle for Mastery*, p. 511. 'He had it in mind': *Annals of Waverley*, from King, *Edward I*, p. 60. 'Now the islanders': Pierre de Langtoft, *Chronicle* (1296), translated in Thomas Wright, *The Chronicle of Pierre de Langtoft* II (1868), pp. 264–6.

219: 'the Scottish people and the Britons': English official (1307), from King, *Edward I*, p. 74.

223: 'These were attempts': Miri Rubin, *The Hollow Crown* (2005), p. 180.

6. Englexit, 1497–1713

231: 'fiscal–military state': Aaron Graham and Patrick Walsh, eds, *The British Fiscal–Military States* (2016).

235: 'the pope's good son': Henry VIII to Venetian ambassadors (1515), from

John Guy, *Henry VIII* (2014), p. 24. 'ungracious dog-holes': Thomas Cromwell, speech to Parliament (1523), from Geoffrey Elton, 'War and the English in the Reign of Henry VIII', in Lawrence Freedman et al., eds, *War, Strategy and International Politics* (1992), p. 16.

238: 'We are so much bounden': Henry VIII to Thomas More (1521), from Guy, *Henry VIII*, p. 31.

239: 'Supreme Head': Act of Supremacy (1534), http://www.nationalarchives.gov.uk/pathways/citizenship/rise_parliament/transcripts/henry_supremacy.htm.

240: 'The poor people': from Derek Wilson, *A Brief History of the English Reformation* (2012), p. 205.

241: 'Christ crucified!' Pilgrimage of Grace (1536), from Perez Zagorin, *Rebels & Rulers, 1500–1600* I (1982), p. 149.

246: 'What king?': Brian O'Connor of Offaly (1528); 'treachery and breach': Chief Governor Sir Henry Sidney (1580); 'to *plant* young lords': Sir Patrick Finglas, chief justice of the king's bench (c.1534); all from Susan Brigden, *New Worlds, Lost Worlds* (2000), pp. 149, 318, 157.

248: 'the strongest wall': Elizabeth I to Parliament (1559), from Nicholas Rodger, *Safeguard of the Sea* (1997), p. 229.

250: 'We are sailing': senior Spanish officer, probably Bernardino de Escalante, to a papal representative (1588), from Rodger, *Safeguard of the Sea*, p. 259. 'I have the body': Elizabeth I, speech at Tilbury (9 August 1588), from Janet Green, '"I My Self": Elizabeth I's Oration at Tilbury Camp', *Sixteenth Century Journal* 28 (1997), p. 443. 'a boy that driveth': William Tyndale, quoted in Foxe's Book of Martyrs (1563).

251: 'Let there be light' etc.: all these, and more, on https://en.wikiquote.org/wiki/William_Tyndale. 'Lighten our darkness': *Book of Common Prayer* (1549), Evensong, Second Collect, for Aid against Perils. 'Once more': William Shakespeare, *Henry V* (probably 1599), Act III, scene i. 'precious stone': Shakespeare, *Richard II* (c.1595) Act II, scene i. 'The King of Great Britain': John Selden, *Mare Clausum* (1635), from Arthur Herman, *To Rule the Waves* (2004), p. 149.

252: 'Our half-doing': Sir Francis Walsingham (1588), from Brigden, *New Worlds*, p. 294.

253: 'joining the two kingdoms' and 'of late so increased': William Cecil, first Baron Burghley (1560), from Jane Dawson, 'William Cecil and the British Dimension of Early Elizabethan Foreign Policy', *History* 74 (1989), p. 209. 'long disputations': James I, speech to the Houses of Parliament (31 March 1607), from Charles MacIlwain, ed., *The Political Works of James I* (1918), p. 291.

254: 'middling sorts': Jonathan Barry and Christopher Brooks, eds, *The Middling Sort of People* (1994).

255–6: 'If we have no Negroes': Malachy Postlethwayt, *The African Trade, the Great Pillar and Support of the British Plantation Trade in America* (1745), p. 2, from David Scott, *Leviathan* (2013), p. 376.

257: 'filthy novelty': James I and VI, *A Counterblast to Tobacco* (1604), http://www.laits.utexas.edu/poltheory/james/blaste/blaste.html.

258: 'warmer, lighter, and larger' and 'there is more of everything': William Hoskins, 'The Rebuilding of Rural England, 1570–1640', *Past & Present* 4 (1953), pp. 50, 49.

259: 'an Englishman's home' (1581): https://www.phrases.org.uk/meanings/an-englishmans-home-is-his-castle.html. 'We have the most part': John Houghton, *England's Great Happiness, or, a Dialogue between Content and Complaint* (1677), p. 19, from Scott, *Leviathan*, p. 342.

260: 'betwixt the Pope and the Puritans': Sir Christopher Hatton, lord chancellor, speech to Parliament (March 1587), from Brigden, *New Worlds,* p. 330. 'prodigality and vanity': Scottish nobleman (*c.*1581), from Thomas Cogswell, *James I* (2017), p. 14.

261: 'Tears, sighs': Girolamo Lando, Venetian ambassador to London (November 1620), from Peter Ackroyd, *History of England* III (2014), p. 70. 'the main end': Cotton Mather, *Magnalia Christi Americana* (1702), I.15.

262: 'strategically incompetent': Brendan Simms, *Britain's Europe* (2016), p. 38. 'Our honour is ruined': Sir John Eliot, speech to Parliament (1626), from Herman, *To Rule*, p. 165.

263: 'Cutting the Liver vein': Proposal for founding a West India Company, from Scott, *Leviathan*, p. 337.

264: 'I have never seen anything': Peter Paul Rubens (1629), from Ackroyd, *History of England* III, 157. 'true religion': Alexander Henderson and Archibald Johnston, *The National Covenant* (1638), https://www.fpchurch.org.uk/about-us/important-documents/the-national-covenant-1638/. 'Parliament is far too nimble': unattributed comment (1641), from Scott, *Leviathan*, p. 158.

265: 'Go, you coward': Queen Henrietta Maria to Charles I (3 January 1642), from Geoffrey Parker, *Global Crisis* (2013), pp. 353–4. 'like to have been torn': Ellis Coleman (5 January 1642), from Parker, *Global Crisis*, p. 354. 'If we beat the King': Earl of Manchester to Oliver Cromwell (1644), quoted in William Hamilton, ed., *Calendar of State Papers, Domestic Series, of the Reign of Charles I, 1644–1645* (1890), p. 151.

266: 'On earth': Job 41:33–4 (King James Version, 1611). 'continual fear': Thomas Hobbes, *Leviathan* (1651), Chapter 17.

267: 'a pulling down': William Walwyn (1648), from Scott, *Leviathan*, p. 193. 'Your great enemy': Cromwell, speech to Parliament (17 September 1656), quoted from Eric Cochrane et al., eds, *Early Modern Europe: Crisis of Authority* (1987), p. 516.

268: 'la[id] a foundation': Nathaniel Worsley, *The Advocate* (1652), p. 2, from Scott, *Leviathan*, p. 342. 'drunkenness, swearing': Major-General Charles Worsley, letter to Secretary John Thurloe (12 November 1656), from Samuel Gardiner, *History of the Commonwealth and Protectorate 1649–1656* IV (1903), p. 36. 'the undoubted Interest': George Villiers, second Duke of Buckingham, *A Letter to Sir Thomas Osborn* (1672), p. 11, from Scott, *Leviathan*, p. 344.

269: "'Tis incredible': Earl of Shaftesbury, speech to Parliament (20 October 1675), from Steven Pincus, 'From Butterboxes to Wooden Shoes', *Historical Journal* 38 (1995), p. 347. 'The want of money': Samuel Pepys, diary entry (30 September 1661), www.pepysdiary.com/archive/1661/09/30. 'The French': John Doddington, letter to Joseph Williamson (27 June 1670), from Pincus, 'From Butterboxes to Wooden Shoes', p. 342.

270: 'altogether Frenchyfied': Edmund Ludlow, from N. Keeble, *The Restoration* (2002), p. 179. 'an adopted daughter of France': *A Relation of the Most Material Matters in Parliament Relating to Religion, Property, and the Liberty of the Subject* (1673), pp. 19–20, from Pincus, 'From Butterboxes to Wooden Shoes', p. 353. 'A colony of French': 'A Dialogue between Britannia and Rawleigh' (1675), from Pincus, 'From Butterboxes to Wooden Shoes', p. 359.

271: 'the French King makes not': Roger Morrice, Entering Book (8 June 1689), from Pincus, *1688* (2009), p. 345.

272: 'There were a hundred thousand': Hugh Trevor-Roper, *Archbishop Laud* (1988), p. 71. "'Tis the press': Roger L'Estrange (1679), from Scott, *Leviathan*, p. 223.

273: 'power of suspending': Bill of Rights (16 December 1689), https://avalon. law.yale.edu/17th_century/england.asp.

274: 'a notoriously difficult subject': Parliamentary Select Committee on Public Administration, Fourth Report (2004), section 3, https://publications. parliament.uk/pa/cm200304/cmselect/cmpubadm/422/42204.htm.

275: 'If Flanders be': Anon., *The Englishman's Choice and True Interest* (1694), from M. Sheehan, 'The Development of British Theory and Practice of the Balance of Power before 1714', *History* 73 (1988), p. 31. 'Credit makes war': Daniel Defoe, *The Complete English Tradesman* (1725), I, Chapter 27.

276: 'the King': Defoe, *A True Collection of the Writings of the Author of a True-Born English-man* (1703), Explanatory Preface, from Scott, *Leviathan*, p. 254.

277: 'When will this bloodshed?' Queen Anne (1709), from Robert Buchholz and Newton Key, *Early Modern England, 1485–1714* (2003), p. 344.

7. The Pivot, 1713–1815

279: 'On trade alone': John Gay, *Fables* (1732), II.8, from W. H. Kearley Wright, *The Fables of Gay* (new edn, 1889), p. 243. 'the peace and tranquillity': Treaty of Utrecht (1713), from Hamish Scott, *The Birth of a Great Power System, 1740–1815* (2014), p. 139. 'We have no eternal allies': Lord Palmerston, speech to Parliament (1 March 1848).

280: 'an honest, dull German': James Stanhope, first Earl Chesterfield, from Scott, *Leviathan*, p. 278.

281: 'lack[ing] the imagination': Scott, *Leviathan*, p. 276. 'while he was speaking': Stanhope, from Scott, *Leviathan*, p. 291.

282: 'The rage of party': J. H. Plumb, *The Growth of Political Stability in England, 1675–1725* (1967), p. 129.

283: 'a very high level': Simms, *Britain's Europe*, p. 60.

284: 'at present' and 'the greatest part': Walpole, speech to Parliament (8 March 1739), in William Cobbett, ed., *The Parliamentary History of England from the Earliest Period to the Year 1803* X (1812), col. 1255. 'Under Queen Elizabeth': William Pulteney, speech to Parliament (9 March 1739), published in Cobbett, *Parliamentary History* X, col. 1298. 'by being absolutely disengaged': Thomas Pelham-Holles, Duke of Newcastle, to Stanhope (20 November 1745), from Brendan Simms, *Three Victories and a Defeat* (2007), p. 336. 'Bawling and huzzaing': Stanhope to Newcastle (25 November 1745), from Simms, *Three Victories*, p. 344. 'But not on Flandria's hostile plain': *Gentleman's Magazine* (1745), from Simms, *Three Victories*, p. 333.

285: 'disregard[ing] all the troubles': Carteret, speech to Parliament (27 January 1744), from Simms, *Britain's Europe*, p. 55. 'When George in Pudding Time': 'The Vicar of Bray', in *The British Musical Miscellany* I (1734), p. 31, from Scott, *Leviathan*, p. 276.

286–7: 'All I know', Arthur Young, 'they have their houses', Madame du Bocage (1720s) and 'not as ours', Pastor Karl Moritz: all from Roy Porter, *English Society in the 18th Century* (1990), pp. 211, 221.

288: 'The number of shops': Guy Miege, *The New State of England under their Majesties K. William and Q. Mary* I (1691), p. 334, from Pincus, *1688*, p. 73. 'the finest in Europe': César de Saussure, letter to his family (1729), from Helen Berry, 'Polite Consumption', *Transactions of the Royal Historical Society* 6th series, 12 (2002), p. 382. 'Piccadilly by the sea-side': William Wilberforce; 'the wives and daughters', *The Connoisseur* (1756); 'I wish', Admiral John Byng; 'the very clergy, Horace Walpole; and 'possessed a vivacity': William Hutton, *The Life of William Hutton* (1816), p. 41, all from Porter, *English Society*, pp. 41, 223, 224–5, 200, 198. 'more common': Miege, *New State* II, p. 42, from Pincus, *1688*, p. 75.

289: 'At first': Defoe, *A Brief Case of the Distillers, and of the Distilling Trade in England* (1726), from Jessica Warner, 'The Naturalization of Beer and Gin in Early Modern England', *Contemporary Drug Problems* 24 (1997), p. 388. 'Drunk for a penny': sign outside a gin dive in William Hogarth's print *Gin Lane* (1751). 'Young creatures': Corbyn Morris (1751), from Peter Ackroyd, *History of England* IV (2016), p. 153. 'this coffee drink': James Howell, quoted in William Rumsey, *Organon Salutis* (1657) sigs. B2–b3; 'Coffee-houses': Sir Thomas Player to Joseph Williamson (10 November 1673), from Steven Pincus, '"Coffee Politicians Does Create"', *Journal of Modern History* 67 (1995), pp. 825, 826.

290: 'a Turkish drink': Thomas Rugg, diary entry (November 1659), from Pincus, *1688*, p. 75. 'When coffee once': *The Character of a Coffee-House* (1665), title page, from Steven Pincus, '"Coffee Politicians Does Create"', pp. 817–18. 'a Cup of

Tee': Pepys, diary entry (25 September 1660), https://www.pepysdiary.com/diary/1660/09/25/.

291: 'vast epistemological effort', Scott, *Leviathan*, p. 270. 'Englished out of Wales': William Richards (1689), from John Davies, *A History of Wales* (2007), p. 294.

292: 'I shall be thought': Alan Brodrick (1712), from Bartlett, *Ireland*, p. 157. 'ridiculous': George I (1719), from Tim Blanning, *George I* (2020), p. 19.

292–3: 'hid[ing] my Head': Edward Burt, *Letters from a Gentleman in the North of Scotland to His Friend in London* I (1754), p. 21; 'at last old Reeky': Margaret, Countess of Panmure, letter to the Earl of Panmure (24 January 1723); 'crowded with men of genius': *Scots Magazine* 25 (1763), pp. 362–3; and 'all the poets': Thomas Sheridan (1762), quoted by James Boswell, *Boswell's London Journal, 1762–1763*; all from James Buchan, *Capital of the Mind* (2003), pp. 12–13, 17, 3, 164.

293: 'If they have no': Philip Stanhope, letter to John, fourth Duke of Bedford (17 September 1745), from Simms, *Three Victories*, p. 340.

295: 'a glass of good wine': Dr Alexander Hamilton (1744), from Richard Johnson, 'Growth and Mastery', in P. J. Marshall, ed., *Oxford History of the British Empire* II (1998), p. 276.

296: 'the American is': Alexis de Tocqueville, notebook entry (15 January 1832), from Arthur Kaledin, *Tocqueville and His America* (2011), p. 327. 'more like a negro country': from Johnson, 'Growth and Mastery', p. 281. 'approached much nearer': Josiah Tucker (1749), from Porter, *English Society*, p. 86. 'unworthy of the name': Benjamin Franklin, 'Fragments of a Pamphlet on the Stamp Act' (January 1766), from Jack Greene, 'Empire and Identity from the Glorious Revolution to the American Revolution', in Marshall, *British Empire* II, p. 225.

297: 'had yet to evolve' and 'profound uncertainty': Linda Colley, *Britons* (2nd edn, 2009), p. 136.

298: 'Commerce is the true source': 'On the Project of the Universal Monarchy of the English' (1748); and 'We must not flatter': Marquis de la Galissonière, 'Memoir on the Colonies in North America' (1750); both from Daniel Baugh, 'Withdrawing from Europe', *International History Review* 20 (1998), pp. 15, 14.

299: 'the First World War': Winston Churchill, *History of the English-Speaking Peoples* III (1967), Book 8, chapter 5.

300: 'It crept into our houses': Daniel Defoe, *Weekly Review* (31 January 1708), from Niall Ferguson, *Empire* (2003), p. 17.

302: 'I am sure': William Pitt, from Scott, *Leviathan*, p. 399. 'wicked madman': David Hume, from Herman, *To Rule*, p. 275. 'I know nobody': Newcastle, from Scott, *Leviathan*, p. 407. 'America . . .': Pitt, quoted by Newcastle, letter to the Duke of Devonshire (9 December 1761), from Simms, *Three Victories*, p. 484. 'However inconvenient': Pitt, from Jeremy Black, *The Elder Pitt* (1992), p. 231. 'No navy': French ambassador to Vienna (1758), from Herman, *To Rule*, p. 284.

303: 'I say' etc.: Admiral Edward Hawke (20 November 1759), from Herman, *To Rule*, pp. 288–9.

304: 'All that could': Hawke to the Admiralty (24 November 1759), from Nicholas Rodger, *The Command of the Ocean* (2004), p. 283. 'all this came': Magon de la Balue, letter to his business partner (5 November 1759), from Daniel Baugh, *The Global Seven Years War* (2011), p. 451. 'our bells': Horace Walpole (1759), from Scott, *Leviathan*, p. 405. 'Come cheer up': David Garrick and William Boyce, 'Heart of Oak', from the pantomime *Harlequin's Invasion* (1759). 'the people have a special character': Giacomo Casanova, *History of My Life* (1789–94), from Everyman's Library edn (2006), p. 843. 'struck such an awe': William Gordon, envoy to Regensburg (1764), from Simms, *Three Victories*, p. 517.

305: 'strategic narcissism' etc.: H. R. McMaster, *Battlegrounds* (2020), p.10, borrowing the term from Hans Morgenthau and Ethel Person. 'Supplying a French army' (1761): from Black, *Elder Pitt*, p. 223. 'a true snake': George, prince of Wales, letter to John Stuart, Earl of Bute (5 October 1760); 'getting rid of him': King George III, letter to Bute (3 May 1762); and 'an alliance': John Montagu, Earl of Sandwich, letter to John Russell, Duke of Bedford (8 September 1764); all from Simms, *Three Victories*, pp. 468, 475, 518.

306: 'far from being': Patrick Henry, speech in the 'Parson's Cause' case, Hanover County, Virginia (1 December 1763); and 'damned rascally': anonymous demonstrator, recorded in the papers of John Adams (5 March 1770); both from Robert Middlekauf, *The Glorious Cause* (2005), pp. 83, 210.

307: 'Long did I endeavour', Benjamin Franklin (July 1776); 'We might have been', Thomas Jefferson (July 1776); 'our unnatural children', Joseph Yorke, ambassador to the Netherlands, to James Harris, ambassador to Russia (13 January 1778); and 'Be the victory', Pitt, letter to Richard Grenville-Temple, Earl Temple (24 September 1777): all from Simms, *Three Victories*, pp. 603, 609, 610.

308: 'other General' (1779): from John Ferling, *Almost a Miracle* (2005), p. 562. 'had increased in proportion': William Pitt the Younger, speech to Parliament (1784), from H. Bowen, 'British India, 1765–1813', in Marshall, *British Empire* II, p. 542.

309: 'the oppression': Warren Hastings, governor-general of Bengal, letter to Henry Vansittart (April 1762); and 'vast exportation of coin': Ghulam Hussain Khan, *Siyar-ul-Mutakherin* (late 1780s), both from William Dalrymple, *The Anarchy* (2019), pp. 169, 211.

310: 'notwithstanding the great severity': East India Company Council, report to directors (February 1771); 'We have outdone the Spaniards': Horace Walpole, personal correspondence (late 1771); 'The riches of Asia': Pitt, speech to Parliament (1771), from Dalrymple, *Anarchy*, pp. 218, 221.

311: 'revenue was absolutely necessary': Charles James Fox, speech to Parliament (1784), from Bowen, 'British India', p. 535. 'gross injustice': Burke, speech in trial of Warren Hastings (4 April 1783).

312: 'I defy': Duke of Leeds (July 1789), from Simms, *Britain's Europe*, p. 82.

'there never was': Pitt (1792), from Rodger, *Command*, p. 367. 'How much the greatest': Fox, letter to R. Fitzpatrick (30 July 1789); 'No Pitt' and 'the most violent': Parson James Woodforde, Weston Longville, Norfolk, diary entry (29 October 1795), from Jenny Uglow, *In These Times* (2014), pp. 13, 147. 'between all the order': Sir Gilbert Eliot, letter to Lady Elliot (7 March 1793), from Rodger, *Command*, p. 426.

313: 'These men have saved': Lord Lieutenant Charles Cornwallis, letter to Major-General Ross (1798), from Robert Hughes, *The Fatal Shore* (1986), pp. 185–6.

314: 'must imply': Alexander Knox, former private secretary to Lord Castlereagh, letter to Castlereagh (9 February 1801), cited from John Bew, *Castlereagh* (2011), p. 178. 'Where is the consolidation?' Henry Grattan, speech to Parliament (1 January 1811), from David Cannadine, *Victorious Century* (2017), p. 97. 'Let us be masters': Napoleon to his generals at Boulogne (July 1804).

315: 'I hate the English': Tsar Alexander I to Napoleon, Tilsit (25 June 1807), from Andrew Roberts, *Napoleon the Great* (2014), p. 457. 'Having occupied': Charles Maurice Talleyrand-Perigord, reported in *The Times* (27 April 1798), from Uglow, *In These Times*, p. 234. 'the geographical key': Napoleon, from Roberts, *Napoleon*, p. 162. 'I never was in': General Gerard Lake (November 1803), from Pradeep Barua, 'Military Developments in India, 1750–1850', *Journal of Military History* 58 (1994), p. 599. 'I fear we are aggrandising': Admiral Sir Edward Pellew (1805), from Michael Duffy, 'World-Wide War and British Expansion, 1792–1815', in Marshall, *British Empire* II, p. 200.

317: 'I will conquer the sea': Napoleon, letter to Louis Bonaparte (3 December 1806); 'No ship coming from England': Berlin Decrees (21 November 1806); from Roberts, *Napoleon*, p. 427. 'the nearest-run thing': Arthur Wellesley, Duke of Wellington (June 1815), from Cannadine, *Victorious Century*, p. 99.

319: 'What overpowering events!': Revd John Stonard, letter to the Revd Richard Heber (15 April 1814); and 'TOTAL DEFEAT': *Morning Chronicle* (22 June 1815); from Uglow, *In These Times*, pp. 599, 619.

8. Wider Still and Wider, 1815–65

320: 'splendidly isolated': George Eulas Foster (1896), from Andrew Roberts, *Salisbury* (2000), p. 629. 'half the world': J. R. Seeley, *The Expansion of England* (1883), p. 12.

324: 'the Great Game': Rudyard Kipling, *Kim* (1901).

325: '*Peccavi*': Sir Charles Napier, telegraph to the East India Company's directors in Calcutta (24 March 1842), from Saul David, *Victoria's Wars* (2006), p. 78. I say 'Legend has it' because some historians believe the supposed telegram was actually a joke invented by Catherine Winkworth, a seventeen-year-old schoolgirl.

326: 'It appears to me': Simon Fraser, British Resident in Delhi, report to Charles Canning, governor-general of India (29 August 1856), from William Dalrymple,

The Last Mughal (2006), p. 114. 'Our Asiatic territories': Charles Grant, from
Dalrymple, *Last Mughal*, p. 61. 'moral regeneration': Lord William Bentinck,
governor-general of India (1829), from Cannadine, *Victorious Century*, p. 189.
'The distant and contemptible manner': Mohan Lal Kashmiri, Delhi English
College (1828); and 'I fear we do not gain': Sir David Octherlony, British
Resident in Delhi, letter to William Fraser (31 July 1820), from Dalrymple, *Last
Mughal*, pp. 69, 70.

328: 'We might annex': James Bruce, Earl of Elgin (1860), from Piers Brendon,
The Decline and Fall of the British Empire (2007), p. 108.

329: 'recolonize' and 'Russia might take California': President John Quincy
Adams, diary (26 November 1823), from Brendan Simms, *Europe: The Struggle
for Supremacy* (2013), p. 191.

330: 'the American continents': President James Monroe (2 December 1823), from
https://avalon.law.yale.edu/19th_century/monroe.asp.

331: 'The deed is done': Canning, letter to Viscount Granville (17 December 1824),
from H. Temperley, 'The Foreign Policy of Canning', in Adolphus Ward and G.
P. Gooch, eds, *The Cambridge History of British Foreign Policy, 1783–1919* II (1923),
p. 74. 'I called the New World': Canning, speech to Parliament (12 December
1826), from http://www.historyhome.co.uk/polspeech/portugal.htm.

332: 'event [. . .] which we all know': T. C. Haliburton, letter to P. Wiswall (7
January 1824), from Ged Martin, 'Canada from 1815', in Andrew Porter, ed.,
Oxford History of the British Empire III (1989), p. 530. 'a few miles': the prime
minister, Lord Aberdeen (1841), from Cannadine, *Victorious Century*, p. 227. 'a
last resource': Lord Gordon to the prime minister, Lord Aberdeen (28 July
1845), from Martin, 'Canada from 1815', p. 528. 'A Colony that is not attractive':
Edward Gibbon Wakefield, *A View of the Art of Colonization* (1849), p. 156. 'that
we have no interest': Sir George Grey, colonial secretary (1830s), from Brendon,
Decline and Fall, p. 73. 'Greater Britain': Charles Dilke, *Greater Britain* (1868).

334: 'increasing hourly': *Boston Recorder* (15 May 1819), from James Belich,
Replenishing the Earth (2009), p. 93. 'a friend and guardian': meeting of northern
chiefs (1831), and 'Ah! Those good old times': from Raewyn Dalziel, 'New
Zealand and Polynesia', in Porter, *British Empire* III, p. 577.

335: 'we are almost always worsted': James Stephens, permanent under-secretary
of the Colonial Office (*c.*1840), from John Darwin, *Unfinished Empire* (2012),
p. 195.

336: 'a vain and unfounded scruple': Sir George Grey, governor of New Zealand,
minute (23 December 1846), from Dalziel, 'New Zealand and Polynesia', p. 580.

340: 'All the people in Great Britain': Henry Fielding, *The Covent Garden Journal*
4 (14 January 1752), p. 683, from Porter, *English Society*, p. 60. 'Free Trade is
implied': Revd William Shrewsbury, *Christian Thoughts on Free Trade* (1843),
p. 40, from Boyd Hilton, *A Mad, Bad Dangerous People?* (2006), p. 504. 'Jesus
Christ is Free Trade': governor of Hong Kong, from Cannadine, *Victorious
Century*, p. 267.

341: 'The vast consumption': Anon., *Mineralogia Cornubiensis* (1778), from David
Landes, *The Unbound Prometheus* (2003), pp. 99–100. 'steam was an elastic body':
James Watt, as told to Robert Hart (1817; the walk took place in 1765), from
Jenny Uglow, *The Lunar Men* (2002), p. 101.

343: 'The spinning jenny': Charles Kingsley, *Yeast* (4th edn, 1883), p. 82.

344: 'North America and Russia': William Stanley Jevons, *The Coal Question*
(1865), from Paul Kennedy, *The Rise and Fall of the Great Powers* (1987), pp. 151–2.
'Cudgels & Sabres': Palmerston, Parliamentary minute (22 April 1860), from
John Darwin, *The Empire Project* (2011), p. 40.

345: 'astounding combination': Lord Russell, speech to the House of Lords (17
June 1850), from Dolphus Whitten, 'The Don Pacifico Affair', *The Historian* 48
(1989), p. 264. 'whether, as the Roman': Palmerston, speech to Parliament (25
June 1850).

346: 'There was a fluttering': *Illustrated London News* (13 June 1868), from
Ferguson, *Empire*, p. 179.

348: 'death by development': Ira Klein, 'Development and Death', *Indian
Economic and Social History Review* 38 (2001), p. 147. 'The earth was made':
Dickens, *Dealings with the Firm Dombey and Son* (1846), Chapter 1.

349–51: 'dirty beyond the usual': G. R. Porter, *The Progress of the Nation* (1847),
p. 533; 'For a growing proportion' and 'basement floor[s]', George Godwin,
Another Blow for Life (1864); 'Picturesque and harmonious', Richard Heath,
The English Peasant (1893), p. 59; and 'labourers seem miserably poor', William
Cobbett, *Rural Rides* I (1821–32); all from John Burnett, *A Social History of
Housing* (2nd edn, 1986), pp. 89, 92, 88, 31.

352: 'a famine of the thirteenth century': Lord John Russell (1848), from
Cannadine, *Victorious Century*, p. 211. 'I have always felt': Benjamin Jowett,
master of Balliol College, Oxford, from James Donnelly, 'The Great Famine':
in John Gibney, ed., *The Great Famine* (2018), p. 124.

353: 'a happiness and a privilege': Anon., 'The First Half of the 19th Century',
The Economist 9 (1851), p. 57. 'crowds of people': Walter Bagehot, *The English
Constitution* (1867), from Asa Briggs, *The Age of Improvement* (1959), p. 449. 'The
Condition of England': Thomas Carlyle, *Chartism* (1839), from http://www.
historyhome.co.uk/peel/rurallife/carlyle.htm.

354: 'our epoch' etc.: Karl Marx and Friedrich Engels, *The Communist Manifesto*
(1848), from David McLellan, *Karl Marx: Selected Writings* (1977), pp. 222, 223,
226, 227, 231.

356: 'God helps those' etc.: Samuel Smiles, *Self-Help* (1859), from Asa Briggs,
Victorian People (1955), pp. 119, 126–7, 123. 'If Europe is a nymph': Juliusz
Słowacki, *Journey to the East* (1836), from Norman Davies, *Europe* (1996), p. 1.
'an imbecile': *The Times* (23 January 1901), from Cannadine, *Victorious Century*,
p. 130. 'They live here': Charles Greville (September 1849), from Christopher
Hibbert, *Queen Victoria* (2000), p. 178.

356–7: 'the pride of sovereignty': Bagehot, *English Constitution*; 'that she is a wife':

Leeds Mercury (11 September 1858); and 'a gentleman at ease': Lord Granville; all
from Briggs, *Age of Improvement*, pp. 459, 450.

357: 'stolid, pipe-sucking manhood': Robert Baden-Powell, *Scouting for Boys*
(1908), from Bill Buford, *Among the Thugs* (1991), p. 12. 'religious and moral
principle' etc.: Thomas Arnold (1830s), from Robert Tombs, *The English and
Their History* (2014), p. 513. 'It is only in England': Matthew Arnold, *Friendship's
Garland* (1871), from Briggs, *Victorian People*, p. 145. 'fresh, brave school-life':
Thomas Hughes, *Tom Brown's School Days* (1858), Chapter 8. 'a book every
English father': *The Times*; and 'Boys who learned': from Tombs, *The English
and Their History*, pp. 513, 514.

358: 'I, Brummell': George Bryan Brummell, from Ian Kelly, *Beau Brummell*
(2005), Fig. 11.

360: 'The English proletariat': Engels, letter to Marx, from Cannadine, *Victorious
Century*, p. 322. 'Wherever cricket': Baron Platt, address to the Lancashire
Assizes (1851), from Neil Tranter, *Sport, Economy and Society in Britain* (1998),
p. 37.

361: 'We thank thee': Revd T. D. Harford Battersby, sermon in St John's Church,
Keswick (26 April 1854), from Orlando Figes, *Crimean War* (2010), p. 163. 'A
Church, Sir': anonymous respondent interviewed by Henry Mayhew (1851),
from Briggs, *Age of Improvement*, p. 466.

363: 'attempt to fasten': Lord John Russell, letter to the bishop of Durham
(November 1850), from Cannadine, *Victorious Century*, p. 264. 'We have reduced
protection': Peel, speech to Parliament (May 1845). 'Why is it': Thomas
Babington Macaulay, diary entry (August 1849), from Hilton, *A Mad, Bad
Dangerous People*, p. 238. 'there never was a period': Palmerston, speech to
Parliament (1832), from Cannadine, *Victorious Century*, p. 186.

364: 'Die, my dear doctor?' Palmerston (18 October 1865), from https://www.
bartleby.com/344/308.html. 'Our quiet days': Sir Charles Wood (1865), from
Cannadine, *Victorious Century*, p. 334.

9. The New World Steps Forth, 1865–1945

369: 'Get a horse!' from Daniel Yergin, *The Prize* (1992), p. 79.

371: 'churchmen, landowners': third marquess of Salisbury, 'Disintegration',
Quarterly Review 156 (1883), from Cannadine, *Victorious Century*, p. 387. 'Far-
called': Kipling, 'Recessional', *The Times* (17 July 1897).

372: 'My beloved submarines': Sir John Fisher, first lord of the Admiralty, private
letter (March 1904); '[with]in three or four years': Fisher (1905); from Nicholas
Lambert, *Sir John Fisher's Naval Revolution* (2002), pp. 83, 123. 'Germany keeps
her whole fleet': Fisher, letter to Louis, prince of Wales (January 1907), from
Robert Massie, *Dreadnought* (1991), p. 500.

374: 'When we inquire' and 'you have the most progressive race': J. R. Seeley, *The
Expansion of England* (1883), from 1971 edn, pp. 12, 15. 'senior partner' etc.: James
Belich, *Replenishing the Earth* (2009), p. 68.

375: 'chimerical if not': Gladstone, quoted by his private secretary Edward Hamilton in his diary (19 November 1884), from Duncan Bell, *The Idea of Greater Britain* (2007), p. 16. 'utter bollocks': Kevin Rudd, former prime minister of Australia, https://www.theguardian.com/australia-news/2019/mar/11/former-australian-pm-kevin-rudd-calls-brexit-trade-plan-utter-bollocks.

377: 'In a splendid isolation': the colonial secretary, Joseph Chamberlain (1902), from Massie, *Dreadnought*, p. 329. 'Hands off the people's food!': Liberal Party slogan (1906), from Peter Clarke, *Hope and Glory* (2004), p. 7.

378: 'to wage implacable warfare': David Lloyd George, budget speech (29 April 1909), https://www.nationalarchives.gov.uk/education/britain1906to1918/g2/gallery2.htm. 'the end of all': Lord Rosebery (summer 1909); and 'We have got them': Lloyd George (30 November 1909); both from Massie, *Dreadnought*, pp. 64, 659.

379: 'mightily concerned': H. G. Wells, *Mr Britling Sees It Through* (1916). 'until further notice': announcement of the closing of the London Stock Exchange (31 July 1914), from Ferguson, *Pity of War*, p. 197.

380: 'business carried on as usual': Churchill, speech at the London Guildhall (9 November 1914), from Winston Churchill, *Complete Speeches* III (1974), p. 2341.

381: 'untenable under any law': US Navy (autumn 1914), from Adam Tooze, *The Deluge* (2014), p. 34.

382: 'peace without victory': President Woodrow Wilson, speech to the US Senate (22 January 1917), from https://www.oxfordreference.com/view/10.1093/acref/9780199891580.001.0001/acref-9780199891580-e-5986. 'I am, I must admit': Wilson to Colonel Edward House (September 1916), from Tooze, *Deluge*, p. 35.

382–3: 'By next June': Chancellor Reginald McKenna, Cabinet discussion (18 October 1916); 'active sympathy': Lloyd George to US Secretary of State Robert Lansing (December 1916); and 'the entire world could not shake': Lloyd George to Edward House (1916); all from Tooze, *Deluge*, pp. 48, 49.

383: 'With our backs': Field Marshal Sir Douglas Haig, 'Back to the Wall' order (11 April 1918), from James Edmonds, *A Short History of World War I* (1951), p. 305.

384: 'a dyke of peaceful': Churchill, from Simms, *Britain's Europe*, p. 150.

385: 'Only national self-preservation': Winston Churchill, *The World Crisis* IV (1929), p. 297. 'shoot hard': Churchill (1920); 'quite mad': Stanley Baldwin (1935); from Lawrence James, *Raj* (1997), pp. 480, 534.

386: 'Britain possessing the finest credit': Churchill (1924), from Peter Cain and Anthony Hopkins, *British Imperialism, 1688–2000* (2nd edn, 2000), p. 458.

387: 'another and more terrible': Wilson to House (December 1918), from Tooze, *Deluge*, p. 268. 'the most intensely dramatic moment' etc.: William Allen White (12 November 1921), from George Herring, *From Colony to Superpower* (2008), p. 454.

388: 'the chief business': President Calvin Coolidge (probably apocryphal, but usually dated to 1925), from David Kennedy, *Freedom from Fear* (1999), p. 34.

389: 'whiff of welfare': Anthony Crosland MP, *The Guardian* (16 June 1971), from Dominic Sandbrook, *Seasons in the Sun* (2012), p. 695. 'red rust' and 'London's creeping': E. M. Forster, *Howards End* (1910), Chapter 44. 'the five giant evils': William Beveridge, 'New Britain', speech at Oxford University (6 December 1942), from John Boyer and Jan Goldstein, eds, *Twentieth-Century Europe* (1987), p. 506.

390: 'turned out nice': George Formby (1941), from https://www.lyrics.com/lyric/4470978/George+Formby/It%27s+Turned+out+Nice+Again. 'less than a Nigger state': Adolf Hitler, speech (30 November 1922), from Brendan Simms, *Hitler* (2019), p. 40.

391: 'the ultimate potential enemy': Defence Requirements Subcommittee (February 1934), from Simms, *Britain's Europe*, p. 346. 'expose to depredation': British chiefs of staff (October 1932), from Niall Ferguson, *War of the World* (2006), p. 321. 'Modern aeroplanes': *Daily Mail* (8 January 1934), from Uri Bialer, 'Elite Opinion and Defence Policy', *British Journal of International Studies* 6 (1980), p. 37. 'We thought of air warfare': Harold Macmillan, *The Winds of Change* (1966), p. 522. 'Every town': J. L. Garvin, *The Observer* (26 February 1933), from Bialer, 'Elite Opinion', p. 43. 'the bomber will always get through': Stanley Baldwin, speech to House of Commons (10 November 1932).

392: 'even more important': United Kingdom chiefs of staff (July 1934), from Simms, *Britain's Europe*, p. 157. 'The old frontiers': Baldwin, speech to House of Commons (30 July 1934). 'an appeaser [a]s one who feeds': Winston Churchill, *Reader's Digest* (December 1954). There is a good chance that this is someone else's reformulation of Churchill's actual words ('Each one hopes that if he feeds the crocodile enough, it will eat him last') in a BBC radio broadcast on 20 January 1940 (https://quoteinvestigator.com/2016/04/18/crocodile/#return-note-13473-3).

393: 'was a racist': Black Lives Matter protesters, Parliament Square, London (7 June 2020), https://www.bbc.com/news/uk-53033550.

394: 'We shall go on': Churchill, speech to Parliament (4 June 1940). 'What is our aim?' Churchill, speech to Parliament (13 May 1940). 'until, in God's good time': Churchill, speech to Parliament (4 June 1940).

395: 'They aren't bust': President Franklin Delano Roosevelt to advisers (November 1940); and 'the silly, foolish old dollar sign': Roosevelt, comments at a press conference (17 December 1940); from Daniel Todman, *Britain's War* I (2017), pp. 526, 528. 'the most unsordid act': Winston Churchill, *The Second World War* II (1949), p. 503. 'a sheriff collecting': Churchill, unsent draft (26 December 1940), from Todman, *Britain's War* I, p. 530. 'Now at this very moment' etc.: Churchill, *The Second World War* III (1950), p. 539–41. 'the world war is here': Hitler, conversation with Nazi regional commanders, Berlin (13 December 1941), from Simms, *Hitler*, p. 443.

396: 'This is not a victory': Churchill, speech from the Ministry of Health building (7 May 1945), from Todman, *Britain's War* II, p. 721. 'People are willing': Ministry of Information report (March 1942); 'There could be': R. J. Hammond, *Food* II: *Studies in Administration and Control* (London 1956), p. 753. 'a plainly marked black line': Eleanor Roosevelt, *The Autobiography of Eleanor Roosevelt* (1962), p. 185–6. 'Thank God for a good King!' anonymous Londoner and King George VI (10 September 1940), from Peter Hennessy, *Never Again* (1993), pp. 50, 51. 'influencing the future': Keynes, speech in the House of Lords (18 December 1945), from Todman, *Britain's War* II, p. 782. 'hopes of better times': Hugh Dalton MP, speech to Parliament (12 December 1945).

10. The Very Point of Junction, 1945–91

399: 'As I look out' etc.: Churchill, speech to Conservative meeting, Llandudno (19 October 1948), from https://web-archives.univ-pau.fr/english/special/SRdoc1.pdf.

401: 'it's no good': anonymous working-class woman to Mass Observation interviewer (Spring 1945), from Todman, *Britain's War* II, p. 760.

403: 'have really done': Hugh Gaitskell, leader of the Labour Party, diary entry, from Dominic Sandbrook, *Never Had It So Good* (2005), p. 65. 'the 'edgerows of experience': Ernest Bevin, British foreign secretary, to George VI (1947), from Hugo Young, *This Blessed Plot* (1998), p. 25. 'the Russians out': Hastings Ismay, secretary-general of NATO (1949). The line is regularly quoted, but has never been traced to Ismay himself.

404: 'We've got to have': Bevin (1946), from John Bew, *Citizen Clem* (2017), p. 420.

404–5: 'We must do it': Churchill to Edwin Plowden, chairman of the Atomic Energy Authority (1952); and 'by threatening to use': internal government report (1957), from Sandbrook, *Never Had It So Good*, pp. 239, 110.

406: 'a new High Authority' and 'the first concrete step': Robert Schuman (9 May 1950), http://europa.eu/abc/symbols/9–may/decl_en.htm.

406–7: 'It's no good': Herbert Morrison, Labour Party deputy prime minister, comments to Cabinet (May 1950); 'just a step': Kenneth Younger, adviser to Ernest Bevin, foreign secretary, diary entry (14 May 1950); 'This is something': Anthony Eden, foreign secretary, speech in New York (1952); and 'There is no attraction', senior civil servant in private conversation (1949); all from Tony Judt, *Postwar* (2005), pp. 160, 158, 164, 159.

407: 'sucked up': Hugh Gaitskell, leader of the Labour Party (1962); 'Britain is not just a small, crowded island': Labour Party National Executive (drafted by Denis Healey), 'European Unity' (1951); from Sandbrook, *Never Had It So Good*, pp. 533, 221. 'to work for the establishment': preamble to paper circulated in advance of the Conference of Messina (May 1955); 'the Old Bailey trial', 'mysticism' and 'appeal to European Catholic federalists': Edward Bridges, head of the home civil service (July 1955); and 'Gentlemen, you are trying to negotiate', words alleged to have been spoken at the Messina Conference by

Russell Bretherton, under-secretary at the Board of Trade (3 June 1955); all from Young, *Blessed Plot*, pp. 80, 78, 91, 93.

409: 'In the beginning': Denzil Batchelor, *Picture Post* sportswriter, in his book *Soccer* (1954), p. 149, from Robert Weight, *Patriots* (2002), p. 261.

410: 'continuation of imperialism': Ronald Robinson, 'Imperial Theory and the Question of Imperialism after Empire', *Journal of Imperial and Commonwealth History* 12 (1984), p. 53. 'Britain has fulfilled': *Pathé News* issue 47/66 (18 August 1947), from Daniel Todman, *Britain's War* II (2020), p. 824. 'could have the United States': Bevin, from W. David McIntyre, *British Decolonization* (1998), p. 87.

411: 'was not the issue': President Dwight D. Eisenhower (August 1956), from David Reynolds, *One World Divisible* (2000), p. 85. 'I know Ike': Chancellor Harold Macmillan, Cabinet meeting (August 1956), from Clarke, *Hope and Glory*, p. 260. 'At all costs': Eisenhower to John Foster Dulles (5 November 1956), from Reynolds, *One World*, p. 85. 'I am not sure', Churchill; 'gravely endangering', Parliamentary motion; and 'There's nobody, in a war', Eisenhower to Emmet John Hughes (all November 1956); all from Sandbrook, *Never Had It So Good*, pp. 26, 29, 28.

412: 'Great Britain has lost': Acheson, speech at West Point (5 December 1962), from Brinkley, 'Special Relationship', p. 601. '*has not so much changed*': Eden, memorandum (28 December 1956). 'an infinite capacity': R. A. Butler, private conversation (1958), from Sandbrook, *Never Had It So Good*, pp. 27, 73. 'We are not a Great Power': Sir Henry Tizard, minute to the Ministry of Defence, from Young, *Blessed Plot*, p. 25.

413: 'a paradigm of national impotence': Bernard Levin, *The Pendulum Years* (1977), p. 130. 'supreme national interests', Nassau Agreement (1962); 'We thought' and 'If we threw away our bombs': A. J. P. Taylor, from Sandbrook, *Never Had It So Good*, pp. 245, 268.

414: 'a British Brigade in Vietnam': National Security Advisor McGeorge Bundy to Johnson (28 July 1965), from Dominic Sandbrook, *White Heat* (2006), p. 124. 'we can't kick': Wilson to Brown (1966), from Kevin Boyle, 'The Price of Peace', *Diplomatic History* 27 (2003), p. 44. 'There are two things': Sandbrook, *White Heat*, p. 26.

415: 'Are these people ready': Macmillan to governor-general of Nigeria (1960), from Sandbrook, *Never Had It So Good*, p. 289. 'The wind of change': Macmillan, Cape Town (3 January 1960), from https://www.oxfordreference.com/view/10.1093/acref/9780191843730.001.0001/q-oro-ed5-00006970. 'cease to play': Denis Healey, minister of defence (July 1967), from Sandbrook, *White Heat*, p. 373. 'For the first time': Macmillan to Seton Lloyd, foreign secretary (December 1959), from Sandbrook, *Never Had It So Good*, p. 527.

415–6: 'grim choice': Macmillan, diary entry (9 July 1960); 'we are not entitled': Wilson, speech to Parliament (2 August 1961); and 'England is insular' etc.:

President Charles de Gaulle, press conference at the Elysée Palace (14 January 1963) all from Sandbrook, *Never Had It So Good*, pp. 527, 536, 532.

416–17: 'life and death': Enoch Powell MP, speech in Parliament (January 1971); 'Fascist bastard!': Reg Freeson MP, debate in Parliament (28 October 1971); 'See the Ambassadors' Gallery?': anonymous attendant, House of Commons (28 October 1971); and 'This is what I have been waiting for': Jean Monnet (28 October 1971); all from Dominic Sandbrook, *State of Emergency* (2010), pp. 164, 166, 165, 167.

417: 'Forty years after': Edward Heath, *The Course of My Life* (1998), pp. 371–2. 'I am not pro': James Callaghan to Robin Day, phone-in interview on BBC Radio 4 (27 May 1975), from David Butler and Uwe Kitzinger, *The 1975 Referendum* (1976), p. 176. 'wished she didn't': Charles Moore, *Margaret Thatcher* I (2013), p. 306.

418: 'to make far-reaching changes': Harold Wilson, speech at the Labour Party conference, Scarborough (12 October 1963), https://web-archives.univ-pau.fr/english/TD2doc2.pdf. 'a bridge and a traitor': Revd Ian Paisley (1965); 'I can get the army in': James Callaghan, home secretary, telephone conversation with Gerry Fitt MP (13 August 1969); and 'Kids were following you': British lance-corporal (14 August 1969); all from Sandbrook, *White Heat*, pp. 356, 754, 756.

419: 'we would have said': General Sir Frank King (May 1974); and 'the police were on the brink': Northern Ireland secretary Merlyn Rees (1974); both from Sandbrook, *Seasons in the Sun*, p. 120. 'A million British citizens': Robert Fisk, *The Point of No Return* (1975), p. 13. 'consider "the unmentionable"': Wilson to Bernard Donoghue (May 1974); and 'the hard men with dark glasses', Kenneth Bloomfield (permanent secretary to the Northern Ireland Executive); both from Sandbrook, *Seasons in the Sun*, pp. 109, 119.

420: 'in danger of being': Dafydd Wigley MP (Plaid Cymru), from Dominic Sandbrook, *Who Dares Wins* (2019), p. 554. 'North Sea oil stands': *Time* (29 September 1975), from Sandbrook, *Seasons in the Sun*, p. 515. 'It's *our* Oil': Scottish Nationalist Party slogan (1973), from Clarke, *Hope and Glory*, p. 323. 'most of our people': Macmillan, speech to Mid-Bedfordshire Conservative Party (20 July 1957), http://news.bbc.co.uk/onthisday/hi/dates/stories/july/20/newsid_3728000/3728225.stm.

421: 'Britain is now': Roy Harrod, letter to Macmillan (11 October 1961), from Sandbrook, *Never Had It So Good*, p. 522. 'Our decline': Nicholas Henderson, British ambassador to France, private dispatch (June 1979), from Young, *Blessed Plot*, p. 311.

423: 'was to settle up': Macmillan, interview at London Airport (7 January 1958), https://www.oxfordreference.com/view/10.1093/acref/9780191843730.001.0001/q-oro-ed5-00006970. 'The simple truth': Peter Thorneycroft, chancellor of the exchequer, resignation speech (23 January 1958); and 'expansion without inflation': Reginald Maudling, chancellor of the exchequer, budget speech (3 April 1963); both from Sandbrook, *Never Had It So Good*, pp. 92, 517. 'If I were a

younger man' and 'The cosy world': James Callaghan, *Time and Chance* (1987),
pp. 326, 425–7 (https://www.youtube.com/watch?v=76ImzIwB1–k).

424: 'the patience of our creditors': Denis Healey, chancellor of the exchequer,
budget speech (15 April 1975), https://www.nytimes.com/1975/04/16/
archives/britain-increases-taxes-assails-unions-demands.html.

424–5: 'stop paying "danegeld"': Anthony Crosland, foreign secretary, comments
in Cabinet (23 November 1976); 'Target for Today': *Daily Mail* headline (2
February 1979); 'means lives lost': Bill Dunn, spokesman for ambulance drivers,
Daily Express (20 January 1979); 'a fucking 'orrible lot', Frank Chapple,
secretary-general of the Electrical, Electronic, Telecommunications and
Plumbing Union, to Bernard Donoughue (January 1979); and 'There are
wreckers among us': Margaret Thatcher, Conservative Party political
broadcast (17 January 1979); all from Sandbrook, *Seasons in the Sun*, pp. 491, 750,
733, 762–3. 'Your country': Edward R. Murrow, 'A Reporter Remembers', *The
Listener* (28 February 1946), from Hennessy, *Never Again*, pp. 18–19.

426–7: 'that nine High Court judges': Levin, *The Pendulum Years*, p. 49. 'One,
[. . .] perhaps two': Macmillan to Ian Macleod (July 1963); and 'nothing
happened except': John Lennon, interview (November 1969); both from
Sandbrook, *Never Had It So Good*, pp. 675, xxiii. 'We love you, Liz!': *The Times*
(8 June 1977), from Sandbrook, *Seasons in the Sun*, p. 633. 'more popular
than Jesus': John Lennon, interview with Maureen Cleave, *Evening Standard*
(4 March 1966), https://www.rocksbackpages.com/Library/Article/
how-does-a-beatle-live-john-lennon.

428: 'as if he was taking part in a demo': Walter Johnson MP, *Daily Mirror* (9
November 1981); 'like the real leader': *Daily Mail* (10 November 1981), from
Sandbrook, *Who Dares Wins*, p. 551.

429: 'irresistible empire': Victoria de Grazia, *Irresistible Empire* (2005). 'the
Eurostomach': E. P. Thompson, *Sunday Times* (27 April 1975), from Young,
Blessed Plot, p. 290.

430: 'the molten curries' and 'well-considered curry': Colonel Kenny-Herbert,
Culinary Jottings for Madras (1885), from David Gilmour, *The British in India*
(2018), p. 352. 'a true British national dish': Robin Cook, foreign secretary,
speech to the Social Market Foundation, London (19 April 2001), https://www.
theguardian.com/world/2001/apr/19/race.britishidentity.

431: 'They just are different': Mick Jagger, *International Times* (17 May 1968),
from Sandbrook, *White Heat*, p. 675. 'You must expect to meet this': Ministry
of Labour, *How to Adjust Yourself in Britain* (1954); 'Poor old Enoch': Ian
Macleod, colonial secretary, private conversation (1958); 'I can't stand those
mad eyes': Macmillan (1960), from Sandbrook, *Never Had It So Good*, pp. 330,
91, 90. 'Like the Roman' etc.: Enoch Powell, speech to the Conservative
Association, Birmingham (20 April 1968), from https://www.telegraph.co.uk/
comment/3643823/Enoch-Powells-Rivers-of-Blood-speech.html. 'the ravings of
a sick hysteric': *Daily Mirror* (22 April 1968), from Sandbrook, *White Heat*, p. 681.

432: 'It is deplorable': *Daily Mail* (5 September 1956), from Sandbrook, *Never Had It So Good*, p. 461. 'the land without music': Oscar Schmitz, *Das Land ohne Musik* (1904), from Dominic Sandbrook, *The Great British Culture Factory* (2015), p. 17. 'we may be regarded': *New Musical Express* (25 June 1965), from Sandbrook, *White Heat*, p. 341.

433: 'Shiny, happy': Tim Adams, *The Observer* (22 March 2009), from Sandbrook, *Culture Factory*, p. 73. 'embraced a new identity': Sandbrook, *Culture Factory*, p. xxv.

434–5: 'We cannot have an international currency': Treasury report (1961); and 'There may indeed': Roy Bridge, adviser to the governors of the Bank of England, from David Kynaston, *Till Time's Last Sand* (2017), p. 452, 453.

436: 'Comrades': Tony Benn MP, speech at the Labour Party conference, Blackpool (29 September 1980), from Sandbrook, *Who Dares Wins* (2019), p. 367.

437: 'give Maggie everything she needs': President Ronald Reagan to Secretary of Defense Casper Weinberger (mid-April 1982), from Moore, *Margaret Thatcher* I, p. 694. 'would mortgage the Washington Monument': Reagan to the US National Security Council (February 1983), from Moore, *Margaret Thatcher* II (2015), p. 25n. 'I stand before you': Thatcher, speech to the Finchley Conservative Association (31 January 1976), http://www.margaretthatcher.org/document/102947.

438: 'the sort of guy': either Charles Powell or Bernard Ingham (both claim the words), to Thatcher, Chequers (16 December 1984), from Moore, *Margaret Thatcher* II, p. 240.

439: 'a matter of profound regret': Thatcher, dinner with the Conservative Group for Europe (1 January 1983), from Stephen Wall, *A Stranger in Europe* (2008), p. 18. 'the most valuable financial agreement': Robin Renwick, assistant under-secretary at the Foreign and Commonwealth Office; 'the golden years': David Williamson, deputy secretary of the Cabinet Office; both from Moore, *Margaret Thatcher* II, pp. 380, 407. 'ostentatiously *communautaire*': Margaret Thatcher, *The Downing Street Years* (1993), p. 548. 'In ten years': Jacques Delors, president of the European Commission, speech to the European Parliament (6 July 1988), from Young, *Blessed Plot*, p. 345. 'Our destiny is in Europe': Thatcher, College of Europe, Bruges (20 September 1988), https://www.margaretthatcher.org/document/107332.

440: 'to achieve what neither Bismarck nor Hitler could achieve': President François Mitterrand to Thatcher, Strasbourg (8 December 1989); 'and then we would': Mitterrand to Thatcher, Paris (20 January 1990); and 'the center of gravity': Robert Zoellick, Counsellor of the State Department, interview; all from Charles Moore, *Margaret Thatcher* III (2019), pp. 502, 507, 223. 'no, no, yes': Douglas Hurd, foreign secretary, from Young, *Blessed Plot*, p. 351. 'No, no, no': Thatcher, debate in Parliament (30 October 1990), https://www.margaretthatcher.org/document/108234. 'I want us to be where we belong':

John Major, prime minister, Bonn (February 1991), from John Major, *The Autobiography* (1999), p. 269.

11. Keep Calm and Carry On, 1992–2103

441: 'Our first objective': Zalmay Khalilzad and Scooter Libby, unpublished draft of the 1992 Defense Planning Guidance (18 February 1992), www.gwu.edu/~nsarchiv/nukevault/ebb245/index.htm.

443: 'The brutal truth': James Baker III, former US secretary of state, from Moore, *Margaret Thatcher* III, p. 621. Canadian forces too: anonymous American officer interviewed by Peter Bergen, Kabul (May 2007), from Peter Bergen, *The Longest War* (2011), p. 189.

444: 'old Europe': Secretary of Defense Donald Rumsfeld, discussion at the Foreign Press Center, Washington, DC (22 January 2003), https://www.youtube.com/watch?v=E0GnRJEPXn4. 'crusades': President George W. Bush, White House South Lawn, Washington, DC (16 September 2001), https://georgewbush-whitehouse.archives.gov/news/releases/2001/09/20010916-2.html; Osama bin Laden (recording broadcast on Al Jazeera, 23 April 2006), https://web.archive.org/web/20070816191154/http://english.aljazeera.net/English/archive/archive?ArchiveId=22235. 'piggy banks': Melanie Phillips, *Londonistan* (2006), p. xx.

445: 'Muslim-only' etc.: Steve Emerson, Fox News Network (12 January 2015), https://www.bbc.com/news/uk-england-30773297. 'a bit bonkers': Birmingham city councillor James Mackay, BBC interview (21 January 2015), https://www.bbc.com/news/uk-england-birmingham-30913393. 'the birthright of all the people of Northern Ireland': Northern Ireland Peace Agreement, Constitutional Issues I.vi (10 April 1998), https://peacemaker.un.org/sites/peacemaker.un.org/files/IE%20GB_980410_Northern%20Ireland%20Agreement.pdf. 'it is always felt': George Orwell, *The Lion and the Unicorn* (1941), p. 48.

447: 'The boom and bust': Gordon Brown, chancellor of the exchequer, budget speech (11 June 1998), from Tombs, *The English and Their History*, p. 850.

450: 'To get rich is no sin': Chairman Deng Xiaoping, speech in Beijing (2 September 1986), from John Gittings, *The Changing Face of China* (2005), p. 103. 'China's displacement': Lee Kuan Yew, from Graham Allison et al., *Lee Kuan Yew* (2013), p. 42.

452: 'import the cancer': US Treasury Secretary Hank Paulson's account of Alistair Darling's comments on the telephone (14 September 2008), https://www.theguardian.com/business/2009/sep/03/lehman-brothers-rescue-bid. 'You'd have had complete panic': Darling, interview with Will Martin (29 May 2018), https://www.stuff.co.nz/business/world/104295018/britain-was-hours-from-breakdown-of-law-and-order-during-gfc-exchancellor.

454: 'After 1989': joke at the G20 summit, London (April 2009), from *The Economist* (23 May 2009), p.47. 'calling on Mayor Sadiq Khan': https://www.

change.org/p/sadiq-khan-declare-london-independent-from-the-uk-and-apply-to-join-the-eu. 'You are now leaving': Dr Laura Lewis's mobile phone (summer 2014).

455: '"London" has become': https://www.telegraph.co.uk/news/politics/local-elections/10852204/Local-elections-The-capital-fails-to-see-the-heartache-and-pain-beyond.html. 'the faceless monster': https://www.telegraph.co.uk/news/politics/local-elections/10852141/Local-elections-The-party-machine-is-what-is-great-about-British-politics.html.

456: 'There is virtually' and 'There are overall signs': Bundesfinanzministerium (4 June 2010), from Adam Tooze, *Crashed* (2018), p. 339. 'do whatever it takes': Mario Draghi, president of the European Central Bank, speech at the Global Investment Conference, London (26 July 2012), https://www.ecb.europa.eu/press/key/date/2012/html/sp120726.en.html. 'To British eyes': Daniel Hannan, *Inventing Freedom* (2013), p. 5.

457: 'opened the door' and 'say they will use': Nigel Farage, leader of the United Kingdom Independence Party, *The Telegraph* (4 September 2015), https://www.telegraph.co.uk/news/politics/nigel-farage/11836131/Nigel-Farage-EU-has-opened-doors-to-migration-exodus-of-biblical-proportions.html. 'banging on': David Cameron, prime minister, Conservative Party annual conference, Bournemouth (1 October 2006), http://www.britishpoliticalspeech.org/speech-archive.htm?speech=314. 'mad, swivel-eyed loons': unnamed senior Conservative (perhaps Andrew Feldman, chair of the Conservative Party), comment to James Kirkup in the Blue Boar pub, Westminster (May 2013), https://www.telegraph.co.uk/news/politics/10065307/David-Camerons-ally-our-party-activists-are-loons.html. 'It is time': Cameron, speech at Bloomberg London (23 January 2013), https://www.gov.uk/government/speeches/eu-speech-at-bloomberg. 'crazy': Nick Clegg, deputy prime minister; and 'I have to do this': Cameron, both from Shipman, *All-Out War*, p. 9. 'reckless beyond belief': Ken Clarke, *Kind of Blue* (2016), p. 473. 'I have no doubt': Iain Duncan Smith, work and pensions secretary, BBC Radio 4 (23 August 2016), from Shipman, *All-Out War*, p. 13.

458: Dinner as opposed to lunch: Nick Clegg, in conversation with the author, Stanford University (8 May 2018). 'modern US presidents': Simon Tisdall, *The Guardian* (28 April 2019), https://www.theguardian.com/politics/2019/apr/28/britain-america-history-special-relationship-highs-and-lows-churchill-to-trump. 'Britain should run' and 'best partner in the West': George Osborne, chancellor, press conference in Beijing (20 September 2015), https://www.economist.com/britain/2015/09/26/the-osborne-doctrine; https://www.bbc.com/news/world-asia-china-34539507. 'They [the Chinese] like George': unnamed British official (late 2015), Michael Ashcroft and Isabel Oakeshott, *Call Me Dave* (2016), p. 455.

459: 'selling our national security': Nick Timothy, adviser to Theresa May, home secretary (20 October 2015), http://www.conservativehome.com/

thecolumnists/2015/10/nick-timothy-the-government-is-selling-our-national-security-to-china.html. 'golden time' and 'golden era': Ambassador Liu Xiaoming and Cameron, respectively, London (17 October 2015), https://www.reuters.com/article/us-china-britain/china-britain-to-benefit-from-golden-era-in-ties-cameron-idUSKCN0SB10M20151017.

460: 'it looks like': Farage (23 June 2016), https://www.independent.co.uk/news/uk/home-news/eu-referendum-nigel-farage-remain-edge-it-brexit-ukip-a7098526.html. 'As a historian': Donald Tusk, president of the European Council, interview with *Bild* (13 June 2016), from https://www.bbc.com/news/uk-politics-eu-referendum-36515680.

461: 'the only politician': Bob Canfield, in conversation with the author, Tucson, Arizona (February 2016).

462: 'the Honourable Member': David Reynolds, *Island Stories* (2019), p. 24. 'leave means leave': Cameron, Royal Institute of International Affairs, London (10 November 2015), https://www.youtube.com/watch?v=gUsKWsPcRXE.

463: 'peaceful development': Binguo Dai, http://china.usc.edu/ShowArticle.aspx?articleID=2325. 'peaceful rise': Zheng Bijian, 'China's "Peaceful Rise" to Great-Power Status', *Foreign Affairs* 84.5 (2005), pp. 14–24. 'When the facts change': there is no direct evidence that Keynes ever said this. It is probably a misquotation of Paul Samuelson (https://quoteinvestigator.com/2011/07/22/keynes-change-mind/). 'hide your capacities': Deng Xiaoping, https://www.economist.com/special-report/2010/12/04/less-biding-and-hiding. 'make China's voice heard': Xi Jinping, speech to China's politburo (December 2014), from Elizabeth C. Economy, *The Third Revolution* (2018), pp. 190. 'strengthening bilateral security': Secretary of State Hillary Clinton, https://foreignpolicy.com/2011/10/11/americas-pacific-century/. 'we'll seek more opportunities': President Barack Obama, address to Australia's Parliament, Canberra (17 November 2011), https://obamawhitehouse.archives.gov/the-press-office/2011/11/17/remarks-president-obama-australian-parliament.

465: 'a bid to enhance': Xinhua News Agency (28 March 2015), https://www.chinadaily.com.cn/business/2015-03/28/content_19938124.htm. 'Whereas World War II': Robert Kaplan, *Asia's Cauldron* (2014), p. 15. 'biggest foe': President Donald Trump, on CBS News (15 July 2018), https://www.cbsnews.com/news/donald-trump-interview-cbs-news-european-union-is-a-foe-ahead-of-putin-meeting-in-helsinki-jeff-glor/. 'strategic autonomy': https://www.consilium.europa.eu/en/press/press-releases/2020/09/08/recovery-plan-powering-europe-s-strategic-autonomy-speech-by-president-charles-michel-at-the-brussels-economic-forum/.

466: 'strategic stability in the region': Commonwealth of Australia, *Defending Australia in the Asia Pacific Century* (2009), p. 43.

467: 'Brexit is an opportunity': Chinese official, Stockholm China Forum (7–8 November 2019), https://www.economist.com/china/2019/11/16/the-west-is-now-surer-that-china-is-not-about-to-liberalise. 'becoming a follower': https://

www.globaltimes.cn/content/1191094.shtml. 'China' etc.: European Commission, *EU–China: A Strategic Outlook* (2019), p. 1. 'the most ambitious agreement': https://ec.europa.eu/commission/presscorner/detail/en/ ip_20_2542. 'Indo-Pacific tilt' and 'China's military modernisation': https:// www.gov.uk/government/publications/global-britain-in-a-competitive-age-the-integrated-review-of-security-defence-development-and-foreign-policy, pp. 29, 66. 'Strategic competition with China': White House Press Secretary Jen Psaki (25 January 2021), https://www.whitehouse.gov/briefing-room/ press-briefings/2021/01/25/press-briefing-by-press-secretary-jen-psaki-january-25–2021/.

468: 'The emphasis in methods' etc.: Valery Gerasimov, Russian Army chief of staff, *Military-Industrial Kurier* (27 February 2013), from https:// inmoscowsshadows.wordpress.com/2014/07/06/the-gerasimov-doctrine-and-russian-non-linear-war/. 'campaigning': Nadia Schadlow, 'Strategy: The Pursuit of Freedom of Action', online Engelsberg Lecture (8 December 2020).

471: 'The audience listened': Kerry Brown, *The Future of UK–China Relations* (2019), p. 2. 'Law of the Fishes': *Mahabharata*, Shanti Parvan (compiled between 400 BCE and 450 CE), 67.16, from Romila Thapar, *From Lineage to State* (1984), pp. 117–18. 'start[ing]' and 'adrift': Mark Malloch Brown (9 July 2020), https:// www.nytimes.com/2020/07/03/world/europe/johnson-brexit-hong-kong. html.

472: 'If we bend the knee': Secretary of Defense Mike Pompeo, Nixon Presidential Library, Yorba Linda, California (23 July 2020), https://www. americanrhetoric.com/speeches/mikepompeochinanixonlibrary.htm. 'so used to your supremacy': Gao Xiqing, president, China Investment Corporation (December 2008), https://www.theatlantic.com/magazine/archive/2008/12/ be-nice-to-the-countries-that-lend-you-money/307148/. Italics in original. 'Chinese interests in the UK': Brown, *The Future of China–UK Relations*, p. 32.

473: 'confined to': Boris Johnson, foreign secretary, Chatham House (2 December 2016), https://www.chathamhouse.org/sites/default/ files/events/special/2016–12–02–Boris-Johnson.pdf. 'Singapore-on-Thames': https://www.theguardian.com/business/2019/dec/17/ uk-singapore-on-thames-brexit-france.

474: 'über-realist power': Robert Kaplan, *The Revenge of Geography* (2012), p. 196. 'the rule of law': Xi Jinping (2014), https://www.lowyinstitute. org/the-interpreter/chinas-rule-law-international-relations. 'We want to be': Ambassador Liu Xiaoming (6 July 2020), https://foreignpolicy. com/2020/08/03/boris-johnson-sinophile-china-hawk/.

475: 'the ability to achieve objectives': https://softpower30.com/what-is-soft-power/. 'Chinese and computer code': https://www.newstatesman.com/ spotlight/2020/01/the-cost-of-britains-language-problem.

476: 'a new kind of tributary state': Brown, *The Future of China–UK Relations*, p. 36.

477: 'England, awake!' Ella Wheeler Wilcox (1910), http://www.
ellawheelerwilcox.org/poems/pengland.htm.

12. Can't Go Home Again, 2017
478: 'in the quiet' etc.: Robert Kaplan, *Earning the Rockies* (2017), pp. 39, 55, 38, 56.
'Brexit Capital': http://www.newstatesman.com/politics/staggers/2017/02/
stoke-central-election-brexit-and-other-issues-could-swing-vote.
479: 'We want our cold nights': https://www.economist.com/united-
states/2021/04/24/why-the-european-super-league-failed. 'Hundreds of Home
Office Civil Servants': https://www.thetimes.co.uk/article/hundreds-
of-home-office-civil-servants-face-being-moved-to-stoke-under-levelling-up-
programme-xv3mmv907.
480: 'Detroit-style impact' and 'routine': Tristram Hunt MP, interview with Tim
Wigmore, *New Statesman*, https://www.newstatesman.com/politics/2015/07/
letter-stoke-how-transform-city-decline.
482: 'a passionate eavesdropper': Kaplan, *Earning the Rockies*, p. 72.

REFERENCES

In both quantity and quality the scholarship on the last ten millennia of British history is simply astonishing. Admitting that he could not possibly list all the heroes who had fought on the Greek side in the Trojan War, the poet Homer said, 'I could not tell them all [. . .] not if I had ten tongues and ten mouths, not if I had a voice never to be broken and a heart of bronze within me' (*Iliad* 2.488–90). Much the same applies to British history. What follows here is therefore selective in the extreme, not only because no individual could ever read every book and article relevant to the topic but also because even if I had managed the impossible, listing them all would have required more end-matter than any publisher could tolerate. All I can do is make my apologies to the many scholars whose work is not acknowledged here.

I begin by mentioning a few excellent, multi-volume surveys of British history that have appeared in recent years, then proceed to the works relevant to specific chapters. For each chapter I start with overviews that I found particularly useful. These document many of the specific claims I make (whenever possible, I cite recent works which have their own extensive bibliographies). Experts argue over almost every detail, but I only reference more specialised studies when the disagreements are particularly strong or new work has added significantly to the more general books. This has happened most often with the archaeology.

Few historians nowadays are bold (or reckless?) enough to write single-authored, multi-volume overviews, but Simon Schama's *History of Britain* (3 vols, 2000–09) stands out, along with Norman Davies's *The Isles* (which, although published in 2000 as one volume, has enough pages to count as two or three books). More often, multi-volume histories of Britain have a different expert writing each book within them. The *Penguin History of Britain* (8 vols since 1996, with one still to come) is consistently accessible and well informed, and the *Oxford History of the British Empire* (4 vols, 1998–99), which has also spun off a series of books on narrower themes, is the standard reference work on its subject.

Before the 1990s historians regularly treated England, Ireland, Scotland and Wales as separate subjects. For reasons I explain in the introduction, I think this obscures more than it reveals, but it has produced some outstanding work all the same. England has received most attention. Peter Ackroyd's *History of England* (6 vols, 2012–21) and Robert Tombs's single-volume *The English and Their History* (2014) are particularly engaging. The ten volumes of the *New Oxford History of England* published since 1983 (four more are awaited) are more academic but often enjoyable. The *Cambridge History of Ireland* (4 vols, 2018–20) and *New Edinburgh History of Scotland* (7 vols since 2004 and 3 still to come) are indispensable. I know of no recent multi-volume Welsh history, but John Davies's *History of Wales* (2007) does a fine job on a smaller scale. I should also mention the *Penguin Monarchs* series, with forty-three slim, learned and entertaining volumes since 2014.

Introduction

Most of the details in the introduction are discussed more fully later in the book, and so I only provide references here for points to which I don't return.

Kenneth Brophy, 'The Brexit Hypothesis and Prehistory', *Antiquity* 92 (2018), pp. 1650–58, discusses how *not* to use prehistory. David Christian's 'The Case for "Big History"', *Journal of World History* 2 (1991), pp. 223–38, and *Maps of Time* (2004) are the classic accounts of big/deep history.

Cato Institute on refugees and terrorists: https://www.economist.com/united-states/2018/04/21/america-is-on-track-to-admit-the-fewest-refugees-in-four-decades.

Hereford Map: https://www.themappamundi.co.uk, with P. D. A. Harvey, *Mappa Mundi: The Hereford World Map* (2010). The latest reference to British body painting is Martial, *Epigrams* 11.53; to tattooing, Claudian, *On Stilicho's Consulship* 2.247, and *The Gothic War*, 416–18.

Mackinder's Map: Halford Mackinder, *Britain and the British Seas* (1902), Figure 3. On commanding the seas, Nicholas Rodger, *The Safeguard of the Sea* (1997), is outstanding.

The Money Map: https://worldmapper.org/maps/gdp-2018/; Parag Khanna, *Connectography* (2016), is excellent on the connections in Figure 0.5. GDP rankings are listed at https://en.wikipedia.org/wiki/List_of_countries_by_GDP_(nominal) and https://en.wikipedia.org/wiki/List_of_countries_by_GDP_(PPP); naval rankings are discussed at http://nationalinterest.org/feature/the-five-most-powerful-navies-the-planet-10610; Nobel prizes are at https://www.nobelprize.org/nobel_prizes/lists/countries.html. Sixty-nine per cent votes to remain (Westminster) and leave (Stoke-on-Trent): https://ig.ft.com/sites/elections/2016/uk/eu-referendum/.

On geography and history generally, Tim Marshall's *Prisoners of Geography* (2015) is endlessly fascinating and informative.

1. Thatcher's Law, 6000–4000 BCE

Many of the best books – such as Richard Bradley's *The Prehistory of Britain and Ireland* (2007), Barry Cunliffe's *Facing the Ocean* (2001), Timothy Darvill's *Prehistoric Britain* (2010), Francis Pryor's *Britain BC* (2003) and, on genetics, David Reich's *Who We Are and How We Got Here* (2018) – are invaluable for Chapter 2 as well as Chapter 1; and Cunliffe's *Britain Begins* (2013) – perhaps the best overview – covers the whole period down to the Norman Conquest. However, the picture is constantly changing, and the best way to keep up to date is by following the journal *Current Archaeology* (https://www.archaeology.co.uk).

For Chapter 1's main topics see: Neil Roberts, *The Holocene* (3rd edn, 2014); Nick Barton, *Ice Age Britain* (2nd edn, 2005); Chris Stringer, *Homo Britannicus* (2006); Andrzej Pydyn, *Argonauts of the Stone Age* (2015); Daniel Zohary, *Domestication of Plants in the Old World* (4th edn, 2013); Stephen Shennan, *The First Farmers of Europe* (2018); and Vicki Cummings, *The Neolithic of Britain and Ireland* (2017).

Happisburgh: Nick Ashton et al., 'Hominin Footprints from Early Pleistocene Deposits at Happisburgh, UK', *PLoS ONE* 9.2 (2014), e88329. English Channel floods 425,000 and 160,000 years ago: Sanjeev Gupta et al., 'Two-Stage Opening of the Dover Strait and the Origin of Island Britain', *Nature Communications* 8 (2017), article 15101; David García-Moreno et al., 'Middle-Late Pleistocene Landscape Evolution of the Dover Strait Inferred from Buried and Submerged Erosional Landforms', *Quaternary Science Reviews* 203 (2019), pp. 209–32. Figure 1.1 is based on https://intarch.ac.uk/journal/issue11/rayadams_toc.html. Neanderthal cleverness: Clive Finlayson, *The Smart Neanderthal* (2019).

Kent's Cavern: Tom Higham et al., 'The Earliest Evidence for Anatomically Modern Humans in Northwest Europe', *Nature* 479 (2011), pp. 521–4; Paviland: Stephen Aldhouse-Green et al., *Paviland Cave and the 'Red Lady'* (2000). Dating: Roger Jacobi and Tom Higham, 'The "Red Lady" Ages Gracefully', *Journal of Human Evolution* 55 (2008), pp. 898–907. Last Glacial Maximum: Miika Tallavaara et al., 'Human Population Dynamics in Europe over the Last Glacial Maximum', *Proceedings of the National Academy of Sciences* 112 (2015), pp. 8232–7. Neanderthal extinction: Tom Higham, *The World Before Us* (2021), pp. 28–47, 128–46, 205–19. Cheddar Man and Adrian Targett: Bryan Sykes, *Saxons, Vikings, and Celts* (2006), pp. 11–12; https://www.dailymail.co.uk/news/article-5364983/Retired-history-teacher-believes-looks-like-Cheddar-Man.html. Cheddar Man's skin and hair: http://www.nhm.ac.uk/discover/cheddar-man-mesolithic-britain-blue-eyed-boy.html. Doggerland: Vincent Gaffney et al., *Europe's Lost World* (2009). English Channel flood *c.*6000 BCE: P. L. Gibbard, 'The Formation of the Strait of Dover', in R. C. Preece, ed., *Island Britain: A Quaternary Perspective* (1995), pp. 15–26; James Walker et al., 'A Great Wave: The Storegga Tsunami and the End of Doggerland?' *Antiquity* 94 (2020), pp. 1409–25. Oldest boats (Noyen-sur-Seine and Pesse): Seán McGrail, *Boats of the World from the Stone Age to Medieval Times* (2001), pp. 172–4. Pacific sailing: Robin Dennell, *From Arabia to the Pacific* (2020), p. 74. Hide boats: Timaeus, cited by Pliny the Elder, *Natural History* 4.104, and McGrail, *Boats of the World*, pp. 181–3. Outriggers: McGrail, *Boats of the World*, p. 172.

Foraging societies: Vicki Cummings et al., eds, *The Oxford Handbook of the Archaeology and Anthropology of Hunters and Gatherers* (2014). British people walking 181 miles per year: http://www.telegraph.co.uk/news/2016/07/28/britain-grinds-to-a-halt-with-average-person-walking-half-a-mile/. Angus Maddison's standards-of-living calculations: https://www.rug.nl/ggdc/historicaldevelopment/maddison/releases/maddison-project-database-2020. World Bank and extreme poverty:

https://www.worldbank.org/en/topic/poverty/overview. Boxgrove butcher: Pryor, *Britain BC*, pp. 23–4. Forager violence: Virginia Hutton Estabrook, 'Violence and Warfare in the European Mesolithic and Paleolithic', in Mark Allen and Terry Jones, eds, *Violence and Warfare among Hunter–Gatherers* (2014), pp. 49–69. Cheddar Gorge cannibalism: Silvia Bello et al., 'Earliest Directly-Dated Human Skull-Cups', *PLoS ONE* 6.2 (2011) e17026; 'An Upper Palaeolithic Engraved Human Bone Associated with Ritualistic Cannibalism', *PLoS ONE* 12.8 (2017) e0182127. Paviland ivories: Pryor, *Britain BC*, pp. 50–56. Bras from Guangdong: http://www.economist.com/news/china/21697004-one-product-towns-fuelled-chinas-export-boom-many-are-now-trouble-bleak-times-bra-town. Star Carr: Nicky Milner et al., *Star Carr* (2 vols, 2018).

Farming and inequality: Amy Bogaard et al., 'The Farming-Inequality Nexus', *Antiquity* 93 (2019), pp. 1129–43. Modern British Gini scores, https://en.wikipedia.org/wiki/List_of_countries_by_wealth_equality, conveniently summarising data from the National Bureau of Economic Research and Credit Suisse. Forager–farmer interaction: Shennan, *First Farmers*, pp. 82–5, 183–206. Coexistence in Germany: Ruth Bollongino et al., '2000 Years of Parallel Societies in Stone Age Central Europe', *Science* 342 (2013), pp. 479–81; in Oronsay, Sophy Charlton et al., 'Finding Britain's Last Hunter–Gatherers', *Journal of Archaeological Science* 73 (2016), pp. 55–61. Counterscarp: Peter Rowley Conwy, 'Westward Ho! The Spread of Agriculture from Central Europe to the Atlantic', *Current Anthropology* 52, supplement 4 (2011), pp. 431–51. Its collapse: Shennan, *First Farmers*, pp. 183–4.

DNA evidence for foragers' replacement by farmers: Selina Brace et al., 'Ancient Genomes Indicate Population Replacement in Early Neolithic Britain', *Nature Ecology & Evolution* 3 (2019), pp. 765–71. Sailing from Brittany to Ireland: Richard Callaghan and Chris Scarre, 'Simulating the Western Seaways', *Oxford Journal of Archaeology* 29 (2009), pp. 357–72. Orkney voles: Natália Martínková et al., 'Divergent Evolutionary Processes Associated with Colonization of Offshore Islands', *Molecular Ecology* 22 (2013), pp. 5205–20.

Hazleton North: Samantha Neil et al., 'Isotopic Evidence for Residential Mobility of Farming Communities during the Transition to Agriculture in Britain', *Royal Society Open Science* 3 (2016), 150522. Charred seeds: Amy Bogaard et al., 'Crop Manuring and Intensive Land Management by Europe's First Farmers', *Proceedings of the National Academy of Sciences* 110 (2013), pp. 12589–94. Early farmers' houses: A. Barclay and O. Harris, 'Community Building', in P. Bickle et al., eds, *The Neolithic of Europe* (2017), pp. 222–33. Size of British homes in 2010s: http://www.dailymail.co.uk/news/article-2535136/Average-British-family-home-size-shrinks-two-square-metres-decade-increasing-numbers-forced-live-flats.html. Monuments: the books by Bradley, Cummings, Cunliffe and Darvill mentioned above have rich details. On violence, R. Schulting and M. Wysocki, '"In This Chambered Tumulus Were Found Cleft Skulls"', *Proceedings of the Prehistoric Society* 71 (2005), pp. 107–38. British rates in 2010s: http://www.worldlifeexpectancy.com. Hambledon Hill: Roger Mercer and F. Healy, *Hambledon Hill, Dorset, England* (2008). Patterns of marriage: Brace et al.,

'Ancient Genomes', although Joanna Brück, 'Ancient DNA, Kinship and Relational Identities in Bronze Age Britain', *Antiquity* 95 (2021), pp. 228–37, raises some questions.

2. Europe's Poor Cousin, 4000–55 BCE

The overviews recommended for Chapter 1 remain relevant here, plus Mike Parker Pearson, *Stonehenge* (2011).

Population trends after 3500 BCE: Sue Colledge et al., 'Neolithic Population Crash in Northwest Europe Associated with Agricultural Crisis', *Quaternary Research* 92 (2019), pp. 686–707. Ranching: Andrew Bevan et al., 'Holocene Fluctuations in Human Population Demonstrate Repeated Links to Food Production and Climate', *Proceedings of the National Academy of Sciences* 114 (2017), pp. 10524–31.

Megalithic missionaries: Chris Scarre, 'Megalithic People, Megalithic Missionaries', *Estudos arqueológicos de oeiras* 24 (2018), pp. 161–73 (http://dro.dur.ac.uk/23764/1/23764.pdf?DDD6+drkocs). New radiocarbon dates: Bettina Schulz Paulsson, 'Radiocarbon Dates and Bayesian Modeling Support Maritime Diffusion Model for Megaliths in Europe', *Proceedings of the National Academy of Sciences* 116 (2019), pp. 3460–65. NG10: Lara Cassidy et al., 'A Dynastic Elite in Monumental Neolithic Society', *Nature* 582 (2020), pp. 384–8. Evangelical Christians: Tanya Luhrmann, *How God Becomes Real* (2020).

Stonehenge burials: Christie Willis et al., 'The Dead of Stonehenge', *Antiquity* 90 (2016), pp. 337–56. Immigrants: David Roberts et al., 'Middle Neolithic Pits and a Burial at West Amesbury, Wiltshire', *Archaeological Journal* 177 (2020), pp. 167–213. Welsh origins of the bluestones: Mike Parker Pearson et al., 'Megalith Quarries for Stonehenge's Bluestones', *Antiquity* 93 (2019), pp. 45–62. Waun Mawn: Parker Pearson et al., 'The Original Stonehenge? A Dismantled Stone Circle in the Preseli Hills of West Wales', *Antiquity* 95 (2021), pp. 85–103. Bluestonehenge: Michael Allen et al., 'Stonehenge's Avenue and "Bluestonehenge"', *Antiquity* 90 (2016), pp. 991–1008. Massive earthwork: Vincent Gaffney et al., https://intarch.ac.uk/journal/issue55/4/full-text.html (2020). Car park totem poles: Parker Pearson, *Stonehenge*, pp. 135–7.

Phil Harding, copper axes and V-shaped cuts: Parker Pearson, *Stonehenge*, pp. 124–5. DNA and Central Asian migrations: Wolfgang Haak et al., 'Massive Migration from the Steppe Was a Source for Indo-European Languages in Europe', *Nature* 522 (2015), pp. 207–11. Migrations into Ireland: Lara Cassidy et al., 'Neolithic and Bronze Age Migration to Ireland and Establishment of the Insular Atlantic Genome', *Proceedings of the National Academy of Sciences* 113 (2016), pp. 368–73. Replacement of 90–95 per cent of DNA: Iñigo Olalde et al., 'The Beaker Phenomenon and the Genomic Transformation of Northwest Europe', *Nature* 555 (2018), pp. 190–96. Mechanisms of demographic replacement: Martin Furholt, 'Massive Migrations? The Impact of Recent aDNA Studies on Our View of Third-Millennium Europe', *European Journal of Archaeology* 21 (2017), pp. 159–91. *Yersinia pestis*: Nicolás Rascovan et al., 'Emergence and Spread of Basal Lineages of *Yersinia pestis* during the Neolithic Decline', *Cell* 176 (2019), pp. 295–305. Amesbury Archer: Andrew Fitzpatrick, ed., *The Amesbury Archer and the Boscombe Bowmen* (2011). Grave with mace: https://www.theguardian.com/uk-news/2021/feb/04/archaeologist-unearth-bronze-age-graves-stonehenge-a303-tunnel-site. Stonehenge Archer: John Evans, 'Stonehenge – The Environment in the Late Neolithic and Early Bronze Age and a Beaker-Age Burial', *Wiltshire Archaeological and Natural History Magazine* 78 (1984), pp. 7–30. I take the Silbury Hill labour requirements from Richard Atkinson, 'Neolithic Science and Technology', *Philosophical Transactions of the Royal Society* A 276 (1974), p. 128. Raunds burial: Timothy Darvill, *Prehistoric Britain* (2nd edn, 2010), pp. 171–2. Sewn-plank boats: McGrail, *Boats*, pp. 184–91; R. van de Noort, 'Argonauts of the North Sea', *Proceedings of the Prehistoric Society* 72 (2006), pp. 267–87. Agriculture: D. T. Yates, *Land, Power and Prestige: Bronze Age Field Systems in Southern England* (2007). Olifant: *Song of Roland* (*c.*1100 CE), line 1764. New religious systems: Kristian Kristiansen and Thomas Larsson, *The Rise of Bronze Age Society* (2015), pp. 251–319. Deliberate disposal of bronze: Richard Bradley, *The Passage of Arms* (2nd edn, 1998).

Coming of iron: Nathaniel Erb-Satullo, 'The Innovation and Adoption of Iron in the Ancient Near East', *Journal of Archaeological Research* 27 (2019), pp. 557–607, reviews the evidence. Simon James, *The Atlantic Celts: Ancient People or Modern Invention?* (1999), shows how heated debates over the Celts can get. Celts and the Danube: Herodotus (*c.*430 BCE), 2.33, 4.49. DNA study: Stephen Leslie et al., 'The Fine-Scale Genetic Structure of the British Population', *Nature* 519 (2015), pp. 309–14. Early origins of Celtic languages: Barry Cunliffe and John Koch, eds, *Exploring Celtic Origins* (2019). Archaeologists debate what hill forts were for (the exchange between Ian Armit, 'Hillforts at War', *Proceedings of the Prehistoric Society* 73 [2007], pp. 25–37, and Gary Lock, 'Hillforts, Emotional Metaphors, and the Good Life', *Proceedings of the Prehistoric Society* 77 [2011], pp. 355–62, is informative). Bog bodies: Miranda Aldhouse-Green, *Dying for the Gods* (2001). There is a list at https://en.wikipedia.org/wiki/List_of_bog_bodies. Druids: Miranda Aldhouse-Green, *Caesar's Druids* (2010).

Origin of governments: the literature is enormous. Allen Johnson and Timothy Earle, *The Evolution of Human Societies* (2nd edn, 2000), pp. 246–312, present the conventional view; James Scott, *Against the Grain* (2017), pp. 116–218, argues against it. East Mediterranean destructions around 1200 BCE: Eric Cline, *1177 BC* (2014). Phoenicians: Glenn Markoe, *The Phoenicians* (2000). Circumnavigating Africa: Herodotus 4.42. Cornwall: Barry Cunliffe, *Facing the Ocean* (2001), pp. 39–45. Greek pots in Britain: Darvill, *Prehistoric Britain*, pp. 284–5. Pytheas: Barry Cunliffe, *The Extraordinary Voyage of Pytheas the Greek* (2001). My examples of *On the Ocean* come from Diodorus of Sicily (40s BCE), 5.21, and Strabo, *Geography* (20s CE), 2.4.1 and 4.5.5. The last known author who claims to have read Pytheas was Pliny the Elder, in the 70s CE (*Natural History* 4.30 and 37.11). Romans in Gaul: Greg Woolf, *Becoming Roman* (1998). Gaul and Britain: Colin Haselgrove and Tom Moore, eds., *The Later Iron Age in Britain and Beyond* (2007). Caesar in Gaul: Adrian Goldsworthy, *Caesar* (2006), pp. 184–356.

3. Empire, 55 bce–410 CE

There are invaluable overviews in: David Mattingly, *An Imperial Possession* (2006); Martin Millett et al., eds, *The Oxford Handbook of Roman Britain* (2016); Guy de la Bédoyère, *Eagles over Britannia* (2001); and Simon Esmonde-Cleary, *The Ending of Roman Britain* (1989). Kyle Harper, *The Fate of Rome* (2017), analyses climate and the empire.

Commius: Caesar, *Gallic War* (55–50 BCE), 4.21; 7.76; 8.6–7, 10, 21, 23, 47–8. Pegwell Bay: https://www2.le.ac.uk/offices/press/press-releases/2017/november/first-evidence-for-julius-caesars-invasion-of-britain-discovered. British campaigns: Goldsworthy, *Caesar*, pp. 269–92. Herod the Great alive two years after Jesus was born: Matthew 2:16.

Charterhouse: Malcolm Todd, *Roman Mining in Somerset* (2002). Prestatyn: Kevin Blockley, *Prestatyn 1984–5* (1989). Boudica's revolt: Miranda Aldhouse-Green, *Boudica Britannia* (2006). Tombstone of Marcus Favonius Facilis, https://romaninscriptionsofbritain.org/inscriptions/200. Early London: Lacey Wallace, *The Origin of Roman London* (2014). Bloomberg site: https://www.theguardian.com/uk-news/2016/jun/01/tablets-unearthed-city-glimpse-roman-london-bloomberg. Roman policy after the revolt: Gil Gambash, 'To Rule a Ferocious Province', *Britannia* 43 (2012), pp. 1–15. Post-Boudican London: Ian Haynes et al., *London Under Ground* (2000). Headless bodies: Gundula Müldner et al., 'The "Headless Romans"', *Journal of Archaeological Science* 38 (2011), pp. 280–90. Drumanagh: Barry Raftery, 'Drumanagh and Roman Ireland', *Archaeology Ireland* 35/10.1 (1996). Inchtuthil: Elizabeth Shirley, *The Construction of the Roman Legionary Fortress at Inchtuthil* (2000). There is an animation at https://www.bbc.co.uk/programmes/p01696lj.

Isotope analyses: generally, Hella Eckardt, 'People on the Move in Roman Britain', *World Archaeology* 46 (2014), pp. 534–50. Gloucester, Carolyn Chenery et al., 'Strontium and Stable Isotope Evidence for Diet and Mobility in Roman Gloucester, UK', *Journal of Archaeological Science* 37 (2010), pp. 150–63; Winchester, Eckardt et al., 'Oxygen and Strontium Isotope Evidence for Mobility in Roman Winchester', *Journal of Archaeological Science* 36 (2009), pp. 2816–25; York, Stephany Leach et al., 'Migration and Diversity in Roman Britain', *American Journal of Physical Anthropology* 140 (2009), pp. 546–51; London, Rebecca Redfern et al., 'Going South of the River', *Journal of Archaeological Science* 74 (2016), pp. 11–22, and Heidi Shaw et al., 'Identifying Migrants in Roman London Using Lead and Strontium Stable Isotopes', *Journal of Archaeological Science* 66 (2016), pp. 57–68. Vindolanda letters: http://vindolanda.csad.ox.ac.uk. On the weather, nos. 234, 343; food, nos. 301, 203; socks, no. 346. Boxing gloves: https://www.archaeology.co.uk/articles/packing-a-punch-boxing-gloves-found-at-vindolanda.htm.

Stature: Gregori Galofré-Vilà et al., 'Heights across the Last 2000 Years in England', *Research in Economic History* 34 (2018), pp. 67–98. Cost of the army: Mattingly, *Imperial Possession*, p. 493. British economy: Michael Fulford, 'Economic Structures', in Malcolm Todd, ed., *A Companion to Roman Britain* (2004), pp. 309–26. Silchester: Thomas Blagg, 'Building Stone in Roman Britain', in D. Parsons, ed.,

Stone: Quarrying and Building in England, AD 43–1525 (1990), p. 39. Towns healthier than countryside: Martin Pitts and Rebecca Griffin, 'Exploring Health and Social Well-Being in Late Roman Britain', *American Journal of Archaeology* 116 (2012), pp. 253–76; Rebecca Griffin, 'Urbanization, Economic Change, and Dental Health in Roman and Medieval Britain', *European Journal of Archaeology* 20 (2017), pp. 1–22. The reverse: Rebecca Redfern et al., 'Urban-Rural Differences in Dorset, England', *American Journal of Physical Anthropology* 157 (2015), pp. 107–20. Consumption levels: Richard Saller, 'Framing the Debate over Growth in the Ancient Economy', in Joe Manning and Ian Morris, eds., *The Ancient Economy* (2005), pp. 223–38.

Country life: Mike McCarthy, *The Romano-British Peasant* (2013). Developer-funded archaeology: Steve Willis, 'A Roman Metamorphosis: The Grey-Literature of the Romano-British Countryside Transformed', *Archaeological Journal* 177 (2020), pp. 408–16, with https://archaeologydataservice.ac.uk/archives/view/romangl/. More than 100,000 sites: Mattingly, *Imperial Possession*, p. 356. Whitton: Michael Jarrett and Stuart Wrathmell, *Whitton* (1981). Marshfield: Kevin Blockley, *Marshfield* (1985). Stowmarket: Kate Nicholson and Tom Woolhouse, *A Late Iron Age and Romano-British Farmstead at Cedars Park, Stowmarket, Suffolk* (2016). Dunnicaer: Gordon Noble et al., 'Dunnicaer, Aberdeenshire, Scotland', *Archaeological Journal* 177 (2020), pp. 256–338. GDP of England and Wales in 2019: https://www.ons.gov.uk/datasets/regional-gdp-by-year/editions/time-series/versions/5. House sizes: Robert Stephan, 'House Size and Economic Growth: Regional Trajectories in the Roman World' (unpublished PhD dissertation, Stanford University, 2013), pp. 55–79.

Plagues: Kyle Harper, *Plagues upon the Earth* (2021), Chapter 5. Parallels between 286 and 2016: https://www.usatoday.com/story/news/world/2016/06/27/britains-first-brexit-286-d/86422358/; https://www.pri.org/stories/2016-06-23/britain-s-first-brexit-286-ad. Christianity: David Petts, *Christianity in Roman Britain* (2003). Coleshill: John Magilton, 'A Romano-Celtic Temple and Settlement at Grimstock Hill, Coleshill, Warwickshire', *Transactions, Birmingham and Warwickshire Archaeological Society* 110 (2006), pp. 1–231. Poundbury: D. Farwell and Theya Molleson, eds, *Excavations at Poundbury, Dorchester* II (1993).

What happened in Britannia after 350 is hotly debated. Neil Faulkner, *The Decline and Fall of Roman Britain* (2000), stresses collapse; James Gerrard, *The Ruin of Roman Britain* (2013), emphasises continuity. For the empire as a whole, Peter Heather, *Empires and Barbarians* (2009), stresses migration; Guy Halsall, *Barbarian Migrations and the Roman West, 376–568* (2007), emphasises stability. Recent DNA and stable isotope analyses include Carlos Amorim et al., 'Understanding 6th-Century Barbarian Social Organization and Migration through Paleogenomics', *Nature Communications* 9 (2018), 3547; Krishna Veeramah et al., 'Population Genomic Analysis of Elongated Skulls Reveals Extensive Female-Biased Immigration in Early Medieval Bavaria', *Proceedings of the National Academy of Sciences* 115 (2018), pp. 3494–9; I. Stolarek et al., 'Goth Migration Induced Changes in the Matrilineal Genetic Structure of the Central-East European Population', *Nature Scientific Reports* 9 (2019), article 6737; and Stefania Vai et al., 'A Genetic Perspective on Longobard-Era Migrations',

European Journal of Human Genetics 27 (2019), pp. 647–56. Magnentius and Paul's purge: Ammianus Marcellinus 14.5. Raiding in 360–64: Ammianus 20.1, 26.4. Barbarian Conspiracy: Ammianus 27.8, 28.3. Honorius' letter: Zosimus, *New History* (early sixth century CE), 6.10.2.

4. The Original European Union, 410–973

The period from the fifth century to the tenth is probably the most controversial in British history. Martin Carver's *Formative Britain* (2019), Aidan O'Sullivan et al.'s *Early Medieval Ireland* (2013) and Helena Hamerow et al.'s *Oxford Handbook of Anglo-Saxon Archaeology* (2011) are superb archaeological accounts. Francis Pryor's *Britain AD* (2005) and Robin Fleming's *Britain after Rome* (2010) are informative and very readable, updated by Marc Morris's excellent *Anglo-Saxon England* (2021) and Matthew Stout's *Early Medieval Ireland, 431–1169* (2017). Chris Wickham's *The Inheritance of Rome* (2010) is strong on the European context.

Hard and soft power: Joseph Nye, *Soft Power* (2004). Gildas: Nicholas Higham, *The English Conquest* (1994). Arthur: Guy Halsall, *Worlds of Arthur* (2013), exemplifies the sceptical approach. Stafford: Martin Carver, *The Birth of a Borough* (2010). Sutton Courtenay: Naomi Brennan and Helena Hamerow, 'An Anglo-Saxon Great Hall Complex at Sutton Courtenay / Drayton, Oxfordshire', *Archaeological Journal* 172 (2015), pp. 325–50. Early Saxon settlements: Carver, *Formative Britain*, pp. 194–207. Berinsfield stable isotopes: Susan Hughes et al., 'Anglo-Saxon Origins Investigated by Isotopic Analysis of Burials from Berinsfield, Oxfordshire, UK', *Journal of Archaeological Science* 42 (2014), pp. 81–92. DNA evidence: Rui Martiniano et al., 'Genomic Signals of Migration and Continuity in Britain before the Anglo-Saxons', *Nature Communications* 7 (2016), 10326; Stephan Schiffels et al., 'Iron Age and Anglo-Saxon Genomes from East England Reveal British Migration History', *Nature Communications* 7 (2016), 10408. Numbers of immigrants: Carver, *Formative Britain*, pp. 51–9. Cadbury–Congresbury: Philip Rahtz et al., *Cadbury Congresbury 1968–73* (1992). Cadbury Castle: Leslie Alcock, *Cadbury Castle, Somerset* (1995). Mediterranean immigrants: K. Hemer et al., 'Evidence of Early Medieval Trade and Migration between Wales and the Mediterranean Sea Region', *Journal of Archaeological Science* 40 (2013), pp. 2352–9. Tintagel and Artognou: Rachel Barrowman et al., *Excavations at Tintagel Castle, Cornwall, 1990–1999* (2007), pp. 199–202.

Christianisation of Britain: Barbara Yorke, *The Conversion of Britain* (2006). Franks settling in England, Bede, *Ecclesiastical History* 5.9; Franks ruling England, Procopius, *Gothic Wars* 8.20.10. Sutton Hoo: Martin Carver, ed., *Sutton Hoo* (2005). Rhynie: Gordon Noble et al., 'A Powerful Place of Pictland', *Medieval Archaeology* 63 (2019), pp. 56–94. Saxon London: Rory Naismith, *Citadel of the Saxons* (2018). Celtic Christianities: Thomas Charles-Edwards, 'Beyond Empire II: Christianities of the Celtic Peoples', in Thomas Noble and Julia Smith, eds, *The Cambridge History of Christianity* III (2008), pp. 86–106. Theodore: Michael Lapidge, ed., *Archbishop Theodore* (1995). Anglo-Saxon coinage: Rory Naismith, *Money and Power in Anglo-Saxon England* (2012).

Vikings: Thomas Williams, *Viking Britain* (2017), is excellent, although rather keen to make the Vikings likeable. Torksey: Dawn Hadley and Julian Richards, 'The Winter Camp of the Viking Great Army, 872–3 CE, Torksey, Lincolnshire', *Antiquaries Journal* 96 (2016), pp. 23–67. Viking DNA in Orkney and Shetlands: Edmund Gilbert et al., 'The Genetic Landscape of Scotland and the Isles', *Proceedings of the National Academy of Sciences* 116 (2019), pp. 19064–70. Vikings in the north and west, David Griffiths, *Vikings of the Irish Sea* (2010). Alfred: Max Adams, *Aelfred's Britain* (2017), is a good account. Loaves story: David Horspool, *Why Alfred Burned the Cakes* (2006). Viking wars: Ryan Lavelle, *Alfred's Wars* (2013). Naval innovations: Rodger, *Safeguard*, pp. 11–17. Angelcynn: Sarah Foot, 'The Making of Angelcynn', *Transactions of the Royal Historical Society*, 6th series, 6 (1996), pp. 25–49. Englalonde: Patrick Wormald, '*Engla Lond*: The Making of an Allegiance', *Journal of Historical Sociology* 7 (1994), pp. 1–24. Unification of England: George Molyneaux, *The Formation of the English Kingdom in the Tenth Century* (2015). Edgar: Donald Scragg, ed., *Edgar, King of the English, 959–975* (2008).

Tenth-century living standards: Christopher Dyer, *Making a Living in the Middle Ages* (2002), especially pp. 13–42. Flixborough: Christopher Loveluck, ed., *Rural Settlement, Lifestyles and Social Change in the Later First Millennium AD* (2007); D. H. Evans and Christopher Loveluck, eds, *Life and Economy at Early Medieval Flixborough* (2009), with John Blair, 'Flixborough Revisited', *Anglo-Saxon Studies in Archaeology and History* 17 (2011), pp. 101–8. Mawgan Porth: Rupert Bruce-Mitford et al., *Mawgan Porth* (1997). Portmahomack: Martin Carver, *Portmahomack* (2008). Yarnton: Gill Hey, *Yarnton: Saxon and Medieval Settlement* (2004). Beginning of English villages: Richard Jones and Mark Page, *Medieval Villages in an English Landscape* (2006). Alfred's London: Julian Ayre and Robin Wroe-Brown, 'The Post-Roman Foreshore and the Origins of the Late Anglo-Saxon Waterfront and Dock of Aethelred's Hithe', *Archaeological Journal* 172 (2015), pp. 121–94. Silk: Robin Fleming, 'Acquiring, Flaunting and Destroying Silk in Late Anglo-Saxon England', *Early Medieval Europe* 15 (2007), pp. 127–58. Wool: Susan Rose, *The Wealth of England: The Medieval Wool Trade and its Political Importance 1100–1600* (2018). Sheep population: N. Sykes, *The Norman Conquest: A Zooarchaeological Perspective* (2007), pp. 28–34. French visitors and Anglo-Saxon sauces: Fleming, *Britain after Rome*, p. 299.

5. United Kingdoms, 973–1497

Starting with this chapter, the relevant volumes of the *New Oxford History of England*, *Cambridge History of Ireland* and *New Edinburgh History of Scotland* become indispensable. Rees Davies's *Domination and Conquest: The Experience of Ireland, Scotland and Wales, 1100–1300* (1990) and his edited volume *The British Isles, 1100–1500* (1988) led the way in treating the Isles as a whole, and Donald Matthew's *Britain and the Continent 1000–1300* (2005) is good on its subject.

Y2k: https://archives.lib.umn.edu/repositories/3/resources/273 has remarkable materials. Y1k: John Howe, *Before the Gregorian Reform* (2019). Aethelred: Levi Roach, *Aethelred: The Unready* (2017). United Kingdom of the North Sea: Timothy Bolton,

Cnut the Great (2017). On Cnut/Canute, Thijs Porck and Jodie Mann, 'How Cnut became Canute (and how Harthacnut became Airdeconut)', *Nowele: North-Western European Language Evolution* 67 (2014), pp. 237–43. Cnut and the tides: Bolton, *Cnut*, 1 n. 1, pp. 214–16.

SS *Black Book*: reprinted as *The Black Book (Sonderfahndungsliste G.B.)* (1989). J. C. Holt, *Colonial England 1066–1215* (1997), pp. 1–24, is particularly good on the Norman conquest of England, as are Rees Davies, *The Age of Conquest* (2000), and Clare Downham, *Medieval Ireland* (2018), pp. 181–344, on Wales and Ireland.

United Kingdom of the Atlantic Coast: Robert Bartlett, *England under the Norman and Angevin Kings, 1075–1225* (2000), is essential. Reassessments of John: Nick Vincent, *John: An Evil King?* (2020). Magna Carta: David Carpenter, *Magna Carta* (2015). Henry III, Sicily and Germany: Björn Weiler, *Henry III and England and the Staufen Empire, 1216–1272* (2012), pp. 147–65; Brendan Simms, *Britain's Europe* (2016), p. 5. Thirteenth-century immigrants: Michael Prestwich, *Plantagenet England 1225–1360* (2005), pp. 93–8.

Eleventh- to twelfth-century economy: Bartlett, *Norman and Angevin Kings*, pp. 287–376. Stature: Galofré-Vilà et al., 'Heights'. Thirteenth- to fifteenth-century economy: Greg Clark, 'Growth or Stagnation? Farming in England, 1200–1800', *Economic History Review* 70 (2017), pp. 1–27. Medieval housing: Ian Mortimer, *The Time Traveller's Guide to Medieval England* (2008), pp. 6–34. Three hundred and thirty-three trees per farmhouse: Prestwich, *Plantagenet England*, p. 14. Wharram Percy: Maurice Beresford and John Hurst, *Wharram Percy* (1991). Robin Hood: J. C. Holt, *Robin Hood* (3rd edn, 2011). Medieval housing: Geoff Egan, *The Medieval Household* (2010). Cuckoo Lane: C. P. S. Platt and R. Coleman-Smith, *Excavations in Medieval Southampton 1953–69* II (1975). Immigration to Stratford, Exeter and London: Rosemary Horrox and Mark Ormrod, eds, *A Social History of England, 1200–1500* (2006), p. 269. Urban food: Miri Rubin, *The Hollow Crown* (2005), pp. 132–6. Drinking holes: Horrox and Ormrod, *Social History*, p. 139. Hardening of identities: John Gillingham, *The English in the Twelfth Century* (2003). Jews: Richard Huscroft, *Expulsion: England's Jewish Solution* (2006).

Edward I: Andy King and Andrew Spencer, eds., *Edward I* (2020). Robert Bruce: Michael Penman, *Robert the Bruce, King of the Scots* (2018). David Green, *The Hundred Years' War: A People's History* (2014), captures the suffering. Black Death: Harper, *Plagues*, Chapter 6, and the website https://bldeathnet.hypotheses.org. Thornton Abbey: Hugh Willmott et al., 'A Black Death Mass Grave at Thornton Abbey', *Antiquity* 94 (2020), pp. 179–86. Covid-19 and wealth inequality: https://blogs.imf.org/2020/05/11/how-pandemics-leave-the-poor-even-farther-behind. Black Death and wealth inequality: Walter Scheidel, *The Great Leveler* (2017), pp. 291–313. Sedgeford: Christopher Dyer, 'Changes in Diet in the Late Middle Ages', *Agricultural History Review* 36 (1988), pp. 21–37.

Fifteenth-century exploration: Felipe Fernández-Armesto, *Pathfinders* (2006). Cabot: Evan Jones and Margaret Condon, *Cabot and Bristol's Age of Discovery* (2016), at https://archive.org/details/Cabotdigital/.

6. Englexit, 1497–1713

As well as the relevant works in the series recommended for Chapter 5, Susan Brigden's *New Worlds, Lost Worlds* (2000) and Nicholas Canny's *Making Ireland British* (1988) are excellent general treatments, as is Steven Pincus's *1688* (2010), which covers far more than the title might suggest. England's pivot towards the Atlantic dominates Chapters 6–8, and has inspired some outstanding books. Among the best, in my opinion, are David Scott's *Leviathan* (2013) and Brendan Simms's *Three Victories and a Defeat* (2007), *Europe* (2013) and *Britain's Europe* (2016). Britain's naval and imperial histories also become central themes in Chapters 6–9. On the former, Nicholas Rodger's *Safeguard of the Sea* (1997) and *Command of the Ocean* (2004) are masterpieces, covering the period to 1815; on the latter, in addition to the multi-volume Oxford history and Scott's *Leviathan*, John Darwin's *The Empire Project* (2009) and *Unfinished Empire* (2012) are especially good. On imperial finance, Peter Cain and Anthony Hopkins's *British Imperialism, 1688–2000* (2002) is magisterial. On the domestic economy, Stephen Broadberry et al., *British Economic Growth, 1270–1870* (2015).

Richard Ameryk: Evan Jones, 'Alwyn Ruddock: "John Cabot and the Discovery of America"', *Historical Research* 81 (2008), p. 238. The link was first suggested in 1910. On Henry VIII, John Guy, *Henry VIII* (2014), has recent bibliography. Wolsey's diplomacy: Simms, *Europe*, pp. 18–19. Charles V's strategic thinking: Geoffrey Parker, *Emperor: A New Life of Charles V* (2019). Diarmaid MacCulloch, *The Reformation* (2004), pp. 106–89, is good on Luther's strategic significance. Englexit's parallels with Brexit: Nigel Culkin and Richard Simmons, *Tales of Brexits Past and Present* (2019), pp. 61–72. Thomas Cromwell: MacCulloch, *Thomas Cromwell* (2018). On the monasteries, Eamon Duffy's *The Stripping of the Altars* (2nd edn, 2005) is unsurpassed. Hugh Willmott's *Dissolution of the Monasteries in England and Wales* (2020) is excellent on the consequences. Hulton Abbey: Peter Wise, ed., *Hulton Abbey* (1985). Digging has continued (William Klemperer et al., *Excavations at Hulton Abbey, Staffordshire, 1987–1994* [2004]). Susan Loughlin, *Insurrection* (2016), has a recent account of the Pilgrimage of Grace. Edward VI's hard Englexit: MacCulloch, *Tudor Church Militant* (2000). John Edwards, *Mary I* (2011), and Helen Castor, *Elizabeth I* (2018), have recent bibliographies.

Elizabethan religious education: Keith Wrightson and David Levine, *Poverty and Piety in an English Village: Terling, 1525–1700* (1995), pp. 13–15. Philip II's strategic thinking: Geoffrey Parker, *The Grand Strategy of Philip II* (2000). Rodger, *Safeguard*, pp. 254–71, has a good brief account of 1588.

Elizabethan English: Robert Tombs, *The English and Their History* (2014), pp. 194–203. Climate and the seventeenth-century crisis: Geoffrey Parker, *Global Crisis* (2013). Witchcraft: Brian Levack, ed., *The Oxford Handbook of Witchcraft in Early Modern Europe and Colonial America* (2013). Great Rebuilding: William Hoskins, 'The Rebuilding of Rural England, 1570–1640', *Past & Present* 4 (1953), pp. 44–59. Early modern houses: Matthew Johnson, *English Houses, 1300–1800* (2010). Cowlam: T. Brewster and Colin Hayfield, 'Cowlam Deserted Village', *Post-Medieval Archaeology* 22 (1988), pp.

21–109. West Whelpington: Michael Jarrett and Stuart Wrathmell, 'Sixteenth- and Seventeenth-Century Farmsteads: West Whelpington, Northumberland', *Agricultural History Review* 25 (1977), pp. 108–19. On Virginian tobacco and Caribbean sugar I recommend two classics: Edmund Morgan, *American Slavery, American Freedom* (1975), and Sidney Mintz, *Sweetness and Power* (1985). Atlantic slave trade: Kenneth Morgan, *Slavery, Atlantic Trade and the British Economy, 1660–1800* (2001).

Foreign policies of James I and Charles I: Simms, *Three Victories*, pp. 9–28. Puritans and New England: David Hall, *The Puritans: A Transatlantic History* (2019).

Civil wars: Michael Braddick, *God's Fury, England's Fire* (2008). Cromwell and the sea: Rodger, *Command*, pp. 1–64. Jenny Uglow's *A Gambling Man* (2009) is a glorious account of the Restoration. Glorious Revolution: Pincus, *1688*. Wars of 1689–1713: Simms, *Three Victories*, pp. 44–76; Rodger, *Command*, pp. 136–80; Pincus, *1688*, pp. 305–65. Act of Union: Allan Macinnes, 'Anglo-Scottish Union and the War of the Spanish Succession', in William Mulligan and Brendan Simms, eds, *The Primacy of Foreign Policy in British History, 1660–2000* (2010), pp. 49–64. The film *The Favourite* is based on Sarah Field, *The Favourite* (2002). Effects of the wars on Leviathan: Pincus, *1688*, pp. 366–99. https://measuringworth.com/datasets/ukearncpi/# discusses the complexities of cross-period calculations like the one I make for William's wars.

7. The Pivot, 1713–1815

Several of the general books mentioned for Chapter 6 remain relevant. John Brewer's *Sinews of Power* (1983) is a classic on the growth of British government, and Linda Colley's *Britons* (2nd edn, 2009) is just as good on the creation of British identities. Among Jeremy Black's many books on eighteenth-century politics, diplomacy and war, I single out *Pitt the Elder* (1992) and *Continental Commitment* (2005). On the rapid changes in English society, Julian Hoppitt's *A Land of Liberty?* (2000) and Roy Porter's *English Society in the 18th Century* (1990) are excellent; on the early history of the East India Company, William Dalrymple, *Anarchy* (2019).

Tory strategies: essays in Jeremy Black, ed., *The Tory World* (2015), pp. 21–62. Arguments over Europe: Stephen Conway, *Britain, Ireland and Continental Europe in the Eighteenth Century* (2011). Britain's wars: Simms, *Three Victories*, pp. 79–383.

Castle Howard and Houghton Hall: Porter, *English Society*, p. 60. Gini coefficients: Peter Lindert and Jeffrey Williamson, 'Reinterpreting Britain's Social Tables, 1688–1913', *Explorations in Economic History* 20 (1983), pp. 94–109. Extraction ratios: Branko Milanović et al., 'Pre-Industrial Inequality', *Economic Journal* 121 (2010), p. 263. Agriculture: Susanna Wade-Martins, *Farmers, Landlords and Landscapes: Rural Britain, 1720 to 1870* (2004). Rural living standards: Craig Muldrew, *Food, Energy and the Creation of Industriousness* (2011). Middle Claydon: John Broad, *Transforming English Rural Society* (2004). Figure 7.4: data from Broad, *Rural Society*, Table 8.2.

Canals: Porter, *English Society*, pp. 207–8. Stature: Galofré-Vilà et al., 'Heights'. Early involvement with India: Dalrymple, *Anarchy*, pp. 1–57. London: for this and Chapters 8 and 9, Roy Porter's *London* (1994) is fascinating. Jenny Uglow's *The Lunar Men* (2002) is wonderful on intellectual life in the provinces. Coffee: Steve

Pincus, '"Coffee Politicians Does Create"', *Journal of Modern History* 67 (1995), pp. 807–34. Beer and gin: Jessica Warner, 'The Naturalization of Beer and Gin in Early Modern England', *Contemporary Drug Problems* 24 (1997), pp. 373–402. Gin craze: Peter Ackroyd, *History of England* IV (2016), pp. 144–55. Clapham's: Craig Cessford et al., '"To Clapham's I Go": A Mid to Late 18th-Century Cambridge Coffee House Assemblage', *Post-Medieval Archaeology* 51 (2017), pp. 372–46. Consumption of tea and coffee: Broadberry et al., *Economic Growth*, Table 7.05. Politeness: Keith Thomas, *In Pursuit of Civility* (2018).

Britishness: Colley, *Britons*. Welshness, John Davies, *A History of Wales* (2007), pp. 285–309; Irishness, T. Moody and W. Vaughan, eds, *A New History of Ireland* IV (2009), pp. 105–22; Scottishness, Bruce Lenman, *Enlightenment and Change* (2nd edn, 2009). Edinburgh: James Buchan, *Capital of the Mind* (2003). American colonies: Alan Taylor, *American Colonies* (2002). American inequality: Peter Lindert and Jeffrey Williamson, *Unequal Gains: American Growth and Inequality since 1700* (2016). Both American scores are for 1774. The English Gini score is for 1751 and the extraction ratio for 1759. American politeness: P. J. Marshall, ed., *Oxford History of the British Empire* II (1998), pp. 289–91. French strategy: Daniel Baugh, 'Withdrawing from Europe', *International History Review* 20 (1998), pp. 1–32. Seven Years' War: Baugh, *The Global Seven Years War, 1754–1763* (2011). American Revolution: Alan Taylor, *American Revolutions* (2017). On India, see Dalrymple, *Anarchy*, p. 133 (extortion, 1757–65), p. 289 (famines of 1769–70 and 1784–6) and pp. 218–9 (profits, 1770–71).

Napoleon, Andrew Roberts, *Napoleon the Great* (2014); the global struggle, Alexander Mikaberidze, *The Napoleonic Wars* (2020); British finances, Roger Knight, *Britain against Napoleon* (2013); the home front, Jenny Uglow, *In These Times* (2014); British, French and American embargos, Ronald Findlay and Kevin O'Rourke, *Power and Plenty* (2007), pp. 366–71.

8. Wider Still and Wider, 1815–65

Many of the works listed for Chapters 6 and 7 remain valuable for the nineteenth century. David Cannadine's *Victorious Century* (2017) provides a good, no-nonsense narrative, and the essays in Chris Williams's *Companion to Nineteenth-Century Britain* (2004) are full of details. On the Industrial Revolution, Robert Allen's *British Industrial Revolution in Global Perspective* (2009) and Joel Mokyr's *Enlightened Economy* (2009) are particularly interesting, and the two-volume *Cambridge Economic History of Modern Britain* (2014) has the facts.

European balance of power: Simms, *Europe*, pp. 176–306. Great Game: Peter Hopkirk's *The Great Game* (1990) is magnificent (the name 'Great Game' comes from Kipling's novel *Kim* [1901]). Crimea: Orlando Figes, *The Crimean War* (2010). Afghanistan: David Loyn, *Butcher and Bolt* (2008), interestingly compares the British, Soviet and American invasions. India: Dalrymple's *Anarchy* and *The Last Mughal* (2006) are absorbing, while Roderick Matthews's *Peace, Poverty and Betrayal* (2021) is unusually even-handed. The insurrection: Saul David, *The Indian Mutiny* (2002). Opium War: Stephen Platt, *Imperial Twilight* (2018).

Britain and the US: Kathleen Burk, *The Lion and the Eagle* (2018), Chapters 1–2. Dominions: Andrew Porter, ed., *Oxford History of the British Empire* III (1999), and Darwin, *Empire Project* and *Unfinished Empire*.

Vets (and other professionals): Boyd Hilton, *A Mad, Bad, and Dangerous People?* (2006), p. 142. England, Bengal and the Yangzi Delta: Robert Allen, 'Agricultural Productivity and Rural Incomes in England and the Yangtze Delta, *c.*1620–*c.*1820' (2006), at http://www.nuffield.ox.ac.uk/General/Members/allen/aspx. Stature and nutrition: John Komlos, 'On English Pygmies and Giants', *Research in Economic History* 25 (2018), pp. 149–68; 'Shrinking in a Growing Economy Is Not So Puzzling after All', *Economics and Human Biology* 32 (2019), pp. 40–55. Free trade: William Bernstein, *A Splendid Exchange* (2008), pp. 280–315, nicely describes the debates in Britain. Unrest after 1815: Robert Poole, *Peterloo* (2019). Coal and its consequences: Vaclav Smil, *Energy and Civilization* (2017), pp. 225–384. Housing: John Burnett, *A Social History of Housing, 1815–1985* (2nd edn, 1986). Irish famine: W. Vaughan, *A New History of Ireland* V (1990), pp. 108–36, 218–331. Death toll: Joel Mokyr and C. Ó Gráda, 'What Do People Die of During Famines?', *European Review of Economic History* 6 (2002), pp. 339–63.

Cannadine, *Victorious Century*, is excellent on mid-century politics. Middle-class culture: Asa Briggs, *Victorian People* (1955) and *The Age of Improvement 1783–1867* (1959), remain classics. Fashion: Ian Kelly, *Beau Brummell* (2005). Wages: Robert Allen, 'The Great Divergence in European Wages and Prices from the Middle Ages to the First World War', *Explorations in Economic History* 38 (2001), pp. 411–48. Consumption: Broadberry et al., *British Economic Growth*, pp. 279–306. Religion: Hugh McLeod, *Religion and Society in England, 1850–1914* (1996).

World-system: Darwin, *Empire Project*. Neither Don Pacifico nor the Magdala campaign has attracted much study; Dolphus Whitten, 'The Don Pacifico Affair', *The Historian* 48 (1986), pp. 255–67, and Frederick Myatt, *The March to Magdala* (1970), remain best. Indian economy: Latika Chaudhary, et al., eds, *A New Economic History of Colonial India* (2015). On balances of trade and payments, Cain and Hopkins, *Imperialism*, pp. 275–302 and Tables 5.6, 5.7.

9. The New World Steps Forth, 1865–1945

The general works listed for Chapter 8 mostly remain relevant to Chapter 9 too, while the twentieth century has generated its own outstanding (and overwhelming) literature. Peter Clarke's *Hope and Glory* (2004) and Robert Skidelsky's *Britain since 1900* (2014) give interestingly different overviews, and Andrew Marr's *History of Modern Britain* (2007) complements both nicely.

Peter Clarke, *Hope and Glory* (2004), pp. 1–76, is excellent on turn-of-the-century Britain, and Robert Massie, *Dreadnought* (1991), tells the story of the 1870s–1910s vividly. Boundary Estate: John Boughton, *Municipal Dreams* (2018), pp. 7–9. Imperial union: Duncan Bell, *The Idea of Greater Britain* (2006). 'British West': James Belich, *Replenishing the Earth* (2009).

Christopher Clark, *The Sleepwalkers* (2014), pp. 448–554, is good on the decision to go to war. Bond markets in summer 1914: Niall Ferguson, *The Pity of War* (1998), pp. 192–7. David Stevenson's *Cataclysm* (2004) analyses the war well, and Adam Tooze's *The Deluge* (2014) is strong on finance and Woodrow Wilson.

Several themes run through this chapter and the next. On Britain and the US, David Reynolds, *Britannia Overruled* (2000), or, for an American perspective, Robert Zoellick, *America in the World* (2020). On finance, Cain and Hopkins, *Imperialism*, and Barry Eichengreen, *Globalizing Capital* (3rd edn, 2019). On the empire, Judith Brown and W. Roger Louis, eds, *Oxford History of the British Empire* IV (1999), and Darwin, *Empire Project*, pp. 305–655.

Versailles: Margaret Macmillan, *Paris 1919* (2002). Post-war India: Kim Wagner, *Amritsar 1919* (2019), and Arthur Herman, *Gandhi & Churchill* (2008). Partition of Ireland: Diarmaid Ferriter, *The Border* (2019). Washington Conference: Zoellick, *America in the World*, pp. 168–98. Britain in the 1930s: Andrew Thorpe, *Britain in the 1930s* (1992). Finance and the Great Depression: Barry Eichengreen, *Golden Fetters* (1992), pp. 297–316. Council Houses: Boughton, *Municipal Dreams* (Dover House Estate on p. 47).

Appeasement: there are interesting revisionist interpretations in Niall Ferguson, *War of the World* (2006), pp. 312–82, and Brendan Simms, *Hitler* (2019), pp. 234–69, 300–46. Worries about bombing: Bret Holman, 'The Air Panic of 1935', *Journal of Contemporary History* 46 (2011), pp. 288–307. Second World War: Daniel Todman, *Britain's War* I (2016) and II (2020). Tonypandy: Martin Gilbert, *Churchill* (1991), pp. 219–21. Churchill's statue: https://www.bbc.com/news/uk-53033550; https://www.theguardian.com/environment/2020/sep/10/extinction-rebellion-protester-arrested-for-defacing-winston-churchill-statue.

10. The Very Point of Junction, 1945–91

The general accounts mentioned for Chapter 9 remain useful. Correlli Barnett's *Audit of War* (1986) is indispensable on Britain's changing international position, and Richard Weight's *Patriots* (2002) is outstanding on identity. This period rejoices in several excellent multi-volume narratives combining politics, culture and social trends. Peter Hennessy's *Never Again* (1993), *Having It So Good* (2006) and *Winds of Change* (2019) cover 1945–64; David Kynaston's *Austerity Britain, 1945–51* (2007), *Family Britain, 1951–57* (2009) and *Modernity Britain, 1957–62* (2014) review 1945–62; and Dominic Sandbrook's *Never Had It So Good* (2005), *White Heat* (2006), *State of Emergency* (2010), *Seasons in the Sun* (2012) and *Who Dares Wins* (2019) provide even more detail for 1956–82. I made excellent use of the early weeks of the Covid-19 lockdown in 2020 by indulging in a binge re-reading of Sandbrook's entire series.

Post-war repositioning: David Reynolds, *From World War to Cold War* (2006). Containment: Reynolds, *One World Divisible* (2000). Nuclear weapons: Richard Rhodes, *Arsenals of Folly* (2007). Post-war Europe: Tony Judt, *Postwar* (2005). Several excellent books review Britain's history with the European Union since the 1950s. I particularly recommend Hugo Young, *This Blessed Plot* (1998), Benjamin Grob-Fitzgibbon, *Continental Drift* (2016), and Stephen Wall, *Reluctant European* (2020). Catholicism and the Six: https://www.politico.eu/article/is-the-vatican-the-cause-of-britains-european-schism/. Canonising Schuman: https://www.telegraph.co.uk/news/worldnews/1469768/Vatican-resists-drive-to-canonise-EU-founder.html. European football organisations: Weight, *Patriots*, pp. 258–63. Decolonisation: John Darwin, *Britain and Decolonisation* (1988). There are many excellent accounts of the empire's disappearance: I particularly recommend Jan Morris, *Farewell the Trumpets* (1978), Piers Brendon, *The Decline and Fall of the British Empire* (2007), and Peter Clarke, *The Last Thousand Days of the British Empire* (2007). Thinking in the 1950s about nuclear war: Sandbrook, *Never Had It So Good*, pp. 248–74.

Northern Ireland: David McKittrick and David McVea, *Making Sense of the Troubles* (2012). Welsh and Scottish nationalism: Weight, *Patriots*, pp. 403–21. British economy: Richard Coopey and Nicholas Woodward, *Britain in the 1970s: The Troubled Economy* (1996). Unpopularity of unions by 1978: MORI poll, from Sandbrook, *Seasons in the Sun*, p. 618.

Cultural changes of the 1960s–70s: Weight, *Patriots*, pp. 355–99, and Sandbrook, *The Great British Dream Factory* (2015), are required reading, while Sandbrook's *White Heat* is a valuable reminder of how much *didn't* change. Liberal laws: Weight, *Patriots*, pp. 361–2, has a convenient list of the major legislation. Theresa May's trousers: https://www.telegraph.co.uk/news/2016/12/03/conservatives-war-theresa-mays-leather-trousers/. Popularity of gardening: 'A Nation of Gardeners', *The Economist* (2 May 2020), p. 44.

Changing diets: John Burnett, *England Eats Out* (2004), pp. 255–319. Fish and chips: Panikos Panayi, *Fish & Chips* (2014). Stir fry and chicken tikka masala: https://www.mirror.co.uk/news/uk-news/stir-fry-now-britains-most-popular-165120.

Margaret Thatcher's legacy remains divisive, but Charles Moore's authorised biography, *Margaret Thatcher* (3 vols, 2013–19), strikes a good tone. Financial reforms: David Kynaston, *The City of London* IV (2001), pp. 415–721. Fall of the Soviet Empire: Robert Service, *The End of the Cold War, 1985–1991* (2015). Britain and German reunification: Patrick Salmon, 'The United Kingdom', in Frédéric Bozo, et al., eds, *German Reunification: A Multinational History* (2016), pp. 153–76.

11. Keep Calm and Carry On, 1992–2103

The general accounts of twentieth-century Britain cover the first parts of this chapter, but I am not aware of any broad history taking 1992 as its starting-point. On American policy, H. R. McMaster, *Battlegrounds* (2020), and Zoellick, *America in the World*, offer interestingly different perspectives.

American strategy after 1989: George Herring, *From Colony to Superpower* (2008), pp. 899–938. Home-grown British terrorists: https://www.thetimes.co.uk/article/focus-blairs-extremism-proposals-attacked-as-the-hunt-continues-for-terrors-new-breed-wvnbz35hm7x. Al-Qaeda affiliations: Peter Bergen, *The Longest War* (2011), pp. 199–201. Calls for sharia law in Britain: https://web.archive.org/web/20110424140110/http://www.muslimsagainstcrusades.com/obeythelaw.php. Polls on Islamist no-go zones in British cities: https://www.independent.co.uk/

news/uk/home-news/uk-no-go-zones-muslim-sharia-law-third-poll-hope-not-hate-far-right-economic-inequality-a8588226.html. Rise of English nationalism: Eric Kaufmann, *Whiteshift* (2018), pp. 137–209. Immigration after 2004: https://web.archive.org/web/20131207074918/http://www.equalityhumanrights.com/uploaded_files/new_europeans.pdf. Reasons for immigration: https://www.the-guardian.com/uk/2010/jan/14/chance-choice-britain-refugees-council-report. Immigration good for the economy: https://www.independent.co.uk/news/uk/home-news/eu-migrants-good-for-uk-economy-1759279.html.

Asian GDP figures from Maddison, https://www.rug.nl/ggdc/historicaldevel-opment/maddison/releases/maddison-project-database-2020. American fears of Japan in the 1970s-80s: Michael Crichton, *Rising Sun* (1992); Ezra Vogel, *Japan as Number One* (1979). American trade with China, https://ustr.gov/countries-regions/china-mongolia-taiwan/peoples-republic-china; rest of world, https://wits.world-bank.org/countrysnapshot/en/USA/textview; British trade with China, https://commonslibrary.parliament.uk/research-briefings/cbp-7379/. Adam Tooze's *Crashed* (2018) is good on financial entanglements, and Jeremy Green's *The Political Economy of the Special Relationship* (2020) on Anglo-American entanglement in particular. Figure 11.8 uses data from Stefan Avdjiev et al., 'Breaking Free of the Triple Coincidence in International Finance', *Economic Policy* 31 (2016), pp. 409–51. China's stimulus: Shahrokh Fardoust et al., *Demystifying China's Fiscal Stimulus* (2012).

Brexit has spawned a huge literature. Tim Shipman's *All Out War* (2016) and *Fall Out* (2017) are my favourites among the fly-on-the-wall accounts, with Harold Clarke et al.'s *Brexit: Why Britain Voted to Leave the European Union* (2017) on the voting patterns and Helen Thompson's 'Inevitability and Contingency', *British Journal of Politics and International Relations* 19 (2017), pp. 434–49, on the actual decision.

Changes in income and assets, 2008–18: https://commonslibrary.parliament.uk/research-briefings/cbp-7950/#fullreport; http://www.smf.co.uk/wp-content/uploads/2015/03/Social-Market-Foundation-Publication-Wealth-in-the-Downturn-Winners-and-losers.pdf; https://www.ippr.org/research/publications/10-years-of-austerity. Impacts of austerity: https://www.ncbi.nlm.nih.gov/pmc/articles/PMC3807771/; Ben Barr et al., 'Suicides Associated with the 2008–10 Economic Recession in England', *British Medical Journal* 345 (2012) e5142. House prices: https://www.globalpropertyguide.com/Europe/United-Kingdom/Price-History. Scottish independence: Tom Devine, *Independence or Union* (2016). Greek tourism revenues: https://data.worldbank.org/indicator/ST.INT.RCPT.CD?locations=GR. Euro-zone and Greece: George Stiglitz, *The Euro* (2016). Ukraine: Lawrence Freedman, *Ukraine and the Art of Strategy* (2019). Refugees: Philipp Genschel and Markus Jachtenfuchs, 'From Market Integration to Core State Powers', *Journal of Common Market Studies* 56 (2018), pp. 178–96. Immigration statistics, 2015–16: https://eua-genda.eu/upload/publications/untitled-67413-ea.pdf. Violent crime: https://www.nytimes.com/2016/01/09/world/europe/cologne-new-years-eve-attacks.html. Terrorism: http://icct.nl/publication/links-between-terrorism-and-migration-an-exploration/. Immigrants and crime: https://www.telegraph.co.uk/news/

uknews/crime/9410827/A-fifth-of-murder-and-rape-suspects-are-immigrants.html. UKIP and Conservatives: Philip Lynch and Richard Whitaker, 'Rivalry on the Right', *British Politics* 8 (2013), pp. 285–312. Conservatives' conflicts over Europe: Philip Lynch, 'Conservative Modernisation and European Integration', *British Politics* 10 (2015), pp. 185–203. Britain and China: Christopher Hill, *The Future of British Foreign Policy* (2019), and Kerry Brown, *The Future of UK–China Relations* (2019) are excellent guides. Osborne's charm offensive: https://www.economist.com/britain/2015/09/26/the-osborne-doctrine. Renminbi bonds: https://www.gov.uk/government/news/britain-issues-western-worlds-first-sovereign-rmb-bond-largest-ever-rmb-bond-by-non-chinese-issuer. Currency swap lines: https://www.gov.uk/government/news/bank-of-england-people-s-bank-of-china-swap-line. Hinkley Point C outcry: http://www.conservativehome.com/thecolumnists/2015/10/nick-timothy-the-government-is-selling-our-national-security-to-china.html. Final go-ahead:https://www.theguardian.com/uk-news/2016/sep/14/theresa-may-conditional-approval-hinkley-point-c-nuclear-power-station. Asia Infrastructure Investment bank: https://www.gov.uk/government/news/uk-announces-plans-to-join-asian-infrastructure-investment-bank. American objections: https://www.ft.com/cms/s/0/0655b342-cc29-11e4-beca-00144feab7de.html. Xi Jinping's London trip: https://www.bbc.com/news/uk-34571436. The Plough at Cadsden: https://www.theguardian.com/uk-news/2016/dec/06/chinese-firm-pub-david-cameron-xi-jinping-pint-plough-cadsden. There is a magnificent video of the two leaders with their beer at https://www.bbc.com/news/av/uk-34608754/david-cameron-takes-xi-jinping-for-a-pint-at-his-local.

Pre-referendum Brexit polls: https://ig.ft.com/sites/brexit-polling/. James Kynge, *China Shakes the World* (2006), describes how co-operation with China looked before it all went wrong. GDP growth, 1989–2015: https://www.imf.org/external/pubs/ft/weo/2018/02/weodata/weorept.aspx. Changes in wages, 1989–2015: https://tradingeconomics.com/united-kingdom/gdp-per-capita-ppp. Chinese competition and Western jobs: David Autor et al., 'The China Shock', *Annual Review of Economics* 8 (2016), pp. 205–40; Italo Colantone and Piero Stanig, 'Global Competition and Brexit', *American Political Science Review* 112 (2018), pp. 201–18. Populism and nationalism: Roger Eatwell and Matthew Goodwin, *National Populism* (2018). Voting patterns in 2016: https://www.express.co.uk/news/politics/1231874/brexit-news-did-wales-vote-for-brexit-scotland-northern-ireland-eu-referendum.

Changes inside China: Elizabeth Economy, *The Third Revolution* (2018). Hardening attitudes since 2009: Richard McGregor, *Xi Jinping: The Backlash* (2019). Belt and Road Initiative: Bruno Maçães, *Belt and Road* (2018). Sino-American trade war: https://www.piie.com/blogs/trade-investment-policy-watch/trump-trade-war-china-date-guide; American strategic rethink: https://foreignpolicy.com/2019/04/20/the-trump-doctrine-big-think-america-first-nationalism/. US-EU relations: https://www.theatlantic.com/international/archive/2021/01/joe-biden-europe/617753/. China and Australia: https://www.lowyinstitute.org/issues/china-australia-relations. Australian 2009 Defence White Paper: www.defence.gov.

au/whitepaper. 2011 ASPI conference: www.aspi.org.au/publications/publica-tions_all.aspx. 16/17+1: Jeremy Garlick, 'China's Economic Diplomacy in Central and Eastern Europe', *Europe-Asia Studies* 71 (2019), pp. 1390–1414; https://thediplo-mat.com/2019/03/chinas-16r-is-dead-long-live-the-171/. Piraeus: https://fortune.com/longform/cosco-piraeus-port-athens/. Italy and the Belt and Road Initiative: https://carnegieendowment.org/2019/05/20/why-did-italy-embrace-belt-and-road-initiative-pub-79149. US lobbying in Europe: https://www.defense.gov/Explore/News/Article/Article/2085573/esper-makes-case-that-china-is-a-growing-threat-to-europe. EU and China: Kerry Brown, 'The EU and China, 2006 to 2016', *Journal of the British Association of Chinese Studies* 8.2 (2018), pp.121–9; https://ec.europa.eu/commission/sites/beta-political/files/communication-eu-china-a-strategic-outlook.pdf; https://www.ecfr.eu/page/-/the_meaning_of_systemic_rivalry_europe_and_china_beyond_the_pandemic.pdf. British policies on China: https://bfpg.co.uk/2020/05/intro-uk-china-strategy/. British opinion poll: https://bfpg.co.uk/wp-content/uploads/2020/06/BFPG-Annual-Survey-Public-Opinion-2020–HR.pdf. Gerasimov doctrine: https://www.politico.com/magazine/story/2017/09/05/gerasimov-doctrine-russia-foreign-policy-215538. China's mili-tary intentions: https://www.prcleader.org/michael-swaine. South China Sea: good summary at https://www.cfr.org/report/military-confrontation-south-china-sea. Freedom of Navigation Operations: https://www.scmp.com/news/china/diplomacy-defence/article/2149062/france-britain-sail-warships-contested-south-china-sea. British views on a Pacific counterscarp: https://bfpg.co.uk/wp-content/uploads/2020/06/BFPG-Annual-Survey-Public-Opinion-2020-HR.pdf, p. 61. RAND war games: 2000s, www.rand.org/topics/taiwan.html; 2010s, https://www.rand.org/pubs/research_reports/RR392.html. Aircraft carriers: https://www.economist.com/briefing/2019/11/14/aircraft-carriers-are-big-expensive-vulnerable-and-popular.

Zeno's dog-and-cart metaphor is mentioned in Hippolytus, *Refutation of All Her-esies* (*c.*200 CE), 1.21, in Anthony Long and David Sedley, *Hellenistic Philosophy* (1987), fragment 62a. Some scholars attribute the story to Cleanthes, Zeno's successor as head of the Stoic school. Social development index: Ian Morris, *Why the West Rules – For Now* (2010) and *The Measure of Civilisation* (2013). Costs of leaving EU, https://www.economist.com/britain/2021/01/14/britains-immediate-economic-prospects-are-grim. Climate migrants: https://www.worldbank.org/en/news/info-graphic/2018/03/19/groundswell---preparing-for-internal-climate-migration. Rising non-EU immigration: https://www.ons.gov.uk/peoplepopulationandcommunity/populationandmigration/internationalmigration/bulletins/migrationstatisticsquarter-lyreport/august2020. Chinese students: https://www.universitiesuk.ac.uk/International/Pages/intl-student-recruitment-data.aspx. Confucian foreign policy: Feng Zhang, 'Confucian Foreign Policy Traditions in Chinese History', *Chinese Journal of International Politics* 8 (2015), pp. 197–218. Rule of law: https://www.brookings.edu/wp-content/uploads/2019/09/FP_20190930_china_legal_develop-ment_horsley.pdf. World Values Survey: https://www.worldvaluessurvey.org/

WVSContents.jsp. Softpower 30: https://softpower30.com. Confucius Institutes: https://www.bbc.com/news/world-asia-china-49511231. Mandarin in British schools: https://www.britishcouncil.org/sites/default/files/language_trends_2018_report.pdf. Britishness: Colley, *Britons*. Scotland leaving UK: https://www.economist.com/britain/2021/01/30/most-scots-want-independence-but-they-lack-the-means-to-get-it; Irish reunification: https://www.thetimes.co.uk/article/northern-irish-back-border-poll-within-five-years-6ndbkz8os.

12. Can't Go Home Again, 2017
A different version of this chapter has been published at https://worldview.stratfor.com/article/left-behind-brexit-capital. 'Routine' jobs: https://www.newstatesman.com/politics/2015/07/letter-stoke-how-transform-city-decline. £1 houses: https://www.bbc.com/news/uk-england-stoke-staffordshire-22247663. Sandbrook, *Who Dares Wins*, pp. 671–90, has a good discussion of journalists' visits to struggling towns, including Stoke.

ILLUSTRATIONS

INDEX

Page references in *italics* indicate images.